THE OFFICIAL HISTORY OF THE BRITISH CIVIL SERVICE

This first volume of the Official History of the UK Civil Service covers its evolution from the Northcote-Trevelyan Report of 1854 to the first years of Mrs Thatcher's government in 1981.

Despite current concerns with good governance and policy delivery, little serious attention has been paid to the institution vital to both: the Civil Service. This Official History is designed to remedy this by placing present problems in historical context and by providing a helpful structure in which others, and particularly former officials, may contribute to the debate. Starting with the seminal 1854 Northcote-Trevelyan Report, it covers the 'lost opportunity' of the 1940s when the Service failed to adapt to the needs of 'big government' as advocated by Beveridge and Keynes. It then examines, in greater detail, the belated attempts at modernisation in the 1960s, the Service's vilification in the 1970s and the final destruction of the 'old order' during the first years of Mrs Thatcher's government.

Particular light is shed on the origins of such current concerns as:

- the role of special advisers;
- the need for a Prime Minister's Department;
- the evolution of Parliamentary Select Committees to resolve the potential tension between bureaucracy and Parliamentary democracy.

This Official History is based on extensive research into both recently released and unreleased papers as well as interviews with leading participants. It has important lessons to offer all those, both inside and outside the UK, seeking to improve the quality of democratic government.

This book will be of great interest to all students of British history, British government and politics, and of public administration in general.

Rodney Lowe is Emeritus Professor of Contemporary History at the University of Bristol. He has published widely on comparative history, and especially on UK government and welfare policy.

WHITEHALL HISTORIES: GOVERNMENT OFFICIAL HISTORY SERIES

ISSN: 1474–8398

The Government Official History series began in 1919 with wartime histories, and the peacetime series was inaugurated in 1966 by Harold Wilson. The aim of the series is to produce major histories in their own right, compiled by historians eminent in the field, who are afforded free access to all relevant material in the official archives. The Histories also provide a trusted secondary source for other historians and researchers while the official records are not in the public domain. The main criteria for selection of topics are that the histories should record important episodes or themes of British history while the official records can still be supplemented by the recollections of key players; and that they should be of general interest, and, preferably, involve the records of more than one government department.

THE UNITED KINGDOM AND THE EUROPEAN COMMUNITY:
Vol. I: The rise and fall of a national strategy, 1945–1963
Alan S. Milward

SECRET FLOTILLAS
Vol. I: Clandestine sea operations to Brittany, 1940–1944
Vol. II: Clandestine sea operations in the Mediterranean, North Africa and the Adriatic, 1940–1944
Sir Brooks Richards

SOE IN FRANCE
M. R. D. Foot

THE OFFICIAL HISTORY OF THE FALKLANDS CAMPAIGN:
Vol. I: The origins of the Falklands War
Vol. II: War and diplomacy
Sir Lawrence Freedman

THE OFFICIAL HISTORY OF BRITAIN AND THE CHANNEL TUNNEL
Terry Gourvish

CHURCHILL'S MYSTERY MAN: DESMOND MORTON
AND THE WORLD OF INTELLIGENCE
Gill Bennett

THE OFFICIAL HISTORY OF PRIVATISATION
Vol. I: The formative years 1970–1987
David Parker

SECRECY AND THE MEDIA: THE OFFICIAL HISTORY
OF THE D-NOTICE SYSTEM
Nicholas Wilkinson

THE OFFICIAL HISTORY OF THE BRITISH CIVIL SERVICE:
REFORMING THE CIVIL SERVICE
Vol. I: The Fulton years, 1966–81
Rodney Lowe

THE OFFICIAL HISTORY OF THE BRITISH CIVIL SERVICE

Reforming the Civil Service, Volume 1:
The Fulton years, 1966–81

Rodney Lowe

LONDON AND NEW YORK

The author has been given full access to official documents.
He alone is responsible for the statements made and
the views expressed.

First published 2011
by Routledge
2 Park Square, Milton Park, Abingdon, Oxon, OX14 4RN

Simultaneously published in the USA and Canada
by Routledge
270 Madison Avenue, New York, NY 10016

Routledge is an imprint of the Taylor & Francis Group, an informa business

© 2011 Crown Copyright

Typeset in Baskerville by
RefineCatch Limited, Bungay, Suffolk
Printed and bound in Great Britain by
CPI Antony Rowe, Chippenham, Wiltshire

All rights reserved. No part of this book may be reprinted or
reproduced or utilised in any form or by any electronic,
mechanical, or other means, now known or hereafter
invented, including photocopying and recording, or in any
information storage or retrieval system, without permission in
writing from the publishers.

British Library Cataloguing in Publication Data
A catalogue record for this book is available from the British Library

Library of Congress Cataloging-in-Publication Data
Lowe, Rodney.
The official history of the British civil service :
reforming the civil service/Rodney Lowe.
p. cm.
1. Civil service reform—Great Britain—History.
2. Civil service—Great Britain—History. I. Title.
JN428.L69 2011
351.4109—dc22
2010032340

ISBN13: 978-0-415-58864-5 (hbk)
ISBN13: 978-0-203-83155-7 (ebk)

CONTENTS

Acknowledgements xii
Abbreviations xiii

Introduction 1

PART 1
The legacy 15

1 **The Northcote-Trevelyan Report and the evolution of the civil service, 1854–1916** 17

    1.1 Introduction 17
    1.2 The Northcote-Trevelyan Report and its implementation 18
        1.2.1 Open competition 20
        1.2.2 The division of labour 24
        1.2.3 Promotion by merit 26
        1.2.4 Unification of the Service 27
    1.3 The historical and comparative context 29
        1.3.1 The political imperative of administrative reform 29
        1.3.2 The changing role of government 31
        1.3.3 The comparative context 33
    1.4 The evolution of the Victorian and Edwardian Civil Service 35
        1.4.1 Conventions 35
        1.4.2 Treasury control and training 38
    1.5 Conclusion 40

2 **The Fisher-Bridges settlement, 1916–56** 42

    2.1 Introduction 42
    2.2 Realising the ideal 44

  2.2.1 *Unification 45*
  2.2.2 *Exclusivity 50*
  2.2.3 *Political influence 59*
  2.2.4 *Missed opportunities 63*
 2.3 *The administrative machine 67*
  2.3.1 *A new despotism? 68*
  2.3.2 *Industrial relations 69*
  2.3.3 *Women and machines 73*
 2.4 *Conclusion 77*

PART 2
The reform momentum   81

3 Modernisation before Fulton, 1956–66   83

 3.1 Introduction 83
 3.2 Pressures for reform 86
  3.2.1 Parliament 87
  3.2.2 The public campaign to 'modernise Britain' 88
  3.2.3 The Fabian Society 92
  3.2.4 The Labour and Conservative Parties 94
  3.2.5 Pressures from within 97
 3.3 The response 100
  3.3.1 The Plowden Committee on the Control of Public Expenditure, 1959–61 101
  3.3.2 Treasury reorganisation 105
 3.4 Conclusion 112

4 The Fulton Committee, 1966–8   114

 4.1 Introduction 114
 4.2 The Report's recommendations 115
 4.3 Fulton's flaws 120
 4.4 Conclusion 127

PART 3
The politics and planning of reform   129

5 Modernisation's moment, 1968–72   131

 5.1 Introduction 131

5.2 Implementing Fulton 135
    5.2.1 Restructuring 138
        (a) June 1968 – March 1970 139
        (b) April 1970 – December 1971 146
    5.2.2 Improving personnel management 151
    5.2.3 Finishing with Fulton 154
5.3 Reorganising Central Government 155
    5.3.1 Pre-election planning and the first 100 days 157
    5.3.2 Central Capability 162
        (a) A Prime Minister's and Cabinet Office 162
        (b) The Central Policy Review Staff 165
        (c) 'Super' ministries 170
    5.3.3 Analytic Capability 172
        (a) The Business Team 173
        (b) Programme Analysis and Review 177
        (c) Hiving off 182
5.4 Conclusion 190

6 The crisis of consensus, 1973–9   193

6.1 Introduction 193
6.2 Preserving the old 196
    6.2.1 Addressing change 197
    6.2.2 Manpower 199
    6.2.3 Pay 203
    6.2.4 Maintaining the momentum of modernisation 209
        (a) The CSD and the centre of Government 209
        (b) Programme Analysis and Review 214
    6.2.5 Halting progress 216
6.3 Pioneering the new 217
    6.3.1 Special advisers and the decline of the CPRS 218
    6.3.2 Cash limits and the rehabilitation of the Treasury 224
        (a) Financial information systems (FIS) 225
        (b) Cash limits 227
6.4 Conclusion 233

7 Mrs Thatcher and the demise of the Civil Service Department, 1979–81   235

7.1 Introduction 235
7.2 Short-term economies 237

7.2.1 Reviewing non-departmental bodies 238
7.2.2 Reducing departmental manpower 240
7.2.3 The Rayner projects 243
7.3 Long-term manpower policy 246
7.3.1 The 630,000 target 246
7.3.2 The Rayner scrutinies 250
7.3.3 Rayner's lasting reforms 256
7.4 The 1981 Civil Service strike 265
7.5 The demise of the Civil Service Department 269
7.6 Conclusion 276

PART 4
Wider issues, 1966–81   279

8 Whitleyism, 1966–81   281

8.1 Introduction 281
8.2 Organisation 282
8.2.1 The staff associations 283
8.2.2 The NSS and CCSU 287
8.3 Collaboration 289
8.3.1 Modernising management 290
8.3.2 Political presence 293
8.3.3 Negotiating pay 296
8.4 Conflict 300
8.4.1 1973: the first national strike 301
8.4.2 1979: the winter of discontent 304
8.4.3 1981: the 21-week strike 306
8.5 Conclusion 309

9 Management Challenges   312

9.1 Introduction 312
9.2 Training 312
9.3 Dispersal 319
9.4 Pensions 324
9.5 Gender and race 329
9.6 Computerisation 340
9.7 Conclusion 346

10 Political Pressures — 348

   10.1 Introduction 348
   10.2 Open government 348
      10.2.1 Reforming the Official Secrets Act 350
      10.2.2 The Crossman Diaries 358
      10.2.3 The press 363
   10.3 Parliament 364
      10.3.1 The ombudsman 365
      10.3.2 Select Committees 368
   10.4 Constitutional change 373
      10.4.1 Europe 374
      10.4.2 Devolution 376
   10.5 Conclusion 379

PART 5
Conclusion — 381

11 Ringing out the old, ringing in the new — 383

   11.1 The challenge 383
   11.2 The response 384
   11.3 The future 386

   Chronology — 388
   Notes — 395
   References — 528
   Sources and Select Bibliography — 529
   Index — 543

ACKNOWLEDGEMENTS

This book has typically taken an unconscionable time to write; and in the course of writing I have benefited enormously from much official and private help. Officially, I have received consistent support from the Histories, Openness and Records Unit of the Cabinet Office (now recast and renamed the Knowledge and Information Management Unit) and, in particular, Tessa Stirling, Sally Falk and Chris Grindall; and from my Project Board and, in particular, Peter Hennessy who from the very start of the project has offered his own unique brand of support and encouragement. I have also benefited greatly from a series of interviews with former officials. A full list appears in the appendix, but I should particularly like to thank Ian Beesley, Sir John Herbecq, Sir John Hoskyns, Peter Jones, John Nethercote, Clive Priestley and John Rimmington for help way beyond the calls of duty. Finally, I should like to thank for their help many record officers and archivists, within and outside Government, and in particular the proactive at Churchill College Archive (Allen Packwood and Andrew Riley) and the long-suffering at the National Archives (Geof Baxter, Julie Ash, Gareth Owen and Marjory George). Long-suffering would also seem to be an apt epithet for Jo Anson who performed the remarkable feat of copy-editing the manuscript without losing her sense of humour – at least permanently. Personally I should also like to acknowledge the (sometimes unintentional) help of Geoffrey Fry, Margaret Jones, Michael Lee, Helen Leiser, Hugh Pemberton, Heather Grant and Jackie Hand as well as Alex, Gini, Billy and Mercury. Many may conclude that the results of the project are tragic. For me personally it certainly started with tragedy, with the death of my then partner, Rebecca. The book is dedicated to her memory.

ABBREVIATIONS

ACAS	Advisory, Conciliation and Arbitration Service
AGSRO	Association of Government Supervisors and Radio Staff
AIT	Association of HM Inspectors of Taxes
AT	Administration Trainee
BIA	British Insurance Association
BNOC	British National Oil Corporation
BP	British Petroleum
CA	Clerical Assistant
CAA	Civil Aviation Authority
C&AG	Comptroller and Auditor-General
CAS	Centre of Administrative Studies
CBI	Confederation of British Industry
CCA	Central Computer Agency (within the CSD)
CCSU	Council of Civil Service Unions (formerly NSS)
CCU	Civil Contingencies Unit
CID	Committee of Imperial Defence (1904–46)
CND	Campaign for Nuclear Disarmament
CO	Clerical Officer
CPRS	Central Policy Review Staff
CPSA	Civil and Public Services Association (formerly CSCA, 1969–98)
CSC	Civil Service Commission *or* (Chapter 9) Civil Service College
CSCA	Civil Service Clerical Association (1922–69, then CPSA)
CSD	Civil Service Department
CSO	Central Statistical Office
CSSB	Civil Service Selection Board
CSU	Civil Service Union
DE	Department of Employment
DEA	Department of Economic Affairs
DES	Department of Education and Science
DHSS	Department of Health and Social Security
DI	Department of Industry (1974–9)
DoE	Department of the Environment)

ABBREVIATIONS

DSIR	Department of Scientific and Industrial Research (1915–65)
DTI	Department of Trade and Industry (1970–4)
DTO	Departmental Training Officers
DVLA	Driver and Vehicle Licensing Agency, Swansea
E	Ministerial Committee on Economic Strategy (1979–81)
EEC	European Economic Community
EIU	European Interdepartmental Unit (within Cabinet Office)
ENA	Ecole Nationale d'Administration
EO	Executive Officer
FCO	Foreign and Commonwealth Office
FDA	Association of First Division Civil Servants
FIS	Financial Information Systems (1976–)
FMI	Financial Management Initiative
FOI	Freedom of Information
GCHQ	Government Communications Headquarters
GDP	Gross Domestic Product
GKN	Guest, Keen and Nettlefolds
GNP	Gross National Product
GOC	Government Organisation Committee (1947–53)
GP	General Practitioner (within National Health Service)
HEO	Higher Executive Officer
HMSO	Her Majesty's Stationery Office
IBM	International Business Machines (USA)
ICI	Imperial Chemical Industries
ICL	International Computers Ltd (UK)
IEA	Institute of Economic Affairs
IMF	International Monetary Fund
IPCS	Institution of Professional Civil Servants
IRSF	Inland Revenue Staff Federation
JAR	Job Appraisal Review
LSE	London School of Economics
MAFF	Ministry of Agriculture, Fisheries and Food
MCA	Ministerial Committee on the Central Capability (1970–4)
MCG	Management Consultancy Group (of the Fulton Committee)
MG	Machinery of Government (Division of the Treasury/CSD)
MINIS	Management Information System (within DoE)
MinTech	Ministry of Technology
MOD	Ministry of Defence
MP	Member of Parliament
MPC	Management Projects Cabinet Committee (1970–1, merged with MCA) *or* (Chapter 10) Major Policy Committee (of the CCSU, 1980–)
MPO	Management and Personnel Office
MSC	Manpower Services Commission

ABBREVIATIONS

NAO	National Audit Office
NATO	North Atlantic Treaty Organisation
NDPB	Non-Departmental Public Bodies ('quangos')
NEC	National Executive Committee (of the Labour Party)
NEDC	National Economic Development Council
NEDO	National Economic Development Office
NHS	National Health Service
NIESR	National Institute of Economic and Social Research
NSS	National Staff Side (of the National Whitley Council, 1920–80, then CCSU)
NWC	National Whitley Council
NWCJC	National Whitley Council Joint Committee (for implementing Fulton)
O&M	Organisation and Methods
OECD	Organisation for Economic Co-operation and Development
OSA	Official Secrets Act
PAC	Public Accounts Committee (of the House of Commons)
PAR	Programme Analysis and Review
PAU	Public Appointments Unit (within the CSD)
PPBS	Planning, Programming and Budgeting System (USA)
PCA	Parliamentary Commissioner for Administration ('ombudsman')
PCC	Policy Coordinating Committee (within the Treasury)
PEO	Principal Establishment Officer
PEP	Political and Economic Planning (1931–78, then Policy Studies Institute)
PESC	Public Expenditure Survey Committee
PFO	Principal Finance Officer
PGO	Paymaster General's Office
PIP	Prices and Incomes Policy
PMD	Prime Minister's Department
PMO	Prime Minister's Office
PRU	Pay Research Unit
PRUB	Pay Research Unit Board
PSA	Property Services Agency
PSBR	Public Sector Borrowing Requirement
PSRU	Public Sector Research Unit (within the Conservative Party, 1966–1970)
RAF	Royal Air Force
SCPS	Society of Civil and Public Servants (formerly SCS, 1976–1988)
SCS	Society of Civil Servants (1930–1976, then SCPS)
SDP	Social Democratic Party
SNP	Scottish National Party
TNA	The National Archives, Kew
TOC	Treasury Organisation Committee (1961–2)
TSU	Technical Support Unit (of MinTech)

ABBREVIATIONS

TUC	Trades Union Congress
V&G	Vehicle and General Company
VAT	Value Added Tax
VED	Vehicle Excise Duty
WNC	Women's National Council

INTRODUCTION

This Official History was commissioned in 2002 at a time when the British Civil Service was the subject of some controversy. Over the preceding decade, both its traditional unity and its future as a career Service had seemingly been jeopardised. The former was as a consequence of the introduction in 1988 of *Next Steps* agencies, in which three-quarters of officials rapidly became employed. Not everyone was convinced by the reassurance that the Service remained 'unified but not uniform'. The phrase, remarked one leading political scientist, was a 'typical piece of "mandarinese" nonsense'.[1] The latter was seen to be threatened by the increasing emphasis on individual employment contracts, performance-related pay and the advertisement of senior posts following the 1994 white paper, *The Civil Service: Continuity and Change*. The values of the private sector, lauded by successive Conservative Governments since 1979, appeared about to trump traditional notions of 'public service'.

The election of a Labour Government in 1997 offered little respite. The granting of executive power over officials to certain unelected special advisers was a major constitutional change and provoked a sustained public campaign for the enactment of a Civil Service Code to protect the Service's traditional virtues of 'integrity, honesty, impartiality and objectivity'.[2] Simultaneously Sir Richard Wilson, on his appointment as Cabinet Secretary and Head of the Home Civil Service, was instructed to concentrate on policy delivery. To many this marked the culmination of the long-frustrated administrative revolution promised by the 1968 Fulton Report: the transmutation of senior officials from 'generalist' policy advisers into 'professional' managers. Fulton had been a self-conscious attempt to adapt the Service to the demands of the twentieth century, as the 1854 Northcote-Trevelyan Report had been seen to adapt it to the demands of the nineteenth century. At the start of the twenty-first century, radical reform was again in the air.

'If you want to reform a great institution', remarked Wilson, 'you must understand it; and if you want to understand it, you need to understand its past.'[3] Hence the commissioning of this History and its primary objective of *directly* enhancing the 'collective memory' of government. Such an objective accords with the original purpose of the Official History Programme, which was established in 1908 to record and learn lessons from the Boer and Russo-Japanese Wars. It also accords

INTRODUCTION

with the objective of a lesser known initiative in 1957 by the then Cabinet Secretary (Sir Norman Brook), who urged all departments to write historical accounts of key policy decisions in order to 'fund experience for Government use'.[4] 'It is a feature of our administrative system', he wrote, 'that we make many forecasts but few retrospects. More post-mortems would be salutary.' Greater efficiency and economy would result, it was claimed, from the placing in historical perspective of the original assumptions and nature of policy decisions and their subsequent modification. Currently, given the commitment to 'evidence-based' policy, the need for such a perspective is as great as ever.

Brook's initiative was not a noted success. Senior officials, so they claimed, were too busy making history to read, let alone write, it. The same might well be said today. Consequently a second, but by no means secondary, objective of this History is *indirectly* to enhance the Government's 'collective memory' through the encouragement of more informed public and academic debate. This objective accords well with the original aspirations of the first general editor of the Civil Series, Official History's first venture into non-military subjects, which was commissioned somewhat courageously in 1941 to learn lessons from the War which was to be won, it was assumed, as much on the home as the military front. Its first editor (the Australian historian, Keith Hancock) was committed to giving 'truth a quick start' by providing others with a quarry of information to which they would otherwise be denied access (indefinitely in his day and then, after legislation in 1958 and 1967, for 50 and then 30 years).[5] It was, in addition, his ambition to enhance this information through a 'new kind of hands-on contemporary history' – the interviewing of officials whilst the ink was still wet on their minutes. Like Brook's later initiative, this ambition proved somewhat unrealistic. Senior officials had more urgent calls on their time. Moreover, there were certain constitutional conventions concerning confidentiality. The importance of oral testimony, however, was acknowledged and when the Civil Series evolved into the permanent Peacetime Programme of Official Histories in 1966, it was supported with conviction by at least one senior official on the grounds that

> an historian working on recent material will be able to fill the gaps, explain discrepancies and produce a continuity of thought and narrative which may be literally impossible in fifty years time when so many of the characters in the drama have disappeared.[6]

Despite – or perhaps as a consequence of – the passage of the Freedom of Information Act in 2000, the need to provide and enrich such a quarry of information remains as great today; and this History will have failed if it does not stimulate informed and independent debate. Its own major contribution to oral testimony is the transcripts of three 'witness' seminars on administrative reform in the 1980s, available since 2007 at http://www.ccbh.ac.uk/witness_civilservicereforms_index.php.

The stimulation of informed debate is all the more important because of current academic neglect of the recent administrative past. Such neglect is surprising given the growing postwar importance of Government and thus of the Civil Service, as the 'black box' through which policy decisions are taken, implemented, and recorded. Government in the UK has typically consumed or redistributed some 40 per cent of GDP and, despite later claims to have 'rolled back the state', greater regulation has further increased its power. Yet the Civil Service's recent history remains a no man's (and no woman's) land between the two disciplines most obviously concerned: history and political science. Historians appear reluctant to enter the adventure playground, which the wealth of records (as left by any bureaucracy) represents despite their ready accessibility at The National Archives. The heyday of administrative history was in the 1960s and 1970s and, even then, the principal focus was on the nineteenth century. Political scientists, for their part, fight equally shy of detailed engagement, despite the predominance of 'historical institutionalism' – a methodology which acknowledges the importance to an understanding of the present of the shaping and reshaping of past institutions by both external shocks and internal dynamics.[7] Why the neglect? The answer is partly chronological. Historians, as a profession, would appear reluctant to advance beyond 1945 whilst even 'historical institutionalists' hesitate to retreat beyond certain stereotypical 'critical junctures' such as 1997 or 1979. It is, however, also methodological; and again this History will have failed if it does not help to bridge the disciplinary gap by, on the one hand, making archival evidence accessible to non-historians and, on the other, by selecting and structuring this evidence in the light of competing theoretical insights.

Of what then should a History of the contemporary Civil Service consist? The nature of both the Civil Service as a whole and of the overall argument used in the book will be discussed later; but some explanation is first required of how so unmanageable a task was made manageable. A history of the Civil Service had been long contemplated but then, perhaps wisely, never commissioned. 'The collection and assimilation of material for a book on a modern Government Department is an immense task', minuted Sir Edward Bridges (the progenitor, as War Cabinet Secretary in 1941, of the Civil Series) of one early proposal – before adding perceptively that 'few if any people . . . would be prepared to undertake such a labour single-handed'.[8] One obvious problem was the sheer volume of documentation which, even after it has been reduced to one per cent for permanent preservation, amounts for the Civil Service as a whole (as opposed to Bridges' single department) to a mile for every year. Moreover, official historians have the right, and duty, to consult the records before the final cull. Even Hancock blanched at the 'devotion that must amount to fanaticism if the historian is not to falter'.

Equally daunting is the size and complexity of the Service itself. This was moderated, to a certain extent, by an early decision to confine coverage to the Home Civil Service. This excluded the Diplomatic Service (as defined after the merger of the Foreign and Colonial Offices in 1966) and the staff of the related Ministry of Overseas Development (merged itself with the FCO in 1979). Excluded also are the Intelligence Agencies (leading to the taunt that this History has been written without Intelligence); the Northern Ireland Civil Service (traditionally omitted even from statistical counts); and industrial Civil servants (who, despite a constant postwar decline, still numbered some 140,000 in 1982).[9] It was also decided that reference should be made to individuals only when developments would otherwise be inexplicable. A complementary text already exists in Peter Hennessy's *Whitehall* (first published in 1989) and neither its style nor popularity, it was agreed, could be rivalled.[10] A further, more contestable, decision was to focus on the reform of the Service rather than the effectiveness of its overall record. To have attempted the latter would have involved the near impossible task of establishing objective criteria against which to measure the relative success of a wide range of policies over an equally wide period of time during which public, political and academic expectation greatly varied. Moreover, despite Northcote-Trevelyan's aspirations and later assurances about its unity, the Service is pre-eminently a federal organisation. Any analysis of its effectiveness would therefore have required the equal treatment of some sixty (or at least fifteen major) departments and, for the 1990s, some hundred agencies.

A concentration on attempts to reform the Service as a whole, by contrast, not only simplified the writing of the History but also enabled its division into two volumes, each centring on what have been commonly regarded as seminal blueprints for reform: the 1968 Fulton and the 1988 *Next Steps* Reports. For reasons given below, the chronological divide was determined at 1981; and this freed space in the first volume for some analysis of the perceived 'golden age' prior to 1966 ushered in by an even more seminal report, against which both Fulton and *Next Steps* were consciously reacting – the Northcote-Trevelyan Report of 1854.

Concentration on reform has many recognised disadvantages. Once again, the central departments (principally the Cabinet Office, the Treasury and, between 1968 and 1981, the Civil Service Department) are to be privileged. So too is activity within Whitehall, to the exclusion of the majority of officials who work outside Inner London and thereby shape the public's perception of the Service, if not that of political commentators or academics. Even the discussion of industrial relations within this volume will concentrate on the national leaders rather than the militant activists who were actually driving change. The silent majority will also remain characteristically silent (see Chapter 8). Moreover a wide range of managerial and political issues, which merit far fuller treatment, have been clustered together in Chapters 9 and 10. In short, the History – despite possible appearances to the contrary – often does little more than scratch the surface, although hopefully it will provide a valuable context for the more detailed case studies which are undoubtedly needed. Once again it will have failed if it fails in this fourth objective: the stimulation and assistance of individual case studies, particularly by former practitioners – whose understanding and experience is much needed, not least as an antidote to the written record, which can be designed to deceive as well as to illuminate.

The nature of the Home Civil Service

There are two ways of conceptualising the Home Civil Service: the popular and the constitutional. The popular, which drove political demands for the modernisation and contraction of the Service throughout the period covered by this volume, typically concentrates on its size and the power of a small, geographically concentrated elite (hence the common equation of the Service with one street in London, Whitehall). The Service at this time was indeed an exceptionally large organisation, dwarfing the biggest private sector companies (such as ICI, which employed less than one-third the number of staff). This underlines the magnitude of the managerial challenge it faced. It also questions the validity of the private sector solutions proffered. On the other hand, the significance of its size should not be exaggerated – as arguably it was in the mid-1970s when many of the country's economic ills were accredited to an overlarge bureaucracy.[11] It admittedly peaked in 1976 and aggregate figures disguise a relentless increase in 'non-productive' at the expense of industrial workers (Table 0.1, columns a and b). Nevertheless, even at the height of its demonisation during the 1979 'winter of discontent', the Service accounted for less than ten per cent of employment in the public sector and three per cent of the national labour force.[12] On this simple statistical basis, its malign economic influence was somewhat exaggerated.

Equally questionable are popular conceptions of the power concentrated in a small elite. The Service, despite frequent protests about its unity, remained essentially a federal body with the 'central' coordinating departments being relatively compact in comparison to such giant departments as the Ministry of Defence (Table 0.1, columns c and d).[13] In short, the Service was not – and did not act as – a monolithic body. The 'open structure', by which the top three grades of officials – Permanent, Deputy and Under Secretary – came to be known after 1971, was similarly compact (Table 0.2, column a, and see Chapter 5.2.1). These grades were, in essence, the elite which were dubbed over-powerful in the 1960s and 1970s. They also became popularly equated with the term 'Civil Service'. Their number was simply too small, particularly in management terms and over the full range of policy, to exert the power attributed to them. The latter allusion was also clearly an illusion.

Two further popular perceptions, however, had greater validity: the Service's geographical and gender bias (Table 0.2 columns b–d). Despite sustained attempts to relocate staff throughout the 1970s, some two–fifths of officials were typically employed throughout the period in the South East of England, a quarter in Greater London and a fifth in Inner London. Given the disproportionate percentage of the population living in the South East, there was some justification for such an imbalance. A crude majority of officials was also employed elsewhere – and many of those working in the South East, it might be argued, were internal migrants. Nevertheless, some Southern bias undoubtedly did persist (see Chapter 9.3).[14] As for gender, the Service as a whole may have provided a relatively plentiful and rewarding source of employment for women; but, once again obscured by aggregate statistics, it was typically concentrated in junior posts. This was particularly well illustrated by the relative absence of women from the 'open structure' (Table 0.2 columns a and b, and see Chapter 9.5). In consequence, of the popular conception of the Service as over-large, over-powerful, over-concentrated and over-male, only the last was incontrovertibly correct.

Table 0.1 The size of the Home Civil Service, 1966–82

	a	b	c	d	e
	Home Civil Service	Non-industrial	Central Depts	Ministry of Defence	DHSS
1966	646 600	430 000	2138	276 000	–
1967	661 000	451 000	2232	275 100	–
1968	677 600	471 000	2319	275 200	–
1969	674 400	470 000	3054	267 400	69 600
1970	689 000	490 000	3860	261 250	70 400
1971	689 800	498 000	4044	255 700	71 816
1972	688 900	496 000	4045	279 300	74 549
1973	679 900	571 000	4976	270 225	76 537
1974	682 000	512 000	4905	267 900	80 940
1975	681 400	524 000	5229	266 500	86 700
1976	732 200	569 000	5567	268 200	91 600
1977	733 800	563 000	5237	261 200	94 500
1978	725 900	560 000	4875	253 300	96 900
1979	721 100	559 000	4966	248 500	97 600
1980	696 000	541 600	4919	241 700	95 400
1981	693 919	536 200	4794	232 800	98 300
1982	665 200	526 400	4474	221 600	96 800

Figures are mainly for 1 January each year and for staff in post. They exclude the Northern Ireland Civil Service and treat part-time staff as 0.5, whilst ignoring casual workers. All, other than column (b), include industrial civil servants where appropriate.

Col (a): Home Civil Service exclude staff in the Diplomatic Service/ FCO (typically 10–11,000) and Ministry of Overseas Development prior to 1980 (typically 2100–2400)

Col (c): Central Departments include the Cabinet Office (whose numbers rose from 408 in 1966 to 554 in 1982, peaking at 685 in 1976), the Treasury (whose numbers rose from 1730 in 1966 to 2582 in 1982, peaking without its CSD responsibilities at 1144 in 1976) and the Civil Service Department between 1969 and 1981 (some 1627 in its first year and 3197 in its last, peaking again in 1976 at 3738).

Source: Annual editions of *Civil Service Statistics*, from 1970.

Constitutionally, the definition of a civil servant on which all statistical series are historically based is that originally provided by the Tomlin Commission on the Civil Service in 1931: 'servants of the Crown, other than holders of political and judicial offices, who are employed in a civil capacity and whose remuneration is paid wholly or directly out of moneys voted by Parliament'.[15] The differentiation from Ministers, judges and the armed forces was uncontroversial; but, as even Tomlin admitted, it was otherwise only a 'working definition' that was neither 'authoritative' nor 'exhaustive'. Its fallibility was confirmed by a major attempt to regularise the position in 1974, occasioned in part by Fulton's call for more accountable management and in part by the computerisation of personnel records (see Chapters 5.3.3c and 9.6 respectively). 'Computers', minuted one frustrated statistician, 'won't stand for . . . the accumulated consequences of years of woolly thinking.'[16] He was, however, destined to remain frustrated as the review concluded that it was

Table 0.2 The Nature of the Non-Industrial Civil Service, 1966–82

	a	b	c	d
	Open structure	Women	South-East	Greater London
1966	–	–	–	–
1967	–	–	–	–
1968	–	–	–	–
1969	–	–	–	–
1970	–	194 655 (40%)	226 700	150 000
1971	500 (3)	200 600	231 900	151 600
1972	718 (13)	–	–	–
1973	771 (22)	–	–	–
1974	817 (24)	216 630	–	–
1975	843 (29)	237 125	228 700	–
1976	774 (29)	–	242 500	–
1977	838 (26)	–	236 000 (42%)	144 000 (26%)
1978	813 (27)	–	234 900	–
1979	814 (28)	–	230 600	–
1980	813 (31)	249 123	222 400	136 300
1981	770 (31)	249 908	217 100	136 800
1982	738 (31)	247 250	211 600	127 700

Gaps in the coverage of officially published statistics before 1980 have been deliberately left in order to illustrate changes over time in the perceived importance, or arguably sensitivity, of each subject.

Col (a): the figures in parentheses are for women.

Source: Annual editions of *Civil Service Statistics* from 1970.

not possible to offer satisfactory definitions of the terms 'Civil Service', 'Home Civil Service' or 'civil servant' . . . The fact that these terms are in common use can lead to the mistaken presumption that they have some clear meaning in their own right; while in practice an exact meaning can only be given to them in a specified context.

Such specified contexts, moreover, frequently produced contradictory results.

Controversy centred on the two terms 'the Crown' and 'remuneration'. Civil Servants had only been separated from the Royal Family's personal staff in the 1830s; and the key legal test for the Service's continuing 'Crown' immunity from taxes (such as rates) and much new employment legislation (such as the 1965 Redundancy Payments Act) was that its officials were 'acting on behalf of the Crown'.[17] Appointment to the Service, moreover, continued to be made by royal prerogative thereby making individuals Civil Servants by virtue of the posts they held rather than, as in continental Europe, as members of a formally defined service. Such legal niceties were matters of considerable import for many during the strikes of the 1970s and the perceived politicisation of the Service.[18] In short, within Britain's unwritten constitution, reference to the 'Crown' was – as one classic constitutional text confessed – a 'convenient cover for ignorance' and the source of much obscurity.[19]

This made Tomlin's other qualification about 'remuneration' all the more important. The hallmark of Civil Servants was that they were paid 'wholly or directly out of moneys voted by Parliament'. This was intended to distinguish them from others paid indirectly from public funds via other organisations (such as National Health Service staff paid via health authorities) or by grants-in aid (such as the museum and gallery staff). Such a distinction was put to the test in the early 1970s when, in the aftermath of Fulton, various attempts were made to 'hive off' executive responsibilities from central government (see Chapter 5.3.3c). In the past when, for instance, the Post Office had become a public corporation, its staff had ceased to be Civil Servants. The same, it was assumed, would be true when, for instance, Civil Servants within the Department of Employment were 'hived off' through their new agencies to the Manpower Services Commission (which principally consisted of representatives of the TUC, and the CBI). 'The presumption must be', concluded CSD officials, 'that when a Commission or other managing body is interpolated between the Minister and executive staff, such a body is not acting on behalf of the Crown unless it is expressly stated in the Statute.'[20] This presumption was based on English case law; but it had been subsequently contradicted by Scottish case law and also by the Treasury Solicitor. In reality, therefore, the situation was as fluid as that concerning the definition of the 'Crown' – as was demonstrated by the withdrawal of civil service status from MSC staff in 1974 and its hurried reinstatement in the following year.

Such fluidity illustrates the fact that the definition of a Civil Servant, and thus of the Home Civil Service, was not a subject of disinterested legal or constitutional deliberation but rather a highly contested political issue, fought out between ministers (publicly committed to reduce the size of the 'Civil Service') and Civil Service staff associations (determined to retain their members and, on their behalf, national negotiating rights over pay and conditions, see Chapter 8). Hence the continuing confusion and the lack of consistency in all historical statistical series relating to the Service. At its core, it is known who are Civil Servants; but at the fringes, some are Civil Servants in certain 'specified contexts' and not in others.

The nature of the argument

Official histories have been criticised in the past for using their privileged access to records to establish 'explanatory frameworks' from which future generations of writers find it hard to escape.[21] This History is no exception in seeking to advance new chronological and explanatory 'frameworks'. Its purpose once again, however, is not to stifle but to stimulate informed and independent debate – by liberating others from the tyranny of existing 'frameworks'. These, such as accounts of the 'implementation' of the Northcote-Trevelyan Report between 1854 and 1870, tend to stress the revolutionary as opposed to evolutionary nature of administrative change (thus creating false norms of rapid change). They also tend to exaggerate the significance of 'critical junctures' in the past such as 1945 and 1979 (thereby creating artificial barriers to understanding).

Three alternative chronological and one thematic 'frameworks' are proposed. The first concerns the existence of a 'golden age' – the period following the Northcote-Trevelyan Report (and ending variously in 1939, 1968 or 1979) when the 'public service ethos' was reputedly predominant and officials had not only the strength but also the political and public respect to enable them to 'speak truth unto power'. The concept of a 'public service ethos' has a distinguished pedigree, based on the work of a range of philosophers from Plato to T.H. Green and of Edwardian political writers. All agreed that it was the moral and – given their role as one of the checks and balances in Britain's unwritten constitution – the constitutional duty of Civil Servants to define and defend their own perception of the 'public interest'. Such an ideal may have been more honoured in the breach, but it was no less powerful for that.[22]

Did such a 'golden age' exist? Before 1914, this was unlikely because, as will be argued in Chapter 1, much of the mystique of Northcote-Trevelyan is founded on myth. Both its recommendations and immediate impact on government were in fact limited. It was, for instance, silent on such core principles as the impartiality and anonymity of officials. Given Trevelyan's own personality, it would have been surprising – and somewhat hypocritical – had it been otherwise. The implications of its actual recommendations, such as the social exclusivity of recruits to senior posts (under the guise of 'open competition') and the oversimplification of management (separating 'intellectual' from 'mechanical' work), also led it to be largely ignored when government started to expand after 1870, in response to a more demanding and democratic electorate. For instance, as will be demonstrated in Chapter 2, the initial pillars of state welfare (the Edwardian innovations of national insurance and labour exchanges) were constructed in defiance of, rather than in accordance with, its recommendations.

Consequently the Report's continuing mystique derives from its implementation not before but after the First World War, and particularly during the period when Sir Warren Fisher (1919–1938) and Sir Edward Bridges (1945–1956) were Head of the Civil Service.[23] Even then, however, its implementation was partial. The final elimination of political patronage may, for example, have consolidated the principle of promotion on merit; but how much was this appreciated in the interwar period by the many women replaced (as in all combatant countries) by returning veterans or by those Keynesians whose careers were blighted by challenging the 'Treasury view' and thus deemed not to be (in the fashionable later phrase) 'one of us'?[24] In addition, several reforms which Northcote-Trevelyan implicitly favoured and could have helped the adjustment of the Service to its rapidly evolving political and administrative role (such as the appointment of outsiders and post-entry training) were quietly buried. There was also a continuing equation of efficiency with economy. Such partial implementation thus effectively betrayed not only the spirit but also the actual letter of the Report.

Such a betrayal, together with the barrage of criticism to which the interwar Service was subjected (first from those who wanted to 'roll back' the state and then from those, such as Keynes, who wanted it expanded), does not, however, preclude the existence of a 'golden age' for four good reasons. First, after 1919 the Service responded more effectively than its counterparts elsewhere to the pressure each experienced internally from democracy and externally from international rivalries. In consequence it was entrusted, by international standards, with exceptional power during the Second World War and repaid this trust by discharging it with relative efficiency. Second, by any standard, it remained financially and politically incorrupt. Third, in comparison to the private sector at that time, it pioneered technological change and good employment practice (see Chapter 2.3.3). Finally, it delivered complex administrative change (such as national insurance before 1914 and the creation of the welfare state after 1945) with an assurance which few later, more explicitly managerial, ages could have rivalled.

Collectively, such achievements incontrovertibly justified the soubriquet 'golden age' and so the British Civil Service could then with some justice regard itself – and be regarded – as the 'best in the world'. Its reputation, however, noticeably depended on *practical* achievements and not the predominance of a 'public service ethos'. For that ethos to flourish in an increasingly democratic and bureaucratic world, as Edwardian commentators had forewarned, a clearer distinction was needed between political and administrative responsibility. Instead, however, an increasingly mystical doctrine of 'ministerial responsibility' was employed by Fisher and Bridges to cloak that distinction. Such evasion could not long survive in an increasingly collectivist and decreasingly deferential postwar world. Thus the 'golden age', which had commenced belatedly around 1919, came to an abrupt halt not in 1945, let alone 1979, but in 1956 with the retirement of Bridges, the invasion of Suez and the advent of more aggressive political reportage as pioneered by commercial television.

The second alternative framework concerns the campaign to 'modernise' the Civil Service after 1956, of which the 1968 Fulton Report has been conventionally perceived as the epitome. As Chapters 3–5 will document, however, there were three simultaneous modernisation initiatives: an internal one, following the 1961 Plowden Report on the control of public expenditure; Fulton; and an alternative Conservative Party programme, fashioned in opposition under Edward Heath, to inject greater business acumen into both the determination and delivery of government policy. Of the three, somewhat ironically given the grounds on which it pilloried senior officials, Fulton was the most amateur. This was true of the quality of both its research and its recommendations. It patently lacked the business expertise of the 1960–2 Glassco Commission in Canada and the gravitas of the 1974–6 Coombs Committee in Australia. Thus the loss of Britain's reputation for administrative excellence at this time owed as much to the failings Fulton displayed as to those it perceived in others (see also Chapter 4). Attempts to implement its recommendations between 1968 and 1972 also consumed, to little effect, an inordinate amount of high-level political and administrative time. Consequently, rather than inspiring much-needed change, it impeded it in two major ways. It halted the momentum of more practicable internal reforms; and confounded with its Fabian assumptions the prescience of Conservative plans which foresaw that, in Britain as elsewhere, efficiency would soon be equated with small government. In other words, Fulton failed not because of a premeditated bureaucratic conspiracy (as asserted by some far from disinterested commentators) but because of its own shortcomings. Allied to this, there was a lack of sustained political support and, perhaps most significant of all, continuing confusion both within Parliament and amongst the public about the proper role – and thus size – of government.

The third alternative framework concerns the managerial revolution, conventionally equated with 'Thatcherism', which was finally effected within Whitehall. As Chapters 6 and 7 will demonstrate, however, the roots of this revolution stretched back long before 1979. To Fulton's frustration, the size of the Civil Service had first been effectively capped in 1968. Simultaneously, under the influence of practice in the USA (as reflected by both Conservative planning and an influx of management consultants into Whitehall) the prevailing assumptions of the 'golden age' had started to crumble and been replaced by the conviction that 'business was best'. Then in 1976, as press and public opinion hardened against the 'privileged' public sector, cash limits were introduced to inject some monetary discipline into the planning of public expenditure (itself a concept, and a system, developed during the first wave of modernisation following the 1961 Plowden Report). They in turn confounded the principle of pay comparability, which determined the overall cost of the Service and underpinned its system of industrial relations – and thus management.

Given the relentlessness of such pressure, it was of little wonder that – contrary to conventional opinion – the election of the Conservatives in 1979 was as much welcomed within Whitehall as viewed with apprehension. As, for example, Robert Armstrong (the politically astute Cabinet Secretary and Heath's former principal private secretary) reaffirmed to Mrs Thatcher in 1980:

> the change of Government last year was felt as a relief from pressures built up under the last Administration and as an opportunity for an improvement in relations between staff and management in the Civil Service.[25]

For its part, the Conservatives' election victory may have presaged a new determination to achieve managerial efficiency with the immediate appointment of Sir Derek Rayner (of Marks and Spencer) to a special unit within No.10. The creation of an 'Efficiency Unit', however, had been first conceived within the Service in 1977 and Rayner himself had previously been a member not just of Heath's Business Team but also of the Pay Research Board, charged with ensuring the integrity of wage negotiations under Labour. Consequently it was not until both sides had fought themselves to the brink of mutual exhaustion during a 21-week national strike and the subsequent closure of the Civil Service Department (created, at the suggestion of Fulton, to drive through the second wave of modernisation) that the 'old order' came to a distinct end. Hence the logic of completing this volume in 1981 rather than 1979.

INTRODUCTION

The final 'framework' is thematic rather than chronological. It is that, important though the Civil Service may be in its own right, it should always be seen – and can only ever be fully understood – as an exemplar of wider forces. Britain was never unique. After the mid-1960s, for example, each Western country was racked by the problem of how – in an increasingly frenzied and then a decreasingly consensual world – political direction could be sustained at the centre of government. Simultaneously, each was striving to determine how, in the absence of the profit motive, managerial efficiency could be sustained in organisations that dwarfed the largest company in the private sector. The need for, and course of, modernisation in the 1960s and 1970s should thus be regarded not as a peculiar cause for national mortification but as a universal challenge. Within Britain, moreover, reform was heavily influenced by changing management fashion within the private sector; changing concepts about the proper role of the state amongst politicians, taxpayers and 'experts' (notably economists); and increasing militancy throughout the whole workforce. The Civil Service is best seen as a reflection of, and not as a scapegoat for the failure swiftly to resolve, these wider challenges.

Bias

Official history in the past has been accused of bias – 'official but not history', in Basil Liddell Hart's tart phrase – and, given the circumstances under which it was commissioned, this History might well be perceived as a pre-emptive case for the defence. To deny the potential for bias would be as foolish as to defend, in the past, the 'value-free' nature of the 'national interest' as conceived by senior officials.[26] This is not least because all official historians are trusted to work within the Official Secrets Act. Moreover, they are guided by a synopsis approved by an official Cabinet Committee, their progress is monitored by an official Project Board and their final manuscript is vetted before publication. More subtly, but arguably of even greater importance, they also work almost exclusively on government records and are thus exposed to the risk of being 'captured' by the assumptions permeating those records.

Suspicions of bias, however, are somewhat exaggerated. 'Capture', for example, is an occupational hazard not unique to official historians, but common to any researcher working on a single large body of material. This was demonstrated, in relation to official records, in 1967 when there was a sudden reduction from 50 to 30 years in the embargo on their release. The quality of scholarship, it is widely acknowledged, temporarily declined because, confronted by this mass of new documentation, it became all too easy to conclude that 'government did all that could be reasonably have been expected of it within the constraints of the time'.[27] To the benefit of the profession as a whole, official history could and should pre-empt such problems by ensuring, as Hancock wished, the early release of a 'quarry of information' and thereby permitting a more gradual acclimatisation. Moreover, particularly in relation to this History, the dual risk of bias and 'capture' is reduced, by the pre-existence of first and second 'drafts of history' composed by investigative journalists and social scientists.[28] They provide an effective check on the validity of its findings. In any case, if this History was intended to be a pre-emptive strike, on whose behalf would this first volume be launched: the pre-1981 generation of officials or their successors, who are amongst its foremost critics? Traditional charges of bias are, therefore, largely outdated. The real challenge to an official historian's integrity lies rather in the location of the most relevant data amongst so large an accumulation of files.

The prime objective of this History, it therefore bears repeating, is not to stifle but to stimulate informed and independent debate. It is also to provide an historical context which will encourage and assist others (particularly past officials, with their inside knowledge) to write more detailed case studies which will either refine or refute its generalities. No historian should rest easy until his or her work has become not the 'last word' but the source of its own obsolescence.

Part 1

THE LEGACY

1

THE NORTHCOTE-TREVELYAN REPORT AND THE EVOLUTION OF THE CIVIL SERVICE, 1854–1916

1.1 Introduction

The reform of the Civil Service in the last third of the twentieth century was dominated by two reports: the Report of the Fulton Committee, published in 1968, and *Improving Management in Government: the Next Steps*, published in 1988. A third report, however, casts a long shadow over this period: the Northcote-Trevelyan Report (or more fully the *Report on the Organisation of the Permanent Civil Service*) published in 1854. The perceived administrative inadequacies of the 1960s were widely accredited to its malign influence. The opening paragraph of the Fulton Report, for example, notoriously asserted:

> The Home Civil Service today is still fundamentally the product of the nineteenth-century philosophy of the Northcote-Trevelyan Report. The tasks it faces are those of the second half of the twentieth century. This is what we have found; it is what we want to remedy.[1]

In direct contrast, the Report was simultaneously perceived – not least by Lord Simey in his formal reservation to Fulton – to have laid the foundations for the high international standing which the Service had long enjoyed. Just as being 'one of us' became the test used by Mrs Thatcher to judge political soundness, so being a 'Northcote-Trevelyan man' [sic] was, and continues to be, the measure of administrative integrity and impartiality.

This chapter briefly looks at the gestation and nature of the Northcote-Trevelyan Report, and its implementation up to 1916. Its popular and academic reputation is mixed. For some it remains 'one of the great state papers of the nineteenth century'; and its 'vision in the middle of the nineteenth century of the sort of civil Service' needed in the twentieth was 'one of the most fortunate things in the history of British government'. Detailed historical research, however, has injected an element of caution. As has been argued, for instance, the Report was not a blueprint for reform. The rhetorical reference to it in the Fulton Report . . . proves on closer examination to be wholly misleading (unless we detach the 'philosophy' of Northcote and Trevelyan entirely from their actual proposals). The Civil Service in the 1960s was the product of many things, but very little of it can be traced clearly and directly back to the report of 1854.[2]

What is myth and what reality? Historically, how far was the Report moulded by the peculiar social and political pressures of its times? How did other countries respond to similar pressures? How were the Report's recommendations, to the extent that they were implemented, reconciled with issues which it did not explicitly address, such as ministerial accountability to Parliament? More generally, as an initiative internal to the Civil Service (like *Next Steps*), does the Report provide any insight into how to effect administrative reform? These questions will be addressed by looking at the implementation of the Report's specific recommendations first in detail, then in their historical and comparative context, and finally in the light of the evolution of the Service as a whole.

1.2 The Northcote-Trevelyan Report and its implementation

The Northcote-Trevelyan Report was brief and blunt. It ran, in its original, to only 23 quarto pages and like Fulton it was gratuitously offensive. Just as officials were caricatured in the 1960s for being wedded to the 'obsolete cult' of the 'amateur' before belated reference was made to the 'Service's very considerable strengths', so in the 1850s the Civil Service was condemned as a magnet for the 'unambitious, and the indolent or incapable' before any acknowledgement was made of 'numerous honourable exceptions'. The litany of failings would not have appeared wholly out of place in the populist campaign against the Service in the 1970s:

> Those whose abilities do not warrant an expectation that they will succeed in the open professions, where they must encounter the competition of their contemporaries, and those whom indolence of temperament, or physical infirmities unfit for active exertions, are placed in the Civil Service, where they obtain an honourable livelihood with little labour, and with no risk; where their success depends on their avoiding any flagrant misconduct, and attending with moderate regularity to routine duties; and in which they are secured against the ordinary consequences of old age, or failing health.[3]

The object of the Report was to remedy this situation by identifying 'the best method of providing [the Service] with a supply of good men, and of making the most of them after they had been admitted'. Currently 'no pains' were taken to appoint 'good men', or to train and motivate them. Indeed, perverse incentives were rife. Promotion was determined by seniority and discipline was lax, so officials knew that 'if they work hard, it will not advance them – if they waste their time in idleness, it will not keep them back'. Hence the Report sought to establish the principle that:

> the public Service should be carried on by admission into its lowest ranks of a carefully selected body of young men, who should be employed from the first on work suited to their capabilities and their education, and should be made constantly to feel that their promotion and future prospects depend entirely on the industry and ability with which they discharge their duties, that with average abilities and reasonable application they may look forward confidently to a certain provision for their lives, that with superior powers they may rationally hope to attain to the highest prizes in the Service, while if they prove decidedly incompetent, or incurably indolent, they must expect to be removed from it.[4]

To realise this ideal, three explicit recommendations were advanced: recruitment by a 'proper system of examination', promotion by merit and the greater unification of the Service. Implicit in the first recommendation was a fourth: a clear distinction should be made between 'intellectual' and 'mechanical' labour.

The examination system should recognise this distinction by generally examining candidates for the 'superior situations' typically between the ages of 19 and 25, and those for the 'inferior offices' between 17 and 21.

What was remarkable about this analysis was not so much its boldness as its narrowness. Wholly unaddressed, for example, were issues such as the political role of officials in relation to both Ministers and the public – or, in other words, the key constitutional issues of ministerial responsibility and official anonymity. These were not just critical for the future. They had already been raised in acute form by, for example, the transformation in 1847 of the Poor Law Commission into the Poor Law Board (to reassert Parliamentary control over policy) and in 1854 by the dismissal of the outspoken Edwin Chadwick from the General Health Board. Equally remarkable for a report widely held to mark an historic watershed in the public administration of Britain, and of the Western world, was its tardy and incomplete implementation. There was, as recommended, no Act of Parliament to implement its proposals and little progress was made until 1870. Even then reform was disjointed and largely surreptitious. It was impelled by undebated Orders in Council, Treasury minutes and a series of public enquiries held not so much to honour the Northcote-Trevelyan ideal but in response to current political pressures: demands for greater economy, discontent within the Service and the relentless growth of government. Indeed, as late as the 1912–14 MacDonnell Royal Commission on the Civil Service, the ideal of 'unity' remained as unwelcome a prospect as ever for many senior officials. Even more seriously, the major expansion of government resulting from new welfare legislation had brought into question the very principle of open competition.

The narrowness of the Report will be examined in Chapter 1.3. This section concentrates on the substance and partial implementation of Northcote-Trevelyan's four principal proposals.

1.2.1 Open competition

The most effective way to end 'the evils of patronage' and thus administrative inefficiency was identified by the Report to be competitive literary examinations, overseen by a Central Board and held at fixed times. For entry into 'superior positions', which required 'intellectual' labour, there was to be a national examination reflecting the highest academic levels. However, it should *not* necessarily 'exclude some exercises directly bearing on official duties'. Subjects such as history, jurisprudence, political economy and geography should be included as well as the 'staples of classics and mathematics'. This would ensure that width and not just depth of knowledge was tested so that 'the greatest and *most varied* amount of talent' would be attracted to the Service. For entry into the 'lower class of appointment', which only required 'mechanical' labour, there was to be a series of district examinations. Their nature was unspecified.[5]

A central board, in the form of the Civil Service Commission, was almost immediately established. It was not, however, established in the spirit intended. Political opposition thwarted the drafting, let alone the passage, of the proposed Civil Service Act to implement the Report. It also contributed to a change in government. Reform was therefore effectively stalled until further evidence of maladministration during the Crimean war led to the formation of the Administrative Reform Association which demanded *inter alia* that, in the appointment of officials, patronage should be replaced by a test of practical, not literary, skills. It was to forestall just such a calamity that the Commission was established in 1855.

The Commission was charged, as the Report wished, with the certification of the age, health, moral character and 'requisite knowledge' of all entrants to the Service. No-one could be employed without such a certificate. There was to be, however, no distinction between recruitment to 'intellectual' and 'mechanical' work, no national or district examinations and no open competition. Candidates could still be nominated by senior politicians or officials and their 'knowledge' tested by an examination jointly set for the occasion by the Commission and the relevant department. There need only be a single candidate although a limited competition between three or so nominees increasingly became the norm. Even this, however, represented little progress since the favoured candidate was often pitched against two of Hayter's 'idiots' (candidates of somewhat limited ability of whom one chief whip, Sir William Hayter, appeared to have a bottomless supply). The initial impact of the Commission was therefore limited. Of the 9826 recruits to the Service between 1855 and 1868, 70 per cent were appointed after no competition, 2763 after limited competition and only 28 as the result of open competition.[6]

The situation finally changed in 1870 when Gladstone as Prime Minister, and more importantly Robert Lowe as Chancellor of the Exchequer, secured by Order in Council the establishment of a national open competition. It was divided into two 'schemes', respectively for graduates and school leavers, and so appeared to consummate the Northcote-Trevelyan ideal. Accordingly 1870 has been conventionally acclaimed as the 'crucial year for enduring Civil Service reform'.[7] The first series of examinations was held in 1871–2, when there were 142 candidates for 10 Class I vacancies and 732 candidates for 95 Class II posts.[8] Appearances, however, can be deceptive. Open competition in fact continued to remain so limited that the MacDonnell Commission on the Civil Service found that only one-third of the 60,000 appointments made before 1910, which fell within its remit, had been so recruited.[9] Why was this?

The majority of exempted posts had no policy implications, although they did reveal the continued existence of widespread patronage. They were either peripheral or very junior posts. Hence until 1885 favoured local MPs were invited to nominate sub-postmasters when a vacancy occurred within the 17,000 strong national network; and until 1912 the Treasury reserved the right to appoint its own nominees as messengers, porters and cleaners within all the revenue departments and national galleries.[10] However, a significant number of appointments to senior posts were also exempted from open competition. This did not necessarily offend Northcote-Trevelyan principles. The Report itself had accepted that senior policy advisers to Ministers (then termed 'staff appointments') should be so exempt, as should posts which required 'special talents and attainments' (such as factory and school inspectors) – although its implicit hope, particularly in relation to 'staff appointments', was that fewer 'strangers' would be appointed. Acts of pure political patronage did duly cease in the 1880s – with, ironically, two of the last practitioners being Northcote himself (who secured a post for his son) and Gladstone (who nominated two of his private secretaries as heads of departments).[11] Nevertheless an increasing number of senior advisers continued to be recruited under various dispensations which exempted from open competition those whose qualifications were 'wholly or in part professional or otherwise peculiar and not ordinarily to be acquired in the Civil Service'.[12] The principal reason for this was a further rapid expansion of government after 1880, particularly into new areas of social policy.

The Board of Trade provides a prime example. It acted as a magnet for social reform after 1880 culminating after 1908, initially under the presidency of Winston Churchill, with the introduction *inter alia* of labour exchanges, unemployment insurance and minimum wages. During this time it established such a tradition of appointing mature experts to senior posts that, of the 13 senior officials advising Churchill on labour policy, none had been recruited by open competition.[13] This tradition was maintained, and typified by, the recruitment of William Beveridge in 1908. He had an unparalleled academic knowledge of, and practice in running, labour exchanges. He had accordingly given detailed evidence to the Royal Commission on the Poor Law and expert advice to the Board on the establishment of a national system. When such a system became a serious possibility Churchill was advised by Sidney and Beatrice Webb (who had already introduced the two) that 'if you are going to deal with unemployment you must have the boy

Beveridge'. A conference was duly held at the Board and Churchill immediately decided to take the Webbs' advice. Beveridge was summoned to the Board to name his terms and the appointment made the following day.[14]

When the first complement of exchange staff was recruited, open competition based on literary exams was similarly waived – with the result, to the disgust of Civil Service staff associations, that three times as many manual workers as serving officials were recruited as exchange managers. The foremost method was a competitive interview with, as a guard against charges of patronage, the First Civil Service Commissioner overseeing the whole process. Churchill, however, decided to preside himself over the appointment of the twelve most senior executive officials (the divisional officers). The safeguard against accusations of patronage was now the requirement, devised by Beveridge in two hours, that each candidate draft a reply to an irate employer. The successful candidates included two trade unionists, two soldiers and a former American gold speculator who claimed to have 'run a labour exchange in Chicago, with a revolver provided as part of the office equipment'. The star, however, was J. B. Adams, Shackleton's second in command in the expedition to the South Pole. He provided the winning answer to Beveridge's test, by inviting the employer to lunch. He also held Churchill in thrall during the interview by tales of his naval exploits. This was adjudged to compensate for his somewhat modest specialist knowledge. When asked his opinion of the Labour Exchange Act, for example, he reputedly replied : 'couldn't understand a word, mate'; and when further asked about what had impressed him most about Beveridge's recently published book on unemployment, he replied 'the price'.[15] Although largely vindicated by its results, this selection process was hardly more rigorous than those pilloried in the 1850s.

Why was there such resistance to open competition both before and after 1870? There were three principal reasons. The first, as with the overall rejection of the Report, was personal: Trevelyan's abrasiveness and the anger generated by his caricature of the existing Service.[16] More substantially, patronage had – and was widely seen at the time to have – many virtues. It was an integral part of the social and political system. Open competition, for instance, could reasonably be described to Queen Victoria as 'republican' because it threatened the traditional means by which the Crown and the aristocracy exercised power. More commonly, electoral and parliamentary politics were both heavily dependent upon the distribution of salaried posts as indeed was family welfare. Could parliamentary government be continued, Sir James Graham asked Gladstone 'on such principles of purity'?[17] Graham was himself a progressive minister and his objection raised the additional point that patronage could actually promote administrative efficiency. It was flexible and could, and had, enabled many talented people speedily to reach influential positions. Trevelyan himself, after all, had been nominated for a place at Haileybury, where he received the necessary training for his early career in India. He had then been appointed as administrative head of the Treasury in 1840, at the age of 32, through the patronage of the Chancellor of the Exchequer and seemingly his brother-in-law, Thomas Macaulay, who was in the Cabinet. Finally, it was argued rather more contentiously that, because of the need to sustain family honour, patronage assured the good moral character and ability of the vast majority of recruits. The refusal by the Civil Service Commission in its first year to certify 309 of 1078 nominations suggests that, at certain levels within the Service at least, such faith was unfounded.[18]

The third reason for resistance to open competition was the proposed examination system and in particular its literary nature. Cramming and pedantry, it was commonly feared in the 1850s, would replace 'character' and the 'moral qualifications' which were 'more important than the intellectual ones'.[19] Placing graduates in government was also as inappropriate as 'putting racehorses to the plough'. Their 'gifts', as Sir James Stephen the highly efficient head of the Colonial Office argued, would be 'ill-suited and even inconvenient to one who is entombed for life as a clerk in a Public Office'. It was here that arguably the prescience of the Northcote-Trevelyan Report was demonstrated because, despite the reservations of contemporaries, the later growth of government undoubtedly did require officials of such intellectual capacity.

What, however, of the nature of the proposed examinations? Edwin Chadwick immediately challenged their predominantly literary nature on the grounds that it would admit 'the gentleman who is, par excellence, an instructor in the abstract sciences and who [has written] articles in the Reviews to show the impracticality of steam navigation across the Atlantic' whilst 'it would . . . exclude those who accomplished the feat'. A similar concern pervaded the Edwardian Board of Trade.[20] It clearly favoured those who wrote learned articles, but the knowledge displayed had to be 'useful' and to be tempered with practical experience. In short, it sought to appoint officials who would be 'problem' rather then 'career' orientated. The latter was an occupational hazard of an exclusive graduate entry – and one realised, for example, in the Victorian Home Office where, as admitted by its historian, 'many clerks viewed their bureaucratic role as a means of securing professional status, a gentlemanly life-style and an entree to the London season'. The Board of Trade did not despise such collegiality but it had to be in a good cause. As its Permanent Secretary, Llewellyn Smith, informed the MacDonnell Commission:

> key posts should not be filled by open competition but be retained for exceptional men attracted by a definite prospect of congenial work of sufficient scope, but not attracted by so nebulous a thing as the Civil Service as a whole.[21]

Llewellyn Smith's evidence to the MacDonnell Commission was not wholly inimical to the Northcote-Trevelyan ideal. Whether through conviction or circumspection, he stressed the need for 'all-round' men (or generalists) in most senior posts. Like the Report, he also considered their recruitment would be discouraged were too many of such posts filled other than by open competition.[22] Nevertheless, historic practice within his department – and the enervation common to its fellow social Service departments – directly challenged both the implementation and, more importantly, the underlying rationale of the Report.

1.2.2 The division of labour

A division between 'intellectual' and 'mechanical' labour was Trevelyan's own principal objective.[23] He had advocated it before the House of Commons' Select Committee on Miscellaneous Expenditure, which started the reform process in 1848. He also pressed for it with rather more success during the Treasury's ensuing *ad hoc* investigations into individual departments.

Trevelyan's goals were twofold: greater efficiency and economy. At the time, all clerks entered departments at the same level and spent their early years, copying, dispatching and filing letters or memoranda from the fair copies passed down to them by their superiors. On the retirement of a senior clerk, a junior one might aspire to make these fair copies himself. Then, on further promotion, he might actually minute the senior 'staff' officials who alone took decisions with Ministers. Such 'staff' officials were typically appointed from outside the Service. The separation of copying ('mechanical') from minuting ('intellectual' labour), so Trevelyan reasoned, would increase *efficiency* in two ways. It would both attract to the Service 'the most promising young men of their day' and ensure that they were not demoralised, and their talent thereby wasted, by stupefying routine. Simultaneously it would be *economic* as departments could be more systematically structured and work allocated to the lowest, and cheapest, level appropriate.

Such a division was not practicable until the introduction of two distinct entry examinations in 1870. Thereafter, it was warmly embraced by successive public enquiries. The Playfair Commission, reporting in 1875, recommended a higher and lower division underpinned by a subsidiary class of temporary boy copyist. A Service-wide 'lower' division was duly established in 1876. Then the Ridley Commission, reporting in 1890, proposed a clearer distinction between a 'first' and 'second' division again underpinned by a temporary class of copyists. Standardised rates of pay and working conditions were immediately announced for the 'second' division; and those whose salaries were 'in excess of those of the second division' were increasingly subject to standardisation, although they resisted incorporation into a 'first' division until after the First World War.[24] Despite such reports and reforms, however, an uncontroversial distinction between 'intellectual' and 'mechanical' labour still remained elusive. Accordingly, the 1912–15 MacDonnell Commission sought yet another restructuring of officials into three permanent classes: the administrative, senior clerical and junior clerical, recruited respectively after university graduation and at the ages of 18 and 16. Why did an effective division of labour prove so elusive?

There were both short-term and long-term reasons. In the short run, as with the attempt to end patronage, it represented too revolutionary a change. Departments depended on the expertise of long-serving clerks who had started at the bottom – not just to remember precedents but also to locate relevant files. Career prospects for existing staff were also based on the principle of seniority, which could not be arbitrarily rescinded. Change, therefore, could be depicted as both injurious and unjust.[25] More fundamentally, there was also found to be no logical division – except at the extremes – between 'intellectual' and 'mechanical' labour. The ideal scheme introduced in the Treasury by Trevelyan in 1853, for example, was soon abandoned; and the distinction became even more blurred after 1870 when, to economise, the Treasury strove to drive responsibility as far as possible down the departmental hierarchy. The Treasury's action was in defiance of Northcote-Trevelyan. It had warned that any division of labour depended for success 'more upon the discretion and management of the chiefs of offices . . . than upon any general regulations that could be made by a central authority'. Confidence was also later expressed that those chiefs would 'take care not to throw upon the supplementary clerks such duties as are likely to make them the most efficient members of the office and, at the same time, debar them from promotion'.[26] Both caveats were ignored. Under Treasury pressure, departments allocated work to both second division and temporary 'assistant' clerks which resulted in their undertaking, on poorer pay and conditions, work remarkably similar to that of their supposed superiors.[27]

The resulting discontent, rather than any positive drive to implement Northcote-Trevelyan, was the direct reason for the successive appointment of the Playfair, Ridley and MacDonnell Commissions. It also illustrated a perverse consequence of attempted reform after 1870: the creation of a unified 'second' division and an assistant clerks grade both of whose members used their collective strength, especially in the increasing militancy of the Edwardian period, to vent common grievances. These included not just deteriorating pay and conditions but also the hypocrisy behind the claim that the Service had become 'open' and 'united'. As the Second Division Clerks' Association argued, for instance, the two-tier examination system – reinforced by the convention that promotion from the second division should be exceptional (see section 1.2.3) – imposed a rigid horizontal barrier throughout the Service. Where was 'unity'? Moreover, when appointments were made to Class I posts, why should practical departmental experience gained by school-leavers after 18 not be equated to the purely academic learning acquired by graduates? How was competition genuinely 'open'? Older assistant clerks were also angered that access to permanent appointments was through an examination system which, on grounds of age, largely precluded them.

The cause of these grievances, of course, was that a clear educational and social divide *was* being deliberately manufactured between the two, or rather three, levels – as Northcote-Trevelyan had intended. Before MacDonnell, the Civil Service Commission advocated 'the broad principle of gathering the natural fruits of the educational system of the country in its various stages as they mature'; and MacDonnell duly constructed its proposed classes around the three principal ages at which education was completed.[28] This made a certain social sense, with the structure of classes in the Service coming to reflect Britain's class structure. It made rather less sense to the rational organisation and efficiency of government departments.

1.2.3 *Promotion by merit*

Once Civil Servants had been scientifically recruited and organised, Northcote-Trevelyan sought to 'encourage industry and foster merit'. This could be achieved by 'teaching all public servants to look forward to promotion according to their deserts, and to expect the highest prizes in the Service if they can qualify themselves for them'.[29]

In the lower divisions, in particular, the right to automatic salary increments and promotion by seniority was to be qualified. Increments were to be made subject to annual reports; and promotion was to depend on a report to the minister detailing the qualities of all potential candidates. Duplicates of such reports were to be held by the Central Examination Board. Such transparency was required because (as with performance-related pay after 1990) the fear was that such promotion by 'merit' would foster favouritism. Further spurs to 'industry and merit' were identified to be 'good Service pensions and honorary distinctions' as well as promotion between, as well as within, departments.

Many of these proposals were realised, at least in principle. Personnel reports were supplied to the Civil Service Commission – although how far the practice of either automatic increments or promotion by seniority was actually modified is debatable.[30] The 1859 Superannuation Act introduced consistent and non-contributory pensions. Permanent Secretaries also started to be knighted in the 1860s, whilst other ranks received lesser honours after the 1880s.

Promotion between departments and divisions, however, remained limited. Northcote-Trevelyan had waxed lyrical about the promotion of career officials in 'superior situations' to 'staff appointments' (such as the post of Permanent Secretary) conventionally reserved for outsiders. The Report, for example, expressed the hope 'that in future, if any staff appointment falls vacant in an office in which there is a deserving clerk well qualified to fill it, his claims will not be passed over in favour of a stranger'. Such a clerk might even be from another department who could then be replaced, on promotion, by a more junior clerk from a third department. This would have the double advantage of 'encouraging public servants, and at the same time introducing fresh blood into an office'.[31]

The number of career officials reaching the top did duly increase although, as the example of the Edwardian Board of Trade demonstrates, this was – with good reason – not universal. Sir Edward Troup, for instance, was the first 'open competition' entrant (and non-barrister) to become Permanent Under Secretary of the highly conservative Home Office in 1908. His, however, was an internal appointment; and this was consistent with the fact that promotion between departments at the highest level did not occur before the First World War. At other levels it was also rare. Equally rare, as the Second Division Clerks' Association rightly noted, was promotion between divisions. Between 1902 and 1911, for example, only eighteen per cent of the 248 recruits into 'Class 1' posts were from the Second Division.[32] This was *prime facie* evidence that the principle of promotion by merit was far from being genuinely accepted.

If merit was not fully fostered, neither apparently was industry. The lax habits of the unreformed Civil Service were immortalised by Trollope's Department of Internal Navigation. As late as the 1890s, however, habits seem to have changed little. According to one witness, for example, staff at the modernised Home Office registry 'used to leave the Office in mid-morning and go for a drink in the "Red Lion". The practice grew to such proportions that on occasion [the superintendent] had to send a messenger to the "Red Lion" to request the gentlemen of the Home Office registry to be kind enough to return and do some work'. The exodus was eventually halted, but only on the understanding that drink could be brought in from the 'Red Lion'.[33]

1.2.4 Unification of the Service

Northcote-Trevelyan's final objective was to end the 'fragmentary character of the Service'. Disunity, it was argued, reduced efficiency in three ways. It encouraged 'the growth of narrow views and departmental prejudices'. It discouraged ambition by limiting an individual's promotion prospects to one department. It also impeded the transfer of resources from overmanned to overstretched departments. The remedies were uniform entry qualifications; the promotion of those engaged in intellectual work to any 'staff' position within the Service; and the transferability of 'lower ranks' between departments.[34]

The establishment of the Civil Service Commission laid the basis for unification. Indeed, it has even been claimed that 'the British civil service dates from 1855'.[35] It gradually introduced more uniform entrance requirements. After 1876 it also oversaw the transfer between departments of an increasing number of 'lower' or 'second division' clerks – amounting to some 489 in 1893. Most importantly, perhaps, its very name gave substance to Trevelyan's aspiration that unity would be advanced by the establishment of an explicit distinction between those paid by the state who had to resign on a change of government and those who did not – or, in the contemporary phrase, between the 'parliamentary and permanent Civil Service'.[36] The use of the term 'permanent Civil Service' by Northcote-Trevelyan (and later of the term 'Civil Service' by Playfair) was indeed in many ways provocative. Far more common at the time were the terms 'public services' or, as employed as late as the 1886–90 Ridley Commission, 'civil establishments'. Both presumed far less unity; and before the MacDonnell Commission a senior official could even object that 'there was no such single thing as the Civil Service'.[37] The Civil Service Commission, by its institutional presence and name, nevertheless marked a genuine watershed in British public administration because it embodied the *belief* that a unified Service was both desirable and practical.

The reality of unity, however, took much longer to materialise – as is apparent from the continuing intensity of departmentalism and the relative absence before 1916 of transferability among more senior officials. The principal impediment was the Treasury, which ironically had the power and seemingly the motive to realise it. Before 1850 it had been made answerable to Parliament for the level of departmental estimates and so it had acquired the right to be consulted on any proposed increase in expenditure. In consequence, Gladstone in the minute setting up Northcote-Trevelyan could describe it as 'the central office for the revision of public establishments'; and in 1872 Lowe had further and, more controversially, alluded to its Permanent Secretary as being 'at the head of the Civil Service'.[38] Each of the three public commissions advocated greater Treasury control over establishment issues; and, after Ridley, a Permanent Consultative Committee was even established briefly to facilitate such control in the same way as the Comptroller and Auditor-General helped to control expenditure. Finally, a flow of Treasury minutes, eventually consolidated by an Order in Council in 1910, confirmed the Treasury to be the effective authority for promulgating and monitoring a common code of practice for all Civil Servants.

However, despite the odd flirtation, Treasury officials declined actively to pursue unity. It was dismissed as both 'undesirable and unattainable in practice'.[39] It was undesirable because the Treasury's first concern was economy. Greater unity, so officials feared, would lead to a levelling-up of pay and conditions, and hence greater expense. Their alternative strategy for restraining expenditure was one of divide and rule, embellished by delay and obscurantism; and this would also be jeopardised by clear principles and uniform procedures. Unification was equally deemed unattainable because of the Treasury's lack of formal powers, particularly over such long-established departments as the Home Office and War Office which both openly regarded the Treasury as no more than *primus inter pares*. As the Treasury's Permanent Secretary minuted in 1884:

> The only mode at present by which uniformity can be introduced into any of the details of the Civil Service is by Order in Council, and even after such an Order has been agreed by the Cabinet (which is necessary if it is to bind Ministers and others at the head of Departments) there is no security for its observance, unless it involves some payment which must be audited by the Comptroller and Auditor General. Probably there are many details connected with the organization of the Civil Service which the Treasury might usefully be empowered to regulate. But at present the Treasury has no such authority and its *advice* has a very limited operation against departmental interest or amour propre.[40]

Such reasoning, however, was disingenuous. There was no reason why, supported by three public commissions, the Treasury should not have sought greater powers. More importantly, existing ones could have been exercised in a manner designed to foster, and not destroy, mutual trust and understanding. The precedent existed in the departmental committees of inquiry, extensively used by Trevelyan between 1848 and 1859, which had channelled even his notorious abrasiveness into constructive collaboration.[41] The consequence of Treasury action, or rather inaction, was the absence of a genuine and generous vision that could have tempered vested interests at the highest level. Indeed it was the departmental interest of the Treasury itself which impeded unification.

There was, however, one area other than the Civil Service Commission where unification proceeded apace, not least because it was consistent with vested interest. This was within the 'lower' or 'second' division. In the 1850s it was not just Trevelyan who had used the term 'Civil Service' for aspirational purposes. It was also junior clerks. They founded the *Civil Service Gazette* in January 1853, which quickly acquired a circulation of almost 75,000. It was but one expression of an increasing sense of mutuality, which also took the form of sports and social clubs, a volunteer corps and a co-operative society. Their explicit objective was to transform 'a concourse of atoms' into a 'living mass with a giant's power' so that the public would 'know and properly estimate their servants'.[42] Hence they favoured Service-wide classes, transferability between departments and uniform rates of pay and conditions.

At the same time, however, they actively opposed two other means by which Northcote-Trevelyan had hoped to attain unification: promotion by merit and competitive literary examinations. The former was rejected because (unlike automatic promotion by seniority) it raised the danger of favouritism. The latter was opposed because in practice such exams restricted promotion for those recruited at 18. This particular objection in fact exposed an unwitting – or perhaps witting – flaw in the Report's logic. Departmentalism (which it decried) may well have raised *vertical* barriers to unification but, as suggested earlier, examinations and division of labour (which it championed) erected equally powerful *horizontal* barriers.

1.3 The historical and comparative context

The nature of both the Northcote-Trevelyan Report and its implementation can be fully understood only in its broad historical and comparative context. Equally it is only in this context that balanced conclusions can be reached about the long-term significance of the Report's proposals (as opposed to those retrospectively ascribed to it). Three issues of particular importance will be examined here. First, the Report was the product of a period of exceptional political interest in administrative reform, unequalled in peacetime until the 1960s. Second, its implementation was shaped by changes in fundamental attitudes towards the role of government, which underpinned two major bursts of government expansion in the 1840s and after the 1880s. Finally, both the Report and its implementation were – and were seen to be – of great international significance because Britain was the first country to confront the political and social, and thus administrative, consequences of 'modernisation' or, more prosaically, industrialisation and mass urbanisation. Uniquely, it did so at a time when the conventions of absolutism, common to all European states, had been replaced by those of Parliamentary government.

1.3.1 The political imperative of administrative reform

The exceptional interest in administrative reform was personified by the Chancellors of the Exchequer who commissioned the Report and introduced open competition: Gladstone and Robert Lowe.[43] Both were passionately committed to the purification and thereby the legitimisation of government. Since Burke's speech in 1780 on 'economical reform' (inspired by the mismanagement of the American colonies) central government had been persistently attacked for being corrupt, inefficient and expensive; and both were impatient to complete the subsequent, attenuated process of reform. In consequence, the Report's drive finally to eliminate patronage was designed to silence three particular sets of critics: those who wanted to end corrupt aristocratic influence (such as the Chartists), those who sought enhanced efficiency (such as the Benthamites) and those who desired greater economy (such as entrepreneurs). Principled disinterest and a public service ethos were to become the accepted and approved hallmarks of public administration.

However, there were two other major objectives. As admitted at the time and frequently noted since, administrative reform was designed not just to legitimise government but also 'as a means of extending, confirming, cleansing and legimitizing' the current ruling elite.[44] Hence the Report's recommendation that recruitment to 'superior positions' should be almost exclusively by literary examination at the age of 21. This deliberately privileged those classes whose sons traditionally attended university. Equally it deliberately excluded both late entrants with business experience (as championed by the Administrative Reform Association) and those who could not aspire to a university education. Gladstone explicitly confirmed that his aim was 'to strengthen and multiply the ties between the higher classes and the possession of administrative power'.[45] Trevelyan concurred; and he also retrospectively admitted an open class bias by revealing that 'the revolutionary period of 1848 gave us a shake, and created a disposition to put our house in order'. Equally, in 1870 Lowe – despite his professed commitment to meritocracy – vehemently defended an 'open' examination system and a strict division of labour which, taken together, effectively excluded non-graduates from Class I posts. As his biographer has concluded by so 'integrating the university-trained, intellectual elite within the Civil Service, Lowe created a safeguard against egalitarianism. It was to prove far more durable than any fancy franchise or constitutional barrier'. Reform, in brief, was deliberately designed to be socially exclusive not inclusive.

The second underlying objective was reform of the education system. After 1850 written examinations were introduced into universities and elementary schools to ensure greater scholastic rigour; and it became an article of faith that such examinations would ensure the best recruits, in terms of ability and personality, for both 'intellectual' and 'mechanical' work. For the graduate, for instance, intellectual attainment was adjudged the best 'moral test' on the grounds that 'the perseverance and self-discipline necessary for the acquirement of any considerable knowledge are a great security that a young man has not led a dissolute life'. Equally, for the school-leaver, competitive entry examinations were seen as an ideal means to test and reinforce character. Successful candidates, so it was argued, would know that they had prevailed 'in an independent manner through their own merits. The sense of this cannot but induce self-respect, and diffuse a wholesome spirit among the lower no less than the higher classes of official men'.[46]

However, competitive entry examinations – especially ones of a literary nature as proposed by Northcote-Trevelyan – were designed to validate not just the choice of recruit but also the new system of liberal education. Northcote-Trevelyan, for example, recommended examination over a wide field of subjects on the grounds *inter alia* that it would 'do more to quicken the progress of our Universities ... than any legislative measure that could be adopted'.[47] Of even greater potential importance was the impact of Class II examinations (and thus entry into a relatively well-paid and secure profession) on the syllabus of elementary schools. Lowe hoped, in addition, that parents would be encouraged to keep their children at school longer as education came to be as valued in England as it was in Scotland. In other words, the exceptional interest in administrative reform between 1853 and 1870 was concerned not just with the welfare of government but also with that of the ruling elite and the educational system. When both ceased to be a political priority, as they quickly did, so too did administrative reform.

1.3.2 The changing role of government

A more persistent influence, particularly on the implementation of reform, was the growing responsibilities of central government. Before 1850 increasing *parliamentary* pressure on Ministers, which required more regular attendance in the House of Commons, had led to an explicit distinction between the work of the 'parliamentary and permanent civil service'. After 1850 the increasing pressure of *departmental* work meant that neither Ministers nor Permanent Secretaries could any longer handle all correspondence personally. Work had increasingly to be delegated and systems devised for its discharge. Britain was becoming bureaucratic in the dual sense that more decisions had to be taken by officials and an increasingly complex administrative machine was evolving with its own particular internal tensions. The number of non-industrial Civil Servants indeed almost trebled between 1851 and 1901 from approximately 40,000 to 116,000 and, as a result of the Liberal welfare reforms, more than doubled again to some 281,000 by 1914. So rapid an expansion, as has been seen, frustrated Northcote-Trevelyan's plan for a clear division of labour (illustrated by the growth of 'intermediary' classes) and the eradication of temporary employment. It also led to the Playfair, Ridley and MacDonnell inquiries turning inward to examine the organisation of the Service rather than broader constitutional issues.

To an extent administrative expansion was self-generating, as suggested by the famous MacDonagh model of government growth which identified five discrete stages: the enactment of a law to prohibit an 'intolerable evil'; the appointment of inspectors and then a central agency to enforce it; the refinement of the law in the light of accumulated expertise; and finally the provision to officials of discretionary powers to ensure more effective enforcement.[48] Not all administrative growth, however, conformed to this pattern. The model also cannot explain the lull in government growth in the mid-nineteenth century and its rapid expansion after the 1880s. There were in fact equally powerful influences, such as the relative power of outside vested interests and the broad philosophical principles (or at least variants of them) which shaped popular attitudes to state intervention.

In economic policy, the prevailing assumption through the nineteenth century was laissez-faire. This inevitably restricted government growth, not least because Treasury officials remained zealously committed to it and, in particular, the principles underlying Gladstone's iconic 1854 budget: the minimisation of government expenditure (to promote *inter alia* the moral virtue of thrift) and the equal sharing of the tax burden (to prevent the political manipulation of competing class interests). This continuing commitment largely explains, and justifies, their innate hostility to any increase in administrative costs particularly when, after 1880, they were incurred to meet particular needs of new working-class voters.

In social policy, the situation was more complex. Before 1854, a combination of administrative reform and innovation could satisfy the conflicting demands of both the entrepreneurial fraction of the emerging middle class (which demanded economy) and its professional fraction (which championed efficiency). The prevailing utilitarian, or Benthamite, philosophy was equally nuanced. State intervention in general was to be abhorred but, as was famously recognised, 'whenever, by the evil thus produced, greater evil is excluded, the balance takes the nature, shape and name of good and government is justified in the production of it'. This was the moral justification for the appointment during the 1840s of a rash of highly interventionist and outspoken officials, such as Horner, Chadwick and Kay-Shuttleworth, to correct proven market failures in such areas as factory working conditions, public health and education. As their ultimately frustrated ambitions demonstrated, however, such officials were soon perceived to pose a practical threat to traditional English liberty and to such 'independent' institutions as local government and voluntary organisation. Hence the rapid inculcation even into each inspectorate of the principle (still engrained in senior Civil Servants after the Second World War) that the role of central government was not to supplant but to support local and voluntary effort.

After 1880, however, such a principle had itself to be qualified. There were many reasons: further evidence of market and voluntary failure (particularly in relation to urban living conditions and destitution);[49] the growing philosophical justification of positive state action by writers such as T.H. Green and Alfred Marshall; the political imperative to satisfy current, and anticipate future, needs of working-class voters (as expressed, particularly in relation to administrative reform, by the Fabian Society); and above all the realisation that, with the intensification of international economic and military rivalry, economy did not automatically equate to efficiency – and in particular to national efficiency. Given such swings in dominant popular assumptions about state intervention, the pace of administrative reform – regardless of the straitjacket the Treasury tried to impose – was inevitably uneven. The ultimate need to expand rapidly into new areas of expertise also exposed, as has been seen in the case of the Edwardian Board of Trade, the limitations of Northcote-Trevelyan as a blueprint for long-term reform.

1.3.3 The comparative context

The mid-nineteenth century reaction within Britain against state intervention was a unique 'liberal' response to the problems of modern society which later, somewhat ironically, underpinned the high international regard enjoyed by the Northcote-Trevelyan Report. The reaction was well summarised by a senior politician in 1850. He deplored the increasing emulation of 'Continental countries, where the government is responsible for everything [and] for whatever goes wrong the government is blamed'. Far better, he argued, was the continued decentralisation of power – and genuine decentralisation because, were independent bodies to be left in practice with little discretion, they would lose interest and 'you will have then to administer the counties by *prefets* and *sous-prefets* and the bureaucratic [machinery] which prevails abroad'.[50] His particular target was France, where the machinery of absolutist government (specifically designed to neutralise aristocratic and other sources of local power) had been adapted to post-Revolutionary society by Napoleon. Under an advisory *Conseil d'Etat* (which was the final authority on administrative law) effective power was directly transferred by Ministers to centrally appointed *prefets, sous-prefets* and finally mayors. Prussia had an equally centralised system of government, with the additional embellishments that the state bureaucracy was clearly regulated (by the General Code passed in 1794) and that all senior recruits were expected to have a university degree in 'cameralistics'. Indeed one of the most damning insults to be hurled at Chadwick prior to his resignation was that he was 'Prussian'.[51]

The fundamental difference in the approach to government, which these institutional differences embodied, was that typically in continental Europe the state was conceived as the ultimate expression of the national interest, in which individual rights were subsumed. In Britain, on the contrary, central government was simply seen as the provider of a constitutional and legal framework within which 'free born Englishmen' (and occasionally women) could exercise their rights. The distinction was well summarised by Jose Harris when she wrote of Victorian society:

> In contradistinction to much continental thought, it saw 'civil society' . . . as the highest sphere of human existence and the arena in which men enjoyed some form of absolute rights. 'The State', by contrast, was an institution of secondary importance and dubious linguistic status (Englishmen generally preferred the concept 'government') which existed mainly to serve the convenience and protect the rights of individuals in private life. . . . The corporate life of society was seen as expressed through voluntary association and the local community, rather than through the persona of the state. More extensive government was widely viewed as not merely undesirable but unnecessary, in the sense that most of the functions performed by government in other societies were in Britain performed by coteries of citizens governing themselves.[52]

The difference was due in large measure to a unique lack of tension in Britain after the seventeenth century between the exercise of power at the centre and in the locality. It was effectively enjoyed at both levels by the aristocracy. There was, therefore, no need for central *experts* to impose their authority on behalf of a king upon the '*gentleman amateur*' who was overseeing local self-government. It was this tradition which Northcote-Trevelyan, by privileging generalist graduates over specialists, was consciously designed to sustain – and did sustain even after the decline in landed wealth after the 1880s.

Legal differences were also important. The British Privy Council had a similar provenance to, for example, the French *Conseil d'Etat*; and an increasing number of outside appointments to 'staff' posts until the 1880s were barristers. The preconditions existed, therefore, for the rigorous development of administrative law and codes, as in continental Europe. Such a development was indeed championed by many Benthamites.[53] The superior status in Britain of common law, however, presented a formidable barrier against such a development. Instead, state intervention grew incrementally through such mundane devices as regulation, licences and Exchequer grants. These gave officials considerable discretion and enabled – and indeed even encouraged – them to exceed their strict statutory authority, so long as their actions were publicly acceptable. 'Confronted with a situation requiring action', as Parris has written, 'an administrator could not plead as a valid excuse for doing nothing that the law did not tell him precisely what he should do. Within the limits . . . of what the law said he must *not* do, he was expected to suggest the course which, in the light of his experience, was most conducive to the general welfare.'[54] As a result, the British official uniquely enjoyed the freedom – and personal responsibility – of being simultaneously above and beneath the law.

Within Whitehall, the regulation of official conduct was similarly entrusted to spasmodic Treasury minutes rather than a General Code, as in Prussia, because they permitted greater latitude and thus the exercise of common sense. A justification typically used in the 1850s was the hypothetical case of passive disobedience by an official. Treasury minutes, so it was argued, would give a minister the effective power (which 'opinion would support him in using') to dismiss such an official 'for misconduct, which it might be impossible for any law to define beforehand, and of which there might be no legal evidence, though there was a moral certainty'.[55] Such pragmatism, as has been seen in relation to Treasury inaction over the unification of the Civil Service, could be enervating because it created a labyrinthine set of precedents (which *might* defy common sense). Its positive purpose, however, was to maximise the autonomy and self-regulation of non-state bodies, such as local government and industry, and even of individual departments within Whitehall.

One final foreign practice which was abjured was the 'spoils system' of the USA. Again, until the final ending of political patronage, there was the potential on a change of government for the replacement of senior officials by those more sympathetic to the new ministry. Such potential, however, was never realised. In part this was because, in eighteenth-century Britain, permanent office came to be regarded as something akin to 'freehold property'. It could not lightly be taken away from the holder. Wholesale change was also less practical than in the USA because there, *inter alia,* appointees were guaranteed a fixed four or eight year term of office. By contrast a government in Britain could fall at any time.[56] The possibility of such a change, however, was only finally removed by the evolution of the conventions of political neutrality and anonymity which accompanied the implementation of the Northcote-Trevelyan Report.

1.4 The evolution of the Victorian and Edwardian Civil Service

The conventions of neutrality and anonymity were but two of the features of the British Civil Service, as it evolved between 1854 and 1916, on which the Northcote-Trevelyan Report remained largely silent. Others included the conventions of permanence and ministerial responsibility, and the practices of Treasury control and training. Any assessment of the Report as a blueprint for the nineteenth, let alone the twentieth, century must take account of such silence.

1.4.1 Conventions

The constitutional conventions of permanence, neutrality, anonymity and ministerial responsibility are interrelated. 'Permanence', as has been seen, historically had a dual meaning. It referred equally to those members of the 'parliamentary civil service' (or, in modern terminology, junior Ministers) who did not resign on a change of government and to the increasing number of 'permanent secretaries' after the 1750s who committed their whole careers to government.[57] By 1854 an effective division had been established between the two, which the Report did little to formalise. Political and administrative careers continued to an extent to be blurred. In the Home Office, for example, successive permanent under-secretaries between 1867 and 1895 had previously stood for Parliament, and a serving MP was actually selected as chief legal adviser in 1885.[58] Similarly Ministers' Private Secretaries remained exclusively political appointments until 1870 and frequently so thereafter, being seen (like special advisers later) as a natural stepping stone to a parliamentary career.

As its title suggested, however, the Report sought to mould the character of the new *permanent* Service. It was to achieve this indirectly by the appointment through open competition of young men with, as has been written, 'their milk teeth hardly shed and the ink hardly dry on their last university papers'.[59] Such recruits would by definition neither have, nor typically have the opportunity to develop, alternative political or business skills – and thus alternative careers. However, the specific measures by which officials were ultimately persuaded to devote their time permanently to the Service, both during the day and over time, were achieved by other means. The principal ones were Treasury minutes, which were usually given the force of Orders in Council, and the 1859 Superannuation Act. The former gradually regulated conduct and most importantly banned, as late as 1890, officials from participating in any other venture requiring attendance outside their office between 10 a.m. and 6 p.m. The latter stipulated that an official should forfeit his pension should he retire early from the Service. Neither the existence nor nature of a permanent Civil Service, in its modern meaning, was therefore ultimately dependent on the Report.

As more officials became permanent and governments came to represent conflicting party policies, rather than factional interest, so the issue of neutrality – or equal commitment to whichever party was in power – arose. This was another issue which the Report evaded and, as Kitson Clark observed, even intensified.[60] Overt support for a political *party* was not encouraged, although officials were only formally forbidden to act as party agents and required to resign on publicly intimating their Parliamentary candidature by Orders in Council in 1883 and 1884. The real issue was rather one of political *influence* or what Sir James Stephen, in his response to the Report, described as officials acting as 'statesmen in disguise'.[61] It was understandable, and inevitable, that specialists (such as early Victorian inspectors or Edwardian labour administrators) recruited *outside* open competition would zealously pursue their own individual policies within Whitehall. They were mature experts, called into government to resolve new and frequently ill-defined problems, and were typically known to be committed to a particular definition of the public interest. The Report, however, effectively encouraged 'generalists' to act in a similar way. Academically gifted, and freed from routine, new recruits would inevitably acquire over time an expertise which, as accepted even by Max Weber, would make politicians look like 'dilettantes'.[62] Moreover their expertise (and their definition of the 'public interest') could not be neutral given their deliberately exclusive social background. With the increasing pluralism of society (as reflected by successive extensions of the franchise), their 'neutrality' became ever more suspect. This was true of both their advice to Ministers and their despatch of particular items of business on which, whether for lack of time or other reasons, Ministers expressed no views.[63] It is here that the Report arguably exacerbated the situation and provided some substance for Fulton's later critique.

Given the reality that officials' views could not be 'neutral', should they be made public? Alternatively, should Civil Servants remain anonymous? As early as 1859, when it was ironically Northcote whom he reproved for disclosing official advice, Gladstone's judgement was that a convention of anonymity existed.[64] Total anonymity, however, was an impossibility. Officials had regularly to appear, then as now, before public inquiries. Revelation of individual assumptions, let alone the occasional outburst, could not be precluded. Moreover there was the question of personality. In particular, zealous social reformers in the mid-nineteenth century felt compelled – and morally justified – to use all means possible to advance the wider public interest, as they saw it. As has been said of Chadwick, for example, 'neutrality would have been meaningless . . . anonymity impossible'. Nevertheless, some restriction and even a measure of self-regulation had been accepted by mid-century – so that even Chadwick himself could claim somewhat unchivalrously that, because they could not effectively respond, attacking an official publicly was equivalent to hitting a woman. Later a Treasury minute of 1875 formally sought to halt deliberate leaks to the press; and even the traditional independence of the factory inspectorate was reigned in. From the privileged position of being required to issue independent reports, they were forbidden from 1879 and 1909 respectively to either publish or deliver papers without prior ministerial consent.

Nevertheless, despite both self-regulation and formal regulation, the convention of anonymity was never fully observed. Such Edwardian 'pro-consuls' as Sir Robert Morant, in the field of education, and Sir George Askwith, in industrial relations, continued to attract public notoriety.[65] This, however, offended no Northcote-Trevelyan ideal. It would indeed have been perverse had it done so because, in his career both in India and the Treasury, Trevelyan himself behaved in a highly political way and was 'the master of the strategic leak'. This was never less so than with the promotion of the Report itself where he orchestrated support and briefed the press in order to neutralise known opposition within Cabinet. As his immediate subordinate (George Arbuthnot) vituperatively wrote, 'the Officer who undertakes the work of reforming the Civil Service sets the example of violating the first duty of a Servant of the Crown – obedience'.[66]

The keystone holding together the concepts of a permanent, neutral and anonymous Civil Service was – as it remains – the convention of ministerial responsibility. It evolved in mid-century principally to fortify the sovereignty of Parliament by making the executive more directly responsible to the legislature. Hence Boards, which had been the pre-eminent agency for effecting social reform, had all been abolished by 1867. They had not typically come under ministerial control and, like later executive agencies, had to some extent shielded Ministers from responsibility for operational policy. After 1867, Ministers became answerable directly to Parliament for all policy formulation and implementation. Moreover, following the successive resignations in 1864 and 1873 of the Chancellor who introduced open competition, Robert Lowe, departmental Ministers appeared to become directly answerable to Parliament for all the actions of their officials, whether they knew of them or not. The corollary of this 'vicarious accountability' was that Civil Servants had no legal or constitutional personality separate from that of the minister. There was, for example, no dissent in 1873 to a backbench assertion that an erring official was of no interest to the House of Commons because

> he is not responsible to us. We ought to look to heads of departments; for if we are to shuffle off these questions by saying a clerk ... however distinguished and disinterested he may be, is to take the burden and the blame on his shoulders, there is an end to parliamentary government.[67]

The convention of ministerial responsibility had two perverse consequences. It frustrated the unification of the Service as desired by Northcote-Trevelyan. This was because it so strengthened the answerability of individual Ministers to

Parliament that, as has been seen, Treasury officials feared to transgress the 'constitutional' responsibility of individual Ministers for the management of their departments. Conversely the development of a proper personnel policy was frustrated by the accountability of Treasury Ministers to Parliament for the Civil Service Commission. They duly had, and exerted, the right to determine policy which reduced the Commission (unlike, for example, its counterpart in Australia) to a mere operational body.[68] The second perverse consequence was that the convention of ministerial responsibility was acknowledged almost immediately to be a constitutional fiction. The growing complexity of government made it in reality impossible for Ministers to oversee all departmental business. Moreover it was unenforceable. Its ultimate test was ministerial resignation enforced by Parliament. Party discipline after the 1870s, however, undermined the independence of the Commons and the evolving concept of collective responsibility shielded Ministers from individual responsibility for specific policy failures. Consequently on departmental, as opposed to personal matters, therefore, Ministers could be – and historically were – only forced to resign on *political* grounds: were they, for example, to lose the confidence of their party or Prime Minister or the government risked losing a vote of confidence. In other words, ministerial responsibility was, in essence, not a *constitutional* convention but an issue of *real politique*. It was thus a very weak keystone to support the concepts of a permanent, neutral and anonymous Service which (although equally unmentioned in the Report) came to be regarded as defining features of the Trevelyan-Northcote ideal.

1.4.2 *Treasury control and training*

The fate of the Report together with the efficiency of the Civil Service depended on two further practical issues: 'machinery of government' reform and training. Unification, as desired by the Report, required not just the introduction of common practices and transferability but also the rationalisation of, and the cauterising of jealousies between, existing departments. As seen in section 1.2.4, there was general agreement at the time that the Treasury alone could achieve this task. Equally it has been agreed in retrospect that the Treasury proved unequal to it. As even its historian has concluded:

> Treasury control was imperfect, both in theory and practice ... An undermanned establishment, strenuously administering a negative principle, seemed well designed to impede, with the maximum of friction, and poorly equipped to collaborate in purposeful government. It was at the same time an over-privileged and over-paid elite, thoroughly permeated by the prejudices of one political party.[69]

The principal theoretical imperfections concerned the lack of political authority to enforce decisions (particularly given the evolving perception of ministerial responsibility) and the essential negativity of the Treasury's administrative power (which permitted the questioning only of increased, and not existing levels of, expenditure and staff). Practical imperfections were largely a consequence of the zealous pursuit by Treasury officials of Gladstonian liberalism. This may not have affected their own salary levels, which were high but it did result in undermanning. Officials consequently lacked not just the inclination but also the time and the expertise to respond purposefully to the immensely complex administrative problems posed not just by reform but also the growth of government in an increasingly pluralistic society.[70]

In such circumstances, the optimum strategy would seemingly have been constructive collaboration and above all the encouragement of trust and self-regulation. This is what Trevelyan himself attempted by holding further departmental committees of inquiry. However because of its predilection for delay and obfuscation, Treasury policy in practice only served to maximise friction. Self-regulation, for instance, was formally advanced by the increasing appointment of Permanent Secretaries as departmental accounting officers; but such an 'advance' was welcomed only when it reaffirmed, rather than contested, Treasury policy. All departments remained closely monitored by a number of central agencies, such as the Exchequer and Audit Department (formally working for the Public Accounts Committee of the House of Commons) and Parliamentary Counsel (which had advance notice of any new legislation that would incur increased expenditure). Each was seemingly independent but each was in fact closely linked to the Treasury. 'We are', as one Permanent Secretary to the Edwardian Treasury bluntly admitted 'branches of the same police force.'[71]

The consequences of Treasury control were duly perverse. Overmanning in long-established departments, such as the War and Home Office, was not effectively addressed. This was because only expanding establishments could be challenged. Moreover, any reduction in the number particularly of Class 1 posts would have offended their *amour propre*, and they had Ministers of sufficient political weight to outface the Chancellor.[72] Meanwhile, new social service departments – established to tackle the most serious social and political tensions of the day – were starved of resources. Their expenditure and establishments were, by definition, expanding and so could be controlled. More seriously, the very rationale for their existence continued to be officially questioned. Hence the Local Government Board, despite its dual responsibility for poor relief and health policy, was denied any Class 1 posts in 1870 because its work was deemed 'mechanical' not 'intellectual'. Its salary levels were also held below the Civil Service norm. In 1890 permission was finally granted to raise them so long as numbers, regardless of new legislation, were cut and expenditure on staff thereby held constant; and in 1904 even this agreement was reneged upon because the Chancellor and his officials concurred that staff were 'not charged with the main responsibility for the decision of great questions of policy'.[73] In short Treasury control failed after 1860 because it ignored Trevelyan's maxim that 'there can be no real economy which is not combined with efficiency and . . . the highest efficiency is generally the best economy'.[74] Greater unification and uniformity may have been slowly achieved, but only in a desultory way. Administrative, let alone national, efficiency suffered.

The final challenge which the Treasury 'failed' was training; and this led subsequently to the denigration of the Northcote-Trevelyan Report on the grounds that it favoured amateurism.[75] Such a charge was unwarranted. The Report, as has been seen did not preclude pre-entry tests 'directly bearing on official business'. Moreover, the presumption behind 'generalist' examinations was that it was 'decidedly best to *train* young men'.[76] The contemporary proposals of Trevelyan's collaborators, Jowett and Macaulay, provide further elaboration of the Report's thinking. Jowett, in a letter which was submitted and published with the Report, recommended four pre-entry examination 'schools' (or sets of examination subjects) to test 'special requirements' and thereby qualify entrants for particular departments. Aspiring entrants for the Treasury and Board of Trade, for example, would have to demonstrate proficiency in commerce, tax and political economy whilst those for the Foreign Office would have to excel in the 'modern languages and history school'. 'Whether immediately wanted for the daily work of the office or not', Jowett wrote, 'all such attainments tend to give an official a higher interest in his employment and fit him for superior positions'.

Macaulay in his Report on the Indian Civil Service, published also in 1854, was less concerned than Jowett about pre-entry qualifications. He supported generalist examinations, deliberately drawn wide to attract genuine all-rounders (rather than narrow specialists in individual arts subjects, which was to be Fulton's *bete noire*). He viewed them positively as a test of character and general intelligence, which in turn provided the best grounding for the post-entry training in specialist subjects (such as jurisprudence, and both Indian language and culture) which future employment would require. After the first examination, he wrote, candidates should be 'considered as having finished their general education ... Their serious studies must henceforth be such as have a special tendency to fit them for their calling'.[77] In short, coincidental to the Northcote-Trevelyan Report, detailed blueprints for pre-entry and post-entry specialism were published; and the Report itself, unlike Treasury policy, was compatible to both. Indeed, taken in historical context, the Report's recommendations – contrary to Fulton's assertions – were consistent with that Committee's predilection for 'relevant' degrees and the establishment of a Civil Service College.

1.5 Conclusion

The Northcote-Trevelyan Report was the product of an exceptional period in British history. Government had to expand rapidly to counteract widespread 'market failure' in the face of rapid industrialisation and urbanisation; the ruling elite sought legitimisation; higher and popular education were being radically reformed; and administrative reform had to be contained within, and advance, the 'liberal' conventions of parliamentary government. The Report's recommendations were naturally shaped by such concerns; and, in the short term, proved too radical. Patronage and promotion by seniority, for instance, were still adjudged essential for the respective working of the political and administrative system.

Implementation was therefore delayed; and when it finally occurred, albeit selectively, much of the original political and administrative momentum had dissipated. Administrative reform was no longer championed as a means to achieve broader *political* ends and, unlike Trevelyan, Treasury officials – upon whom implementation depended after 1870 – failed to appreciate the clear distinction between economy and efficiency. In consequence, the Report became somewhat frozen in time. It also increasingly began to appear outdated. The deliberately exclusive nature of recruitment, for example, sat awkwardly with the increasing pluralism of the political system; and the division between 'intellectual' and 'mechanical' labour was made increasingly artificial by the complexity of late Victorian and Edwardian administration. Three subsequent public inquiries failed to adapt the Report's vision to changed circumstances.

Placing the Report in its historical context reveals it to be both broader and narrower than conventionally depicted. It is broader because it had a clear *political* purpose (which dated it). It also left open several options (which makes it more compatible than commonly inferred with some reforms after 1968). It acknowledged, for instance, that 'under any circumstances' it would always be necessary to fill some senior posts from outside the Service; and, placed in the context of simultaneous proposals by Jowett and Macaulay, it was far from inimical to either 'relevant' pre-entry skills or to post-entry training. However, at the same time – and perhaps more disconcertingly – the Report is more narrow than commonly perceived. It either remained silent on (or at least did not explicitly address) many of the key issues, which were later taken to be the defining characteristics of the British Civil Service. These included the conventions of permanence, impartiality, anonymity and ministerial responsibility. There is, therefore, a very real difference between what the Report said and what it was later perceived to have said; and this rift between reality and myth was, as will be seen, deliberately fashioned by a bowdlerisation of the Report in the 40 years after the First World War.

Finally, does the Report offer any insights into how administrative reform may be effectively achieved? Its tardy and incomplete implementation suggests not. Political commitment, and a wider political agenda, were clearly essential both for the commissioning of the Report and for the partial introduction of open competition in 1870. However, Gladstone's excess of zeal in trying to eradicate all patronage in 1853, against the advice of both Trevelyan and Northcote, was counterproductive. So too was the abrasiveness of the Report, albeit that it was an internal document. Most damaging of all, however, was the lack of constructive purpose displayed by Treasury officials after 1870. Their failure exemplifies the inherent difficulty of effecting the reform of any administrative body through that body, unless there is an overriding popular demand and consistent, committed political direction.

2
WAR AND PEACE: THE FISHER-BRIDGES SETTLEMENT, 1916–56

2.1 Introduction

The period between 1916 and 1956 may be seen as the apogee of the 'Northcote-Trevelyan' ideal. It opened with the belated establishment of a central machine for the effective exercise of political and administrative power.[1] The Cabinet Secretariat was established in December 1916 formally to record and monitor the implementation of Cabinet decisions for the first time. Then in 1919 the Permanent Secretary of the Treasury was officially recognised as Head of the Civil Service, with explicit responsibility for the structure, pay and conduct of 'His Majesty's Civil Establishments'. Building on these reforms the Service, by common consent, enjoyed its finest hour with the orchestration of the War effort between 1939 and 1945. 'We have in Britain', concluded a 1947 Fabian study, 'what is probably the best civil service in the world.'[2] The 'golden age' then concluded with the retirement of Sir Edward Bridges as Head of the Civil Service. He has justifiably been described as 'the twentieth-century incarnation of the Victorian ideal'; and his retirement was swiftly followed by the Suez debacle, which fatally undermined both within and outside government the conventional morality and respect for authority upon which that ideal was based.[3]

Despite frequent references to 'the best civil service in the world', however, there was at the time little sustained perception of a 'golden age'. Criticism of the Service was as passionate and as pervasive as it was to become after the 1960s. Following the First World War, for example, there was a vicious 'anti-waste' campaign; and following the Second, in a throwback to the Napoleonic wars, officials were attacked as 'a particularly odious breed of state spies with sealed lips and the proud motto, "Stealth, Secrecy, Snooping"'.[4] During the interwar period there had also been a series of legal assaults on bureaucracy, the most notable of which was by the Lord Chief Justice (Lord Hewart) in his 1929 polemic *The New Despotism*. Such attacks were frequently a surrogate for a fundamental hostility to increased state intervention. Equally damning, however, were the critiques by those sympathetic to it of the inefficient use of interventionist powers particularly in relation to German aggression and mass unemployment. As J.M. Keynes, for example, wrote in relation to the latter in 1939:

the civil service is ruled today by the Treasury school, trained by tradition and experience and native skill to every form of intelligent obstruction . . . We have experienced in twenty years since the war two occasions of terrific retrenchment and axing of constructive schemes [1922 and 1931]. This has not only been a crushing disappointment for all who are capable of constructive projects, but it has inevitably led to the survival of those to whom negative measures are natural and sympathetic.[5]

What more sweeping condemnation could there have been of the new *esprit de corps* which the first official Head of the Civil Service (Sir Warren Fisher, 1919–39) in his extended term of office had sought, and claimed, to have achieved?

Bridges' headship of the Service between 1947 and 1956 was attacked with equal venom. His eulogy to Treasury control in the 1950 Stamp lecture, for example, ended with the aside: 'no doubt some Stamp lecturer of 1977 or 1980 will find much cause for amusement in our present arrangements'. The reckoning came far sooner than anticipated but, like Queen Victoria, it was not amused. 'It really is an abuse of language', fulminated the House of Commons' Estimates Committee in 1958, 'to speak of a "system" of Treasury control, if by the word "system" is meant methods and practices that have . . . been deliberately planned and instituted.' Similarly, the generalist 'training and tradition, outlook of mind and aspirations', celebrated in Bridges' *Portrait of a Profession*, became a prime target for increasingly vituperative attacks on the 'Establishment' in the early 1960s.[6]

The repudiation of the Fisher-Bridges era as a 'golden age' has been sustained retrospectively. Principally this is because the nature of administrative reform, ostensibly based on Northcote-Trevelyan principles, has been adjudged diametrically opposed to what was actually needed. As G.K. Fry was the first to note, there was a curious paradox. When in the nineteenth century 'administrative work had been relatively simple and homogeneous, it had been treated as if it needed departmental specialization'. Then in the twentieth, when it became 'more complex and might well need more specialization, it was thought of as homogeneous'. The failure after 1945 to retain the wartime mix of 'insiders' and 'outsiders', generalists and specialists to discharge government's radical new responsibilities in relation to welfare and economic management has likewise been condemned as 'the greatest lost opportunity in the history of British public administration'.[7]

This chapter will examine the Service's chequered reputation during this period. Was it or was it not a 'golden age'? More specifically, was reform driven by the Northcote-Trevelyan ideal or merely a variant of it? If the latter, to what extent was such a variant justified either by shortcomings within the Report or by changed circumstance? Alternatively, were the very differences between the Report and this variant the root of the Civil Service's perceived failings? Initially the perspective, like that of most contemporary and current commentators, will be 'from above'.[8] Then there will be a brief examination 'from below' of the pressures generated by the growth of government, and thus of the Service. Were they, as in the late Victorian and Edwardian period, the ultimate determinant of change?

2.2 Realising the ideal

The First World War provided a better opportunity than 1870 fully to implement the Northcote-Trevelyan Report. Until 1914, the principles of unification and open competition continued to be contested. Total war, however, demanded the optimal use of national resources. Only central government, so it was eventually acknowledged, could ensure this; but the chaos and corruption which attended the resulting improvisations at both a political and administrative level were patently wasteful. As in 1854, the need for efficiency and economy coalesced in a demand for administrative reform.

Peacetime developments also demanded efficient central administration. Universal manhood suffrage (established in 1918 and succeeded in 1927 by the granting of votes on similar terms to women) provided the necessary democratic precondition, as defined by Weber, for the development of a 'rational' bureaucracy.[9] More prosaically, it created an electoral demand for minimum levels of subsistence which traditional relief agencies such as local government and voluntary bodies were unable uniformly to guarantee. In addition, during the Second World War, there arose a demand for a more comprehensive and universal welfare system. This resulted in the 1942 Beveridge Report and the evolution of a welfare state after 1945. The growing social role of central government, and thus of the Service, was matched by increased economic intervention. In the interwar period, rapid technological change and the intensifying international competition required a fast and fundamental restructuring of industry, which the market appeared unable to deliver. Greater intervention was initially resisted but was finally endorsed in the wartime Coalition's 1944 *Employment Policy* white paper. This led first to economic planning under the postwar Labour Governments (1946–1951) and then to the management of the economy along broadly Keynesian lines.

These developments reflected a curious paradox. Total government expenditure grew relentlessly, as a percentage of GDP, from approximately 12 per cent in 1913 to 26 per cent in 1937 and to 37 per cent by 1956. Simultaneously, the number of centrally-employed Civil Servants expanded from approximately 281,000 to 375,000 and finally to 639,000 by 1956. Nevertheless, there remained a deep-seated political and popular suspicion of government growth. This was particularly true in the interwar period, as epitomised by the Geddes and May Reports on national expenditure in 1922 and 1931; but it also continued after 1945 and accounted for the emasculation of economic planning. As the Labour Government's *Economic Survey for 1947* admitted, for example, totalitarian regimes might subordinate individual need to that of the state and indeed

> such methods may be necessary even in a democratic country during the extreme emergency of a great war. Thus the British people gave their wartime Government the power to direct labour. But in normal times, the people of a democratic country will not give up their freedom of

choice to their Government. A democratic Government must therefore conduct its economic planning in a manner which preserves the maximum possible freedom of choice to the individual citizen.[10]

Such historical tensions over the role of government, and thus the Service are matched by historiographical ones. These concern not just the long-recognised shortcomings of historians themselves, such as the misinterpretation of official advice (tailored to meet Ministerial needs) as statements of personal belief. Rather they concern the evaluation of both contemporary and retrospective criticism. The former, by definition, is usually partial. It should not be taken as a statement of objective fact and any criticism of the Civil Service should be set against a much larger whole, or system of 'governance', of which it is but just a part. Retrospective criticism may be equally partial. It is necessarily based on either explicit or implicit assumptions; and when such assumptions change, so too should its conclusions. Until the 1980s, for instance, it was conventionally assumed that Keynesian demand management could ensure full employment and that welfare policy should be both centrally financed and delivered. Both assumptions were then revised. So too should have been conventional criticisms of interwar officials for resisting any possible move towards demand management and their simultaneous defence of a mixed economy of welfare. Now that presumption of Britain's relative economic decline has been similarly challenged, and so too should be the critique of officials' alleged complicity.[11]

Innumerable historical and historiographical difficulties, therefore, beset any analysis of the 'administrative golden age'. Here it will be examined through the prism of the Northcote-Trevelyan Report, tracing the greater unification of the Civil Service (which the Report overtly wanted), its increasing exclusiveness (which it surreptitiously wanted) and then its political influence (on which it remained silent). There will be a final subsection on the 1918 Haldane Report on the Machinery of Government and the extensive inquiries into the machinery of government between 1942 and 1952 to determine whether, in practice, there was any alternative to the path taken.

2.2.1 *Unification*

It was the establishment of the Cabinet Secretariat and the formal strengthening of Treasury control between 1919 and 1926 that laid the basis for greater unity within the Home Civil Service. The full consequences of these two initiatives were worked out whilst Sir Warren Fisher was Head of the Service between 1919 and 1938. They were then tested first by war and thereafter by the major expansion of government, whilst Sir Edward Bridges was Head between 1945 and 1956.

The Cabinet Secretariat's initial contribution under Maurice Hankey (Cabinet Secretary, 1916–38) was to standardise departmental submissions to Cabinet, and formally to record and disseminate Cabinet decisions. This made a greater reality, both politically and administratively, of *collective* responsibility.[12] Then an extended system of Ministerial and official Cabinet committees was developed under Bridges (Cabinet Secretary, 1938–47) and Brook (Additional Cabinet Secretary, 1945–47; Cabinet Secretary 1947–63). The purpose of Ministerial committees was to resolve second order issues and thereby relieve pressure on Cabinet. That of the shadowing official committees was of greater political and constitutional significance: the reaching, wherever possible, of a common *administrative* view prior to political discussion. The acceptance of this system was symbolised by the distribution to all Ministers in 1946 and again in 1949 of a document which over time was to assume ever greater importance: *Questions of Procedure for Ministers*. This was known colloquially as the Prime Minister's rule book, although the conventions it contained had been devised by Hankey and elaborated by Brook.[13]

The growing influence of the Cabinet Secretariat (working after 1920 within a Cabinet Office) was subject to continuing Parliamentary and press attack, not least in 1922 when it was accused of being the nucleus of a Prime Minister's Department.[14] Both its staff and international role were then reduced, but its fortunes soon revived. Given its strategic position in Whitehall, this was inevitable. The composition of the Cabinet agenda and minutes, for which it was responsible, could never be wholly disinterested. Its officials alone attended Cabinet and serviced all Cabinet committees and so acquired unrivalled administrative and political intelligence.[15] The Cabinet Secretary was also in contact with the Prime Minister more regularly than any other official and, given strong personalities and views, the opportunity was not wasted. In the 1920s, moreover, it was staffed by 'irregular' Civil Servants, at least one of whom acted as a 'political adviser' to successive Prime Ministers. This was Thomas Jones (Assistant, then Deputy Cabinet Secretary 1916–30) to whom Stanley Baldwin appreciatively wrote:

> You don't let me forget or ignore the whole range of ideas that normally I should never be brought up against if you were not in and out of this room. You supply the radium . . . Every Tory P.M. ought to have someone like you around the place.[16]

Of longer-term significance was that the Cabinet Office also acted as a magnet for the 'Central Capability' which, so it was gradually recognised, Ministers needed both to maintain an overview of policy and to obtain 'more authoritative guidance in technical matters than any individual department could readily command'.[17] In the interwar period, it serviced two bodies of outside experts commissioned, in accordance with the principles of the Haldane Report, to bring 'continuous forethought' to policy: the Committee of Civil Research (1925–30) and the Economic Advisory Council (1930–39). Then, after 1940, it actually housed these experts itself in the newly-formed Central Statistical Office and the Economic Section. Hankey had sought to deflect criticism of his perceived influence by stressing the apolitical nature of his Office. Bridges and Brook, faced with similar criticisms about the power of the Office's central experts, employed a different tactic. To prevent too powerful and permanent a body of central officials, the main posts in the Office were staffed exclusively by those temporarily seconded from other departments. In reality, of course, such a policy reinforced their Whitehall network and thus strengthened the Cabinet Office as a potential rival to the Treasury.

The formalisation of Treasury control occurred simultaneously. The Treasury itself was radically reorganised in September 1919, with each of its main responsibilities (finance, supply and establishments) assigned to a 'controller' under the general command of a Permanent Secretary, who was unambiguously designated 'Head of the Home Civil Service'.[18] Four momentous decisions followed. First, in February 1920, agreement was reached in the National Whitley Council over the establishment of six Service-wide classes. For the interwar period at least, this achieved the Northcote-Trevelyan ideal of an effective division between 'intellectual' and 'mechanical' work.[19] Second, after March 1920, the Prime Minister's consent (on the advice of the Head of the Civil Service) was required for any appointment to, or dismissal from, the four senior posts in each department: Permanent Secretary, Deputy Secretary, Principal Establishment Officer (PEO) and Principal Finance Officer (PFO). The latter two posts were new and designed to instil greater control and uniformity into departmental practice. Their authority needed to be protected from attack by departmental 'zealots'.[20] Control over appointment to the other two posts realised the Northcote-Trevelyan ideal of a Service-wide Administrative Class. Third, in July 1920 the Treasury's unequivocal authority to regulate staff costs and numbers in all other departments was confirmed; and its control over departmental expenditure as a whole was similarly confirmed by a flurry of circulars around the appointment of the first Labour Government in 1924, which pronounced that all memoranda proposing increased expenditure should be submitted to Cabinet at least five days in advance. Ministers, and more importantly Treasury officials, would thereby be able to assess the impact on public total expenditure. Finally, and arguably most significantly, in 1926 all Permanent Secretaries were appointed departmental accounting officers answerable directly to Parliament for departmental expenditure. This ensured that those with ultimate official responsibility for policy could no longer disown its financial consequences.[21]

These reforms generated an irresistible momentum for greater unity. Organisationally, for example, PEOs and PFOs met regularly in their respective standing committees to discuss and identify common solutions to common problems; and after 1945, Bridges held weekly meetings of Permanent Secretaries or, in his own words, the 'greybeards'. Even more potent, however, was the appointment of an official Head of the Civil Service. As was argued in a major internal review in 1945, it gave the Service 'someone to whom they may look with confidence to represent and interpret feelings and traditions to the Ministerial Head' or, in other words, the Prime Minister. Equally, it gave 'the Prime Minister someone to whom he in turn can look with confidence to ensure that the evolution of the Service, its spirit and its adjustment to its task, are in accordance with [the Government's] wishes'.[22] The first role was particularly valuable in ensuring that the Service was properly defended against political and press attacks.[23] The second, for better or worse, discouraged undue Ministerial interference in administrative matters.

More specifically, a common culture was forged, in their different ways, by Fisher and Bridges in their lengthy tenures as Head of the Service.[24] Mercurially, Fisher sought to establish the Service alongside the three armed forces as a 'fourth service', with a distinctive *esprit de corps* based on efficiency, team spirit, high moral values, disinterest and a devotion to public service. His focus was on the whole Service, as demonstrated by his commitment (in the wake of junior clerks in the 1850s) to the development of social and sports facilities. Bridges furthered this ideal through force of moral example and public speeches – although he focused very much on the elite or, in his own words, those who 'gained an intense satisfaction and delight in the accomplishment of difficult tasks, a delight which has much in common with scholars and even on occasion by artists'.[25] Neither translated these values into a formal code of conduct, concurring with nineteenth-century Treasury officials that this would only detract from the individual moral responsibility. However, after two scandals – the 'Francs' case in 1928 and Crichel Down in 1954 – each did circulate a memorandum defining individual responsibility. In 1928, Fisher pronounced that:

> the first duty of a Civil Servant is to give his undivided allegiance to the State at all times and on all occasions when the State has claim upon his services . . . [In addition] the Service is entitled to demand that its servants shall not only be honest in fact, but beyond the reach of suspicion of dishonesty . . . Practical rules for the guidance of social conduct depend . . . as much upon instinct and perception of the individual as upon cast-iron formulas; and the surest guide will, we hope, always be found in the nice and jealous honour of Civil Servants themselves. The public expects from them a standard of integrity and conduct that is not only inflexible but fastidious.[26]

This homily was recirculated by Bridges in 1954 with an additional injunction that Civil Servants should be civil. The obligation to each citizen should be so honoured that his 'personal feelings, no less than his rights as an individual, will be sympathetically and fairly considered'.

Despite the setting of this high moral tone, however, the post of Head of the Civil Service came to be bitterly attacked both within and outside Whitehall. There were three principal reasons: its perceived power, the way in which that power was exercised and its identification with the 'negativity' of Treasury control. *Politically*, it was attacked immediately by Ministers and then in three Parliamentary debates (in 1926, 1927 and 1942) as unconstitutional. Denying a Minister his choice of senior officials was, so it was argued, an infringement of Ministerial responsibility. To this there were two obvious responses. First, a reduction in Ministerial responsibility was necessary to break down departmentalism and thus a precondition for collective responsibility. Second, the power to make any appointment was constitutionally the Prime Minister's. The Head of the Service, whatever his influence, had the power neither to nominate senior officials nor indeed to issue orders to them once appointed.[27] *Administrative* apprehension about over-centralisation was more justified. In 1922, for example, Fisher fought – albeit unsuccessfully – both to eliminate a potential rival and to add to its own formidable 'police' force by making the Cabinet Secretary a 'fourth' controller within the Treasury. He also long sought to make the Treasury the general staff of his 'fourth service'. It should, as he argued in 1935, recruit only from other departments and thereby form a '"corps d'elite" . . . to which departments in turn would look to fill their top posts. Such a state of affairs would greatly facilitate the proper filling of the posts of Head and deputy Heads of Departments'.[28] No one, in short, would be able to reach the top of the profession without first having been scrutinised at close quarters within the Treasury.

Such ambitions were made less palatable by Fisher's erratic and often deliberately unconventional behaviour, particularly towards the end of his tenure. 'He was given', as Bridges diplomatically admitted, 'to quick enthusiasms, both for people and causes.'[29] Both could also be dropped with equal rapidity. In reaction, Bridges deliberately 'soft-pedalled' the use of the term 'Head of the Home Civil Service'. Nevertheless, as has been remarked, he 'did not soft-pedal his exercise of the role'. He dominated by his very presence. 'Without imposing *any* conformity', as one senior official later recalled, 'he could not help making us into a team by his example and personality'. More perniciously, any variation within that team from the norm (such as an instinct to respond enthusiastically to the expansion of postwar government) was typically smothered in endless consultation and committees. As Bagehot had predicted, bureaucracy 'elated by sudden success, and marvelling at its own merit' had started, so it appeared, to confuse routine with results.[30]

Such criticisms of negativity might more justifiably be levelled against Treasury control in general rather than against the Head of the Service in particular – and indeed they were. The list of perceived failings remained remarkably consistent from the 1860s to the 1960s and, as summarised by the Machinery of Government Committee in 1945, included over-detailed control ('minor cheeseparing'), deliberate delay, innate suspicion (undermining any move to genuine departmental self-regulation), lack of management expertise and, above all the lack of any broad or constructive vision.[31] Consequently at the start of the century, and again in the 1940s there was a call for a separate 'civil service department', possibly through a return to the Civil Service Commission of powers forfeited to the Treasury in 1870. Such a suggestion was emphatically rejected in 1945 although, as will be seen, it was finally to be acted upon in 1968 following the Fulton Report. Such criticisms of Treasury control in practice was all the more telling because of the consistent support for it in principle. It was advocated by all public inquiries, from Playfair to Tomlin including the iconic 1916–18 Haldane Committee. It was also championed by a succession of highly critical Parliamentary inquiries between 1917 and 1946 and, rather less surprisingly, by Treasury dominated internal reviews such as the 1918–19 Bradbury Committee on the Organization and Staffing of Offices. The Bradbury Report was, in its way, as iconic as Haldane and provided an occasion, not for the last time, for the Treasury perversely to benefit from a crisis of its own making. Exposed during the First World War as impotent to provide administrative leadership, it nevertheless emerged in 1919 with its authority enhanced. As a bonus, there was also a classic definition of Treasury control:

> What is essential, if efficiency and economy are to be secured, is identity and unity of action throughout the Public Service, and these conditions will be fulfilled only if there is genuine cooperation between the Treasury and other departments, inspired by a sense of trusteeship and responsibility and informed by the constant interchange of experience and ideas.[32]

Treasury officials did not survive wholly unscathed in 1919. To their shock an unconventional 39-year-old outsider was appointed as their head. This was Fisher who, given his personal experience, was determined to 'break the pride and prejudice of the Treasury'. He was also publicly commissioned to 'jerk the service out of [its] reactionary and niggling ways' in order to realise Lloyd George's 'visionary outlook'.[33] That its traditional weaknesses persisted, and even intensified, was a measure of his failure.

Fisher's failure was one reason why, despite the potential of the 1919–26 reforms, Northcote-Trevelyan's goal of unification was – on Fisher's own admission –never fully achieved. Plentiful evidence survives of continuing interdepartmental rivalries as well as games of bluff and counterbluff between the Treasury and departments. The Treasury's claim in 1945 that 'stock comments about "the dead hand of the Treasury" and "Treasury cheeseparing" . . . would not nowadays be generally endorsed by . . . Departments' was simply not true – as confirmed by the strictures of the *Official* Committee on the Machinery of Government.[34] The informed view of one senior insider in 1952, moreover, was that even in relation to the machinery of government, where the opportunity and incentive was greatest for co-operation, permanent secretaries showed 'little interest in problems which did not affect their departments, and had taken an extremely departmental line on those which did'.[35] Such disunity did not mean, however, that there was no advance towards the Northcote-Trevelyan ideal. The very concept of a united Service had, after all, been openly challenged before the MacDonnell Committee; and between 1914 and 1918 it had been openly defied. Three major advances were the Whitley Council standardisation of classes, the creation of an interservice Administrative Class and, above all, the forging of a common ethos by Fisher and Bridges. The consequence was that, although internal divisions remained, to the outside world the Service presented a united front. This in itself, however, was dangerous because of the concerns raised about its exclusivity and corporate political influence.

2.2.2 *Exclusivity*

Increasing unity brought greater homogeneity and thus both a risk and accusations of exclusivity. There were two principal accusations. The first was that recruitment was educationally and hence socially biased. (This, as has been seen, was an implicit objective of the Northcote-Trevelyan Report.) The second was that the *esprit de corps*, fostered by Fisher and Bridges, was based on generalist values to the exclusion of managerial and other specialist skills; and that it was increasingly introspective. In consequence, officials were neither representative nor responsive to the needs of the new democratic electorate. Moreover they lacked the expertise to develop and deliver the interventionist policies required to counteract market and voluntary provision failure. Such accusations were, by definition, levelled not at the Service as a whole but at the Administrative Class.[36] To what extent were they justified; and to what extent – if at all – did they expose the increasing anachronism of the Northcote-Trevelyan ideal?

The educational and social bias of the Higher Civil Service was the more crude, if undeniable, charge. In 1955, R.K. Kelsall published the first serious statistical study of the Higher Civil Service. He concentrated in particular on the social background of those above the rank of Assistant Secretary in 1929 (121 officials), 1939 (179) and 1950 (332).[37] As a result of the Second World War, he noted, there had been some broadening. Nevertheless, there remained an undue predominance of those educated at Oxbridge and at private schools. For instance, although Oxbridge typically accounted for a third of honours graduates and of first class degrees, the proportion of its graduates in these posts was 69 per cent in 1929 and still 60 per cent in 1950. In contrast, graduates from London University and from Scottish universities had been consistently under-represented at around six to seven per cent and four to seven per cent respectively, whilst graduates from all other English and Welsh universities (which produced 46 per cent of all postwar honours graduates) remained as low as three per cent. A similar predominance was enjoyed by those educated at private boarding and day schools (which, by the broadest definition, accounted for a quarter of secondary school pupils). They had filled 72 per cent of posts in 1929 and still filled 59 per cent in 1950. Such educational statistics clearly represented a class bias. Indeed Kelsall calculated that in 1929 four-fifths of relevant officials had been born into the Registrar General's Social Classes 1 and 2 (the solidly middle-class professional and 'intermediate' grouping which accounted for under one-fifth of the population). In 1950 the figure was still 70 per cent. Moreover, as Kelsall further established, the higher the position within the Service the greater the bias. In 1939, for example, 70 per cent of Permanent and Deputy Secretaries had been educated at Oxbridge and 76 per cent at private schools.

Why, if at all, did such a bias matter? After all, the goal of Northcote–Trevelyan and that of many other reforming institutions (such as the Fabian Society which blunted crude class assaults on the Service within the Labour Party) was a meritocracy. 'Social representativeness' did not matter: quality not equality was the aim. However, as Kelsall remarked, was it credible that administrative talent was so concentrated in private schools, Oxbridge and the top two social classes?[38] Oxbridge undoubtedly attracted a disproportionate number of talented students and so its graduates might reasonably expect, as in other leading professions, to hold a disproportionate number of senior posts. So *pronounced* a bias, however, suggested that other sources of talent were not being adequately tapped. In short, there was a *prima facie* case for concluding that recruitment procedures were no longer in step with best educational practice, as Northcote-Trevelyan had intended.

Recruitment practice, as reflected by the Civil Service Commission's policies and procedures, supports such a conclusion. In the early 1950s, the CSC was highly respected nationally and internationally because of the perceived fairness of its examinations and its reputation, after the wartime introduction of the Civil Service Selection Board (CSSB or Method II), for being 'at the forefront of personnel selection procedures'. However, by its own admission, this reputation was undeserved.[39]

Increasing conservatism within the Commission is best illustrated by the implementation of a key Northcote-Trevelyan recommendation: the open examination for the Administrative Class.[40] Despite the growth of provincial universities, the proportion of successful candidates who were Oxbridge graduates actually rose in the 1930s from 80 to 89 per cent; and even after the resumption of normal recruitment in 1949 it remained at 74 per cent. A major reason was that following the introduction, after the First World War, of a fifteen minute interview and, after the Second, of a range of practical exercises and extended interviews (the 'country-house' CSSB selection process), the importance of the written examination was downgraded. The interwar interview was particularly flawed. Its purpose was to remedy a weakness which, as has been seen, had been instantly recognised in the 1850s: written examinations tested book-learning and not 'personal effectiveness'. However, as a new First Commissioner (Sir Percival Waterfield, appointed in 1939) immediately recognised, its conduct was too 'slapdash and amateurish' to be effective. Hence he introduced CSSB.[41]

Waterfield's instincts were confirmed by Kelsall's research. In 1938, for example, it was shown that 24 per cent of successful candidates owed their success to the interview which enabled them to leap-frog over those with higher examination scores. This was no case of 'positive discrimination' as the CSC sought to adjust its intake to changing social circumstance causes. Rather the majority of those displaced had been educated in local authority schools and came from the lower social classes, whilst a disproportionate share of the beneficiaries had boarding school and Oxbridge educations. The explanation provided was that the latter were more articulate as a result *inter alia* of their 'residential' education. The former, on the other hand, were disadvantaged by an interview style which was as much influenced by the predominance of Oxbridge personnel as was the setting and marking of the original written examinations. Having overcome one hurdle, they consequently fell at the second. To this extent, CSSB was no great improvement. In 1955, for example, eight of the nine group chairmen and eleven of the twelve observers on the CSSB final selection panels were Oxbridge educated.[42]

Such 'biased' recruitment procedures reflected an inherent prejudice within the Commission and indeed the Treasury, which retained ultimate responsibility for policy. Two examples, from 1937 and 1955, must suffice. In 1937 the relative weighting of the interview (300 points), despite its flaws, was increased significantly by a reduction in maximum score for written examinations from 1800 to 1300 points. This revision followed detailed academic discussion – but only with

Oxbridge. Its advice, so it was agreed with Fisher, might be 'taken as representative of general well-informed opinion'; and so no discussion should be opened with other universities until 'a substantial measure of agreement has been reached between the Commissioners and the two older universities'. Likewise in 1955, when it was declared policy to court non-Oxbridge students, Bridges approved a system of liaison officers between the Commission and universities. Twenty were allocated each to Oxford and Cambridge (so that individual colleges might be covered). A mere ten was considered sufficient to cover all other universities. The reason for such an imbalance was clear. As the secretary of the Commission privately minuted, in direct contradiction to stated policy: 'we don't want to stimulate the interest of provincial universities in the Administrative Class'. The Executive Class was the proper summit for their graduates' ambitions.[43]

In short, the continuing educational and social exclusiveness of the Administrative Class was no accident. Was it, however, the result of a conscious or deliberate bias? Despite concerns about unrepresentative recruitment voiced from the MacDonnell Commission onwards, there long remained a widespread public and academic belief that the quality – and readiness to apply – of Oxbridge graduates justified such unrepresentativeness. The attitudes of the Commission and Treasury were therefore not atypical at the time. Two things, nevertheless, are certain. First, the nature of the selection process ensured that its results were as biased as if, in Chapman's measured phrase, there had been an 'intended preference towards candidates with certain social and educational backgrounds'. Second, such a process reflected a mindset that was becoming increasingly out of touch with the evolving needs and values.

As the Service became more unified, this mindset was reinforced by the common, generalist culture encouraged by both Fisher and Bridges and by growing introspection. This introspection was intensified by two particular developments: the evolution of the concept of Ministerial responsibility and the operation of the Official Secrets Act.

With regard to Ministerial responsibility, Fisher sought to persuade successive Prime Ministers (Baldwin and Chamberlain) in 1936 that since time 'immemorial . . . under the Constitution Parliament has no cognisance of individuals comprising the four Crown Services: for Parliament it is Ministers alone, whether as individuals or as the Government, who formally exist. Anonymity so far as it is humanly possible should be the guiding rule for official advisers of Ministers'.[44] Bridges concurred; and in 1954 (the centenary of Northcote-Trevelyan) drafted its classic definition. Were Parliament, he argued, to take exception to any action by an official there were four options. Were the official 'carrying out the explicit order of his Minister' or 'acting in conformity with [agreed] general principles', then that Minister should accept full responsibility. Were the official guilty of maladministration on a minor matter, the Minister should again accept responsibility but take 'corrective action'. Finally, were the official guilty on a major matter of acting in a way of which the relevant Minister 'strongly disapproves and had no prior knowledge', then that Minister should inform Parliament of 'what had occurred and render an account of his stewardship'. This would include an explanation of why existing procedures had failed and what disciplinary action, if any, was to be taken. For the Service, however, the key point was that in none of these situations should any responsibility be publicly attached to a named official.

Politically, Fisher's 'quasi-theological' musings and Bridges' memorandum had little effect. Bridges' memorandum, for instance, was drafted for the Conservative Home Secretary, Maxwell Fyfe, at the end of the Crichel Down affair. The then Minister of Agriculture (Sir Thomas Dugdale) had resigned following the questionable treatment by his officials of a Dorset farmer over the buying of some land which had been compulsorily purchased during the War. A committee of inquiry had breached official anonymity and concluded that the relevant officials had not been corrupt (as commonly assumed) but inefficient. They had also been somewhat economical with the truth. This deeply concerned Bridges who, as noted earlier, duly issued a circular re-emphasising the need for high moral standards.[45] Dugdale's resignation, however, was forced less by constitutional principle, as enunciated by Bridges, than by political necessity: he had lost the confidence of his backbenchers and ultimately the Cabinet because, despite pre-election promises, he had failed to reverse 'socialist' policy on compulsory purchase. His officials, therefore, may not have conformed to the highest ethical standards. They had, however, taken no action of which the Minister could 'strongly disapprove or had no prior knowledge'. In short, the most significant impact of the memorandum was that it entrenched still further in official and Ministerial minds the right of individual Civil Servants to be insulated from public attack.

This insulation was reinforced by the operation of Section 2 of the 1911 Official Secrets Act. This sequel to the original 1875 Treasury circular on leaked information was draconian, making it illegal to reveal not only any official document but also any information acquired in the course of official work. The Act was frequently honoured in the breach, especially during the battle over rearmament in the 1930s. In the best traditions of Trevelyan, Fisher himself primed both Parliamentary committees and the press on various issues; and, in briefing Lord Woolton in 1938 on the shortcomings of the aircraft industry, he notoriously broke down in tears protesting that 'the protection of the country was more important than a rigid adherence to the regulations that should govern his conduct as a civil servant'.[46] Likewise, Bridges and Brook sanctioned the release of classified material, and even ghost-wrote some of the material, for Churchill's history of the Second World War. Their justification was that it was in the national interest to counter alternative versions of the truth emanating largely from the USA. Despite such high-level breaches, however, the Act was enforced at a lower level – with, for example, the prosecutions of Compton Mackenzie and Edgar Lansbury in 1932 and 1934. Such prosecutions were designed *pour encourager les autres*, but they served only to intensify the sense of isolation amongst those junior officials who, like Fisher and Bridges, wished to serve the 'national interest'.

Such introspection was particularly damaging because it hobbled the Administrative Class when it was approached for, and sought, information. As

Richard Chapman has written, for example, it acted 'rather arrogantly' when deciding, on a very imperfect knowledge of the outside world (or at least the world outside Oxbridge), with whom to co-operate. In consequence, 'relations with citizens interested in Whitehall and its workings were seen as both time-consuming and irritatingly unwelcome by busy officials. They . . . had more important things to do than satisfy . . . at best idle curiosity . . . and more often the troublesome interference of busybodies intent on causing embarrassment'.[47] It was such attitudes that prompted public perceptions of complacency and denied officials the understanding of the world beyond Whitehall which was increasingly required.

More serious than such public relations failures was a reluctance to engage with outside expertise in policy delivery and development, which intensified the Administrative Class' generalist ethos and thus sense of exclusivity. With regard to policy delivery, both the 1919 Bradbury Report and the 1929–31 Tomlin Commission had stressed the need for better management. An Investigations Section was duly set up in the Treasury in 1919; and during the interwar period, as will be seen in Chapter 2.3.3, there were some successful examples of large-scale mechanisation. However, it was not until the formation of the Organisation and Methods Division at the Treasury in 1941 that management specialists within Whitehall increased from a mere four to some 356 (by 1955); and even they tended to be within the Executive rather than the Administrative Class. The disdain of the latter was well illustrated by their continuing ambivalence towards the body which offered an optimum forum for a discussion of best practice, the Institute of Public Administration.

The Institute had been founded in 1922, under the presidency of Lord Haldane, to advance the practice and study of public administration – and in particular the principles of its president's 1918 Report. It quickly became a natural meeting place for officials and both a sponsor and disseminator of research. Fisher and Bridges, as Head of the Service, became its vice president *ex officio*. Both, however, remained distinctly ambivalent towards it. The substantive reasons were spelt out in a letter by the Treasury's controller of establishments (Sir Russell Scott) in 1922, rejecting the Institute's initial request for financial support. Administration was a practical skill, he wrote, not one that could be learnt through theoretical study. Moreover, with no constitutional personality other than their Minister's, Civil Servants – unlike other professions, like doctors – could not develop a formal, self-regulated code of conduct. 'I do not like your scheme', he concluded, 'because it seems to be a glorification of the bureaucracy. We are unpopular enough already, God knows, but I tremble to think how we should be regarded if we consciously assumed the air of superior persons.'[48] Beneath such protests, there also lay two less worthy reservations. First, the Institute was an outside initiative, which ultimately could not be controlled. Second, the independent research it sponsored could be both 'subjective and highly political' and therefore potentially embarrassing. This danger was all the more real because the research was typically executed outside Oxbridge, particularly at LSE, and was associated with such 'left-wing' organisations as the Fabian Society, which favoured greater state intervention.

In relation to policy development, the Administrative Class was equally hostile to outside expertise. As part of the NWC unification process, for example, the recruitment of mature experts – as had occurred during the rapid expansion of welfare policy in Edwardian Britain – was banned. Consequently, when there was a parallel expansion after 1945, there was no similar influx. Experts, having been temporarily recruited during the Second World War, left rather than joined Whitehall. Even more damagingly, both departmental expertise and specialists working within Whitehall (such as trained scientists, engineers and accountants) were disparaged. The former was classically justified by Fisher before the Tomlin Commission. 'Let us guard ourselves against the idea that heads of departments should be an expert', he warned, 'he should not be anything of the kind.'[49] Bridges concurred. He was more respectful of the 'store of knowledge and experience' within departments. Yet, to maximise unity, he continued Fisher's policy of 'musical chairs' in his recommendations for promotion to senior posts. To minimise public expenditure, he also passionately defended the right of Treasury generalists to control departmental experts. 'The Treasury clerk is a layman dealing with experts', he admitted, but 'it is his business to form a layman's judgment on whether the case presented . . . can be allowed on a common sense judgment'.

Bridges' generalist stance attracted considerable controversy. It was widely accepted that any centralised promotion policy would give the Treasury a potentially dangerous degree of patronage but that it was based on such principles meant that policy advice to Ministers might be sub-optimal for up to two years – whilst a new Permanent Secretary 'read himself in'. On the other hand, it was argued, 'musical chairs' was the only way to enhance efficiency by breaking down departmentalism and promotion blockages. It therefore accorded with Northcote-Trevelyan (although, as has been seen, both authors had later relented and pronounced that 'the regular course of promotion' should be within department). In any case, it was further argued, any new Permanent Secretary *would* be expert – in 'the workings of the government machine'. This was a positive, transferable skill and enabled him, in theory at least, to operate efficiently at both an administrative and political level.[50]

The disparagement of internal specialists was more serious and substantial. In general, they were denied direct access to policy-making for two reasons. First, were a specialist formally to transfer at a late stage into the Administrative Class, his 'technical experience and training' would be lost without any guarantee that he would make a good administrator. Indeed it was likely that he would not, given that he lacked the early training in the 'workings of the government machine' which would have imbued him with 'that sense of proportion and that recognition of the political, financial and practical limitations which every administrator must learn'.[51] Second, there was a danger that, on transfer, specialists might become highly conservative. 'A body of quasi-experts', the Tomlin Commission was warned, 'would grow up in the secretariat who would tend to press their views in technical matters, possibly in opposition to those in technical departments.' Outdated expertise, in short, would be narrowly pursued. This conviction was all the more powerful for being endorsed by leading academic scientists, who tended not to hold fellow scientists working within the Service in the highest regard.

Specialists were not uniformly scorned. The Service ministries, for example, enjoyed a 'board' system by which policy advice was pooled, openly discussed and not channelled exclusively to Ministers by a single Permanent Secretary. Government-employed scientists consequently enjoyed considerable influence over armaments policy – and thus over a sizable percentage of the country's research and development expenditure.[52] The board system, moreover, was extended to the Post Office in 1932. This followed a recommendation of the Bridgeman Committee of Inquiry into the Post Office, which had been appointed because even the Tomlin Commission had been appalled that engineers had so little influence in so technological a department. No engineer, indeed, had ever been admitted to the Administrative Class.

Such specialist influence, however, was exceptional. The 'board' system was not formally adopted by other ministries and the proportion of senior administrative posts held by transferees from the specialist classes fell to a nadir of 5.4 per cent in 1950. Bridges strove to place the specialist classes on a regular Service-wide basis and to raise both their status and pay.[53] This, however, was in response not so much to their proven indispensability during the War but to a tightening labour market. Moreover, it served to reinforce their division from the Administrative Class which, so critics argued, jeopardised efficiency. Specialist advice was likely to be bowdlerised or even ignored in policy submissions to Ministers. Even more perniciously neither specialists nor administrators had any incentive to widen their horizons. Any acknowledgement or display of specialist expertise, for example, was more likely to retard than advance an administrator's career.

Given government's new responsibility for economic management after 1945, however, what particularly exercised the more vocal critics and led ultimately to the appointment of the Fulton Committee was the marginalising not of technological but statistical and economic expertise. The importance of such expertise had been recognised during the War by the creation in 1941 of the Central Statistical Office and the Economic Section. The former, in an international context, was hardly revolutionary. Belgium had had such a body for 100 years and France for over 50. In Britain, statistical excellence had also been long recognised as a prerequisite for effective policy. Therein lay the rub. Statistics had the power to challenge the assumptions of generalists. Since the 1880s they had been typically used to expose market and voluntary sector failure, and thereby justify further state intervention. That, for example, was a major reason why – under the guise of economy and in defiance of the Haldane Committee – statistical divisions had been either closed or etiolated throughout Whitehall after 1919.[54] Economic expertise was feared for similar reasons. Before 1939, Keynesian policies were rebuffed on what has politely been termed 'anti-intellectual' grounds; and between 1945 and 1961, despite its government's huge new responsibilities, there were never more than twelve economists employed in Whitehall. Major economic ministries, such as the Board of Trade and the Ministry of Labour, had none.[55]

Between 1919 and 1956, therefore, the Service – and the Administrative Class in particular – undoubtedly became more exclusive and introverted. There was one way in which this could have been countered: through an effective post-entry training programme, as advocated by Macaulay in the 1850s. The possibility was belatedly examined in 1943 when, under strong parliamentary and political pressure, the Assheton Committee on the Training of Civil Servants was appointed. However it merely confirmed conventional Whitehall wisdom that there was no substitute for practical experience. It did recommend a short central course to enable recruits to place this experience in better context but this was rejected, in turn, by the Treasury. It sought instead to generalise interwar best practice by requiring each department to offer recruits a five-year job rotation programme, culminating with a posting as a Private Secretary. In consequence Bridges' Headship of the Service saw the apogee of a training policy affectionately known within Whitehall as 'sitting with Nellie'. Outside Whitehall, however, it was disparaged as highly amateurish. It neither encouraged recruits to challenge the rationale of traditional 'departmental views' nor imparted specialist skills – unlike the three-year training programme run by the *Ecole Nationale d'Administration*, from which French officials were seen to emerge – to the delight of Whitehall's critics – as 'social scientists in action'.[56]

Growing exclusivity was thus the consequence of both pre-entry and post-entry factors. In accordance with Northcote-Trevelyan, recruitment was educationally and thus socially exclusive. In contrast to the Report's implicit intentions, however, there was neither an effective training programme nor the encouragement of departmental expertise to provide the necessary leaven. Despite radical political and social change, the flexibility permitted by Northcote-Trevelyan was deliberately rejected. In the short term, such inflexibility could be justified. Given the relentless increase in the power of government and the equally relentless suspicion of it, a culture of self-contained self-denial was arguably the only way in which the public could be reconciled to an enlarged Service. This is what lay at the root of its reputation as the 'best civil service in the world' – in comparison with bureaucracies abroad which, in response to similar challenges, became either corruptly linked to business or job-creation agencies for political parties. Accordingly, as David Vincent has written, 'while to some contemporaries and many later critics, Whitehall as a whole and the Treasury in particular were in this period of crisis turning away from the modern world, the leaders of the civil service were convinced that their combination of selfless efficiency and inner-disciplined integrity placed them on the leading edge'.[57] Problems, however, were being stored up for the long term – as underlined by a significant change in the meaning of the term 'administration'. As employed in the 1922 letter to the Institute of Public Administration it meant an 'awareness of Ministerial responsibility' – or, in other words, an expertise in the 'working of the government machine' and the dispatch of parliamentary business. 'The first duty of the higher official', as H.E. Dale concluded in his classic description of the interwar Service, 'is to save his Minister.' By the 1950s, however, it was being used in a very different sense: the direction and management of government's greatly enlarged responsibilities. 'What we need in the Service is a better concept of leadership', Brook (Bridges' successor as Head of the Home Civil Service) wrote in 1957, 'I am sure that members of the Administrative Class are not sufficiently alive to the great responsibility which they should carry in management duties.'[58] To the critics, this lack of awareness was not a neutral but a deliberate political stance.

2.2.3 Political influence

Political neutrality was an ideal with which the term 'Northcote-Trevelyan' became synonymous but, as noted earlier, it was not one which the Report explicitly addressed. In fact, its recommendations in some ways made it more difficult to achieve. By the 1880s, the separation of the 'parliamentary' from the 'permanent' Civil Service was essentially complete and official involvement in party politics had started formally to be restricted. Nevertheless, as Sir James Stephen had warned, the reservation of 'intellectual' work for gifted graduates recruited through open competition threatened the creation of a permanent cadre of 'statesmen in disguise' and, to many, this threat became a reality after 1919. Consequently, the Fisher-Bridges era has been commonly seen not as the apogee of political neutrality but as the time when the Higher Civil Service 'reached the height of its corporate influence'.[59]

There are three principal justifications for such a view: a reversion to the practice of officials becoming Ministers; the perceived power of successive Heads of the Service; and the pervasive influence of the Administrative Class on policy. The first was the more surprising since it was not the committed social reformers, recruited at a mature age in the Edwardian period, who attained political power. Their public careers, like those of their Victorian predecessors, were actually cut short by growing conformity. Rather, of the four appointments, the greatest prominence was achieved by two open competition entrants: Sir John Anderson (the former Permanent Secretary of the Home Office, who was Lord President and then Chancellor of the Exchequer between 1940 and 1945) and Sir James Grigg (promoted from official to Ministerial head of the War Office in 1942).[60] Their appointment can be explained in part by the exceptional conditions of war and coalition government; but it was also a premonition of the increased managerial role which Ministers were to be expected to play.

Contemporaries, as signified in Chapter 2.2.1, were most perturbed by the power of successive Heads of the Civil Service. Each was seen to have immense powers of patronage and to use that power to encourage uniformity. Prospects of promotion, for example, were not noticeably enhanced by challenging the Treasury view on balanced budgets before 1940 or enthusiastically embracing state intervention thereafter.[61] Each was also believed to have unduly influenced policy. Hence Fisher was attacked (incorrectly) for promoting appeasement whilst Sir Horace Wilson, whom one contemporary described as 'more powerful ... than almost anyone since Cardinal Wolsey', actually did.[62] Working from his office next to the Cabinet room in No. 10, Wilson even appeared to assume the role of Deputy Prime Minister. Here was another premonition – of the charges to be levelled against Sir William Armstrong in 1974. Bridges was aware of the inherent danger. 'One, if not two, of my predecessors', he wrote to Clement Attlee in 1946, 'gained the reputation of seeking to exercise more influence or power (I am not sure which is the right word) than was right for a civil servant. It would be bad for the civil service if that came to be said about me.' Nevertheless it was. Soon after his retirement Thomas Balogh vehemently attacked 'the power of the headships of the Treasury and the Civil Service' as a 'menace [to] the future of the country'.[63] This was because, in his view and that of many others, the success of the postwar management of the economy depended on an appropriate institutional framework and official attitudes. This Bridges appeared either unwilling or unable to deliver. Instead, because of his peculiar moral presence, he set himself up as a rather conservative 'guardian of the constitution', in which capacity 'he could call on Ministers and tell them they were behaving badly'.[64] The taking of necessary initiatives to make interventionist policies work was equated all too often with bad behaviour.

However, it was the third charge – that of excessive corporate influence – that was the most substantial. Given the increasing complexity of departmental business, which Ministers no longer could be expected to master, such influence was to an extent inevitable. Delegated legislation, in particular, gave officials considerable discretion in the implementation of policy (where, in practice, the principles of policy were often determined). As Stephen had predicted, however, their relative expertise also enhanced their influence over formal policy-making. 'No attempt should be made to formulate a new policy', Bridges pronounced, 'without the fullest consultation with those who have practical experience in that field and with those who will be called upon to carry it out.' In consequence it was 'the duty of a civil servant to give his Minister the fullest benefit of the storehouse of departmental experience ... and to let the waves of the practical philosophy wash against ideas put forward by his Ministerial master'.[65] Given increasing uniformity and in particular the role of Bridges' official committees, Ministers by the 1940s were being confronted by a veritable tsunami.

Moreover, even were they impartial in the narrow party-political sense, these 'waves of practical philosophy' were not unbiased. Any definition of the 'public interest' can but rest on a set of implicit, if not explicit, assumptions; and, as a result of the educational and social exclusiveness, there was a clear class bias to official advice. This was admitted at the time and has been demonstrated since. Dale, for instance, acknowledged that 'having gained by their talent a right to enter a social class [the upper middle class] above that to which they were born', senior officials 'more or less deliberately exercised that right' with the result that 'while there may be no conscious departure from previous convictions on politics and economics there is likely to be some, perhaps much, alteration in the general tone of ... beliefs, habits and prejudices'. An even more nuanced conclusion has been reached by an historical examination of four interwar welfare ministries. It is that:

the interplay of institutions and individual experience systematically linked class to power. The Ministerial culture that developed within each government office established a 'normative order' that presumed and drew upon a system of class relations. Official behaviour in turn reconstituted and enacted these social relations by the implementation of policies bearing its imprint. Civil Servants acted purposefully in this respect, even though their articulation of goals does not reveal anything so arrogant, so grandiose, or so tidy as a self-conscious and class-conscious conspiracy. Nevertheless government officials cannot be relegated to a mere walk-on role in some elaborate social and political coincidence. Civil Servants knew what they were doing and what they did often made a difference.[66]

The particular difference they made, particularly after Lloyd George's flirtation with a 'development state', was the discouragement of any political urge fundamentally to alter the balance between government and civil society.[67] Within interwar Whitehall the neo-classical 'Treasury view' provided as unchallenged and unchallengeable a policy framework as, on William Armstrong's testimony, neo-Keynesianism became in the 1960s.[68] True to Gladstonian principles, it championed the balancing of budgets at the lowest practical level in order to maximise individuals' freedom to spend their own money and to stem politicians' natural profligacy. In consequence, faced with clear evidence of market and voluntary sector failure (in the shape of mass unemployment and poverty), greater state intervention was instinctively opposed. Neither central government nor Ministers had the capacity to supplant, as opposed to support, civil society. Such principled reservations about the capacity of Ministers in particular hid an in-built bias and indeed a fundamental contradiction, in official thinking: an 'immense deference to the Ministerial office' and simultaneously an equal 'contempt for the holder of it'. References to Ministers as 'our political liabilities' sat uneasily with Fisher's and Bridges' elaborations of the constitutional convention of Ministerial responsibility.[69] Self-deprecation also became self-fulfilling. 'A policy of "do-nothing" in the fond – and jejune – hope that a negative absolves them from any positive responsibility' lay, according to 'modernisers' in the 1960s, at the heart of officials' culpability for Britain's relative decline.[70] State intervention, for its success, required the positive commitment of state officials.

Officials at the time vigorously rebutted such charges. As Bridges classically responded to an outspoken attack (triggered by the Labour Government's failed experiment in economic planning) on the Higher Civil Service as not just statesmen but Conservatives in disguise:

> The experience and training of Civil Servants generally led them to adopt a view of political matters different from that of politicians of either Party. We looked at matters from the point of view of their effect on administration and, from this standpoint, there were things in the programmes of both the major parties which we disliked and others equally that we liked. Our attitude therefore became one apart from party and although, of

course, we took great interest in political matters, we were not filled with the suppressed desire to push politics either to the Right or the Left.[71]

This provided a firm rebuttal of political partisanship, although revealingly it evaded the issue of surreptitious class bias. The precise criteria on which the effect of Party policy on administration was 'liked' or 'disliked' were left unspecified. Nevertheless – in Dale's equally classic judgement – the issue was largely immaterial because, in contrast to most other commentators, he adjudged that the Service's effective influence was decreasing. This was because open competition had drawn in recruits of a lower social standing than the typical Minister; and because the constant pressure to pass exams had equally extinguished that 'animal spirit . . . which, more than wisdom, gave weight to a man's advice and made the strongest Minister hesitate before rejecting it'. In consequence there was an increasing preponderance of 'yes-men'. Moreover, whatever the opportunities, he was adamant that – in defiance of the assumptions of later political choice theorists – officials were not interested in self-aggrandisement. 'Bureaux have grown', he insisted, 'but not bureaucracy'.[72]

In any case, to what extent was 'negativity' a proper constitutional response to popular and Parliamentary pressure? As Dale continued, 'timidity, rigidity, slowness of decision and action, red tape, evasiveness, fear of responsibility are the convex . . . of the concave represented by close obedience to law and the will of Parliament, loyalty to Ministers . . . and . . . the desire to meet the varying demands of the public and the House of Commons.'[73] Both Fisher and Wilson, it should be remembered, had started their careers by advocating greater state interventionism. Fisher was determined to correct the Victorian's neglect of destitution and Wilson to ensure that the 'public interest' was better represented in industrial disputes. Both, however, were defeated and (at least in Wilson's case) forced, like the rest of the Service, into a 'stoical realism'.[74] Equally it is likely that the Service's most vociferous critics after 1930 (and, in particular, Keynes) would have welcomed its increased 'corporate influence', had that influence been exercised in a way of which they – rather than the majority of the electorate – approved.

The Northcote-Trevelyan Report had anticipated a political role for a permanent Civil Service. It was seeking the high quality officials to 'advise, assist, and to some extent, *influence*, those who are from time to time set over them'. In the late nineteenth-century Treasury, as has been seen, such influence had been exercised by officials in a highly partisan way. After 1916 it was not, but it was none the less biased. This was because, as the Fabians correctly argued in 1964, it was impossible for policy advisers to be 'non-political'.[75] Judgements reflected values; and the success of postwar interventionism, even more than that of predominantly regulatory policy of the interwar period, depended on genuine commitment. After 1919, growing exclusivity and unity seemed to intensify, as well as blind officials to, this bias. Ultimately they were impervious to interwar critics of government growth because they shared the critics' basic instincts and only condoned an enlargement of government (as with unemployment relief by the 1930s) when it was validated by public and political demand. By contrast, in the changed circumstances of postwar Britain, they were both temperamentally and technically far more vulnerable to attack from their fellow professionals.

2.2.4 Missed opportunities

Could the Civil Service have adapted more effectively to such a period of rapid change? A formal opportunity was provided by two further Royal Commissions – Tomlin and Priestley, held respectively between 1929–31 and 1953–55. The former enjoyed a traditionally broad remit, received a traditionally wide range of evidence and produced a traditionally narrow set of recommendations. Its report, broadly endorsing the *status quo*, has been adjudged historic because it 'marked and recorded the culmination of the changes that were recommended by Northcote and Trevelyan'. However, it also overlooked both the historically specific challenges with which Northcote-Trevelyan had been faced and, more importantly, its essential flexibility which could have allowed its recommendations to be adapted to changed circumstance. The opportunity was consequently lost to question Fisher's stewardship. The Priestley Commission, in contrast, had a restricted remit. 'Somewhat smugly', a Treasury official minuted, 'we doubt whether there is much practicable in the way of [organizational] reform' and so it was confined to a consideration of pay and conditions. It did, as will be seen, achieve some stature by further entrenching the principle of 'fair comparison' between public and private sector pay – a principle that was to be unilaterally abandoned by the Thatcher Government, thereby provoking the major strike of 1981. Typically, however, its report was dismissed as 'unreadable and unread'.[76]

Consequently the optimum opportunity for adaptation was provided by two other initiatives, both the products of wartime tension: the 1917–18 Haldane Committee on the Machinery of Government and the 1942–45 Cabinet Committee on the Machinery of Government (together with its peacetime successors). The former has been heralded as the 'first serious attempt since Bentham to analyze British central government in terms of systematic administrative theory';[77] and its Report greatly influenced both academics and practitioners (including Fisher and Bridges). Its two guiding principles were simple. 'Investigation and thought' should always precede action. Each organisation should also have – and retain – a clear purpose. In practice, this meant that both government as a whole and individual ministries should have a 'general staff' (in the respective shape of a Ministry of Research and 'statistical and investigation' divisions) to ensure 'enquiry, research and reflection before policy is defined and put into operation'. Each ministry should also be organised by discrete function (such as employment or education) rather than the 'persons or classes to be dealt with'. These two principles were key to the attainment of efficiency and economy. Better administrative coordination, however, was also needed. Herein lay an admitted danger. Coordination could best be achieved by the recording and implementation of Cabinet decisions (through a Cabinet Secretary) and by administrative standardisation (through specialist Finance and Establishment Officers working in each department under Treasury guidance). The danger was that any such increase in efficiency might 'expose the State to the evils of bureaucracy'. To counter this, it was swiftly affirmed that no policy should be exempt from 'those safeguards which Ministerial responsibility to Parliament alone provides'. Moreover Parliament's investigatory powers should be strengthened, particularly by the appointment of departmental select committees.

The reasons for the Report's attraction to, and continuing influence on, Fisher and Bridges are transparent. It provided, in place of rampant departmentalism, a vision of government that was politically and administratively united. It also identified a Cabinet secretariat and the Treasury as the principal agents for change. Haldane, moreover, later argued that Civil Servants should develop an *esprit de corps*, based on principle of public service, in order to set democracy an example. As he proclaimed, in his inaugural address as President of the Institute of Public Administration:

> It is not only by rendering highly skilled services to the public . . . that the civil servant of the future may serve the public. The Civil Service, if itself highly educated, may become one of the greatest educative influences on the general community. It may set a high example and may teach lessons which will have far-reaching influence . . . It should set this ideal before itself as one which is of immense practical importance in its tendency to raise the standards in business and in life generally.[78]

The Report, however, was never debated by Cabinet. In consequence, its recommendations were only selectively implemented and the *esprit de corps* (on which unity was indeed built) isolated the Service from, rather than integrated it with, the rest of society. This danger had, to an extent, been anticipated. Greater unity, the Report had warned, would only succeed were Treasury control over other departments matched by 'a corresponding obligation' on the Treasury 'not to assume a negative attitude in the first instance towards suggestions for improving the quality of a service or the efficiency of the staff which administers it'. This obligation was clearly not honoured. Departmental statistics and investigation divisions, for example, fell victim to the postwar anti-waste campaign and their revival thereafter discouraged. So too was the implementation of other recommendations designed to moderate exclusivity. They included the appointment of advisory committees ('to make available the knowledge and experience of all sections of the community affected by the activities of the Department') and of Ministerial boards (to ensure that 'the heads of any professional or technical branches' had a direct input into policy). Equally, no new Parliamentary select committees were established.[79]

Why were Haldane's recommendations so selectively implemented and its spirit betrayed? There are three conventional explanations. The first is that, in the short term, the Report was impracticable. In 1919, Whitehall was overstretched by the needs of reconstruction and such radical changes would have been too disruptive. Then, in the early 1920s, political priority was economy and not the enlargement of government (on which, like the later Fulton Committee, the

Report's recommendations were largely predicated). Second, it failed fully to correlate administrative and political need. Administrative efficiency might require small cabinets and functional ministries. Politically, however, greater scope was needed to accommodate political ambitions, manage parliamentary majorities and satisfy vested interests. Third, the Report contained a fundamental flaw. Desperate to pre-empt any charge that they condoned 'bureaucracy', its authors had instinctively endorsed the convention of Ministerial responsibility.[80] Formally, this may have made officials democratically accountable but in practice, as has been seen, the convention was being made increasingly impracticable by government growth. It was also, as several contemporary commentators noted, becoming increasingly pernicious. Officials who could have responded constructively to the challenge of greater state intervention were being forced into 'stoical realism', whilst those committed to economy were able to disguise their very real influence. In other words, for very little real gain, administrative initiative was discouraged whilst both Parliamentary and public debate were truncated.

Just as the Institute provided an ideal forum for informed debate, however, so – on balance – the Report fused with remarkable skill solutions to the administrative, political and constitutional issues raised by the advent of democracy. Although by no means flawless, it provided far more *pragmatic* long-term solutions to the challenges facing governments worldwide than were available elsewhere – and especially in the USA. The tragedy, for the longer term, was that this double opportunity was missed.

The Haldane Committee had been commissioned in 1917 in reaction to wartime chaos, accentuated rather than relieved by Lloyd George's appointment as Prime Minister. A similar concern with maladministration was voiced in Parliament by the Committee of National Expenditure during the darkest days of the Second World War in 1942; and it was duly exploited by Churchill's one serious rival as Prime Minister, Sir Stafford Cripps. The result was the appointment of a Ministerial Cabinet Committee on the Machinery of Government, chaired by the Lord President (Sir John Anderson) and shadowed by an official committee. Both were wound up in 1945. The initiative, however, did not wholly die. Parliamentary pressure provoked a flurry of official working parties, under very loose Ministerial leadership. Then, following a highly critical report by the Estimates Committee during Labour's 'annus horribilis' of 1947, an official Government Organisation Committee (1947–53) was appointed under Bridges' chairmanship. It was supported within the Treasury by an enlarged Organisation and Methods Division which, to demonstrate the seriousness with which such matters were now being treated, included for the first time a discrete section handling 'machinery of government' questions.[81]

For over a decade, therefore, there was a unique opportunity radically to review the Service's management and structure as well as the political context within which it worked. The lessons of wartime improvisation could be digested and then applied to the challenge of administering government's greatly enhanced responsibilities. The improvisations with greatest peacetime potential included the devolution of power from Whitehall (to either regional offices or authorities), the granting of executive powers to coordinating committees (which had been used to expedite international decisions, particularly with the USA) and the growth of a Central Capability (particularly with the creation of the CSO and the Economic Section). The particular peacetime challenges demanding attention were the better functional division of responsibilities between departments (particularly in relation to economic policy); the reduction of Cabinet to a more manageable size (possibly through the appointment of 'overlords'); and an assurance that Parliament had both the time and expertise to debate legislation and monitor the Executive.[82]

Given their remit, it is unsurprising that most of the proposals which were later to dominate administrative reform were either aired before or debated by these committees. For example, in anticipation of the 1961 Plowden Report, Bridges called for joint forecasts of public expenditure and government income to 'bring Ministers to a sense of real responsibility about finance' before major policy decisions.[83] In anticipation of Fulton, there were demands *inter alia* for a separation of the financial and management responsibilities of the Treasury, unified grading and the creation of a civil service college. Even in anticipation of Thatcherite reforms, there were proposals for a greatly increased number of Parliamentary select committees, less uniform treatment of individual citizens in the interests of efficiency (one of Rayner's proposed lasting reforms) and, albeit in relation to nationalised industries, a clear differentiation between Ministerial responsibility and executive independence. The fact that such proposals continued to dominate postwar debate is, however, evidence of the failure of the Anderson Committee and its successors to seize a unique opportunity to modernise the Service in anticipation of future need. Rather its record was a 'melancholy tale of ineffectual inquiry and recommendation'.[84]

A major reason for this failure was beyond the control of officials. This was a continuing absence of political leadership without which no major administrative or constitutional change can be effected. During the War, Churchill was understandably uninterested whilst, within the Coalition, the very different attitudes of Conservative and Labour Ministers towards state intervention stifled debate.[85] Its continuing absence after the Labour government election was rather less excusable. Failure fundamentally stemmed, however, from Anderson's initial persuasion of Cripps in 1942 that any inquiry should be internal. This was a measure of how increasing exclusivity had narrowed officials' perceptions – and particularly those of Anderson as a former civil servant. Indeed, despite its acknowledged influence on Fisher and Bridges, the Haldane Committee was conventionally cited within Whitehall as a prime example of the ineffectuality of outside inquiries. Such inquiries, so it was argued, lacked 'the first hand experience to make immediately applicable recommendations'. In the longer term, their recommendations were also generally impracticable because they ignored the impact of contingency (such as individual personality) on organisation – a fact that could never be admitted in public. In addition, and rather less creditably, they were bound to fail because they aroused 'a defensive frame of mind' amongst those being reviewed, which would impair implementation.[86] Consequently, while officials felt confident that they could emulate 'outsiders' by keeping abstract principles in mind, they were equally certain that they would not – and should not – let theoretical considerations interfere with the practical realities of administration. The Service, in Anderson's words, best developed 'organically'; and as Bridges minuted Brook in 1952: 'if those of us who have lived all our working lives in Whitehall and have studied the Whitehall organization give up as hopeless all attempt to reform it from inside, then what hope is there of any reform in our time?'[87]

The problem was that the 'practitioners' equivalent to Haldane', as the Anderson Committee and its successors became known, was even more flawed. This was largely because, in Michael Lee's words, it was bedevilled by a 'special mixture of ambiguity in definition and ambivalence in discussion'.[88] The Anderson Committee itself, for instance, had no formal terms of reference, Bridges successfully insisting that its purpose would be best 'served by good sense, not by definition'. Subsequently confusion reigned over whether it should plan for or beyond reconstruction and indeed what the long-term role of government would be. Likewise the remits of later official committees were unclear as to whether their prime purpose was to remedy existing in efficiencies or to tackle new problems efficiently. Such confusion was compounded by Bridges' determination to achieve a practical consensus through exhaustive interdepartmental negotiation and a distillation of the wisdom of Permanent Secretaries. Hence his obsession with 'tactics and personality' and yet his simultaneous inability, particularly in relation to economic planning, to break down the traditional impediments of Ministers 'reserving their position' and officials defending departmental interests to the death. Coordination of policy, Anderson had argued, could best be achieved by Cabinet committees rather than by 'overlords'; but this presupposed that, as Haldane had urged, the functional divisions between departments were rational.[89] Similarly interdepartmental official committees were only effective if their purpose was clear and the will existed to resolve, rather than evade, problems. Neither condition was met between 1942 and 1953. 'A separate outside body', officials had insisted in 1949, 'could be justified only if it were contended that the reforms needed were so radical that Civil Servants could not be expected even to consider them, let alone recommend them'.[90] The need was 'so radical' and, in addition, given the practical experience of wartime 'temporaries' and the Service's high prestige, the time also propitious for open debate. To the Service's long-term detriment, however, this seemingly ideal opportunity for reform was missed.

2.3 The administrative machine

Powerful though the Administrative Class has been as a magnet for attention, it represented only a small fraction of the non-industrial Civil Service. The typical Civil Servant, and thus the embodiment of government growth, was the executive, clerical, scientific and professional official. Between 1929 and 1956 the Administrative Class doubled from approximately 1100 to 2500. Simultaneously the Executive Class more than quadrupled from 15,400 to 68,200, the Clerical Classes tripled from

66,100 to 184,400 and the professional/scientific classes more than quintupled from 18,500 to 99,000.[91] Such an escalation raised questions about the growth of bureaucratic power. It also required government, as the largest employer of white-collar workers, to pioneer new methods of industrial relations and work – including, not least, the replacement of the archetypal Victorian male clerk with women and machines. These are the subjects of the following section.

2.3.1 A new despotism?

An early manifestation of government growth was the increased use of delegated legislation (with officials being entrusted by Parliament to determine in detail how legislation should be implemented) and administrative justice (whereby, as in the case of the interwar Court of Referees and unemployment insurance, a body other than a court of law adjudicated on appeals against administrative decisions).[92] Both developments theoretically undermined Parliamentary sovereignty and the rule of law; and they were most famously attacked for so doing in 1929 by the Lord Chief Justice, Lord Hewart, in his polemic *The New Despotism*. This attack was quickly dismissed by the 1932 Donoughmore Committee on Ministerial Powers (on which both Anderson and Fisher served). There was, it concluded, 'nothing to justify any lowering of the country's high opinion of the Civil Service or any reflection on its sense of justice, or any ground for a belief that our constitutional machinery is developing in directions which are fundamentally wrong'. As a result, amongst even the most conservative lawyers 'the cloak and dagger view of bureaucratic conspiracy faded quietly away'.[93]

Certain safeguards were nevertheless recommended by Donoughmore and were belatedly incorporated into a somewhat prosaic programme of reform in the 1940s. A specialist Parliamentary select committee, for example, was appointed to scrutinise delegated legislation and to alert Parliament to issues requiring debate. The 1946 Standing Instruments Act also sought to standardise such legislation and thus make it more intelligible. These reforms reflected continuing tension between Parliament and the Executive. Remarkably, however, the earlier suspicions of the judiciary had evaporated. Despite Whitehall's assumption during and after the War of exceptional administrative powers (in relation, for instance, to rationing and town and country planning), judges leant over backwards 'almost to the point of falling off the bench' in order to be accommodating.[94] Planning inspectors' reports, for example, were permitted to remain secret (despite the assumption of 'natural justice' that they should be open to all interested parties). 'Ouster' clauses in delegated legislation, which forbade judicial review, continued to be condoned despite their condemnation by Donoughmore. Most famously, a series of legal judgments after the Liversidge v Anderson case in 1941, ruled that courts had no right to interfere in the exercise of administrative power by a Minister (or more realistically by an official) if he or she could claim to have acted 'reasonably'. The criterion for 'reasonableness' was to be determined by the relevant ministry; and, following a 1948 legal judgment, all the courts required was a tautological assurance that official action had not been 'so unreasonable that no reasonable body should so act'. In short, despite an underlying suspicion of increased state intervention (as reflected in the Crichel Down affair) government and its officials were judicially granted an immense 'zone of immunity'.[95]

The fundamental reason for this immunity was a pragmatic acceptance of the inevitable. Parliament had neither the time nor the technical expertise to scrutinise effectively 'the kind and quality of legislation which modern public opinion requires'. Delegated legislation was, therefore, unavoidable.[96] Administrative tribunals also tended to be speedier, cheaper and less forbidding for the claimant than traditional courts of law. Finally, as the Donoughmore Committee stressed, parallel developments were occurring in most Western countries (including the USA) to enable governments to satisfy democratically expressed needs. As in so many other areas of government, however, the typically pragmatic British response led to peculiar problems. It created a haphazard accumulation of precedents, which led to contradictions and confusion. In his despair, Hewart was tempted even to defy his mentor, Dicey, by arguing that a system of administrative law (as in France) would be preferable to a state of administrative lawlessness (as was developing in England). Similarly W.A. Robson consistently championed administrative law, albeit for very different reasons. Dicey had been wrong, he insisted, to assert that the *droit administrative* gave the French state arbitrary and irresponsible power. Rather, it benefited individual citizens by giving them 'superior guarantees of justice and better facilities for redress'.[97] Inevitably so radical a change was never contemplated with the result that, when both public and informed opinion began to swing against authority in 1956, government was left unprotected. Judges started once again to reassert the supremacy of the common law over Parliament and the Executive; and, to its considerable embarrassment, 'the protective wall' surrounding government gradually collapsed.

2.3.2 *Industrial relations*

The rapid increase in the size of the Civil Service during the First World War inevitably created new problems for its management. Before the War, falling real wages and a constant downgrading of work had generated considerable unrest. This was exacerbated particularly in 1916 by the Treasury's unilateral attempt to increase the working day (without compensation) and its continuing refusal to raise wages in line with inflation (in order to set the private sector a good example). Increased militancy, however, extracted a significant concession. A Civil Service Arbitration Board was appointed which not only sanctioned a series of cost-of-living bonuses but also, by giving them official recognition, made staff associations within the Service respectable.

There followed an exceptional period of collective organisation. The number of associations increased between 1913 and 1919 from 80 to 194. Conversely, and rather more importantly, they started to amalgamate. The most significant merger was that of eleven major associations, representing some 16,500 officials, to form the Civil Service Clerical Association (CSCA) in 1922. It became the most powerful interwar union under the charismatic, if somewhat maverick, leadership of W.J. Brown and by 1956 represented all but 6000 of the 155,000 strong Clerical Class. Other major developments were the founding in 1918 of the Association of First Division Clerks to represent the nascent Administrative Class; the formation of the Institution of Professional Civil Servants a year later, uniting the myriad of small associations representing individual specialisms; and the rebranding of the Society of Civil Servants in 1930 to represent Executive Class officials (including those formerly represented by the Second Division Clerks Association). Interwar unity was further enhanced by the combination of all major unions within the Civil Service Confederation.[98]

Between 1916 and 1922, collective organisation was principally driven by antagonism towards government. After 1922 it was not. The driving factors then were a desire to increase density of membership (which, in contrast to other areas of white-collar employment, reached 90 per cent by the 1950s) and demarcation disputes (particularly over women, temporary and ex-service officials). The catalyst for reduced antagonism towards government was the introduction in 1919 of Whitleyism and, in particular, the subsequent division of officials into four broad classes – the administrative, executive, clerical and writing assistant classes (supported by two further classes of 'manipulative' workers, namely typists and shorthand typists). Assimilation of existing staff into these classes and the representation of their particular interests became the principal determinant of both union structure and action. The earlier ideal of one all-Service union was lost.[99]

The establishment of Whitleyism was a triumph of rank-and-file militancy. The reconstruction plan of 1917 to improve industrial relations by creating joint councils of managers and workers at a national, district and workplace level had originally been restricted to private industry. Clerical associations, however, demanded its extension to government. Then, when the creation of the National Whitley Council (NWC) was being negotiated in June 1919, they ensured – against the Government's expressed wishes – that it had real power. Remarkably, given the Treasury's long history of using the conventions of Ministerial responsibility and Parliamentary sovereignty to evade decisions, the NWC constitution made explicit that it was an executive (not a mere advisory) body and that its decisions became operative once they had been reported to Cabinet.[100] Rank-and-file pressure was equally instrumental in the setting up of the NWC Reorganisation Committee which, once again with remarkable speed, agreed by January 1920 the standardisation of classes into which all officials were to be fitted. The actual process of reorganisation took longer and provoked further threats of militancy. It was complete, however, by 1924 – as was the establishment within each ministry of the supplementary tiers of departmental and unit committees. Within five years, therefore, a formal mechanism had been established which could, and duly did, foster co-operation and trust both within the associations (who formed the 'staff side' of the NWC) and between them and the 'official' side (consisting mainly of senior Administrative Class officials under firm Treasury leadership).

Whitleyism reflected many wider trends. The new service-wide classes, for example, accorded with Northcote-Trevelyan's principles of unification and of the division of labour. It also contributed to the Service's growing exclusivity: rank-and-file grievances were no longer aired in petitions to MPs and so generated less public controversy. Officials also assumed the gratifying, if rather anomalous, role of both employer and employed. It also successfully replaced the disorganisation, mutual resentments and rising militancy of the late Victorian and Edwardian era by providing the mechanism by which both the unions and the Treasury could marshal their arguments and address issues rationally without undue confrontation. Its true worth was demonstrated during the Second World War when – often through complex, informal negotiations similar to those within the contemporary Cabinet committee system – it effectively resolved issues (such as the payment, dispersal and eventual redundancy of staff) which had generated considerable conflict during the First World War.[101] Such co-operation was not inevitable, although it did accord with the changing temper of industrial relations throughout the country between 1921 and 1956.

Whitleyism, however, far from provided a panacea for all industrial relations problems. During the economy cuts of the early 1920s, for example, anger was generated by a unilateral cut in wartime bonuses and the abolition of the Conciliation and Arbitration Board between 1922 and 1925. Thereafter the National Whitley Council descended into what has been termed a mix of 'starch and dynamite' – increasing rigidity and formality enlivened by sudden emotional outbursts from union leaders such as Brown. Preliminary discussions between the unions also descended on occasion into physical violence (as Brown and the leader of the Post Office workers, G.H. Stuart-Bunning, sought to resolve sectional differences by more traditional methods).[102]

Such discord at a national level meant that the opportunity was lost to discuss ways of adapting the interwar Service to social and political change. Longer standing issues, such as pay and civil rights, were also not fully resolved. On pay, for example, the Treasury – under Parliamentary pressure – continued to seek to minimise costs by downgrading work. Moreover, the recommendation of the Tomlin Commission in 1931 that 'fair' wages should also reflect the 'economic condition of society' was seized upon as a pretext to renounce the government's role as model employer and to follow, or rather lag behind, market rates in a largely unorganised sector of private industry. Real levels of pay for established Civil Servants duly plummeted. As a result of militancy they had risen considerably for the lower grades between 1916 and 1920. Those of higher grades had followed suit in the 1920s. Thereafter, they both fell uniformly, with one commentator even concluding chillingly that 'all grades except clerical officers and women clerks were receiving less in real wages in 1950 than they were in 1875'.[103] This was the problem the Priestley Commission was established to resolve.

The issue of civil rights was equally contested and had particularly exercised the MacDonnell Commission. How was the impartiality of officials to be reconciled to their democratic right both to be members of trade unions and to participate actively in politics? The 1926 General Strike brought the first issue to a head. Several major unions, including the CSCA and the Association of Officers of Taxes (headed by the future Labour Cabinet Minister, Douglas Houghton) were affiliated to the Labour Party and the TUC. Consequently their leaders instinctively promised to place their resources and members at the TUC's disposal. This shocked not only many of their own members but more especially the leaders of those associations representing senior grades. They took the alternative – and arguably contradictory – stance that, to remain impartial, Civil Servants should not strike and that, out of loyalty to the state, they should even volunteer to undertake additional work. The result was that co-operation between the associations temporarily ceased. More significantly, the 1927 Trade Disputes and Trade Unions Act forbade established Civil Servants to be members of, or affiliates to, any organisation which either included persons other than those 'employed by or under the Crown' or had explicit political objectives. Consequently, until the legislation was repealed in 1946, Civil Servants could be members of neither the Labour Party nor TUC, nor indeed of many professional and international organisations.[104]

The more fundamental civil rights issue, however, was the extent to which Civil Servants should participate in national and local politics. Throughout the period, the 1884 decision held firm that no working, non-industrial Civil Servants could be adopted as a prospective Parliamentary candidate. The situation concerning local politics and canvassing, however, remained confused and, belatedly Bridges sought its resolution in 1948. The Masterman Committee was appointed and duly recommended that a line be drawn between the clerical and 'manipulative' classes to distinguish those who were politically 'free' from those who were 'restricted'. Staff associations were outraged. The right to participate in local politics (which was their main concern) had, in their judgement, been curtailed. Moreover no government, let alone a Labour Government, should have accepted such a recommendation without discussion. Exhaustive negotiations on the NWC ensued and eventually a compromise reached whereby an 'intermediate' group of officials would be allowed, at their department's discretion, to participate in all political activity other than Parliamentary candidature. This was a reversion to a nineteenth-century tactic of evading clear statements of principle and was equally bound to generate anomalies and contradictions.[105]

Despite its unquestionable success, therefore, Whitleyism between 1919 and 1956 begs two important questions. First, given plummeting rates of pay (particularly after 1932 when the NSS was at its most compliant), would greater militancy have reaped greater material rewards? Whitleyism, after all, may have strengthened the staff associations, but did it not strengthen the Treasury even more? It used Whitleyism to reassert its authority rapidly over Ministers (for whom it acted as proxy), outside interests (whose representatives were soon excluded from the Official Side) and other departments (whose members 'like witnesses to a medieval charter' tended not to participate actively at the NWC but just 'lend weight and dignity to the proceedings'). After 1920, consequently, Treasury control was rarely compromised. Once again, having started from a position of considerable weakness, had it emerged from a bout of radical reform with its powers enhanced? At the height of militancy in 1917, Brown had thundered that 'nothing less than the elimination of Treasury control will do'. By the mid-1920s, however, the reality was that 'the Staff Side may say what they like ... but the Official Side ... do what they like'.[106]

The second fundamental question is whether Whitleyism compromised managerial efficiency. By structurally entrenching the sectional interests of staff associations, for example, did it impede change? Alternatively, did it generate such 'complex and delicately balanced agreements' that managers dared not question them? Did the reaching of such agreements become an end in itself? In other words, like Bridges' other creation – the system of Cabinet and interdepartmental committees – had Whitleyism by the mid-1950s started to become an impediment rather than a spur to good government? This was a question which the Fulton Committee was directly to address.[107]

2.3.3 Women and machines

Whatever the changes to administrative law and industrial relations, the most visible – and arguably fundamental – transformation in the Civil Service was the replacement of the male copyist by machinery and women. In 1916, British government, like British industry, was a technological laggard. One of the last in the West to mechanise its most daunting administrative task (the census), it had installed by the end of the War only one-quarter the number of the comptometers (punched card machines) that were available in the USA to the federal Inland Revenue Department alone.[108] The extreme wariness with which earlier innovations, such as the typewriter in 1880s and the telephone in 1890s, had been accepted also remained a perverse source of departmental pride.[109] In 1911, however, a bridgehead had been established by the mechanisation not only of the census but also of the records of some eighteen million people covered by the new National Insurance Act. This bridgehead was extended by wartime demands such as demobilisation and the payment of war pensions; and thereafter both the routine and capacity of government was revolutionised. New technology (such as duplicating, calculating, franking and punched card machines) was applied to standard tasks (such as the payroll and the collection of statistics) and, even more importantly, to the extension of policy (including the delivery of ever more complex social services). Indeed, the Civil Service in many areas began to lead the private sector. The Post Office Savings Bank, for instance, mechanised far faster than private banks; and, in a significant reversal of roles, delegates from the USA to the Old Age Pensions offices at Kew in the 1930s expressed amazement at how much could be achieved by so few.[110] A personal example was even set by Walter Desborough, a boy clerk appointed to the Home Office in 1903, who rose to head the Treasury's Investigating Section (established in response to the 1919 Bradbury Committee to ensure 'business efficiency' in Whitehall). Permitted an exceptionally public role as chairman of the Office Appliance Trade Association in the 1920s, he ultimately left the Service in 1931 to become the general manager of Powers, one of the two leading British manufacturers of punched card machines.

The public sector's lead was maintained and even extended after 1939. Emergency wartime legislation, such as national registration and rationing, posed huge logistical challenges. So too after 1945 did the introduction of, by international standards, a highly centralised welfare state. By 1951, for example, the office of the Ministry of National Insurance at Newcastle alone held the records of some 28 million people and was processing over 40 million payments a year. The response to these challenges, together with the discharge of more routine tasks (such as the updating of equipment) was initially controlled by the Treasury which, smarting from Parliamentary criticism in 1941 and 1948, had enlarged and rebranded its Investigating Section as the Organisation and Methods Division. By the 1950s, however, the dual demands of complexity and capacity demanded more radical action. That was provided by the adaptation to office work of wartime experiments in computerisation, pioneered by code-breakers at Bletchley Park. Once again the Civil Service took the lead. While private firms such as the Prudential (to which the earliest tasks of card-punching had been contracted out in 1911) faltered, computers were used for the first time in 1955 on clerical work within Whitehall (the calculation of PAYE tax changes). Then, to launch an ambitious programme designed by a new interdepartmental Standing Committee on Automatic Data Processing, the payroll of the Ministry of Supply and National Assistance Board was computerised in 1958.[111] Having been a laggard in 1916, the British Civil Service by 1956 had become technologically not just a national but an international pioneer.

It was not, however, the employment of machines that initially caused the Service the greatest problems. It was the employment of women. The two were closely related. For instance, the three lowest Service-wide classes approved by the NWC in 1920 – typists, shorthand typists and writing assistants – were the ones which principally operated new technology ('writing assistants' being the somewhat inappropriate term used for those operating *inter alia* punched card and calculating machines).[112] They were exclusively female. This raised no fundamental problem in itself. Rather, it provided the Treasury with an ideal solution to the problem which had been exercising it: the reconciliation of declining morale with the need for greater capacity. Before 1914, the spectre had been looming of an ever-growing army of militant male copyists, increasingly recruited from the lower social classes and disenchanted by limited career prospects. This was allayed by the employment of women. Given universal education and limited alternative employment, there was a pool of women who were typically better-educated and socially superior. Allied to their perceived 'natural' qualities (such as greater patience and attention to detail), this promised high levels of efficiency and trustworthiness. It also promised economy. Women's wages were lower; they were traditionally less militant; and their typical wish to leave work on marriage both kept average wages down and limited pension liabilities – as well as solving the problem of limited career opportunities. The fundamental dilemma facing the

Treasury, therefore, was not whether to employ women at this level but whether to recruit them also into the Clerical, Executive and Administrative Classes.

The First World War provided an opportunity to resolve this dilemma. Prewar prejudice was exposed by the relatively successful employment of women at all levels within the Service. Indeed the 1918 Haldane Committee even argued that the previous absence of women had 'deprived the public service of a vast store of knowledge, experience and fresh ideas, some of which would, for particular purposes, have been far more valuable and relevant than those of even the ablest of men in the Civil Service'.[113] Following the enfranchisement of women over thirty, the 1919 Sex Disqualification (Removal) Act also appeared to outlaw discrimination. It stated that 'a person shall not be disqualified by sex or marriage from the exercise of any public function, or from being appointed to or holding any civil or judicial office or post'. Almost immediately, however, residual fears resurfaced about the propriety of men and women competing for and within employment (which, to an extent, were condoned by the new feminist ideal of 'separate spheres'). There was also an understandable sense of obligation towards ex-servicemen. Consequently barriers to the employment of women, particularly on equal terms to men, were quickly re-erected.[114]

In the clerical and executive grades, the employment of women was immediately impeded by the 'substitution' in 1919 of temporary clerks by ex-servicemen. In addition, there was also an implicit assumption that women should be confined to the three 'sub-clerical' classes (or at least to their supervision). Then, when these temporary posts were made permanent, the core Northcote-Trevelyan principle of open competition was suspended from 1919 until 1925 (for women) and 1927 (for men). The alternative 'reconstruction' competitions were restricted to existing temporary staff and gender-segregated. They thus favoured the newly 'substituted' male and, under escalating political pressure, they increasingly advantaged him: examinations were made easier, those who failed were encouraged to re-apply and those who persisted in failing were eventually made permanent.[115] By such means, over 31,000 ex-servicemen were permanently recruited into the Clerical Class. By contrast, the examinations for women were made progressively harder and those who failed were not encouraged to re-apply. Only 6,500 were recruited. Consequently, the proportion of Civil Servants who were women (which had peaked at 56 per cent in 1918) only marginally rose from 21 to 27 per cent between 1914 and 1938. Simultaneously the percentage of ex-servicemen rose from 8 to 50 per cent. This did not, on the Treasury's own admission, represent a gain in operational efficiency.

In the Administrative Class, the efficiency gains anticipated by the Haldane Report were also largely lost. Women were formally excluded from some departments. These included the Foreign, Colonial and Dominions Offices (where they might have had to deal with foreigners) and the defence ministries (where they might have had to deal with officers). They were excluded also from a discrete range of other jobs in, for example, the Ministry of Agriculture and law departments (where, even more embarrassingly, they might have had to grapple with such subjects as animal breeding and sexual offences). In addition, they were excluded from all but one of the reconstruction examinations – and from that only four candidates emerged successful. Thereafter the traditional routes of entry, via open competition and promotion, proved scarcely more profitable. Only 7.5 and 8.5 per cent of the respective entrants between 1925 and 1938 were women. As with the relative failure of non-Oxbridge candidates, disappointment was accredited by many to the interview; and, to give credence to such suspicions, in 1937 women attained three of the top four places in the written examination, only to be downgraded after interview. As with non-Oxbridge graduates, however, a more fundamental explanation would appear to have been the social pressures which discouraged women from applying. Disconcertingly, these trends continued after 1945.[116]

In addition to the barriers against the employment of women, their employment on equal terms to men was discouraged. There were two specific impediments: the marriage bar and unequal pay. In theory, the former had been outlawed by the Sex Disqualification (Removal) Act. In practice, however, it was strengthened. In a prime example of delegated legislation, the application of the law to the Civil Service was left to regulation; and the Order in Council, duly issued in August 1921, restricted posts to unmarried women or widows. Disingenuously, the Treasury argued that a negative right (that a women should not be disqualified from holding certain posts) did not amount to a positive entitlement to hold such posts. So long as the 'spirit of the act' was honoured by generally increasing employment opportunities for women, 'a certain amount of discretion' was permissible in the way the Act was implemented.[117] Despite so blatant a subversion of the law, the marriage bar nevertheless induced little protest. At senior levels, the real bar to marriage was the absence of eligible men following the slaughter on the Western Front. Were the prospect of marriage to loom, the actual vows rather than employment could be – and frequently were – foregone. Alternatively, after 1938, exemption could be sought. At a lower level, single women tended to appreciate the greater opportunities afforded by the exclusion of married rivals and their immediate right to a marriage gratuity (as opposed to a minimal, delayed pension). The bar was finally raised by the Labour Cabinet in 1946, but even then the Staff Side of the NWC supported retention.

Unequal pay aroused stronger passions. Arguably this was because it not only raised women's sense of injustice but also men's fear of being undercut. Motions were regularly passed in the House of Commons from 1920 to 1952 demanding equality; but as late as 1946 a Royal Commission on Equal Pay could provide a formidable list of reasons why it should be denied. Among these were women's 'natural' inclination to greater absenteeism and inflexibility, the cost (and, after 1945, the inflationary effect) and the inadvisability of advancing too far ahead of public opinion and private practice. Agreement was finally reached on the NWC in 1954 for the staged implementation of equal pay by 1961. Rather than being a resounding endorsement of a principle, however, this was something of a damp squib. The principle had been conceded (costlessly) by the Labour Government in 1947. Then the principal motivation behind its promised implementation was an (unsuccessful) attempt by a Conservative Chancellor to enliven a dull budget.[118]

The manner in which machinery and women were accommodated within the Service after 1916 might appear, in retrospect, to have been highly conservative. Indeed the special treatment of ex-servicemen in the interwar period, by placing political obligation before operational efficiency, could be presented as a reversion to the evils of patronage which Northcote-Trevelyan had reputedly exorcised. Placed in a contemporary context, however, practice within the Service often preceded that in the private sector and, more importantly, public opinion. Before 1945, for example, this was true of comparable occupations such as banking, and after 1945 more generally in relation to computerisation and equal pay. Formally, therefore, the Service appeared frequently to be in the van of progress. Whether in practice this was so, or whether it meant very much – as demonstrated, for instance, by the evasion of the Sex Disqualification (Removal) Act – is another matter.

2.4 Conclusion

Were the years between 1916 and 1956, as in later collective memory, a 'golden age'? To the extent that they were, how far was this – as again suggested by collective memory – a legacy of the Northcote-Trevelyan Report? Certainly, it was at this time that the British Home Civil Service established its international reputation as the best in the world. This provides a valuable criterion for assessment because it encourages the measurement of performance not against some ideal type but against the contemporary response of other bureaucracies to the dual challenge of democratic politics at home and intensified economic and military competition abroad.

In many respects, the Service's reputation was justified. It exuded financial and political integrity. Scandals such as the Francs case and Crichel Down were minor by international standards, as was any involvement in party politics. The ability, and conscientiousness, of individual officials was typically high. Despite the interwar preference of ex-servicemen over women and the increasing bias towards Oxbridge graduates in senior posts, officials *at all levels* represented – in a commonly used phrase – 'the cream of the education system'.[119] Most importantly, despite the inevitable and innumerable instances of interdepartmental rivalry, the system as a whole enjoyed an unrivalled operational unity and flexibility. This was a triumph for the development after 1916 of Service-wide classes, the committee system and the encouragement of a common ethos under the leadership of the Treasury and the Cabinet Secretariat. The Service's integrity duly ensured that it was entrusted, with few qualms, with the ever-increasing power which central government in all Western democracies was accruing. Its relative efficiency was proven by its performance in the Second World War.

Nevertheless, as has been seen, the Service was subject to continuing contemporary criticism, first from those who opposed government growth and then from those who advocated it. How can such seemingly contradictory views be reconciled? Contemporary criticism, it should be remembered, was not disinterested. Its validity has, therefore, to be assessed in the light of the historic constraints imposed on the Service both by public opinion and the relative weakness of the other two requirements for good government: political leadership and an effective Parliament. Lloyd George's administrative improvisations may not always have been benign; but they were at least preferable to the succeeding political neglect of administrative reform. This was particularly pronounced after 1945. Moreover, Parliament was not strengthened after 1916 to the extent that, for instance, the Haldane Report wanted. As a result economy could still be publicly confused with efficiency and the need for government growth, as democratically demanded, denied by anti-waste campaigns. The Service, not for the first or indeed the last time, was being used as a scapegoat for the failings of others.

Given this context, the Service's record between 1916 and 1956 appears wholly creditable. In the adoption of technology and equal pay, for example, it preceded – so far as was politic – both public opinion and private practice. In the development of administrative law and Whitleyism, it also drew the early venom of both the judicial system and the trade union movement. This provided a unique opportunity to forge an informed consensus on how, administratively, democratic government should evolve. To the Service's discredit, however, it was squandered. Those most culpable were the Higher Civil Service which demanded, and was duly entrusted with, responsibility for reform immediately after the Second World War. The common ethos of self-denial and public self-effacement may have earned its initial trust. In the absence of a powerful and independent political counterweight, however, this ethos soon descended into self-regard and self-righteousness. As demonstrated by the reception of Keynesianism, the discussion – let alone the formulation – of alternative views was actively discouraged. 'The gentleman in Whitehall knows best', became the ruling assumption, 'and the gentleman who dares to question Whitehall is no gentleman'.[120] In short, intellectually and temperamentally, it was ill-equipped to respond constructively to the radical change of government – to which it should have been fully alerted by the steady growth of the interwar administrative machine beneath it. By 1945 the challenge, and definition, of 'administration' was irrevocably changing from an 'awareness of the Minister's mind' to the active management of interventionist policy.

Both the strengths and weaknesses of the Higher Civil Service during this 'golden age' have been accredited to the Northcote-Trevelyan Report. On the one hand, the Report was seen as a blueprint for integrity, unity and high intellectual attainment. On the other, it was deemed responsible for its exclusiveness and inherent 'amateurishness'. In its quest for efficiency, Northcote-Trevelyan had certainly encouraged educational and social exclusivity. At the time this was perfectly logical; but would its authors have so ignored later educational advance and intensified social bias, through the addition of an interview to the selection procedure? What is incontrovertible is that they did not favour 'amateurism', as alleged by the Fulton Committee. The Report neither opposed the appointment of outsiders to senior posts nor privileged generalist above department expertise. It implicitly favoured post-entry training. Moreover, it expressed a ruthlessness in its intention to promote the able and remove the incompetent that was not always employed by later regimes. Many of the weaknesses attributed to the Report's legacy, therefore, were not the result of its actual recommendations but of adaptations to, or the non-application, of them.

There was one key issue, however, that Northcote-Trevelyan had not adequately addressed. This, ironically given later collective memory, was the issue of political neutrality. Party political allegiance may have come to be suppressed over time but the problem of officials acting as 'statesmen in disguise' had been potentially increased by open competition. As government grew, the problem grew ever larger. The Haldane Committee failed to address it. It was then intensified when both Fisher and Bridges, in their supposed implementation of Northcote-Trevelyan, endorsed and further refined the increasingly impracticable convention of Ministerial responsibility.

Part 2

THE REFORM MOMENTUM

3

MODERNISATION BEFORE FULTON, 1956–66

3.1 Introduction

The Fulton Report, commissioned in February 1966 and published in June 1968, was a deliberate attempt to make good the 'lost opportunity' of postwar administrative reform. Within and outside government, its recommendations immediately became the benchmark for measuring the Service's *institutional* capacity to discharge its increased responsibilities. However, its significance – if not the frisson of excitement its publication generated – soon faded. There were two main reasons. First, by the mid-1970s the *inherent* capacity of government to resolve society's problems was once again being questioned following a resurgence, at all levels of society, of that instinctive individualism which had both compromised the Haldane Report and encouraged Bridges to resist reform. This cast doubt on the Report's underlying assumptions and hence its proposals. Second, the Report came to be seen not as the culmination of, but rather as an idiosyncratic contribution to, a vigorous post-Suez debate about the 'modernisation of Britain'. This debate – which, like Fulton, took as axiomatic the beneficence of greater state intervention – is the subject of this chapter.

The debate was facilitated by decreasing deference and fuelled by a conviction of 'national decline'. The Suez invasion, through its perceived political incompetence and amorality, discredited the 'establishment' (a term coined in 1953, popularised in 1955 and refined by 1962 to describe a cluster of elite groups believed to hold effective power).[1] Combined with greater individual confidence, arising from increasing affluence, this led to its more aggressive treatment in the media and ridicule by the satire 'movement'.[2] Commercial television, for instance, had introduced a more aggressive form of political reporting by 1956. *Beyond the Fringe* was also first staged in August 1960 and *Private Eye* first published in October 1961; and, reaching a far wider audience, *That Was The Week That Was* was briefly transmitted from October 1962 to December 1963. The Higher Civil Service was inevitably identified as part of the 'establishment'; and the veil of secrecy, as well as the aura of principled integrity and disinterest, so carefully constructed by Fisher and Bridges, was duly compromised.

Suez had also exposed Britain's inability to act, militarily and economically, independently of the USA. Succeeded by a period of rapid decolonisation and a dawning awareness of faster economic growth in other European economies, the conviction consequently grew that Britain was in a state of *avoidable* national decline.³ Whether such a 'boom in gloom' was justified is questionable. Britain's economic growth rate, for instance, was at an historical high; and comparative European rates were temporarily boosted by an influx into industry of underemployed agricultural workers and, statistically, by their calculation from a much lower base due to wartime devastation. The critique also contained a fundamental contradiction. On the one hand, relative economic decline was attributed to low domestic investment as the result of an 'indefensible' misallocation of scarce resources to overambitious military and colonial commitments ('global overstretch'). On the other, any reduction in such commitments would have confirmed for many Britain's decline as a world power.

Whatever its justification, 'decline' became (as it has tended to remain) the predominant political discourse; and because it was deemed avoidable, a culprit had to be sought. Conservatism throughout society was typically targeted, with the favoured remedies being trade union and, above all, educational reform. 'The old privileged values of aristocracy, public schools and Oxbridge', wrote Anthony Sampson, for instance, in his path-breaking *Anatomy of Britain* in 1962, 'have failed to provide the stimulus, the purposive policies and the keen eye on the future which Britain is looking for.'⁴ All 'establishment' institutions (including the City and industry) were attacked; but, as in Sampson's own analysis, the principal focus all too easily became the Government and, even more narrowly, the Treasury. Responsible for the management of both the economy and the Civil Service, it was a convenient scapegoat for the perceived failures of both.

Politicians and officials reacted speedily to this demand for modernisation. Until 1958 there had been continuing attempts to 'roll back' the state, such as Operation Robot in 1952 and Peter Thorneycroft's attempted expenditure cuts of 1957. However, the defeat of Robot and Thorneycroft's resignation as Chancellor, together with that of his whole ministerial team, were evidence that such attempts failed. This was, as it continues to be, for neo-liberals a 'lost opportunity' of equal significance to that sustained, according to advocates of state intervention, by Bridges' failure to reform postwar Whitehall.⁵

After 1958, the Labour Party – convinced of both the reality of relative decline and the Conservative Government's culpability – championed major institutional reform. This resulted, after its election victory in 1964, in the creation *inter alia* of the Department of Economic Affairs (to counteract the Treasury's alleged short-termism) and the Ministry of Technology (to harness scientific expertise more effectively to industry). The commissioning of the Fulton Committee fitted naturally into this pattern. The preceding Conservative Governments, however, had been far from idle. The political will to modernise had, for instance, been expressed with typical panache by Harold Macmillan in October 1962. In Cabinet, he begged the question:

> Do we, or do we not, set out to control the pattern of events, to direct development, to plan growth, to use the instruments of Government to influence

and determine private decisions. Believe that this is inevitable. Forces at work now too complicated, risks of set back too great to leave to market forces and laisser faire. Dirigisme. But it must be creative dirigisme.[6]

Preceding this speech, there had been a major institutional innovation: the creation of the tripartite National Economic Development Council (NEDC), with an independent secretariat (the National Economic Development Office, NEDO), to coordinate and stimulate growth. Succeeding it, an ambitious public expenditure programme was adopted to provide the perceived preconditions for growth. Not least amongst these was the 1963 Robbins Committee's recommendation that the number of students in higher education should be doubled within ten years.

Attitudes and working practices within Whitehall had been simultaneously adjusted. In a typical Macmillan ploy, a leading critic of the Treasury (Sir Frank Lee) had been appointed its Permanent Secretary in 1960; and the consequent creative thinking was epitomised by the official report, *Economic Growth and National Efficiency*, which recommended a rich combination both of public and private, as well as economic and social, action. It later provided the foundation for NEDO's 'orange' book, *Conditions Favourable to Economic Growth*, which many still regard as one of the most penetrating analyses of Britain's postwar economy.[7] This 'great reappraisal' penetrated the highest administrative levels, as is well illustrated by the contrasting views of Norman Brook and his successor as Cabinet Secretary, Burke Trend. In the early 1950s, Brook had bemoaned the failure of the postwar 'Socialist' government to wield a new Geddes Axe and had once described rent control as a 'standing relic of the fool's paradise' in which the country was living. In contrast, when the cost of the Conservatives' modernisation programme began to concern Macmillan's successor (Alec Douglas-Home) in 1964, Trend minuted:

(a) an increase in public expenditure – and therefore in tax – is not necessarily a bad thing, in so far as it provides better social benefits for the less fortunate members of the community and eliminates the grosser disparities of wealth.
(b) by any reliable criterion of value for money, it is not always public expenditure that needs to be reduced. The private sector, particularly consumption, may be the villain of the piece.[8]

Such changes in official attitudes were matched by changes in organisation. Of central importance here was the Plowden Committee on the Control of Public Expenditure, commissioned in 1959 and making its final report in 1961. It was important in three particular ways. First, it inspired the creation of the Public Expenditure Survey Committee (PESC), which provided an unprecedented oversight of total public expenditure. As such it was soon to be described as 'the most important innovation in this field in any western nation'.[9] Second, a private letter from Plowden to the Chancellor recommended a clear differentiation of role between the three most senior administrative posts – the Cabinet Secretary (as the Prime Minister's closest adviser), the Head of the Treasury (with ultimate responsibility for economic policy) and the Head of the Civil Service (with ultimate responsibility for administrative efficiency).[10] Such a division was implemented in January 1963 on Brook's retirement, thereby opening a long-running debate (common to all Western countries) which was only to be partially closed after 1982 by the re-merger of the posts of Cabinet Secretary and Head of the Civil Service. Finally, Plowden underlined the need within the Treasury for greater professionalism in relation to both economic policy and management. This led directly to the establishment of an official Treasury Organisation Committee (TOC) and the Treasury's subsequent radical reorganisation on functional lines, with the relocation of over 1300 officials and some half a million files. In 1964, Harold Wilson was to boast that within 48 hours his incoming government had produced 'the biggest revolution in Whitehall since Lloyd George'.[11] Arguably such a revolution had already occurred under the Conservatives.

The specific purpose of this chapter is to examine these 'revolutions'. Given the prevailing consensus that government had the *inherent* capacity to modernise Britain, had the basis been laid by 1964 of its *institutional* capacity to achieve this end? If so, was the reform programme of the incoming Labour government, including Fulton, essentially counterproductive? Consequently, should the Fulton's *selective* implementation be seen not as the result of some self-interested bureaucratic conspiracy but rather as the rational continuation of an earlier and more effective reform programme? To answer such questions, the full range of reforms designed to 'modernise' the Service will be examined and then the nature of the administrative response gauged.

3.2 Pressures for reform

The proposals for administrative reform generated during the post-Suez 'modernisation' debate were eclectic and partial. They had five interrelated objectives. The first was the creation of a greater strategic capability within government to direct and co-ordinate intervention. Hence, mirroring the Haldane Report, there were calls for smaller Cabinets and planning units within each department. There was also support for a stronger Prime Minister's department (a proposal that was thereafter to dominate reform in Britain as in other Western nations). Second, there was a drive to reduce the 'influence' of officials by the introduction of political advisers and a reduction in the Treasury's powers of patronage. Third, there was an attempt to break the perceived exclusiveness of administrative class by *inter alia* improved training, enhanced promotion prospects for specialists, greater interchange of staff with industry and other public services, and reduced secrecy. Fourth, there were proposals to increase economic and management expertise through, for example, the revival of another Edwardian idea: the dismemberment of the Treasury. A separate Ministry of Finance, so it was argued, could hone economic skills whilst another body (possibly a strengthened Civil Service Commission) concentrated on administrative efficiency. Finally, there was an increased emphasis on personnel management to attract and retain, in a tight labour market, high quality staff. A new professional attitude to management was being adopted by industry, as symbolised by the arrival in London in 1959 of the American management consultants, McKinseys. It was hoped, as it had been by Haldane in 1923, that Whitehall would not just follow but set industry an example.

These proposals tended to focus narrowly on the higher administrative class and the Treasury. They had, however, a wide range of advocates. These included Parliamentary select committees, individual modernisers, the Fabian Society and both main political parties. Civil servants themselves were also proactive. Individually, they privately encouraged and advised each outside initiative. Collectively, as will be seen, they also urged, drafted and implemented many reforms.

3.2.1 Parliament

As in 1917 and again between 1942 and 1947, it was the House of Commons which somewhat surprisingly precipitated reform. In particular, it was reports from its Estimates Committee in July 1958 and August 1965 that prompted the respective appointment of the Plowden and Fulton Committees. The constant probing of its Public Accounts Committee, most notably during the Ferranti scandal in 1964, also forestalled complacency.[12]

The Estimates Committee, with three major reports, provided the most sustained public scrutiny of administrative practice during this period. None was overly critical. Its 1958 report (*Treasury Control of Expenditure*) for example concluded that the 'system appears to work reasonably well'. The succeeding *Treasury Control of Establishments* in 1964 was even more positive. There was, it concluded, 'a greatly increased emphasis in the Treasury on what may be broadly called management. The reorganisation of November 1962 was designed to achieve this, and it has succeeded to a remarkable extent in a comparatively short period'. Such praise, however, was somewhat less pronounced in its 1965 report, *Recruitment to the Civil Service*. 'This country', it admitted, 'has gained inestimable benefit from the ability and integrity of the civil service. Its fine tradition is still very much alive today. But both its structure and public image need to be reviewed in the light of modern needs.' It then confidently added that the Service should emerge from such a review 'strengthened both in its ability to discharge the great responsibilities entrusted to it and in its place in public esteem'.[13] This prediction was not exactly to be fulfilled in the wake of the resulting Fulton Committee.

Despite their relative blandness, however, each report did contain particular reservations. The most momentous were in the 1958 report, which asserted that:

> It really is an abuse of language to speak of a 'system' of Treasury control, if by the word 'system' is meant methods and practices that have at one time or another been deliberately planned and instituted. What is called 'Treasury control' is better described as a complex of administrative practice that has grown up like a tree over the centuries . . . The question here at issue is whether such a 'system', many features of which emerged in

times when Government expenditure played a relatively small part in the national economy, is appropriate to the middle of the twentieth century.

Such a criticism infuriated senior Treasury officials. It appeared to be unsupported within any of the 400 pages of evidence and the Report then blithely confirmed that the 'system' appeared to work well. The Report, however, proved impossible to ignore – not least because it had been largely prompted by other officials (both inside and outside the Treasury).[14]

Reliance on such internal prompting exposed a fundamental weakness of the Committee (and Parliament in general) as a constitutional check on the Executive and thus on the Service. It had no research budget, was served by generalist clerks (with administrative skills similar to those of the administrative class) and relied heavily on the 'native wit' of its members. In consequence, investigations tended to be poorly planned, the questioning of witnesses amateurish and recommendations frequently contradictory. Hence the inconsistencies within the 1958 Report and, for example, the conflict between its call for greater delegation by the Treasury (to achieve greater efficiency) and its demand in 1964 for continuing central control (to enable the Committee itself, as a watchdog, to remain fully informed). Its reports were also rarely read, followed up or debated in Parliament.

Such ineffectuality reflected a wider constitutional failing. The adversarial nature of the House of Commons discouraged the non-partisan approach required to sustain serious inquiries. Backbenchers' careers, for example, were not notably enhanced by criticism of their own Government's administration or praise of their opponents. Moreover, assessments of administrative efficiency required judgements about the objectives of policy and the alternative means by which they might be attained. Select committees were, however, precluded from discussing policy. Under the convention of ministerial responsibility, Ministers alone were accountable to Parliament. The example of the USA, frequently cited by modernisers, was therefore irrelevant. It was because of Congress' *independent* legislative role that its well-resourced select committees could dispute the Executive's actions and even vet Presidential appointments.

Such weaknesses were increasingly to provoke debate and experiment, particularly after faith in 'big' government started to wane in the 1970s. In the meantime, however, the essential role of the Estimates Committee remained – in the words of a leading contemporary political scientist – not to 'provide blueprints for improvement but to explain in lay terms what is being done and to stimulate the departments into self criticism'.[15] Did the public or officials listen?

3.2.2 The public campaign to 'modernise' Britain

The persistent public charge against the Service, particularly when identified with decline, was one of amateurishness. This could be defined in one of three ways. It could mean lack of economic expertise which denied it an understanding of the need for, let alone the ability to implement, economic planning. It could mean lack of scientific knowledge which prevented it from helping to forge, in Harold Wilson's famous 1963 phrase, a modern Britain in the 'white heat' of a technological revolution. Alternatively, it could mean simple backwardness in relation to Europe. The leading proponents of these views were Thomas Balogh in 'The apotheosis of the dilettante' (1959), C.P. Snow in *The Two Cultures and the Scientific Revolution* (1959) and Brian Chapman in *British Government Observed* (1963). Their conclusions were somewhat modified at the time by Anthony Sampson in *Anatomy of Britain* (1962) and by Samuel Brittan in *The Treasury under the Tories* (1964).[16]

Balogh's attack on the Civil Service ranged widely over the past century but particularly focused on the 'lost opportunity' of the Attlee Government. This, he insisted, must not re-occur. 'In conditions where the nation's will to live awakens and demands positive action', he insisted, 'the mandarins must be displaced. They are a hindrance to survival.'[17] Their exclusivity and lack of economic expertise denied Ministers the 'facts' and necessary framework for positive action. One remedy was improved recruitment and training. For example, no more than a quarter of recruits should be permitted to be generalists and permanent establishment should be made conditional on the completion of a one-year training course (heavily weighted towards the social sciences). Within departments, the 'board' system should become standard so that Ministers might receive a full range of advice.[18] In addition, to break Whitehall's 'political' hold, the Head of the Civil Service's powers of patronage throughout the whole public sector should be curtailed. Within departments, Ministers should also be assisted by expert special advisers recruited from outside. Finally, to enhance the strategic capacity of government, a Ministry of the Budget should also be created. This would both inject professionalism into the planning of public expenditure and free the Treasury to plan the economy with equal professionalism.

For C.P. Snow, economic planning was insufficient to halt decline. Industry had also to be revolutionised. Likewise, administrative reform alone was insufficient. An expansion of scientific and technological education, especially within universities, was required to transform the culture of the political and industrial, as well as the administrative, elite. Nevertheless, as a former Civil Service Commissioner, he unhesitatingly endorsed Anthony Sampson's conclusion that the Service represented the 'most troubled frontier' in the 'apartheid . . . between amateurs and professionals'.[19] Insufficient scientists (who had 'the future in their bones') were being recruited and the fortunate few were then segregated in specialist grades. Consequently their advice was either ignored or misunderstood by a scientifically illiterate administrative class. The exclusiveness of this class had to be broken; new scientific expertise and method (and, in particular, operational research) embraced; and the interventionist capacity of the state enhanced by the creation, for example, of a Ministry of Technology.

Chapman's pamphlet proved equally controversial. The rejection of Britain's application to join the Common Market in 1963 marked for him a nadir in the country's 'international prestige'. How, within ten years, had the strongest nation in Europe become the weakest? His answer was simple. Britain's 'policy-making institutions' were inadequate for the 'needs of the complex modern state'. On continental Europe, strong states committed to 'public service' had both the expertise and drive to resolve all political (and not just economic) challenges. In contrast, at the 'very heart of British government' there was 'a luxuriant amateurism and voluntary exclusion of talent'. Typically this resulted in slow and ineffective decision-making and an over-readiness to entrust the implementation of policy to semi-autonomous bodies (such as nationalised industries) where government was 'constantly outwitted by groups they were notionally expected to control'.[20]

His solution was equally simple. It was not in the implementation of policy that the fault lay. In the Post Office and welfare departments, such as the Ministries of Labour and Pensions, the work of the executive class was efficient and humane by European standards. The fault was in policy formulation. The exclusiveness of the administrative class had to be broken (by, for example, the advertisement of senior vacancies). Its political influence had to be openly admitted and even encouraged (by, for instance, the incorporation of 'high-fliers' in policy-making ministerial *cabinets*, as in France). Individual responsibility had also to be clarified by reduced secrecy, the ending of the myth of ministerial responsibility and, more particularly, the creation of executive directorates (or hived-off boards, as in Sweden) whereby management could be held clearly to account. Such reforms would greatly increase the power of the state but democratic control could be maintained by the reinforcement of both Parliament and the system of legal redress (including, if not a full-blown system of administrative courts as in France, at least an ombudsman as in Scandinavia).

Superficially these critiques appeared identical. They identified the administrative class (rather than the Service as a whole) as the principal cause of national decline and exclusivity as the principal cause of its amateurism. However, they offered few common remedies. Was, for example, exclusivity to be broken by the appointment of more experts at a young age (as suggested by Balogh and Snow) or of proven administrators at a later age (as proposed by Chapman)?[21] Was the influence of the administrative class to be diluted by the appointment of expert special advisers to ministerial *cabinets* or reinforced by the appointment of administrative high-fliers to these very same *cabinets*? Was it greater economic or scientific expertise that was required? Finally, if greater strategic capacity was to be created in government, to what precise end should it be employed? Was decline to be halted by better economic planning (as sought by Balogh), the regeneration of industry (as advocated by Snow) or the state's commitment to 'public service' across the board (as demanded by Chapman)?

The only feature which the critiques, in fact, had incontrovertibly in common was a disregard for administrative and political reality. Administratively, each demanded less secrecy but simultaneously appeared ignorant of the information readily available *inter alia* in Select Committee reports. Chapman, for instance, despite his proclaimed concern about the constitutional position of nationalised industries, was unaware of the very existence of the Select Committee overseeing them. Snow also turned a blind eye both to the extent of Research and Development sponsored by government (which was exceptionally high by international standards) and the effective power enjoyed by scientific 'experts' in the service ministries.[22] Politically, decline was similarly attributed too readily to government rather than to other 'governing' institutions. In relation to the financial sector, for example, the Service might have been presented as exemplary. Elite 'training' at the Bank of England, after all, still consisted largely of copying documents 'with meticulous accuracy' – a habit abandoned in Whitehall some hundred years before. In direct contrast to Balogh, moreover, Sampson found his apotheosis of the amateur 'in the "old boy nets" of insurance companies or joint stock banks'.[23] Finally, and arguably most importantly, too little thought was given to the fundamental problem of how an increasingly powerful bureaucracy could remain responsive to ministerial and Parliamentary control.

One attempt to correct these lacunae, not least because it was partly inspired by Whitehall, was Samuel Brittan's *The Treasury under the Tories*.[24] It openly acknowledged the power of the Treasury and hence its culpability for past economic failings. Its officials 'provided the framework of thought within which the Government acted', which Ministers had neither the capacity nor competence to challenge. The basic failing, however, lay not in the administrative but the political system. 'It was', concluded Brittan in a reversal of Chapman's analysis, 'precisely because the British Civil Service is not a ruling bureaucracy that economic policy has been so uninspired. The Whitehall administrators are meant to be amongst the checks and balances of the British constitution' and for the system to work Ministers had to lay down the 'guiding lines of policy'. They had not. Consequently 'Treasury knights' had had to 'step into the vacuum, and . . . make essentially political decisions for which they neither had the background nor the training'.[25]

Brittan's recipe for better government was to strengthen Ministers and reinvigorate Whitehall. Ministers should have *cabinets*, or 'brains trusts' of technical experts and political advisers, to help them challenge the assumptions underlying official advice. In addition, the objectives behind economic planning could be crystallised by hiving off from the Treasury responsibility for the management of both public expenditure and the Service. Other strategic objectives could be clarified by a strengthened Prime Minister's Office. Administrative reinvigoration, in turn, could be best achieved not by the influx of more specialists (who tended to be blinkered) but *inter alia* by more openness, less exclusiveness (through increased interchange with staff outside Whitehall and fuller training), and better personnel practices (such as faster promotion). Brittan welcomed recent reforms, such as the creation of the Centre of Administrative Studies. Critics, he acknowledged, were already 'speaking to the half converted'. He had, however, residual doubts about whether such reforms were sops to 'keep the reformers at bay'. Was administrative reorganisation, particularly at the top, merely a 'substitute for the reorganisation of ideas which was really required'?[26]

Similar proposals and doubts also characterized the other major blueprint for 'modernisation' drafted in collaboration with practising officials. This was the report from the Fabian Society entitled *The Administrators* which, despite its rejection of the need for a further inquiry 'to tread the ground again', crystallised Labour Party thinking and formed the basis of its submission to the Fulton Committee.[27]

3.2.3 The Fabian Society

In a somewhat belated response to Balogh, the Fabian Society mounted its own enquiry into the Civil Service in June 1962. In the following May, the preliminary conclusions were shown to a small group of serving officials, who collaborated in their redrafting. As a result, the balance and attention to detail in the final report – published in June 1964 – anticipated Brittan rather than reflected Balogh. Its conclusions were based on a simple proposition: 'Is the civil service . . . the best we could have to meet the needs of today?' The answer was 'emphatically no' because it was 'plainly out of touch with the times' and so 'unfitted to more positive government'. Officials were as guilty as Ministers for past errors because if 'they had possessed, or obtained, more expert knowledge of the subject and if they had looked farther ahead' such errors could have been prevented. Reform was thus a 'pre-requisite to enabling a Labour government – or any other government – to carry through the modernisation of the country'.[28]

Two particular reforms, so it was argued, were urgently needed. First, the familiar problems of exclusivity and amateurism of the administrative class had to be addressed. To reduce exclusivity, there had to be a genuine attempt to recruit other than Oxbridge arts graduates and to encourage greater movement in and out of the Service. At and above Assistant Secretary level, posts had to be opened to specialists (who should be merged with generalists into a 'Senior Civil Service') and some 'grit' added by permitting up to a fifth of posts to be filled by outside candidates. As a result, administrative class officials would no longer be able to luxuriate under the illusion that they were a member of a 'closed and protected . . . monastic order'.[29] Then, to enhance expertise, there should be an initial two-year training course modelled on the French Ecole Nationale d'Administration. This was to be of sufficient quality to attract the highest qualified graduates, whether or not they intended to stay within the Service – but the best would be attracted to stay by the promise of careful career planning (ensuring *inter alia* responsibility at an early age and the opportunity to specialise in a given policy area). To ensure their vigour, such personnel policies were to be transferred from the Treasury to a new department centred on the Civil Service Commission.

The second set of proposals dealt with an equally familiar issue. This was the alleged power of the administrative class. Consistent with Stephen's instinctive reaction to the Northcote-Trevelyan Report (see Chapter 1.4.1), the Fabians dismissed the notion that there could be 'non-political advisers on policy'. No-one could switch wholeheartedly between competing policies – least of all as they became older, more senior, and thus more influential. Yet wholehearted commitment was essential 'if a new government on coming to power' was 'to have vitality and . . . to succeed in devising, presenting and executing new policies'. There were two principal remedies. Reduced secrecy would encourage open and informed debate, particularly on long-term policy. Outside experts and political aides should also be appointed to ministerial *cabinets*. It was, in short, 'high time that an end was put to the error of pretending that governments can change but none of their servants or advisers should'.[30]

The Fabians, like Brittan, recognised that many of their proposed reforms already existed in embryo. However, they were equally unconvinced about the commitment to them. Above all, they sceptically regarded the Treasury's reorganisation as 'another game of musical chairs with most of the same people circulating round the old jobs, some slightly regrouped under new names'.[31] Such scepticism was reinforced by the serving officials. 'The much trumpeted reorganisation of the Treasury', wrote one, 'does not go far enough on the "establishment" and "management" sides because not enough of the people now concerned know anything practical about management from experience in departments that actually do it.' Training in some departments might be good but 'by far the weakest spot' was the Treasury's Training Division, which was 'terrible'.

Impressive though the Report was considered at the time, and has been considered since, it had two major defects. First, as the product of a major inquiry into administrative reform within a Party committed to greater state intervention, it engaged few leading figures. Of its initial 'star-studded' membership, Anthony Crosland, Balogh and Shirley Williams (during a lengthy stay in the USA) were notable for their absence. Regularly absent also were two future Permanent Secretaries rumoured to have contributed (Alan Neale and Leo Pliatzky).[32] Second, it was narrow. On its own admission, it focused exclusively on the administrative class. It was also preoccupied almost exclusively with the Treasury and economic policy. Moreover, the key issue was evaded of how to harmonise more effective, centralised planning with the political realities of ministerial responsibility and democratic accountability.

This narrowness was due in part to the initial conception of the inquiry, which was simply 'to discuss policy-making on economic questions in the higher ranks of the civil service'. After its scope had been widened, however, it also reflected a tendency – so despised when displayed by officials in interdepartmental committees – to circumvent inconvenient facts and fudge contested issues. Four examples must suffice. First, the Report made no reference to the authors' acceptance that management practice (such as promotion procedures and training below the topmost level) was generally superior in the public sector to that in the private. Second, there was no reference to the initial riposte to Balogh's critique that the real impediment to effective economic planning was not the Treasury but 'obsolete industries, obsolete institutions and obsolete people' throughout society.[33] Third, although the need for ministerial *cabinets* was acknowledged to have arisen because of the declining quality of planning within political parties, the reason for this decline was not examined (despite, or arguably because of, the Fabians' long history as a research institution for the Labour Party). Finally, the Report failed to resolve an on-going internal disagreement over the relative merits of generalists and 'professionals'. Several of its members had argued that, by fulfilling the 'middleman role between politicians, experts and the clients', generalists (who might be better termed experts in the 'working' of government) were essential to effective policy-making. This went unacknowledged.

Such failings tarnished the Report. So too did its admonition that 'officials should not . . . respond too unanimously to fashion'.[34] This barb was directed at Treasury officials who had too readily embraced the free market 'Robot' scheme in 1952. The Report's authors, however, lacked sufficient self-awareness to recognise that they themselves were equally gullible. As they were warned, their proposed reforms held a hidden danger. They could – and later would – empower not just those championing 'big government' but also those vehemently opposed to it.

3.2.4 The Labour and Conservative Parties

How did the two main political parties affect the momentum of reform? The Fulton Committee has been termed a 'Labour' committee because of both its appointment by the Wilson Government and its members' sympathy towards the Party's known agenda.[35] That agenda reached back to the Party's foundation, had been revitalised by Balogh in 1959 and had then further developed in *The Administrators*. Its best assimilation, however, was in the Party's submission to Fulton. The general premise of this submission was that postwar society had been transformed by a scientific and education revolution. Consequently what was required was a different type of government (actively to manage the new 'techno-industrial society') and a different type of official (both willing and able to identify with the relevant problems and help to resolve them in a 'professional, adaptive and creative way'). Hence the need to break down the current exclusiveness of senior officials by such familiar means as the integration and relevant training of all classes. Such measures would, moreover, simultaneously resolve current problems of low morale and recruitment. Finally, the 'power' of officials was to be countered by two types of temporary political appointment – experts to help implement 'particularly controversial or . . . radical changes' in policy, and 'personal assistants' based in a ministerial *cabinet* 'to act as an extra pair of eyes and ears' and thereby 'stimulate' Ministers.[36]

Two new variations were added to these familiar themes. The first was a frontal attack on officials' power. Information, it was claimed, was withheld from Ministers in order to make them the 'tools of their department'. Equally, interdepartmental committees were used to 'undermine the authority' of Ministers. In consequence, there was a 'need to strengthen the Minister, the "temporary politician", in his department in relation to the "permanent politicians", his Civil Servants'. Wilson immediately renounced such allegations. Second, in contrast to *The Administrators*, there was an attempt to define 'management'. It meant, it was argued, two different things: 'in relation to the Civil Service as a whole it means improving its structure and organisation, seeing that it is manned by the right people of the right quality and that the best possible use is made of them. In relation to the individual departments it . . . also denotes a new positive approach to the planning and execution of policy'. In this second sense, management had been badly neglected; but then – apart from an allusion to the subdivision of ministries into 'bureaux' – it compounded the problem by neglecting it itself.[37]

These variations did little to resolve the tensions within the Party's traditional policy on administrative reform which had always had four potentially incompatible objectives: greater executive efficiency, reduced bureaucratic power, effective democratic accountability, and a less class-biased mandarinate.[38] The active management of a complex 'techno-industrial society', indeed, risked an accentuation of these incompatibilities. For example, were an increased number of 'professional and expert' officials to be employed in specialist 'bureaux', would not the 'temporary politician' heading the department be further marginalised? If, in compensation, ministerial power were reinforced by politically chosen experts and *cabinets* would not the power of the Executive be strengthened and democratic accountability thereby reduced? On the other hand, were either Parliamentary or ministerial control enhanced, would not that jeopardise any 'efficiency gains' resulting from any advantage to be gained by officials' increased expertise or sense of individual responsibility?

Wilson's swift renunciation of his own Party's submission was testimony to such unresolved tensions. In government, however, action had to be taken – and was, with the appointment of many 'irregular' civil servants and the establishment of new ministries.[39] Many of the irregulars were appointed to provide particular technical expertise and thus continued wartime practice (as well as peacetime practice within the Scientific Class). What was novel was the appointment, mainly of economists, as partisan experts explicitly to counteract officials' perceived power. How were they to be deployed? To galvanise officials, should they have shared responsibility for the immediate execution of policy? Alternatively, to challenge underlying assumptions, should they be concentrated in a planning unit or a ministerial *cabinet*? Moreover, should such *cabinets* also include non-expert personal aides upon whose loyalty and political judgement an overloaded Minister could instinctively rely?[40] Wilson's answer to such questions was to favour experts over aides and to employ them outside *cabinets*.[41] Their improvised deployment, however, brought a new set of problems. Administratively, for example, the appointment of Neild (the principal author of *The Administrators*) as Chief Economic Adviser to the Chancellor was potentially counterproductive because it threatened the future of the Treasury's Economic Section. This was the body which, since 1940, had provided successive governments with expert technical advice and whose staff moved regularly in and out of Whitehall – in short, representing two of the very characteristics which modernisers claimed were missing from the permanent Civil Service. Politically, the ban on the discussion of devaluation made a nonsense of the appointment of leading 'special advisers' (such as Balogh at No. 10 and Nicholas Kaldor at the Treasury). As a result, the Fabian Society in particular despaired and in its own submission to Fulton emphasised the need for a sustained 'infusion of talent' and its professional deployment. The current 'lack of systematic approach leaves the impression', it complained, 'that the Government is content to have manned up its new departments and sprinkled a few extra irregulars over certain established departments and now wishes this *ad hoc* expedient to develop no further'.[42]

The 'new departments' to which the Fabians referred were principally the Department of Economic Affairs (DEA) and a Ministry of Technology (MinTech), established in October 1964 to satisfy modernisers' calls for greater economic planning and industrial intervention.[43] Both embodied the belief that vested departmental interests had to be broken if new policies were to be vigorously pursued; but, as with the introduction of 'irregulars', herein lay a hidden danger. Energy and ingenuity expended on the establishment of new administrative structures and relationships could not, by definition, be spent simultaneously on the vigorous pursuit and attainment of new policy objectives. The new ministries might offer presentational and political advantages but (particularly given the demise of the DEA and MinTech in 1969 and 1970 respectively) did they deliver any long-term administrative benefits?[44] Whilst advancing the reform agenda, therefore, Labour did little – in theory or practice – to resolve its inherent contradictions.

The Conservatives, for their part, made no formal submission to Fulton but the mid-1960s were nevertheless an unusually fertile period for their consideration of administrative reform. Whilst in office, as has been noted, traditional indifference had been replaced by institutional innovation; and in opposition the subject was adjudged, from the leadership down, to have 'political sex appeal'.[45] In the past reform had been typically equated with either the greater involvement of businessmen (as after the Crimean War) or the eradication of 'waste' (as after both World Wars). Both were in essence surrogate calls for a 'rolling back' of the state. The 1966 manifesto appeared to conform to this pattern. It promised, for example, 'a war on waste in Government' and the establishment of a 'Cost Effectiveness Department to introduce new management techniques into all Government Departments'.[46] Moreover, both pledges were prompted by an embryonic Public Sector Research Unit (PSRU) which, as will be seen in Chapter 5.3.1, was later to champion both the latest management techniques from the USA and teams of businessmen to oversee their implementation. The essential objective of the1960s (and even of PSRU), however, was wholly alien to traditional values – which were to reassert themselves after 1975. It was neither to roll back the state nor to denigrate officials. Rather it was to identify which national problems could be best resolved collectively; and then to ensure that, where collective action was needed, the machinery for *political* decision-making could optimise the work of both Ministers and officials. In short, as Heath informed Fulton, the Party's essential concern was 'defects in the machinery of government rather than the men [sic] who served it'.[47]

To this end, a study group had been established in December 1964 and its report in April 1967 recommended the creation of 'giant' departments, on the model of the MOD (which the Conservatives had created in 1964).[48] By cutting the number of Ministers, such departments would reduce Cabinet to a more effective size. By cutting the number of interdepartmental committees, they would also produce less 'fudged' advice. What about the definition of, and continuing adherence to, an overall policy strategy? The final answer here, which emerged in 1968 from a new advisory committee chaired by Dame Evelyn Sharp (the former Permanent Secretary of the Ministry of Housing and Local Government), was that the Cabinet Office should become a fully-fledged Prime Minister's Office. Not only should it continue to serve the Cabinet and coordinate advice to the Prime Minister, it should also help to determine overall priorities and so control the 'machine' that it could ensure effective implementation.[49] It was at this point that the proposal dovetailed with PSRU's proposed Cost Effectiveness Unit.

Once provisions for a clear strategy had been established, there was little perceived need for concern about officials. 'Trained minds' were needed and the subject of an individual's first degree was irrelevant. Ministers did not need *cabinets*. Indeed, in sharp contrast to Labour, such an innovation was regarded as dangerous since it might dilute the robustness of official advice. 'It should be the primary task of the Civil Servant', Heath informed Fulton, 'to show the Minister the results straight thinking produced; it was then up to the Minister to bend it if he had to.'[50] Moreover, doubts were expressed over whether policy implementation could be hived off to executive agencies because of the issue of Parliamentary accountability. Accountability, however, proved – as so often – to be an Achilles heel. The initial study group had been instructed in 1964 to consider the Parliamentary context and constraints within which the government machine worked. It failed to report on the subject.

3.2.5 *Pressures from within*

For all the outside demand for modernisation, the most persistent, knowledgeable and ultimately effective advocates of reform came from within the Service itself. Covertly, as has been seen, individual officials advised both the Fabians and the Conservatives. They also, as will be seen, drove through reform both on and after the Plowden Committee. More overtly, the Royal Institute of Public Administration became, as had been Haldane's initial ambition, a forum for debate on current and best practice.[51] A genuine public dialogue, from which Bridges had shrunk, was also joined by William Armstrong (his former private secretary) through, for example, his collaboration with Samuel Brittan. Finally, as befitted more liberated times, junior officials felt freer to air their grievances and to suggest remedies.

The most conservative of these 'internal' critics were, not unnaturally, those retired officials who advised the Conservative Party. Norman Brook, for example, rejected fashionable attacks on the Administrative Class. It was, he protested, as well qualified to process expert advice for lay Ministers as Powell wished. 'Government by technocrats' was dangerous and long-term planning impossible given the reality of short-term political pressures. Were the Service to have any weaknesses, they were in its 'lower echelons' where there was a need for a reduced 'sogginess in attitudes and procedures' and for increased mechanisation. Such a view directly contradicted not only outside commentators such as Chapman (who, as has been seen, praised executive officers) but also the Treasury's own management expert, who claimed with some justification that government led industry by example, having been 'conspicuously bold and venturesome in the use of sophisticated equipment'.[52] It also contradicted the view of another senior retired Treasury official, Sir Thomas Padmore, who claimed that 'for a generation the Civil Service had been in the van of progress in the application of managerial techniques'.

Padmore's claim admittedly bemused the audience to which it was addressed – a PSRU seminar in 1968 designed to inject more business rigour into Whitehall. Nevertheless, official advice and action continued to be respected. Indeed, one of the seminar's principal organisers (David Howell) explicitly stated that its purpose was not to declare 'war on the Civil Service. The aim is to change the routines and procedures in which Civil Servants are trapped'.[53] A new advisory group of retired officials was then commissioned to identify the necessary changes and, as has been seen, it advocated the creation of a Prime Minister's Office. It also recommended a smaller Cabinet (willing and able to take a strategic lead); giant departments (eliminating the inevitable 'fudging' of difficult decisions by interdepartmental committees); and the relief of overloaded Ministers (possibly by hiving off blocks of work to executive agencies). Such recommendations were not a denial of the need for changes in official behaviour. Rather, they distilled Whitehall's wisdom about the political and constitutional changes needed to maintain the momentum of internally generated reform. The Fulton Committee was, of course, precluded by its terms of reference from addressing such issues (see chapter 4.3).

The chair of the advisory group was Dame Evelyn Sharp. Before her retirement, she had long been a leading protagonist for reform – frequently to Brook's discomfort. In 1959, for example, she had been instrumental in instigating the first 'Sunningdale' conference, a meeting of Permanent Secretaries to discuss issues of mutual interest (which thereafter became an annual event). For the first meeting she also succeeded in extending the agenda from the 'well-being' of the Service (as favoured by Brook and the Treasury) to its 'efficiency'. In particular she sought to learn from industry how management could work 'as a team' and from colleagues how to 'avoid being immersed in Ministerial business, policies and casework' so that she could concentrate on 'running her department'. Brook vetoed outside speakers but the 'problems of higher management' were frankly discussed in a final open session. Unanimous agreement was reached, to the confusion no doubt of contemporary critics (had they known), that Permanent Secretaries should make sufficient time to 'attend to the essential problems of management and organization'.[54]

Sharp simultaneously collaborated with Sir Frank Lee in orchestrating complaints within Whitehall against Treasury control; and, once a member of the Plowden Committee, she ensured that the Committee fully addressed the Treasury's shortcomings. These shortcomings related not just to the amateurishness of its control but, more importantly, to its failure to rise to Fisher's challenge that it become a general staff for a unified Service. To ensure good departmental management throughout the service, she argued, the Treasury should devolve effective power to departments and act itself simply as an expert adviser and ultimate enforcer of good practice. To ensure effective leadership, it should also guarantee proper career planning for all 'fliers'. There was at present 'too much reliance on people whose experience has been gained largely in the Treasury and too little regard . . . paid to the value – we think the near necessity – of departmental experience as well. There ought to be a long-term plan for the people who are to go to the top'. The key was a radical change in personnel. Higher quality officials should be appointed to manage the Service, preferably on secondment (as in the Cabinet Office) and possibly located outside the Treasury in a separate Establishment Department.[55] The latter suggestion was rejected by Plowden, but the subsequent reorganisation of the Treasury owed much to Sharp's persistence.

One of Sharp's colleagues on the Committee was the Treasury official, Sir Richard (Otto) Clarke. Just as Sharp forced the pace of reform in relation to Treasury reorganisation, so he forced it in relation to public expenditure control. Together they thereby substantiated the chairman's claim that the Committee was in essence a 'Whitehall operation'. Subsequently Clarke accepted responsibility for the implementation of many of its recommendations, such as the Public Expenditure Survey Committee. This was established in 1961 – before the major public debate on modernisation had started – and, eschewing secrecy as it later advocated, Clarke delivered three lectures on the subject, including the 1964 Stamp lecture.[56] The latter, particularly when contrasted to Bridges' Stamp lecture of 1950, illustrated just how far the Service had modernised itself, for it addressed three far from esoteric questions: 'Is the public sector of the right size? Is every part of it designed to give the best possible social value for the resources which are needed to provide it? Are these resources in the event efficiently used?' There then followed an expert analysis, which few outsiders could have matched.

In the Stamp lecture, Clarke even concurred with Sharp's demand for greater decentralisation. 'Instead of being a back-seat driver,' he agreed, 'the Treasury's job is to ensure that every Department has the best possible cars and drivers and is properly equipped with maps.' How far he personally succeeded in realising such an ambition has been questioned. As a Treasury official, he was noted for relaxing central control and, as a Permanent Secretary at MinTech, he was reputedly – like Sharp – not the most effective of managers.[57] However the trails blazed by such pioneers laid the basis on which more 'rounded' administrators (such as Burke Trend and William Armstrong) could build. Combined with the report inspired by Sir Frank Lee on *Economic Growth and National Efficiency*, submitted to Cabinet simultaneously with the final Plowden Report, they also demonstrate that outside critics were typically ill-informed. Even within their particular *bete noire*, the Treasury, there was both a willingness and a capacity to modernise.

At a more junior level, the legacy of the 'missed opportunity' of the 1950s arguably lingered longer. Rather than the appetite for reform being dulled, however, it was in many cases whetted. This was apparent from the assistance given to the Fabian Society. It was apparent also in the critique somewhat daringly submitted by four 'young Principals' in the Treasury to Brook in 1962. Echoing Sharp, it argued that morale was low within the Treasury because inefficient organisation wasted 'educated manpower'. In consequence, some of their work was 'nugatory, some ill-done, and some valuable work is missed'.[58] They offered three remedies. First, there should be a clear definition of the Treasury's core role (which might lead, they admitted, to the creation of a separate Bureau of Establishments). Second, the Treasury should be reorganised to reflect its new responsibilities (with the supply divisions, for instance, being matched to the new PESC expenditure categories). Finally, as advocated by Clarke, the Treasury should adopt a 'back seat' role. This would permit it to perform its pre-eminent task, providing authoritative advice both to departments on management and Ministers on spending priorities.

Other junior officials (both serving and recently resigned) gave evidence to Fulton. They stressed the difficulty of discharging a 'positive' role within traditional constitutional constraints. 'Those who now criticize the civil service as obsolete and unimaginative', one particular group argued, 'must ask themselves how far they are ready to risk sacrificing any of the traditional values.'[59] The diversity of the Service and thus the inappropriateness of a uniform panacea were also emphasised. Above all, however, it was agreed that low morale could only be raised by a clear demonstration that both government and individual officials mattered. On the one hand, there should be better strategic planning to ensure state intervention succeeded. Younger officials, for example, should be employed – as Haldane had wished – in departmental planning units with, as a corollary, Permanent Secretaries relieved of 'the day-to-day pressure imposed by the political system'. They might then concentrate on management.[60] On the other hand, through a mixture of training and career planning, individuals from the start of their careers should be encouraged to develop specialist knowledge and skills. 'If the individual was able to stay longer in particular posts', so it was argued, 'to develop expertise for coping with a particular range of problems, to work in team and individual projects which he [sic] would follow right through and if senior officials and Ministers were more willing to accept and reach decisions on vigorously disagreed proposals . . . then his energies and talents, enthusiasm and loyalty could be fully engaged.' This, in sum, was the vigorous internal response to outside critiques of the 'permanent politicians'.

3.3 The response

Preceding the outside modernisation campaign, there were – as has been noted – two major internal attempts to reform Whitehall: the appointment of the Plowden Committee in 1959 and the reorganisation of the Treasury in 1962. They were, in part, driven by wider social change. In particular, coherent reform had previously been precluded by an ideological battle between 'socialist' planning and the free market, to which senior Civil Servants were not immune. By the late 1950s that had largely been resolved in favour of planning. The importance of management was also coming to be acknowledged (as illustrated by the summoning of the first 'Sunningdale'). Moreover a tightening of the labour market, particularly in 'educated' manpower, was perceived as a threat both to the recruitment and the retention of high quality staff within the Service. It was this that particularly concerned Brook and the Treasury, and prompted the Estimate Committee's 1965 Report which, in turn, led to the commissioning of the Fulton Committee. To what extent had the basis for effective reform been laid by these two initiatives? Was it then disrupted, rather than advanced, by the Labour Government in general and Fulton in particular?

3.3.1 The Plowden Committee on the Control of Public Expenditure, 1959–61

The Plowden Committee, like Fulton, was not a royal commission (as some had wished) but an internal 'mixed' committee. Four of its members, including the chairman, were 'outsiders' although each had experience of working within Whitehall. The other five were serving officials, two of whom held senior positions in the Treasury; and a further 72 officials were co-opted onto its eight subcommittees.[61] The Committee was appointed just before the 1959 election and, following a flurry of confidential interim reports, published a Final Report (Cmnd 1432) in June 1961, which focused on two main issues: the control of expenditure through long-term planning and improved management within Whitehall.

In relation to the control of expenditure, the Final Report has been described as a 'milestone' in modernisation. Its critical recommendation in this respect was that 'decisions involving substantial future expenditure should always be taken in the light of surveys of public expenditure as a whole, over a period of years, and in relation to the prospective resources'.[62] Administratively, this was to be achieved by the Treasury agreeing each summer with other departments a five-year expenditure programme on an official committee (the Public Expenditure Survey Committee or PESC). This programme was then to be reassessed later in the year in the light of a Treasury survey of prospective resources. Politically, so a confidential interim report recommended, a permanent Ministerial Group on Public Expenditure should oversee this second phase; and its members thereafter support the Chancellor of the Exchequer in Cabinet against electoral or Parliamentary pressure to spend more. In short, a sophisticated means was proposed for the rational control of public expenditure based on an informed assessment of both its *affordability* and *aggregate* economic impact. In this respect, the Report was a 'great conceptual achievement'.[63]

Was such planning, however, practicable? After 1961 the PESC met annually and, in an attempt to accentuate 'joined-up' government, analysed expenditure in seven broad categories rather than by department. It was not able immediately to supplant the games of bluff and counterbluff traditionally employed by the Treasury and departments to agree budgets.[64] Similarly, an *ad hoc* Ministerial Group met between December 1960 and March 1961, and in the summers of 1962 and 1965; but its spasmodic meeting and *ad hoc* nature (except briefly in 1965) bore testimony to the fact that it too was not wholly successful. A plausible explanation for such disappointments was provided by Burke Trend, as Cabinet Secretary. As he advised the Prime Minister in 1964, PESC presupposed that it is feasible for the government to consider all their forward commitments together; to arrange them in ideal order of priority; and to keep their development thereafter under tight control. In practice this is not possible. The government can rarely, if ever, consider their commitments comprehensively; and even if they could, unforeseen events can make hay of the most careful planning exercise. The control of Government expenditure is not a static exercise; it is a moving process which has to adapt itself continuously to changes in circumstances over which the Government have little, or no control.

No departmental minister is ever willing, for obvious political reasons, to allow himself to be put into a financial strait jacket for years ahead. Nor can the government as a whole afford to forego, for merely financial reasons, a reasonable degree of political flexibility.[65]

Did such a political reaction represent mere teething problems or a more fundamental impediment to 'rational' planning?

The Report's immediate acceptability was certainly adversely affected by certain shortcomings of both the Plowden Committee and the Treasury, on whom the implementation of the Report rested. Committee members, for example, acknowledged that the political behaviour, as identified by Trend, would not change until Parliamentary procedure and public opinion did so also. The subcommittee investigating Parliamentary procedure, however, swiftly sub-contracted the task to the Treasury in the full knowledge that little could be expected from that source. Similarly, the Final Report acknowledged that even 'the best system and the most up-to-date techniques' could succeed only were public opinion 'actively stimulated and enabled to take a balanced view of the alternative uses of national resources'.[66] It offered, however, few concrete suggestions and actively discouraged the publication of annual public expenditure white papers (which were actually issued in 1963 and 1966 in the hope of fostering informed opinion).

The suspicion also arose that, as in 1919, the Treasury was using an attack on its competence to reinforce its power rather than to mend its ways. This was suggested, for instance, by the making of the Ministerial Group a Treasury, rather than a Cabinet Office, Committee. This meant that it could be attended solely by Treasury officials (serving the Chancellor rather than the Cabinet as a whole). It was also possible to withhold papers from spending Ministers and deny them attendance at the Group, even when their departmental interests were being discussed. As the sympathetic Heclo and Wildavsky later confirmed: 'the entire rationale of the Plowden Committee was an attempt to find a basis on which the Treasury could not be defeated'.[67] Moreover, its renewed power was to be put to a covert purpose. Richard Clarke, the official who drafted the Final Report and who oversaw the initial PESC process, had earlier sought – and remained on record as seeking – to cap expenditure permanently at a given percentage of GNP. His declared purpose was to prevent any further rise in taxation; but this, as Iain Macleod angrily countered at the first Ministerial Group meeting, was in reality a mere proxy for the traditional Treasury view that public expenditure was 'inherently undesirable'.[68] Such a view not only contradicted government policy but also the more sympathetic attitude to state intervention evolving elsewhere in the Treasury and shortly to be published, coincidentally with the Final Report, in *Economic Growth and National Efficiency*.

Such conflicts might be seen as teething problems, which could be and – as with the expenditure white papers – frequently were remedied. There were, however, more fundamental technical and political problems. Technically, for example, the long-term survey of resources relied on new computer techniques and economic modelling which, as even its progenitor (F.R.P. Vinter) admitted, often made it little more than 'a bluff'. The Final Report admitted such difficulties but then, totally inconsistently, asserted that the survey was 'technically practical'.[69] The political objections, identified by Trend, also remained unresolved. Ministers, having initially accepted the necessity for PESC then objected to it in practice. Rather than making 'the theory of collective responsibility a reality' (as the Report claimed), so Macleod argued, it actually degraded 'the function of the Cabinet in the determination of public policy' by effectively forcing it to take decisions on far from disinterested evidence. Enoch Powell was even more critical. With some prescience, he predicted that PESC would become 'an exercise in escapism' through the convenient assumption of too fast a rate of economic growth. Tough decisions would thus be evaded. There was 'only one key to the control of public expenditure. That is for government to wish it'. Clarke's response to such criticism was, however, equally forthright. The 'nature of political life', he admitted, was that final decisions would always be determined by 'push and pull, threats and cajolery, bluff and counterbluff'. However, as a result of PESC, politicians would at least be 'talking and bargaining about all the right questions . . . making real choices not artificial ones . . . This is the real gain . . . and an important one'.[70] Could administrative reform on its own achieve more?

The development of PESC monopolised the Plowden Committee until June 1960 and thereafter its principal attention was turned to management. The omens were not good; and the Final Report duly concluded that there was 'no evidence of serious strain in the relationships between Departments and the Treasury: the system seemed to us to be working reasonably well'.[71] This flew in the face of the damning testimony provided *inter alia* by Sir Frank Lee and Evelyn Sharp – the accuracy of which was privately admitted by Treasury officials. Lee, for instance, placed on record the conviction from all his years at the Board of Trade that '*detailed* control by the Treasury is nearly always a mistake, a waste of effort and a cause of frustration' and even this denunciation, he then confided to Plowden, far from fully represented the 'strength of my feeling about the waste and folly of the present system'.[72]

A similar tension attended the Final Report's expressed wish that throughout Whitehall, in a phrase reminiscent of Sir Warren Fisher, there should be an increased sense of 'joint working together in a common enterprise'. The expectation was raised that, within the total estimates agreed at PESC, there might be – as Lee wished – a 'delegation to Departments of *complete* freedom of expenditure on projects or services'.[73] The Report, nevertheless, still insisted that 'submissions on individual expenditures' should be made so that the Treasury could 'form a judgement on' departmental efficiency. Similarly, in relation to establishments, it was agreed that departments be responsible for their own efficiency; but then the prospect of greater autonomy was dashed by the assertion that the Treasury would still have to remain 'sufficiently familiar with the internal organisation of other Departments to be able to detect, and co-operate in remedying, defects and shortcomings'. It was also to 'take the initiative' in promoting new managerial techniques not only in the Service but throughout the public sector (where, as with local government or the NHS, there had historically been effective decentralisation). As a famous spoof parodied the Report's apparent message:

> It should be made perfectly clear in future that this is not to be regarded as a game between equal players . . . The functions of policy-making are now concentrated in the Treasury, and it has been given ample powers to keep lower management in its place. It is in the hands of the Treasury alone to measure the efficiency of management, and to apply rewards and sanctions by posting and promotion.[74]

Why, in relation to reform management, did the Committee apparently so disappoint expectation? There were three interrelated reasons. The first was that the Committee's work was incomplete. One of its (unpublished) remits was to examine the efficiency in departmental administration 'right down the line'. This was never achieved. On its own admission, for example, the subcommittee on management services had time only to acquire a 'bird's-eye view' and so its conclusions were based on 'only the most general impression from evidence which may be quite unrepresentative'.[75] Second, the part-time 'outsiders' on the Committee were preoccupied by external interests, whilst Treasury members were obsessed by the long-term surveys, to the exclusion of management issues.[76] Finally, there was the role of the Treasury itself which, as its officials frequently boasted, effectively 'steered' the Committee. One of its prime steering mechanisms was an internal committee (formed in the spring of 1960, with the same secretary as the main committee) the purpose of which was to agree a 'departmental' view as both a guide to Treasury officials on the Committee and a means of co-ordinating other departments' evidence. In consequence, it was hardly surprising that the Committee received far from disinterested evidence; and the few criticisms of the Treasury that slipped into the confidential interim reports were then largely excised from the final, public one.[77]

The fate of the Eighth Interim Report, amalgamating the recommendations of the sub-committees on the control of establishments and management services, typified this neutering process. It acknowledged, for example, that Treasury control could appear 'irksome' to departments and that the quality of Treasury staff had to be improved if they were to be accepted as 'collaborators in a common purpose'. To this end, it was strongly recommended that they should be selected for their 'temperamental suitability' as much as their 'intellectual ability'.[78] None of this was replicated in the Final Report, except in the most veiled way. In contrast, extracts from the interim report's appendix were included – when they were to the Treasury's advantage. In relation to computerisation, for example, it was noted that Whitehall was 'in the forefront of national progress'. Any failings admitted were exclusively those of other departments.[79]

Such apparent flaws in both the Committee's methods and its Final Report antagonised contemporary opinion within and outside Whitehall. The Treasury's reluctance to acknowledge past failings, to specify how they were to be remedied, and to accord equal treatment to spending departments did not augur well for the effective modernisation of Whitehall. However, such flaws served a positive, if covert, purpose. Plowden had from the start considered the Committee's primary role to be 'to allow and indeed compel the civil service to think through their own problems'.[80] This, in his judgement, was the more effective way to achieve genuine change than the pillory later provided by Fulton. The Treasury admittedly presented a peculiar problem. As Sharp (and earlier Haldane) had recognised, it alone could direct reform; and yet, of all departments, it needed reform the most. How could it be persuaded to change its spots? Not by confrontation, it was concluded, but by self-improvement. The Final Report, therefore, was allowed only to hint at the need for its wholesale reorganisation; but once the 'milestone' of PESC had been agreed (with all its flaws, which were presumed to be remediable) this was precisely what Plowden – as will be seen – was most determinedly fighting for *in private*.

3.3.2 Treasury reorganisation

As evidence of a possible change of spots, the Treasury was reorganised with remarkable speed and efficiency. An internal Treasury Organization Committee (TOC) was appointed in December 1961 and its report, submitted in June 1962, was implemented (somewhat appropriately) on 5 November. Simultaneously, there was a radical change of structure at the very top of the Service. It was agreed that there should be three distinct posts held, for the first time, by three different people: a Cabinet Secretary and Joint Secretaries at the Treasury – one to head its economic and financial side, the other to take responsibility for establishments policy as Head of the Civil Service. The new holders of these posts were intended to take office on 1 January 1963, and this was when Trend succeeded Brook as Cabinet Secretary. Due to illness, however, the other two appointments were expedited. William Armstrong succeeded Lee as head of the Treasury on 1 October whilst Sir Lawrence Helsby assumed the Headship of the Home Civil Service from Brook on 19 November.[81]

Important though these changes were in their own right, they had an added significance because it was they (rather than Fulton) that ignited three major debates that were to dominate civil service reform until at least 1981. Should the Treasury's responsibilities for establishments be formally split from its economic and financial role and entrusted to a Public Service Board, as in some Commonwealth countries, or a Civil Service Department? Should there, as in the USA, be a Bureau of the Budget (uniting the supply and establishments side of the Treasury) distinct from a Ministry of Finance (discharging the Treasury's other responsibilities)? Finally, what was the optimal relationship between the Treasury and the Cabinet Office? Should the Cabinet Secretary (possibly as head of a Prime Minister's Office) assume greater powers as both the Prime Minister's principal adviser and Head of the Service? Such questions had long been flirted with.[82] Now was the time for action.

Changes to the 'top posts' were precipitated by a confidential letter by Plowden to the Chancellor of the Exchequer on 9 June 1961. Its recommendations were accepted in principle by the Prime Minister in September and then debated by Brook and three senior colleagues (Lee, Padmore and Trend) outside the formal TOC machinery before a final decision was taken in March 1962.[83] Plowden's overriding objective was to ensure the 'more positive management of the civil service under a strong central authority'. He identified the Treasury as that 'authority' but recognised that its responsibilities were too diverse for a single head. Moreover, he recognised that – as in the past – economic and financial policy, because of the urgency with which decisions had typically to be taken, would always take precedence over management. Consequently he recommended that, in addition to a Cabinet Secretary (whose responsibilities he did not specify), the Treasury should have joint permanent secretaries. One, to be designated Head of the Service, was to be concerned principally with management: the career progression of senior staff, the development of management training, the proficiency of departmental management, and the updating of lists for public appointments. However, he admitted, such a post would pose a fundamental dilemma. Wholly divorced from day-to-day policy, would its holder be able to retain *authority* over colleagues (directly responsible to Ministers for the enactment of policy) and would he be *competent* to 'make an informed judgement' on both the relationship between policy and management, and the relative promotion potential of particular officials? Plowden thought not. To be effective, the Head of the Service would have to retain some policy responsibility, and he recommended that he should be *ex officio* chair of the Budget Committee.

In their subsequent debate, Brook and his senior colleagues reopened the question of whether the Treasury should have a single Permanent Secretary. This, after all, had been the practice in Sir Warren Fisher's day (when the 'economic and financial' side was largely delegated to a deputy) and it was sound business practice for an organisation to have a single head. This option, however, was firmly rejected on administrative, political and managerial grounds. Administratively, Brook confirmed the range of responsibility had grown so inexorably since the War that it was 'too wide for any single man'. Politically, it was foreseen that the Chancellor would wish to 'rely mainly on the deputy [and] resent the occasional "interventions" of the Permanent Secretary' who, as Head of the Service, would also have a dual loyalty to the Prime Minister. Managerially, the business parallel was inappropriate since it was Ministers not Permanent Secretaries who were ultimately the head of a department.[84]

What about Joint Permanent Secretaries? Here the validity of Plowden's reservations was accepted. As Brook confirmed:

> one cannot be confident that a Permanent Secretary who is neither in constant touch with Ministers, nor in charge of the central financial department of government, nor concerned any longer with the formulation of policy, would command sufficient authority to deal effectively with all the problems of Civil Service management.

Lee, more graphically, predicted that he would become a 'pale unhappy ghost'. His preferred solution, rather perversely, was to transfer the Service's management to a 'separate organization outside the Treasury'. From this independent position, he argued, a Head of the Civil Service could act as the 'Prime Minister's general adviser and factotum' – and thereby remain at the heart of policy-making. Brook demurred, if only for personal reasons. As Cabinet Secretary, in Plowden's vivid phrase, he had been Macmillan's effective 'chef de *cabinet*' and he was determined that the Cabinet Secretary should remain 'the principal official adviser of the Prime Minister'.[85]

Another alternative was then proposed by Padmore. Following Balogh and anticipating Brittan, he suggested that future Heads of the Civil Service could maintain policy contact as head of a Bureau of the Budget within the Treasury, overseeing both public expenditure and manpower. Politically, this would be uncontentious because the organisational split would simply mirror the new division of responsibility between the Chancellor and the Chief Secretary. On expenditure control, for instance, the Head of the Service would report largely to the Chief Secretary, whilst the Chancellor could enjoy exclusive contact with the 'economic' joint secretary. Managerially, the sound 'business' principle (later endorsed by Derek Rayner) would be attained of uniting financial and manpower control over the Service. Padmore's suggestion, however, also fell victim to vested interest. It would, so it was finally agreed, 'destroy the unity of the financial and economic work of the Treasury, and would on this account run counter to the recent trend of development in Treasury reorganisation'.[86] In other words, primacy within the Treasury was still being accorded over management to economic and financial policy (as traditionally conceived).

How was the dilemma to be resolved? Brook dismissed as a 'profound mistake' Plowden's proposal that the Head of the Service should chair the Budget Committee because it would, amongst other things, 'blur' his colleagues' responsibility for economic policy and sully his relationship with the Chancellor. Brook himself, however, could offer no alternative other than the minimisation of risk by the appointment to the post of 'a man of seniority' who had 'an established reputation based on his performance in another important task'. Such authority 'might prove a wasting asset; but it may well last out the remaining five or six years of his service'. Brook's pessimism was arguably a product of his own lack of interest in, and neglect of, administrative reform – and it deeply offended Sir Lawrence Helsby – the first incumbent of the re-designated post between 1962 and 1968 – when he belatedly heard of Brook's views. Particularly at a time of rapid administrative change, he argued, the position carried with it 'in a very real sense, its own authority and standing'. Personally he had never felt his authority to be under challenge or a 'wasting asset'. Whether such confidence was justified for Helsby, or his successors, is an open question.[87]

The success of the Treasury's reorganisation in 1962 is equally open to question given that, within two years, for example, economic planning had been transferred to the Department of Economic Affairs and, with a further two, a separate Civil Service Department created. Such a haemorrhaging of responsibilities and of staff did not exactly suggest success. Did reorganisation, therefore, fail or did it simply appear to fail because, not least as a result of the vehemence of demands for 'modernisation', it was denied the time to succeed? If the latter, does this represent yet another 'lost opportunity'?

Structurally, reorganisation went further than Plowden had suggested. The Treasury's financial and economic side was divided into three 'Groups', with the Finance Group taking responsibility for monetary policy, the National Economy Group for the coordination of economic policy, and the Public Sector Group for the control of public expenditure. The National Economic Group was the major innovation, not least because it contained (as modernisers wished) a mix of economists and generalists.[88] The Public Sector Group, headed by Sir Richard Clarke, also had some innovative features. For instance, its new Public Income and Outlay division, servicing PESC, was given responsibility for overseeing aggregate expenditure and resources. Its other five divisions had the more traditional responsibility of controlling departmental expenditure, but they were no longer to be organised by individual but rather by related groups of departments.[89] A semantic change explained the reason. They were to be named 'expenditure' divisions (to reflect the positive role public expenditure could play in stimulating growth) rather than 'supply' divisions (with its association with Parliamentary estimates and 'cheese-paring').

On the management side two further Groups were created: Pay and Management. The latter included divisions on discrete subjects such as training but there was also to be a new Management Services (General) Division to meet Plowden's wish that the Treasury should promote new management techniques and keep 'an oversight over the management practice of all the Departments'. In other words, its officials – in Ian Bancroft's inimitable phrase – were to be both 'crusaders and narks'. It was this Division that provoked the most debate in TOC and – as will be seen – posed the greatest problems thereafter.[90]

Reorganisation was designed to provide the Treasury with a 'functional specialism' which, in turn, was to ensure greater efficiency throughout the Service.[91] Did, however, Treasury officials have – or could they acquire – the requisite skills? The exclusion from TOC of 'outsiders' (as recommended by Plowden) boded ill; and continuing allusions within the Public Sector Group to the purpose of PESC showed little change in either administrative or political attitudes. In 1962, for instance, Clarke reassured colleagues that PESC was not to increase departmental autonomy but was rather to be 'an instrument to convey the Treasury's policies to the departments and to secure their support and cooperation'. Then, as if to confirm Macleod's and Powell's worst fears, a major PESC survey was introduced in 1965 as an 'essay in Whitehall knowing best'.[92] Nevertheless, as Plowden had hoped, PESC did gradually lead to a moderation and maturing of views both within and outside the Treasury. The public expenditure programme of 1965, for example, was finalised within the agreed estimate of prospective resources, despite the special pleading of such powerful spending Ministers as Crossman and Castle. The Treasury's holy grail of a permanent Ministerial Expenditure Committee was also briefly attained. No administrative reform could succeed in so 'political' an area without such a lead; and so its abandonment immediately after the 1966 election was a major cause for concern. This, however, was a political not an administrative failure.[93]

The crucial test for reorganisation, in fact, lay within the Management Group. Treasury officials had long neglected management issues; and as a confidential report, written before the commissioning of TOC, admitted: 'many of these issues, if they are to be dealt with adequately, involve innovation and call for a fresh mind and an enthusiastic approach – whereas the Assistant Secretary and at least two of the Principals in the division primarily concerned are without doubt some of the weakest members of those grades'. This weakness was not immediately redressed, as serving officials testified to the Fabian inquiry, largely because the Management Group enjoyed neither the high profile nor high-level support of the National Economy and Public Sector Groups. Not until December 1965 (three months before the commissioning of Fulton) was a serious bid made for the employment of management experts with the requisite skills.[94]

Confusion also continued to reign over the objectives and style of management policy. The development of particular techniques, such as Organisation and Methods, was unproblematic. But should they be promoted? TOC itself could provide little guidance for, as was somewhat ironically noted:

> one of the spheres in which management services could be introduced with advantage is the organisation of the papers concerned with the subject of "Management Services". They are as many, as varied and as unclassifiable as the different categories of management services themselves.

One of the more important of these papers was written by W.W. Morton, who was later to head the Group. He wrote somewhat disparagingly of Plowden's proposals (which had, of course, been drafted within the Treasury) and advocated instead the comparative study of departmental management techniques in order to build up a 'store of general knowledge' and to 'spread knowledge of the best practices'.[95] Accordingly, studies were commenced on financial control over R&D contracts and administration within local social security offices (each weighing in at four volumes).

The advantage of this comparative approach was that it did not infringe the autonomy of, and thereby antagonise, other departments. Its disadvantage was that it neither seized the initiative in identifying new techniques (as Plowden had wished) nor significantly changed departmental practice (in line with the private sector). As a result, a major policy reappraisal was commissioned in the autumn of 1965. Within the Management Group it was agreed that active consideration should be given to new techniques such as cost-benefit analysis and cost-effectiveness (as pioneered by Macnamara in the US Defense Department) and Operational Research (as practised in the some UK defence departments). However, any initiative would have to have prior departmental approval and its objective should not be to 'investigate or teach new techniques' but rather to ensure their better funding. To many others in the Treasury, this was wholly inadequate: Management Group officials, in effect, were to be neither crusaders nor narks. In their opinion, designated units should be set up within the Group to become expert in new managerial techniques, to extol their merit and then to 'father' similar units within each department to ensure their successful implementation.[96]

This conflict exposed a continuing fissure within the Treasury between expenditure and manpower control, which reorganisation had accentuated and which was to bedevil the next two decades. In TOC's original vision, once PESC had determined the aggregate size of departmental budgets, the core concern became their efficient expenditure on which the Management Group could provide technical expertise. In practice it could not. Moreover, it was the Public Sector divisions which were the Treasury's effective 'eyes and ears', identifying where management was defective. Moreover, they alone also had the financial 'clout' to ensure change. As the dilemma was succinctly summarised in 1965:

> the policy problems on which the new techniques can be exercised are to be found in the programmes handled by the Public Sector divisions; moreover [these divisions] are in a position to encourage (and on occasion insist upon) the use of new methods. The task of developing techniques, explaining and "selling" them to departments and, eventually, training departmental staff to use them is one which belongs more naturally to the management side.[97]

How was this fissure to be bridged? TOC had recognised that 'functional specialism' might create such tensions and urged close 'day-to-day consultation'. This was attempted. For instance, the Management Services (General) Division agreed to act essentially as an agency for the expenditure divisions, investigating problems which they had identified but lacked the resources to address.[98] There were also formal joint mechanisms such as Operation Vigilant, established in November 1963, which accumulated information about financial control systems in individual departments before recommending specific changes to their respective Permanent Secretaries. In December 1965, a joint Management Accounting Unit was also planned to provide a focus for a new range of expert troubleshooters.

Such expedients, however, did not prevent too many problems 'slipping' into, and then disappearing within, the fissure. This was in part because of a divergence in operational styles. As was ruefully pointed out by Clarke as head of the Public Sector Group, 'the function of Management Services divisions is intrinsically to provide services for departments at the latter's request and not as a key element in the apparatus of Treasury control'. Such a divergence had been anticipated by TOC; and it had informed its decision that, although the natural 'roots' of the Management Services were in the expenditure divisions, it should not be 'brigaded' with them for fear of impairing its 'neutrality'.[99] In other words, TOC wholly endorsed the constitutional convention that, under the doctrine of ministerial responsibility, departments were essentially autonomous. They were not, despite Fisher's earlier ambitions and Clarke's current ambitions, part of a unified service to which the centre could issue orders.

The failure to bridge this fissure led to a realisation within the Treasury that it might have three rather than two 'sides', with the Public Sector Group needing to secede from the Financial and Economic side because of its 'natural' links with Management. This might even lead to the creation, as earlier suggested by Padmore, of a Bureau of the Budget. Clarke in fact visited the United States in 1964 and was duly impressed by the Bureau of the Budget there.[100] However, in part because of the dislocation caused by TOC and the creation of the DEA, there was no longer the stomach for radical change. Reorganisation, in any case, became frozen within an alternative debate (fuelled by the commissioning of the Fulton Committee) over the establishment of a separate Civil Service Department.

Such a proposal, of course, had been early mooted by Sharp and – within the Treasury – by the Principals who wrote to Brooke in 1962. It had also been explicitly rejected in early 1962 by senior officials both within and outside TOC, with William Armstrong (somewhat ironically given his later headship of the CSD) concluding that: 'to split the Treasury into two quite separate groups would create far more problems than it would solve'. The issue was revisited by an internal Treasury committee in 1966. Its report, after two meetings with outside Permanent Secretaries, was eventually submitted to Fulton under the title 'Central management of the Civil Service'. There was, it maintained, virtually unanimous support for the *status quo*. Its principal justification, however, was alarmingly superficial. As Helsby persuaded other Permanent Secretaries to agree, the problem was essentially one of presentation:

> the restrictionist image of the Treasury, and indeed the name "Treasury" were, however undeservedly, hindrances to the effective discharge of the Pay and Management function, and the only argument of substance for making a change.[101]

This simply was not true, as continuing tensions within the Treasury confirmed. That such an argument was advanced, however, epitomised the excessive – and damaging – defensiveness into which the Service had been pushed by the vehemence of external demands for modernisation.

The Treasury's reorganisation, as demanded and then recognised by Plowden, was a qualified success. 'I am delighted', he wrote in 1963, 'with the reorganisation of the Treasury and with the appointments. I do not think they could be better.'[102] An *administrative* framework for the planning of public expenditure had been established, which was recognised to be amongst the best in the world. This was a precondition for a genuine decentralisation of responsibility, without which there could be no effective improvement in departmental management or efficiency. However, the Treasury enjoyed rather less success as an initiator of, and pace-setter for, improved managerial practice. Other areas of reorganisation received priority. The Management Group was denied the number and quality of staff Plowden had regarded as essential. The respective ability of the two new Joint Secretaries was also not without significance. Most importantly, however, the 1964 election – and, in particular the creation of the DEA – halted serious planning for a year whilst senior staff were monopolised by, and more junior staff were continually moved to, other tasks. Enforced modernisation from outside the Service cauterised the instinct to reform within.

3.4 Conclusion

The decade after Suez was a frenzied decade from which the Civil Service could not be insulated. Indeed, as part of the 'Establishment' with a perceived responsibility for national 'decline', it provided a focus for this frenzy. Moreover, it was an easier target than other potential 'culprits' such as the financial sector and industrial management (which were more secretive and elusive) or Parliament and the political parties (which begged even more fundamental questions). The frenzy was initially contained within the Service by means of the Plowden Committee which, more than realised at the time, was a vehicle for internally driven reform. It also achieved results which, even at the time of the Kennedy administration in the USA, were radical by international standards.

However, little credit was thereby gained. This was largely because of the legacy of the past. Postwar complacency (which had prevented a professional response to the changed role of government) had, under a veil of secrecy, cultivated an air of principled integrity and disinterest. Once this veil was lifted, criticism knew no bounds. 'It was the very height and strength of the dam', as one contemporary analysis has concluded of the broader collapse in deference, 'which ensured that, when it was finally breached, the explosion should come with such bitter violence.'[103] This is what presented Helsby with his irresolvable presentation problem. The modernisation movement outside Whitehall was typically ill-informed, contradictory and, above all, impervious to reason.

This did not mean that Whitehall had a monopoly of wisdom. Nor did it mean that internally generated reform would have been sufficient to modernise the Service. Genuine doubts remained about how much attitudes had changed, particularly within the Treasury, as well as the commitment to, and the speed of, reform. 'We cannot rely', as even one of the more conservative commentators remarked, 'on the inevitability of gradualness.'[104] In addition, there were unresolved managerial issues, particularly in relation to the proselytising of best practice (hence the tension within the Treasury), personnel policy (hence the continuing disillusion of junior officials) and the projection of 'public service' (as sought by Chapman). There seemed no longer to be, as in Haldane's day, an acceptance that management of the public sector was not only different from that of the private sector but also, in many areas, superior. This was indeed a significant sea-change.

Such outstanding issues could not be resolved by administrative action alone. Enhanced economic performance required improved governance as much as improved government; and improved government required effective political leadership. This, however, appeared a receding hope when the Minister most intellectually engaged by constitutional issues (Richard Crossman) professed – and displayed – ignorance about how government actually worked. Party political interest in administrative reform, even in its heyday, could also be startlingly naive. When seeking outside consultants, for example, the Conservatives' principal management adviser drafted a definition of whom he wanted: 'the sort of man who makes a first class salesman . . . probably under 25, keen on politics and prepared to put in six months hard work for the hell of it. A young journalist might be the ideal candidate'.[105] Was this a portent of the future?

4
THE FULTON COMMITTEE, 1966–8

4.1 Introduction

The Fulton Committee on the Civil Service was appointed and first met just before the March 1966 general election, at which the Labour Government increased its majority from two to 96. It reported in June 1968 in rather less propitious circumstances. In the previous November, the pound had been devalued and Britain's second application to join the EEC had been rejected; George Brown, as Deputy Prime Minister, had resigned in March and mounting tension within Cabinet reputedly left Wilson as Prime Minister vulnerable to a coup.[1] A further examination of the Service, as seen, had been deemed unnecessary by the Fabian Society. The House of Commons' Estimates Committee, however, disagreed. Its report in August 1965 on recruitment had concluded that the quantity and quality of applicants would only improve were there significant changes to the Service's structure and management. It was on the basis of this report that the Fulton Committee was appointed and its terms of reference – to 'examine the structure, recruitment and management, including training, of the Home Civil Service' – determined.

The Estimates Committee, however, was less successful in determining the nature of the new inquiry. On the advice of two leading academic witnesses (Professor W.J.M. Mackenzie and D.N. Chester), it had recommended a two-stage process. First a 'mixed' committee, similar to Plowden, should initiate a research programme to clarify, particularly in the light of international experience, how government could best respond to 'modern' conditions. The government could then either accept a particular set of recommendations or refer the matter to a Royal Commission for more open deliberation. Senior Treasury officials (including the new Joint Secretaries, Helsby and Armstrong) strongly opposed any new inquiry. Their somewhat contradictory justification was that the current internally-driven reform programme needed time to reach 'fruition' and that, since government was in a 'particularly fluid state', no current set of recommendations was likely to last 'for the next hundred years'.[2] However, once the Estimates Committee had reported, such opposition evaporated. The hope now was that the success of the Plowden Committee could be repeated, albeit more publicly, and the fashionable frenzy for modernisation cauterised.[3]

In the event, the Fulton Committee combined the role of both the intended research committee and a Royal Commission. However, it neither replicated the success of Plowden (as Treasury officials hoped) nor enhanced the Service in 'public esteem' (as the Estimates Committee had anticipated). This latter failure was in no small part due to what its Secretary (Richard Wilding) later termed the 'misconceived hand grenade' of its opening paragraph, which condemned the Service as the 'product of the nineteenth-century philosophy of the Northcote-Trevelyan Report', and the subsequent attack on the 'obsolete cult' of the 'amateur (or "generalist" or "all-rounder")'.[4] The Service's reputation was irretrievably damaged both at home and abroad.[5]

What, however, of the Fulton Committee's own reputation? It self-consciously strove to be as radical and as historic as the Northcote-Trevelyan Report.[6] Was it successful on either count? The answer to this question divided its signatories and commentators at the time, and has divided practitioners and academics ever since.[7] On the one hand, for example, one of the Committee's consultants (John Garrett) maintained that it was 'the most radical document on postwar public administration'; and in the 1980s a major reformer (Derek Rayner) agreed, calling the Report a 'brilliant analysis of some important weaknesses' in the Service. On the other hand, a signatory (Sir James Dunnett) claimed that it was 'neither a radical nor a revolutionary document'; and the contemporary press (which had eagerly welcomed the Committee's appointment) tended to agree. As the *Spectator* trenchantly commented, for instance, its recommendations were 'worlds away from the root and branch' remedies required, were the apocalyptic diagnosis of the opening two chapters to be believed. Rather than being radical, they were merely presented with 'bogus radical aplomb'. Retrospectively, this is also the judgement of the best-informed academic commentators. G.K. Fry, for instance, has argued that it would be 'an abuse of language to call Fulton radical' whilst Peter Hennessy, albeit for different reasons, has denied that the Report was 'ground-breaking'.

Despite such scepticism, however, the Report's place in history would appear secure. For Garrett again it was a 'landmark in the study of public administration' and academic commentators at the time and since (such as D.N. Chester and Peter Barberis) have used identical terms. Since 1979, a succession of senior practitioners have also agreed with Robert Armstrong that it was a 'milestone'; and the principal author of *Next Steps* has even described it as a 'model of careful analysis, clear thinking and sensible solutions' which made an indelible impression abroad. How can such differences between people and between judgements be reconciled? This is the conundrum which this chapter will address, by analysing first the Report's recommendations and then its methods.

4.2 The Report's recommendations

The Fulton Committee, despite its specific focus, was more alert than most within the 'modernisation' movement to the broad context within which it was working. 'Our proposals for the reform of the Civil Service', it acknowledged, 'need to be seen as part of the more general reappraisal that is being made of our inherited forms of government and social and economic organisation.' Nevertheless, its overriding message was that government – and hence the Civil Service – must play an active role in the promotion of the 'country's well-being'. Thus officials had to deliver 'well-prepared innovation' and, for this, they needed both impeccable interventionist and political skills. As its Report specified, a modern Civil Service

> must be able to handle the social, economic, scientific and technical problems of our time, in an international setting. Because the solutions to complex problems need long preparation, the Service must be far-sighted; from its accumulated knowledge and experience, it must show initiative in working out what are the needs of the future and how they might be met. A special responsibility now rests upon the Civil Service because one Parliament or even one Government often cannot see the process through.[8]

Success, so the Report continued – contrary to the wisdom of later advocates of managerial reform – depended on the Service remaining 'uniform' (as well as united) and there being permanent Civil Servants (as well as a permanent Civil Service).[9] Uniformity was required because 'emerging problems' had to be 'tackled systematically and comprehensively and on the basis of common major hypotheses'.

Equally career civil servants were needed in the majority of posts (including most 'top jobs'). There were four principal reasons. 'Long experience and accumulated knowledge' were essential for a 'truly professional' Service. Morale might suffer were top jobs – as in the USA – awarded consistently to outsiders. Forthright advice might not otherwise be offered to ministers. Finally, corruption had to be obviated. In this respect, it was of the highest importance that 'civil servants should not come to think of those who do business with their departments as their prospective employers, and that firms, which are increasingly required to reveal their technical and financial affairs to government, should be able to do so in confidence'.[10]

It was in this broad context that the Committee settled to its principal task: the drafting of a blueprint for a 'fully professional and dynamic Service'. It defined 'professional' in two ways. One was 'being skilled in one's job – skill which comes from training and sustained experience'. The other was 'having the fundamental knowledge of and deep familiarity with a subject that enable a man [sic] to move with ease among its concepts'. The need for such professionalism was clear:

> civil servants who are more at home with the machinery of administration than with its content tend to be cautious – sometimes, even negative; a few, reacting the other way to what they do not fully understand, may well be rash. . . . Well-prepared innovation is more likely to come from those whose grasp of their subject gives them a sure awareness of its possibilities as well as its limitations and from those able to talk with experts in their own language.[11]

How was such professionalism to be achieved, particularly at the top? There were again two ways. First, 'specialists' (such as scientists, engineers and economists) should be recruited 'in the right numbers and of the right type and quality'. They should then be given an early training in management so that – as in industry – they could assume, when appropriate, the most senior positions. Second, 'administrators' should cease to be generalists and, in a given area of policy, should 'acquire and develop the appropriate body of knowledge with its associated conceptual framework and analytical tools'. The Committee identified two such areas: the economic and financial, and the social. The former included economic planning and the financial control of major expenditure programmes. The latter included housing, education, race relations and (rather bizarrely) personnel management. Mobility within and between departments was still to be encouraged, but movement should normally be within an administrator's existing area of specialist expertise.[12]

There was some dispute within the Committee over how administrators might best gain their expertise. Least controversial was the creation of a Civil Service College (for which, as will be seen in chapter 9.2, ambitious plans were advanced). 'Administrators' should complete a two-year probation within their departments and then receive further training at the College in their specialism, in management techniques and in 'the machinery and practice of government'.[13] More controversial was the question of whether, during recruitment, preference should be given to graduates with 'relevant' degrees. Eight Committee members thought that it should. 'To give preference for relevance', they argued, 'is to adapt to the needs of today the old principle that the Service should seek to recruit those it believes best equipped for work in government'. Universities and the most committed students were increasingly concentrating on the 'problems of the modern world' and they wanted the 'Service to attract its full share of young people motivated in this way'. Moreover, like Northcote-Trevelyan, they hoped that the educational system as a whole would benefit from a demonstration of their 'special interest' in 'modern' subjects. Four members, however, remained unconvinced. In a tight labour market, they argued, such favouritism would artificially restrict recruitment – given, in particular, that many students had effectively to specialise at the age of 13. Like Macaulay, they preferred to recruit those with the most 'rigorous and disciplined habit of mind' which could be 'imparted by "irrelevant" as well as by "relevant" studies'. Specialist knowledge could be gained thereafter through post-entry training.[14]

Professionalism was only one of the two qualities Fulton sought to instil in the Service. The other was dynamism. How was that to be achieved? The principal solutions suggested here were better personnel management and the more efficient organisation of work. In relation to personnel management, the Estimates Committee's original instinct was confirmed that recruitment, training and subsequent career development should be 'parts of a single process to be as closely integrated as possible'. As with Northcote-Trevelyan, the overall objective should be to attract the most talented recruits and then ensure that 'the exceptionally able' moved 'rapidly up the system'. In the past, so it was alleged, such progress had been frustrated by inexpert and 'stuffy' Establishment Departments. They should now be renamed 'personnel and organisation' divisions and their status enhanced so that they could attract staff 'capable of rising to the highest posts'.[15]

In relation to the organisation of work, the Report recommended in particular 'accountable management' and the 'hiving off' of discrete blocks of executive work to autonomous public boards. The specific object was 'to enable responsibility and authority to be defined and allocated more clearly [so that] individuals and units could then be called to account for performance which is measured as objectively as possible'. These initiatives were to be supported by what became the Report's most controversial recommendation: unified grading. Officials were currently divided into 47 general service classes and some 1400 departmental classes, each with its own range and levels of responsibility. All such classes, it was argued, should be abolished and replaced by a continuous grading system. The advantage was that, in the absence of rigid class barriers, all posts could be graded and filled on an evaluation of the actual job to be done. This would permit staff to be used more flexibly. 'The practice of assigning duties to individuals by reference to their particular classes', the Report fulminated, 'is at best an irrelevant distraction and at worst a serious obstacle to the kind of job evaluation which is needed'.[16]

Exceptionally, unified grading was to affect not just senior but also junior staff whose 'potential talent', so the Committee alleged, the Service had been 'mis-using and stultifying'. There should, above all, be an 'open road to the top'. Newly appointed executive and clerical officers, for example, should be regarded as trainees for their first three or four years. Were they to show particular talent, they should then be placed on a 'fast promotion route', from which they could expect to secure advancement within two years 'without regard to the claims of seniority'.[17] Greater fluidity was assured because expectations would be raised by the abolition of classes. 'The word "class" and the structure it represents', as the Report noted, 'produce feelings of inferiority as well as of restricted opportunities.' Moreover, with the introduction of unified grading and job evaluation, 'a man's experience and qualification to do a job at a higher level' would become 'the main factor in promotion decisions' and 'full weight' could be given to past performance. Nevertheless, there was to be no free lunch. Were efficiency to be rewarded, then inefficiency should be penalised. Annual pay increments, for instance, should be withheld as well as being accelerated; and probation should be made more rigorous. Moreover, a guarantee of a lifetime career (implied by an 'established' post) should also be terminated as it encouraged complacency. Officials should instead be placed on contracts terminable at up to six month's notice. Even pensions (made more liberal to facilitate mobility in and out of the Service) should become contributory.[18]

Senior staff in particular were to be galvanised by a further four recommendations. First, to alert them fully to both the world outside Whitehall and 'the new ideas and methods which are developing in universities, in business and in other walks of life', they were to become 'more representative, geographically, educationally and socially of the nation at large'.[19] Second, 'new ideas and relevant experience' were to be injected by a mix of late entrants, short-term appointments, nominees from industry and academia, and special ministerial advisers. Third, a greater sense of personal accountability was to be generated by an emphasis on 'management by objective'. 'Problem solving' would thereby replace 'buck-passing' and the replacement of 'parallel' by 'unified' hierarchies (by the breaking down of 'vertical' barriers between the Administrative Class and specialists) would at last mean specialists could be 'on top' and not just 'on tap'.[20] Finally, there was to be a greater accent on youth, as in France or Sweden, with 'the most able, vigorous and suitably qualified' of younger officials being grouped into 'Planning Units' where they might have an early and direct impact on policy-making. This would necessarily break the monopoly of policy advice to Ministers traditionally enjoyed by Permanent Secretaries. However Permanent Secretaries should, it was finally agreed, retain control over their departments – although their primary concern should become management. As the Report explained:

> our proposals for accountable management and for enlarging the role of departmental personnel and organisation divisions will inevitably add still further to the burdens of the Permanent Secretary. He will have to devote more time to his managerial function – to be the spearhead of the constant drive to improve the efficiency of his department at all levels and among the various accountable units; and, with the greater emphasis on career management . . . the Permanent Secretary's responsibility for the selection and movement of staff will become even more important and demanding.[21]

What of the institutional changes to underpin the delivery of 'well-prepared innovation' by this new professional and dynamic Service? The Committee, as will be seen, was implicitly forbidden to trespass onto questions concerning the 'machinery of government'. Nevertheless, within departments, it did recommend such institutional innovations as hiving off, planning units and new personnel and organisation divisions. In addition, and in concert with the earlier demands of the Treasury's Public Sector Group, it favoured the creation of a 'Management Services Unit' in each department to ensure that it 'keeps its organisation up to date, conducts a regular audit of its efficiency, and constantly applies the best available methods and techniques to its tasks'. Other fashionable suggestions, such as formal boards of advisers (as suggested by Balogh) and ministerial *cabinets* (as suggested by Chapman and Brittan) were, however, rejected. Planning Units, it was deemed, made them unnecessary.[22]

However one major institutional change, long favoured by reformers for the centre of government, was vigorously advocated: the creation of a separate Civil Service Department. 'The central management of the Service', the Report maintained, was 'not, under modern conditions, an appropriate function for the central finance department'. It could, and had, led in the past to an undesirable bias in the appointment of senior officials. Officials within a single department were incapable of mastering so diverse and complex a mix of responsibilities as economic and personnel management. Moreover it was essential that the 'central management' of the Service

> should be positively and creatively concerned with maintaining and improving the standards . . . It should therefore be a separate institution with a single-minded devotion to its own professional purpose; and should be in a position to fight, and to be seen fighting, the Treasury on behalf of the Service'.[23]

To achieve these ends, so the Report continued, the CSD had to have the authority of the Prime Minister at its head. Its staff had to be representative of all major occupations within the Service and be management experts. Above all, it had to have 'the appropriate degree of ultimate authority' (which, it admitted, the Treasury had never formally enjoyed). Troubled relations with other departments, the Treasury and staff associations were foreseen; and in an astute premonition (as will be confirmed in chapter 5) the Report particularly warned that Whitleyism, as in the past, would impede 'effective management', were not the 'pattern of joint consultation' to 'reflect' rather than 'determine the results of the changes we propose'.[24]

4.3 Fulton's flaws

Coherent though the Report's recommendations might appear, their effectiveness as a blueprint for reform depended in practice on the extent to which they were well researched, well argued and well directed. Their effectiveness, in short, depended on the Committee exhibiting the same qualities it demanded of a reformed Service – professionalism and dynamism. However, these were the very qualities which – by common consent – it lacked. As one of its signatories confirmed, its proceedings were characterised more by 'anarchy than strategy'; and another confessed that, of the many reports he had signed, it was undoubtedly the 'worst'.[25] Why was Fulton so flawed? Amongst the more common explanations are its low status as a departmental committee, its restricted terms of reference, poor chairmanship, personal antipathy amongst its members and a lack of sustained political support.

That Fulton was a departmental committee, rather than a more prestigious Royal Commission, was of little importance. The decision was reputedly taken so that it could contain a mix of insiders and outsiders (like Plowden) and report quickly. Such reasoning, were it true, was confused. Earlier Royal Commissions (such as MacDonnell) had included serving officials and others (including the Tomlin and Priestley Commissions on the Civil Service) reported faster than Fulton.[26] In any case, a departmental committee did not necessarily lack prestige. The Northcote-Trevelyan and Haldane Reports, after all, were the products of such committees.

The restricted terms of reference were another matter. In announcing the Committee's appointment to the House of Commons, Wilson had insisted that

> the Government's willingness to consider changes in the Civil Service does not imply any intention on their part to alter the basic relationship between Ministers and Civil Servants. Civil Servants, however eminent, remain the confidential advisers of Ministers, who alone are answerable to Parliament for policy; and we do not envisage any change in this fundamental feature of our parliamentary system of democracy.

The Committee, in addition, felt itself debarred from discussing changes to the machinery of government.[27] Why were such restrictions imposed and accepted? One reason for their imposition was a belief that, were so fundamental a constitutional convention as ministerial responsibility or so important an area of the Prime Minister's prerogative to be examined, a far weightier committee would be required. Its deliberations accordingly would take longer than the Government wished. More conspiratorially, the restrictions were explained by the Report's main author (Norman Hunt) as a deliberate device introduced by the 'mandarins' to stall unwanted reform on the grounds – which they indeed subsequently used – that 'until "machinery of government" questions had been settled, you could not really know what sort of civil servants you needed and how they should be organized'. Hunt dismissed such arguments as 'nonsense'. 'The tasks of government were to be pretty much the same', he maintained, 'however many departments you had, or whatever their size.'[28] This in itself was nonsense because, as was becoming clear in 1968 and was transparent by the time he was writing (1980), there was a diminishing consensus about what the proper 'tasks of government' should be. Nevertheless, the restrictions under which Fulton laboured were real and prevented it from being 'ground breaking'. Unable to address the same fundamental constitutional and organisational issues as either Northcote-Trevelyan or Haldane, it could but be a 'one-dimensional . . . rather than the three-dimensional investigation that was needed'. This, however, merely begs another question. Why did not Fulton exceed its terms of reference? Earlier committees had certainly done so, most notoriously the 1941–2 Beveridge Committee. It was certainly encouraged so to do – not least by some of the 'mandarins' who submitted evidence.[29]

A prime reason for the lack of such initiative was the quality of its chairmanship. Fulton was no Beveridge. He appeared ideally suited for the job. A former Oxford fellow in philosophy and politics, he was a close friend of the Prime Minister with whom he had famously shared fire-watching duties whilst a temporary Civil Servant during the War. He had then specialised in university administration and become the first Vice-Chancellor of the University of Sussex (1959–67). Thus he had both an academic and practical knowledge of the Service as well as proven administrative skills. By general consent, however, he was an 'appalling' chairman, with a 'grass-hopper' mind, little control over the Committee and even less command of the subject.[30] Moreover, such failings could not be countered – as they were on other committees – by a strong secretariat.[31]

The other Committee members appeared equally well qualified. There were two leading industrialists (Sir Norman Kipping, the recently retired Director General of the Federation of British Industries; and Sir John Wall, the managing director of EMI and a former member of the Plowden Committee); one trade unionist (Walter Anderson of the National Association of Local Government Officers); two MPs (Sir Edward Boyle, the chair of the Conservative's study group on government, and Shirley Williams (who was quickly replaced by Robert Sheldon on her appointment as a Minister); and two academics (Norman Hunt, an Oxford fellow in politics, and Lord Simey, Professor of Social Science at Liverpool University). In addition there were four serving officials – two 'administrators' (Sir Phillip Allen, then head of the Pay and Management Group at the Treasury; and Sir James Dunnett, Permanent Secretary of the Ministry of Labour), one 'specialist' (Sir William Cook, the Deputy Chief Scientific Officer at the Ministry of Defence) and one temporary special adviser (Robert Neild, the Economic Adviser to the Chancellor of the Exchequer and erstwhile chair of the Fabian Society enquiry). Each was well respected and the majority had first-hand knowledge of the Service.

There were, however, four fatal flaws. First, amongst those who had no specialist knowledge of the Service were the two academics. Hunt, despite being a fellow in politics, was essentially an historian who had lately specialised in the eighteenth century; and Simey, despite being an authority on social administration, never regarded administrative reform as 'really his subject'.[32] It was unfortunate that neither of the two leading academic experts on public administration was appointed – Sir Norman Chester (the 1964–5 Estimates Committee's special adviser) or W.J.M. Mackenzie (its most forthright witness). Second, those with the most specialist knowledge became preoccupied elsewhere. Neild, for example, became heavily involved in the devaluation crisis. Following his appointment as the Post Office's Deputy Secretary in 1966, Wall (whose contribution to the Plowden Committee had, in any case, been somewhat irregular) became increasingly distracted by its transformation into a public corporation. In 1966 Allen was also promoted to Permanent Secretary of the Home Office, where he became immersed in Roy Jenkins' highly controversial social reform programme (including the legalisation of homosexuality and the 1967 Abortion Act). Likewise Dunnett was transferred to the Ministry of Defence where he helped to mastermind Britain's planned withdrawal from 'East of Suez'. Third, some of those who did have the time (such as Boyle and Cook) showed little inclination to use it. Finally, interpersonal relations were poor. 'They were a nasty lot of people', recalled the Secretary, 'and they did not like each other. There was lots of ill temper.' His judgement has been questioned but it was certainly, and perhaps inevitably, true of the two academics. It was no secret that Simey 'just could not stand Hunt'.[33] This was a major factor behind his increasing withdrawal from the Committee and the issuing of his formal 'reservation' to the first chapter.

Such tensions contributed to two of the Report's fundamental weaknesses: its intemperate language and its lack of substance. In the first instance, a troika of Neild, Hunt and Sheldon was determined to condemn the Administrative Class as comprehensibly as had become the fashion – not least in the Fabian inquiry (which Neild himself had chaired). In the body of the Report, both its perceived exclusiveness and amateurism tended only to be criticised by inference; but it was explicitly attacked in the opening two chapters, which were designed to provide a broad overview of the Service's current shortcomings and future requirements. Such an imbalance was essentially the consequence of an initial intention to publish the overview chapters separately, with the more detailed recommendations and supporting evidence to follow in later volumes. Short and pithy, they were designed to have as powerful an impact as Northcote-Trevelyan; and to this end, Neild drafted the notorious opening sentence for Chapter 1 and, with equal zeal, Hunt listed the Service's six major failings. No modification was thereafter permitted by Sheldon even when – in tacit acknowledgement of the lack of agreed radical measures – it was belatedly decided to merge the two chapters with the detailed recommendations.[34]

Prominent amongst those seeking some modification were, not unnaturally, the two Permanent Secretaries. For the reasons cited in Simey's reservation, they maintained that the opening chapters wilfully ignored both the Service's past achievements (particularly during the War) and the political constraints within which it worked (such as the need to serve 'generalist ministers ... a generalist Parliament and a generalist public').[35] Both, however, were preoccupied by their departmental responsibilities; and Dunnett's protests, at least, were moderated by a measure of sympathy for some of the proposed reforms (such as an enhanced role for specialists and better management training). Most importantly, however, both were reluctant to press harder for modification for fear that sustained dissension – let alone a minority report – would spark rumours that the Service opposed all change. This might have provoked an even more radical majority report or, given the expected re-election of Labour in 1970, radical action. Both Hunt and Fulton, after all, were known frequently to see the Prime Minister and it was presumed they had his full backing.[36]

The Permanent Secretaries' reticence and thus the Report's continuing acerbity were, as is well known, counterproductive. Outside the Service, the opening paragraph and charges of 'amateurism' offended informed opinion. Even the erstwhile moderniser and Labour minister, C.P. Snow, expressed his 'regret that this absurd stereotype was not criticised out of existence during the process of drafting'.[37] Within the Service, there was equally deep resentment even amongst those who had earlier voiced similar criticisms (see chapter 3.2.5), not least because of the damage done to the prospects of serious reform – be it internally or externally driven.[38] Yet unanimity could be reached on one score: Fulton had at least proved itself the equal of Northcote-Trevelyan in its gratuitous offensiveness (although readers had to wait for the twenty-second – rather than eighth – paragraph to balance the initial onslaught against a list of the 'Service's very considerable strengths'). Plowden's approach had been very different. So too, significantly, was that of the Management Consultancy Group, upon whose report (as will be seen) Fulton relied heavily for its radicalism. It listed the Service's 'distinctive strengths . . . at the outset' before proceeding to dissect its weaknesses.[39]

Lack of substance also limited the Report's effectiveness. This was the consequence of three principal shortcomings: the randomness of the evidence collected, the inadequacy of commissioned research, and the absence of sustained debate – and informed agreement – during its drafting. A major concern about the inquiry being a mere departmental committee had been that it would lack the authority to 'send for persons and papers'. In the event, there was a surfeit rather than a shortage of oral testimony; but, on the Secretary's admission, its collection wasted an 'awful lot of time'.[40] No attempt was made, for example, to ensure its representativeness and it was not properly recorded. Exceptionally for such an inquiry, there was no initial attempt, and thereafter only a sporadic one, to keep verbatim minutes. This resulted in a somewhat damning paradox. Just as the authors of *The Administrators* had condemned officials' anonymity whilst choosing to remain anonymous themselves, so Fulton attacked official secrecy whilst being one of the few public inquiries not to publish its evidence.

The research programme was equally amateurish. Varying numbers of Committee members made three foreign visits – to the USA, France and Sweden – between September 1966 and February 1967 but such visits were admitted to be 'too brief to be of much utility'. Certainly they, and follow-up enquiries, produced a rather flawed understanding of 'unified grading' in the USA; and, given the attack on the social exclusivity of the Administrative Class, the unqualified praise heaped on the equally elitist French *grand corps* was somewhat inconsistent. Within Britain, research was equally flawed. Funds were available for a full-time director of research (as on the concurrent Redcliffe-Maud Commission) but no such appointment was made. In consequence, of the eleven projects whose findings Fulton published, five had actually been commissioned by other bodies (four by the Estimates Committee and one by the 1965–70 Public Schools Commission). A sixth simply expanded existing work at the Civil Service Commission; and two others (Chapman's 'Profile of a Profession' and Pickering's survey of the careers of unsuccessful candidates in the 1951 open competition), albeit of a high standard, were the result of chance remarks or contacts – and the authors were never invited to discuss their findings.[41]

The two research projects, actually initiated by the Committee, which had the longest-term impact were A.H. Halsey's 'Social Survey of the Civil Service' and the report of the Management Consultancy Group. Even they had been commissioned less out of conviction for their intrinsic worth than for fear that the Report would appear 'naked' were such fashionable forms of research ignored. The Social Survey, for example, was only belatedly agreed in November 1966 when Fulton blatantly overruled majority opinion at the key Committee meeting. Moreover, it was completed too late to have any significant impact on the Report. Early drafts were circulated to the Committee but they were largely ignored, not least because (as one Committee member admitted) they contained 'mistakes of fact, logical errors, obscurity, turgidity of expression and . . . showed insufficient understanding of the Civil Service'.[42] Significantly the speaker was not one of the Survey's critics, but one of its more committed supporters – Norman Hunt.

The Survey's importance, therefore, was mainly in the long term (see, for example, Chapter 9.5); and so the only practical exception to Fulton's 'amateurism', despite the serious overrunning of both its budget and deadline, was the report of the Management Consultancy Group (MCG). The Group consisted of one businessman (E.K. Ferguson from BP), one management consultant (John Garrett who later, as a Labour MP, became Fulton's staunchest advocate) and one Treasury official (S.D. Walker, the Chief Executive Officer in charge of the O&M division, whom Garrett described as 'the best management consultant I ever knew'); and its report was based on the investigation of 23 blocks of work within twelve departments, selected by Dunnett and Allen, to determine how and by whom the work was done and the potential for greater efficiency.[43] Its investigations may not have been as thorough as those of the contemporary Glassco Commission which had examined the Canadian Civil Service between 1960 and 1962. It may also have failed to follow the full market logic of its analysis, as did Glassco with its overriding message of 'let the managers manage'.[44] It nevertheless laid the groundwork for many of Fulton's more radical proposals such as 'accountable management' and unified grading. Equally important, it also amassed an unparalleled range of detailed information about management practice within the Service; and, by comparing it less favourably than hitherto with business practice, challenged conventional wisdom. It thus made good the deficiency within the Treasury of managerial expertise (which, as has been seen, survived Plowden) and paved the way for the managerial reforms of the 1980s.

The MGC owed its existence, as did most other research initiatives, to Norman Hunt, who was the most energetic member of the Committee and the principal author of the final Report. On sabbatical leave from Oxford and in close contact with the Prime Minister, he had both the time and the apparent authority to replicate Otto Clarke's role on Plowden or to become, at the very least, an effective *de facto* director of research. Unfortunately, however, he lacked not only specialist knowledge of the Service but also the requisite managerial experience and sociological training. Thus, despite two weekend conferences and a series of dinners for the 'inner core' in order to deepen understanding of key issues, Fulton was condemned to appearing irredeemably amateurish in relation to similar inquiries abroad – not just Glassco but also the earlier Hoover Commissions in the USA and the subsequent Coombs Commission in Australia.[45]

Such amateurism was, of course, not solely the fault of one individual but of the Committee as a whole. It was also the result not just of personal animosity (of which evidence has already been provided) but a lack of common purpose. The fundamental issue, for example, was never resolved: was the Committee's prime objective to professionalise the Administrative Class (to whom the Fabians looked to ensure the successful expansion of collectivist government) or to secure the better management of a machine which, as described in Chapter 2.3, had grown relentlessly throughout the century (the logic of the MCG report). Without agreement, in the words of the Committee's Secretary, the final Report became a 'kind of a sandwich with a piece of Fabian rye bread on top and a piece of managerial white bread underneath'.[46] The filling, he might have added, was also rather insubstantial. In addition, and regardless of Simey's formal reservation, there were an exceptional number of recorded disagreements on detailed points covering, for instance, recruitment ('preference for relevance' and the abolition of Method I) and terms of employment (job evaluation and performance pay).[47]

There were no openly recorded disputes over 'technical' managerial issues, but there were many private ones. The most significant concerned 'unified grading'. Initially no one supported it. The Treasury had immediately recommended the abolition of the 'horizontal' barrier between the Administrative and Executive Class (which the MCG characterised as the true 'management group').[48] It was also agreed, against the advice of the businessmen on the Committee, to assimilate the Clerical Class. What, however, of the 'vertical' barriers between the Administrative, specialist and departmental classes? Should they be removed down to the level of Under Secretary, Principal or (as was eventually agreed) throughout the Service? The basic dilemma which the Committee faced was how to remove the multiplicity of classes (to enhance personal ambition and work flexibility) whilst maintaining the recruitment levels and the *esprit de corps*, which specialist and departmental classes were believed to encourage. Its final solution was a combination of unified grading with the rather indeterminate concept of 'occupational groupings'. Was this a practicable solution or merely a face-saving formula? Time alone could tell; but the lengthy contest over the decision, the tactical reasons for its ultimate acceptance and unanswered doubts about its practicability provided legitimate grounds for later reservations.

Lack of common purpose also led to the total evasion, or serious underexamination, of some key issues. It was never resolved, for instance, whether the final Report should simply propound key principles or be a detailed action plan In the event it fell between two stools, with many principles remaining undeveloped and the resolution of many details left either to the Treasury or (later) the CSD. Leaving decisions to the Treasury might appear compatible with Plowden's non-confrontational approach. In fact, however, it led frequently to the compromising of the Committee's professed principles. The eventual concordat between the Treasury and CSD, for example, did little to clarify how the latter could attain an 'appropriate degree of ultimate authority'.[49] Likewise the adoption, albeit unacknowledged, of the Treasury's training plans scotched any prospect of an anglicised Ecole Nationale d'Administration, which many on the Committee regarded as essential. Of the principles left undeveloped, the two most glaring concerned audit and the proposed Planning Units. The creation of a strong external audit body and well-developed departmental systems of budgeting and expenditure control, for example, was implicit in the MCG report; and yet neither was recommended. Similarly, the constitutional implication of Planning Units (key to the Fabian conviction that state officials should be responsible for 'well-prepared innovation' regardless of changes in government) were, on the admission of one signatory, 'never thought out'. The 'rapid and effective implementation' of the Report's recommendations, as Garrett later admitted, 'depended on the clear and precise specification of change, yet the Committee left confusion surrounding most of its proposals'.[50]

Fulton's flaws might have been modified by strong, external political leadership. Wilson as Prime Minister did regularly meet Fulton and Hunt; but these meetings seem to have been arranged more out of curiosity than concern and led, despite the trepidation of the Permanent Secretaries, to no directives from on high. Indeed Wilson appeared torn between genuine respect for the Service (as a 'civil servant *manqué*', in the view of his political secretary, Marcia Williams) and an antipathy towards its elitism (as regularly reinforced by his Principal Private Secretary, Michael Halls).[51] Ultimately, it might be concluded, it was the image rather than the substance of a reformer that he sought, particularly when his leadership came under attack in June 1968. Consideration of other Ministers' interests then became paramount; and they patently did not include administrative reform. Wilson's most powerful political allies were Richard Crossman and Barbara Castle. Both were highly suspicious of the 'permanent politicians' but they were nevertheless uninterested in serious reform. Prior to the Cabinet on 20 June 1968 at which the Report was first discussed, for instance, Crossman notoriously struck a deal with Roy Jenkins to support the Chancellor's request for a delay in publication in return for a postponement to cuts in social service expenditure and support for House of Lords reform. Castle, for her part, actually left that Cabinet early – but not before making known her view that, were any additional expenditure to be agreed, equal pay should have preference over unified grading. Jenkins himself was Wilson's chief rival and, given that the Report recommended the division of his department, was somewhat aggrieved – with some justice – that he had not been forewarned of its contents. He consequently sought to sabotage it. At a time of almost unprecedented popular and political interest in administrative reform, therefore, the opportunity seriously to discuss it at the highest level degenerated into 'a lever for quick deals on other issues and the lightening conductor for paranoia and rivalry'. 'Such is the nature of high Cabinet politics!', as Peter Hennessy has written in exasperation.[52]

4.4 Conclusion

Fulton's place in history ultimately depended on the extent to which it enabled government to make good the opportunity 'lost' by Bridges immediately after the War. Concern then, in most Western countries, had been over government's increasingly interventionist role – as demonstrated by the appointment of major inquiries such as the Hoover and Glassco Commissions. By the time Fulton itself was commissioned, however, attention was turning to the efficiency, rather than the size, of government – as was to be the case later with the appointment of the Coombs Commission in Australia. Fulton was thus on the cusp of two very powerful political and popular concerns which posed two very different, if related, questions. The first was how senior civil servants, as policy advisers, could acquire both the specialist skills and the constitutional legitimacy expertly to direct interventionist government. This was an issue that had long concerned the Fabian wing of the Labour Party and had informed both the Haldane Committee and Sir Warren Fisher's initial reform plans in 1919. The second was how the ever-growing government machine could best be managed. Government until the 1960s had prided itself on providing a model for the private sector. Now that British industry was under increased competitive pressure, it was developing an interest in managerial efficiency and was particularly receptive to new techniques from the USA. Had the private sector something to offer government? This was the question which was to dominate the next four decades.

In relation to the first question, Fulton's restricted terms of reference and some of its members' animosity towards the Administrative Class restricted its radical impact. Plans for greater professionalism and accountability may have boosted morale at the more junior levels of the Administrative and Executive Class (which Plowden had culpably neglected). However, the issue of how much initiative senior officials could take, given the convention of ministerial responsibility, remained unresolved; and the Report's intemperate language pandered to, rather than corrected, public prejudice about their 'amateurism'. In relation to the second question, the Management Consultancy Group certainly injected into the debate some of the knowledge and managerial expertise patently lacking within the Treasury, even after Plowden. Questions remain, however, over how well the Group's recommendations were handled by the main Committee; their applicability to the special circumstances of the public sector; and even whether they represented best private sector practice. In addition, Fulton's commitment to big government (and thus to a permanent and united Civil Service) limited the degree to which, by the predominant ideological criteria after 1976, its recommendations might be termed radical.

Fulton's inability to produce authoritative answers to such questions raised, and has continued to raise, doubts about its own professionalism. On the Report's publication, for instance, the *Economist* commented that it represented little more than 'an assault on the whole-time gifted amateurs of Whitehall by a part-time group of gifted amateurs, gathered together in the most nineteenth-century British institutional mechanism, an *ad hoc* investigation by a number of uncommitted gentlemen meeting about once a week for three years'.[53] Whether all its members were 'uncommitted' is, as has been seen, open to question. Some, from the start, were committed to an assault on the Administrative Class. Whether all were gentlemen, on the Secretary's evidence, is equally open to question. The charge of amateurism, however, sticks. In comparison to parallel inquiries abroad, the Committee failed to commission serious research; in comparison to Haldane it failed to provide a forum for sustained debate; and in comparison to Beveridge, it lacked a bold vision and clear direction. To win acceptance for its recommendations, it also opted for the abrasiveness of Northcote-Trevelyan rather than the emollience of Plowden. Thus the fact that, unlike Northcote-Trevelyan, it had to wait less than fifty years for partial implementation owed more to good luck than to good judgements.

Part 3

THE POLITICS AND PLANNING OF REFORM

5
MODERNISATION'S MOMENT, 1968–72

5.1 Introduction

Between June 1968 and December 1972 modernisation's moment had seemingly arrived. First the Fulton Report was published. Then, following the election of June 1970, the Heath government published a white paper (*The Reorganisation of Central Government*) which was the fruit of much detailed research during the Conservatives' years in opposition. In consequence, an exceptional amount of time and thought was devoted to administrative reform at all levels within the Service. In its intensity it equalled, and arguably surpassed, the years immediately after the First World War.

There was, in addition, a potentially powerful engine for change: the Civil Service Department (CSD), established in November 1968 in response to Fulton. The Prime Minister, as recommended, became its titular head (with day-to-day responsibility delegated to another Cabinet Minister) and so – in theory at least – it had the political muscle to drive through reform. It also had the administrative capacity, given that it was manned by first the Treasury's former 'pay and management' staff (freed from their traditional restraints) and then an influx of hand-picked officials from throughout Whitehall. Equally important was the appointment of Sir William Armstrong as its first Permanent Secretary and Head of the Civil Service. Unlike Fisher in 1919, Armstrong was a Treasury 'insider'. He was, however, equally charismatic. Having helped to mastermind the Treasury's reorganisation in 1962 and committed to a policy of greater openness, he was also a proven reformer. Harold Wilson could consequently assure the staff associations in July 1968 that he was no 'unwilling draftee'. Rather, he was determined to 'fight for them as well as for change'.[1]

Despite such positive auguries, however, the perception persists that during these years a mountain of effort produced only a mouse. Modernisation's moment, in short, was missed. Is this correct? Did the reforms of Fulton and Heath go largely unimplemented? Worse still, by halting internally driven reform in its tracks, was the pace of change actually reversed? Alternatively, was this period one of substantial reform, the full extent of which has been obscured by unfavourable comparison with idealised versions of certain contemporary blueprints – advanced by their far from disinterested authors?

Norman Hunt, the driving force behind the Fulton Report, established himself as the leading exponent of the view that modernisation's moment had been missed and his explanation was simple: reform fell victim to a bureaucratic conspiracy. In a somewhat Faustian deal with Harold Wilson's Principal Private Secretary (Michael Halls), he had been granted a room in No.10 and full access to papers in 1969 so that he could monitor Fulton's implementation; and, even under the Conservatives, he continued to be briefed on developments – not least in 1972 when he was forewarned of the abandonment of Fulton's 'ark of covenant': unified grading. At the time he was reported as being 'a bit disappointed but no more'.[2] Having served as both a special adviser and Minister in Wilson's final administration, however, he adopted a far more aggressive stance. In a co-authored book pointedly entitled *The Civil Servants: an Inquiry into Britain's Ruling Class* (published in 1980), he devoted a chapter to explaining in detail 'how Armstrong defeated Fulton'. 'Civil servants', he concluded, 'win by a cumulative advance of small steps – each one, on its own, a barely perceptible (and presented, therefore, as non-controversial) move, but in aggregate causing a decisive shift of direction. So it was with Fulton.' Such suspicions were equally entertained by David Howell, the leading advocate of reform within the Heath Government, who remained convinced that not only Fulton but also his own reform plans were sabotaged within Whitehall.[3]

In their self-promotion such accounts tend to disregard the extent to which reform was actually achieved and explanations, other than bureaucratic conspiracy, for perceived 'failure'. The extent of reform achieved will be examined in the following chapter. Of the alternative explanations for 'failure', there are at least five. The first was a loss of political urgency behind the demand for reform. Other priorities came to dominate politics, most notably the state of the economy (following devaluation in November 1967), industrial relations (with the publication of *In Place of Strife* in January 1969 and the Conservatives' Industrial Relations Act of August 1971), Northern Ireland (with troops first committed in August 1969 and 'Bloody Sunday' in January 1972) and the EEC (with entry finally secured in January 1973). As Harold Wilson admitted, 'with so many urgent problems at that time, I was not able to give my mind to it sufficiently . . . the sheer rush and pace of Government . . . has prevented as much being done on this as I think should be'.[4] Heath was similarly distracted; and, even when the reformers themselves enjoyed a measure of power – with Howell himself (between 1971–2) and then both Sheldon and Garrett (in 1974) holding Ministerial posts within the CSD – they were unable to reverse the situation.

A second explanation, despite the creation of the CSD, was a lack of administrative resources. In January 1968, just before Fulton's publication, Civil Service numbers had been capped. Then, in September 1968, a group of businessmen (the Bellinger Committee) was commissioned to advise on the eradication of waste in government. This Committee may not have menaced Armstrong as the Geddes Committee had menaced Fisher in the early 1920s but it was nevertheless a token of escalating concern about the size of government, which was later to burgeon under Conservative backbench pressure into planned manpower cuts in 1970 and 1972.[5] In his first address as Head of the Civil Service to departmental Establishment Officers (upon whom the success of any reform programme ultimately depended), Armstrong admitted that implementing Fulton would initially have to be a 'case of making bricks without straw'. He was insistent, however, that 'the Service could not for very long be expected at one and the same time to reform itself, increase its training and reduce its size'.[6] This, however, is precisely what became expected of it.

A third explanation for the 'failure' of reform was escalating resistance 'from below'. Staff association leaders, in their collective guise as the National Staff Side (NSS) of the Whitley Council, may have remained in constant and constructive communication with the CSD. This was despite the projected abolition of classes (which the associations' organisation reflected) and the hiving off of work to the private sector (which implied reduced membership). Nevertheless, they were ultimately answerable to their members and they could but reflect increasing militancy outside the Service, caused *inter alia* by successive prices and incomes policies and attempts at industrial relations reform. In addition, there were tensions peculiar to the Service. These included anger at the 'staging' of pay awards in 1968; anxiety over plans to disperse government offices from London; increasing alienation generated by the Conservatives' creation of 'super' departments; and frustration with a perceived worsening of working conditions.[7] Whatever their leaders' instincts, therefore, staff associations began to flex their muscles. They started to adopt strike policies and, for the first time since the early 1920s, to affiliate with the TUC (see Chapter 8). Then the first ever one-day national strike was held in February 1973. Such tension was not conducive to consensual reform.

A fourth explanation relates less to contingency but to the reform process itself. Were the recommendations of both Fulton and the Conservatives just impracticable? This, unsurprisingly, was an argument employed by those accused of mounting a bureaucratic conspiracy against reform. Armstrong, for example, responded to Hunt's goading that he was deliberately sabotaging unified grading by accepting that its introduction was 'in one sense, of course, . . . practicable right across the Service at all levels . . . we [could throw] all the grades together on the nearest approximation of their present pay-scales'. But then, he countered, 'in the other sense of an economical and durable scheme which would help rather than hinder the efficient organisation and manning of the work, there are some real questions to be resolved'.[8] The use of such 'practical' objections, of course, was – as it remains – a trusted bureaucratic tactic to stifle unwanted reform. However, in this instance it would seem to have had some substance particularly given the dysfunctional way in which Fulton's recommendations were reached. Likewise, many of the Conservatives' reforms were to be resisted on the grounds that they were based on management theories that had been insufficiently applied in the private, let alone adapted to the needs of the public, sector.

The final explanation of 'failure' is more damning of the CSD, although it stops well short of conspiracy. Even had circumstances been propitious and the blueprints practicable, would not reform have been stifled by a lack of managerial skill? To implement Fulton, for example, Armstrong erected an immensely complex committee structure.[9] To win the minds of Permanent Secretaries, he established a Steering Committee, which met some 20 times between July 1968 and October 1971. Beneath it, there were appointed five specialist subcommittees to identify – in league with the regular monthly meeting of Establishment Officers – practical solutions to the more intractable problems. Simultaneously, to win the hearts and minds of the rank-and-file, a Joint Committee of the National Whitley Council was established. This ultimately became the forum at which, following intense informal as well as formal negotiations, four joint reports were agreed. Published each spring between 1969 and 1972, prior to the annual conferences of the various staff associations, their preparation – not wholly to the amusement of the Steering Committee – became the key stimulus for, and the means of recording progress towards, the achievement of Fulton's goals. The objective behind such complexity was to maximise consensus. However, as Hunt feared, it tended instead to foment three latent sets of antagonism – between the CSD (as a central, reforming department) and individual departments (jealous of their autonomy); between departments (particularly when represented by their Establishment Officers) and staff associations (to whom, it was considered, management's prerogatives were being surrendered too readily); and between the staff associations themselves (with their very different vested interests). As a result, any final consensus had a tendency to be the lowest common denominator.

Such enervation might have been avoided by greater centralisation. The CSD, in short, needed to acquire an 'appropriate degree of ultimate authority' (as Fulton had recommended) and staff associations had either to become a single union or to surrender more autonomy to the NSS (as its Secretary General urged).[10] Greater centralisation, however, proved impossible. In relation to the CSD, as has been seen, the requisite political leadership was lacking and, administratively, all depended on Armstrong.[11] In his general role as Head of the Civil Service, his initial prestige did not (as Brook had feared in 1964) become a 'wasting asset'. In his particular role as an administrative reformer, however, it did. After November 1971 he became so preoccupied by his role as Heath's policy adviser that he came to be dubbed 'Deputy Prime Minister'. Even before then, however, his lack of managerial experience had arguably been exposed. As Frank Cooper was later to testify, the essential criteria for successful reform were not only 'hard driving attention from the Prime Minister of the day' but also 'the permanent attention of a tough, mature and experienced manager rather than an outstanding intellectual'.[12] Neither condition was met.

The purpose of this chapter is, therefore, to examine the record of the period between 1968 and 1972 as the apex of 'modernisation'. These years had the potential to be as radical as those following the First World War. Was this potential realised? If not, why not? Was it, as alleged at the time, due to bureaucratic conspiracy or rather to contingency (such as declining political interest, limited administrative resources and rank-and-file resistance), impracticable blueprints and poor management? These questions will be addressed first in relation to the implementation of the Fulton Report and then of *The Reorganisation of Central Government* white paper.

5.2 Implementing Fulton

On the publication of Fulton, Harold Wilson committed his Government to the implementation of three of its major recommendations: the CSD, a Civil Service College, and unified grading. Politically, this represented an extraordinary exercise in Prime Ministerial power since it preceded any consultation with the Minister most closely involved (Roy Jenkins as Chancellor), let alone any Cabinet discussion.[13] Administratively, the reaction to each may be taken as a proxy for Whitehall's reaction to the Report as a whole.

Three reactions were possible. First, the Report might have been accepted in full. This is clearly what Hunt expected. As he wrote, for example, to Armstrong in February 1970 at the height of the controversy over the extension of unified grading: 'the remit to the Civil Service Department is to devise a practicable scheme . . . The remit is NOT to see whether such a practicable scheme can be devised'.[14] This expectation survived even changes of government and administrative priorities. Any deviation from the letter of a Fulton recommendation was *prima facie* evidence of a conspiracy.

Second, Wilson's action might have been welcomed as an explicit political commitment to reform and thus, at minimum, a means to breaking residual resistance to the internal programme of post-Plowden reform. This provides some explanation for William Armstrong's departure from the Treasury, which so astounded his colleagues. It was, in short, not a negative reaction to the battle over devaluation and his uneasy relationship with the new Chancellor, but rather a positive move to associate himself closely with the Prime Minister in forging a more efficient and responsive administrative machine.[15] He had long been considering how officials might simultaneously be 'active in policy and neutral in politics', as modernisers appeared to demand. Accordingly he had, for example, championed the creation of executive agencies (to encourage 'accountable management') and the identification of officials behind policy proposals in 'green papers' (to encourage more informed debate, especially on Parliamentary Select Committees). He was thus sympathetic to many of Fulton's recommendations but feared – with, as has been seen, some justice – that their consequences had not been fully thought through. 'The cumulative effect of accepting in full the recommendations as they stand', as he advised Wilson on reading the draft Report:

> would over a period undoubtedly change the character as well as the internal structure, organisation and efficiency of the Service. We would become a much more open Service, with staff interchanging on a much greater scale with the private sector and being at liberty to speak their mind on government business more freely and, coupled with the wider

expansion of political appointments ... on the lines recommended by the Committee, the Service might be expected to develop more on current American lines. Some move in this direction is desirable, but the move would be much more marked than Ministers collectively and the public would want if we accept the report as it stood.

Hence, in his judgement, Fulton neither covered all the necessary ground nor 'should be regarded as a bible for the part of the ground which it did cover'.[16]

The third possible reaction, particularly given both the opening sentence and what the *Whitley Bulletin* called its many 'sweeping and unsupported generalisations', was a stiffening of resistance to reform. This would appear to have been the reaction of several Permanent Secretaries and Establishment Officers (long jealous of their department's autonomy). It was also the initial, collective reaction of the staff associations which, regardless of any sectional interest, were genuinely concerned about many of the proposals for restructuring. In sharp contrast to Hunt, they consequently saw the Report not as a practicable blueprint but merely as an 'outline sketch, the full details of which will have to be slowly and painfully hammered out'.[17]

Of Wilson's three commitments, the first to be realised on 1 November 1968 was the establishment of the CSD. The manner of its establishment, however, accentuated fears of a conspiracy. Fulton had recommended that, to prevent reform being frustrated, no top posts should be filled from inside the Treasury or even Whitehall. The CSD, in short, should be 'in a position to fight, and be seen fighting, the Treasury'. In the event, however, all senior posts went to Treasury officials (whose opposition to the Report's more radical proposals was on record); and the 'concordat' signed by the Treasury and the CSD on 25 October stressed that it was 'essential that there should be the closest contact, both formal and informal, between the two departments'.[18] Did this amount to a conspiracy? As has been seen, following devaluation, both manpower and public expenditure had been capped. Consequently, this was an inapposite moment to make – let alone pay the enhanced salaries to attract – outside appointments. Nor was it an apposite time to make wholesale staff changes for, as Armstrong explained to Wilson: 'too radical a reorganisation <u>at this stage</u>, when the department is understaffed to carry out its functions, would weaken the total effort because it would result in too many people doing work which was new to them'.[19]

An act of collective political will could, of course, have released additional resources but – as demonstrated by the Cabinet's initial discussion of Fulton – no such will existed in 1968. Nor did it exist in 1969, as demonstrated by the battle over the accommodation of the CSD's 365 executive and administrative staff. Armstrong insisted that, were the CSD to succeed, it had to develop a corporate identity. This meant *inter alia* that it should be physically separated from the Treasury and housed in one building (rather than the existing ten). A Ministerial Cabinet Committee was appointed in March 1969 to resolve this superficially trivial issue but, even after seven meetings, it failed to do so. A single central location was then identified through less formal channels, only for the Minister of

Public Buildings and Works to veto the cost of relocation. Such, in hard economic terms, was the *political* priority accorded to administrative reform.[20] In contrast, there was a demonstrable *administrative* commitment. Based on an understanding that 40 per cent of its staff should be seconded from other departments, Armstrong immediately trawled Whitehall and assembled an exceptionally able team. In addition, contracts were signed with both management consultants and individual businessmen to improve *inter alia* recruitment procedures and personnel management.[21] Where did the lack of leadership lie?

Wilson's second commitment, the creation of a Civil Service College, was also honoured – although expenditure cuts, ironically, delayed its opening until after the 1970 election so that it became the first public duty of Heath as Prime Minister. The manner of its establishment and subsequent development, however, further disillusioned Hunt. 'Though the building stands', he concluded in 1980, 'its main purpose has been lost'. As Fulton had wished, its first head was an outsider (the demographer, Professor Eugene Grebenik). Specialist courses for the Administrative Class and management training for specialists and junior staff were also introduced (see Chapter 9.2). What particularly aggrieved Hunt was the failure to develop the College's research role which, it had been hoped, would both breach Whitehall's secrecy and generate informed debate. This ambition, as will be seen, was vigorously opposed by a variety of vested interests. To Hunt, however, blame lay exclusively with a conspiracy led by Armstrong (which somehow managed to survive his retirement, the return of Wilson as Prime Minister in 1974 and even Hunt's own appointment as a Minister). 'Wilson announced one thing', he concluded, 'Armstrong wanted something different. And as with unified grading, Armstrong won'.[22]

Unified grading, Wilson's third commitment in 1968, was the most contentious. There was common agreement that the existing number of classes into which officials were divided was, in Armstrong's words, 'patently absurd'.[23] What provoked controversy was the ultimate objective of reform. For Wilson's closest advisers (Halls and Hunt) it was essentially *political*. They sought, like Fulton, to construct an 'open road to the top' by which non-graduates and specialists could challenge and break the monopoly on policy advice held by a socially exclusive and largely Oxbridge-educated elite. The removal of class barriers was thus conceived as much in sociological as in managerial terms. Allegedly this was also Wilson's objective. For him, as Hunt recalled, a commitment to unified grading was 'a *cri de coeur* about the way working class lads became undervalued professionals or executive or clerical officers, while the nobs became administrators and acquired the power'.[24] Such an objective accorded fully with the greater egalitarianism of postwar Britain. It also represented an explicit assault on the perceived elitism of Northcote-Trevelyan which, as has been seen, had deliberately reserved policy work for those with higher educational qualifications – and hence social status.[25]

Administrative Class officials within the CSD, as elsewhere, unsurprisingly bridled at this assault on their values and alleged exclusivity. To sustain the former, they strove to maintain the flow of 'high flying' recruits and sustained a vigorous debate on the 'character' of the Service, which peaked with Armstrong's lecture to the British Academy during the 1970 election campaign.[26] In relation to the latter, they were insistent that – given that some 40 per cent of officials within the Administrative Class were not direct entrants – the rigidity of class barriers had been somewhat exaggerated. Nevertheless, they did accept the *managerial* need for change. The current system, they agreed, did discourage ambition, reduce flexibility and overcomplicate personnel management, particularly in relation to pay. Like the staff associations, however, they doubted whether placing all staff on a single grading structure was the answer. Would efficiency, and in particular the recruitment and retention of specialist expertise (which modernisers demanded), really be enhanced by the costly and disruptive process of placing some 500,000 non-industrial officials into one amorphous organisation?

Unified grading thus epitomised the tension between the political and managerial goals at the heart of demands for 'modernisation'. Accordingly it came to dominate, and to dictate the pace of, the initial attempts to implement Fulton. It will similarly dominate the following analysis, which concentrates first on the attempted restructuring of the Service and then on the 'alternative' strategy of enhanced personnel management. So selective an approach provides a less than rounded picture of reform. There were, for example, simultaneous changes to training and superannuation which were both important in their own right and which – by facilitating, for instance, promotion and the mobility of staff into and out of Whitehall – were essential preconditions for the achievement of Fulton's wider goals.[27] Nevertheless it was unified grading which provides the key test of the ultimate balance struck between the three possible administrative responses to Fulton.

5.2.1 *Restructuring*

Whatever the other motives, there was one common objective behind the call for restructuring: the provision of the maximum flexibility with which officials could move – and be moved – between jobs. This required in particular the removal of all barriers which previously had, either physically or psychologically, impeded individual ambition. Politically, for those who attributed Britain's relative decline to the shortcomings of the administrative elite, increased flexibility provided the means for its replacement. Managerially, for those concerned with efficiency and economy, it offered an assurance – in Fulton's words – that the 'best man for the job' could always be appointed and that the organisation of work could be determined by the 'best way of doing' that job.[28] Such political and managerial advantages were not, of course, mutually exclusive.

In the event, restructuring took two forms. First, there was an 'interim' programme by which some 260,000 officials were organised into three broad vertical groupings – the General, the Science, and the Professional and Technology Categories (formed respectively in January 1971, September 1971 and January 1972). This 'interim' programme had two major shortcomings. It affected only half of non-industrial officials and largely left untouched staff in the majority (94 per cent) of departmental classes.[29] More seriously, whilst the horizontal barriers to promotion *within* each category were removed, the vertical barriers *between* categories were potentially reinforced. Both shortcomings were to be made good during the second stage of restructuring: the introduction of a permanent system of unified grading by which, as advocated by the MCG, all officials would be subjected to a rigorous programme of job evaluation and then assigned to some 20 to 25 common grades. All class barriers would thereby be removed and total freedom of movement assured.

A measure of unified grading was introduced in January 1972 when, as recommended by Fulton and long-favoured by the Treasury, a Senior Policy and Management Group was formed covering the most senior 700 officials (at and above the level of Under Secretary, or its equivalent). A year earlier, however, a decision had been taken not to extend unified grading below the level of Principal; and a year later a further decision was taken not to extend it to the level of Assistant Secretary.[30] Why was unified grading thus abandoned? Was it the fault of officials nominally responsible for reform or of those who were responsible for persuading Wilson to make the initial commitment?

(a) *June 1968 – March 1970*

The period leading up to Christmas 1969, when unified grading for the whole Service was abandoned, was the more contentious – not least because it occurred exclusively under a Labour Government. Whilst Fulton was in draft, Armstrong had warned Wilson of the inherent dangers but, galvanised by Hunt and Halls, the Prime Minister nevertheless demanded an 'unequivocal' public commitment. Accordingly, as equivocal a statement as possible was drafted. The Government, so Wilson announced in Parliament in June 1968, accepted

> the abolition of classes within the Civil Service and will enter immediately into consultations with the staff associations with a view to carrying out the thorough-going study proposed by the Committee, so that a practicable system can be prepared for the implementation of the unified grading structure.[31]

Such a compromise statement permitted, as Armstrong intended, a continuing examination of the 'practicability' of unified grading whilst simultaneously committing the CSD to both a preparatory programme of job evaluation and the principle of 'classlessness'. Both commitments were honoured. First an Investigating Team was appointed in March 1969, which duly confirmed in October that job evaluation and unified grading both were practicable down to the level of Assistant Secretary and possibly Principal.[32] In the meantime, in September 1969, the *Whitley Bulletin* had announced 'the abolition of classes' following an agreement between the CSD and NSS to merge the Administrative, Executive and Clerical Classes into an 'Administration Group'. The elite Administrative Class, Fulton's particular *bete noire*, was formally consigned to history.

Such apparent success, however, only served to arouse Halls' suspicions and he duly called upon Hunt for advice. This he provided with relish and there followed a vituperative battle between No. 10 and both Armstrong and Lord Shackleton (the Minister in day-to-day charge of the CSD) which, although only of cursory interest to the Prime Minister, contributed to the tension which caused Halls' fatal heart attack in April 1970.[33] The crux was the drafting by the CSD of the second joint progress report with the NSS (*Fulton: a Framework for the Future*). The NSS refused to commit itself, as the CSD wished, to the extension of unified grading down to Assistant Secretary. Such, as Shackleton reported in a key letter to Wilson on 16 January 1970, was the price to be paid for good industrial relations. He then significantly added:

> we are of course quite clear that what we have to examine is the extension of unified grading to cover the whole service at all levels. I am however bound to report to you that we cannot yet determine whether this will prove practical ... The Fulton objectives – the abolition of classes and complete freedom of movement – are universally accepted, and we are confident that they can be achieved. But, I am also convinced, the difficulties in the way of achieving them by means of a grading structure that is completely unified at all levels are very real.[34]

This directly defied a request from Wilson two days earlier (drafted by Halls) for both an explicit commitment 'to implement a unified grading structure' and an agreed timetable.

The 'very real' difficulty to which Shackleton principally referred was pay. If, as implied by unified grading, pay scales were to be determined by comparable levels of responsibility (or 'internal relativities'), how would it be possible to recruit those with scarce skills who could command a higher market wage? Moreover, how could the Priestley principle (of 'fair comparison' with the pay of 'outside staffs employed on broadly comparable work') be honoured? Fulton, after all, had acknowledged that its retention was 'necessary to the efficiency as well as the contentment of the Service'.[35] Such a dilemma had been foreseen by Armstrong as early as June 1968 when he had warned Wilson that any premature commitment would 'risk either losing the goodwill of staff associations, which is vital, or saddling ourselves with a nonsense, or both'.[36] He had recommended instead a threefold strategy: the commissioning of further research into the practice of unified grading elsewhere; the identification of its prospective cost; and the resolution of the latent tension, in Fulton's face-saving formula, between unified grading and 'occupational groupings'.

Armstrong himself initiated the research by leading a delegation to North America in September; and its main findings were published in May 1969.[37] Unified grading, Fulton had argued, was being increasingly adopted by big businesses and lay behind the greater dynamism of the US Civil Service (and in particular its better integration of specialists). Both assertions were challenged. On the one hand, the validity was questioned of applying to a 500,000 strong Service a system used in 'big' business where rarely more than 10,000 were employed in any one firm. On the other hand, unified grading in the US Civil Service was found to be costly. Each grade was paid the 'average' rate of analogous jobs in the private sector, with 'scarcity allowances' for those with rare skills. Thus everyone was paid either at or above the 'average market' rate; and the wage bill was accordingly inflated, regardless of 'classification creep' (the continual up-grading of jobs where scarce skills were in demand). Constitutionally, moreover, there was an impasse: pay rates in the US were determined by government regulation, whereas in the UK they were freely negotiated and subject to independent arbitration. Staff associations simply would not accept the determination of 'average' payments or the allocation of 'scarcity payments' by government fiat. Other international experience was equally damning. In Canada, for example, the Federal Government had specifically rejected the Glassco Commission's recommendation of unified grading, whilst in Australia the Commonwealth Civil Service was currently abandoning an analogous system.

Attention was then turned to Armstrong's second concern: the prospective cost. The MCG had assumed that unified grading would ultimately save money because job evaluation would reduce staff numbers. In June 1968, however, the Cabinet was warned that the cost of restructuring might be £10 million per annum; and by March 1969 this had been revised upwards to ten per cent of the annual wage bill, or £31.5 million, by 1976/7. This was not an example of bureaucratic scaremongering, but a calculation based on experience within the private sector. At a time when Shackleton was locked in battle with the Chancellor over restricting the total annual cost of 'implementing Fulton' to under £10m, so great a risk of increased expenditure was clearly unacceptable.[38]

The third strand in Armstrong's strategy was an examination of the new scheme's 'durability'. Unified grading, it was concluded, was inherently unstable because wage levels were to be determined by 'internal relativities'. However, fluctuations in the scarcity of their skills might at times enable certain 'occupational groups', in accordance with Priestley, to demand a higher market rate. Armstrong's solution was to introduce unified grading not *en bloc* to the whole Service, as recommended by Fulton, but by 'slices' from the top.[39] Above the level of Under Secretary, pay scales could be uncontroversially based on 'internal relativities' – and thus unified grading introduced immediately – because common levels of administrative responsibility outweighed differences in specialist expertise. On the same grounds, common pay rates were thought to be *technically* feasible at the level of Assistant Secretary and even a possibility at the level of Principal. Below that level, however, it was self-evidently impracticable.

How then, as both Fulton and the Treasury desired, were existing pay scales to be simplified? The 'interim' answer was the creation of three vertical 'categories' (General, Scientific and Works).[40] Each was to have a common pay and grading structure into which all officials in the relevant 'general' classes and related departmental classes could be assimilated. The merger of the generalist Administrative,

Executive and Clerical Classes into the Administration Group in September 1969 was the first step in this 'interim' programme. It was to form the core of the new General Category.

The logic behind this creation of categories was that it established 'the smallest number of pay and grading structures ... consistent with the principle of fair comparison with outside pay'. They thereby resolved one major contradiction within Fulton; but they simultaneously failed to resolve another. This was the managerial need to recruit, train, career-manage and maintain the morale of specialist officials (tasks for which, against Northcote-Trevelyan wishes and to Fulton's annoyance, departmental classes had evolved). Armstrong had been made immediately aware of this problem in 1968 when a meeting of specialists (who, somewhat ironically, were supposed to be amongst Fulton's principal beneficiaries) had warned him that 'any general merging of the classes into an undifferentiated mass in which professional labels disappeared would be anathema'.[41] Fulton had, of course, in its face-saving formula tried to resolve this dilemma through the suggestion of 'occupational groupings'; and it was to achieve such a solution that led Armstrong into innumerable confrontations throughout 1969 with Permanent Secretaries on the Steering Committee. No generic 'occupational grouping', they insisted, could ever satisfy managerial needs or departmental differences. Equally, they politely enquired, what would happen when a member of an occupational group in one 'category' had – for managerial reasons – to be transferred to a lower-paid one? If it entailed a pay cut, would this not discourage the very mobility Fulton was seeking? Alternatively, if the higher salary were to be retained, would this not make a nonsense of the common pay and grading system in the new 'category'? In short, it became increasingly apparent that increased efficiency, as envisaged by Fulton, required both greater mobility *and* specialisation. The optimal delivery of each, however, required very different and potentially incompatible structures.[42]

During this stand-off, the practicability of unified grading was being examined by the Investigating Team. This was a labour-intensive task. To establish comparative levels of managerial responsibility, for example, the creation of the Senior Policy and Management Group required interviews with 180 of the 815 people potentially involved; and its extension to the 16,700 posts between Assistant Secretary and Principal required 1800 questionnaires (with 240 follow-up interviews).[43] Such enquiries increasingly frustrated Permanent Secretaries and Establishment Officers because, at a time of capped manpower, it diverted scarce resources from 'operational' policies. More seriously, attention was also diverted from alternative and cheaper means (such as improved personnel management) of achieving the same goals. The investigators, however, plodded on. Fulton had predicted that research would take up to five years; and Armstrong agreed that was there was 'no short-cut by which ... a comprehensive answer which is both economical and durable' could be reached.[44] Hence his defiance in January 1970 of No. 10's demand for a categorical commitment to, and timetable for, unified grading. The problem, he might have added, was not of his making. It was rooted in the Government's rejection of the 1965 Estimates Committee's recommendation that research should precede prescription, and then in Fulton's own flawed research.

There was one final element in Armstrong's three-stranded strategy which antagonised his fellow Permanent Secretaries – and ultimately Halls and Hunt. This, somewhat ironically, was his determination to ensure the 'durability' of any reform through its acceptability to the whole Service. His construction, as has been noted, of the complex mix of formal committees and informal negotiations (centred on the Steering Committee and the NWCJC) was one consequence of this.[45] Another more novel one was the forging of a close relationship between the CSD and the staff associations (whose annual conferences Armstrong, in contrast to his predecessors, was only too willing to address). The early drafts of most proposals were shown, in the strictest confidence, to the General Secretary of the NSS (Leslie Williams) and to an 'inner circle' of association leaders; and the responses often led to the reversal of decisions taken by the Steering Committee. Permanent Secretaries and Establishment Officers were not amused by such a challenge to their managerial authority. Halls, despite his professed desire to redress the balance between senior and junior staff, also objected. Indeed his resentment peaked in December 1969 when the NSS vetoed a commitment (which the CSD was ready to give) to the extension of unified grading below the level of Under Secretary. However, Armstrong was as adamant as Shackleton. In the state of industrial relations following *In Place of Strife*, the goodwill of the NSS was essential were the Service ever to accept 'fundamental change'.[46]

Armstrong's strategy was designed, superficially at least, to deal with the consequences of Wilson's three original commitments which, in his continuing judgement, were based on bad advice. In return, the 'bad' advisers (Hunt and Halls) simultaneously condemned his every move as evidence of bad faith. As Halls vituperatively minuted Wilson, for example, in 1968: 'if we are really turning our backs on Northcote-Trevelyan, let us turn our backs on the "Ministers without Portfolio and without Ministerial responsibility" – the Warren Fishers of the Civil Service'. A year later he was still warning:

> the danger is (and Norman Hunt and I are at one over this) that William is pretending to move towards a unified grading structure when in fact all he is doing is [a] much more limited operation.[47]

Hunt, if anything, was more Machiavellian. Focusing on the formation of the Administrative Group in 1969, for example, he admitted that it advanced egalitarianism by removing 'horizontal' class barriers; but then, in a significant change of tack, he argued that egalitarianism should not be the priority because there was already a 'great deal of upward movement' within the generalist classes. Rather, the priority should be the involvement of specialists in management and policy advice (as the Fabians had traditionally demanded). Such 'sideways' movement, he noted, would now be impeded by the rigidity of the three new 'interim' categories. As to the *secondary* objective of egalitarianism, job evaluation was the key because it would place the right people in the right jobs, whatever their backgrounds. Regrading within categories, however, was proceeding without job evaluation and its results were unlikely to be revised in the near future. In short, the creation of categories was a deliberate retreat from – not, as Armstrong protested, an advance towards –Fulton's objectives. This led him to urge Wilson in January 1970 to demand a renewed commitment to, and a timetable for, unified grading.[48]

Were the suspicions of Halls and Hunt justified? Arguably not. Armstrong had been explicit in his criticisms before Fulton was published; but, once the political commitment had been made, he fully accepted Shackleton's view that it 'was essential for the CSD to be seen to be going for a full unified grading system until such time as it might be knocked off this course by the weight of contrary evidence'.[49] Hence the launching of the job evaluation programme in May 1969 with a genuinely open mind – as was later confirmed during a confrontation with the staff associations. The NSS, so it was reported:

> wished to rationalise the present structure into three main blocks covering Treasury grades, scientific and works personnel. The CSD wished to study the problem objectively before committing ourselves objectively to an outcome. Pressure from the Staff Associations for early moves partly represented an attempt to push us off a radical look at structure.[50]

In the event, the NSS triumphed and the 'three main blocks of work' formed the basis of the 'interim' categories. It had, however, first to promise publicly that it would not use the interim changes to block unified grading. The creation of 'categories' also reflected Armstrong's judgement that reform could not be frozen for five years, as Fulton had implied. It would be inexcusable, he argued, were the external expectation of, and internal readiness for, change wasted.[51] 'Categories' at least immediately removed the horizontal impediments to greater flexibility. Likewise, by neutralising problems of pay comparability, 'top slicing' permitted immediate action. Because it involved relatively few posts, it also only placed limited demands on other departments for further information.

Some scepticism, admittedly, had started to surface within the CSD by December 1969. Officials began to become aware that their repeated request for information was putting other departments under undue pressure. They were also increasingly sympathetic to the view – first expressed by Armstrong before Fulton's publication – that the managerial objectives of unified grading could be achieved by simpler and cheaper means. Such scepticism, however, was quickly scotched by Richard Wilding (the former secretary of the Fulton Committee who was now directly responsible for the reform programme and the drafting of the NWC Reports). He begged the fundamental question:

> Why do we propose unified grading at all . . .? Is it purely and simply because Fulton said so and the Government said so too – provided that it is practicable? Or do we also believe that it actually has some merit?

Having admitted that 'the Emperor's clothes are a bit translucent', he then insisted that there was

> something more than nakedness. The difficulty is that the arguments are impalpable and have more to do with the attitudes and practices which class differences have encouraged than with concrete facts about barriers to movement.[52]

In other words, he was defending the spirit as well as the letter of Fulton by acknowledging that, if not physically then psychologically, the old class system had impeded flexibility and needed to be reformed. Moreover, the absence of such doubts – even expressed confidentially – in the earlier written record of the CSD is testimony to the fact that allegations of bad faith are ill-founded.

Indeed, were anyone to be accused of bad faith, it would seem that it should be Halls and Hunt themselves. Halls was the self-proclaimed champion of junior officials. Yet, as has been seen, he discounted the views of their elected representatives. Hunt's change of tack on egalitarianism has also been noted and such revisionism was later extended to pay. 'If the Priestley principle is an obstacle to the introduction of a unified grading structure below Assistant Secretary level,' he proclaimed at the peak of the restructuring battle, 'then the sanctity of the Priestley principle should be called into question.'[53] This directly contradicted an explicit Fulton commitment. Just how it would have endeared an increasingly militant rank-and-file to reform was also left unclear.

If not bad faith, was bad management then responsible for the abandonment of unified grading? Superficially, no. As early as February 1969 Wilson was writing in glowing terms of the first joint NWC report: 'I would not have thought there was so much to say, or so much done by this stage'. A year later Peter Shore, when asked by Wilson to adjudicate between the rival claims of Hunt and the CSD, also paid testimony to 'the momentum and the range of the CSD's work in its short and active life'.[54] There was even some grudging praise in Hunt's own memoranda. On a more detailed level, however, Wilding later conceded that 'if it had really wanted to' the Civil Service 'could have slotted all the existing grades into a new grading structure within 12 to 18 months, and sorted the anomalies over a period of years thereafter'.[55] Both decision-making and decision-taking unquestionably lacked incisiveness. In relation to the former, for example, the Investigating Team – charged with the critical task of adjudging the feasibility of job evaluation – was given only eight staff (compared to the two hundred employed on a similar inquiry in Canada) and their over-academic approach was scathingly attacked by Permanent Secretaries. Such alleged shortcomings could be defended. A small team was appropriate because only the grades above Principal were to be investigated (not the whole Service, as in Canada). The Permanent Secretaries' alternative proposal of a high-powered committee of experienced officials (namely themselves) would also, as Armstrong countered, typically favour 'hunch' over objectivity.[56] Nevertheless the work and quality of the Investigating Team did, as will be seen, create problems for the future. The personnel director at BP (S. Mullally) also criticised the CSD as a whole for its overcomplexity. Every anomaly, he noted, was welcomed as an intellectual challenge rather than being regarded as a problem to be rapidly resolved.

As for decision-taking, a senior CSD official openly admitted in November 1969 that 'frankly I doubt whether any one of us can say offhand just at what stage we are at any one time in this whole complex business'. Armstrong's decision to make the annual progress report both a major statement of policy and a joint NWC document was also criticised. As Wilding argued whilst opposing the original decision, for instance, the report should have been a 'management programme with which we intend to associate the staff as fully as we can; not a joint programme, with the implications of action limited to the higher common factor of agreement'.[57] Yet just such a restriction was accepted with the result, as has been seen, that in December 1969 the CSD's preferred policy was stalled. In the given state of industrial relations, such a concession may well have been necessary; but it tended to substantiate Cooper's judgement that what the situation required was a 'tough, mature and experienced manager', not an 'outstanding intellectual'.

The period between June 1968 and the Spring of 1970 (when unified grading for the whole Service was formally abandoned) might, therefore, appear to vindicate Armstrong's initial reaction to Fulton. The fears which he then expressed, most notably about 'losing the goodwill of the staff associations . . . or saddling ourselves with a nonsense', appeared justified. So too did his alternative proposals. In the event, no significant reform was achieved beyond what the Treasury (itself the guardian of the post-Plowden reform programme) had been already prepared to concede. Was this, as Hunt claimed, the preordained result of a deliberate strategy? The evidence would suggest otherwise. Was it the result of bad management? There is some evidence of this but its root cause was a lack of adequate resources to effect so fundamental a reform. In other words, bad management reflected in essence a lack of *political* will; and given that the ultimate objective behind unified grading was political, should not Halls and Hunt have halted their somewhat obsessive (and inconsistent) campaign? In short, it was neither bad faith nor bad management but rather bad political advice which fundamentally stalled restructuring under Labour.

(b) April 1970 – December 1971

With the change of government in June 1970, the political commitment to unified grading diminished further; and in November 1971 Heath agreed to abandon its extension below the level of Under Secretary (despite the CSD's acceptance only two years before that it was both feasible and desirable). Armstrong underlined the finality of this decision in an address to the Joint Whitley Committee. It was, he insisted:

> important that the possibility of further extending unified grading should not hang over the Service . . . It would be wrong to give the impression

that a decision on [it] had merely been postponed; the important thing now was to emphasise the positive aspects of the [alternative] programme.[58]

This alternative programme was the one of improved personnel management, which he and departments had long championed – and which embraced many of Fulton's managerial (as opposed to politically-driven) recommendations. December 1971, accordingly, became the 'moment of truth' for both the modernisation of the Service and the CSD's ability to deliver it.[59]

Finality took a long time to deliver, with agreement not being reached with the NSS on the principles of the 'post Fulton' programme until March 1972 and on its detailed implementation a year later. In the meantime many of the 'interim' reforms, first mooted in 1969, were finally introduced. These included the establishment of the Senior Policy and Management Group in January 1972; the creation of the third and final 'category' (Professional and Technology); and the 'rational simplification at minimum cost' of the organisation of small occupational groupings, such as economists and statisticians, within the Administration Group. In addition, a measure of egalitarianism (as sought by Fulton) was achieved within that Group by the introduction of an administration trainee scheme by which potential 'fliers' could be 'fast-tracked' to positions of responsibility. These officials might be newly appointed graduates (as in the past) or school-leavers with some years of office experience (which was new).

Why, in 1971, was unified grading abandoned below the level of Under Secretary and thereby all attempts to restructure the Service along Fultonian lines? Had the 'weight of contrary evidence', in Shackleton's earlier words, simply grown too great?

Armstrong had certainly sensed that this was so when he asked the CSD to 'draw a line under Fulton' in January 1971. Both his anticipated fears (that unified grading would damage industrial relations within the Service and saddle it with a 'nonsense') appeared increasingly prescient.[60] On the one hand, the staff associations were sliding – in the words of the NSS Secretary General – into a state of virtual 'civil war'. The Institute of Professional Civil Servants (representing 'specialists') championed the introduction of unified grading down to Principal whilst the Society of Civil Servants and First Division Association (representing the old 'generalist' Executive and Administrative classes) adamantly opposed any further extension. Accordingly 'the only prospect of consensus' appeared to lie in aborting the whole reform process.[61] On the other hand, the CSD's increasingly convoluted attempts to standardise levels of managerial responsibility were made to look more nonsensical because they diverted skilled personnel managers from more effective means of attaining the same ends at less cost. It was thus with some conviction that Armstrong could inform the Joint Whitley Committee in November 1971 that

> he was ... very much in favour of all the effort which had gone into the improvement of personnel management. ... The good progress made in

these areas was very much more important than the rather slow progress made on structure. The diversion of effort needed to implement unified grading [would] delay progress towards the real goals.

Not only Heath but also Labour's shadow Ministers and the House of Commons' Expenditure Committee concurred with this judgement.[62]

Nevertheless the CSD's change in policy does appear to have been effected with unseemly haste. As late as April 1971, for example, senior officials had still been distinguishing between a 'best' and a 'worst' scenario. The former involved 'a more or less complete remodelling of the Civil Service structure which put into practical form the spirit of the Fulton recommendations'. This entailed the extension of unified grading to the level of Principal and the incorporation of all departmental classes into the three new 'categories'. 'Class', staff association conferences could then be assured, was 'an obsolete word'. The 'worst' scenario was that reform would 'fall well short of what Fulton intended'. Unified grading below Under Secretary would be abandoned along with the incorporation of departmental classes; and the defence mounted that 'the spirit of Fulton depended more on improvements in personnel management . . . than on structural reform'.[63] This is in fact precisely what happened, as evidenced by Armstrong's address to the Joint Whitley Committee in November 1971. Why had the CSD so precipitately embraced its own 'worst' scenario?

Part of the answer undoubtedly lay in the 'weight of contrary evidence'. Part, however, lay elsewhere. First, there was the nascent scepticism first expressed in December 1969 and triggered by pressure from other departments. Even before the Conservatives' election victory, therefore, it had been admitted to assembled Establishment Officers that 'much of the emphasis of the CSD to date had been on the implementation of Fulton' and an assurance given that the focus would now be on 'the long term so as to be as helpful as possible to other departments'.[64] Second, after the June election, Armstrong's own interest waned, not least because he was constitutionally obliged and personally inclined to favour the Conservatives' alternative plans for *institutional* restructuring. Third, within the CSD restructuring became the responsibility not just of planners (alive to Fulton's broader objectives) but also of officials in administrative divisions, such as Pay and Manpower (with more pragmatic, short-term interests). Key planners with a commitment to Fulton, such as Richard Wilding and Philip Rogers, were also promoted to posts outside the CSD.[65] Finally, in July 1971 there was the publication of the 'disastrous' Bird Report on job evaluation, after which planners were overwhelmed with a vengeance by 'management' considerations.

Why was the Bird Report (the final product of the Investigating Team established in 1969) so disastrous? It had reported, after a lengthy exercise in job evaluation, that unified grading down to the level of Assistant Secretary was practicable. It then, however, had made the fatal mistake of admitting that any final analysis, assessment and, above all, allocation of specific posts to specific grades must ultimately be 'subjective'. In addition, further sampling was needed. Permanent Secretaries and departmental Establishment Officers were not amused. Under protest, they had committed scarce resources to an exercise, which had palpably failed to provide the objective criteria on regrading they needed to minimise conflict with the staff associations. Moreover, they were irked by the tone of the Report which, even to planners within CSD, appeared 'esoteric' and 'unnecessarily complex'.[66]

Such a disaster reflected badly on the quality of the Investigating Team. More generally, however, it reflected badly on the managerial competence of the CSD, which had accorded the team limited resources and a low priority (despite, or arguably because of, the importance attached by Fulton to job evaluation). Moreover the majority of its officials not only treated the Report with open scepticism but also structural reform with increasing disingenuity. This was demonstrated by a CSD memorandum to the final Steering Committee in October 1971, strongly recommending the abandonment of unified grading below the level of Under Secretary on the grounds that 'the collective weight of management, pay and cost considerations' was 'formidable in terms of upheaval, problems with the pay regime . . . the tendency to distort future work patterns by attempting to make them conform to the same mould, and the resources to make the transition'.[67] Even on the memorandum's own evidence, none of these arguments was sustainable. 'Problems with the pay regime', for example, referred to the long-recognised conflict between internal relativities and pay comparability; but, as was admitted, 'fair comparisons have not been by any means a universal method of fixing pay . . . in the past' at the level of Assistant Secretary. The argument, therefore, could not be 'pushed too far'. The 'distortion of work patterns' referred to the equally long-standing fear of grade proliferation (and, in particular, the creation of an additional grade between Under and Assistant Secretary, to be called Assistant Secretary +, to incorporate non-generalist officials who had what were euphemistically termed 'direct management' responsibilities); but the potential number of Assistant Secretary + posts amounted to no more than 350 and so hardly posed an insurmountable problem for effective managers.[68] Finally, the concern over 'upheaval' centred on the perceived problems of regrading all officials within departmental classes; but the NSS was prepared to expose such perceptions as grossly exaggerated. Consequently, as the 'worst' scenario had predicted, the weightiest 'managerial' argument against restructuring was that it would divert scarce expertise within personnel management divisions with the result that the 'further pursuit of unified grading might take us further away from the essential Fulton purposes rather than nearer to them'.

The fracas over the Bird Report also epitomised the innate tension between the CSD and other departments. Such tension was perhaps inevitable, given the federal nature of the Service and the shortage of resources. Was it, however, exacerbated by poor management? After its somewhat frenetic first year, as has been seen, the CSD had been obliged to be more 'realistic' but it was still criticised for its lack of appreciation of the very real constraints under which 'operational' departments worked. As the Bird Report exemplified, repeated requests for detailed information typically appeared to produce results whose value was in inverse proportion to the effort expended in its collection. In 1971 a major internal inquiry then concluded that communications with other departments continued to lack clarity and consistency, and were thus a cause for confusion. For example, Estacode – supposedly the undisputed authority on any contested point – was widely disparaged as 'a mixture of a bible, legal exposition and tips by a racing tipster'.[69] The keenest source of tension, however, was the CSD's ever-closer relationship with the NSS. It was essentially a question of power. Establishment Officers were resentful of any reduction in managerial prerogative, while the staff associations – not least to control their members – sought regular consultation and concessions. More particularly, Establishment Officers sought maximum flexibility in the interpretation of central guidelines so that they might adapt them to their department's perceived peculiarities. Staff associations, in contrast, demanded maximum conformity both to prevent departments from evading the guidelines' objectives and to prevent any compromise (painfully reached between themselves) from unravelling.[70] The known divisions between staff associations, so Establishment Officers countered, should have been more ruthlessly exploited. So too should have been their ultimate willingness collectively to reach compromise solutions (if only to have a justification with which to defend collaboration to their respective conferences). Whether such 'tougher' tactics would have worked, given greater militancy amongst the rank-and-file which boiled over into the first national strike in February 1973 (see chapter 8.4.1), is a moot point. However, as Frank Cooper testified, it was never really within the CSD's competence.

Was the abandonment of unified grading, therefore, ultimately the result of bad management, bad faith or bad advice? Bad management, particularly in relation to the Bird enquiry, played its part. There was also an element of bad faith in the growing scepticism about Fulton after December 1969 and the disregard for its political objectives thereafter. However, there is plentiful evidence – in private and in public – that both CSD officials and Armstrong himself genuinely believed that, in the given political circumstances, the 'weight of contrary evidence' was too great and that Fulton's *managerial* goals could best be achieved by an 'alternative' programme. As Armstrong, for example, argued before the Joint Whitley Committee in November 1971:

> Going back to first principles, the object of the exercise was to abolish classes, remove all artificial barriers to the flexible development of staff, and introduce instead a regime which would enable people to move freely both outwards and upward ... This much was common ground ... In his own view, the crucial factor in obtaining the Fulton objectives was the personal care and attention which would have to be given to the deployment of staff by all concerned.[71]

This is why December 1971, when the CSD directed departments to implement the alternative programme of enhanced personnel management, was genuinely the 'moment of truth'.

5.2.2 *Improving personnel management*

Modernisation's final moments in relation to Fulton duly focussed on the achievement of greater flexibility through 'non-structural' means; and, following exhaustive negotiations with departments and the staff associations, culminated with detailed plans for the implementation of a 'Post-Fulton' programme being submitted to the NSS in December 1972 and endorsed by the Joint Whitley Committee in February 1973.[72] Because of the outstanding commitment to abolish 'classes' and to simplify management, structural reform could not be wholly abandoned. The CSD, however, had formally removed it from its list of priorities by the summer of 1973.

The attenuation of structural reform was somewhat demeaning. The professed intention was that categories should become a 'nucleus' for the assimilation into larger, more manageable units of staff currently employed in the myriad of smaller classes. Before the ink was dry on the final NWC Report of March 1972, however, the future of categories was already being questioned within CSD; and by July it was agreed that they were 'meaningless' and that their further development would be 'so much wasted effort'.[73] The favoured alternative was the amalgamation of the remaining classes into smaller 'occupational groups'. The problem was once again pay. Categories had been conceived as a more stable alternative to unified grading, because all assimilated classes would be linked to a 'foundation' group, whose pay scales could be fixed by pay research based on the Priestley principle of comparability. In reality, however, market rates for many small professional classes varied in relation to those of the 'foundation' group; and, were they to gain (on the Priestley principle) an anomalous pay increase, they would have necessarily to leave their category. In other words, categories were just as unstable as unified grading itself.

In the event, categories did survive but mainly on account of contingency and managerial laxity. The introduction of an incomes policy in November 1972, for example, prevented staff associations from using restructuring to gain surrogate wage increases; and the threat of a national strike concentrated minds and accelerated acceptance by the NSS of the 'Post-Fulton' programme. Meanwhile CSD officials were 'less than fastidious' in their planning and avoided difficulties by sanctioning eight new categories. The results were consequently, on their own admission, rather 'superficial'.[74] This was a distinctly mangy mouse to emerge from five years of mountainous effort.

Resources, in terms of both money and manpower, were transferred instead to personnel management. This had always been the preferred option within Whitehall and was fully consistent with the internal post-Plowden reform programme. The General Personnel Manager of Shell Mex and BP (John Drake) had indeed been appointed as an adviser in late 1969 and accordingly 1970 had been internally heralded as 'personnel management year'. The unexpected Conservative election victory almost ended such ambitions, but Drake proved his worth by an impassioned defence of his specialism, which was forwarded to the Prime Minister. It did not equate, he argued, as rumoured to '(a) bureaucratic systems devised by personnel departments for personnel departments, or (b) frivolities'.[75]

What precisely did it equate to? In May 1971, Drake outlined the basis for a new policy which built on, but also distanced itself from, Fulton. He dismissed it as inadequate because its Fabian-inspired obsession with central policy-making left it with 'extraordinarily little to say' on policy delivery. Since 70 per cent of officials worked outside London, he maintained, the real challenge of personnel management lay in tackling the 'remediable dissatisfactions' of middle and lower ranking officials, who dealt mainly with the public and upon whom (despite the temporary diversions by modernisers) the Service's popular reputation thus depended.[76] This reorientation of policy was welcomed, partly out of vested interest, by the staff associations; and so Armstrong's words fell on receptive ears at the final Joint Whitley Committee in February 1973, when he admitted that 'the Fulton Report had almost ignored the problem of junior staff' and proclaimed himself 'very ready to stop referring to Fulton if this was no longer helpful'.[77]

Drake's policy concentrated on improvements to staff appraisal, both to enhance managerial efficiency (by providing a 'rationalised amount of information about a person's experience, talents and prospects') and individual fulfilment (by providing 'tangible evidence' of management's interest and concern).[78] The main innovation was the Job Appraisal Review (JAR), which required line managers to discuss with each of their subordinates the nature of their current job, any changes needed for its better performance, and promotion prospects. JARs were to be supplemented by traditional annual reviews as well as less regular career interviews (at which personnel officers could offer more expert advice than line managers on promotion prospects). The information gathered was also to be fed into more centralised schemes of 'career development', designed to ensure – as recommended by Fulton – a greater degree of 'administrative specialism' for generalists and enhanced managerial opportunities for specialists.[79]

Impressive – and arguably excessive – though such plans were, they had one obvious failing: they remained just plans. A timetable for the implementation of each scheme had been agreed within CSD by January 1972; and it was presented first to Establishment Officers and then, after exhaustive discussion and amendment, to the NSS in September 1972. Even after it had formed the basis of the agreement endorsed by the Joint Whitley Committee in February 1973, however, grave concerns were still raised about the vagueness of, and the inordinate delay in honouring, the various commitments. Little progress, for instance, had been achieved in relation to lateral movement and opportunity posts – two crucial reforms on which hopes for the achievement of the Fultonian goals of enhanced equality and efficiency had been pinned when unified grading had been abandoned.[80] Because of the added burden on line managers, the introduction of JARs was also to be generally delayed until mid-1974 and as late as 1977 in major departments such as the MOD.[81] In short, by the end of 1972 it was not just structural reform which appeared to be running into the sand but also the 'alternative' programme of improved personnel management. Why?

CSD officials could not be criticised for bad faith. Their plans had been finalised by January 1972 and thereafter they sought to force the pace, first with other departments throughout the Summer of 1972 and then with the staff associations over Christmas. They were impeded, however, by three countervailing forces: Establishment Officers' obduracy; a renewed drive by Government to cut Civil Service numbers; and the conservatism of the NSS. Establishment Officers' obduracy was illustrated by the passive disobedience of even Ian Bancroft, in a brief sojourn away from the CSD as Establishment Officer of the Department of the Environment (DoE). He expressed a 'deep sense of unease' at the CSD's assumption that departments had sufficient resources to introduce 'more intensive personnel management'. This was certainly not true in the DoE, he argued, where a small increase in establishment staff had been either swallowed up in part by further restructuring or looked 'likely to disappear under the blows of your Parliamentary Secretary's hatchet'.[82] This was an allusion to the greater priority being accorded to 'hiving-off' (such as the creation of the Property Services Agency, see Chapter 5.3.3(c)) and to further manpower cuts (endorsed by Cabinet in August 1972).

Staff associations were equally intransigent. Progress on lateral movement and opportunity posts, for example, was criticised as 'slow and disappointing' by the General Secretary of the NSS. The principal reason, however, was that both had been consistently opposed at national and departmental level by one of his constituent associations, the SCS, which feared its 'generalist' members would suffer at the hands of specialists. Moreover the associations collectively insisted that, on the grounds of egalitarianism, career interviews and training places should be as available to most junior as to senior officials. This delayed access to these services to those who could most benefit, whilst simultaneously raising unrealistic expectations and causing dissatisfaction for the others. It also diverted scarce resources from other programmes, such as the enhancement of job satisfaction, which might have benefited non-mobile officials more.[83]

Given such constraints, the CSD tended to herald any department's agreement to a timetable (however vague) and any expenditure of additional resources on personnel management as 'major breakthroughs'.[84] Could more substantial breakthroughs have been achieved? During the Spring of 1972 there was the inevitable debate within the CSD over the desirability of having the power to instruct, rather than merely to exhort, other departments. It was, however, never granted an 'appropriate degree of ultimate authority' as recommended by Fulton. Hence, faced by Establishment Officers' protests in June 1972, its officials could but 'smooth out the over-precise commitments' in its original programme (which caused the 'vagueness', of which the NSS were to complain) and jettison the 'more formal and detailed monitoring' of departmental performance (as demanded by the NSS). At the same time, they had to be equally emollient towards the NSS itself, eschewing Fulton's more punitive recommendations (such as compulsory redundancy and the ending of 'established' posts).[85] Such 'laissez-faire' attitudes inevitably raise questions about the CSD's managerial ability to rise to the two fundamental challenges posed by the modernisation of personnel management.

The first was the delicate task of cleansing the Augean stables, into which some departments had fallen after years of neglect. The second was the need to resolve those conflicts which were part of the 'inescapable fabric of personnel management'.[86] These included the simultaneous need to plan individual careers whilst 'plugging' sudden administrative gaps; to train staff whilst delivering over-pressed services; and to ensure consistency in the treatment of individuals (for the sake of equity) whilst encouraging decentralisation (to maximise sensitivity). It was the magnitude of such problems which somewhat tarnished the 'moment of truth'.

5.2.3 Finishing with Fulton

Amongst Armstrong's initial reactions to the Fulton Report had been a concern that 'premature acceptance "in principle" could plunge us into months of sterile argument and delay the real work'.[87] This proved prescient. Much 'real work' on recruitment and training continued; but the modernisation of personnel management was seriously delayed by the 'months of sterile argument' over unified grading.

Was such sterility, as alleged by Hunt, the result of a premeditated conspiracy? Certainly Fulton did not enjoy the blind loyalty of officials. As a draft Cabinet memorandum prepared within the CSD in November 1970 to explain past policy declared, for example, there was

> no question of automatically implementing the Committee's specific proposals as if they formed part of an accepted blueprint . . . Proposals based on the Committee's recommendations have been adopted only when they were considered to be fully justified on their merits and in relation to the cost and work involved.[88]

It was, admittedly, CSD officials who typically made the value judgement on whether a particular recommendation was 'merited'; but in private as well as public, there was no question of the zeal with which they pursued Fulton's key *managerial* goal of greater flexibility first through structural reform and then, after 1970, through 'non-structural' means. Fulton consequently bore concrete results. Coming from industry, Drake noted the pre-existence of an internal reform programme but then concluded that 'like any consultancy report, the Fulton recommendations provided an acceleration'. This was confirmed by Richard Wilding, who later admitted that 'without the accelerator, a number of reforms already beginning to move before Fulton would quite probably have been stopped in their tracks'.[89] Even the 'sterile' battle over unified grading can be credited with some positive outcomes. Would, for example, so many class mergers or personnel management reforms have been implemented, had not Establishment Officers viewed them as an 'escape' from something far worse?

If zeal was not lacking within the CSD, then arguably the requisite management skills were. This was unsurprising. The size of the task exceeded anything attempted in the private sector. Central management, after decades of neglect and arcane developments, was venturing into the relatively unknown world of specialists and the 'lower' grades. The Plowden Committee ten years earlier had deliberately evaded such a challenge. The resources and power, which Fulton deemed essential, were lacking. Manpower restrictions, as has been seen, were imposed on the Service even before the Report's publication; and successive governments denied the CSD the 'appropriate degree of ultimate authority' to drive reform through. Finally, industrial relations were deteriorating so fast that Fulton's insistence that 'the pattern of joint consultation should reflect, not determine the results' of the changes it recommended became ever more unrealistic.[90] Just as, in a federal system, the support of establishment officers (however obdurate) was indispensable for the implementation of reform, so too was the co-operation of staff associations (however frustrating) for the compliance of the rank-and-file. This was the lesson which Hunt and Halls failed to learn in January 1970.

At root, therefore, it was neither bad faith nor bad management which principally frustrated Fulton, but rather contingent factors and a lack of political will. There was, in addition, the question of bad advice. Because of its perceived emphasis on management Fulton has acquired a posthumous reputation as the precursor of radical reform in the 1980s. However, its principal objectives were in fact 'big' government, the unity of the Civil Service and its reorganisation within a straitjacket of unified grading. This actually places it in direct conflict with later managerial reforms, such as *Next Steps* which included amongst its major findings that:

> The Civil Service is too big and too diverse to manage as a single entity ... It is an enormous organisation compared with any private sector company and most public sector organisations. A single organisation of this size which attempts to provide a detailed structure within which to carry out functions as diverse as driver licensing, fisheries protection, the catching of drug smugglers and the processing of parliamentary questions is bound to develop in a way which fits no single operation effectively.[91]

That is precisely the same conclusion reached by those detailed to implement unified grading – and who were subsequently pilloried for failing to deliver.

5.3 Reorganising Central Government

The Conservatives' election victory in June 1970 changed the direction but not the intensity of modernisation within Whitehall. Fulton had sought to enhance the efficiency of an expanding Service by realising the full potential of its officials. The Conservatives, in contrast, sought to increase efficiency within a contracting Government by better strategic direction and more forensic analysis. Having jettisoned unified grading with extreme wariness in 1971, they were not unsympathetic to the 'alternative programme' of improved personnel management.

However, their differing agenda crowded it out in terms of both time and resources.

Before the election, David Howell had expounded the new agenda most fully as head of the Public Sector Research Unit (PSRU); and, as a junior Minister at the CSD between 1970 and 1972, he had the opportunity to implement it. In *The New Style of Government*, published in May 1970, he identified the 'real issue' as the 'capacity of an elected government to control a massive bureaucracy, to reduce its functions and responsibilities and to direct its attention swiftly to the matters which should concern government in the 1970s as against those which preoccupied them in the 1940s and 1950s'.[92] The principal objective was, therefore, political: to revive democracy by reversing the 'steady bureaucratisation of life'. Politicians, once in office, had to retain a strategic vision and continually subject every government activity to the same test: should it continue, be hived off or privatised? They had also (in anticipation of Mrs Thatcher's call for Minister-managers) to involve themselves more deeply in the 'methods, machinery and procedures by which public policy is made'. This might be 'anathema' to them and officials alike, but 'the capacity to undertake this kind of analytical penetration of the bureaucratic labyrinth' was key to 'establishing the new style of government'.

The key institutional recommendation was the creation of a more compact Cabinet through the restriction of its membership to the heads of a smaller number of larger departments. It was also to be given a greater 'analytical capability' (possibly in the shape of a Bureau of the Budget reporting direct to the Prime Minister) and its greater power counterbalanced by more effective Parliamentary scrutiny. Neither the earlier growth nor inefficiencies of government was blamed on civil servants. Rather 'one of the more heartening developments' was the number of senior and middle-ranking officials who recognised 'the desperate need for a change in the pattern of accountability in order to bring modern management methods to bear and to establish new and healthier lines of contact with Parliament and the public'. Nevertheless, the introduction of such management methods would require a revolution in Whitehall culture. 'Whereas in the Whitehall structure of today', Howell concluded, 'the main characteristic is the departmental divisions of responsibility with heavy emphasis on departmental interests and departmental cohesion, the main requirement would be the capacity to create organisations swiftly to deal with specific objectives and functions – and to dismantle them equally swiftly when the objectives in question have been achieved'.[93] To achieve this, a considerable number of outside appointments would have to be made.

By March 1972, when Howell was transferred from the CSD to the new Northern Ireland Office, none of these aims had been achieved. There then followed an enlargement of government, the u-turn in economic policy (with a reflationary budget and the Industry Act in May) and a return to arbitrary manpower cuts in August. Had the Conservatives' 'new style of government' been frustrated by bureaucratic conspiracy, as Howell (in imitation of Hunt) later alleged? Alternatively, should blame once again be laid on contingency, inadequate planning or bad management (of which Howell himself might be guilty)?

The Conservatives' attempts to construct a 'central' and an 'analytical' capability will be examined successively in the light of such questions. First, however, it is necessary to examine the Party's pre-election planning and its reception in Whitehall prior to the seminal *Reorganisation of Central Government* white paper in October 1970.

5.3.1 Pre-election planning and the first 100 days

There were, as seen in chapter 3.2.4, two strands in Conservative pre-election planning. The first, largely informed by retired civil servants, reflected an administrative desire for clearer and more coherent political leadership. Thus a series of reports, drafted under the chairmanship of Dame Evelyn Sharp, recommended the creation of 'giant' departments (to reduce the size of Cabinet and facilitate 'joined-up' government) and of an Office of Prime Minister and Cabinet (which, in addition to servicing the Cabinet, would determine strategic priorities and oversee the management of the Civil Service). The second strand was driven by the PSRU, of which Howell was head and of which Mark Schreiber (the CSD's political adviser throughout the Heath government) was a director.[94] It did not disagree with Sharp's recommendations, but added a strong political commitment to smaller government and (heavily influenced by both the public and private sectors in the USA) the use of new management techniques.

The PSRU's plans became the more predominant, particularly after the Sundridge Park conference in September 1969. Senior managers were thereafter seconded by private companies to assist in the 'preparation for government' under the leadership of a joint team of politicians and businessmen, headed by Lord Carrington and Richard Meyjes (the Marketing Coordinator of Shell International). Seven joint 'action groups' were formed to identify major policy areas which might be 'hived off' and run 'as much like business entities as possible'. Due to a lack of information, political direction and businessmen's time, however, the focus soon shifted to a general discussion of how to define strategy and execute policy more efficiently.[95] Hence when the PSRU submitted its 'urgent action dossier' (the so called *Black Book*) to Heath on 3 June, just before the election, its key recommendations were the establishment of a 'Central Capability' and a Ministry of Programmes. The former (a mixed body of senior officials, businessmen, political advisers and expert 'evaluators') was directly to advise the Prime Minister on how to clarify strategic goals and then devise the means of delivery and 'progress chase'. Thereby it would provide the overarching '*analytical capability* to identify redundant resources and to derive new objectives', whilst the Ministry of Programmes would provide the necessary '*action capability*' to deliver results. To be modelled on the US Bureau of the Budget, it would be formed by a merger of the Treasury's public expenditure and the CSD's manpower divisions; and it would require all departments to use 'output budgeting' (as used by Macnamara in the USA Defense Department) to analyse all their expenditure rigorously in the light of the government's overall strategy. In such a way, the *Black*

Book maintained, a new 'logic and ruthlessness' could be achieved and a more compact government could 'do its real job, concentrate on those things which it alone can do, and do them efficiently at low cost'.[96]

After the election, however, neither a 'Central Capability' nor a Ministry of Programmes was established. Why? The reason was partly political and partly administrative. Politically, there was an immediate series of meetings between the authors of the *Black Book* and CSD Ministers which culminated in an *ad hoc* Cabinet Committee and the submission of a paper to the full Cabinet on 14 July. Their cumulative result was the rejection of the concept of a Ministry of Programmes; agreement that the Business Team should initially be attached not to the Prime Minister as part of a new 'analytical capability' but to the CSD as mere 'consultants'; and a firm decision that the main 'analytical capability' should remain within departments.[97] Simultaneously, to honour an election pledge to cut public expenditure, a programme of 'crash cuts' was commissioned by Heath four days after the election. It did lead to some contraction of government but the savings (estimated by the Treasury in October at some £1600m) owed nothing to the analytical rigour for which the *Black Book* had called, and everything to traditional horse-trading.

A contraction of government was similarly sought through a review of departmental responsibilities commissioned by Heath immediately after the election. This duly resulted in a Cabinet commitment on 22 September to cut Civil Service numbers by 5 per cent within two years; but it nevertheless aroused Howell's ire because, in direct contrast to his pre-election plans, it explicitly excluded Ministerial involvement. On its completion, he and his immediate superior (Lord Jellicoe) had to urge Heath both to let senior Ministers consider its findings (as finally occurred on 11 September) and to publicise the consequent recommendations.[98] This was the origin of the white paper, *The Reorganisation of Central Government* (finally published on 15 October).

This white paper was regarded at the time, and has been regarded since, as placing an official stamp on the Conservatives' 'new style' of government. However, to Howell's dismay, it literally was an 'official' stamp. Ministers once again were largely excluded from its drafting; and in consequence, it was dominated by Whitehall's managerial concerns about the restructuring of government departments and, in particular, the projected creation of two 'giant' departments (as recommended by Sharp) – the DTI and the DoE. The PSRU's more radical political objectives were confined to the introduction and conclusion. Admittedly the former tellingly summarised the Conservatives' objectives as 'less government, and better government, carried out by fewer people'. The latter also anticipated the maintenance of a more 'clear and comprehensive definition of government strategy' by a Central Policy Review Staff as well as the introduction of 'output budgeting' through Programme and Analysis Review – although it had yet to win Cabinet approval (see respectively Chapters 5.3.2b and 5.3.3 b). There was little of substance, however, to justify Howell's original title for the paper which had been: 'The Reorganisation *and Contraction* of Central Government'.[99]

Why were the PSRU's pre-election plans so swiftly stifled? Bureaucratic conspiracy is a plausible explanation because the CSD's own planning had been as – and arguably even more – thorough than the PSRU's. It had been inaugurated by Armstrong in October 1969 partly as an antidote to Wilson's 'gimmickry' but, more positively, as an attempt – in tandem with the implementation of Fulton – to maintain the internal post-Plowden modernisation programme.[100] Its recommendations formed the basis of the briefs submitted to Heath immediately after the election and greatly influenced his initial decisions. In the minutes of the key Cabinet Committee meeting of 3 July, for instance, it was recorded that 'the general nature of the central analytical capability as now envisaged coincided largely with the development of official thinking in recent months'. The review's recommendations also formed the basis of the white paper.[101]

The review was a 'ten paper' Machinery of Government exercise. Most of the papers were concerned with the functional division of responsibilities between departments and strongly favoured the creation of 'giant' departments. One paper, however, focused on the concept of a Prime Minister's Office – not so much because a Conservative election victory was anticipated but because, as illustrated by the Sharp Committee, there was a shared recognition of the need for a clearer determination of priorities and the more effective modernisation of management. Its initial draft, written 'with rebellious thoughts from my sickbed' by one of the CSD's more outspoken assistant Under Secretaries (T.H. Caulcott) favoured a 'Big Prime Minister's Department'.[102] To provide the Prime Minister with expert advice, this was to contain the No.10 secretariat, the Cabinet Office and common services (such as the Central Statistical Office); but more significantly, it was also to include an effective 'ministry of programmes' to ensure, and if necessary enforce, agreed priorities for public expenditure and managerial efficiency. Over the next few months, however, three critical flaws were gradually exposed in such a proposal and an alternative fashioned.

The first flaw was the impracticality of a Ministry of Programmes, be it within or outside a Prime Minister's Department. Politically, the second most powerful figure in government (the Chancellor of the Exchequer) was unlikely to welcome the dismemberment of his department. Administratively, it was impolitic to divide responsibility for management of the economy from one of its major tools (the control of public expenditure) – especially as, following the final demise of the Department of Economic Affairs, the two had just been reunited within the Treasury. The second flaw was that the transfer of management controls from the CSD would only be logical were they to be reunited with the Treasury's controls over public spending. Were the Treasury to remain undivided, they should properly stay with an independent CSD; and it was logical that, should any outside management experts be appointed, they should be accommodated there rather than in a new 'Central Capability'. The third and conclusive objection, however, was constitutional. Not only, argued the Cabinet Secretary (Burke Trend), should the Prime Minister act as a neutral chairman but there was also a latent conflict between the two cardinal principles:

(a) individual Ministerial responsibility, i.e. the need for each Minister to be – and feel that he can genuinely be – accountable to Parliament . . . for the acts and policies of his department.
(b) collective Ministerial responsibility, i.e. the need for each Minister to be assured that he can rely on his colleagues to support him in Parliament . . . on the basis that all the members of the Government share the accountability for the totality of the Government's policy.

The latter required a clearer definition of strategic objectives than was currently provided by the 'centre'; but should – and could – such objectives then be *imposed* on individual Ministers? The solution which was eventually agreed was the continuation of a trend (so to speak) towards the appointment of a small number of expert 'support staff' within a neutral Cabinet Office, who could guide interdepartmental committees towards the highest rather than (as currently) the lowest common denominator. Were their responsibilities to coincide with the 'blocks' of expenditure used by PESC, then there would be the additional advantage of drawing ever nearer to the Plowden ideal of 'making collective responsibility a reality'.[103]

Even before Howell and Schreiber were installed in the CSD, therefore, a reasoned rebuttal of the PSRU proposal for a Central Capability existed. Did this alone, however, account for its non-implementation or were the failings of pre-election planning and post-election management of equal, or greater, significance? Despite the Heath Government's reputation for being well prepared, this was demonstrably not true in relation to administrative reform. Pre-election planning, as viewed by one senior Conservative insider (Brendon Sewill), had been highly divisive with 'private armies' vying for influence. Moreover, senior opposition leaders were not enamoured of modern management techniques. 'What's all this balls we're having dinner about at the Carlton tonight?', was Reginald Maudling's considered reaction to one of Howell's initiatives, 'I cannot understand what it's all about.'[104] Most importantly, Heath himself remained torn between the virtues both of big and small government and of consensual administrative and divisive political advice. This led him 'unreservedly' to dismiss any idea of a Ministry of Programmes or a Prime Minister's Office in his pre-election meeting with Armstrong (before official advice could have exerted any influence). In addition, he was highly sceptical of any promises to contract government, being fully aware that many manifesto commitments (such as greater selectivity, or means-testing, in the social services) were highly labour intensive.[105]

Such contingencies were accentuated by the PSRU's own failings. The *Black Book* itself admitted that it was only an 'impressionistic' guide to action. This was partly because the election was called much earlier than expected. It was mainly, however, because of the ineffectuality of the Action Groups – and, on Meyjes' evidence, of some businessmen involved.[106] There was also a serious underestimation of the time needed to create a Central Capability and to assemble a team of businessmen. Even more serious was the lack of understanding about how government actually worked and, in particular, how any new 'Central Capability' would relate to the existing system of control over public spending represented by PESC. This had become apparent during a succession of pre-election meetings between Schreiber and officials. Mr Schreiber, noted one Treasury official, was 'clearly an intelligent young man, well up with modern management methods' but he was 'substantially out of touch with the way in which Ministers operate and indeed with the sophistication of Government administration'.[107] Such a view was clearly condescending and partial; but it coincided with reservations earlier voiced within the Conservative Research Department, where Schreiber had been based.

This 'amateurishness' (as Fulton might have termed it) was further exacerbated by poor political management after the election. Schreiber and Meyjes, for instance, battled for control over the Business Team.[108] Jellicoe was frequently unaware of what Howell was doing. The proceedings of Howell's working group (to which Heath entrusted first the coordination of the Business Team's 'projects' and then the collation of Ministerial replies to his September request for a review of the 'activities of government') were also chaotic and antagonistic. Departmental Ministers, as well as officials, grew so suspicious that a senior member of the Cabinet Office had to warn his counterpart in the CSD that:

> it would be only kind to the Parliamentary Secretary to point out . . . that it is a matter of human nature, which no instruction from the Prime Minister will change, that no departmental Minister worth his salt will tolerate any discussion behind his back on any matter for which he is departmentally responsible in Parliament. To fly in the face of this will not only do the Parliamentary Secretary considerable harm but will also wreck the working group's chances of obtaining an objective analysis of particular issues.[109]

This was no way to disarm opposition to radical administrative reform.

The *Black Book* had anticipated many of these problems. 'When you take over government', it had warned the incoming Prime Minister, 'it will be in some ways analogous to an entrepreneur taking over a tired and badly run company which contains many underused assets.' Releasing those assets would be more difficult than their identification. It would be

> highly political and there is quite likely to be a ganging up between some of your Ministers, their officials, Parliament and . . . interest groups. . . . If you leave the problem to negotiation through the usual channels we suspect you will get too little too late.[110]

Were, however, the 'usual channels' to blame or was it the reformers' own shortcomings that persuaded Heath that the pre-election planning of the CSD was more professional and practical than that of the PSRU? The first 100 days, leading up to the publication of *The Reorganisation of Central Government*, were clearly critical; but what was to happen over the next two years, as the commitment to Fulton faded, to the projected creation of a 'central' and an 'analytical capability'?

5.3.2 *Central Capability*

A stronger 'Central Capability', as has been seen, was widely acknowledged to be necessary to provide the Prime Minister with more expert advice and to sustain a government's strategic vision. Pre-election plans had included the creation of a Prime Minister's and Cabinet Office, a central 'analytical capability' staffed in part by 'outsiders' and – to facilitate a smaller more strategically minded Cabinet and the better coordination of policy – 'giant' or 'super' departments. The first had been immediately rejected; the second was partly satisfied by the creation of the CPRS; and the last was fully implemented. Why was there such a selective response?

(a) A Prime Minister's and Cabinet Office

The creation of an expanded Prime Minister's Office (PMO) was soon to become the norm in many countries with a 'Westminster model' constitution; and having been rejected within Whitehall in 1970, it was reconsidered by the press in August 1972.[111] Armstrong once again briefed against it. A PMO, it was argued, could never have the same depth of expertise as specialist departments and so would have to be either reliant upon or forever second-guessing them. This would lead to an overlap of responsibility and, inevitably, friction. Moreover with the Cabinet Secretary, Head of the Civil Service and, by now, the CPRS at his effective command – whatever the constitutional niceties – the Prime Minister had all the personal power he needed. Somewhat perversely the creation of a PMO, by making explicit his sources of power and thereby begging some awkward constitutional questions, might actually weaken his authority.

Heath was not amused by Armstrong's negativity. 'This solves none of the problems' he minuted angrily. The 'problems' were the perceived lack of expert advice and effective policy levers for a Prime Minister who, as has been widely recognised, was a 'managerial, rational, problem-solving' leader and 'hankered after a French-style Civil Service with highly trained officials not afraid to take a strong line'.[112] In such circumstances an obvious alternative to a PMO was a chief of staff, charged with the coordination of advice and 'progress-chasing'. Such a position had in fact been recommended by the Sharp Committee and was raised by Heath in his pre-election meeting with Armstrong on June 7, when he was then advised (in accordance with post-Plowden discussions) that all his requirements would be satisfied by the triumvirate of Cabinet Secretary, Head of the Civil Service and head of the Treasury.[113] In 1972 Armstrong, somewhat ironically, maintained his opposition. Such a post, he claimed, had effectively been held by Norman Brook as Cabinet Secretary between 1956 and 1962; and the consequence, on Brook's own admission, had been that a preoccupation with policy had crowded out concern for managerial efficiency. The CSD, he admitted, might now exist to promote the latter; but its head, and indeed the Cabinet Secretary, would be deprived of the 'standing and authority they need finally to resolve really important questions with their fellow Permanent Secretaries' should an appeal over their heads always be possible to a chief of staff.

The irony within this advice was that although the post-Plowden discussions had identified the Cabinet Secretary as the Prime Minister's 'principal official adviser', Armstrong (as Head of the Service) slowly assumed that position, given his greater sympathy with Heath's style of government. By the Spring of 1971, for example, he had gained the regular meetings which Wilson had denied him and, in the following Autumn, he was appointed to head a secret task force to develop a more proactive response to rising unemployment.[114] As the economic and industrial relations crises deepened, Trend's retirement in September 1973 and his replacement by Sir John Hunt (who was explicitly charged with forging a more proactive Cabinet Office) made little difference. Armstrong in effect became Heath's *chef du cabinet* (a position which he had always opposed) and acquired a 'political' influence in the manner of Sir Horace Wilson (an 'overstepping of the line' which he had always feared). This resulted in his being dubbed 'deputy Prime Minister' in January 1973 and ultimately in his nervous breakdown a year later.[115]

Whilst this administrative tragedy played out, what has been little recognised is that –in the first years of government at least – there was an alternative to Armstrong as chief of staff. This was none other than the CSD's Parliamentary Secretary and leading protagonist of the 'new style of government', David Howell. He was given three opportunities to develop the role. The first was at the end of July 1970, when Heath commissioned him to set up an official working group to draw together the Business Team's advice or, more formally, to provide

> a focus for bringing before Ministers ideas as to government policies and procedures that needed early investigating, with regard to the government's general strategy, the improvement of decision-making, the improved management of government activities and the prospect of reducing government expenditure.

It was to report to a high-powered Management Projects Cabinet Committee (MPC) chaired by the Prime Minister. Despite the expectation that this Committee would meet fortnightly, however, it met only once (on 15 September 1970) for an allegedly 'desultory' discussion. In November, the working group was then charged with collating Ministerial replies to Heath's request for a Ministerial review of the 'activities of government'. It submitted two reports (on 21 December and 27 January 1971) before being required to produce an action plan, which was to provide the basis for a second, important white paper. Howell, therefore, had a belated opportunity to produce his 'Reorganisation and Contraction of Central Government' white paper; but the action plan was so thin that the paper was ultimately abandoned and the working group was disbanded in September 1971.

For the last five months of his tenure, Howell then chaired the Parliamentary Secretary's Organisation Group. This was designed to progress chase and 'draw any necessary organisational implication from the Government's developing overall strategy'. However, it met only three times and its sole purpose, so it was alleged, was to maintain Howell's *amour propre*.[116]

Why, as a putative chief of staff, did Howell fail? His purpose, in tandem with Schreiber and as trailed both in *The New Style of Government* and the *Black Book*, was explicitly political. In fighting for the original working party, for instance, Schreiber urged that its role must be to ensure that 'the political motivation and thrust should not be lost'. Its staff must be 'entrepreneurial' and the MPC encouraged, in a seminal phrase, 'to think the unthinkable'. Howell equally returned from an audience at Chequers on 31 December 1971, convinced of the 'firm political will' to reduce the size of government; and he immediately drafted a letter to the Prime Minister to that effect. Hence the plans for a second white paper. Accordingly he was infuriated when, because of the largely official membership of the working group charged with drafting this paper, Armstrong referred to its work as a 'staff exercise'. It was, he fulminated, 'precisely because the working group had been able to introduce a political and policy element into their examinations . . . that the exercise has been of value. It is just these qualities which Mr Heath feels need to be perpetuated'.[117]

Did Armstrong deliberately impede Howell's attempt to introduce 'political motivation and thrust'? He was certainly unsympathetic, having over the past two years developed an alternative programme of structural change (based on the 'ten paper' review) and improvements to personnel management (based on Fulton). Were government to be made more efficient, he clearly believed, this was the way forward. He was also on record for doubting whether the political will existed to reduce the role of government. 'It is possible that a Government or a series of governments might reverse the postwar trend', he admitted to the British Academy in June 1970, but it was most unlikely to 'happen overnight'. Armstrong's major objection to Howell's initiatives, however, concerned not their political motivation but their method. Under pressure from Howell and Jellicoe, as has been seen, the principle had been established in the autumn of 1970 that individual Ministers were constitutionally responsible for administrative reorganisation. By inference, they should also be responsible after that for the contraction of their own department's activities. Armstrong was therefore appalled when, in December 1970, 'the considered replies' of Ministers to Heath's September minute were subjected to criticism 'by a group containing officials . . . without either being formally known or Departments being given any opportunity for taking part'. This was not the way to do business, let alone achieve results.[118] CSD officials took their lead from him and in February 1971 they resisted Howell's request to bombard other departments with requests for further information. This information, they had to be duly reminded by the working group's secretary, was requested by a Minister and 'we need to do our duty'. A year later, however, no such duty was recognised. 'We don't take' recommendations from the Parliamentary Secretary's Organisation Group, minuted another official, 'as an order for action'.[119]

Did such action – or inaction – amount to a bureaucratic conspiracy? In two ways it did not. First, it was a conditioned response to wishes of the Prime Minister who, at best, gave only sporadic support to Howell and Schreiber. Hence his reluctance to reconvene the MPC; the inordinate delay in his response to Howell's post-Chequers letter of 12 February; and his readiness to abandon the second white paper in November 1971. From March 1971 there was a steady escalation in the belief amongst Ministers as well as officials that Howell had lost the Prime Minister's trust.[120] Second, official 'recalcitrance' was often little more than a rational response to Howell's perceived managerial shortcomings. The meetings of the working group, for example, were chaotic. There was little prioritisation of agenda items and, in consequence, an absence of detailed briefing and reasoned discussion. His approach to other departments, as has been seen, could be equally ill-disciplined and counterproductive.[121] Were anything to be achieved, alternative methods had to be adopted.

The creation of a PMO after 1970 was, therefore, never a practical proposition. Consequently, the real tension centred on the appointment of a chief of staff. This was a post which Heath's style of working clearly favoured and had been considered within Whitehall before the election. It had then been rejected because, in Ian Bancroft's inimitable phrase, the holder was doomed to become 'either an ineffective pain in the neck to executive Ministers, or . . . effectively Deputy Prime Minister'.[122] Howell was privately perceived to become the former. Armstrong was publicly accused of becoming the latter.

(b) *The Central Policy Review Staff*

The Central Policy Review Staff (CPRS) was one of the Conservatives' more 'colourful' initiatives and continued to enjoy a 'heady moment of creative energy' until the Autumn of 1973 when its head (Victor Rothschild) fell into disgrace and, due to pressure of outside events, its innovative biennial strategy sessions at Chequers were suspended.[123] As a 'Central Capability', however, the CPRS was a very different body from the one envisaged by the PSRU; and this was reflected in its fraught origins between July 1970 and February 1971.

Pre-election planning by the CSD and the PSRU, as has been seen, was convergent but not congruent. Senior civil servants had long recognised the 'hole in the centre' of government, which denied the Prime Minister a source of 'independent' (non-departmental) advice. It also denied the Cabinet an opportunity to articulate a collective strategy against which individual actions of departments might be measured.[124] Hence the CSD's initial advocacy, like the Sharp Committee, of a Prime Minister's Office. By the Election, however, the views of Armstrong on administrative practicality and Trend on constitutional propriety were predominant. Accordingly Heath was advised not to establish 'any extra capability' designed either to 'duplicate' the current system for controlling expenditure or 'to harry departments in carrying out *their own* functions' (italics added). The Prime Minister, in other words, should have no increased executive or political power.

There was, however, an 'admitted need for an extra capability at the centre to provide advice to Ministers ... on priorities'. Even Trend (despite suggestions to the contrary) recognised the fallibility of the current Cabinet Committee system. 'It puts a premium on departmental differences', he admitted to Armstrong, 'and results too often in a conclusion which is little more than a lowest common denominator of agreement'. Nor, as it pretended, could the Treasury be a central analytical capability because it had a 'negative' departmental interest in minimising public expenditure rather than maximising policy effectiveness. Departments had accordingly developed a 'profound resistance' to providing it with information. Hence Heath was strongly advised to endorse Trend's earlier suggestion to reinforce the existing 'series of specialist staff' within the Cabinet Office. Working to senior Ministers chairing Cabinet Committees, they could provide 'neutral' and 'objective' advice on priorities within and between blocks of expenditure. Thus they could help to ensure that both current and future policy was cost-effective and consistent with an agreed strategy.

The PSRU shared the same critique but not the same administrative and constitutional concerns. For it, the rationale behind a 'Central Capability' was to give the Prime Minister increased executive and political power. Aided by business experts, it would enforce 'output budgeting' on all departments to ensure that their expenditure accorded to clearly defined policy objectives. It would then both ensure that each of these objectives was consistent with the Government's overall strategy. Finally it would monitor subsequent departmental submissions to ensure that they were 'technically sound' and that the Prime Minister's 'personal political evaluation in terms of priorities and constraints' had been taken into account. In short, it was to be the vehicle by which the Prime Minister could impose on colleagues and Whitehall alike both the minimisation of government and the maximisation of managerial efficiency.[125]

Following the meetings on the *Black Book* between 29 June and 3 July, the battle between these two concepts was fought out over the definition and, then, over the appointment of the head of the new 'Central Capability'. The initial move was the establishment – to the deliberate disadvantage of the PSRU – of a distinction between its managerial and political function. The Cabinet memorandum of 14 July, heavily reworked by Armstrong, confirmed that the 'Business Team' would be responsible to a Cabinet Committee (not directly to the Prime Minister) and act as 'consultants' within the CSD (not a PMO). The Cabinet Committee (to be called the Management Projects Committee or MPC) would have the power to authorise or initiate management projects but they were to be implemented by and within departments. The first was to be the development within the Treasury of a system of output budgeting (Programme Analysis and Review or PAR). The issue of the more political role of the 'Central Capability' was sidestepped although there was an allusion to the creation of another body, possibly located in the Cabinet Office, to which businessmen might have 'a contribution to make'.[126]

Battle was then joined over this second 'political' body and, after a furious exchange of memoranda, another *ad hoc* Cabinet committee appeared largely to endorse the Whitehall concept. Trend was instructed to draft a Cabinet memorandum, which duly recorded that the principal purpose of the new body was to develop a 'coherent Government strategy' although it was not to duplicate the work of other departments. Rather, 'working in close co-operation with departments' it would

> seek to reconcile differences in the analysis of interdepartmental problems; to clarify points of significant disagreement between departments; to identify the real issues for decision and the considerations which should be taken into account in deciding them; to set the issues in the context of the Government's strategy and priorities; and to report to Ministers collectively on an objective and non-departmental basis.

To emphasise its responsibility to the Cabinet as a whole, it was to be overseen by yet another Cabinet Committee (later known as the Ministerial Committee on the Central Capability or MCA).[127]

This memorandum, however, was intercepted by Howell on its way to Heath; and, despite his membership of the *ad hoc* Committee, he vehemently opposed it on three grounds – all of which and, despite his chairmanship of the *ad hoc* Committee, Heath upheld. Howell's first objection was that the memorandum underplayed the 'crucial working link' between the 'new capability' and the 'budgetary and analytical capability within the Treasury' (reinforced by PAR). In other words, Howell envisaged the new body using PAR to impose within all departments a new ruthlessness towards both the role of government and managerial efficiency. This underlined his second objection, which was that the quintessential political purpose of the new body had been ignored. The draft, Howell complained

> states that the new capability will be 'objective'. If this means not grinding departmental axes, that is fine; but if it means analytically objective and free from prejudices, that is a nonsense. The whole point of this capability is that it should enable the political wishes of the Prime Minister and his colleagues to be translated into programmes; and for [that] bias . . . to be strongly and continuously fed into the work of the capability.

Finally, the new body's 'most crucial function' had been overlooked. This was the monthly monitoring of departmental action against the Government's agreed strategy and an annual presentation to Cabinet of the 'overall strategic picture'. Such presentations, Howell asserted, were 'at the heart of the new style of government'.[128]

The definition of the new unit's role was consequently deferred whilst, rather incongruously, a search was mounted for its first director. Schreiber made plain his desire for an 'intensively political' head and suggested either Peter Goldman (the pre-eminent thinker in the Conservative Research Department) or Charles Schultz (the former head of the US Bureau of the Budget, despite his being a US citizen).

To ensure an injection of 'tough business experience', Howell suggested Meyjes. The CSD, on the other hand, favoured an academic economist with practical experience within and outside Whitehall. In the final event, however, personal rapport with the Prime Minister was considered crucial and Heath expressed a preference first for Kit MacMahon (who declined to leave the Bank of England) and then Professor Hugh Ford, an engineer at Imperial College, London (who accepted but then retracted after a week, citing his other 'wide-ranging commitments').[129]

Then Victor Rothschild serendipitously passed through Downing Street on other government business. Trend pounced and found him to be both acceptable to Heath and willing to accept. It was, by general agreement, 'an inspired choice ... one of the best appointments Heath ever made'. Rothschild was charismatic, independent, iconoclastic and fearless and, moreover, had an extensive network of outside contacts. These were qualities widely deemed essential for the job. Nevertheless he was – as Howell later made explicit – 'not at all the sort of person' that he and Schreiber had wanted.[130] He had little business experience or economic expertise; lacked any interest in modern management techniques; and most damningly, was a long-standing Labour Party supporter rather than a political partisan champing at the bit 'to take the British system of government by the scruff of the neck and open the way for a decisive defeat of the big government philosophy ... which prevailed not in Britain but virtually throughout the world'. Indeed, despite his alleged iconoclasm, he was fully wedded to the assumptions of Keynesian economics and the 'ideals of the welfare state'.

Rothschild's appointment in late October did not conclusively determine the nature of the CPRS. He received, and continued to receive until March 1971, encouragement from Howell and Schreiber to reintegrate the managerial and political sides of the 'whole' new Central Capability, and to serve the Prime Minister personally. On the way to winter in Barbados, he also visited *inter alia* Charles Schultz in Washington. Before formally taking up office on 1 February, however, he had been closeted for over three days in Barbados with a Cabinet Office official (John Mayne) and had met most senior Permanent Secretaries. When in March 1971, therefore, he was required to define his guiding principles for maximising 'the quality and effectiveness of the Government's collective decisions', it came as little surprise that he explicitly stressed that 'the CPRS is not a "Bureau of the Budget" or an "Office of the President"'. Rather, as Trend's earlier draft had averred, it would work with and through other departments to provide 'impartial and expert advice' on issues requiring collective decision.[131]

The nature of the small staff he assembled reflected this bias. It contained neither the partisan politicians nor the businessmen of proven management experience, which Howell and Schreiber had envisaged. Rather, despite being a mix of insiders and outsiders, its members largely reflected the traditional character of the Administrative Class (intelligent, white, male Oxbridge graduates). Indeed only in the early age at which they gained influence might they be described as atypical. This was nevertheless sufficient to generate an 'intellectual excitement quite different from the rest of Whitehall' and, given Rothschild's personality, enabled awkward questions to be asked of both policies and people. The fact could not be disguised, however, that its approach to – as distinct from its presentation of – problems was 'not outstandingly innovative'. Analysis owed 'more to common sense and quite a lot to applied economics' than to the more modern managerial techniques. Moreover, its assumptions faithfully reflected those of the 'liberal intelligentsia'.[132]

How, and how successfully, did the CPRS operate in its first two years? It chose to concentrate on four distinct roles, and in all but one its record remains open to question. Its principal task, long advocated by senior officials, was to help the Cabinet to develop and maintain a coherent strategy. To this end, it mounted two strategy reviews which formed the basis for successive meetings of Ministers in October 1971 and May 1972. These meetings were certainly an innovation and, in the judgement of Heath's political secretary, highly successful because they 'rubbed Minister's noses in the future'.[133] This was perhaps the very reason why others, such as Jellicoe, were less appreciative. Claims of 'success' also have to be tempered by the fact that the Heath government notoriously failed to honour its manifesto commitments (not least with the 1972 economic u-turn, to which the CPRS arguably contributed by espousing a prices and incomes policy in its second review). The prevention of such eventualities had been the intention behind its second initiative: the institution of an 'early warning system' to alert Ministers to impending crises which might throw their agreed strategy off course. This was acknowledged to be an unmitigated failure and was discontinued in 1972. The CPRS was incapable of sufficiently transforming traditional Whitehall culture to make officials routinely think ahead and the Treasury, in particular, disclose 'sensitive' information.

The other two roles were more routine and designed to fulfil the long-standing wish within Whitehall to make Cabinet decisions more informed and rational. These were the mounting of special inquiries and the writing of collective briefs. The former examined 'neglected' policy areas and the latter were produced to enable the Cabinet to see beyond special departmental pleading. Individually both tasks were performed well. Amongst the triumphs of the special inquiries, for example, was the identification of the impending oil crisis. Collective briefs were also widely adjudged to have prevented individual Ministers 'from steamrolling his colleagues through his own unexamined assertions'. Collectively, however, they were less successful because they exhausted the CPRS's very limited resources. Special inquiries, for instance, prevented the CPRS from providing a comprehensive set of briefs and the coverage of the special inquiries themselves was extremely uneven. As a later Parliamentary inquiry concluded, it was a 'butterfly system which flies from one thing to another, looking at them, making interesting reports, not really following them up, and then moving on to something else'. This, two leading CPRS members later agreed, was 'fair comment'.[134]

The early contribution of the CPRS to the modernisation of Whitehall was, therefore, somewhat less than has been sometimes rather romantically portrayed. Was this because it had been emasculated during the protracted dispute over its establishment? The short answer is no. Between the PSRU and Whitehall there was, as Trend later admitted,' a quite remarkable coincidence of diagnosis'.[135] Each, however, had developed quite different remedies. The more radical ambitions of Howell and Schreiber for a 'Central Capability' were undoubtedly thwarted; but the essential reason for this was they were adjudged by Ministers, as much as by officials, to be impractical. The CSD's pre-election planning was once again proved to be the more professional and realistic. Nevertheless, both Armstrong and Trend were pushed further than they wished to go. The CPRS, for example, was a single unit rather than a series of staffs serving a range of Cabinet Committees – a fact that potentially threatened the Cabinet Secretary's authority and undoubtedly discomforted Trend. Their concept of constitutional propriety was also offended by strategic reviews (which effectively gave officials working within the CPRS a partisan political role) and PAR (which enabled the CPRS to intervene in responsibilities for which departmental Ministers alone were answerable to Parliament). The early role of the CPRS was thus far from an unalloyed 'bureaucratic' triumph. On the contrary, it exposed the limits of bureaucratic power by demonstrating, particularly in relation to its strategic role, that the modernisers' political ambitions for such a 'Central Capability' could never be met. In short, the case had been made for the establishment of a Policy Unit in No. 10, answerable directly to the Prime Minister.

(c) 'Super' ministries

The third, and superficially the most successful, means by which the 'Central Capability' was enhanced was the creation of 'super' or 'giant' departments. They had been universally championed in pre-election planning. For the Sharp Committee, for example, they provided the opportunity to secure a smaller, more strategically minded Cabinet and to minimise interdepartmental compromise. For the PSRU, they embodied current management thinking that big was beautiful. For the CSD, they reflected organic change within the Service following, for example, the creation of the unified MOD under the Conservatives in 1964. Accordingly when two such departments – the Department of the Environment (DoE) and of Trade and Industry (DTI) – were established in October 1970, they were broadly welcomed.[136] To what extent did they realise the conflicting hopes they raised?

The Reorganisation of Central Government white paper restated many of these hopes. Strategically, the new departments would help establish 'clearly defined and accepted objectives' both for the government as a whole and in their own specialist fields. If, in the latter, there was any conflict, it would be resolved 'within the line of management rather than by inter-departmental compromise'. Their greater functional unity would also enhance both management and open government (given that a Minister could be more easily identified with a specific policy). Nevertheless, there were potential dangers. Politically, collective responsibility might be eroded if debates became internalised within the ministries. Whilst avoiding the 'parochial' interests of smaller departments, 'super' ministries – and thus government – might also become less responsive to outside opinion. Administratively, there was a danger of size. As the CSD pre-warned Heath, were there sufficient Ministers and Permanent Secretaries with the skills to manage such departments efficiently? Might not remoteness from Ministers and an initial lack of corporate identity alienate staff? Finally, Heath was warned, public administration was not solely a matter of managerial efficiency: political personality and priorities had also to be accommodated.[137]

In its pre-election planning, CSD officials had worked hard to minimise each of these dangers. In relation to responsiveness, for example, they rather optimistically hoped that each 'super' ministry would

> adopt (or somehow be compelled to adopt) a different style of policy-making within itself, and an acceptance of a new responsibility for admitting other departments at an early stage to its own internal policy-forming processes – often before its own departmental line has even formed. This also implies a readiness on the part of the Minister to abstain from the full use of what the Americans would term the "political clout" of his department in his dealings with others.

More realistically, they emphasized the need for more authoritative and well-briefed Cabinet Committees to rein in over-powerful Ministers and to ensure, at the highest level, joined-up government. To encourage managerial efficiency, specific responsibilities might also be delegated to either junior Ministers or 'accountable managers' – although, because of the need for Parliamentary accountability, any 'hiving off' of specific blocks of work to the private sector or to 'autonomous' public bodies (as suggested by the PSRU) was rejected.[138]

Did the two new 'super' ministries improve the 'Central Capability'? The Department of the Environment, for a variety of reasons, was initially the more successful. It had been long planned. It was less involved with controversial legislation, so that both the Minister and senior officials could concentrate on organisational issues. Moreover, the Minister (Peter Walker) had the requisite business skills to be a Minister-manager. His daily 'prayer meetings' with junior Ministers, for example, ensured that policy was coordinated and thus a clear sense of direction ensured.[139] By 1976, however, the prize goal of uniting local government and transport planning within an 'infrastructure' department had been lost with the creation of an independent Ministry of Transport.[140] As originally conceived, therefore, the DoE survived for less than five years, the period conventionally regarded as the minimum for achieving the full benefit from organisational change.

The DTI fared far worse. The concept of a Ministry of Industry (uniting the main responsibilities of the Ministry of Technology, Board of Trade and Department of Employment) had been first floated by management consultants commissioned by PSRU; and it was endorsed by Howell in the *New Style of Government*. Simultaneously, some rationalisation had been planned by CSD although its intention was always to retain the three ministries – as was the expectation of the relevant Permanent Secretaries as late as September 1970.[141] Unlike the DoE, therefore, the DTI was neither well planned nor supported within Whitehall. The Secretary of State (John Davies), as a businessman rather than a politician, then had the greatest of difficulty in blending together a very heterogeneous group of responsibilities and Ministers and, in any case, was immediately distracted by a major political crisis (the impending bankruptcy of Rolls-Royce). Consequently, the DTI soon started to disintegrate. Further political pressure led to the appointment of a second Cabinet Minister within the department in 1972 (Geoffrey Howe as Minister for Prices and Consumer Protection) and the hiving off of the Department of Energy in January 1974.

As a means of strengthening the 'Central Capability', therefore, neither 'super' ministry was an immediate success. This was unsurprising because, as the CSD had warned, the disadvantages of disruption inevitably preceded the advantages of greater functional unity.[142] The omens, however, had never been good. The delegation of 'executive blocks of work . . . to accountable units of management', which all pre-election planners had regarded as essential to their efficient management, was slow to develop (see Chapter 5.3.3(c)). As feared by the CSD, the impersonality of 'vast departments' was soon associated by staff associations with plummeting morale and thus administrative efficiency. Most significantly of all, however, Howell became disillusioned with their political purpose. As rethinking started in 1975, following Mrs Thatcher's election as leader, he confessed:

> I supported super ministries because I thought it would lead to a smaller Cabinet less cluttered with day to day problems. But I was wrong. We need a big cabinet so that everyone feels they've got a line to it . . . The idea of a smaller Cabinet was meaningless and positively harmful.

In relation to super ministries specifically, he then admitted that

> neither the public nor Parliament understands them. The public and the press and MPs want lots of Ministers with lots of labels whom they believe to be "responsible". Otherwise they go for the top man and make his burden intolerable.[143]

His changing views accorded with changing trends in management theory: small was again becoming beautiful.

5.3.3 *Analytic capability*

Initially, as has been seen, the PSRU did not distinguish between a 'central' and an 'analytic' capability: indeed the *Black Book* referred to the Central Capability as the 'analytical capability'. It, together with its executive arm (or 'action capability', the Ministry of Programmes), was to come under the Prime Minister's direct control and be served by a team of businessmen with proven managerial (or 'analytical') expertise. As will be seen, a team of businessmen was established. So too were several management initiatives, most notably output budgeting (PAR) and 'hiving off'. As with the CPRS, however, each was a pale reflection of what the PSRU had originally intended. Why?

(a) The Business Team

A six-man team of businessmen was appointed in July 1970, to be supplemented in 1971 by two further members (Herbert Cruickshank from the builders, Bovis, and Timothy Sainsbury from the eponymous supermarket giant). Individuals left on the completion of their original tasks and the team was disbanded in September 1972, when the contract of its head (Dick Meyjes from Shell International) expired[144]. The team's major achievements were the introduction of PAR and the establishment of two departmental agencies (the Procurement Executive and the Property Services Agency, the first of which was initially headed by one of the original complement of businessmen – Derek Rayner of Marks and Spencer). These initiatives will be examined in the following sections. What, however, was the team's broader significance?

The role of the Business Team aroused controversy even within the PSRU. It was agreed that it should cover both analysis (the improvement of the government's decision-making process) and action (the management of specific activities). For Howell and Schreiber, however, the ultimate goal was the contraction of government. As Schreiber, for instance, wrote to Jellicoe on 3 July 1970:

> The emphasis on introducing outsiders into the Government machine is not to attempt to make the Civil Service more efficient – civil servants are thoroughly aware of the need for efficiency and indeed they are extremely intelligent, hard working and in every way competent – but it is to question the policy assumptions on which so many activities are based.

For Meyjes, on the other hand, the role was 'entirely non-political': the improvement of the 'basic analytical system'.[145] Hence the tension over the separation of the managerial from the political elements of the proposed 'Central Capability' between July and August 1970. Meyjes was ready to accede. Schreiber and Howell were not.

This did not mean, however, that Meyjes was at one with the plans of the CSD. As Head of the Civil Service, Armstrong had consistently supported the import of managerial expertise into Whitehall. In 1968, for example, he had encouraged the appointment of an eight-man team of businessmen under Sir Robert Bellinger to cut waste. Six industrialists had recently been appointed to executive posts (such as the chief executive of the Dockyards) and a further two as advisers within the CSD. In addition management consultants had been contracted to undertake more than 60 commissions.[146] Far from being opposed, therefore, a further influx of businessmen was regarded as 'welcome and highly important'; and within a week of the election, plans had been laid for a fourteen-strong team. That only six were appointed was solely the consequence of the limited number of 'projects' to be supervised by businessmen, identified by Meyjes in his letter to Heath accepting the appointment.[147]

Where were the six to be accommodated? The CSD proposed that where a project involved only one ministry, the relevant businessman should be embedded within it; and where it was interdepartmental, he should be located in one of the central departments (the CSD, Treasury or Cabinet Office). Meyjes, however, resisted so close an embrace. As he protested to Heath, the team could not

> function effectively without a special and independent status which gives them the ability to generate ideas and carry out projects across the whole of the Government structure with the direct support and encouragement of the Prime Minister.[148]

They had, therefore, to be fully independent of departments and answerable only to him. Armstrong baulked at such demands on practical and constitutional grounds. Businessmen working on a single department project, he maintained, had to work where the administrative expertise and Ministerial accountability to Parliament lay; and even those working within a central department had to be responsible to the Cabinet as a whole, not just the Prime Minister.

Meyjes' additional demand that his team should be a part of the 'decision-making process' concerned Armstrong even more. Policy-making, he argued, was exclusively for Ministers.[149] This was a point Meyjes, given his essentially apolitical stance, readily conceded. He had only made the demand, he confessed, because of the 'unhappy history of past attempts to inject businessmen into the Government machine'. The Bellinger committee, for example, had been appointed by Labour Ministers and then almost wholly ignored. So long as he was guaranteed that the Business Team's initiatives would be evaluated by Ministers, and thus be part of the decision-making process, he was content. Accordingly in mid-July he accepted, despite Howell's misgivings, the team's supervision by a Cabinet Committee (the MPC) rather than the Prime Minister. Likewise he accepted its location in the CSD rather than a Prime Minister's Office – so long as it was answerable to Heath and Jellicoe, not to officials. Thus a compromise was reached between Meyjes' concept of a central 'independent' business team and the CSD's constitutional concerns.

Unfortunately this compromise did not work, as was well illustrated by the frustration vented in the Business Team's first report. The original objective, it protested, had been to 'undertake a series of short investigatory projects leading rapidly to a definition of executive jobs in Government into which members of the team could be redeployed'.[150] Such posts, however, did not materialise and so the team was employed on a number of smaller diagnostic cases, for which its members were ill-equipped. Within a year, four of the original team had duly left or been redeployed, whilst the remaining two (Robin Hutton and Meyjes) had become underemployed. No new major projects were authorised (not least because the MPC met only once) and the concept of a business 'team' became discredited. By

May 1972, minds were concentrated by the impending expiry of Meyjes' two-year contract. Should the experiment continue? Unsurprisingly Howell advocated this, so that Ministers (who, contrary to his initial plans, had neither the time nor temperament to become Minister-managers) might benefit from some 'managerial common sense'. 'Fresh outside minds', he maintained, would provide 'valuable advice and stimulate straight thinking'. This was a view ultimately adopted by Meyjes himself and Jellicoe, albeit in the more modest form of a single business adviser. Located within the CSD, argued Jellicoe, such an adviser could

> advise on machinery of government and organisational questions and bring a business view to them; watch over the work that the present Business Team has set in hand; take a special look at particular problems ... and generally provide a source of independent and experienced advice from the business world.[151]

Armstrong opposed his Minister's view. 'The real place for businessmen', he countered, was 'now in departments on the basis of particular men for particular jobs'.[152] Their recruitment and the provision of general advice could be handled in house, supported – where necessary – by management consultants. Businessmen, in other words, should once again be on tap but not on top. Armstrong's view prevailed. An effective decision taken in October 1971 neither to authorise new projects nor to make the Business Team permanent was not reversed; and in January 1973, after considerable wavering, Heath also vetoed the appointment of a senior business adviser.

Why did the experiment fail? Opposition in Whitehall was clearly a partial cause. The team's first report may have praised Armstrong for his 'most valuable encouragement' and accredited resistance not to 'men' but the 'system'– such as the 'perfectionism', 'fairness' and risk aversion demanded by Parliamentary accountability. As has been seen, however, Armstrong was implacably opposed – to the extent of briefing against his own Ministers – both to the original concept of the team and to later attempts to give Ministers independent managerial advice. Other CSD officials were even more vitriolic. As, for example, the outspoken Tom Caulcott minuted in January 1971:

> The Business Team have exactly two achievements to their credit. These are:
>
> (1) they have increased the number of civil servants
> (2) they have delayed the carrying forward of government policy.

This was because, in their disorganisation, they were bombarding officials for obtuse information and, in their ignorance, they were reopening issues which had already been exhaustively examined and were simply awaiting political decision. In short, the challenge to both official methods and authority was deeply resented.[153]

Important though such bureaucratic resistance was, however, the Business Team's failure lay also in its lack of political support and its own fallibilities. Heath had initially been reluctant to appoint Meyjes. His preference was for someone 'weightier', such as Sir Val Duncan (of Rio Tinto Zinc) or Jim Slater (the former partner of the new Secretary of State for the Environment in Slater Walker Securities). Significantly he was also recorded as not having 'in mind to consult the Lord Privy Seal or Mr David Howell' before making his decision.[154] Moreover, his refusal to call more than one meeting of the MPC, a five-month delay between his agreement to meet and his actual meeting with the team in December 1971, and the further postponement of a further meeting on its future in May 1972 signified a lack of commitment. The 'direct support and encouragement of the Prime Minister', which Meyjes had identified as crucial on his appointment, was patently lacking. So too was the support of other Ministers. Tensions had dogged pre-election planning because of the extent to which managerial change was seen to infringe upon policy. For this reason, two potentially sympathetic Ministers (Keith Joseph and Robert Carr) had respectively delayed the initiation of projects on the NHS and the employment services. Furthermore, the team was stunned by the Cabinet's initial rejection in November 1970 of its first major report, *Improved Expenditure Decisions*, which advocated the introduction of output budgeting (see Chapter 5.3.3(b)). Frustration within the Business Team's first report was, therefore, aimed as much at Ministers as officials, with the hope expressed that the 'fresh, uninhibited but experienced view' it could bring to 'major and intractable issues' would soon be better appreciated by them.[155] It never was.

This lack of appreciation stemmed also from the team's own shortcomings, which were soon the subject of a scathing attack from the head of its support unit within the CSD (Nigel Forward), the CSD official working most closely with it. In *his* frustration, he wrote:

> whatever may have been the advantages to be expected from bringing in people with wide ranging business experience and pre-election familiarity with the aims and aspirations of members of the future Administration, the idea was marred in the event by the quality of people chosen.

There then followed a series of character assassinations before the conclusion was reached that:

> only one member of the team (Rayner) has shown the talents and ability to work with the system that would be expected of an outstanding person from the business world, and only one other ... has shown himself as even moderately well equipped with the general skills necessary to acquire an effective influence over the conduct of public business. The others have proved inadequate to the tasks for which they were selected. Meyjes must ... stand convicted of having grossly misjudged either the

task, as being appropriate for mediocrities, or the men, as being the bright stars they are not.

Such an attack might be dismissed as a vendetta, but its substance was corroborated by others. The Chief Secretary to the Treasury, for example, in seeking to terminate the contract of the businessman redeployed to the Treasury to implement PAR criticised him on precisely the same grounds. Rayner, it was reported, also had a 'scarcely disguised contempt' for the majority of his colleagues.[156]

The Business Team failed, therefore, due to a mixture of bureaucratic resistance, lack of political support and its own imperfections. In retrospect, however, its very concept came to be questioned even by Rayner. On his premature retirement in 1972, for instance, he confirmed that businessmen were best employed in a specific executive rather than a general diagnostic role. Since senior men of the requisite quality would be difficult to recruit, he recommended the secondment of 35-year-old managers on one-year contracts to undertake a specific, well-specified task. Surprisingly, given his own relative success, he opposed the appointment of businessmen as the chief executives of 'hived off' agencies. Such posts, he argued, required continuity and a greater familiarity with Whitehall's ways than any outsider, on a time-limited contract, could offer. A businessman's proper place was, therefore, as a deputy to a chief executive (who should be a Civil Servant) driving through an agreed programme of management reform.[157] This, however, was all for the future. In the short term, the tragedy was that mutual misunderstanding impeded the very change in managerial culture that Armstrong himself was seeking throughout Whitehall. On the one hand, businessmen (other than Rayner) failed to appreciate the constraints under which the public sector had to work. On the other, officials failed to appreciate the urgency with which (within revised constitutional conventions) they were now expected to work. To what extent did PAR and 'hiving off' resolve, or deepen, this misunderstanding?

(b) Programme analysis and review

PAR represented, and thus held the key to, all that was hoped from the Conservatives' 'new style of government'.[158] Its development was the first project assigned to the Business Team; and after widespread discussion in Whitehall a report (*Improved Expenditure Decisions by Government*) was agreed, which was duly considered by Cabinet in November 1970. It recommended that each department should produce an annual series of 'programme reviews'. A 'programme' was defined as an area of policy, entailing expenditure of no less than £10 million, which had to be considered as a whole were rational decisions to be made; and the reviews, up to 25 pages in length, were to be divided into four standardised sections. They were:

1 Review of current situation, impending changes and major decision issues
2 The policy and purposes of the department

3   Recommendations for the particular programme
4   Action required

Each October the reviews would be submitted to the Treasury and, once agreed, to the relevant Ministerial Cabinet Committee. That Committee's conclusions would then be fed upwards to Cabinet (to inform the Government's overall strategy) and back to departments (to reinforce cost-effective implementation). It was essential they be synchronised with the established PESC machinery for medium-term planning.[159]

PAR was therefore designed to achieve three specific objectives: the robust examination within departments of policy in 'output' terms; the explicit statement of each policy's objectives so that it might be 'tested' against, and simultaneously refine, Government strategy; and the reinforcement, through the analysis of existing policy, of PESC (which was largely concerned with new expenditure commitments). As such, it potentially satisfied a wide range of interests. For departmental Ministers, it represented a means of attaining 'control' over all the policies for which they were formally responsible. For Cabinet Ministers collectively, it provided the information needed to maintain a clearer and more consistent strategy. This was the holy grail of many modernisers. Finally, for the Treasury it promised more effective control over public expenditure (through a strengthening of PESC) and more rigorous departmental planning (for the achievement of which its own officials had flown to Washington to study output budgeting). It was particularly delighted by the report's promise that 'the public expenditure divisions of the Treasury will concentrate on PAR each Autumn, as a preliminary to PESC in the following Spring. PAR will become the beginning of PESC'. Such a strengthening of PESC had been long sought.

Given these multiple advantages, the surprise was that PAR was not immediately endorsed by Cabinet.[160] Full approval was in fact delayed until January 1971 and so not only the first but also the second programme of PARs (to be commenced in November 1971) had to be improvised. Consequently it was only in January 1973 that a three-year rolling programme, geared to key strategic themes and covering some 50 per cent of public expenditure, commenced.[161] By this time the economic u-turn had occurred and so both analytical rigour and strategic coherence had become all the harder to attain. What caused the delay and to what extent did it indelibly tarnish PAR's reputation?

There were technical, operational and, above all, political explanations. Technically, the limitations of output budgeting had been increasingly exposed in the USA and Canada; and even the Business Team's report to Cabinet had acknowledged the 'dangers in relying excessively on analysis, in going into absurd detail, or trying to value the invaluable'.[162] Cost-benefit analysis or the measurement of 'outputs', for example, were wholly inappropriate in policy areas where the benefits were largely qualitative. So too was comparative costing for evaluating the various hypothetical ways by which an agreed strategy might be achieved. Meyjes duly assured Jellicoe that, in forgoing a rigid system imposed from above, his team's recommendations were 'basically quite different in approach to the US system'. Moreover, he acknowledged that an immediate shortage of expertise should not be made good by a 'large scale importation of outside analysts'. This was because in his judgement – and no doubt to the amusement of his official support team – they might 'plunge into action without comprehension of the government machine'. Instead, the necessary skills should be developed in-house by a Service-wide training programme.

The trouble with such reasonableness was that, shorn of their intended rigour and a sufficient complement of skilled analysts, the majority of departmental PARs lost most of their purpose. Responsibility for PARs, so it was noted, fell typically over time 'to generalist administrators best known for their consummate skills as essayists. Thus the final product was just that – an essay with little evidence of rigorous appraisal or of prescription for action'.[163] At a time of manpower constraint, was it justifiable (especially in the absence of the promised training programme) to divert senior staff – or indeed any staff – to such planning exercises from 'operational' work? Certainly little new 'analytical capability' was developed 'from below'.

Departmental doubts were intensified by an initial lack of clarity over the operational purpose of PARs. Was it to complement PESC (and thus reinforce control over public expenditure) or to inform strategic planning? For Howell and Schreiber, there was no conflict between these objectives. Strategic planning, they assumed, would lead to a contraction of government and thus ineluctably to reduced public expenditure. The Treasury, with good reason, was less sanguine. Given electoral pressures, it feared that PARs would be used to support increased expenditure on *individual* programmes and thereby either pre-empt or challenge existing PESC decisions on the limitation of *total* public expenditure. Therefore, it insisted that all PARs should not only 'work within PESC limits' but also be subject to its own officials, performing their 'normal functions' in relation to any 'departmental document which could have significant resource implications'.[164] The Business Team, embedded within the Treasury during the preparation of its report, concurred. 'As at present', its report read, 'expenditure decisions will be taken within the PESC procedures: as at present, these decisions will be taken within the context of total available resources'.[165]

Departments, however, were inevitably perturbed – as were departmental Ministers throughout the Winter of 1970–1. For them, PAR represented a significant potential increase in the Treasury's power because, whereas it had traditionally been concerned only with the totality of departmental expenditure and with new policies, now it was to be empowered to 'crawl' over all a department's activities and to question existing, politically agreed, policy. These fears, moreover, were confirmed by an internal Treasury document which admitted that whilst

> it could be argued that the Treasury assuming these functions would carry too far the process of making the Treasury a central department, rather than just one amongst many each with its own spheres of responsibility . . . in reality, the Treasury has been a central department for decades.[166]

This was the administrative and political nub; and one which was addressed as soon as the CPRS was fully operational. Should the CPRS (with its responsibility to develop a 'coherent Government strategy') or the Treasury (the 'abominable no-man' in relation to public expenditure) ultimately control PAR? The Treasury, it was agreed, should remain in operational control because it alone had the requisite staff to check departmental submissions. Its Chief Secretary should also chair the new coordinating Cabinet Committee. The CPRS, on the other hand, should have the right to help select the annual programmes (to ensure their strategic relevance); to comment independently on the reviews when they were submitted to the sectoral Cabinet Committees (to correct any Treasury bias); and collate both those Committees' reports for Cabinet and the Cabinet's subsequent comments (to ensure a continuing emphasis on strategy). The irony of this concordat was that it made departments even more subject to centralised control; and in time they even expressed a preference for the 'known evil' of the Treasury. After all, it was with its officials that they had to negotiate daily over expenditure whereas the pay-off for accommodating the CPRS was uncertain. Moreover with its emphasis on interdepartmental and long-term policy, the CPRS potentially posed an even greater threat to their autonomy.[167]

Such bureaucratic politics and power-play could have been ended swiftly by decisive political leadership. That too, however, was lacking. Over the years, Heath sporadically sought to revive PAR to clarify strategy and rationalise expenditure. Repeated efforts were also made to involve both junior and senior Ministers.[168] However, both within departments and Cabinet, Ministers declined to change their habits. Junior Ministers typically exhibited little desire to become 'Minister managers'; and even so managerialist a Minister as Peter Walker, the Secretary of State for the Environment, was riled by requests from the centre to expend scarce departmental resources on reviews that were not his first choice.[169] Such requests, it was implied, begged fundamental constitutional questions of the proper balance between individual and collective responsibility.

Just such a conflict, as has been seen, had been identified by Trend before the election and had reportedly been used in Cabinet on 17 November 1970 to oppose the introduction of PAR. However, by January 1971 – when Cabinet finally approved its introduction – the dilemma had seemingly been resolved. As Armstrong briefed Heath:

> The central point is that issues which fall within the individual responsibility of a single Minister must eventually, if they are sufficiently important, be considered by Ministers collectively. There is nothing new in this, which is and has been the essential limitation on the responsibility of individual Ministers.[170]

The constitutional path to collective Ministerial action may have been smoothed, but many mundane obstacles remained. Ministers, for example, remained reluctant – and genuinely lacked the time – to read the 'detailed' PAR reports. 'Depth of analysis was unimportant', as Gray and Jenkins concluded, 'Ministers preferred superficiality'. There was also the issue of political brokerage. Meyjes, for example, had noted that in the USA output budgeting threw 'light into dark places and many of the participants prefer reaching decisions in an atmosphere of undercover political bargaining'. The same was true in Britain. 'I'm not poking holes in their programmes', one Minister reputedly confessed, 'and I certainly hope they are not poking holes in mine.' Rational planning, in short, was seen to impair the short-term bargains and initiatives upon which party politics depended. For Ministers collectively, therefore, PAR represented not a golden opportunity to modernise government consistency but a 'distinctly fringe activity'.[171]

The many retrospective analyses of PAR have regarded its rapid demise as inevitable. It was 'slow, top-heavy and the victim of a relentless interdepartmental grind', as one of the more authoritative has concluded; and one senior Treasury official was even so moved as to dismiss it as an 'excrescence'.[172] Such judgements are necessarily based on its full history. Was it so flawed in its first two years, and if so why?

Contingency certainly played a part in its early 'failings'. PAR's gestation preceded the creation of the CPRS (its natural champion) and even after February 1971, Rothschild was uninterested.[173] This left it at the mercy of the Treasury and vulnerable to bureaucratic gamesmanship. Its introduction also coincided with a major drive to restrict manpower, which denied it the requisite number of trained analysts. In addition, the two main businessmen involved in its conception and launch were commonly acknowledged to be temperamentally ill-suited to conflict resolution and detailed implementation.[174] Finally, PAR only became fully operational after the economic u-turn of 1972, which made both strategic planning and expenditure control inestimably harder. Damaging though such contingencies were, however, they could not disguise fundamental administrative and political design faults. The former was best summarised by Heath's own political secretary (Douglas Hurd) who recalled:

> the arguments against abandoning any particular programme were fiercely sustained by people who, by virtue of their position, knew more of the details than their critics. The truth is that a party which believes in reducing the power of the state will always face serious problems with civil servants at all levels.

Conversely the latter was best identified by a serving official (Leo Pliatzky), who insisted that:

> there was a lack of reality about the idea that the whole organic process of policy formation could somehow be subordinated to a mechanical review procedure.[175]

In short, there was no meeting of political and administrative minds over PAR; and it was just such an accommodation that was vital were, in the allocation of national resources, state intervention ever to prove itself superior to the market. By its failure, therefore, PAR prepared the way for the contraction of government – albeit in a very different way from that planned by Howell.

(c) Hiving off

Hiving off was the final, and given the later establishment of *Next Steps* agencies, potentially the most important reform pioneered between 1968 and 1972. Once again each set of modernisers favoured it, although their ideas did not coalesce. The common goal was greater efficiency. By assigning responsibility to specific officials for discrete blocks of work, so it was argued, specialist expertise and high morale would be assured within Whitehall. Moreover, relieved of routine responsibilities, Ministers – particularly in the new 'super' ministries – would be able to concentrate on strategy. Where consensus broke down was over whether such blocks of work could – and should – be removed from Ministerial, and thus Parliamentary, control. Should they be hived off to the private sector as advocated by Howell? Should they be hived off within the public sector to what Sharp had termed 'semi-independent agencies' and Fulton 'autonomous public boards'? The transformation of the Post Office into a public corporation in October 1969 provided a precedent here. Alternatively, should they be hived off to 'visibly distinct' organisations within the parent department, after the fashion of the Board of Inland Revenue within the Treasury? By the 1970 election, the latter had become the preferred choice of the CSD's Machinery of Government division and consequently formed the basis of its advice to Heath.[176]

No conclusive agreement, however, was reached even within the CSD until the Autumn of 1971. Then, coincidentally with the abandonment of unified grading and the 'moment of truth' in relation to personnel management, the terminology was at least standardised and a new term, 'departmental agency', coined. 'Hiving off' was defined as:

> a process whereby a current activity for which Ministers are fully answerable to Parliament, carried out at their direction by civil servants, financed directly from Votes, within the departmental framework, is *either* transferred to an autonomous public body not staffed by civil servants, and not financed directly from Votes, for whose actions Ministers are not fully answerable to Parliament *or* is removed from the public sector altogether.

It covered, therefore, the proposals both of the PSRU and of Sharp and Fulton. By contrast, a 'departmental agency' was:

> an organisational entity, under its own executive head, either part of a government department or a corporate body within the departmental

framework, acting at the direction of a Minister who is answerable to Parliament for its activities, and staffed by civil servants ... but distinguished from the conventional pattern of departmental organisation by having its own executive head, and accounting officer, and by a large degree of freedom in staff management.[177]

This reflected the CSD's ideal. Why had this terminological clarification taken so long and what, if any, impact did it have on policy?

Delay was the result of continuing conflict between four sets of protagonists. Within the Civil Service, there was Armstrong and the CSD's Machinery of Government Division, whose overriding aim was to enhance efficiency through 'accountable management'. Increasingly they favoured the creation, where appropriate, of departmental agencies. Other officials within the CSD and, more particularly, those within the Treasury, remained wedded to the *status quo*. They feared the loss of traditional financial and manpower controls over public expenditure as well as other conventions, such as the primacy of Permanent Secretaries within departments. Outside the Service, politicians of both Parties sought to reduce the size and – in the Conservatives' case – the role of the Service. There was also the Business Team which – like Fulton's Management Consultant Group – sought to inject both outsiders and modern management techniques into government.

The evolving views of each will be examined in turn but there were two generic concerns: political accountability and 'accountability for performance'. The former reflected the need not only for hived-off bodies to remain responsive to political direction but also for Ministers to remain answerable to Parliament. In the late 1960s there was a growing public and Parliamentary demand for control over the Executive, as exemplified by the demand for an ombudsman and the strengthening of Select Committees. Hiving off, as the disbandment of non-Ministerial agencies in the 1850s testified, was its exact antithesis (see Chapters 10.2 and 1.4.1 respectively). In relation to the accountability, even Fulton had acknowledged that accountable management could only be introduced where 'measures of achievement can be established in quantitative or financial terms, and individuals held responsible for output and costs'.[178] Given the belated introduction of PAR and of JARs, such measures typically did not exist in the early 1970s and thus the scope for increased managerial flexibility (on which increased efficiency depended) was limited. Flexibility was also threatened on another front: the staff associations. In principle, they favoured accountable management because of the improved job satisfaction and standards of public service it promised. In practice, however, they were distinctly wary – at a time of rising unemployment and militancy – of any deterioration in pay or working conditions that withdrawal from national pay agreements or loss of Civil Service status might entail.

The contest over hiving off was most fierce within the Civil Service. The first phase preceded the 1970 election. Armstrong had responded positively to Fulton's recommendation that there should be an inquiry into the 'delegation of responsibility to autonomous public boards' and suggested it should cover three types of government activity. These were the commercial, where (as with the Royal Mint or the Forestry Commission) performance could be measured by profit; the quasi-commercial (such as education and housing) which required large capital expenditure, planning beyond the term of one government and a considerable measure of management expertise; and 'large administrative' tasks (such as the payment of social security benefits) which had long been regarded as purely managerial. Such an inquiry, he suggested, could result in a 'drastic' change in the size and character of the Service and bring it closer to current Swedish practice or Howell's hopes in *The New Style of Government*.[179]

Following resistance from Permanent Secretaries on the Fulton Steering Committee, however, these plans had had to be modified. Issues of principle were remitted to the Organisation Subcommittee, whilst detailed planning for commercial activities (where the prospects for hiving off were greatest) was entrusted to a Hiving Off Steering Group, chaired by the Treasury (where enthusiasm was least). Progress was thus stalled, hence the post-election brief to Heath that there was 'no easy solution to the problems of government through hiving off'. However, it was noted – as was to be repeated in *Reorganisation of Central Government* – that 'the application of accountable management to some blocks of work' might relieve administrative and Ministerial overload in the new 'super' ministries.[180]

Such conservatism was principally justified by the unresolved problem of Parliamentary accountability. In a placatory circular to Permanent Secretaries in August 1969, however, Armstrong also acknowledged other impediments, including potential rigidities in relation to staff pay and conditions. In addition, he acknowledged the danger of increased inefficiency (rather than efficiency) were services to become fragmented, staff no longer interchangeable, and charges levied by one agency or department on services for another.[181] Another acknowledged impediment was the shortage of Parliamentary time. The initial intention had been to introduce a general enabling bill; but each decrease in accountability, so it was later argued, had to be justified individually to Parliament. This would inevitably confound the legislative timetable.

Were such objections genuine? Undoubtedly they provided a cover for much deep-seated resistance to reform. Semantic games, for example, were played throughout Whitehall over the term 'accountability' – with accountable management, because of the potential loss of Parliamentary control, being branded as 'newspeak for non-accountable management'. The Treasury also typically used the Hiving Off Steering Group to strengthen, rather than relax, its financial control over other organisations. In addition, there were 'highly emotional' reactions to each suggestion that a block of work should be severed from its parent department.[182] Most importantly, however, it soon became apparent that the CSD was simply using the threat of hiving off to beat departments into acceptance of Fulton's lesser evil of accountable management. This was implicit in Armstrong's circular to Permanent Secretaries. As he explained, he did not expect hiving-off to provide a specially easy route to achieve the benefits in terms of more efficient resource use and improved management which accountable management is intended to confer. Accountable management ... in the long run will ... inform the public service at large, whereas hiving-off is necessarily limited in its scope by our political and constitutional arrangements.

Such ingenuousness was counterproductive in that it bred cynicism and prepared the way for a further downgrading of accountable management into Fulton's even lesser evil of 'management by objective' (which enabled departments to evade all restructuring).[183]

The second phase of in-fighting lasted from the 1970 election to 1 February 1971, when Armstrong chaired a major strategy meeting within the CSD. 'Emotional protests' throughout Whitehall continued, as did Treasury caution. The CSD was also buffeted by Howell's demand for privatisation and the Business Team's interest in entrepreneurial management. The weight of pre-election thinking and investigatory committees initially countered such challenges; but the *ad hoc* nature of policy nevertheless began to concern CSD officials. Accordingly in November 1970 the first draft was composed of the paper which, a year later, was to standardise terminology. Simultaneously, two substantial memoranda (on common services and hiving off) were also drafted, questioning the extent of potential efficiency gains. First, there was the issue of charging for common services, deemed essential to 'motivate people towards economy'. Would not the processing of transaction costs waste resources? Moreover, to what extent should 'autonomous' agencies be free to supply and receive services from the private sector? Secondly, there was the question of staffing rigidities. Would not common standards of pay, grading and promotion have to be maintained were, to win NSS support, hived-off staff either to remain Civil Servants or to be guaranteed either no worsening of their conditions or 'a return ticket' to the Service? If so, would this not hobble entrepreneurial management? Significantly for the future, it was also concluded that each accountable unit should have its own contract making explicit both its objectives and its degree of freedom in both staffing and finance.[184]

The third, and most creative, phase lasted from March to December 1971. It was conterminous with the review of departmental functions ordered by Heath (which, as has been seen, was intended to culminate in a second white paper) and with the Business Team's promotion of common service agencies (including the establishment in May 1971 of the Procurement Executive). The ingrained resistance to change, of which the *Black Book* had warned, was transparent. Throughout the departmental review, for example, neither officials nor Ministers identified any significant functions as either redundant or ripe for privatisation; the NSS simultaneously voiced its disenchantment with the 'continuous change' which was undermining its members' morale; and the Treasury marshalled its reconvened Steering Group to defend, in particular, the role of Permanent Secretaries as departmental accounting officers (through whom financial control might be exercised).[185] In vain Armstrong protested that the enlargement of government made institutional modernisation imperative. 'Nominal and real responsibility' had to coincide because, as he pointedly remarked:

> we all <u>know</u> that in practice a Permanent Secretary, especially in a large department . . . cannot and does not in practice 'control' the details of the management of expenditure; while we go on pretending that he does, real responsibilities are blurred and concealed – and may not be properly provided for.[186]

Accordingly CSD officials decided in July to be more proactive. Despite the continuing support of Ministers and the Business Team for hiving off in its purest form, they dropped it as their prime objective and instead developed (despite earlier reservations) a 'philosophy' and a 'model' of a departmental agency. It was this which informed their final memorandum on 'the development of government organisation', which was collectively approved by Permanent Secretaries and then by the Cabinet in December 1971. A clear distinction, as has been seen, was drawn within this memorandum between hived-off agencies (which were not staffed by civil servants) and departmental agencies (which were). The activities to be transferred to the former were strictly limited. They were those which

> are, or can be made, commercial to such a degree that the organisation could be wholly or largely financially self-supporting and its level and quality of output determined by the price mechanism . . . There should be little or no policy-making component and little or no significant discretionary authority vested directly in the body concerned which could affect the liberty or economic activity of the citizen except in a minimal way.[187]

All other activities could be transferred only to departmental agencies.

However, agreement on terminology – even at Cabinet level – did not equate to agreement on policy. Conflict continued both within and outside the CSD throughout 1972. Within, departmental agencies were opposed by those with day-to-day responsibility for management and pay, who wished to retain traditional controls over other departments. They were also critical of MG officials' proselytism. 'Permanent Secretaries are jealous of their responsibility for organising their own departments', they complained, 'and if they feel the CSD is trying to bounce them, they will put up the shutters'.[188] The shutters closed anyway, as evidenced by the limited response to Armstrong's letter in January 1972 encouraging change and the continuing opposition of Permanent Secretaries at their October Sunningdale. 'The underlying principles of personal accountability', they protested, 'clearly owed much to the business environment' and it would be a mistake to draw too facile a comparison with the private sector. Bogus performance indicators could lead to excessive costs and, more generally, it would be regrettable if the cultivation of business techniques led civil servants to adopt some of the more abrasive business attitudes.[189]

Such a reservation deeply frustrated those in the CSD who wanted hard decisions in selected areas where departmental agencies were patently appropriate; and this frustration intensified when delay led to a renewed interest in 'management by objectives' (with its gradual, often painfully gradual, development of managerial responsibility). Just as improved personnel management had first been advanced in 1971 as an alternative to unified grading and then been greatly modified itself, so it was with departmental agencies as an alternative to hiving off. The 'moment of truth' for neither was particularly glorious.

The failure to develop a consistent policy was in no small way the fault of Ministers, for whom the pre-eminent motivation for hiving off became the capping of Civil Service numbers in order to assuage backbench pressure. This had, for example, particularly aroused Harold Wilson's interest – although, for ideological reasons, privatisation was out of bounds even when (as in the case of the state-owned public houses) it was entirely logical. Moreover, after June 1970 Jellicoe made it his mission to establish a 'plimsoll line' of 500,000 non-industrial civil servants, which led him to work in tandem – if not precisely in unison – with Howell, with his ideological commitment to privatisation. Both were constrained to some extent by the latent tensions within the Conservative Party manifesto. Jellicoe had to be reminded of the commitment to labour-intensive reforms (such as VAT), just as Howell was reacquainted with Parliamentary fears of an overpowerful Executive – which duly diverted him into consideration of how Parliament might become an 'intelligent critic' of government, encouraging rather than inhibiting efficient management.[190] Nevertheless, continuing pressure from both led hiving off to be precipitately pursued in areas which were not entirely appropriate and where there were no adequate performance measures (as demanded by Fulton). Hiving off, it was finally agreed in November 1971, should only be pursued where 'it appeared right, rather than merely expedient in order to reduce numbers'.[191] In the meantime, however, officials had critically been denied Ministerial help in both the formulation and implementation of policy.

The final set of protagonists was the Business Team. Initially they strongly advocated privatisation and, where services had to be government-provided, an injection of entrepreneurial leadership (which they expected to provide themselves).[192] In July 1971 they broadly welcomed the concept of departmental agencies although they remained unconvinced that such agencies were the only 'practicable alternative' to privatisation. Meyjes had been convinced, however, by the time of his retirement in September 1972. Hiving off, he conceded, provided a 'much more limited solution to the overall organisational problem than was first thought' and 'super' ministries had 'seriously aggravated' the 'dangerously' low level of managerial efficiency throughout the Service. Accordingly, the only way forward was an increased number of departmental agencies, in which chief executives enjoyed untrammelled managerial responsibility and Parliamentary accountability. These chief executives, he continued, should also act as a team, meeting regularly on a policy committee chaired by the Permanent Secretary – who, in turn, should accept a diminution of his control over operational work. Was Meyjes' vision viable? One of his former colleagues, Derek Rayner, in his own post-retirement letter, thought not. The tasks of, and the constraints on, government departments were far greater than any experienced by a private company and many 'real difficulties' remained unresolved.

Rayner's views were the more persuasive because, having been the businessman selected before and after the 1970 election to examine procurement policy, he had become in May 1971 head of the Procurement Executive (which his earlier report had advocated).[193] This was one of two departmental agencies established under Heath on the advice of the Business Team, the other being the Property Services Agency (PSA) established in May 1972, with Sir John Cuckney (the financier and former chairman of the Mersey Docks and Harbour Board) as its first chief executive.[194] How well did these new agencies do? The Procurement Executive achieved many of its objectives. It integrated a large number of previously independent procurement bodies both inside and outside the MOD. It encouraged, as Fulton had recommended, individual responsibility and specialism. Moreover Rayner expressed himself well-satisfied by the modernisation of routine procedures (such as the speeding-up of cash flow for contractors, albeit at the cost of £45m to the defence budget). However, its structure was extremely complex. Beneath the Chief Executive there were four controllers (of sea, land and air weapons, and of guided weapons and electronic systems) who were also accounting officers. In addition there were four others (for policy, finance, personnel and sales) who were not. They also reported to the Secretary (as the Chief Executive's principal adviser) rather than to the Chief Executive himself. In consequence, there was no blending of specialists and generalists into a 'unified hierarchy', as Fulton had sought. On the contrary,'a sharper distinction' between policy work and management was trailed as one of the Executive's major attractions (because it enabled 'generalists' to be drawn back into the MOD). In addition, traditional 'political' constraints remained (such as the embargo on the common business practice of 'preferred suppliers' whose reliability was guaranteed), as did problems long-associated with technological advance. 'I should be less than frank', Rayner admitted in his resignation letter, 'if I held out any prospect that . . . we shall be able to solve a problem which no-one in any country has yet succeeded in solving – the accurate estimating of the future cost of equipments on which little actual work has been done.'[195] Thus the establishment of a departmental agency did not, at a stroke, provide a universal panacea.

Given its belated establishment, December 1972 is too early a date by which to adjudge the managerial efficiency of the PSA – although it was significantly to gain notoriety as the source of all the maladministration cited in Leslie Chapman's book, *Your Disobedient Servant*, which so incensed the public (and particularly

Mrs Thatcher) in the late 1970s. In the short term, however, its creation did significantly heighten interdepartmental tension. The core issues were the degree to which 'common services' should be responsive to, or used to control, departmental demands and whether, to encourage genuine managerial autonomy, the cost of such services should be charged directly to departmental budgets.[196] The CSD and the Business Team argued that they should; but they were opposed by the Treasury and the DoE, which maintained that such transactions would be artificial (because there was no effective choice) and costly (because of increased bureaucracy). Armstrong's final ruling was that there should be 'a presumption in favour of payment', although he left sufficient caveats to accommodate old habits. There was also an ongoing political battle over the respective powers of the new Chief Executive and his Permanent Secretary. In direct opposition to Meyjes, Peter Walker (as Secretary of State for the Environment) insisted that the PSA could not be as autonomous as the Procurement Executive on such issues as the career planning of senior staff.[197] This raised real questions about managerial freedom. As with PAR, the Minister and Permanent Secretary of the best run 'super' ministry were seeking to neutralise a reform deemed indispensable for both its own efficiency and that of government as a whole.

There was one further major initiative, conceived neither by the Business Team nor the CSD: the creation in 1972 of an Employment Service and a Training Services Agency. Such bodies had featured in the Business Team's pre-election planning for a National Manpower Commission, but their actual creation was the achievement of officials within the Department of Employment. The Employment Service Agency aroused particular controversy. In the long term, it may have promised a better public service and the more efficient use of national manpower. In the short term, however, it represented for the Treasury a huge increase in public expenditure given that employment exchanges (with their 'dole' image) were to be transformed into professional and market-orientated Jobcentres. Moreover it threatened joined-up government. Job placement, for example, would be separated from the payment of social security benefits and thus from the associated checks for fraud. Did this amount to a cost-effective use of aggregate resources? Most seriously, Department of Employment officials also continued to flirt with the 'genuine' hiving off of these agencies to an autonomous public body (the Manpower Services Commission or MSC, on which the TUC, CBI and the educational establishment would be represented). This, to Ministers' delight, might remove 19,000 officials from the manpower count; but, to backbenchers' and the Treasury's dismay, it would also remove some highly sensitive discretionary powers and some £76 million of public expenditure from Parliamentary control. The MSC was eventually established in January 1974 and later assumed control of both agencies, thereby providing a wholly new justification for hiving off: the involvement of representative bodies in the provision of government services in order to make them less remote from, and thus more responsive to, public need.[198]

Given the positive response of staff in both the Procurement Executive and the Department of Employment to increased managerial autonomy, did so limited an experiment in hiving off represent yet another 'lost opportunity'? By May 1971 many CSD officials were indeed becoming frustrated. 'We need to consider', bemoaned one,

> why we have made so little progress on hiving off and accountable management when these are policies approved in principle by both the last Labour administration and perhaps even more by the present Conservative administration ... Of course it's all very difficult. But it remains a sad reflection on our efforts that after all this time our only firm decision is to sell the state pubs.[199]

They did not bear the guilt alone. Politically, they were denied the effective leadership to neutralise the vested interests which any radical reform must necessarily excite. Constitutionally, despite Fabian assumptions, central departments were also denied the power to impose their will on the rest of the Service. Those awaiting reform could only be persuaded, not ordered, to accept it. However, on their own admission, they lacked the requisite hard-edged administrative skills. Without prior management experience, they remained dependent for operational knowledge on – and thus at the mercy of – those most likely to resist reform. Moreover, as with unified grading, reform was allowed to become unnecessarily over-complicated and thus fatally compromised.

5.4 Conclusion

The years between 1968 and 1972 were not the desert of administrative reform as in collective memory, but rather ones of exceptional fecundity. A wide range of ideas continued to be aired within both major Parties, as they were within the Service itself where the post-Plowden reform programme was being carried forward by a specialist department (the CSD) under a new, powerful, and initially committed Head of the Civil Service. Major reforms resulted. As Fulton had recommended, the Administrative Class was abolished and an open Senior Policy and Management Group established. Personnel management and training started to be transformed and a new emphasis placed on managerial expertise (not least through the embedding of individual businessmen and management consultants within departments). Apart from the CSD itself, there was also the creation of 'super' ministries, the CPRS and, perhaps most significantly of all, new departmental – or executive – agencies. In addition, PAR was also introduced to enhance efficiency and economy. Why then does so negative a collective memory persist? One explanation is the transient nature of many of the reforms. The 'super' ministries, for example, started to disintegrate almost immediately. PAR was formally disbanded in 1979, the CSD itself in 1981 and the CPRS in 1983. More potent is the determination of the original modernisers, in order to preserve their own reputations, to distance themselves from such 'failures' – despite each having earlier warned that, as past experience had confirmed, each innovation would need at least 20 years fully to mature.[200] Herein lay the origin of the myth of a bureaucratic conspiracy.

As with most persistent myths, it contained an element of the truth. Unquestionably there was considerable atavism throughout the Service, particularly at levels (such as Establishment Officer and even Permanent Secretary) where active support for reform was most needed. Such atavism frustrated modernisers within as much as those outside the Service. Were not, however, the 'internal' modernisers themselves frequently guilty of resisting 'external' reforms? This again is unquestionably true, but usually it was because – as with the CSD's Machinery of Government Review – they had their own well-developed concept of reform. By comparison external programmes were too often (to coin a phrase) 'amateurish'. They demonstrated little understanding of how government actually worked and overlooked, in particular, the constitutional constraints – such as the federal nature of government (which meant that neither the Prime Minister nor central departments could unilaterally impose their will) and Parliamentary accountability (which meant that private sector management techniques were often inappropriate). Such constraints had either to be fully respected, as they were – arguably to a fault – by modernisers within the Service, or openly challenged from outside. They were not.

The fundamental cause of the relative failure of both the Fulton Report and the *Black Book*, therefore, was not bureaucratic conspiracy. Neither was it contingency nor management failure (of which there were both many). Rather these blueprints failed because of their own shortcomings. Moreover, they lacked essential political support. Representing only a minority view within each Party, their authors enjoyed the unreserved support of neither the Cabinet nor successive Prime Ministers. Despite the frequent congruence of their recommendations, their political purpose was also diametrically opposed. Fulton, for example, sought to increase the efficiency within 'big' government whilst Howell strove to contract government.[201] This inevitably eroded their aggregate impact. In the meantime, the electorate – and thus majority opinion in both main Parties – swung, somewhat dishonestly, between calls for increased state intervention and a capped Civil Service. This presented the Service with a further dilemma. To justify its current (let alone an extended) range of responsibilities, it had to demonstrate its superiority over the market. Could politicians respond more sensitively to changing demand and the Civil Service deliver services more efficiently? PAR provided the test case and, both politically and administratively, it failed.

In both deeds and words, therefore, the years between 1968 and 1972 anticipated most of the reforms that were to change the nature of the Service over the succeeding decades. To this extent at least they represented modernisation's moment. They also marked two historic watersheds. The first was international. Fulton's critique and the halting nature of reform thereafter so tarnished the Service's reputation that, even in relation to those countries which adhered to the 'Westminster model', the administrative lead was taken by others. The second concerned the dynamics of reform. The 'disappointment' of modernisation's highest hopes made plain that, to succeed, reform could no longer be self-generated (as presumed particularly in the 1940s) but required sustained political commitment (preferably from the Prime Minister). During the rest of the 1970s interest in administrative reform waned whilst, to the detriment of 'big' government, postwar consensus shattered. Then, following this period of gestation, political circumstances were ripe for reform with a vengeance.

6
THE CRISIS OF CONSENSUS, 1973–9

6.1 Introduction

By December 1972, modernisation's moment was over. Administratively, William Armstrong had lost interest and so the internal post-Plowden reform programme lost momentum. Politically, Howell had been transferred to the Northern Ireland Office and Heath's interest in administrative reform had equally waned. The House of Commons' Expenditure Committee sought to keep modernisation alive with an inquiry into the Civil Service (the English Committee) between 1976 and 1978; but, as Prime Minister, James Callaghan showed as little sustained interest in reform as had Wilson.[1]

Other issues took precedence, particularly the rising power of trade unions and the declining economy. Trade unions came to be perceived as all-powerful as a result of their emasculation of the Industrial Relations Act and the success of the 1972 miners' strike. There followed, in anticipation of a second miners' strike, the three-day week between January and March 1974; the election of March 1974 on the issue of 'who governs Britain?', which the Conservatives unexpectedly lost; and finally, following the breakdown of the 'Social Contract' between the Labour Government and the TUC, the 'winter of discontent' which contributed to Labour's electoral defeat in May 1979. So great indeed was the perceived threat of the unions that the Conservatives mounted in the late 1970s an inquiry into 'the authority of government'. Based on the prediction, advanced by many leading political scientists, that liberal democracies were 'likely to pass away in the lifetime of adults now alive', it did little to lift the gloom. No strengthening of civil contingency planning, it conceded, could defeat determined union action. Britain was becoming ungovernable. 'In the last analysis', it concluded fatalistically, 'the authority of government in a civilised country rests on a thin shell of belief which lawyers call "legitimacy" and political scientists call "consent" but which in practice includes quite an element of bluff'.[2]

Similar pessimism pervaded analyses of the economy and appeared fully justified when the Labour Government had to seek a $3.9 billion loan from the IMF in late 1976. The immediate need was to halt a collapse in the value of sterling. The more fundamental one was to halt the perceived collapse of the economy.

The quadrupling of oil prices in 1973 had provided a shock to all Western economies but, for long-diagnosed if unresolved reasons, the United Kingdom was most seriously affected. In 1975 inflation had risen to the unprecedented level of 27 per cent and unemployment had peaked at over 1.5 million. Such 'stagflation', according to Keynesian theory, was impossible and so the fundamental economic assumptions underpinning policy had also to be revised. Such a revision was initially attempted in the budget of April 1975 (which rejected the use of contra-cyclical expenditure to reduce unemployment) and by Callaghan's speech to the 1976 Labour Party Conference (which argued 'in all candour' that it was not possible to spend one's way out of a recession). However, it was the major public expenditure cuts – demanded by the IMF and agreed after some nine full Cabinet and a further seventeen ministerial meetings in November and December 1976 – that provided the overt proof of a crisis in postwar consensus. The joint memory of interwar depression and the planned wartime economy was fading. No longer was Beveridge's assertion automatically accepted that social expenditure was a necessary precondition, rather than an impediment, to economic growth. Nor was Keynes' assumption that state intervention (or at least the mixed economy) was more efficient than the market. Monetarist theory was gaining support outside government as was a renewed emphasis on the creation, as opposed to the distribution, of wealth.

Such tensions presented the Civil Service with a major challenge. As one of the most unionised sectors of the workforce, it could not remain immune to industrial militancy. This had serious consequences for the delivery of services. As the provider of policy advice, it had also helped to shape – and in turn been shaped by – the very consensus which was now under attack. How could, and should, it react? This would have been a difficult question to resolve in the most favourable circumstances; but, given the lack of political stability and the growing hostility to 'big' government, circumstances were far from favourable. The strategic coherence, for which modernisers had striven between 1970 and 1972, was a chimera and government was no longer seen as the potential solution to Britain's problems but their principal cause.

Political stability was particularly fractured in March 1974. No Party emerged from the election with an overall majority and at the succeeding October election, the Labour Government gained an overall majority of only 3. This left it vulnerable in Parliament to backbench revolts – as was to be demonstrated in March 1976 when a major programme of expenditure cuts was defeated and had to be salvaged by an immediate vote of confidence. As the result of adverse by-elections, even this nominal majority had evaporated in 1976 and the Government's majority was thereafter tenuously dependent on agreements with the Liberal Party. This instability was intensified by Labour's lack of internal unity. Under Wilson, No.10 was notorious for discord and for near paralysis prior to his resignation in March 1976. More fundamentally, both the Wilson and the Callaghan Governments were embarrassed by the decisions taken by the Party, whilst in opposition, to strengthen the policy-making powers of the National Executive

Committee and to endorse an alternative economic strategy (which, in the words of *Labour's Programme* in 1973, sought to achieve 'a fundamental and irreversible shift in the balance of power and wealth in favour of working people'). Such 'democratisation' created, as was intended, a tension between Cabinet Ministers' individual responsibility to the Party and their collective responsibility to the Government. This directly led to the unprecedented decision to suspend collective responsibility prior to the referendum on continuing membership of the EEC in March 1975 and to regular altercations thereafter between Tony Benn and his colleagues. For officials, such dual loyalty was unsettling because it confused lines of responsibility. Moreover, as will be seen in Chapter 10.4, their unease was deepened by constitutional uncertainties emanating from both accession to the EEC and by the spectre of Scottish and Welsh devolution (which was not allayed until the adverse referenda results of March 1979).[3]

The Service was threatened even more seriously by the growing hostility at all levels of society. The common impression of senior officials as elitist, amateurish and conservative was reinforced by the publication of first-hand accounts of the first Wilson governments in Marcia Williams' *Inside No.10* (1972) and, most notoriously, in the Crossman diaries (1975–7). Such accounts were seen to provide empirical backing for the theories of the 'public choice' political scientists in the USA.[4] Popularised in Britain by the Institute of Economic Affairs (IEA), their principal premise was that officials, if only unconsciously, sought to expand government to improve not the public good but rather their own careers and salaries. Such theories dovetailed well with the principal premises of monetarism, (also promoted in Britain by the IEA) that 'big government' was a principal cause of both inflation and industry's declining profitability. The Public Sector Borrowing Requirement had constantly to be increased to cover the gap between government expenditure and income; and, equally constantly, the manpower and the money required for private investment, and thus economic growth, was 'crowded out' by the needs of the public sector.

Such elite convictions paved the way for more popular attacks on big government in general and the Civil Service in particular. The 'crowding out' thesis, for example, was quickly taken up by small employers, resentful that they could no longer match the level of public sector pensions and other 'good' employment practices (introduced, ironically, in response to earlier modernisation campaigns and, particularly, Fulton). It was further popularised in 1976 by the press serialisation of *Britain's Economic Problem: too few producers* by Robert Bacon and Walter Eltis. Moreover, the press was not reticent in using such issues as inflation-proofed pensions and job security in the public sector to foment resentment amongst taxpayers, who enjoyed neither; and such resentment was augmented by its sensationalist coverage in May 1978 of the allegations of bureaucratic inefficiency in Leslie Chapman's *Your Disobedient Servant*. Consequently, the increasing militancy of public sector workers, culminating in the 'winter of discontent', merely provided a final nail in the coffin. The Civil Service as a whole – not just as an elite provider of policy advice – had become the common target for political, academic and popular contempt.[5]

Could this crisis have been, as argued at the time and in retrospect, ridden out under Callaghan's determined leadership?[6] The Labour Party became more disciplined, a major strike by firefighters was defeated in January 1978 and over half the IMF loan had been repaid by October 1978. Inflation fell, as did unemployment. The postwar consensus, it seemed, was not yet dead. 'Normality' could be restored. A reality check, however, was provided by the rejection of incomes policy by the Labour Party conference in October 1978 and the subsequent 'winter of discontent'. As Callaghan was later famously to remark, there was 'once every thirty years a sea-change in politics'.[7] Such a sea-change had occurred – and it did not favour the postwar consensus.

For its part, could the Civil Service have ridden out the storm unscathed? To do so, it required strong political and administrative leadership; but it enjoyed neither. As the Minister directly responsible for the Civil Service, Lord Jellicoe had to resign on personal grounds in June 1973.[8] He was succeeded by Lord Windlesham and then, under Labour, by Ted Short (in 1974), Lord Shepherd (from October 1974 to September 1976) and finally Lord Peart. Only Short and Peart were seasoned politicians; and the former was preoccupied by his other duties as Lord President whilst the latter, by common consent, was past his peak by 1976. Administratively, Armstrong was diplomatically permitted to retire as Head of the Civil Service in June 1974 and complete a long-planned move to the Midland Bank. His replacement was Sir Douglas Allen, who had earlier succeeded him as the Treasury's Permanent Secretary.[9] A non-Oxbridge economics and statistics graduate, with original views fearlessly expressed, he appeared the ideal Fulton appointee. However, he had little personal interest in management (which, he complained, appeared to be conducted in 'mid-Atlantic Cherokee') and was unable to forge the close partnership with senior colleagues at the centre, which Armstrong considered the key to good government.[10] Allen's own successor in January 1978 was Ian Bancroft who, having masterminded the Treasury's reorganisation in 1962 and the creation of the DoE in 1971, was a proven manager. In addition, he had an intimate knowledge, and the trust, of the NSS. From the start, however, there were doubts about his 'toughness' and these were intensified when he soon became seriously ill with cancer.[11]

The crisis of consensus outside Whitehall was thus matched by a crisis of authority within. How successfully could the Service parry the widespread attacks upon it and preserve the best of the old? And between 1973 and 1979 what significant innovations – if any – were pioneered? These two questions will be examined in turn.

6.2 Preserving the old

The crisis of consensus, and the consequent confusion of values, placed a premium within the Service on damage limitation. This resulted in the regular analysis of change at the highest level and an active defence of the levels of manpower and pay deemed necessary to ensure efficient government. In addition, earlier reforms were propelled forward by their remaining momentum.

6.2.1 Addressing change

The initial pressure for change came from within, not outside, the Service. The one-day strike in February 1973 alerted Ministers and senior management alike to the depths of rank-and-file discontent, which had the power not only temporarily to halt government but permanently to block specific policies.[12] A substantial pay award was rapidly granted and a 'Wider Issues' review launched to examine the 'workaday problems of the middle and lower grades'. The pay award, because it was sanctioned under the 'anomaly' regulations of the existing incomes policy, fuelled the later belief that the Civil Service had received special treatment. The Wider Issues review in its final report (*Civil Servants and Change*) of January 1975 recommended a wide range of pragmatic improvements such as the upgrading of accommodation, the acceleration of personnel management reform and enhanced communication (through the 'fullest and most effective use of Whitleyism'). Wilson was impressed and duly affirmed in Parliament that:

> a stable, loyal and efficient Civil Service is part of the fabric of an ordered society. Civil servants must be fairly treated, and there should be no discrimination against the public service as compared to other sectors.

He then issued two personal minutes, in June 1974 and February 1975, reminding senior colleagues that civil servants should be 'treated as reasonably as other employees, not forced to serve as examples which we hope other employers will follow'. They should also be collectively defended when 'unjustifiably attacked for doing the job that we or Parliament have required'.[13]

Such homilies, however, were soon forgotten. When external criticism started to escalate, Wilson met with CSD Ministers and Allen in January 1976. Albeit armed with positive suggestions from normally hostile sources within No.10, his contribution was 'just a blank boredom'; and no coordinated ministerial defence of the Service ever materialised.[14] This *volte face* was in part due to the deteriorating economic situation. In August 1975, the Cabinet had finally agreed to plan major public expenditure cuts (amounting eventually to £3.6 billion). Part of the planning process was 'fundamental review of the growth of bureaucracy'; but the clear conclusion of the relevant Committee, when it reported in December, was that there could be no contraction without a parallel reduction in either the 'work to be done' or standards. Nevertheless, at Cabinet on 11 December when the details of the economy package were finalised, this is precisely what was agreed. To balance the books, and to forestall ministerial resignations, Wilson resorted to the time-honoured expedient of recommending a cut in Civil Service costs (amounting to £140 million by 1978/9) without any matching reductions in policy or standards. The Cabinet reportedly heaved 'a deep collective sigh of relief' and concurred.[15]

Such a *volte face* disillusioned senior officials with not just the Labour Government but also the state of the country as a whole. Their disillusion was most overtly expressed at the annual conferences of Permanent Secretaries at Sunningdale and was placed in context by a speech by Allen in October 1975. Even on his own admission, it was somewhat apocalyptic.[16] There was, he argued, a 'profound lack' of 'national consensus' or 'common purpose' due to unrealistic and thus frustrated public expectations. No national institution, therefore, could any longer be truly representative; and this was particularly damaging for the Service because officials 'at all levels could increasingly come to feel that they were working either to no purpose or at cross-purposes, leading to acute frustration or complete cynicism'. Already its traditional character as both a national institution and a permanent career service was threatened. Greater loyalty was being shown, especially by junior staff, to sectional or regional interests. The demand for more political advisers or appointees was also growing because the traditional 'political neutrality' of officials was being equated to 'political insensitivity or even opposition' to government policy. How, Allen questioned, should the Service react? Should officials speak out and open a 'real debate' in order to 'get unreal expectations out of our system'? This would certainly secure 'more general understanding of the constraints within which governments have to operate'. However would it not also 'highlight the impracticalities (in the eyes of Civil Servants) of some Party manifestos' and thus, by breaching the conventions of anonymity and political 'neutrality', undermine the very character of the Service they hoped to preserve?

The collective response to Allen's speech was more measured than earlier Sunningdale debates, in which Scottish and Welsh nationalism had been identified as prime examples of the 'break-down of respect for the national parliament . . . and of an increase in divisiveness and self-seeking'.[17] Alarmist pictures had been drawn of future mass civil disobedience (on the pattern of the 1974 Ulster strike, which had brought down the power-sharing executive) and even of extremists blowing up oil and water pipelines. By 1976, however, the debate had again become febrile. The multiple levels of supranational, national, regional and local government were seen to reflect and reinforce public dissatisfaction which, in turn generated pressure for further change, which typically reflected not 'the real merits' of a particular proposal but rather frustration with 'the existing pattern and institutions of government'.[18] Even worse, democracy itself was threatened by 'powerful sectional interests . . . moving into seats of public authority where they can serve their interests rather than the public interest generally'. Could government in general and the Civil Service in particular buck such trends and again become 'trusted as the guardian of the national and public interest'? Little optimism was immediately expressed but then, as passions cooled, some was offered in 1977 and 1978. In his farewell address, for instance, Allen recommended greater congruence between officials and Ministers. The former, he argued, should specialise and contribute more to public debate, whilst the latter should involve themselves with management and thus gain a better understanding of the limitations of government. This theme was further developed in 1978.

What is ultimately most striking about the Sunningdale debates is not their expression of disillusion but their confounding of 'public choice' theory. This is because what they reveal is a beleaguered, rather than an all-powerful, bureaucracy and one that was only too aware of its limitations. In Allen's words, it was 'less confident . . . than at any time in the postwar period'.[19] What the debates also reveal is a significant identity of interest, as in the 1960s, between senior officials and their leading critics. Further state intervention, for example, was unanimously opposed. As Allen summarised the general tenor of the 1976 proceedings:

> what emerged was a very strong feeling of over-government in the UK; interventionism in this country had (it was felt) gone too far, and it is no longer possible for anyone to do anything without finding some bureaucrat on his back, if it is not more than one from different parts of the government machine. This was at any rate part of the reason for a great sense of disillusionment among the public with government generally, a disillusion which could not be completely ascribed simply to poor economic performance.

Government growth was also opposed on more pragmatic grounds, suspiciously similar to the 'crowding out' thesis: there was only a 'finite stock' of graduates and, should government monopolise it, the 'productive' sector would suffer. Given that senior officials were used through PESC to seek an optimum balance between public and private resources, such a concern was perhaps unsurprising – except to political scientists from the USA.

6.2.2 Manpower

As the 1975 Cabinet debate suggested, maintaining the size of the Civil Service became and remained a major preoccupation within Whitehall throughout the 1970s. This represented not just vested interest but also a genuine concern for the quality of service provision. Moreover, it did not contradict senior officials' antipathy to over-government. Over-government was perceived as an essentially political phenomenon – the response of Ministers to electoral demands for more and better services (which lay somewhat uneasily with simultaneous demands for less government). The size of the Service was thus a consequence, not the cause, of over-government. Nevertheless, it had been a target for attack since devaluation in 1967 and, as the economy declined further, so political hostility was stiffened by ideological conviction. Channelled, in particular, by Conservative backbenchers into the reports of the House of Commons' Public Accounts Committee, this generated the Parliamentary pressure to which Wilson was arguably responding when he reverted to the 'numbers game' in December 1975.

Pressure on numbers also reopened a major fissure within Whitehall. Ever since the 1968 concordat, there had been an awkward division between the Treasury (with its continuing responsibility for the overall cost of staffing) and the CSD (with its responsibility for the 'scale' of staffing).[20] With a rapidly expanding PSBR, the Treasury grew ever keener to cut public expenditure by the simple expedient of cutting numbers. The CSD opposed such crudity. Its preference, in the absence of any reduced workload, was to minimise manpower by maximising productivity. Moreover, its officials argued, attention should focus on not just numbers but also 'total' manpower costs which included 'manpower substitutes' (such as overtime and the employment of both consultants and casual staff) by which departments typically evaded central quotas.[21]

This conflict was given added edge by the fact that the Treasury, with its responsibility for Customs and Excise and the Inland Revenue, was the second largest departmental employer of manpower. It could not, therefore, be insulated – as the CSD constantly reminded – from the impact of its own policy. Some officials acknowledged the policy consequences (that, for instance, the tax system could not be so finely tuned in future). Ministers, however, were less obliging. The Financial Secretary complained of some economies in February 1975, for example, that:

> I would not apply either of the phrases 'greater efficiency' and 'good housekeeping' to this cut. There may be some scope for such savings – but most of the cut will mean giving up useful work and reducing standards of advice and support to Treasury Ministers.[22]

Such a comment revealed, at a political level at least, that the prejudice which had earlier dogged the Treasury's management of the Service was not yet dead. 'Useful work' and policy advice in other departments, so it was implied, would be undamaged by parallel cuts.

Initially, as has been seen, the Labour Government was sympathetic to the Service and agreed that its size should be determined solely by its workload.[23] This was, in part, a reaction to growing union militancy but it also reflected Wilson's tactical appreciation that the Conservatives' power to embarrass him was limited by record in office. They may have honoured the letter of their 1970 manifesto pledge to cut Civil Service numbers. The 'headline' number of staff in post had fallen from just under 702,000 to just under 700,000. So marginal a reduction, however, betrayed the spirit of the manifesto. Moreover, the figures disguised a significant increase in 'non productive' non-industrial staff (from 496,000 to 520,000) and owed more to good luck than good planning. Recruitment difficulties, especially in London, had held numbers some 18,000 below complement; and the approved estimate for staff in 1975 was in fact 735,000.[24]

For Labour, this artificial shortfall represented an unexploded time bomb and its detonation was brought ever nearer by the decision – under NSS pressure – to bring the 20,000 staff employed by the hived-off Manpower Services Commission back into the Civil Service in 1976. By late 1975, in short, the Labour Government was under potential political attack for having 'enlarged' the Civil Service by some 50,000. Such, as the CSD had warned, was the sterility and artificiality of the 'numbers game'. Nevertheless, as has been seen, it was just such a game which Wilson decided to play in December 1975 when he persuaded Cabinet to cut Civil Service costs by £140 million (or some 35,000 staff) by 1978/9. In retrospect this cut was dismissed as a mere 'balancing item' and a typical Wilson 'gimmick' to maintain Cabinet and Party unity.[25] Nevertheless, at the time it was embedded in the 1976 public expenditure white paper and thus became a firm commitment against which the credibility of both the Wilson and the succeeding Callaghan Government was judged. Consequently it consumed inordinate amounts of administrative and political time at the highest level until July 1976 when, after three heated Cabinet debates, defeat was finally acknowledged and a reduced package of £95 million (or 26,000 staff) accepted.

The essential sterility of this exercise was demonstrated by the ever-changing nature of the target. The basis of Wilson's 'back of the envelope' calculation was that, given a projected shortfall in economies of some £140 million and that the average cost of an official was £4000, a five per cent cut in Civil Service numbers was the answer.[26] By May, however, the target had risen to ten per cent for two reasons. First, the largest department (the Ministry of Defence) had to be excluded since it had already agreed to major cuts. They could not be double counted. Second, as a result of increasing unemployment and inflation, an extra 16,000 staff had had to be employed in mainly 'demand-led' services. A ten per cent cut clearly required major policy changes. Moreover, to seek such a cut for 1978/9 was becoming increasingly surreal when, to meet a deteriorating economic situation which was ultimately to lead to the appeal to the IMF, immediate cuts were being sought of a further £1 billion.[27] Albeit for very different reasons, therefore, the political relief at the abandonment of the exercise in July 1976 was as palpable as it had been at its start in December 1975.

The relief was also administrative. Treasury officials had long insisted that the reason for the cut was financial: to reduce the PSBR. It was therefore 'lunatic' to cut its own revenue-raising staff; but their own 'lunacy' was exposed by a suggested simplification of the tax system which temporarily became a *cause celebre*: the replacement of Vehicle Excise Duty (VED) by an increased tax on petrol.[28] This, so the CSD calculated, would save 3000 staff. It also had the backing of a majority of Cabinet Ministers. Nevertheless it was rejected. It would, so the Treasury countered, infringe its traditional prerogative on tax. More pragmatically, it would have encouraged the purchase of smaller cars which, reputedly, the British car industry was unable immediately to supply. Import penetration would therefore have been increased (to the detriment of the balance of payments) and the heavily subsidised British Leyland disadvantaged (to the detriment of the PSBR). Such a Cabinet defeat, of course, confirmed the earlier realism of the CSD when drafting the report of its Cost of Central Government Committee. 'Efficiency savings' of one per cent a year, it was agreed, were possible but 'the basic fact' was that, if a reduction in staff was genuinely required, a new 'tone' would have to be set 'at the top'. Ministers and Permanent Secretaries would have to make explicit that 'economy in the use of manpower and other administrative resources must play a much more significant part in the choice of policy options and the way they are put into effect. There is no easier or less painful way'.[29] Nevertheless, it was just such an 'easier and less painful way' that Ministers sought both in December 1975 and July 1976.

There were both positive and negative consequences to the £140 million cuts exercise. Positively, it was one of the means by which a potential increase in manpower (feared at one time to be 100,000 over the Labour Government's term of office) was halted. As demonstrated by Table 6.1, numbers were kept in line with the original ambitions of the exercise and well within the projections of the 1976 Public Expenditure Survey. Indeed, if artificial additions (as explained in the table) are excluded, the size of the Service in January 1979 was comparable to that in January 1975. 'The Treasury tell me that the story is a good one', Callaghan was reassured by his Private Secretary in June 1978, 'the CSD has done well'.[30]

On the negative side, industrial relations within the Service were unnecessarily damaged by uncertainty — not least in South Wales where the new DVLA at Swansea was to be responsible for VED.[31] Moreover, the administrative and political weakness of the CSD became increasingly exposed. To prevent an across-the-board percentage cut and thus 'equal misery' for all departments 'regardless of either the pressure of demand or the Government's own priorities', it requested each to draft varying proposals for a 5, 10 or 15 per cent cut in numbers (an expedient that was again to be used by Mrs Thatcher).[32] Laudable though such rationalism was, it ignored the reality that the threat of *unequal* cuts raised vital issues of relative ministerial and departmental prestige, and thereby generated much political and administrative ill-will. The CSD's own lack of analytical rigour was also exposed by its categorisation of departmental submissions on little more than their

Table 6.1 The size of the Home Civil Service, 1973–9

	a	b	c	d
	Staff in post 1 January	Non-industrial staff 1 April (estimates)	£140m cuts projection 1976	Public Expenditure Survey projection 1976
1973	692 700	509 000		
1974	694 400	574 000		
1975	712 500	526 800	739 000	
1976*	745 100	571 000	754 000	754 000
1977	746 200	573 000	754 000	773 000
1978	738 000	569 000	735 000	753 000
1979	733 200	568 000		740 000

Notes
*Figures increased by the re-inclusion of 20,000 staff of the Manpower Services Commission within the Civil Service and the 'regularisation' of many casual staff.

Figures in columns (a) and (b) are both for full-time equivalents but are not wholly compatible. Column (a) records contemporary figures for staff actually in post; the totals in column (b) are retrospective, taken from the historical series in *Civil Service Statistics, 1977* and are based on Estimates. The distinction between industrial and non-industrial officials was formally abandoned in 1971, in part to mask the rise of the latter as the former declined.

tone of language (or, in the Treasury's derogatory phrase, 'prose'); and the political weakness of the Lord Privy Seal, in relation to the Chief Secretary to the Treasury, likewise when concessions had to be solicited from colleagues. In short, as will be confirmed in Chapter 6.3.2, the joint failure of the CSD and its 'options' programme smoothed the way for a revival of Treasury control and the cruder, but more effective, instrument of cash limits. Once again, the Treasury had snatched victory from the jaws of defeat.

A final reason for the CSD's increasing disrepute is well illustrated by two rather extreme memoranda by the No.10 Policy Unit submitted to the Prime Minister in the Autumn of 1976. Fuelled perhaps by the impending economic crisis and Bacon and Eltis' version of 'crowding out', they demanded a moratorium on recruitment to, and pay increases within, the public sector. This would save, so it was argued, up to £2 billion a year and 'be welcomed by everyone outside the public sector and have excellent confidence effects'.[33] Such an assertion begged many questions. Would, for instance, everyone – including the unemployed – really have 'welcomed' such an initiative? Would not the more likely reaction have been a resort, at best, to civil disobedience? Would this, in turn, have really boosted financial confidence? Moreover, would not being singled out for an enforced pay cut have adversely affected the efficiency of those remaining within the public sector? Finally, had not a strong public sector been traditionally seen as an essential mechanism for achieving Labour's goals? The real significance of the memoranda, however, was the irrational antipathy it demonstrated towards the Service, even at the heart of government and amongst typically well-informed and politically astute policy advisers. Gone was the earlier reality that the Civil Service (as distinct from the public sector as a whole) accounted for only 3 per cent of the workforce and that its size was a function of its executive responsibilities. Gone too was an honesty about the political impediments to reform (as demonstrated by the defiance of majority Cabinet support for the abolition of VED).[34] Rather, draconian action was demanded because 'the Civil Service had failed to find even £140m in savings'.

6.2.3 Pay

Pay was an even more politically charged issue than manpower; and, given that the period opened with the first nationwide Civil Service strike and ended in the 'winter of discontent', epitomises the tensions within postwar consensus.[35] The core problem was an incompatibility between the principle of 'comparability' (enshrined in the 1955 Priestley Commission, which was designed to take Civil Service pay out of politics) and successive incomes policies (which re-politicised pay negotiations).

Priestley had recommended that pay should be based on a 'fair comparison with the current remuneration of outside staffs employed on broadly comparable work, taking account of differences in other conditions of service'; and a complex system of 'pay research' had been duly established to ensure settlements were 'fair' not just to officials but also to the wider community, be it as taxpayers (who would not be asked to fund excessive wage claims) or as the users of state services (who could be assured that the quality of services would not be jeopardised by low pay and thus under-manning).[36] However, incomes policy – be it statutory, as under the Conservatives, or voluntary, as under Labour's Social Contract – had destroyed the resulting equilibrium by overriding free collective bargaining and, more importantly, was seeking to break the vicious circle of inflationary pay awards. 'Comparability' in the Civil Service context was not inherently inflationary because it was, in essence, a 'catching up' exercise designed to match – not exceed – earlier wage increases in the private sector. Nevertheless, because it involved so many people, any award was expensive. It duly affected the PSBR. Despite being retrospective, it could also trigger further demands in both the public and private sectors. Government was expected to set an example; and it was accordingly tempted to make an example of its employees.

Incomes policy had first angered staff associations in 1968 when, for the first time, a pay award was 'staged'; but it was the Conservatives' statutory pay freeze in 1972, and above all its restrictive Stage II (at the introduction of which William Armstrong had been dubbed 'Deputy Prime Minister') which seriously provoked them.[37] Although the full research-based award for 1973 was eventually allowed in November, under an 'anomalies' ruling by the Pay Board, some ten months' salary increase was nevertheless lost. The incoming Labour Government was determined to avoid similar trouble and so it signed a new National Pay Agreement with the NSS (which, in its guise as Committee A of the National Whitley Council, was the staff associations' joint negotiating body) in December 1974. This allowed for research-based increases on an annual, rather than a biennial, basis. To assist management, it also advanced the pay date from January to April and, to appease the associations, included a one-off adjustment to compensate for the lag between the time research data were gathered and the increases paid. The trouble was that when the 1975 award was agreed in March these two adjustments effectively transformed it into a fifteen-month award and turned an annual pay increase of eighteen per cent (which was deemed reasonable) into one of 32.5 per cent (which was not). It was a decision that Government strove until the last minute to avoid but eventually honoured because the NSS warned that they were sitting on 'a powder keg of militancy'.[38] Nevertheless, it was a decision that they came bitterly to regret because, allied to Priestley and the anomaly ruling, it consolidated in the public mind the conviction that the Service was being unduly favoured.

The 1975 award became all the more anomalous because in July the Government published a white paper, *The Attack on Inflation* (Cmnd 6151) which, with the agreement of the TUC, immediately introduced a voluntary pay policy. Pay increases were limited to £6 a week for those with an annual income under £8500, and all increases – including increments – banned for those on higher salaries. It thus explicitly suspended the National Pay Agreement, on which the ink was scarcely dry, and froze – or, in real terms, reduced – the income of senior officials. As with all incomes policies, the critical question then arose of how to return to 'normality'.

In the best administrative tradition, this issue was first remitted to an official working group in July 1976 and then to an *ad hoc* committee of Cabinet Ministers (GEN 64), which eventually reported in June 1977. The options considered included the establishment of a new pay regime, the appointment of a public inquiry to supersede Priestley and the revision of the existing system. It was the latter which was recommended by the official group; and on the basis of its report, Lord Peart (who had replaced Lord Shepherd as head of the CSD the previous September) felt able to reassure the Prime Minister in January 1977 there was 'no firm evidence' that the Priestley system had 'over-indulged' the Civil Service. Indeed all the available evidence seemed to suggest 'the opposite'. Its abolition would thus not only remove a proven restraint on wage inflation but also provoke confrontation. He then added menacingly:

> There has been an enormous growth of trade union power generally and it has been demonstrated all too often that that muscle is what counts. The Civil Service trade union movement is now much more likely to adopt militant tactics and has the power, at no great cost to its members, to embarrass the government, and if need be, to stop essential activities ... A return to the comparative anarchy of the pre-Priestley regime would, in the circumstances of the 1970s, have incalculably adverse consequences for Civil Service management and the efficiency and health of central government.[39]

Such rhetoric cut little ice with the head of the No.10 Policy Unit. Nor did it convince the Treasury (which was resigned to the likelihood that research-based awards would always conflict with incomes policy and, more especially, its recently introduced cash limits); the Cabinet Secretary (who did not wish to lose the option of a 'quite different system'); or the Prime Minister's Private Secretaries (at least one of whom favoured an independent inquiry). Nevertheless Peart's letter achieved its principal purpose. With a greater knowledge of the trade union movement than his close advisers, the Prime Minister agreed that 'any different system will cause a hell of a row and may well not give better results'. Accordingly he sanctioned the appointment of the ministerial committee to make specific recommendations.

This Committee, whilst also confirming that Priestley did not unduly favour the Service, recommended certain technical and presentational improvements.[40] It fully accepted the technical integrity of the independent Pay Research Unit (PRU). Nevertheless, it maintained, the system was vulnerable to charges of bias. The PRU, for example, was responsible to a Steering Committee consisting of CSD officials and Whitley Council representatives – all of whom were potential beneficiaries of awards based on its findings. The analogue firms, with which pay comparisons were made, were also mainly large well-organised firms, rather than the medium and small ones which were currently bearing the full brunt of the recession. Moreover the translation of the crude research data into a mean 'true money rate' (averaging out differences between the analogues and incorporating other factors, such as the 'value' of inflation-proofed pensions and job security) was a subject not for PRU but for negotiation between the CSD and the NSS – and typically occurred before the start of serious negotiations, under ministerial supervision, on the actual size of the award. Finally, the conclusions of pay research could always be qualified by internal relativities (or, in other words, awards could be increased when the pay rates of those with comparable responsibilities within the Service were higher than those in parallel private sector posts). This was in fact the means by which senior scientists in the public service – to growing public concern – were able to enjoy considerably higher pay than those in the private sector. All such technical 'frailties', the Committee recommended, should be removed. They should also be seen to be removed. Hence its three major presentational recommendations: the replacement of the Steering Committee by a Management Board, of whom the chair and at least one-third of the members should be from outside the Service; the publication of an annual report containing the maximum possible amount of factual information; and an increased weighting for non-monetary benefits.

These recommendations were broadly accepted and in November 1977 formed the basis of a revised National Pay Agreement under which, within the terms of the prevailing incomes policy, a relatively uncontroversial ten per cent pay increase was awarded in the following April. The 'reactivation' of research-based pay, however, proved far from uncontroversial. It provoked a half-day strike by the Society of Civil and Public Servants (SCPS) on 8 November 1977; a mass demonstration by all unions some three weeks later; and, for the first time since 1950, a meeting of the full National Whitley Council (NWC) on 1 December. The overt reason for such provocation was the Government's failure to reintroduce research-based awards in 1978 (although, given the complexity of the research, this was privately acknowledged to be impractical). The real cause, however, was the 'duress' under which the NSS had felt itself placed during the negotiations and, above all, the fear that Stage IV of the incomes policy would make research-based awards impractical even in 1979.[41] Such suspicions, as the 'winter of discontent' was to prove, were well-founded.

For its part, the Government was provoked in two ways. First, the Institution of Professional Civil Servants (IPCS), representing scientific and professional staff, sought to remain outside pay-based research because, as was well recognised, this advantaged its members. The Government insisted, however, that pay research should cover all Civil Servants or none. Second, in the Autumn of 1977, the traditionally compliant Inland Revenue Staff Federation (IRSF) demanded special bonuses for the processing of a change in tax coding. 'This is blackmail and shows a break down in discipline ... it stinks', riposted the Prime Minister (a former official of the Federation). The Treasury was nevertheless ready to concede until the CSD intervened. 'Good for the CSD', Callaghan noted, 'I hope the Chief Secretary [to the Treasury] is ashamed'. His Principal Private Secretary agreed. 'The much maligned CSD', he minuted, 'are much tougher on this issue than the "tough" Treasury'.⁴² Tension was thus as great within Whitehall as within the staff associations. This boded ill for the future.

In the negotiation of the 1979 pay award, as anticipated, pay research proved incompatible with incomes policy. It suggested a 25 per cent increase, whilst incomes policy (and thus cash limits) permitted only five per cent. As the Prime Minister somewhat revealingly admitted: 'I think there is some lack of clarity in our policy towards the Civil Service (if we have one!)'.⁴³ The five per cent limit was treated as dismissively by the staff associations as it was by the rest of the Labour movement. During the subsequent 'winter of discontent', however, they all went their own way. None joined the public sector unions' day of protest on 22 January. Instead the two associations which had struck in 1973 (the SCPS and the CPSA) held a one-day strike on 23 February and then opted for a highly effective programme of selective action (see Chapter 8.4.2). The seven other associations did not strike until 2 April, and then only for a day. This was sufficient, however, to encourage an escalation of selective action by the SCPS and the CPSA; and with an increasing threat *inter alia* to front-line military services and to Easter travel (by air traffic controllers), as well as the proximity of a general election, a 25 per cent pay deal was finally brokered. There was to be an immediate down payment of nine per cent plus £1 (so that the Government and NSS could claim credit respectively for a 'single figure' settlement and a bonus for the low-paid). The rest was to be paid in two stages by January 1980 (earlier than the Government wished but as demanded by the NSS in order to ensure that the 1980 pay research exercise was not compromised).

This deal did not reflect the reasoned argument which both Priestley and the revised 1977 Pay Agreement had sought. Rather it was the result of 'costly disorder', resulting from the ever-increasing number of Ministers and thus departments involved.⁴⁴ This had two particularly adverse consequences. First, negotiations became enmeshed with those for other public sector workers who (like local authority manual workers and police) had been promised either full comparability awards or assured that their full award would be paid within a year. With their long tradition of comparability awards and detailed work on their current claim having been started in 1977, the associations were offended by the perceived 'discrimination' against them. The consequent sense of injustice persuaded the SCPS and CPSA executives to give their more militant members their head in January.

Second, in an eerie premonition of what was to occur under the Thatcher government, the main ministerial committee responsible for public sector pay (incited by the No.10 Policy Unit) started to renege on the letter as well as the spirit of the 1977 Pay Agreement.⁴⁵ The objectivity of the PRU and the validity of its findings, for instance, were openly questioned and the award based on its findings dismissed as 'much too generous'. Contrary to earlier ministerial statements, it was also agreed that full comparability should only be re-established over three years. As was minuted by a normally hawkish Cabinet Office official (Peter Le Cheminant) who attended the key meeting, it was doubtful whether 'Ministers fully understood the facts of the . . . situation or indeed the changes which have occurred in the outside world'. Certainly they exhibited 'a deep distrust and indeed dislike of Civil

Servants'. This distaste and Ministers' willingness to renege transmitted itself to the NSS and formal negotiations ended abruptly. 'Those who had held back', Ministers were informed, felt betrayed and the Government was accused of deliberate 'deceit in reactivating pay research in 1977'. This impasse led directly to all associations striking on 2 April. It also led later to an extra £23 million being added to the Cabinet's 'final' offer. As Callaghan's Principal Private Secretary noted, it was a 'high price' to pay and, at root, totally unnecessary. From the start CSD negotiators had known, and as late as 28 March the Cabinet Secretary had tried to reassure the Prime Minister, that there was 'at bottom . . . little real difference between the Cabinet's fall back position and the ambitions of the staff'.[46] Steps, it was urged, should be taken to ensure that such disorder never happened again.

Such conflict belied the reality that, particularly in relation to the private sector, pay negotiations within the Service throughout the 1970s were remarkably orderly and mutually beneficial. For the staff associations, the result was that the level of pay was – in the words of the 1977 Working Group on Pay Research and as confirmed in Figure 6.1 – 'as up-to-date as it has ever been'. Likewise the Government and the general public were well served. As the typically hostile *Financial Times* conceded, for example, on its demise in 1981 'the despised pay research system actually did the job it was supposed to do' by keeping 'Civil Service pay broadly in line with pay outside the Service'.[47] So much for the tales of rags and riches peddled respectively by the

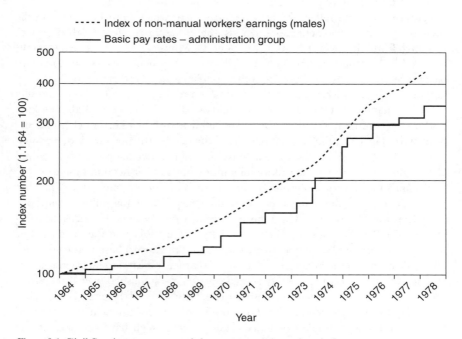

Figure 6.1 Civil Service pay rates and the non-manual earnings index.

NSS and the No.10 Policy Unit. Such mutual benefit, moreover, was achieved by a system of industrial relations – Whitleyism – which, more than any other, embodied the ideal of industrial democracy currently advocated by the Bullock Committee.[48] The NSS acted, to breaking point in March 1979, as a constraint on its more militant members (see Chapter 8.1.2). Similarly the CSD strove to constrain the destructive mix of aggression and appeasement which had traditionally characterised – and, as seen in 1977 in relation to the IRSF, continued to characterise – the Treasury's approach to industrial relations. The tragedy was that, due to political failings, greater advantage was not taken of so effective a system.

6.2.4 Maintaining the momentum of modernisation

Whilst the size and pay of the Civil Service demanded immediate action, the reforms initiated under the Fulton and PSRU modernisation programmes also continued to require attention. Elements of each, such as unified grading (as proposed by Fulton) and the embedding of a business team in Whitehall (as initiated by the Conservatives), had already been abandoned. Others, such as hiving off and super ministries, were in the process of being disowned.[49] It was, therefore, the strengthening of the 'Central Capability' (as sought first by Plowden and then, in the shape of the CSD, by Fulton) and of the government's 'analytical capability' (as represented by PAR) to which attention was principally turned.

(a) The CSD and the centre of government

The focus for the debate on the government's 'Central Capability' was the inquiry into the Civil Service mounted by the House of Commons' Expenditure Committee. Chaired by the Labour MP, Michael English – and thus better known as the English Committee – it started taking evidence in May 1976 and reported in September 1977. A Government response was issued in March 1978 (Cmnd 7117), which was so bland that it exceptionally prompted a further collection of evidence and a second report.[50]

The Committee exemplified not only the tensions within the existing consensus but also the seductive similarity of proposals emanating from radically different ideological standpoints. Labour's two leading members were John Garrett (a former member of Fulton's Management Consultancy Group) and Brian Sedgemore (recently dismissed as Tony Benn's Parliamentary Private Secretary). Their overriding objective was to see Fulton fully implemented, with Sedgemore even drafting an alternative introduction to the first Report making overt Fulton's covert assumption that radical change was being stifled by an elitist and amateurish bureaucracy. In sharp contrast, two of the leading Conservative members were Nicholas Ridley and Nigel Lawson. Both were simultaneously members of Opposition planning groups dedicated to rolling back government and thus their priorities were to keep alight the flame of *Black Book* and, in Lawson's words, to 'restore Treasury meanness'. At the onset, the chairman had described the Committee's purpose as being to examine the Civil Service's 'intended functions and what they should be, in relation to their cost and what that should be'.[51] Such issues clearly went to the heart of Party politics and so, typically, could not be resolved by a Select Committee (see Chapter 10.3.2). Instead some superficial consensus was sought in a common assault on the Civil Service.

This assault had two principal, interrelated targets: the Service's failure fully to implement Fulton and the perceived ineffectuality of the central departments. In relation to Fulton, the CSD argued in vain that four-fifths of the Report's recommendations had been 'substantially implemented'.[52] The Committee responded, with some reason, that only the letter of Fulton and not its spirit was being honoured. A dispute over training reinforced its point. The Committee wished to abolish the new fast-track Administration Trainee (AT) scheme and make promotion to posts above Assistant Secretary dependent on performance on a new 'higher management' training course. Its classic Fultonian purpose was to halt a system which seamlessly transformed 'Oxford historians into crown princes' and to replace it with a genuine 'road to the top' for proven managers under the age of 35. The CSD's counter-proposal, to modify the AT scheme and strengthen mid-career training for officials over 35, may have eradicated some vestiges of earlier bias but its purpose was clearly more limited.

Was the presumption correct, however, that Fulton was being frustrated by a bureaucratic conspiracy? As argued earlier, and as indeed acknowledged during the discussion of the Committee's remit, Fulton's full implementation would have conflicted with other Government priorities. Improvements in personnel management and training, for instance, were costly in terms of manpower and public expenditure. Both at the time were capped. Likewise the implementation of unified grading, for which Garrett continued relentlessly to fight, would have breached successive incomes policies. In short, political rather than administrative impediments frustrated reform.[53] Nevertheless, the vestigial anger of Labour members drove them to be complicit, somewhat surrealistically, in the demand for the abolition of a major innovation directly attributable to Fulton. 'We do not believe', the initial report argued

> that the CSD in its present form has a permanent part to play at the centre of Government. It was the product of the post-Fulton boom; with the evaporation of Fulton enthusiasm and the virtual shelving of the Report it has lost its raison d'etre.[54]

Such complicity was manna from heaven for the Conservative members, who wanted greater central coordination for a very different reason: tighter control over public expenditure. They believed that the division of responsibility for manpower (ceded to the CSD in 1968) and finance (retained in the Treasury) had reduced the traditional 'clout' of Treasury control, thereby giving spending departments a freer rein. Their reasoning was also flawed. As has been seen, for example, the CSD's eventual delivery of the £140 million manpower cuts programme was to be widely recognised to be a 'success story'; and it would have been more expeditiously achieved had Cabinet agreed the abolition of VED.[55] In short, it was political rather than administrative will that was again lacking. Moreover, a re-concentration of power in the Treasury demanded a leap of faith. After all, it had been the Chancellor who opposed the abolition of VED and the revenue departments were not well managed. This should have served as a warning to the Conservative members – just as past managerial failings (which had prompted Fulton's appointment) should have concerned their Labour colleagues.[56]

Whatever the English Committee's shortcomings, it nevertheless re-ignited an internal debate about the structure of the 'centre of government' and the related issue (last fully examined after the Plowden Committee) of the role of the Head of the Civil Service. In relation to restructuring, Callaghan – having masterminded the Cabinet discussions over the IMF package – was already considering the replacement of Dennis Healey as Chancellor. He wished above all to open economic policy to collective discussion which, he considered, had for too long been debated solely within the Treasury and then 'bounced' on Cabinet. Accordingly, he was instinctively attracted to a proposal advanced both by Sir John Hunt (as Cabinet Secretary) and Sir Douglas Allen (as Head of the Civil Service) not to re-concentrate power in the Treasury but rather to divide it into a Ministry of Finance and a Bureau of the Budget. The proposal was not new. It had been previously suggested by Otto Clarke and reiterated in the Conservatives' *Black Book* (which had championed a Bureau of the Budget in the guise of a Ministry of Programmes).[57]

The proposal withered, however, on exposure to the Treasury. Its Permanent Secretary (Sir Douglas Wass) argued *inter alia* that sound Cabinet decisions required 'well prepared not rival papers'. More potently, Healey asserted that in the aftermath of the IMF visit such radical surgery would undermine international confidence – before characteristically adding that it was 'unwise to carry out an appendix operation on a man while he was lifting a grand piano'.[58] Consequently structural reform was shelved and instead, to reinforce both Cabinet discussion and public expenditure control, the Chief Secretary to the Treasury (Joel Barnett) was promoted to the Cabinet. As in 1919 and again in 1961, the Treasury had turned an attack on its competence to its advantage. The spotlight then fell on the CSD. Its weakness was widely acknowledged. Having been created as a 'power for change', as the Prime Minister was warned, its 'first head had over-publicised his role and lost the confidence of the Civil Service'. Consequently it was 'now insular and weak and held in no high esteem'. It could be 'outgunned' by all the larger departments and 'no up-and-coming civil servant would want to go there'.[59]

English's recommendation that the CSD should be abolished, however, was never seriously entertained. Rather, when the 'big three' (Allen, Hunt and Wass) were summoned to a 'council of state' by Callaghan in October 1977, their only alternative to the division of the Treasury was minor adjustment to the *status quo* (a policy irreverently known within the CSD as the '*status quo* with knobs on'). This remained the position during the planning for the next election. The 'Red Centre' brief, prepared for a returning Labour Government, contained detailed plans for a Bureau of the Budget; and, had the election been held in the autumn of 1978, David Owen and Edmund Dell were respectively in line to become Minister of finance and of public expenditure, with Healey elevated to Foreign Secretary. However, in the absence of any guidance for the Conservative opposition, the 'Blue Centre' brief simply advocated minor modifications to the *status quo*.[60]

Why was the reorganisation of the centre so intractable? Politically, there was the need to accommodate personalities and to balance the factions into which both major Parties were falling. The principal reason, however, was the absence of a viable solution. The centre was responsible for four major policy areas: public finance; economic and industrial planning; public expenditure; and the management of the Civil Service. Together they formed both a 'seamless web' and too great a burden for one department, let alone one Minister. Public finance included the levying of taxes and so was inextricably linked to public expenditure. They, therefore, could not be divided. Public expenditure, however, was a major instrument of demand management and both its size and efficiency depended on the quality of Civil Service management. This in itself was a specialist task and, moreover, had at its core the issue of pay, which *inter alia* affected any incomes policy upon which economic and industrial planning might depend. The interdependencies, in short, were boundless.

Any solution, it was consequently agreed in Whitehall, had to meet three preconditions. First, the Treasury should not be overloaded. Politically, for instance, 'only a titan' like Mr Healey (who had been rehabilitated speedily after February 1977) could be expected to master its current range of responsibilities. Second, the CSD should not be reduced to a rump. This would weaken it in relation to other departments and further retard the improvements to personnel management. It would also offend the NSS and thus worsen industrial relations. Finally, to sustain the 'clout' of the centre, the Treasury and CSD should co-operate – and be seen to co-operate – rather than engage in internecine warfare (as, for example, over VED).[61] By such criteria the English recommendations were exposed as wholly impractical. Were the CSD to be abolished, for instance, the Treasury would have to assume its responsibility not just for manpower and personnel management but also for pay and computerisation (which were intricately linked to grading and enhanced productivity). The Treasury would thus be even further overloaded.

Consequently it was agreed that the best solution in the circumstances would be, as in other countries, the creation of a Ministry of Finance (which would at least allow its Minister time to think) and a Bureau of the Budget (which should strengthen the centre's grip over public expenditure). The link with public expenditure and taxation (which Wass continued to describe as 'desperately important') would be broken; but there would be two equally powerful and functional departments, which would permit – and thus meet as an acknowledged 'part of the objective' – greater direction of policy by both a more proactive Prime Minister and Cabinet Office.[62] This was the reasoning behind the 'Red Centre' brief.

The only alternative, as advanced at the 'council of state' and then in the 'Blue Centre' brief, was 'the *status quo* with knobs on'. Each knob was designed to strengthen the CSD. The most imaginative was Allen's concept of an Efficiency Unit', headed by an outsider, to identify 'accretions' to policy which might readily be removed. Such an initiative was designed to strengthen the CSD and increase efficiency. However, it had the additional advantage of providing a convenient response to English's recommendations that there should be regular 'surveys on the possibilities of reducing costs by policy changes' and that the monitoring of officials should no longer be exclusively by other officials. Allen's suggestion was not uniformly welcomed in Whitehall but the ultimate reason for its rejection was once again political. Whilst Allen remained in post, the Prime Minister prevaricated. Then, when his successor (Bancroft) revived the idea and suggested its first task might be to review VED, Callaghan's considered response was 'balls; the Cabinet has had three goes at that!' A 'very positive rebuff' was then issued.[63]

The debate on restructuring the 'centre' was made all the more urgent by the imminence of Allen's own retirement as Head of the Civil Service. The post's future was by no means assured. During the CSD's management review (completed in August 1976) Allen himself had questioned it because, despite his seniority, he felt constantly outgunned by the holders of two other posts (which Plowden had correctly identified as potential rivals). His advice to the Prime Minister, even on the machinery of government, was frequently refined by the Cabinet Secretary and 'the final authority on any given pay settlement' (which Fulton had assigned to the post) had been assumed, on the introduction of cash limits, by the Permanent Secretary of the Treasury.[64]

Five potential roles were eventually identified for a Head of the Civil Service. The first, which Frank Lee had advocated in 1961, was as 'the Prime Minister's general adviser and factotum'. This is what Allen, following Armstrong's experience of 1972–4, had anticipated although he soon recognised that such a role (as Brook had counter-argued in 1961) fell more naturally to the Cabinet Secretary, because of his daily contact with the Prime Minister. The next two roles were the provision of advice on senior administrative appointments and changes to the machinery of government. Divorced from the pressure of everyday policy, the Head of the Civil Service alone had the time and – in the shape of the CSD's personnel and MG divisions – the expertise to discharge such responsibilities; and it was here where, it was widely agreed, the 'real power' lay. Fourth, there was the role which Plowden had regarded as pre-eminent: the management of the Civil Service. Since 1971, this may have lost some of its attraction and it was not one to which Allen personally warmed. Yet, as his suggestion for an Efficiency Unit and its later adoption by Mrs Thatcher demonstrated, it still had considerable potential. Finally there was the representational role. This meant, in part, defending the Service in the face of mounting political and public criticism – although, arguably, this better befell a Minister. Again it was something to which Allen, unlike Armstrong, did not warm. However, it also meant providing a professional lead to what might easily fracture into a disunited, federated body. This was the role which Allen, through his weekly Wednesday morning meetings with senior colleagues, did perform with considerable success. Armstrong's monthly meetings, in contrast, had been 'pretty deadly and not gone well'.[65]

It was to develop these five roles, and not simply to block Hunt's predatory instincts or the reassertion of Treasury control, that Allen developed his own programme for institutional change.[66] This involved the division of the Treasury into a Ministry of Finance and a Bureau of the Budget, with the Head of the Civil Service as a free-floating Permanent Secretary of the latter (rather like Warren Fisher) delegating to two deputies the reunified responsibility for financial and manpower control. It also envisaged more regular meetings with the Prime Minister so that the Service might be continually refashioned in the ruling Party's image. His programme, however, did not find political favour. Just as Heath had brought the headship of the Civil Service into disrepute through excess interference, so Callaghan undermined it by neglect. As he candidly admitted in 1977, he 'did not recognise any function' which made 'sense' of the post. Then, somewhat disingenuously, he responded to a rather poignant retirement letter from Allen by apologising for not arranging more frequent meetings and promising that this oversight would be corrected 'under your successor'.[67] It was not.

All this planning was overshadowed, and to some extent outdated, by an independent development elsewhere: the relentless growth of the Cabinet Office. Since succeeding Trend in 1973, Sir John Hunt had ruthlessly delegated work in order to make time – as Heath had wished – to act as the 'Prime Minister's general adviser and factotum'. The Office's capability was also greatly strengthened by the inclusion of CPRS (which provided an alternative source of economic advice to the Treasury) and the European and Constitutional Units (which, as will be seen in Chapter 10.4, gave it an interventionist rather than just a coordinating role in the two critical policy areas, the EEC and devolution). Callaghan may have referred to the Office as 'a waste paper basket' into which he 'threw things that he did not know what to do with'.[68] Its growth, however, was well choreographed. Moreover, although Hunt persistently protested that he had no ambition to create a Prime Minister's Office, there was an element of protesting too much. His conviction was on record that such a development was inevitable; and the tide was fast turning in this direction in other 'Westminster' style democracies such as Canada and Australia. The die, in short, had been cast.

(b) Programme analysis and review

The other major legacy from modernisation's moment, which required enhancement, was PAR. Designed to strengthen government's 'analytical capacity', its teething problems had seemingly been resolved by 1973 with the introduction of a three-year rolling programme of reviews. It was to cover over half of public expenditure; clarify the objectives of existing, as well as new, policies; measure outputs, wherever feasible; and check the relevance of each policy to the government's overall strategy. In short, at a time of polarising opinion – particularly over the relative virtues of the market and the state – PAR offered a means of ensuring and providing proof of the efficiency of public provision. It also provided, as the English Committee recognised, a means of delivering one of its principal recommendations: the reduction of 'costs by policy changes'.[69]

PAR had initially been dogged by technical, operational and political problems. Technically, there were insufficient experts and analytical tools. Operationally, the Treasury had clashed bitterly with the nascent CPRS over whether the principal objective should be to cut expenditure or clarify strategy. Politically, junior Ministers had resisted the temptation to become Minister-managers. Likewise, Cabinet Ministers had been unenthusiastic about exchanging horse-trading for a rational discussion of strategic goals. Accordingly PAR had become a fertile field for administrative and political gamesmanship and doubts had started to grow about its ability to deliver the expected benefits – particularly given failure of its inspiration (Planning Programming and Budgeting Systems in the USA).

Such doubts recurred over the next six years, particularly at times of political transition. In 1974, for example, many Labour Ministers challenged the continuation of a Conservative innovation on the somewhat optimistic assumption that two election manifestos would guarantee strategic coherence. In 1976, following the succession of Callaghan, warfare again erupted – even within the Treasury – over whether short-term needs should take precedence over strategic coherence. Finally in 1978 when, in the shadow of an impending election, the Treasury realigned itself with the CPRS to champion the programme's revitalisation, it was collectively rebuffed by departmental Permanent Secretaries at Sunningdale on the grounds that PAR had 'outlived its usefulness'.[70] In other words, doubts were never doused and the viability of PAR never fully established.

The conventional explanation for failure was, in the characteristically earthy words of its leading antagonist within the Treasury (Leo Pliatzky), that it was a 'bloody excrescence'. Translated into rather more delicate language by the Cabinet Secretary, this meant that 'high powered staffs were wasting valuable time providing useless reports'.[71] Why was this permitted to continue? Part of the reason was the need, which even the Permanent Secretaries at Sunningdale recognised, for 'some way of escaping from the restrictions of the established pattern of public expenditure and the tendency of the Public Expenditure Survey exercise to examine only the margins of expenditure'. PAR potentially provided that 'way'. Ideally, it encouraged Ministers to take a coherent forward look at, and collective decisions about, the totality of public expenditure. Administratively, it also enabled the central departments to persuade their big-spending counterparts to re-examine core programmes and to initiate, in the interest of 'joined-up government', reviews of policies involving more than one department. In addition it encouraged greater analytical sophistication throughout Whitehall, as demonstrated by the proliferation of departmental planning divisions. As a summary of the Sunningdale debate concluded, there continued to be an agreed need for 'a minimum capability to deal with inter-departmental issues and to think the unthinkable'.

The etiolation of PAR, however, continued. This has commonly been explained by administrative attrition. Spending departments, so it was argued, were antagonised at being 'put into semi-permanent commission' by overambitious review programmes imposed on them by the centre and the diversion of their most able staff from policies (and policy reviews) to which they accorded greater importance. Accordingly they adopted a policy of 'damage limitation', volunteering only peripheral policy areas for review and then belatedly producing defensive reports. Such stalling tactics generally succeeded, as the head of the CPRS lamented, because of a fundamental flaw in the UK constitution: 'the existence of strong Departments without the countervailing pressures of a strong centre'.

Why, however, were such tactics allowed *politically* to continue? The basic reason was that, given the convention of ministerial responsibility, departmental autonomy was as much a matter of ministerial as of administrative concern. As Hunt had admitted when helping to launch PAR as a Treasury official, 'some Ministers feel their departmental prerogative is being intruded upon. The short point is that it is'. Nevertheless, he had hoped that such Ministers would be reconciled by a demonstration of 'how the PAR system can help them in running their own departments', the building of more rational programmes 'from the bottom up' and 'improved management information/planning/control systems'.[72] Ministers, however, no more welcomed such systems than the corporate planning of Heath's Business Team. Likewise, it was they who demanded that PAR should be shrouded in the secrecy which, to the fury of the English Committee, pauperised public debate. Once again administrative attrition merely reflected political intransigence.

6.2.5 Halting progress

By 1979, therefore, the momentum of reform inspired by Fulton and the PSRU had largely dissipated. Many planned reforms had quickly imploded, but two key ones survived. The first was the CSD (conceived by Fulton as the essential vehicle to initiate and sustain a managerial revolution); the second was PAR (the epitome of the PSRU's desire for the tauter management of more selective state services). By the mid-1970s, the future of both was clearly endangered. Even those who remained faithful to Fulton were demanding the closure of the CSD. Simultaneously, Permanent Secretaries were baying for the abandonment of PAR because even if its ends were justified, its means were not. Consequently there was a very real danger of counter-revolution: that attitudes and practices within Whitehall might revert to what they had been in the early 1960s – when, to ensure the more professionalism, Plowden had recommended PESC and the appointment of a discrete Head of the Home Civil Service.

More mundane reforms, it is true, continued to evolve. The work of the CSD's staff inspectors in eliminating waste, for example, won universal praise; and a wide range of modern management and personnel practices was also introduced. Their impact, however, was limited. The number of staff inspectors was capped at 40 and the cost-effectiveness of the other measures came to be seriously questioned.

In 1975, for instance, the head of the Treasury duly warned Allen: 'The CSD was launched with a distinct belief in some form of professionalism in management. We have to ask now . . . whether we have seen enough return from it'. His concern may well have been partial; but his suspicions were confirmed by a retrospective admission by the head of the CSD's key Management Services Divisions that 'in many of our efforts to improve Civil Service management, there was a disproportion between the size of the resources that were put into a given project (visible and large) and the size of the improvement actually achieved (invisible and perhaps quite small)'.[73] Progress, in short, was halting in both senses of the term.

Why was this so, given that in the 1970s a generation of Civil Servants was coming in to its own for whom (in Bancroft's classic phrase) 'everything was possible'? There were many administrative reasons, which the English Committee was only too willing to catalogue. The fundamental reason, however, was political. The English Committee itself epitomised the growing lack of consensus over the 'proper' role of the state. In consequence the meaning of modernisation changed – or at least became contested. This destroyed the clear sense of political direction without which, given their respect for constitutional propriety, officials were powerless to make anything 'possible'. In addition, Ministers individually failed to take policy delivery seriously and collectively baulked at both acknowledging changed reality and ensuring strategic coherence. Increased responsibilities were expected to be discharged by decreased numbers and, at a time of rising militancy, pay agreements were readily reneged on. Successive Prime Ministers were also culpable. Heath, in seeking to implement the PSRU's vision of corporate planning, wilfully ignored constitutional convention and the federal structure of Whitehall, both of which prevented government from being run like a business. At his behest, William Armstrong tested the water in relation to greater independence for 'accountable managers' and a more autocratic role for the 'centre'. He drowned.[74] For their part, Wilson and then Callaghan carried the flame for Fulton but successively failed to give the CSD (for which they were officially responsible) either strong personal support or a strong ministerial head. In such circumstances, no rising generation of officials – whatever its relative strengths and weaknesses – could have sustained or successfully modified modernisation.

6.3 Pioneering the new

Modernisation, as conceived in the 1960s, may have stalled in the mid-1970s but there were two significant innovations for modernisation, as it was later to be conceived. The first was the regular appointment of ministerial special advisers and, in particular, the establishment of the No.10 Policy Unit. At one level, this was a natural reaction to Labour's ingrained suspicion of bureaucracy. At another, however, it was an implicit acknowledgement that the *political* task of ensuring strategic coherence could not – as the creation of the CPRS had implied – be discharged 'in house'. Consequently, as the role of special advisers expanded, so the CPRS contracted. The second innovation was the introduction of cash limits in 1976. By reverting to pre-Plowden practices, and even flirting with monetarism, it too signified the end of an earlier ideal: 'rational' planning as exemplified by PESC and later PAR. It also marked the start of the Treasury's rehabilitation and thus threatened the CSD's future.

6.3.1 Special advisers and the decline of the CPRS

The regular appointment of special advisers in Whitehall was the major constitutional innovation of the 1974–9 Labour Government. There were two separate, albeit related, developments: the establishment of a Policy Unit within No.10 and the granting to each senior Minister of the right to appoint a maximum of two 'political' advisers. Both were natural developments from the past. The No.10 Policy Unit had been foreshadowed during wartime by Lloyd George's Garden Suburb and Churchill's Statistical Section and, between 1964 and 1970, by Balogh's embryonic Economic Secretariat. Likewise, expert advisers had long been appointed to make good any perceived lack of specialist skill amongst generalist officials. Hence, during the 1964–70 Labour Governments, Brian Abel-Smith (an established professor at LSE) had provided regular advice on social security whilst Christopher Foster (then a far less experienced Oxford economist) had been appointed by Barbara Castle to modernise the Ministry of Transport and, in effect, sideline its Permanent Secretary (Sir Thomas Padmore). The Policy Unit, by its provision of independent advice directly to the Prime Minister, was designed to fill the 'hole in the centre of government' (which, as has been seen, was widely acknowledged to exist) and to provide the 'intensely political' support for the Prime Minister as the 'guardian of the manifesto' (as deemed necessary by the PSRU). Meanwhile, the 'non-expert' political advisers were expected to counter the alleged 'dulling' of Ministers' political instincts by the volume of departmental work and officials' control over their diaries. As Wilson elaborated at a Commonwealth Heads of Government Conference in 1975:

> The political adviser is an extra pair of hands, ears and eyes and a mind more politically committed and more politically aware than would be available to a Minister from the professional neutrals in the established Civil Service. This is particularly true for a radical reforming party in government, since 'neutralism' may easily slip into conservatism with a small 'c'.[75]

Special advisers – and in particular the No.10 Policy Unit – were broadly welcomed by senior officials. Despite some early suspicion and tensions within particular departments (later immortalised in the television programme *Yes Minister*, to which officials and special advisers fell over themselves to contribute), the principal objections either came from backbenchers or, as will be seen, were the product of a *political* refusal to clarify their terms of employment. The resulting misunderstandings consumed an inordinate amount of time, generated much ill-feeling and even led Callaghan, as Prime Minister, uncharacteristically to encourage officials to 'obfuscate'.[76] Thus although, as in other countries, the growing role and complexity of government made special advisers inevitable, in the event their appointment was poorly planned. Similarly, although their appointment became regularised during the 1970s, in practice the conditions on which they were employed remained highly irregular.

The No.10 Policy Unit was the greater success. Its establishment was far from planned; but speedy agreements were reached between its new head (Bernard Donoughue, a reader in politics from the LSE), the Cabinet Secretary (Sir John Hunt) and the No.10 Private Office (in the person of Robert Armstrong, the Prime Minister's Principal Private Secretary). Hunt and Armstrong needed the Unit as an antidote to the increasingly erratic behaviour of Marcia Williams as Wilson's Political Secretary. Donoughue, in turn, was sufficiently shrewd – unlike Balogh before him – to realise he needed Hunt's 'papal blessing' were he to gain access to vital committees and papers. Equally, the trust of the Private Office was essential were he to remain well informed about developments within No.10 (and not least of the content of the Cabinet Secretary's briefing notes before Cabinet).[77] This was, for example, to prove crucial in June 1975 when a combination of Williams and the Treasury sought to freeze the Unit out of the consideration of incomes policy. Actively supported by Ken Stowe (who had replaced Robert Armstrong), the Unit was able to persuade Ministers to honour the manifesto commitment to voluntarism – a victory which, at least in Donoughue's judgement, unequivocally established the Unit's value 'in the eyes of the Prime Minister and its credibility in Whitehall'.[78]

Nevertheless its future was called into question when Callaghan succeeded Wilson in April 1976. This was not just because all special advisers had to resign on a change of administration but also because the new Prime Minister's values and working habits were, on his own admission, far less congenial to Donoughue. However, the Unit survived to provide a source of 'fresh ideas and perspectives' as well as Prime-Ministerial leverage with Cabinet colleagues. An example of the former was the Ruskin Hall speech on the maintenance of educational standards in the autumn of 1976 (which well reflected Donoughue's personal commitment to individual 'rights and responsibilities'). An example of the latter was the defeat, during the IMF crisis, of both Benn's alternative strategy and the Treasury's initial letter of intent (which conceded far more than Cabinet had agreed).[79] The Unit was arguably most effective when Donoughue was the conduit for the ideas of experts (and in particular the Oxbridge economists, Andrew Graham and Gavyn Davies) and rather less so when Donoughue's own instincts were to the fore.[80] Until 1979, however, it consistently displayed the intellectual distinction and partisan commitment for which it had been designed; and, although she too was remiss in her pre-election planning, the innovation was to be safe in Mrs Thatcher's hands.

The rise of the Policy Unit, however, paralleled the decline of the CPRS. This was, in part, for personal and organisational reasons. In September 1974, Rothschild resigned as its head and was succeeded by Sir Kenneth Berrill who, but for a longstanding academic feud with the Chancellor's new special adviser (Nicholas Kaldor), would have remained within the Treasury as the Government's chief economic adviser. Berrill had neither Rothschild's extensive contacts nor his flamboyant iconoclasm and, as an administrative insider, tended towards caution. This was particularly apparent during the economic crisis of June 1975 when his reserve drove Donoughue to despair. 'I don't see how you can run a Think Tank, as an originator of original and uncomfortable ideas, on this basis', he confided to his diary, 'a long way from Victor Rothschild – and not in the right direction!'[81] When he was finally tempted from the Treasury's embrace it was only into that of the Cabinet Office, thereby supporting Hunt's ambition to become the Prime Minister's principal 'adviser and factotum'. This was a mixed success and so, under Callaghan, the CPRS's impact on policy tended to be 'detached and episodic'. It was not helped by an own goal, almost as spectacular as the opening sentences of Fulton: its 1977 report recommending the radical reform of the Diplomatic Service, which set the 'Tom-Toms of the Establishment' beating and drove the Government into a hasty retreat.[82] In truth, however, the CPRS' fate had been effectively sealed earlier. Its original brief to 'think the unthinkable' was simply incompatible with the domestication forced upon it by Trend and William Armstrong.

In contrast to the Policy Unit, the record of individual ministerial advisers varied. This was perhaps inevitable given the variety of conditions under which a variety of advisers was appointed for a variety of reasons. Two of the issues which generated the most conflict (and which, somewhat unfairly, further sullied the CSD's reputation) were their pay and political freedom. By 1976, considerable antagonism had arisen with regard to pay, not least because of the low salaries paid to two advisers at the FCO and Home Office. 'I find', Callaghan's respected Political Secretary, Tom McNally, complained angrily

> that the CSD, having successfully boxed David Lipsey and Roger Darlington into a grossly unfair and anomalous position, their situation is now quoted to set other salary standards. If Ministers are going to be able to attract worthwhile people to serve in a job which has no career prospects, and is subject to instant dismissal, then the rigid application of Civil Service salary scales is impossible.[83]

He then threatened to publish the relative responsibilities and salaries of permanent officials.

Such a threat was itself both anomalous and grossly unfair. Special advisers had consistently objected to the publication of their own salaries, to the frustration of both Parliament and the CSD.[84] Moreover, the CSD had long striven to end the pay 'shambles' but had been defeated by successive Prime Ministers and incomes policies. Wilson had initially ruled that Ministers should determine the salaries of their own advisers on an *ad hoc* basis, with due regard to their 'market' value. The CSD's sole responsibility was to remind departments of the 'rules'. When it then sought to clarify those rules, however, Wilson was somewhat vague and rejected as too 'generous' a common age-scale based on Principal and Assistant Secretary grades within the Service.[85] This rejection occurred in 1975 just before the introduction of the voluntary incomes policy which, so Callaghan argued on becoming

Prime Minister, disqualified Lipsey and Darlington from increased 'responsibility' payments (which the CSD wished to award). These payments were sanctioned a year later, but only on condition that they should not be made public. Such secrecy cloaked the consistent, and frequently liberal, attempts by the CSD (and, in particular, by Allen) 'to get a bit of reason into the system'.[86]

The other contentious issue was the degree of political freedom which special advisers should continue to enjoy. Following advice from William Armstrong, a senior ministerial committee (chaired by Wilson) agreed on 3 April 1974 that no-one paid from public funds should either participate in national and local politics or contribute regularly to the press.[87] This ruling, however, was disputed by an unholy alliance of Barbara Castle and Roy Jenkins (not least because their chosen advisers, Jack Straw and Matthew Oakeshott, were – and wanted to remain – local councillors). Cabinet supported their objection and, given the proximity of an election, agreed also that advisers could become prospective Parliamentary candidates. This required legislative change (an amendment to the 1960 Servants of the Crown (Parliamentary Candidates) Order), of which the House of Commons was duly informed on 27 June. Uproar ensued, as both the Conservatives and the Labour backbenchers reacted angrily to a perceived increase in patronage. Consequently a Cabinet Committee (MISC 34) was convened, which reviewed *inter alia* the Conservatives' proposal that advisers should be paid from the same fund that was to be set up to subsidise opposition Parties. Special advisers would thus become the employees of the ruling Party rather than temporary Civil Servants. Such a proposal, however, was rejected on legal advice (that the Executive could not be so subsidised) and pragmatic grounds (that it was 'premature' to codify, and thus set in stone, any new regime). Estacode, the administrative rulebook governing Civil Servants' behaviour, was adjudged sufficiently flexible to permit further extemporisation. Hence the circulation by Robert Armstrong on 12 December 1974 of a revised 'memorandum of arrangements for the appointment of special advisers' with its classic statement that Estacode 'will *normally* apply to special advisers *without exception*'.[88]

As with pay, the CSD's objective was always logical consistency. Before the February 1974 election, it had suggested the creation of a 'special regime' (which would have made advisers 'servants of the crown' rather than temporary Civil Servants) and Allen fought tenaciously for its acceptance throughout 1974.[89] It was fully accepted that it was a nonsense to subject temporary appointees, whose very purpose was to be partial, to rules designed to safeguard the impartiality of permanent officials. The concept of regime change was then revived in 1976 by another 'virtual u-turn' by Wilson. Having decreed in late January that 'the rules should be tightened' to exclude advisers from 'political activities in general and Party committee meetings in particular', he then agreed in March to their participation in Party committees revising *Labour's Programme*.[90]

The appointment of a new Prime Minister, it was hoped, would clarify the system; and a meeting was immediately convened between Allen and Stowe (representing the permanent Civil Service) and Donoughue and McNally (representing special advisers). In its wake, Allen drafted a memorandum which confirmed the official view that the strict application to special advisers of Civil Service rules 'would make it impossible for them to perform the function for which they have been appointed'. The solution was now seen not to be a 'special regime' (which might require contentious legislation) but an explicit set of exemptions from Estacode (including the right to participate in local politics and Party policy committees so long as it was only to explain, and not to contest, Government policy). Allen's memorandum was not submitted to Callaghan for almost a year. This was in part because of the IMF crisis but also because of an outbreak of 'trench warfare' between No.10 and the CSD, which forced Allen into a number of other concessions.[91]

Even after the revised memorandum had been approved by Callaghan, however, peace did not break out.[92] The approach of another election encouraged special advisers to seek Parliamentary seats and McNally (who, as a prospective candidate himself, was hardly disinterested) bitterly attacked the CSD for sticking rigidly to the earlier ruling that, on selection, advisers must resign from publicly funded posts.[93] Then, in 1978, a problem arose which Allen had long foreseen: several advisers were approaching the maximum of five years' service which temporary appointees were permitted before they had to be certificated by the Civil Service Commission. The Commission belatedly conceded that there was no legal basis for such a convention and thus no problem. This, however, was not before Ken Stowe (normally a sympathetic ally of Donoughue) had dismissed as 'nonsense' some of his insinuations about the CSD's motivation for raising the issue.

Why, despite the illogicality and consequent tensions, was the retention of Civil Service status for special advisers regarded as so important? The overt reasons diverge significantly from the covert. Overtly, it was argued – particularly by Sir John Hunt, Robert Armstrong and the majority of Permanent Secretaries in 1974 – that the existing arrangements were working well.[94] Any change in the 'status' of advisers (as wanted by the CSD) might well prompt a Parliamentary outcry, as in July 1974 – particularly after 1976 when Labour, under staff association pressure, had had to appoint the Armitage Committee to clarify the political rights of permanent (let alone temporary) Civil Servants.[95] Covertly, however, Ministers were concerned that advisers in one department might openly criticise the policies of another and feared that, given the ideological divide within Cabinet, they might mount a challenge to Government policy inside the Party. Just such a challenge was indeed mounted in April 1975 when, in conjunction with his advisers (Francis Cripps and Frances Morrell), Tony Benn unveiled his alternative industrial strategy to an NEC subcommittee; and Wilson's contortions between January and March 1976 arguably reflected his concern that there might be a repeat performance during the redrafting of *Labour's Programme*.[96] In such circumstances, the ability to impose *political* discipline through the Civil Service rule book appeared highly attractive. For their part, senior officials – as was confirmed by Hunt in a key letter – were convinced that advisers would be 'easier to control if they were bound by Estacode' and if permanent secretaries had some 'locus' in their appointment and deployment. Their numbers could also be more easily controlled. Moreover, as the contemporary example of the Whitlam Government in Australia appeared to confirm, there was a danger that a 'psychological barrier' might arise between advisers and permanent officials were each to be employed under different 'regimes'.[97]

Why, however, did special advisers themselves comply? Many, after all, spent much of their time defying their terms of appointment whilst simultaneously excoriating the CSD. Some were also deliberately less discreet than permanent officials in their use of confidential material.[98] The answer would appear to be that their employment under a 'separate regime' would have exposed them to the full rigours of a House of Commons which, despite McNally's assertion, remained highly hostile to patronage. Consequently, their numbers and cost might have been subject to greater control. In short, despite their pyrotechnics, they recognised that employment as a temporary Civil Servant was the softer option.

Despite such distractions, did the more regular appointment of special advisers achieve its prime objective of improving departmental policy-making? Undoubtedly there were successes particularly where, as in the past, additional expertise was injected into a department. Such was the case at the DHSS (under Abel-Smith's continuing guidance); at the Home Office (where Anthony Lester drafted the 1975 Sex Discrimination Act); and at the DoE (where the transfer with Crosland to the Foreign Office of his special adviser, David Lipsey, allegedly left its Permanent Secretary distraught). Lipsey in particular fulfilled the early CSD hope that advisers would assist officials by 'giving them an increased awareness of political considerations which might not otherwise be accorded their proper weight'.[99]

However, by general agreement, the collective impact of special advisers was marginal. In part, this was because they varied in quality and remained few in number. Donoughue wanted a critical mass of some 40–60, but neither Ministers nor officials were so enthusiastic. Moreover, they also failed to form an effective network for either policy promotion or mutual support. This could not be blamed on the CSD, which had expressed the hope before the February 1974 election that one might be formed to complement the Private Secretary's network and thereby ensure that 'politically significant information' was not lost 'in the press of daily Departmental business'.[100] In part it was also undoubtedly due to bureaucratic resistance. Senior officials, for example, strove to ensure that special advisers should be employed 'outside the hierarchy' so that they could not (like political appointees in the USA) issue orders to permanent officials. Equally they opposed their being corralled into ministerial *cabinets*, where – as in France and indeed Australia – they might have created a barrier between permanent officials and the Minister. Instead they were restricted to being just an alternative channel of advice. At root, however, the real reason for their lack of collective success was the natural tendency for individual 'non-experts' to fight their own Ministers' corner and the frequent incompatibility of their views. After all, six – including McNally – were later to join the SDP whilst Morrell, for instance, became active in the Labour Party's Rank and File Mobilising Committee.[101] Such discordance was evidence that much about their role, let alone their regulation, still remained unresolved in 1979. Like the Policy Unit, the principle that they should be appointed was well-established; but their effectiveness was not.

6.3.2 *Cash limits and the rehabilitation of the Treasury*

The principal target of special advisers, and in particular the No.10 Policy Unit, was the Treasury which – as the economy deteriorated – became widely regarded as '*the* scapegoat department' because of its perceived lack of control, competence and candour. Its loss of control over public expenditure dated from the 1973 Barber boom and was seen to peak in 1975 with the 'lost £5 billion' – the amount by which a former Treasury adviser, Wynn Godley, calculated (to Parliamentary and public outrage) public spending in 1975 had unaccountably exceeded its planned total in real terms.[102] Its technical competence was questioned because of the seeming inaccuracy of its computerised forecasts. Finally, its candour became suspect because officials reputedly agreed policy amongst themselves and then 'bounced' it on not only other departments but also the Chancellor. This minimised the political acumen with which policy changes were introduced and, more importantly after April 1976, deeply angered the Prime Minister (as an ex-Chancellor).

This low esteem was not wholly of the Treasury's own making. Loss of control over public expenditure, for instance, was abetted by the creation of a separate CSD, which demystified and thereby dissipated the traditional awe in which 'Treasury control' had been held. Moreover, the peculiar political circumstances of 1972–4 (the Conservatives' u-turn and Labour's electoral politics) made an explosion in public expenditure almost inevitable. Likewise, in relation to technical competence, the crisis in consensus removed the common assumptions on which postwar economic policy had been based and exposed Treasury officials (who remained broadly Keynesian) to the jibes of a growing minority of monetarists.[103] Low external esteem, however, was exacerbated by low internal morale. This resulted in part from demoralisation at persistent economic decline and 'shell-shock' at the display of naked trade union power. Nevertheless, it was also a consequence of poor management. The Fulton revolution singularly failed to penetrate Great George Street.[104]

The Treasury reputedly reached its nadir in December 1976, when the Prime Minister seriously considered the replacement of not just the Chancellor but also its Permanent Secretary.[105] Both the economy and the Chancellor's reputation were soon to revive; but this had little to do with the IMF agreement. The seeds of recovery had been sown earlier by the Treasury's own radical reorganisation and two policy initiatives: Financial Information Systems (FIS) and cash limits. Reorganisation was precipitated by a Management Review between October 1974 and July 1975 (ironically mounted with the help of the CSD) which not only greatly improved personnel management but also policy coordination.[106] Consequently departmental morale was sufficiently high by December 1976 to ward off plans to re-divide it into a Ministry of Finance and a Bureau of the Budget.

Simultaneously the diplomatic introduction of – and the more effective use of computers by – FIS helped to re-establish the Treasury's reputation for administrative and technical competence. Cash limits were then introduced with rather less finesse (as arguably befitted the effective restoration of Treasury control) but their success contrasted sharply with the short-term failure of the CSD to cut manpower. The future shape of modernisation had been determined.

(a) Financial information systems (FIS)

FIS was the first initiative to emerge from a flurry of committees designed to improve economic management. The initial committee, the Cash Flow Group, was established under the Conservatives in February 1974 to identify, somewhat ironically, the reasons for the chronic underspending of departmental budgets.[107] The agreed solution was to enhance the Treasury's monitoring of aggregate expenditure through improved management information systems within departments (as PAR was simultaneously seeking to attain) and the better pooling of data. This, however, required departments to standardise their expenditure returns; and so a FIS Study Group was appointed in September 1974 to study international practice. It was impressed by the extent of computerisation in the USA but more especially by the speed at which aggregate data was processed in West Germany as a result of central payments to a department being taken as a proxy for that department's expenditure.

To its 'surprise', therefore, the Study Group discovered that 'exciting possibilities for getting really quick information' already existed in the shape of the computerised system installed at the Paymaster General's Office (PGO).[108] 'Really quick' action then became possible when the explosion of public expenditure in 1974–5 placed cash limits firmly on the political agenda. To be effective, they clearly required expenditure flows to be closely monitored both in departments and by the centre. Following the reorganisation of the Treasury, therefore, detailed plans were laid to introduce in April 1976 a standardised system by which each department could make speedy monthly returns to the Treasury ('Proposal 1') and by which, after April 1977, these returns could be then matched every three months against an agreed 'profile' of expenditure ('Proposal 2').

FIS was thus, in essence, a policy-neutral exercise to standardise the recording of expenditure so that departments might manage their own programmes, and the centre monitor aggregate public expenditure, more effectively. Inevitably it raised major technical and tactical problems. The former were epitomised by the need to determine a uniform price basis for the returns. Should it be, for example, the original survey price, the price level at the start of the financial year, current prices or outturn prices? The choice was important because it went to the heart of the problem which rapid inflation posed for the control of public expenditure: the conflict between the planned volume of services, costed in the Public Expenditure Survey at constant prices ('funny money') and the current (cash) cost of those services as sanctioned by Parliamentary estimates. Moreover, even the use of current prices was problematic because the deflators used by the Treasury to estimate the overall rate of inflation were often inapposite for the particular mix of manpower and other inputs consumed by individual departments.[109]

Other technical problems were inherited. One reason for the lack of control over public expenditure in the early 1970s, for example, was the historic use of four different control systems. Departments had, of necessity, to observe the Parliamentary Estimates because they alone gave their expenditure legal authority and Parliamentary sanction. The coverage of 'vote subheads' in the Estimates, however, differed radically from the economic classifications used in forecasting (on which postwar planning had been based), from Public Expenditure Survey programmes (on which planning had been based since Plowden), and from the 126 'blocks' of expenditure (on which cash limits were to be based after April 1976).[110] How could the requirements of each system be reconciled in one return? Likewise there had been, often quite deliberately, a wide diffusion of computer hardware and software systems adopted in Whitehall. How could greater standardisation be achieved?[111]

The greater problem, however, was not technical but tactical. How could departments be persuaded to accept a Treasury initiative? Friction peaked in the autumn of 1975 when PFOs fiercely opposed the introduction of the PGO system.[112] Such resistance was, to an extent, justified because FIS conflicted with much departmental 'best practice'. For example, to improve internal control, the MOD had just introduced a new accounting system which made faster returns than the PGO system – but with which it was incompatible. The assumption that payments by the PGO were synonymous with immediate expenditure was also confounded by the practice of 'suspense accounts' by which, to ensure administrative flexibility (for the payment, for instance, of contractors) departments often temporarily deposited the money in commercial banks. Moreover, the enforced diversion of staff to yet more managerial 'refinements' was deeply resented at a time of capped manpower. The real cause of friction, however, was the perceived threat to departmental autonomy. This was not just because of the link between FIS and cash limits (which was as yet unknown), but because the PGO method meant that the Treasury would receive raw information direct from a department's spending divisions – whereas traditionally it had been processed by its Finance Division. PFOs feared that this would both undermine their authority and give the Treasury the evidence it had long sought to interfere more extensively in policy. Somewhat perversely, many senior Treasury officials sympathised. Ever since the early 1920s, they recognised, Treasury control had been vicariously exercised by the 'self-discipline' within departments by PFOs and Permanent Secretaries in their role of accounting officer. Any weakening of such internal discipline might well be counterproductive.[113]

PFOs were eventually won over to FIS because they realised that – were they to comply with cash limits – the efficient monitoring of expenditure was imperative.[114] Initially, however, the link with cash limits was tenuous and, right up to April 1976, there were serious doubts about whether the Labour Government had the political will to impose them. The early success of FIS was, therefore, attributable to other factors – and the greatest amongst these were technical expertise and adept diplomacy. The former was first exhibited by the joint Treasury-CSD

Operational Research team, led by Peter Turner, which completed the final FIS Report in July 1975.[115] The latter was personified by Sir Douglas Henley, the Second Permanent Secretary with ultimate administrative responsibility for FIS's introduction. Atypically, he never stood on ceremony to deny current Treasury failings and continually stressed the mutual benefits that would result from 'more efficient management and the more economical and better-organised interchanges' between departments and the Treasury. Moreover, he was always prepared to go, and to encourage those below him to go, to considerable lengths to accommodate departments' genuine concerns.[116]

After the Treasury's reorganisation, the baton was passed to the FIS implementation team headed by Robin Butler (as Assistant Secretary) under the general direction of Patricia Brown (as Under Secretary). For both Proposal 1 and 2, frequent pilot studies and 'dry runs' were undertaken to test forms and procedures; departmental concerns were painstakingly argued through, not least by dedicated liaison officers; and evolving successes were never oversold (Pliatzky's lust for immediate publicity being successfully countered by Brown's maxim that you should 'never say you are pregnant until after the first three months').[117] Such exemplary behaviour by Treasury officials also brought the best out of others. PGO staff, for example, rose to so unexpected a challenge and the team of consultants from Arthur Andersen (which designed the software for the central Treasury computer) won nothing but praise from Butler.[118]

With good reason, therefore, FIS was regarded at the time as a model of implementation; and, once Proposal 2 had been introduced in April 1977, the original implementation team was disbanded. How well did their legacy stand the test of time? Ominously, the system's first major appraisal in January 1978 concluded that it was 'not working as well' as hoped.[119] Within its narrow – albeit far from negligible – task of profiling and monitoring departmental expenditure, it was performing satisfactorily. The earlier chaos had also been reduced and a further diffusion of departmental practice and computer systems moderated. However, a rigidity of design (arguably caused by the 'rush' to meet the needs of cash limits) had dashed the initial hope that departmental management information systems would more generally be improved. Consequently, another FIS study group had to be convened in 1979 'to examine the current requirements of interested parties for a computer based system to process data for PES, Estimates and Treasury FIS'. Only the Department of Industry was deemed to have an adequate system and, even more tellingly, only five other departments declared themselves to be 'interested parties'. Much work was left to be done, therefore, by another joint Treasury-CSD initiative – the Financial Management Initiative of 1982.[120]

(b) Cash limits

If the Treasury's rehabilitation started with FIS, its political reputation and administrative power were fully restored by cash limits. Politically, they were accredited with capping public expenditure, whilst administratively they were instrumental in the reimposition of Treasury control. Initially the concept of cash limits had only been advanced tentatively by Treasury officials; but once the Chancellor had 'jumped the gun' by announcing their imminent introduction to Parliament on 1 July 1975, planning and negotiations with other departments started with a vengeance. Modifications were promised in the light of experience but, as the economic crisis deepened throughout 1976, so they came to be regarded – in the Cabinet Secretary's words – as the 'touchstone of the Government's commitment to hold down expenditure'. Any modification, therefore, might be construed as a 'loss of nerve' and undermine international confidence.[121] The promise was consequently broken, and both they and Treasury control became entrenched.

Cash limits, as announced in a white paper in April 1976, were based on the division of 'voted' government expenditure (other than that on 'demand-determined' services, such as social security) into some 126 'blocks'.[122] At the start of the financial year each block was to be given a cash budget, which included an allowance for anticipated inflation. It was not 'normally' to be exceeded unless Ministers collectively agreed to expand the relevant policy. The scope for such expansion, however, was limited given that any additional expenditure had to be financed out of the Contingency Fund – which for 1976/7 amounted to only £700 million, or 1.5 per cent of the total vote. Crucially the white paper then warned that, should the allowance for inflation prove inadequate, spending departments could not 'rely, as they have in the past, on supplementary provision if this would take their total provision for the year beyond the cash limits'. In short, the burden of inflation was no longer to be met by the PSBR but out of existing budgets. Departments would have to prevent any escalation in their costs, be it on staff or other inputs. Alternatively, they would have to find a more economical means of delivery or cut services.

Cash limits were, therefore, essentially an instrument of administrative control. They were underpinned, however, by two small but significant political innovations. The first was the convention that Treasury Ministers could no longer be outvoted in Cabinet Committee over expenditure. Were a dispute to arise, the onus was to be on the spending Minister to bring the proposal for increased expenditure to Cabinet, where the Chief Secretary could – and routinely did – calculate the consequences for the Contingency Fund. Second, as the Estimates Committee demanded with increasing force, cash expenditure on each block was to be published at the end of each financial year so that Parliament might adjudge the outcome.[123] Individually and collectively, therefore, Ministers were left with little room for evasion.

The white paper, however, left unresolved two of the inherent difficulties which had initially caused Treasury officials to hesitate. The first was the potential conflict between the *volume* of planned services (as enshrined in the Public Expenditure Survey and still regarded as essential for the optimum use, in the medium term, of available resources) and the *cash* cost of each service (as specified in Parliamentary Estimates and needed, in the short term, for expenditure control). The white paper hinted strongly, but did not categorically state, that cash should have precedence over volume. The second major issue was the tenuity of any allowance for future inflation. This was particularly important in relation to public sector wages, where such allowances (particularly when they reflected government targets – or, in other words, wishful thinking – rather than economic forecasts) threatened to conflict with pay research and the principle of comparability to which, as has been seen, the Government was still publicly bound. In the short term, this did not matter. Under the first two stages of the Government's incomes policy, both the TUC and the NSS accepted that wage increases should be contained within the agreed norm. Wage inflation was thus calculable. Conflict, however, became inevitable when – as was to occur in 1978 – norms could no longer be agreed.

So irreconcilable did such conflicts appear that Treasury officials initially opposed cash limits. A report in August 1974 acknowledged that, as a 'monetary sleight of hand which appears to avoid the necessity for explicit and painful decisions to cut real programmes', they would have a 'recurring appeal to Ministers'.[124] In economic crises, in other words, politicians could opt to cut expenditure piecemeal (as the money ran out) rather than logically (within an objective planning process). Nevertheless, cash limits were 'blind and irrational' because they were based on a 'gamble' about the future rate of inflation. They could consequently lead to 'unpredictable and unplanned cuts'. Moreover, because departments would be under even more pressure to hold back expenditure until the end of the year for fear of exceeding their 'limit', spending patterns would be distorted. Finally, because only selected services would be covered, there would be inequity. This would make them impractical because whilst 'departments will go a long way with the Treasury on the basis of "Fair do's" . . . they will fight every inch of the way if the "do's" are manifestly unfair'. The emphatic conclusion, therefore, was that 'bluff is a less than rational tool of management'. It should not be used.

Such negativism was directly challenged by the unprecedented size of the supplementary estimates in November 1974, which confirmed that public expenditure was seriously out of control. As has been seen, a Cash Control Group was consequently formed within the Treasury, under the previously sceptical Sir Douglas Henley, to consider the introduction of cash limits as an emergency measure. This was rejected because of a range of unresolved – and seemingly irresolvable – technical difficulties; but it was agreed in principle that they could be introduced at some time in the future. The Group's report was endorsed by the Treasury's Policy Coordinating Committee on 27 February 1975 but, because of panic over the budget, it was not submitted to Ministers until 13 May. By that time, some of the technical concerns had been eased by the realisation that FIS could monitor expenditure and so forewarn of overspends. More significantly, however, the Chancellor had been alarmed by the magnitude of the recent 32.5 per cent Civil Service pay award. Hence the nature of his Parliamentary statement on 1 June, which took the majority of his officials by surprise. 'We propose', he announced, 'to fix cash limits for the wage bill in the public sector so that all concerned may understand that the Government are not prepared to foot the bill for excessive settlements through subsidies or borrowing or by loading excess costs on the public through increases in prices or charges.' Then, as something of an afterthought, he added that cash limits would be employed 'more generally as a means of controlling expenditure in *the short term*'.[125]

Healey thereby opportunistically exploited the tentative change in officials' attitudes and, more fundamentally, their growing disillusion with the Plowden planning system.[126] Plowden was still greatly revered for having ended the chronic short-termism of the 1950s. It was even still regarded as invaluable for the control of expenditure. Ministers were obliged to plan realistically in the light of available resources. 'Real control points' were provided at which projects could be aborted before their expenditure escalated out of control. Moreover, departmental managers were guaranteed the necessary stability to optimise their use of resources. In a period of rampant inflation, however, its implied commitment to a given volume of services – regardless of actual cost – aroused concern because it created a 'false baseline' for spending programmes which, in Treasury officials' opinion, the economy simply could not afford. Particularly when settling wage claims, Ministers had to be made aware that money was limited and that 'excessive' settlements would have to be offset by cuts elsewhere. Likewise managers had to realise that the increasing cost of their programmes could not be met indefinitely 'for free'. Cushioned against inflation, they were doing nothing to counter and were arguably even feeding it. The discipline of annual cash limits was, therefore, urgently required. As a welcome bonus, they also meant a reversion to cash accounting and the 'greater precision and incisiveness of control' that would entail. Britain, in short, would be brought back into line with practice in continental Europe where 'a healthy respect for the discipline of annual budgetary procedures in cash terms with the emphasis on expenditure/revenue balance' had never been lost.

Such a modification to Plowden inevitably caused prolonged soul-searching within the Cash Control Group. Significantly, however, a small minority of officials was sufficiently emboldened to advocate an even more proactive role for the Treasury. They recommended, for instance, the restoration of its pre-1968 control over manpower and pay (which had been ceded to the CSD) in order to make it more 'economical'. A more direct influence over policy was also sought. As one explained:

> the question to my mind is not so much whether we seek to use cash control to cut programmes 'by stealth', or to provide what is objectively judged sufficient to buy a predetermined block of resources ... it is whether the cash control is to be active or passive. If it is to be active, we shall say, as someone in the private sector would say, that at a certain level we will do without the resource, or alternatively review our other expenditure to see what else we should give up to make room for it.[127]

It was just such cuts and the restoration of Treasury control that other departments most feared.

As with the introduction of FIS, cash limits were introduced with unwonted diplomacy via an Interdepartmental Group on Cash Control (between June 1975 and May 1976) and two meetings with Permanent Secretaries (on 6 August 1975 and 8 January 1976).[128] Nevertheless departmental fears were well-grounded. To the end, official policy was that cash limits would always be sufficient to 'buy' the volume of services sanctioned by Ministers in the planning process. Within the Treasury, however, it was admitted from the start that such a guarantee was empty.[129] The ultimate purpose of cash limits was to reimpose financial discipline. To succeed, they would thus have to be tight and, given the unpredictability of inflation, they would inevitably at times be insufficient. When this occurred, it was essential that they should have 'primacy' and a shortfall in volume would occur. That shortfall, were credibility to be retained, would then have to be made permanent, with spending Ministers actively prevented from reverting in future years to the original planning totals. The logic of cash limits, therefore, even for those officials who were not committed to a reduction in public expenditure for its own sake, was that there would be effective cuts.

Likewise with the restoration of Treasury control, Permanent Secretaries were assured in January 1976 that the 'Treasury has neither the resources nor the desire to increase its involvement in departmental affairs'.[130] This, however, was belied by the operating rules which were ultimately adopted. To determine the appropriate cash level for each programme, for example, its cost at current prices had to be translated into an estimated average of prices throughout the financial year. The basis for this calculation was the forecast increase in the Retail Price Index; but, to allow for the peculiar mix of staff and goods in each programme (its relative price effect), certain additional 'revaluation factors' were employed. Traditionally the range of such factors had been wide and their calculation had been entrusted to the relevant department. After April 1976, however, only 22 standard 'revaluation factors' were permitted; and each was to be centrally determined and their use closely monitored. This represented a significant, if surreptitious, increase in the Treasury control.

The story was the same in the third area of potential conflict: pay. The NSS was assured in May 1976 that there was 'no intention that cash limits should prejudice a decision on the re-introduction of a pay system based on fair comparisons'; but a year earlier Sir Douglas Allen had demonstrated the impossibility of honouring such a commitment.[131] The two principal reasons were expounded by the CSD throughout the summer of 1975, to the Treasury's mounting irritation. First, at a time of increasing militancy, the principle of comparability was not an extravagant luxury but a prerequisite for industrial peace. Second, the logic was that if 'excessive' pay settlements pushed staff costs through their relevant 'limit', numbers should be cut. However, as the Cost of Central Government Committee was simultaneously arguing, this would be impossible without a parallel cut in 'functions'– which Ministers would find equally unpalatable. In addition, recent employment legislation made redundancy neither quick nor cheap.

The power of such arguments was acknowledged by some within the Treasury, who concluded that the gains for which they had been hoping were 'illusory'.[132] This did not deter others, but it did flush out their ultimate objective: to end the essential 'irresponsibility' of negotiators who had no budgetary responsibility for the deals they signed. In other words, freed since 1968 from the 'discipline' of having to negotiate themselves with the NSS and to manage the Service, some Treasury officials were seeking a return to the pre-1955 world when all public pay negotiations – and arbitration awards – were subject to a political judgement of what was economically in the 'national interest'. Given the crisis of consensus, and in particular changing attitudes towards 'big' government, such a demand was bound to escalate. The days of comparability were numbered.

As late as their introduction in April 1976, cash limits continued to be advanced with caution. In part this was due to continuing conflicts within the Treasury. In the main, however, it was due to continuing doubts over whether Cabinet had the collective will to impose, and spending Ministers the intention to comply with, such restrictions.[133] The replacement of Henley by Pliatzky as head of the new Public Services Sector in February 1976 provided the necessary administrative resolution, just as the replacement of Wilson by Callaghan ensured the political will. Practices and attitudes consequently tightened as the economic situation deteriorated. Between July and September 1976, for example, it was agreed that the latitude afforded departments to offset anticipated overspends (such as the right to vire between CSD and Treasury blocks of expenditure) should be restricted in order to achieve 'what one suspects was an intention of cash limits i.e. that they should bite on volume'. 'Failing' PFOs were also to be 'exposed' rather than covered.[134] The real crunch, however, came in November, just before the arrival of the IMF. Earlier the Chief Secretary – with the Cabinet Secretary's support – had sought definitely to deny compensatory increases in cash limits should inflation be higher than forecast. Callaghan demurred, correctly identifying the change as a 'significant policy proposal' on which Cabinet should explicitly agree. Agree, to the Treasury's relief, it did; and so the Chief Secretary was able both to announce the further restriction to Parliament and implement it immediately in relation to the impending 'winter' supplementary estimates. Simultaneously, the Treasury had to negotiate the cash limits for 1977/8 with departments. Because of the earlier sleights of hand, it was feared that PFOs would be obdurate. Again to the Treasury's relief, they were not; and their continuing compliance resulted in an underspend in 1977/8 – even on limits which had been kept artificially low – of 2.9 per cent (or £809 million).[135] This was even larger than the underspend in 1976/7 and helped to account for the first real-term fall in welfare expenditure since the War.

Cash limits, therefore, effectively restored Treasury control and installed within the Treasury a new generation of officials driven by assumptions and objectives which, as recently as 1974, would have been openly ridiculed. This was essentially an administrative revolution. Initially Treasury Ministers may have forced the pace; but Healey's initial Parliamentary statement only referred to 'controlling expenditure in *the short term*' and cash limits were only accepted, in principle, by Cabinet 'by default' and, in detail, when No.10 was paralysed by Wilson's resignation. Even when they faced their critical test in November 1976, they were dismissed by Callaghan as 'dreary stuff'.[136] Nevertheless, their political significance was immense. By questioning the principle of pay comparability, they challenged an assumption upon which the modernisation of Civil Service management had been based for a generation. More fundamentally, by asserting the primacy of cash budgets over the planned volume of services, they challenged the long-standing and all-party commitment to planning. They, therefore, truly epitomised the contemporary crisis in consensus. So potentially revolutionary a change were they that Treasury officials advanced with extreme caution, fearful that – as predicted in 1974 – their bluff would be called by the Cabinet, by spending Ministers or at least by outraged PFOs. Somewhat ironically, however, it was Callaghan (the embittered ex-Chancellor) who provided the discipline that enabled the Treasury to restore its control; and in their compliance PFOs reflected the lack of self-confidence and concern for over-government earlier voiced by their Permanent Secretaries at Sunningdale. Indeed, it was only the NSS that sought to call the Treasury's bluff – and that led ultimately to the 'winter of discontent', which did not notably advance its members' interests.

6.4 Conclusion

For the Civil Service, it was the 1970s rather than the 1930s that was the 'devil's decade'. The revolution in its postwar responsibilities for economic and social policy had remained unmatched by any parallel revolution in the role either of Parliament (the ultimate scrutineer of its efficiency and effectiveness) or of Ministers (who remained wedded to the outdated convention of 'Ministerial responsibility').[137] The postwar consensus, which had validated the increase of state intervention, then came under serious ideological and electoral attack. Consequently, at the very time that the Service's capacity was capable of major expansion – with computerisation and the coming of age of a generation of officials for whom 'everything was possible' – it was constrained and suffered, at the top at least, a serious loss of confidence. The tension which had always existed between democracy and the Fabian concept of bureaucracy (which had most recently dogged the Fulton Committee) had been finally and fully exposed.

The meaning of modernisation changed in Britain, as in other Western countries. Key to its old meaning had been a commitment to rational planning (symbolised by the 1961 Plowden Committee and the subsequent creation of PESC) and efficient management (symbolised by the creation of the CSD in 1968). The former was challenged by the introduction of cash limits and, symptomatic of the confused values of the times, they resulted – under a Labour Government – in an underspend of departmental budgets which, when initially planned under a Conservative Government, it had been their express purpose to prevent. Symptomatic too of the confusion was the demand by Fulton's remaining adherents – in concert with their ideological opponents – for the CSD to be reabsorbed within the Treasury. Fulton had urged its creation for the very reason that it could 'fight, and be seen fighting, the Treasury' for greater efficiency. A third harbinger of change was the appointment of special advisers. The monopoly of policy advice, for which officials had long and jealously fought since 1854, had finally been breached.

The devil's decade was not decisive. Cash limits did not immediately replace volume planning. The CSD was not abolished. Special advisers were contained. What was lacking, as during modernisation's moment, was the sustained political will to establish a new consensus and adjust the machinery of government accordingly. That will was soon to be felt throughout the Service.

7
MRS THATCHER AND THE DEMISE OF THE CIVIL SERVICE DEPARTMENT, 1979–81

7.1 Introduction

By 1979 the time was ripe for radical administrative reform. Political and popular expectations were high. Initially, Fulton had popularised elite concerns about the efficacy of postwar Government; and the flood of memoirs from participants in the Wilson Governments, culminating in the publication of the Crossman *Diaries*, had deepened doubts. With the Heath Government, the focus of attack had then changed. Under the influence of 'public choice' theorists and monetarists in the USA, 'big government' had come to be seen as the cause of – not the potential solution for – Britain's relative decline. Criticism focused instead on the self-aggrandising nature of the public sector and its tendency to crowd out private investment. As the economy declined, so public anger simultaneously concentrated on the 'privileges' of officials, such as guaranteed employment and inflation-proof pensions. Further evidence of incompetence (as dramatised in 1978 by Leslie Chapman's *Your Disobedient Servant*) merely rubbed salt into the wound.

Such a political and popular frenzy demanded – and secured – reform. During the period of 'big government', for example, an attempt had been made to enhance professionalism through structural change (such as the nominal abolition of the Administrative Class) and a greater emphasis on management and training. Senior Ministers had also been permitted to appoint special advisers to prevent their political instincts being dulled by bureaucrats. Then to reduce 'big government', cash limits had been introduced to reinforce the cap on numbers; and they, in turn, had challenged the principle (pay comparability) on which industrial relations within the Service, and thus the power of staff associations, were based. This change in emphasis from expanding to contracting government had caused some embarrassment. The recently signed national pay deal, for example, had to be abruptly abrogated in 1975. On the other hand, some reforms satisfied both camps. 'Accountable management', for instance, had initially been promoted by Fulton to encourage greater professionalism but was eventually introduced, in the form of departmental agencies, by the Conservatives to increase efficiency and contract government. Similarly, opposing factions on the English Committee in 1977 could view with equanimity the possible replacement of the Civil Service Department (intended by

Fulton to enhance professionalism) by a Bureau of the Budget (designed to impose more rigorous control on public expenditure and administration). The prospect was even more widely welcomed because of the potential for the new Bureau to work in tandem with a strengthened Cabinet Office and thereby form an embryo Prime Minister's Office, which would strengthen 'top down' control.

How well prepared was the incoming Government under Mrs Thatcher to capitalise on such propitious circumstances? Its manifesto, it is true, promised major savings from 'the reduction of waste, bureaucracy and over-government' and the restoration of 'responsible pay bargaining'.[1] Such platitudes, however, were commonplace and had been uttered frequently in the past. Consequently they aroused little interest, and few expectations, amongst officials at the centre. Rather, as with the Heath Government, Ministers were known to disagree diametrically about the 'proper' role of government and were confidently expected to be distracted by other priorities, notably industrial relations and the economy. These were the issues which had monopolised pre-election planning whereas, in sharp contrast to the 1960s and despite its relevance to the desired 'cultural' change, administrative reform had been relatively neglected.[2] Thus Geoffrey Howe's musing on the eve of the election about the creation of a Bureau of the Budget (which caused a certain panic within the CSD) was essentially extemporised. Whitehall could also rest assured that Mrs Thatcher herself had little personal experience of, or interest in, management.[3]

Initially, therefore, the Thatcher Government set about exploiting the exceptional opportunity for change with little more than rhetoric and the 'gut instincts' of the Prime Minister. The vacuity of the former (which had already aroused intense anger within Whitehall in relation to pensions, see Chapter 9.4) had been further exposed by the manifesto commitment to save £1.2 billion on the administration of tax and social security. Such 'economy' measures had already been examined and shown to be potentially self-defeating because of the likelihood of falling revenue and a rise in fraudulent benefit claims. The susceptibility of the Prime Minister's instincts was similarly exposed by her insistence at an informal ministerial meeting on 8 May that all Ministers should accept personal responsibility for the promotion of efficiency and the elimination of waste in their departments.[4] The concept of minister-managers had also been already tried and had not proved a notable success either during the Heath Government or with PAR. It was to prove equally unpopular with her colleagues. Her simultaneous, and sudden, delegation of responsibility for the assault on 'waste and bureaucracy' to a small 'Efficiency' Unit headed by Sir Derek Rayner (the joint managing director of Marks and Spencer) also appeared somewhat conservative. The creation of such a unit had been previously advocated by Douglas Allen; and Sir Derek Rayner, as has been seen, was a former member of Heath's business team and head of one of the first departmental agencies (the Defence Procurement Executive). Currently he was a member of the Board overseeing the much-reviled Pay Research Unit. Moreover, he was well-known for holding most Civil Servants in high regard.[5]

Consequently the initial programme of administrative reform was characterised by a curious mix of conviction and caution. This, as will be seen in Chapters 7.4 and 7.5, was borne out by the two major developments (the 1981 Civil Service strike and the abolition of the CSD) which signalled the end of the old order and, in retrospect, acquired the aura of emblematic 'Thatcherite' achievements. Before the strike, conviction was displayed by the imposition of cash limits on Civil Service pay in the Spring of 1980 and the unilateral suspension of the national pay agreement in the autumn. This, it might be argued, did little more than mimic the Labour Government's actions between 1975 and 1978. However, whereas Labour had buckled during the winter of discontent, Mrs Thatcher – as will be seen – rode out the subsequent storm of a 21-week strike. Its length and cost may well have been increased by her tactics but, having arguably lost the battle, she incontrovertibly won the war. By contrast, her one major structural initiative (the abolition of the CSD in November 1981) was characterised by caution. Its fate had earlier elicited an uncharacteristic series of 'u-turns' for, having initially agreed its closure in July 1980, she then reversed that decision before changing her mind yet again during the strike. Even the process of actual closure prompted further hesitancy and, somewhat ironically, the decisive actions had to be taken by the officials involved.[6] Whatever the nature of her decision-making, however, both the strike and the closure of the CSD were highly symbolic. The one marked the end of Whitleyism and thus the power of staff associations within the Service. The other required the effective dismissal of both the Head of the Home Civil Service (Sir Ian Bancroft) and his deputy (Sir John Herbecq).

In 1981, therefore, the opportunity for radical reform was belatedly seized and two major initiatives provided an impression of decisiveness. Both initiatives were, however, essentially negative – clearing the way for, rather than actively promoting, reform. Meanwhile, to provide an impression of activity – and to give some substance to political rhetoric and satisfy public expectation – a series of expedients was enacted. On a more positive note, to make good pre-election neglect –and thereby give substance to Mrs Thatcher's instincts – the Efficiency Unit hastily prepared a programme of 'lasting' reforms. The nature of these short-term economies and long-term plans will be examined in turn.

7.2 Short-term economies

The three principal expedients adopted in 1979 – the culling of quangos, the emergency reduction of manpower, and the initial programme of Rayner projects – differed little from past practice and were, in essence, mere holding operations whilst other priorities (such as economic strategy) were resolved and long-term objectives clarified. They were however, particularly significant in that they further discredited the CSD and so contributed directly to its demise. Such an eventuality was the more surprising since the titular head of the CSD was the Prime Minister and it thus had the potential to be – as was initially envisaged by some – the vehicle through which she could impose her stamp upon the Service. Particularly in relation to the preceding Labour Government, it also had a strong ministerial team headed by Lord Soames. As Churchill's son-in-law and a former Ambassador to France and European Commissioner, he was unquestionably a political heavyweight – although his other duties as Lord President meant that he could devote only half his time to departmental duties and, as Governor General in Rhodesia overseeing Zimbabwean independence between December 1979 and April 1980, he was wholly absent. There is also some doubt as to whether he was ever fully reconciled to so relatively humble a post or prepared to master what, particularly in negotiations with the unions, must have appeared 'footling' details. However, his tactical skill, intellectual powers, and integrity were greatly appreciated by his officials. 'If inclined to judge the service harshly', as his Second Permanent Secretary (Sir John Herbecq) recalled, 'he recognized that it had a vital role to play in the effective government of the country; he never treated it with contempt'. His fundamental problem was that he had a 'terminal lack of sympathy' with the Prime Minister's economic policy and, particularly during the discussion of the seminal 1981 budget, was at no pains to disguise it.[7] Soames' deputy was Paul Channon who, having been born (as well as marrying) into the Guinness family, was equally well-connected. Extremely hard working and approachable, he perhaps lacked public charisma but – despite his exclusion from the Cabinet – he displayed consummate tactical skills within Whitehall and Westminster, especially when substituting for Soames. He was ultimately promoted to Minister for the Arts in 1981, to be replaced by Barney Heyhoe. Soames himself was noisily dismissed in September 1981 at the end of the Civil Service strike and replaced by Lady Young. When the CSD was abolished, therefore, and its responsibilities divided between the Treasury and the new Management and Personnel Office (MPO) attached to the Cabinet Office, it represented not just an administrative but also a ministerial watershed.

7.2.1 *Reviewing non-departmental public bodies*

The first economy measure to be fully completed was the review of 'quangos' or non-departmental public bodies (NDPBs). It was self-contained but nevertheless epitomised the nature of administrative reform before 1982. It was entrusted not to Ministers or the CSD but to a favoured individual – in this case Sir Leo Pliatzky, the Treasury official responsible for the initial implementation (but not the planning) of cash limits, who had recently retired as Permanent Secretary of the DTI. It was impelled by a vociferous Party and press campaign which the final *Report* (Cmnd 7797) exposed as exaggerated and unrealistic. Instead of making a major contribution, as trailed, to a £2000 million reduction in public expenditure, the *Report* merely recommended the abolition of 247 (out of the existing 2115) NDPBs with a direct saving of £11.6 million. It was nevertheless praised by the Prime Minister as 'a remarkable feat'.[8] It also made some detailed procedural suggestions, as was certainly not the Prime Minister's initial wish, which the CSD then sought to turn into a code of best practice but whose circulation was typically delayed so that it might be made more robust by the Efficiency Unit. This was a final humiliation for the CSD which had all the necessary information at its fingertips (following the 1978 Bowen Committee on fringe bodies), had recommended Pliatzy as head of the inquiry, and had duly alerted him to the impracticality of certain Efficiency Unit suggestions (such as consultation with all NDPB members). However, it was unable to translate (or prevented from translating) such expertise into effective action.

The review was also dogged by a fundamental confusion of purpose. Before 1979, the attack on NDPBs had had three overriding objectives: to reduce public expenditure; to restrict patronage; and to reverse the expansion of government. Public expenditure, it was argued, was increased not just by the bodies' own costs but also by the spending programmes they validated and the cost of departmental monitoring. As the *Daily Telegraph* inimitably put it on 19 June 1978:

> The new breed of tax-eater, placeman and sinecurist is infinitely more pernicious than those whom Burke excoriated and the Victorian reformers abolished. They voted and picked up their pay – no more. The new class . . . appropriate public wealth as though it were their own and waste it as though it was someone else's. For every million in fees and perks, they waste a billion to justify their existence.

Patronage was similarly abhorred as a source of backdoor influence – particularly for trade unionists. Finally the New Right sought to contract NDPBs, and especially new high-spending bodies such as the Manpower Services Commission, in order to reverse the corporatism of the Heath Government.

In government, however, the target simply became a high 'body count' – with any reduction in public expenditure as a bonus. This was made plain to Pliatzky at his first meeting with the Prime Minister on 28 August, to which he robustly replied that he would have to mount a thorough factual survey both to inform his conclusions and to counter Party polemics. Such a prospect appalled the Prime Minister. Eventually, however, she relented, conceding that 'Sir Leo approached his assignment in a way which differed from her own views. They would doubtless respect one another's integrity.' He also warned that there might only be moderate savings because there were 'limits to how much he could pull up government policy from the roots in the guise of reviewing quangos'.[9] Consequently Pliatzky's brief, as announced to Cabinet on 30 August, was less crude than originally planned. All Permanent Secretaries were to be circulated with a list of criteria against which every NDPB for which they were responsible was to be judged. The list read:

1 Is the function which is being carried out essential? or
2 If not, is it valuable enough to justify the time and money spent on it?
3 If the answer is that the function is either essential or sufficiently valuable, is it best carried out by the non-Departmental body in question rather than by another means?

4   Is it being carried out well and economically?
5   Conversely, would there be any substantial loss or disadvantage if the body were wound up?

Departments were to provide the answers; Pliatzky was to interview the Permanent Secretaries; and then decisions were to be taken with the agreement of Ministers.[10]

The circular made two things apparent. First, arguably because the Conservative Party was now making the appointments, the issue of patronage had lost its urgency. Rather, the *Report* paid tribute to the many 'worthy people who gave their services free' and who had been besmirched by the polemical attack on quangos.[11] Second, a new ruthlessness towards state intervention was required – not least because in response to incessant demands for manpower cuts, Ministers were surreptitiously transferring departmental responsibilities to quangos. This angered both Mrs Thatcher and Pliatzky who demanded, and was given, the right to investigate all organisations 'hived off' under Heath.[12] He found none to cull but the *Report* nevertheless contained the warning that 'we should not think in terms of a further considerable extension of "hiving off", to echo the Fulton Committee's phrase, as an instrument for securing improved efficiency and economy'.[13]

The *Report's* inability to identify any major candidate for abolition was significant because, having established that 20 bodies were responsible for 87 per cent of expenditure, six had been singled out for particular scrutiny (including, at Mrs Thatcher's request, the MSC and the Health and Safety Commission and Executive). The need for each was duly confirmed. Instead, the *Report* concentrated on greater prudence and accountability. New bodies should be established only as a last resort and, wherever possible, with a finite remit; the value of existing ones should be kept constantly under review; and to maximise Parliamentary and public scrutiny, all financial records should be accessible to the Comptroller and Auditor General and detailed annual reports published. These were the guidelines which the CSD was then instructed to codify.[14]

The review, therefore, demonstrated the essential barrenness of totemic reform driven by Party and public rhetoric. The number of NDPBs may have halved by December 1981 but this was largely the result of expedients (such as amalgamation) and so illusory. Ideologically, little was gained. As early as 1983, indeed, complaints were being voiced about not only the creation of a new generation of NDPBs but also those which had 'survived the 1979 purge ... [including] quite major ones like the National Economic Development Council'.[15] A new initiative was duly launched and stricter guidelines issued in 1984 and 1985 respectively. By then the critique was more soundly based and the objectives more ambitious.

7.2.2 Reducing departmental manpower

Whilst non-departmental bodies were being reviewed, so departmental manpower was also subjected to four major initiatives. The first Cabinet instructed the CSD to freeze recruitment in order to reduce immediate manpower costs by three per cent. On 31 May 1979 the CSD then launched an 'options' exercise (as in 1976) to cut the Service by up to 20 per cent. In June 1979 the Efficiency Unit instituted a series of departmental 'projects' to identify specific areas of waste. Simultaneously, the Treasury tentatively and then, in February 1980, more firmly imposed a cash limit on manpower costs.

With so many initiatives, the potential for confusion was as great as it had been during the NDPB review. Was the prime objective to reduce numbers or public expenditure? The two were not synonymous, as has been seen, because a reduction of DHSS anti-fraud officials or of tax collectors could respectively increase expenditure or decrease revenue. Was the priority to cut waste or to reduce the role of government? Again the two were not synonymous; and were it the latter, should not any action have been preceded by a review of policy (or 'functions')? Alternatively was the objective simply the crude meeting of monetarist targets? The Conservatives, as was widely acknowledged, had received a 'dreadful inheritance', with Labour having unrealistically budgeted for a mere two per cent increase in public expenditure.[16] Consequently, without major manpower cuts, they could not honour two of their central manifesto commitments: a reduction in the Public Sector Borrowing Requirement and tax cuts. As with the NDPB review, however, Ministers collectively were either unwilling or unable to resolve such confusion.

In addition, the resulting tension further exposed the fault line between the CSD and the Treasury, with their respective responsibility for manpower control and public expenditure, as well as condemning the CSD in the eyes of Mrs Thatcher. The initial freeze on recruitment, which lasted from 9 May to 27 July 1979, foreshadowed many of the later political tensions. In order to set the tone for the whole administration and to oblige both Ministers and officials to confront stark choices, Mrs Thatcher demanded a six-month freeze and a cut of five per cent. This provoked a Cabinet revolt as early as 17 May on the grounds that such an indiscriminate freeze could be counterproductive. It could, for example, reduce operational efficiency in regions (such as London) and in specialist areas (such as computing) where turnover was high. It could, as has been seen, frustrate monetary targets were there to be a rise in either benefit fraud or tax evasion. Unions would also be antagonised and morale (and thus efficiency) impaired. Above all, Cabinet rejected the premise, derived from Leslie Chapman, that no policy changes were needed because waste was so excessive.[17] Typically, the Prime Minister succeeded in maintaining a freeze but, atypically, she was defeated on two major counts. As desired by the CSD, the target for reduced manpower costs remained 3 per cent rather than 5 per cent (with 2.7 per cent, or the loss of 21,000 jobs, being eventually achieved); and the ban was to be lifted after only three months (when cash limits were scheduled to be introduced).

The exercise with which the CSD sought to replace the freeze was the 'options' programme, which required each department to specify how it would reduce manpower by 10, 15 or 20 per cent (as opposed to 5–15 per cent in 1976). It was intended to be provocative because, as Soames wrote to fellow Ministers, 'too much government over too many years had created the habit of mind that regards every activity as essential and the expectation, among the public no less than among civil servants, that it will continue'.[18] It was, however, a failure. Three progress reports were considered in Cabinet, on 13 September, 1 November and 22 November but when the programme's final results were announced in Parliament on 6 December savings of only five per cent (or 39,000 posts) had been identified – of which 11,000 were the result of contracting out, rather than genuine savings. Privately and in Cabinet, Soames expressed incredulity that Ministers should consider 95 per cent of the activities of the previous 'Socialist' Government to be essential; and Mrs Thatcher had originally anticipated a reduction of at least ten per cent. What had gone wrong?

One impediment was the immediate disinterring of departmental 'horror comics' which demonstrated how civilisation, as it was known, would collapse were there anything more than marginal cuts.[19] By such tactics, the three largest departments which employed 64 per cent of officials – the Ministry of Defence, the Treasury (with its 'sub-departments', the Inland Revenue and Customs and Excise) and the DHSS – justified proposals for respective cuts of only 3, 4.2 and 1.8 per cent. There were, however, more substantial reasons for failure. As Francis Pym (the Secretary of State for Defence) argued, not wholly disingenuously, a sounder strategy was to 'build upwards from the facts rather than downwards from arbitrary targets'.[20] Before committing himself to any cuts, he thus wanted to complete the internal policy reviews he had already ordered. Many projected cuts were dependent on controversial policy changes (such as, to reduce DHSS manpower, the payment by employers of the first six weeks of sick pay), for which Parliamentary approval was required. Moreover, the threat (if only for effect) of a 20 per cent cut had so provoked a rash of unofficial strikes that an emergency Cabinet Sub-committee (E(CS)) had had to be formed to draft contingency plans. Finally, and arguably most damaging of all, was the conflict provoked by the reduction of numbers through the contracting out of services to the private sector. Mrs Thatcher and Michael Heseltine went on record as supporting it, even if it increased public expenditure (and thereby undermined monetarist targets). Soames opposed such an eventuality in Cabinet and Channon boldly ruled it out in Parliament.[21]

By Cabinet on 1 November Mrs Thatcher was clearly exasperated by the CSD's ineffectuality and the Lord President's bluster, and instead seized on the Rayner 'projects' which had recently been completed (see Chapter 7.2.3) and the virtues of Michael Heseltine's management control system (MINIS) by which he claimed – like Chapman – that manpower could be cut without any policy changes.[22] Consequently, she abandoned the 'options' initiative and thereby the CSD. This was the more unfortunate because, with Soames in Rhodesia, Channon simultaneously embraced cash limits as the means to secure results. Correctly anticipating a gap between the future cash limit on manpower costs (14 per cent) and the pay rise to be recommended by PRU (18.75 per cent), he eschewed a crude numbers game and recommended that all departments cut their manpower costs by five per cent. When this drew the inevitable response, he appealed first to the relevant Cabinet

Committee and then to the full Cabinet on 28 February 1980. The latter endorsed his logic if not all his proposals. The pay award had to be honoured, it was agreed, otherwise 'we should, unlike any previous government, have enlisted behind the militants the great bulk of the loyal staff'. On the other hand, Party activists would be antagonised were there to be no cuts at a time when private industry was being forced to shed labour. A cut in manpower costs of 2.5 per cent was finally agreed, which led to a further saving of 15,000 posts.[23]

In his memorandum to Cabinet, however, Channon had made a significant admission. 'Time', he confessed, 'simply does not permit a more sophisticated course.'[24] Rayner concurred but simultaneously expressed dismay that, rather than a coherent manpower policy, there were only 'sporadic squeezes when other factors require them'. This criticism was directed as much at the Prime Minister as the CSD – as was demonstrated later by his explicit rejection of her preferred policy of 'nil recruitment, nil redundancy'. However, by satisfying her wish for practical action, he managed to maintain her confidence. The ideal way forward, therefore, appeared to be for Rayner and Channon to collaborate on the development of a longer-term manpower policy. This, as will be seen in Chapter 7.3.1, is precisely what happened. First, however, it is necessary to examine the means by which Rayner won Mrs Thatcher's confidence.

7.2.3 The Rayner projects

Derek Rayner, as has been noted, was appointed somewhat peremptorily as Mrs Thatcher's unpaid personal adviser on 'the promotion of efficiency and the elimination of waste' five days after the election. His initial position, however, was by no means clear or secure. As joint managing director of Marks and Spencer (responsible both for expansion into Canada and maintaining harmony on the board between warring family factions) he could devote no more than half his working time to Government. Considerable concern was also expressed in Whitehall about the location, at the Prime Minister's insistence, of his Efficiency Unit (which initially comprised simply an Under Secretary, Clive Priestley, and an economic adviser, David Allen) in No. 10 rather than the Cabinet Office.[25] Equally difficult was his initial relationship with the Prime Minister. Meetings were typically on his rather than her initiative and, as late as June 1980, one of her Private Secretaries admitted that the Prime Minister 'tended to test out Derek's ideas on whatever is at the top of her mind rather than allowing the conversation to pursue the topics for which [the meeting] was set up'.[26]

One major problem was that, in opposition, Leslie Chapman had been Mrs Thatcher's efficiency adviser; and both she and Keith Joseph thought he still had much to contribute. Rayner saw him on 30 May, when Chapman turned down the chance to address the first 'Rayner's raiders' (all of whom had been issued with copies of *Your Disobedient Servant*) on the eve of their first departmental inquiries; and he was finally sidelined in September when he somewhat disgraced himself by attacking Rayner's anti-waste programme on the grounds – not wholly unjustified – that it was a 'joke' and would save a mere £30 million out of a potential £500 million. Rayner found Chapman 'a mixed blessing, intellectually and personally'. He agreed with many of his ideas, including – somewhat ironically – his opposition to arbitrary cuts (as favoured by Mrs Thatcher). On the other hand, he disliked the concept of a 'private army' of between 200 and 400 lawyers, accountants and management consultants aggressively auditing departments, preferring instead to instil good management practices into existing officials. Personally, Chapman also appeared boastful and too publicity conscious.[27] However, as will be seen, it was for positive rather than negative reasons that Rayner gained Mrs Thatcher's trust.

Pre-election planning and consultation over Rayner's role were limited, as is evident from Hunt's early allusion to 'Raynor' and Rayner's own reference to 'Shannon'. Hunt, however, soon offered forthright advice. Rayner should be a 'hatchet man who will go for the things that the normal PESC process will miss'. These included 'functions that can be cut, wasteful work systems [and] unnecessary demands on the public (forms, surveys etc.)'. Less perfectionism, or 'rougher justice', in administration should also be encouraged.[28] Rayner himself was equally forthright. He would focus on neither policy nor *ad hoc* anti-waste projects but rather on 'the way in which the civil service manages its work and the framework of organisation and control within which it operates'. His role should be advisory, with Ministers and their officials making – and taking responsibility for – all changes. To raise cost-consciousness and thereby defend taxpayers' interests, however, he hoped that amongst the new practices would be departmental payment for 'common services'.

All Rayner's objectives were matched to the aspirations identified at the first Cabinet to produce a programme for action, which was agreed with the Prime Minister on 31 May and 16 July. Whilst responsibility for certain initiatives (such as the culling of quangos) was to be passed to others, his 'main campaign' was to effect 'lasting reforms' to the 'general practices and convention' which were 'barriers to the effective management of business and resources' within departments.[29] This campaign was to be sustained throughout the whole administration. At the same time the Efficiency Unit was to assume from the CSD (which Mrs Thatcher dismissed as the 'sick lamb' of the Civil Service) prime responsibility for the coordination of all current anti-waste initiatives. Most significantly, a series of 'projects' was also to be launched by which in each department an energetic and able junior official – or team of officials – would radically examine a particular activity or function to determine whether it could be performed more effectively or efficiently.[30]

The projects were intended to be a one-off exercise, lasting up to six months and illuminating common problems which the 'main campaign' could then address. Mrs Thatcher was initially sceptical. She feared they would either 'sink into the time – and staff – consuming style' of PAR (which she had immediately cancelled) or concentrate on such small issues that they would make little difference.[31] As a result of her misgivings, certain refinements were made. The number of 'examining officers', for example, was minimised and they were to report direct to Ministers, with no intermediary supervising committee of senior officials. They should also last no longer than 90 days. When the first findings were brought to the Prime Minister's attention in the October recess, however, her scepticism evaporated.[32] She was excited by the potential savings and, in particular, by the graphic presentation of the two projects, by Clive Ponting of the MOD and Norman Warner of the DHSS; and insisted that the presentations, uniquely, be repeated in Cabinet. Given their less than heroic record as 'minister-managers', she reasoned, its members had much to learn from those on the front line. As the same time, the projects were rebranded 'scrutinies' and made a permanent feature of government.

As with the Pliatzky exercise, it was the style of the Rayner projects as much as their actual achievements which attracted the Prime Minister. In a narrow sense, the projects – like the later scrutinies – were failures. The potential annual savings from the first round of projects were initially calculated at £80 million with a further £53 million in one-off savings but were revised down to no more than £20 million plus £12 million in one-off savings.[33] Chapman's scepticism, therefore, seemed fully justified. One reason for the disappointing results, as foreseen by Mrs Thatcher, was delayed implementation. The projects, launched in July, had been completed by 30 November but as late as April 1980 six of the 29 'action plans' were still outstanding. The overriding reason, however, was – as again anticipated by Mrs Thatcher – the modest size of most projects. Major savings were consequently dependent on the success of a few major ones which, in the event, proved politically contentious.

The foremost example was the DHSS project, which had been the subject of Warner's presentation to Cabinet and was for Rayner the 'bedrock' of the programme.[34] It recommended, in line with European practice, the fortnightly rather than weekly payment of benefits and the provision of an option for payments directly into banks rather than through a post office. The Post Office Chairman inevitably feared a major loss of business and orchestrated a campaign by 15,000 sub-postmasters and mistresses (typically the mainstay of local Conservative Party associations) to protest against the consequences for small – and especially rural – communities and the most vulnerable. A tortuous series of Cabinet meetings, Parliamentary debates and Parliamentary Select Committee investigations then followed before a compromise was eventually agreed in May 1981. To extend consumer choice, direct bank payments were to be introduced; but, although a preference for monthly payments for pensions and child benefit was made explicit, existing beneficiaries and the vulnerable groups were to be permitted to collect weekly payments. The Post Office was to be compensated for a potential five per cent loss of business and given the right to offer other public services (such as energy stamps and bus passes). Such belated concessions, however, cost the Government much political goodwill as well as much Ministerial and official time. They also reduced potential annual savings from £50 million to £32 million.

If the Rayner projects were no more – and arguably less – successful than the CSD's short-term economy measures, they nevertheless had other virtues. They focused, and kept focused, attention (and particularly Prime Ministerial attention) on administrative reform. This marked the first, albeit tentative, step towards the acceptance by Ministers and officials alike of a management 'culture'. They gave junior officials an unparalleled opportunity to display initiative and to demonstrate, as Rayner never tired of telling Mrs Thatcher, the latent ability, energy and dedication within the Service. They also identified a range of generic problems, such as the need swiftly to accept 'modern methods' (such as computers) and the excessive monitoring of business and local government.[35] Finally the projects precipitated specific service-wide initiatives such as the charging for common services (which, as has been seen, was one of Rayner's initial interests). In other words, the importance of the projects lay not so much in the short-term economies they achieved but in the basis they laid for more lasting reforms.

7.3 Long-term manpower policy

Mrs Thatcher's first year in government was permeated by a sense of *déjà vu*. Rhetorical attacks on the Service by both the public and Party had proved as empty a guide to effective reform as they had during 'modernisation's moment'. There may have been no formal enquiry (such as Fulton), major policy statements (such as *The Reorganisation of Central Government*) or ambitious blueprints (as with unified grading) but, beset by similar economic and political pressures, equal amounts of energy were expended to bring forth an equally mangy mouse. There were, however, two crucial differences. First, unlike Wilson and Heath, Mrs Thatcher had retained her reforming zeal. Second, the failings of pre-election planning had been gradually made good by the development of a long-term policy which was presented to Cabinet on 1 May 1980 – almost a year, to the day, after the election. It had three elements. The first, driven by the CSD, was the planned reduction of the Service to its smallest size since the War (630,000). The second, fostered by Rayner, was the encouragement of a new managerial culture throughout the Service by means of annual scrutinies and a programme of 'lasting reforms'. The third, the particular concern of Michael Heseltine as Secretary of State for the Environment and building on the bridgehead established by FIS, was to embed within each department an effective management information system (such as his own MINIS) which would finally make the concept of minister-managers a reality.[36] At the last minute, the Prime Minister persuaded Heseltine not to wax lyrical about MINIS in Cabinet, but to inform his colleagues of it by letter. Ministerial discussion was in fact to be delayed until February 1982, and so it will be discussed in the next volume. Accordingly, this section will deal with only the first two elements of long-term policy.

7.3.1 *The 630,000 target*

The CSD's final foray into the numbers game was rooted, somewhat ironically, in dissatisfaction with past performance. Most importantly, Rayner had soon concluded that previous economy campaigns had been characterised by 'agonised parings of the Civil Service ... followed by expansions of work, so that the automatic response to each new "cut" is a cynical expectation that what has been taken away with one hand will soon be replaced with the other'. As a result, there had been mere 'skirmishes on the frontiers of most departments [whilst] the heartland within was rarely penetrated'. What a 'long-term manpower policy for a reforming administration' really needed was an attainable target towards which consistent progress could be made over a number of years. This would require a year to plan.[37] Mrs Thatcher, however, wanted immediate results. Consequently, at a somewhat confused meeting with Rayner and Channon at Chequers on 9 April 1981, it was agreed that the effective choice for long-term policy lay between 'asking Ministers to agree at once to a specific target or asking them to spend some time in their departments, somewhat like the Secretary of State for the Environment, in considering in reasonable detail what contributions they could make'.[38] Consequently, the CSD directly set about defining, and determining the means to achieve, the 'specific target'.

The resulting memorandum, which it submitted to Cabinet on 1 May, went through four drafts and its key recommendations were finalised by Mrs Thatcher, Channon and Rayner in consultation with two senior Ministers (Whitelaw and Howe) on 22 April.[39] There was to be a 12.5 per cent cut in manpower, cumulatively achieved by an annual 2.5 per cent cut in each department. This would reduce numbers to 620,000 for the delivery of existing services and permit a contingency margin of 10,000 for additional work (arising, for example, from increased unemployment). The exercise was to be overseen by the CSD, not by a 'special commissioner' or 'special adviser' (as Rayner originally wanted) and was to focus on increased efficiency (rather than policy changes) and cuts in senior posts (which had so far been reduced by only 1.5 per cent). Channon anticipated ministerial resistance to such a strategy but, as he sought to demonstrate to Mrs Thatcher, he was determined to succeed. 'Some may say', he admitted to her, that

> the target of 2.5% for 3 years is too high. I do not believe – nor incidentally do CSD officials – that the target is too high.... Some colleagues may argue that we ought not to set an arbitrary across the board percentage cut, but to look at functions first and accept that there may be wide variations between departments.... But we simply must have a target. Otherwise we shall have nothing worthwhile to announce and no firm objective. We did a 'functions review' last year. It yielded only 4% then. It would ... probably yield much less now.[40]

In the event the 630,000 target was accepted by Cabinet. However, after a heated debate, the exclusive focus on efficiency, the cutting of senior staff by ten per cent within two years and equal misery for all departments were rejected in favour of greater flexibility between departments and over time. Cabinet, in brief, willed the end but not the means.

The new programme was, nevertheless, immediately launched by the Prime Minister in tandem with two uncharacteristic initiatives. The first, a dinner she hosted for all Permanent Secretaries on 6 May, has entered Whitehall folklore as 'one of the most splendid disasters of the Thatcher years' (see Chapter 7.3.3).[41] The second was a Prime Ministerial announcement in Parliament on 13 May. This was equally disastrous because it exposed her to the scorn of both the Labour Party and her own right-wing backbenchers. The 630,000 target had been repeatedly leaked and doubts had been expressed, equally repeatedly, about its practicality. The statement contained no concrete suggestions. Accordingly, it was attacked by Labour as being at best 'flatulent and empty' and at worst 'pandering to the worst prejudices' against the public services in her Party.[42] Meanwhile those 'prejudices' were not satisfied because no ritual sacrifice, such as the abolition of the CSD, was promised. Under such an attack Mrs Thatcher faltered, even asserting at one point that manpower reductions were on course and that the 'extra target' did 'not require a great deal more decision-making on functions'. This, as has been seen, directly contradicted Cabinet policy. Exceptionally she also defended the CSD, arguing that the size of the Service was the result not of poor management but of past Governments which had 'loaded extra tasks on to it and seemed . . . to encourage the retention of as many people as possible'.

The programme's implementation inevitably intensified Ministerial opposition. On 4 June, Soames (who had assumed prime responsibility from Channon) requested a provisional summary of their department's cuts within a month. When the returns then revealed a shortfall of 25,000, he instinctively demanded an alternative across-the-board cut of ten per cent. The Cabinet rejected this but did agree the returns should be revised.[43] These still revealed a 17,000 shortfall – or 22,000, were the contingency reserve to be expanded, as was now thought prudent, given the intensifying economic downturn. Soames decided to allocate the additional cuts unilaterally. This again won Cabinet support but, on the insistence of the Chancellor of the Exchequer, the minutes recorded that each department's target represented not a commitment but an aspiration 'which each departmental minister would do his utmost to secure'. However, once published – as Mrs Thatcher wished in order to defuse Parliamentary and public criticism – would not such 'aspirations' in effect become binding?

Detailed departmental figures were finally published on 27 November, but they provided little respite because departmental estimates for 1981–2 simultaneously revealed that –rather than decreasing – manpower was due to increase. Soames' instinct this time was to ban all recruitment, but he was dissuaded by yet another promise to revise departmental programmes. When this proved abortive, the CSD was empowered to make unilateral cuts.[44] Nevertheless, this 'effective handing over of authority on their staffing levels to the Lord President' angered Ministers and turned covert non-compliance into overt defiance. Mrs Thatcher consequently abandoned the 'target' programme and it was surreptitiously merged with the PESC exercise (which had by now been placed on a cash rather than a volume basis). This realised Rayner's ideal of uniting the control of manpower and expenditure (which had informed his desire to remerge the CSD with the Treasury), whilst Soames was left to combat the Civil Service strike and to draft the anodyne white paper, *Efficiency in the Civil Service* (Cmnd 8293).

Ministerial disenchantment with the CSD's manpower campaign was not fully justified because, despite intense pressures, there was no u-turn and the target of 630,000 was ultimately attained by its target date of April 1984. Meanwhile, however, the Government sustained considerable damage. Outside Whitehall, the scorn displayed in Parliament was reinforced by the Treasury and Civil Service Select Committee. 'The May 1980 announcement', it concluded with some justice in August 1980, 'appears to have been a mainly political decision based on intention rather than on calculation ... The inability to express the 102,000 net contraction in the size of the Civil Service in terms of tasks either to be cut or reduced represents a weakness in the Government's policy.'[45] So too, it argued, was the inability to calculate the likely economic and social costs of the programme. The Civil Service unions were also incensed by the disdain for public service implicit in the cuts and the readiness to embrace contracting out, whether it saved money or not. In response, many Ministers and advisers (including Keith Joseph and Rayner) constantly urged the Prime Minister to express some public appreciation of the Service. 'Something positive needs to be said about the value of the Civil Service and about its pay and conditions', urged one of her main protagonists, Francis Pym, 'It is not clear to me how you get the best out of people if you appear all the time to be lambasting them in public'.[46] Appreciative references, as included in the draft of the 13 May Parliamentary announcement, nevertheless continued to be excised. This all contributed to the anger which spilled over in March 1981 into the Civil Service strike.

The more substantial damage, however, was sustained within Government. Before the debate on 1 May, the Cabinet Secretary had warned of 'signs of ministerial revulsion, if not revolt' and, as has been seen, once the cuts began to bite resistance stiffened further.[47] In September 1980, for example, John Nott led the opposition to the enforced introduction of an information management system such as MINIS. 'Unhesitatingly', he proclaimed, 'I see myself as a politician not as a staff-manager.' Peter Walker voiced another common concern. 'We must avoid giving to arbitrary targets for manpower', he asserted, 'such a degree of priority as to confer on them absolute power to determine policies and functions.' A third grievance was then expressed most trenchantly by Lord Hailsham who denounced 'arbitrary reductions which have no necessary relationship either to efficiency or expense'. 'I cannot believe', he concluded, 'that we are engaged on an exercise which is purely cosmetic in intention and otherwise counterproductive in effect.' Such rhetoric was transformed into outright defiance after Christmas 1980, as the cuts started to bite into policy. When so requested by the CSD, for example, both Jim Prior and Patrick Jenkin (at the Department of Employment and the DHSS respectively) refused to implement the recommendations of the Rayner scrutiny on the payment of benefit to the unemployed. Supplementary benefit, Jenkin reminded Soames, was 'a benefit to which people are entitled by law and we cannot decide whether or not to deal with a claim'. Precipitate action would also render relations with the unions on the Manpower Services Commission 'a farce'.[48] Even more serious was the recalcitrance of the Chancellor of the Exchequer. The Treasury (somewhat ironically given the managerial responsibilities Mrs Thatcher and Rayner wished to bestow on it) had been one of the most dilatory economisers. In February 1981, however, Howe dug in his heels over the suggestion that, in order to save manpower, the taxation of unemployment benefit should be deferred. An annual saving of £35 million, he protested, would deny Government an estimated £400 million in revenue.

The Chancellor's protest at last brought home to Mrs Thatcher the potential contradictions in her pursuit of the 630,000 target and she consequently withdrew her support – as in November 1979 – from the CSD. This was serious for the Department because, despite their collaboration (over, for example, the payment of benefit to the unemployed), it was well known that Rayner and the Efficiency Unit was planning its demise (see Chapter 7.5). The initial adoption of the 630,000 target had been a major triumph for the CSD; but thereafter Rayner and his staff had constantly cast doubts, in Mrs Thatcher's presence, about its ability to deliver. Senior officials were dismissed as being insufficiently 'robust and manly', each initiative disparaged as 'worryingly ad hoc' and Soames' letters to Permanent Secretaries (which the Unit had repeatedly to sharpen) ridiculed as 'pious and exhortatory'.[49] Given the Prime Minister's obsession for quick results, Bancroft at the CSD had typically been able to deflect such criticisms. Such triumphs, however, ultimately turned out to be pyrrhic.

7.3.2 *The Rayner scrutinies*

The Rayner scrutinies ran parallel to, and informed, the CSD's manpower programme and were – as noted earlier – a permanent product of the 'one-off' Rayner projects of 1979. They duly became both the 'cutting edge' and the most popular manifestation of 'Raynerism'.[50] In 1980, 39 departmental scrutinies were commissioned and in 1981 a further 40, together with two 'multi-departmental' scrutinies (each covering some eight departments). Their broad purpose was outlined to Cabinet by Rayner on 4 October 1979. The 'reduction of waste, bureaucracy and over-government' which had been promised in the manifesto, he argued, could not be achieved 'by wishing it or by magic: [it] must be by a conscious exertion of Ministerial will, not once and for all, but sustained throughout the Administration'. Accordingly every year each department was to appoint a junior official, reporting directly to a Minister, to 'consider the efficiency of their operations by examining why and how selected blocks of work are carried out, seeking simplification and, if appropriate, the elimination of some activities'.[51]

Three specific objectives were thereby to be achieved. Particular instances of waste and inefficiency would be identified and removed. By bypassing senior officials (whose commitment to reform was suspect) and supervisory committees (which were typically mechanisms for delay) the latent ability within middle management would be unleashed. Finally Ministers themselves would become involved, as 'minister-managers', in the 'sharp end' of policy.[52] In addition, Rayner hoped that individual scrutinies would identify solutions to generic problems which, in Marks and Spencer's jargon, could be 'read across' to other departments; pioneer initiatives to improve managerial practice (as was to be the case in the Department of the Environment with the development of MINIS); and popularise new concepts (such as charging for 'common services').

The implicit assumption behind scrutinies was, therefore, that, Civil Servants had 'the knowledge, competence and integrity to be radical on behalf of Ministers who make plain their determination to improve their administration'; and that by working with, rather than against, the departmental grain they would permanently raise the managerial skills of officials and ministers alike.[53] In the long term, they would thus be far more effective than another report like Fulton (which might remain unimplemented) or an inquisition by outside auditors or management consultants (as favoured by Chapman and, sporadically, by Mrs Thatcher). The spirit of co-operation in which the scrutinies were to be implemented was spelt out in a note of guidance drafted by Rayner. 'The reasoning behind the scrutiny programme', it read,

> is that ministers and their officials are better equipped than anyone else to examine the use of the resources for which they are responsible. The scrutinies therefore rely heavily on self-examination. The main elements are the application of a fresh mind to the policy, function or activity studied, *unfettered by committees or hierarchy*; the interaction of that mind with the minds of those who are expert in the function or activity; the supervision of the Minister accountable to Parliament for its management and the resources it consumes; and the contribution of an outside agency in the shape of my office and me.

The examination was, nevertheless, to be rigorous. All activities were to be subjected to four fundamental questions: 'Why is this work done at all? Why is it done as it is? How could it be done more efficiently and effectively at less cost? . . . . What value is added?' No answers were to be assumed and the principal source of information was to be officials 'on the ground', who should never be approached with the attitude of a 'Smart Alec'. Moreover, quality of analysis was not enough. The provision of a practical 'action plan' to rectify all identified weaknesses was a prerequisite.[54]

The scrutiny programme flourished, initially at least, because it served different interests. It was welcomed by the media, as it was by Mrs Thatcher, because it gave a human dimension to the abstract concept of administrative reform and thereby injected a heroic element into the battle against bureaucracy. The publication of the more important reports provided an unusual instance of open government (see Chapter 10.2.1) – although press reluctance to treat each as an exposé of a new 'scandal' rather than an example of a new professionalism did little to encourage further openness.[55] Officials within the CSD were also enthusiastic, and particularly those working in the new Division (Functions and Programmes) which had been established in October 1979 'to shadow and support' the Efficiency Unit. After years of frustrating rebuffs, particularly under Labour, the programme offered a 'rare opportunity' to penetrate other departments with strong Ministerial backing. By matching ends with means, it also had the potential to fill the void between the two conventional investigative tools of PAR (which dealt with ends) and managerial review (which was concerned with means).[56] Finally, and most importantly, the programme initially won Ministerial support. At a time when departmental resources were fully stretched by manpower cuts, it employed a minimum of staff. It offered a welcome alternative to 'crude cuts'. It also appeared to preserve departmental autonomy because it was for Ministers to choose the subject for scrutiny, appoint the scrutineer, and act on its findings. Not only were outside agents, such as management consultants, but also the 'central departments' to be kept at bay.[57]

Nevertheless, despite all these advantages, the first rounds of scrutinies were not an unqualified success. Very little 'inefficiency and waste' was actually eliminated. The 1980 round alone, for example, identified a potential 9500 posts to be cut by December 1982, but the number of cuts agreed for the *whole* programme was a mere 21,000, of which only 12,000 had been made. The agreed reduction in annual savings also totalled only £400 million, of which only £180 million had actually been achieved.[58] These figures, in themselves, were not necessarily disappointing. Rayner, for example, had persistently stressed that his principal object was to instil a management culture into officials and Ministers alike. This, in time, would achieve far greater economies than individual scrutinies. The disappointing results, however, were evidence of two inherent weaknesses within the programme. The first was growing Ministerial resistance, provoked by the increased emphasis on management and the extent of centralisation (which had not been immediately apparent).[59] This resistance was rarely overt but was expressed in the selection (as with PAR) of marginal rather than 'significant and characteristic' policy areas for scrutiny and a reluctance to accept or endorse 'action plans'. In the light of such resistance, Rayner posed the question in December 1980: 'should we be content with the scale on which the programme is operating and its apparent effectiveness?' 'The answer', he concluded, 'must be No.'[60]

The second weakness, to which Ministers were responding, was the programme's inherent naivety. To an extent this reflected the ingenuousness of individual scrutineers, who (like the young Turks in the CPRS) were typically youthful generalists with little managerial experience; but, more fundamentally, it reflected the insensitivity of Rayner, as an unelected businessman, to political reality. In the drive for administrative simplicity, for example, the broader political purpose behind policy was sometimes ignored. The ability of vested interests to frustrate reform was also underplayed – as in the case of the Post Office and social security payments. 'Particular interest groups', Rayner complained bitterly, 'have in effect a preference for inefficiency or for levels of service to which they have grown accustomed, the cost of which is borne by the anonymous "State"' or, in reality, the taxpayer. The constraints of Parliamentary procedure were similarly underplayed. To implement an 'action plan', for example, Rayner often demanded immediate legislative change. 'If the idea gained currency', he asserted, 'that savings reliant on legislation were less graspable than those which were not, the steam would go out of the Government's drive for administrative reform.' The response from the leader of the House, Francis Pym, was forensic. 'It is of course', he countered, 'in the very nature of our Parliamentary system that legislative time is scarce and that savings reliant on legislation are bound to be less graspable . . . This consideration is something which . . . we need to have very much in mind when looking at the . . . most efficient ways of achieving the staffing improvements which are our common objective.' Rayner's belief that lessons could be 'read across' from one department to another, as between Marks and Spencer department stores, also betrayed a serious overestimation of the homogeneity of the Service and the tasks for which it was responsible.[61]

The relative strengths and weaknesses of the early scrutiny programme are best illustrated by three scrutinies carried out in 1980: the joint Department of Employment/DHSS examination of unemployment benefits (as representative of a 'single' departmental scrutiny); the review of the Government's Statistical Service (as representative of a Service-wide inquiry, 'reading off' lessons from an earlier scrutiny); and the annual scrutiny of departmental running costs (as representative of a multi-department initiative). On the surface, the DE/DHSS study was exemplary. It covered a major area of public administration, employing some 26,000 staff and expending each year some £1298 million of taxpayers' money on over one million claimants. It also recommended some radical changes. Several labour-intensive but ineffective practices (such as compulsory registration and proof of availability for work) should be eradicated and the administration of benefit greatly simplified (mainly by the merger of the three offices which claimants, to their considerable inconvenience, had typically to attend).[62] In return, more money should be spent on the employment of more fraud investigators (given the greater potential for abuse) and refurbishment (to make the one-office concept practical). In short, conditions for both claimants and staff should be permanently improved, at a net saving of 5000 staff and up to £80 million a year.

These recommendations did not wholly fall on stony ground. Voluntary registration, for example, was introduced in October 1982 and annual savings reached £31 million by 1984. However, modernisation was far slower than expected and the 'one-office' concept was completely lost. Why? The conventional culprit is departmental vested interest.[63] The management and unions at the DHSS, for example, resisted the transfer of some 10,000 staff to the new 'one-single office', because it was to be run by the DE; despite Rayner's mantra of 'spend to save', the PSA declined to commit its limited budget to the project; and the Treasury baulked at increasing the number of fraud investigators when, in its judgement, greater rewards could be reaped by an equivalent number of new tax inspectors. There was also, as has been seen, widespread Ministerial reluctance to create the necessary Parliamentary time. As a No. 10 official consequently lamented, 'the collective interests of Ministers rapidly turn[ed] a small team's thoroughbred stallion into an extremely lumpy camel'. Outside vested interests, however, were also to blame. For example the TUC (with its responsibility via the MSC for jobcentres) was reluctant to accept any job cuts and vigorously opposed any increase in fraud investigation. So too, despite compensatory improvements for claimants, did single-issue pressure groups such as the Child Poverty Action Group. Such obduracy may be explained by political contingency. Soaring unemployment had soured relations with Government and, even more pertinently, Conservative Party rhetoric – particularly on fraud – had fomented distrust. Here the Prime Minister herself was culpable. She rejected, for instance, the Treasury's special pleading on the somewhat contentious grounds that 'to claim unemployment benefit <u>fraudulently</u> is to get money <u>out</u> of the state . . . it seems to me much worse than the problem of [non-payment of] income tax or VAT'. She then vetoed the recommendation that once a year claimants be allowed to miss a fortnightly registration to go on holiday. 'There would be outrage if the holiday was beyond Britain's shores', she claimed, 'we should be providing more money to increase jobs overseas'.[64] Administrative reform may have remained one of her priorities, but practical measures to achieve it foundered on such mutual suspicions.

The review of the Statistical Services generated similar problems.[65] It too appeared exemplary. Prompted by the success of the Department of Industry's 1979 project, some 90 per cent of its 700 recommendations were ultimately accepted (resulting in a 20 per cent reduction in staff, at an annual saving of £17 million). It was bedevilled, however, by a simultaneous excess of ambition and lack of vision. The Efficiency Unit's lack of capacity to oversee all 22 departmental investigations was exposed; and when one recommended few economies, the relevant department was ordered to repeat it – thereby suggesting that the true objective of the exercise was not cost-effectiveness but cost-cutting. Such a suspicion inevitably aroused professional concern. As long as statistics were regarded as a prerequisite for effective planning within the public *and* private sector, so it was assumed that Government had a duty to collect them. With the commitment to 'roll back the state', this assumption had had to be qualified; but to the extent that they were collected, statistics– so it was argued – were still a public good and any attempt to make 'customers' pay for their collection, as suggested by the scrutiny, was anathema because it threatened their integrity. Anger was also generated by the apparent hypocrisy behind the incessant rhetoric concerning the lifting of the 'burden' of form-filling from private enterprise. Not only did this equate the collection of statistics to an act of overindulgent bureaucracy, but it also contrasted sharply with equally strident demands from 'reformers' themselves for ever more precise statistics with which to manage and monitor that same bureaucracy. The review, in short, exemplified the scrutiny programme's circumscribed vision, promoting 'narrow' managerial needs above broader political goals – let alone the principle of public service.

A similar narrowness of focus also affected the concurrent annual scrutiny of departmental running costs. It was a far more invasive exercise, agreed by Cabinet on 4 October 1979 almost in a fit of absent-mindedness. The annual administrative cost of Government was £6000m, a figure which exceeded revenue from VAT. Ministers, Rayner duly insisted, could not abdicate responsibility for so large a block of expenditure – although they might delegate it to senior officials (so long as they were properly trained and could identify down the line precisely where the expenditure was being incurred). A pilot scrutiny was launched in February 1980 and supervision entrusted to the CSD, which completed it in full and on time.[66] Fatefully, however, it revealed – in a year of manpower cuts and 18 per cent inflation – an apparent rise in costs of 25 per cent.[67] Both Rayner and Mrs Thatcher were infuriated and Soames sought to quell their anger at Cabinet on 29 January 1981 by promising to investigate the reasons. His subsequent report on 11 May, however, merely served to re-ignite it. Rayner complained that it gave him 'no real feel . . . for the effectiveness of departments at keeping costs down and achieving specific savings'; and Mrs Thatcher's Private Secretary damned it as 'further evidence that the CSD is failing to get to grips effectively with major management issues'.[68] The scrutiny for 1981, it was agreed, had to be more robust. Innovations considered included Prime-Ministerial interviews with recalcitrant Ministers (bilaterals); full publication of all returns so that Parliamentary Select Committees might probe more deeply; a greater use of management consultants; and the universal use of the management information systems, as pioneered by Michael Heseltine. Although Rayner had initially dismissed MINIS as 'more akin to the approach of small business' and his relationship with Heseltine was strained, it was the latter option that was adopted.[69]

This scrutiny of running costs was an attempt, in Rayner's words, to coax Ministers into accepting that management was a 'policy in its own right' and to 'quicken the professional conscience' of officials.[70] Both Ministers and officials, he argued, should have readily accessible information to monitor and control all departmental expenditure – including not just direct costs (such as salaries) but also those carried on other departmental votes (such as stationery and accommodation) and nominal costs (such as pensions contributions). Ministers were incensed at such a suggestion. The 1980 pilot scrutiny, they argued, had been bedevilled by technical shortcomings, especially in relation to the calculation of nominal costs. Departmental comparisons were also invidious and frequently misleading. The Prime Minister's Office, for example, had had hastily to excuse an excessive 35% rise in costs on the grounds that it had an atypical number of 'policy' staff and that Mrs Thatcher's style attracted an exceptional amount of public correspondence.[71] Two objections, however, were paramount. The first, surprisingly voiced by the No. 10 Policy Unit, was that the scrutiny was over-elaborate. At a time of severe retrenchment it was an 'annual bureaucratic jamboree which consumes more resources than it will ever save'. The second, again voiced by John Nott, was that Ministers were being reduced to 'staff managers'. To a chorus of approval he protested that he was a politician, responsible for policy and the mobilisation of public support; his Permanent Secretary was better qualified to take management decisions; and if he were not, he would ask the Prime Minister to replace him. These comments provoked an angry response from Rayner. Over the first point he scrawled: 'Rubbish. Abdication of responsibility'; over the second 'Try sample examination. No drive, no success'; and over the third 'When did this last happen?'[72] This outburst epitomised the conflict of principles and perception which characterised the attempt to impose a new management culture on Whitehall.

The scrutiny programme, in short, confirmed Rayner's worst fears. It provided irrefutable proof, in his judgement, of the managerial ineptitude of senior officials and of the 'disdainful reluctance' of Ministers 'to take seriously items costing millions because government budgets run into tens of millions'.[73] However, the CSD was the particular butt of his scorn. In the face of spiraling costs, it had remained calm – whereas it should have 'seized and acted upon the returns' to drive home reforms by, for instance, issuing directives on how to contain cash-limited expenditure or by the zealous dissemination of best practice. The shortcomings the scrutinies revealed, in other words, made his 'lasting reforms' the more urgent.

7.3.3 Rayner's lasting reforms

On his appointment, as has been seen, Rayner's stated objective was not to interfere in policy or mount *ad hoc* anti-waste initiatives but to revolutionise 'the way in which the civil service manages its work and the framework of organisation and control within which it operates'. This required a radical and comprehensive programme; and one was haltingly drafted over the following year.[74] Described as a review first of the 'general practices and conventions which are barriers to the effective management of business and resources' and then of Whitehall 'philosophy' or conventions, it finally assumed the title of 'lasting reforms' when submitted to Mrs Thatcher on 31 March 1980. She approved and commissioned work from it before it was endorsed by Cabinet on 1 May 1980.

The reason for halting progress was principally the scale of the task. There were, however, political impediments. Immediate manpower reductions took precedence until, arguably, February 1981. Rayner himself was also distracted by the tension generated by his projects and scrutinies – not least because, given his limited administrative resources, he was dependent for the success of both on the very Whitehall machine he was seeking to reform. Similar tension also pervaded the 'lasting reforms' programme itself because it relied heavily on the co-operation of the CSD which, as was well known, Rayner was trying to close down. Consequently it was unsurprising that, on his own admission, the programme's objectives were far from realised by December 1983 when he formally retired from Whitehall, let alone as early as November 1981.[75]

The legendary demonstration of the tension generated was the dinner hosted by Mrs Thatcher for all Permanent Secretaries on 6 May 1980. Its purpose was to inform them of the major decisions taken by Cabinet on 1 May; to elicit 'constructive suggestions on priorities for action which will improve the effectiveness of the management of the civil service at all levels'; and to 'seek ideas' on how to overcome union resistance.[76] The drafts for Mrs Thatcher's address provided respectively by Sir Ian Bancroft, as Head of the Home Civil Service, and Clive Priestley, on behalf of Rayner, epitomised the tension. Bancroft advised Mrs Thatcher immediately to admit that Conservatives had 'policies and an approach to management' fundamentally different to previous administrations and that this required an equally fundamental change in official attitudes. The 'key test' would be the persistent cost-consciousness of line managers 'on their own initiative'; and that, in turn, required all Ministers to support and implement central directives. Unions, he advised from his vast experience of dealing with the NSS, could be best mollified by a commitment to minimise compulsory redundancy.

Priestley's draft, particularly in its longer version, was apocalyptic and more abrasive. 1980, it claimed, marked 'a turning point in the history of the civil service'. 'Government', it argued in a phrase reminiscent of the *Black Book* in the early 1970s, 'should do only what it must and do it superbly well'; and so the fundamental challenge was:

> to lead the Service to update its priorities, equip it for the modern world and fight for simplification – less paper, fewer rules, more reliance on individuals. Build on the best of the existing foundations to devise first-class Government operations and practices for the 1980s and 1990s. Show the way to other public sector employers.

Ministers should manage, but Permanent Secretaries could best 'help them by being more radical in their thinking than they will know how to be in theirs' – particularly in the specialist task of 'resource management'. 'I do not rejoice in generalism', Mrs Thatcher rather gratuitously was primed to announce. Such a display of leadership would re-establish the Service as 'unmistakably the best in the world' and, by restoring morale, would outflank union militants. A mailed fist, however, lay behind such blandishment. Permanent Secretaries might have the 'power of action and inaction, enthusiasm and coldness', the draft continued, but they could not hold the government to ransom. Procrastination could be circumnavigated by the appointment of a 'young progress chaser'. Moreover, inefficient PEOs and PFOs should be immediately retired and, since they did not 'live in a private world', all officials should be judged on their management record. Only in this way could the relentless tide of political and public criticism be stemmed.

In retrospect Mrs Thatcher and many Permanent Secretaries regarded the dinner as a total disaster. As Mrs Thatcher recalled, it was 'one of the most dismal occasions of my entire time in government', serving up 'a menu of complaints and negative attitudes' which 'etched into her soul' the impossibility of changing attitudes *en bloc*.[77] Officials, in turn, remembered the Prime Minister's late arrival, flushed from congratulating the SAS on lifting the Iranian embassy siege, and the hectoring tone in which she demanded their help in beating 'the system'. 'But', responded Bancroft somewhat imprudently, 'we are the system'. The reality, however, may have been rather different. Consistent with the nature of their earlier Sunningdale debates, many Permanent Secretaries welcomed the commitment to a 'smaller and more efficient Civil Service' and consequently declared themselves, in

Sir Patrick Nairne's phrase, 'enthusiasts' on the Prime Minister's side. Nevertheless, they had to speak truth unto power.[78] Success depended, they argued, on the Government being committed consistently to take 'hard-nosed political decisions' – a commitment that had been noticeably absent not just before 1979 but also afterwards, as illustrated by the sub-postmasters' veto of DHSS reforms. It also had to be acknowledged that rising unemployment and increased indirect taxation, required more – rather than less – manpower; and that efficiency was dependent on morale, and thus both on working conditions (which were often 'downright bad') and Ministers' readiness to rebut unwarranted attacks on the Service (to which, as has been seen, Mrs Thatcher herself appeared temperamentally averse). Finally Sir Frank Cooper spelt out the contradiction between the decentralisation required to empower line managers and the centralisation which the Prime Minister typically favoured. In other words, rather than serving up a 'menu of complaints' at the dinner, it could be argued that Permanent Secretaries were merely seeking to ensure success in a conventional way by alerting the Prime Minister to practical difficulties and political inconsistencies which might later impede reform. To Mrs Thatcher, however, such premeditation smacked purely of negativism, as she swung between a desire (encouraged by Rayner and Priestley) to rebuild a world-beating Service and her instinctive contempt for 'senior civil servants as a breed'.[79]

Unlike Mrs Thatcher, Rayner was generally sympathetic towards the Service. 'I have a high regard', he insisted

> for many senior officials . . . whom I regard as amongst the most dedicated, hard-working and effective people I know. Equally, the junior staff I have encountered . . . convince me the Government is the fortunate employer of a wealth of talent and enthusiasm for the public good. However there is no gainsaying the fact that permanence, privacy, a certain lack of definition of roles, the steady accretion of pay and rewards, excellent pension arrangements and the 'easy come, easy go' attitude of the nation over the past 25 years or so cannot fail to make bureaucracy a comparatively comfortable place to be . . . Galvanization is needed.'[80]

Galvanisation, therefore, was what the lasting reforms programme was designed to achieve.

The programme had four main objectives: to reduce the scale of government; to strengthen the management of resources both collectively and within departments; and to alter permanently the 'culture' of Whitehall.[81] Initially, the first was not pronounced. Rayner was insistent that his role was solely administrative, although (as has been seen with the payment of benefits) the implementation of policy could verge on the political. However, his advice could not be value-free; and it was clearly based on the assumption that, in Priestley's words, 'government should only do what it must'. This did not mean, as some Party activists wished, a return to the 1930s. 'It would be foolish', he maintained, 'for our Government to stand back from areas where other governments were active, especially if this adversely affected our economic performance. It was no longer simply a matter of keeping things ticking over.'[82] Nor did it mean further hiving off or privatisation. Rather he wished to reduce the scale of *existing* Government by minimising the excessive monitoring of outside bodies and the excessive layers of bureaucracy within Whitehall. This aim was more succinctly summarised, in a phrase redolent of the 1970 *Reorganisation of Central Government* white paper, as 'less government, using fewer staff better'.[83]

In the event, the minimisation of outside monitoring and the bureaucratic hierarchy, was entrusted to the CSD as part of its task of applying more generally 'generic lessons' learnt from the 1979 projects. The latter, in particular, was a far from happy experience. First, the trade unions prevented an examination of the Administration Group (covering grades from Assistant Secretary to Clerical Assistant). Then, when the Wardale Report on the Chain of Command (covering the Open Structure, or the top four grades) was published in April 1981, it was savaged by Rayner as 'non-quantitative and non-forensic' because *inter alia* it contained no detailed costings and was over-reliant on evidence from interested parties.[84] Moreover its principal conclusion, that no grade should be abolished (although not every grade needed to be used in every Ministry) was dismissed as unacceptable. Rayner wanted to abolish three administrative grades (and in particular the 591-strong Under Secretary grade) and to reduce the Open Structure to its size in 1965 (equivalent to a 35 per cent cut). Unacceptable too was Wardale's proposed 'action plan': a 'stringent review' by departments, supported by a team of former Permanent Secretaries, to eliminate superfluous posts. Former Permanent Secretaries, as Rayner tartly remarked, were precisely the people who had permitted such posts to proliferate in the first place. The Report, in short, confirmed the instinct of both Mrs Thatcher and Rayner that the CSD was pathologically incapable of either analysing problems rigorously or devising radical solutions.

Rayner's criticisms were themselves rebutted by CSD officials. They were also challenged, on a political level, by Soames (who wished to implement the Report) and by other senior Ministers, including Whitelaw and Hailsham, who regarded a 35 per cent cut – somewhat ironically, given Rayner's past condemnation of manpower targets – as arbitrary and unattainable. It was also, they argued, poor reward for the loyalty displayed by senior staff during the recently concluded Civil Service strike (see Chapter 7.4) as well as boding ill for their co-operation over future reforms. Mrs Thatcher duly relented, so that when the 'stringent reviews' (steeled by the presence of Rayner himself and several management consultants) were ultimately launched in November 1981, the 35 per cent cut was downgraded – in a familiar ploy – to a mere aspiration. Rayner's outburst had nevertheless exposed the mailed fist, at which Priestley had hinted. Senior officials, as a group, were no longer characterised as 'dedicated, hard-working and effective' but condemned as 'an amiable coterie of cynics . . . who know nothing of management and despise those who do'.[85]

The second aim of the lasting reforms programme, the strengthening of the collective management of resources at both a political and administrative level, was the most sensitive and so was responsible for the majority of amendments between its first and final draft. The general objective remained constant: 'to update the Plowden concept of partnership between the spending and central departments to take account of modern circumstances'; and 'modern circumstances', so it was argued, needed the more efficient calculation and overall allocation of public expenditure, a better balance between central and spending departments in relation to the monitoring of performance, and the existence in each department of an effective management system.[86] What was controversial, and prompted the amendments, was the increased degree of central control this new 'partnership' implied. In particular, a stronger centre was to be created by the merger of the CSD with the Treasury and the establishment of a new post of Inspector General. 'The balance of power between the "spending" and "central" Ministers', one excised passage read, 'must be further redressed in favour of the centre . . . The mass of Ministers and departments must always be anti-centre [and] for the centre to divide itself in face of this seems . . . like a self-inflicted wound'. The merger itself will be analysed in Chapter 7.5; but the battle over both the Inspector General and the imposition of new management systems on departments are, in themselves, instructive.

The appointment of an Inspector General, reporting directly to the Prime Minister, posed the greatest threat of increased centralisation. The post was intended to provide 'a sustained cutting edge' for reform through the dissemination, maintenance and monitoring of best practice.[87] Once it had been agreed in principle at a dinner at Rayner's house attended by Mrs Thatcher and the Cabinet Secretary on 8 July 1980, however, objections immediately started to proliferate. Rather than strengthen central departments, it was claimed, it would simply create another layer of bureaucracy; and, rather than encourage the self-criticism and self-improvement (the supposed key to lasting reforms), it would force officials in both central and spending departments to act defensively. Moreover, were the Inspector General to use either central staff to sustain initiatives or departmental officials to investigate public complaints, Ministers' constitutional and managerial responsibilities would be seriously infringed. The post, it was thus argued, might be valuable *within* an existing central department – especially were the CSD to be abolished and management to become again a peripheral Treasury interest. Otherwise it served no purpose unless, as Bancroft pointedly observed, 'the objective were to provide the Prime Minister with an official machine for checking on what central Ministers were doing'. This, he added, 'would be a major constitutional innovation and not . . . a happy one'.[88] Bancroft's suspicions had some foundation. Rayner was seeking to make his Efficiency Unit permanent and to ensure Priestley as his successor (although the latter was duly modest about his ability to live up to the acronym for the alternative title of the post, Head of the Efficiency Review Office). Mrs Thatcher was at the same time seriously considering the creation of a Prime Minister's Department. In the event, the opposition proved too strong and the post of Inspector General, like a PMD, was not established.

The attempt centrally to impose management systems on departments was a more public battle and took two forms. The first became enmeshed in a backbench campaign to strengthen the Comptroller and Auditor-General's Department, which led eventually to the creation of the National Audit Office in 1983 (see Chapter 10.3.2). The principal objective, was to increase Parliamentary control over public expenditure, and thus the Executive; and the highlight of the campaign was a bitingly critical report by the Comptroller and Auditor General on departmental audit systems, which excited the attention of both Rayner and Mrs Thatcher.[89] For them, it was confirmation of a 'serious neglect of duty' and the heads of the Treasury and CSD were consequently obliged to write immediately to all Permanent Secretaries urging reform. 'Internal audits', they reminded their colleagues, 'were a potent weapon to help us control our business, look after our assets and secure value for money'. The letter, however, far from mollified the Prime Minister who – prompted by Priestley – was scathing about its lack of urgency, expert guidance and, above all, any 'action plan'. It indicated, she concluded, 'all that is wrong with the civil service approach' and foreshadowed the dismemberment of the CSD by sanctioning the transfer of its Accountancy, Finance and Audit Division to the Treasury to provide a nucleus for a more powerful central unit.[90]

The second initiative was prompted by a Treasury scrutiny of its Supply Divisions and ultimately resulted in the Financial Management Initiative of May 1982 (which required all departments to adopt approved management information systems). After lengthy consultation, a Cabinet memorandum was circulated on 2 June 1981 (in the middle of the Civil Service strike) entitled *Control of expenditure: departmental responsibilities*. Despite the title, its essential objective was to reinforce Treasury control; and that it was likely to revive historic tensions was well recognised, as illustrated by its assertion that

> in recent years the emphasis has been on decentralisation and on the responsibility of the spending departments for their own efficiency. We have no intention of detracting from, or in any way undermining, the responsibilities of the spending departments. But we believe that, in partnership with spending departments, and as a complement to their work, the central departments should be more active and more positive in setting standards and seeing that they are observed.[91]

As initially planned in 1920, PFOs and PEOs were accordingly to act as Treasury agents within departments ensuring compliance with directives and forewarning it of any untoward development.

Permanent Secretaries took exception to such proposals, as did Ministers when – to expedite reform – Mrs Thatcher held a presentation on 8 September 1981 on what by then was termed 'financial management'. A range of political, technical and personal objections were voiced. It was argued, for example, that a maximum return on resources (which a businessman might require) could never be achieved because of contradictory political priorities (such as equity and economy); that reliable costings were often unattainable; and, above all, that officials within the central departments currently lacked the requisite skills to develop or monitor departmental management. The latter objection was supported by David Wolfson, as her Chief of Staff, and almost led Mrs Thatcher to abort the whole initiative. Rayner assured her, however, that 'the Treasury and the CSD are now hard at work inventing the wheel of "financial management", the former ... with some enthusiasm and the latter I suspect with rather less'.[92] The initiative therefore continued, although the CSD had been further disparaged.

The attainment of the third objective of the lasting reforms programme, the strengthening of the management of resources *within* departments, clearly depended on the success of the central initiatives. There remained, however, the question of how to make the management systems work once they had been installed. This raised technical and personal issues. Technically, Rayner had sought since his appointment to encourage greater cost-consciousness through direct departmental payments for 'common services'; and, as has been seen, their cost had been attributed to 'user' departments in the annual scrutiny of running costs. For Rayner, however, there was a 'world of difference in management terms between knowing what it costs somebody else to provide you with goods and services and having to find the money for these from your own budget'. Moreover, he maintained, payment would 'strengthen the customer-supplier relationship' and thereby ensure a more 'responsive and flexible' service.[93] As a result of his exertions, HMSO and the Central Office of Information had placed their services on a full repayment basis by 1981. So too, after a heated battle between Rayner and Heseltine, as Secretary of State for the Environment, over the more radical option of privatisation, had the PSA (in relation to the provision of accommodation and maintenance). The most prominent exception was the Civil Service College (see Chapter 9.4). Departments (working within ever stricter cash limits) resented not only the transaction costs but also the principle of paying for the training of officials from which other departments might ultimately benefit. A compromise was therefore finally reached whereby they were required to pay for 'job specific' training whilst the CSD paid for the rest (as the 'central consumer for the training ... necessary in the interests of the long run efficiency' of the whole Service). Such a compromise could be construed as a pretext for shielding an inefficient College from competitive pressure – and was so construed by Mrs Thatcher. It thus became another stick with which to beat the CSD.[94]

With regard to the fostering of greater personal commitment to financial management, Rayner particularly sought a clearer definition of the 'managerial authority' of Ministers, the role of Permanent Secretaries as departmental accounting officers, and the 'authority, responsibility and requisite qualifications' of PEOs and PFOs (whom he termed Permanent Secretaries' 'right hand men'). Little initial progress was made because of Ministerial resistance. As the Cabinet Secretary correctly predicted, Ministers opposed so 'critical and far-reaching' a recommendation because:

> under present arrangements Ministers can, if they choose, to a degree hide behind their accounting officers when things go wrong. New definitions which make it clear that the ultimate authority is the Minister will increase Ministerial vulnerability to Parliament and to Select Committees.[95]

Accordingly, the proposal was excised from the programme's first draft. The requirement that all PFOs should be professionally qualified was also disparaged as an example of the programme's myopia. PFOs, it was argued, required vision and political sensitivity as much as formal accountancy training.[96] Nevertheless, by November 1981, the Civil Service College was primed to offer new courses in financial management for existing officials – although Rayner was still demanding a more rigorous 'crash programme' and the appointment of outside experts.

The fourth and final objective of the lasting reforms programme was the transformation of the generalist Whitehall culture in order 'to drive home the fact that managing activities efficiently is of equal merit to thinking through policies and analyzing issues'.[97] Rayner had been equally determined to transform ministerial culture but, in anticipation of Cabinet resistance, specific recommendations were excised from the draft initially submitted to the Prime Minister. The focus was, therefore, once again on officials. Rayner had two interrelated goals: the promotion to senior positions of officials with proven managerial skills and the encouragement of such skills throughout the Service. The first was belatedly addressed by the introduction in February 1982 of a formal succession policy. Each department was required to indicate annually who would succeed to senior positions in the 'normal course of events', who could succeed if the positions 'were unexpectedly vacated', and who should be 'in the field for the next but one succession'.[98] All potential candidates were then to be given the requisite training and experience.

The broader encouragement of managerial skills involved the removal of disincentives and the provision of rewards. Disincentives included an over-lengthy hierarchy (which stifled individual responsibility), the 'disproportionate' promotion of generalists to senior posts (which discouraged the ambitious from developing managerial rather than 'political' skills) and the 'cost of democracy' (the collective term used to cover a number of perceived sins, such as the 'excessive' cost of answering Parliamentary Questions and the creation of an 'alibi consciousness' amongst officials in reaction to Parliament's preference for finding fault rather than praising success). The first two were tackled respectively by the Wardale inquiry and succession policy. To correct the third, a serious attempt was made to limit the supply of information to Parliament. CSD officials were initially appalled, with a future member of the Efficiency Unit (Elizabeth Thoms) complaining that answering MPs' enquiries fully was a 'fundamental piece of our constitution and ought not to be considered in the same light as' other lasting reforms. Nevertheless Rayner, supported by successive Cabinet Secretaries, continued to argue for 'less perfectionism' and succeeded in persuading Cabinet in May 1980 to mount an inquiry.[99]

The provision of rewards included honours and pay. Honours involved Prime Ministerial prerogative and so their reform was never referred to Cabinet.[100] However, proposals for performance-related pay (earlier considered by the Callaghan Government) were revived. Arguing that it was common in the private sector and would boost morale, Soames sought to introduce it successively for

Under Secretaries in 1981 and Assistant Secretaries in 1982. Officials were divided. As the Cabinet Secretary (Robert Armstrong) minuted:

> there are those who see it as out of keeping for a public service, inconsistent with the traditions of the Civil Service, and liable to introduce considerations of competitiveness to a degree which could affect the dispassionateness and even integrity with which the duty of advising Ministers on policy is discharged. Others – of whom I am one – think that it will be a good thing ... there is no reason in principle why it should not introduce a healthy element of incentive ... and, if it is properly controlled, it should quickly become apparent that attempts to qualify for merit pay by unmeritorious means do not pay.[101]

Ultimately Ministers, again led by Whitelaw and Hailsham, rejected the measure on the grounds that it could politicise the Service and offend the natural collegiality of public service. Many practical objections were also cited, such as the additional bureaucracy required to monitor and determine payments. Accordingly on 15 January 1981 Cabinet replaced it with a programme of accelerated promotion and early retirement (which itself was later compromised by further manpower cuts and trade union opposition).

To Rayner, the lasting reforms programme was his core contribution to administrative reform; but, as has been seen, it was neither as well organised nor as well received as his scrutiny programme. On the one hand, it was far more eclectic and, by focusing exclusively on management issues, ignored critical political and constitutional realities. On the other hand, Ministers were as antagonised by its threat of further centralisation as they had been in relation to the CSD's manpower policy. It also stifled latent support within Whitehall. Rayner, after all, was well known to be broadly sympathetic and most of his proposed reforms (in their objectives, if not their precise detail) had been championed by the CSD.[102] What had always hamstrung the CSD, however, was lack of strong Prime Ministerial backing. This Rayner patently enjoyed but he was unable to marry it to the expertise of the CSD – be that the fault of the CSD (which arguably remained too wedded to the generalist culture), the Prime Minister (who lacked organisational skills and certainly showed no desire to manage her 'own' department) or Rayner himself (with his penchant for a particular managerial and rhetorical style, and his exasperation at the discordance between public and private sector management). By November 1981, however, the programme had enjoyed some notable successes. It had prevented a u-turn on administrative reform, when Ministers had grown restless in 1980. It had instilled into officials a new concern for management. Above all, although it actually opposed the most radical initiatives (such as hiving off and privatisation) and evaded others with which it had initially flirted (such as open government), it had also laid the groundwork for a wide range of later reforms. These reforms could then be the more swiftly enacted following two seminal events: the 1981 Civil Service strike and the demise of the CSD.

7.4 The 1981 Civil Service strike

The 1981 Civil Service strike started with a one-day walkout on 9 March and lasted for 21 weeks. The immediate cause was the Government's unilateral abrogation in the previous October of pay comparability and its stated intention to contain all future pay awards within predetermined cash limits. As previously under the Labour Government, the unions construed this as a fundamental threat to free collective bargaining and thus to their future. Equally the Government felt threatened by the strike, not just because of its length (which exceeded, at that time, that of any other national dispute since 1926) but also because, as in opposition, it feared its authority might be undermined by administrative paralysis. There were only two further mass walkouts (on 1 and 14 April) but selective action, rarely involving more than 5000 officials, was taken against carefully chosen targets. In particular, revenue collection was disrupted (to upset monetary targets) as was defence (which angered the US intelligence services). Consequently, by July both sides were anxious to settle. Moderate union leaders, mandated by their members to call an all-out strike, feared the cost and unpopularity of such an action as well as the militancy it might unleash. Government, in turn, was increasingly concerned by escalating costs (estimated by the Treasury at £130 million in lost revenue and £500 million in increased interest charges) and the political danger of entering a Parliamentary recess without any guarantee that the payment of social security benefits would continue. There were also contingent pressures. The Toxteth riots exploded on 8 July, Mrs Thatcher's popularity fell to a nadir of 25 per cent and the Cabinet was bitterly divided over the budget (which did not reflate the economy in the expected Keynesian way).

Given such mutual anxieties, the conventional wisdom is that the honours were evenly divided. For the Government, for example, Geoffrey Howe concluded that the strike 'could not be seen as a famous victory, though it fell well short of disaster'.[103]

Its short-term objective of keeping the 1981–2 pay settlement within its six per cent cash limit was attained. So too was its long-term objective of replacing – or at least qualifying – comparability as the determinant of pay. An independent inquiry (the Megaw Committee), with a carefully controlled remit and membership, was appointed to reconsider 'the principles and the system by which the remuneration of the non-industrial civil service should be remunerated' and it duly recommended a move towards a fuller recognition of market forces. The unions, however, were not without their own successes. Against the Government's initial wish, the new pay system was to be openly debated rather than covertly imposed. Pending the Committee's report, pay was also to be negotiated outside predetermined cash limits and subject, if necessary, to arbitration. This meant, in principle, that the cost of the following year's pay settlement could still exceed Government estimates of what the country could afford. It was this potential danger which led Mrs Thatcher to assert, on several occasions, that the Government was making all the concessions and gaining nothing in return.[104]

The strike will be examined fully in Chapter 8.3.1 and the Megaw Committee in Volume 2. Administrative reform was, however, directly affected by the strike in two ways. It provided the pretext for Lord Soames' dismissal and exposed the incompatibility between the Treasury and the CSD. In the first instance, Soames found himself in an impossible situation. The CSD remained formally in charge of industrial relations within the Service and, as such, he was the Government's leading negotiator with the unions. As a negotiator, however, he enjoyed little freedom of action – and, as a policy maker, even less. The Treasury had effectively controlled pay policy since May 1979 (if not before) because monetary targets and cash limits dictated the size of public expenditure and thus of pay settlements. This was made explicit by the Chancellor's chairing of the Public Sector Pay Subcommittee of the crucial Economic Strategy (E) Committee, whereas Soames himself only chaired the Civil Service Subcommittee on discipline. Moreover, were the Treasury to falter, the No 10 Policy Unit and Conservative Party activists (intent on 'deprivileging' civil servants) provided a bulwark against concessions. The Policy Unit, for instance, had helped to stiffen the Chancellor's resolve when the key decision was taken in June 1980 to keep the 1981–2 pay settlement within cash limits. Its intervention was also crucial in Cabinet on 9 April 1981 to the defeat of an interim formula designed to secure an early settlement; and again on 19 May, when Cabinet decided to escalate the dispute in order 'to win'. Then, when a majority within Cabinet favoured a settlement in early June, the strength of Party opinion reputedly persuaded Whitelaw to rally support for the Prime Minister (who had threatened to resign on the issue).[105] To add to such constraints, Soames then had to negotiate with six major unions which, as will be seen in Chapter 8, were far from united.

Such a cocktail of constraints would almost certainly have defeated the most skilled of negotiators; and so Soames' dismissal on 14 September for his alleged mishandling of the strike has been widely adjudged unfair. This was the view held particularly by those in a position to know that his proposed settlement in June would most likely have resolved the dispute on better terms for the Government and at less cost to the economy. 'His being right cost him his job', was Ian Gilmour's barbed comment, 'her being wrong cost the country £500 million'.[106] In truth, however, the reasons for his dismissal were more fundamental and reflected, as earlier noted, major personal and political differences with the Prime Minister. In particular, his attitude to the strike was coloured by his non-dogmatic economic views. For him, as for CSD officials, good government required harmonious working relations within Whitehall; and they could be best achieved by working within the current pay system, surreptitiously supporting moderate union leaders against the militants (and thus being ready to make timely concessions) and minimising provocative action (as favoured by the Policy Unit). To his more dogmatic colleagues, convinced that good government (and thereby a sound economy) depended on a strict adherence to cash limits and market discipline, such views were anathema. His dismissal was not, therefore, as surprising as has been suggested. Indeed, what arguably is the more surprising, given the importance Mrs Thatcher attached to administrative reform, was his being given the post in the first place and the fact that he held it so long.

The independence of the CSD was similarly undermined. This was because the strike highlighted policy differences between it and the Treasury and thus the illogicality of a divided 'centre'. Such differences intensified in April 1981 when an Official Committee, under CSD chairmanship, was commissioned to devise an alternative pay system as a basis for reopening negotiations with the unions. No agreement could be reached because, as the Chairman reported, of an irreconcilable difference of opinion. This divergence became even more explicit at the Permanent Secretaries' Sunningdale conference in October 1981, one of Bancroft's last initiatives as Head of the Home Civil Service.[107] The crux, it was agreed, was the extent to which – if at all – collective bargaining should be 'structured'. The Treasury favoured a 'fluid' system governed by 'market factors' and the 'Government's ability to pay' (defined as 'the level and taxation which Ministers judge to be acceptable and compatible with the health of the economy' and to be embodied in a predetermined cash limit). During the strike, therefore, it opposed the appointment of an independent inquiry or an interim commitment to arbitration (two concessions eventually won by the unions) on the grounds that Government might lose control over the level of public expenditure. By contrast, the CSD interpreted the 'principle' of 'ability to pay' as a simple desire to 'get away' with as little as possible. Consequently, it wanted a more structured system which permitted genuine negotiation in order to ensure both union co-operation and fairness (defined as the assurance that Government would treat its employees no worse, and no better, than workers in the private sector).

There was some common ground. Both sides agreed that the current system of pay comparability was not working. Since the early 1960s, awards based on pay research had constantly fallen foul of incomes policy or cash limits – although, equally constantly, comparability had been sustained by periodic 'catching up' awards (as in 1975). Here, however, the views of the Treasury and CSD perceptions again began to diverge. Such awards, the CSD contended, had typically been achieved by militant action and, were arbitrary cash limits permanently to determine pay levels, such militancy would become institutionalised. Why not have a structured system, topped by genuine arbitration, which might theoretically weaken government control over public expenditure but would, in practice, maintain comparability without the unquantifiable cost of strikes and low morale? 'King Canute was right', its spokesman concluded, 'there are forces which it is beyond the power of government to control and it is foolish for it to try'.

Such divergences exposed the illogicality of a divided centre. First, pay and manpower policy needed to be coordinated. In the private sector, the Treasury had long argued, pay negotiations had to 'proceed with responsibility, negotiators on both sides being constrained by the knowledge of the consequences which the financial framework will impose if settlements are excessive'.[108] Pay increases, in short, had to be balanced against potential job losses. This should be equally true in the public sector (as indeed Channon had accepted during the 1980–1 pay settlement, see Chapter 7.2.2). Second, there was a need to coordinate pay policy and managerial reform because, in order to exploit local labour markets, the Treasury was seeking to decentralise wage bargaining and this required a revolution in the structure, expertise and attitudes of local management.[109] Finally, there was an equal need to coordinate pay and discipline. One of the more notable discordances during the strike had been the Treasury's demand for ever more draconian measures to end disruption to its Inland Revenue and VAT offices, whilst CSD officials feared such action would escalate the dispute. Soames' Subcommittee had duly vetoed draconian measures (such as the wider use of Temporary Relief from Duty orders to suspend people without pay).[110] Just as the strike undermined Soames' political position, therefore, so it undermined the administrative justification for an independent CSD.

The strike, as well as reviving the very issues which had caused the original division of the CSD from the Treasury, also highlighted the extent to which circumstances had changed. The unions, as will be further discussed in Chapter 8, had grown more powerful. This was in part because of the general increase in militancy and dependency on technology. It was also because of the Government's increasing acceptance of the unions' right to wide-ranging consultation – a right which the CSD had had a role, and even a vested interest, in developing. Mrs Thatcher was incensed when this 'right' was used to block managerial reform (as, in her judgement, during the Wardale inquiry); and such behaviour was equated, not least by Rayner in an early draft of the lasting reforms programme, to 'Luddism'. In many ways, however, union action was less a show of strength than a symbol of frustration at the lack of genuine consultation and at continuing polemical attacks on the Service.[111] The leadership had, for example, been particularly angered by the 630,000 manpower target, which it regarded as arbitrary (preceding any decision on a reduction of functions), illogical (encouraging 'hiving off' even when it was more expensive) and highly damaging to morale and thus efficiency. As the Secretary General of the NSS then berated Bancroft in April 1980, following leaked reports of the lasting reforms programme:

> What on earth is going on? Are these merely public relations exercises designed to placate the Government's wilder supporters? Or, is there a real possibility that the Civil Service will be subjected to still further butchery . . . ? The Staff Side deeply resent hearing about possible developments of a serious and radical nature in this way . . . [and it is] not prepared to be bypassed whilst issues of this importance are in the air. We have a right to put a point of view and to ensure there is a balanced debate about what are, as they currently stand, one-sided and ill-considered proposals.[112]

'No loyalty', another General Secretary argued rather more succinctly 'could be given to political prejudice.'

Such widespread anger and distrust sustained solidarity throughout the strike far longer than had been anticipated. Stiffened in their resolve by the Policy Unit, however, the Prime Minister and Chancellor remained resolute. The imposition in 1980 of a six per cent cash limit, when inflation was running at seventeen per cent, had been deliberately designed to change public expectation, with a tough public sector pay settlement demonstrating to the private sector that – if economic decline were to be halted – there was no alternative to cuts in real living standards.[113] The subsequent search for an alternative pay system was similarly designed to serve notice on Civil Servants that the cosy world of comparability was dead. Once the strike had started, attention was concentrated on breaking the prevalent 'strike culture' 'We believe as a general rule', Hoskyns minuted Mrs Thatcher on 8 April when both the CSD and the Cabinet Secretary were seeking a settlement, 'that the only way to end the strike culture is to let it [the strike] happen . . . concentrating all our efforts on just one thing – mobilising public opinion to win the battle for us'. Again in early June, during another CSD bid for peace, he instead encouraged escalation. 'We should', he urged, 'be using this dispute to challenge and then start to shift the conventionally woolly-minded thinking of so many commentators.' It was, he continued, lamentable that 'everyone has become accustomed over the years to the idea that only the union side may behave unreasonably, while the employer – and certainly Government as an employer – must be gentlemanly right through to defeat'.[114]

Hoskyns' advice was not fully followed. In July, as has been seen, the Government was as anxious as the unions to settle. In effect, however, it was the unions' bluff, rather than the Government's, which had been called. For reasons that will be discussed in Chapter 8, their leaders were unable (or perhaps unwilling) to force further concessions from a divided and unpopular Government. Except in the very shortest of terms, therefore, the honours from the strike were anything but even. Indeed the strike can best be seen as part of a process, which included the Permanent Secretaries' dinner in May 1980 and later confrontations such as the miners' strike, by which the privileged influence of professional groups and trade unions was gradually broken. The power of the Civil Service unions, which had steadily accreted since Fulton, had been dramatically checked. It was then to be even more seriously jeopardised by the abolition of the CSD.

7.5 The demise of the Civil Service Department

Shortly after the end of the strike, on 7 September 1981, Mrs Thatcher announced her decision finally to abolish the CSD in a meeting with Rayner and Robert Armstrong. There followed Soames' dismissal on the 14th September and what, by mutual agreement, was an 'unhappy' audience with Bancroft on 24 September before the reorganisation was announced to Parliament on 12 November, became operational on 16 November and fully legal on 7 December. A brief Parliamentary debate was held on 20 January 1982, at which the Labour Party (contrary to its representatives' urgings on the English Committee) sought to reverse the decision; but the motion was easily defeated. The CSD's abolition was simultaneously expected and unexpected. As has been seen, it had been widely canvassed since the mid-1970s and was a core 'lasting reform'. Both the Efficiency Unit and the

Prime Minister had also criticised it relentlessly, despite the former being largely dependent on it for administrative support and the latter being its nominal head. On the other hand, Mrs Thatcher had taken an earlier decision to abolish it in July 1980. Press notices and Parliamentary statements had even been prepared. She had then, however, performed an uncharacteristic u-turn.

It was her readiness to perform yet another u-turn which took Bancroft by surprise on 24 September and resulted in a certain heat permeating the characteristic iciness of their formal meetings.[115] One obvious cause of his 'unhappiness' was the inference that the timing of the change had been dictated by personal considerations. Had that been, abolition would surely have been delayed until the retirements, in May and December 1982, of Sir John Herbecq (Bancroft's deputy) and Bancroft himself. Immediate action, given their well-known aversion to accepting sinecures, meant that both were effectively being made redundant. Moreover, Bancroft claimed, the timing could hardly have been worse given that so many reforms (such as the Financial Management Initiative) were at a critical point in their planning or implementation. Bancroft's principal concern, however, was for the morale of the Service. Handing back 'the jugular vein of pay and numbers' to the Treasury, whose Ministers were regarded as 'hostile to its interests', threatened to revive the very antagonism that Fulton had been designed to end. More particularly, the abolition of the CSD so soon after the strike would be taken as further proof that the Government was 'hostile to its own employees'. The Prime Minister angrily denied this latter charge, insisting somewhat disingenuously that 'Ministers were not hostile to the Civil Service, though she did feel disgust at the resistance which she had encountered to her efforts to bring about greater efficiency. This she did regard as disloyalty.'

Why had the abolition of the CSD been so persistently demanded? And why was Mrs Thatcher's initial u-turn so swiftly reversed? Abolition was justified on both institutional and personal grounds. Institutionally, as has been seen, the English Committee had concluded that, with the effective abandonment of Fulton, it had lost its 'raison d'etre'. Rayner was equally dismissive, albeit on the very different grounds that the separation of the CSD from the Treasury was 'neither justified in principle or by experience'. As in business, he argued, the optimum use of money and manpower efficiency required united control over both.[116] Moreover, experience – not just during the strike – had shown that a divided centre was a weak one. The current experience of spending departments, in the fighting talk of Robert Armstrong, was a bit like being 'slugged' by two boxers from the left and right without the coordination of punches one pair of hands might achieve. As a result, it was a 'little easier to dodge the punches'.[117]

Personally, as the Cabinet revolt in October 1979 demonstrated, the CSD Ministers and officials alike were widely perceived to be interventionist. Rayner, again, took a rather different line. CSD personnel, he argued, were indeed – and needed to be – interventionist; but, currently, they were so only in a petty way. Consequently they were signally ineffective in prescribing and monitoring, let alone enforcing, reform. In part, this was a result of their sensitivity to the constitutional independence of other departments but, in the main, it was because senior staff were insufficiently 'seized by the importance of management' and lacked the requisite 'background and success in management'. Consequently they were 'cautious, introspective and self-conscious' and (in Priestley's rather injudicious phrase, given the Prime Minister's gender) 'ladylike'. Some CSD officials were admitted to be very good; but it was made clear in the summer of 1980, by a series of private and semi-public remarks, that no senior figure was adjudged sufficiently 'manly' to become the projected 'Inspector General' to drive through the lasting reforms programme.[118]

These perceived weaknesses could have been resolved in one of four ways, each of which (as will be seen) was summarised by Robert Armstrong in his evidence to the Treasury and Civil Service Select Committee when (as the Conservatives' answer to the English Committee) it mounted in 1980 a formal Parliamentary inquiry into the future of the CSD. However, when in due course an attempt was made to select an option, each raised such difficulties that abolition of the CSD – hardly surprising given the compelling reasons for its creation scarcely ten years before – proved far more complex than assumed. It was such complexity that, at root, forced Mrs Thatcher into her uncharacteristic u-turn and resulted in CSD's demise only at the third attempt.

The first possible solution, identified by Armstrong, the rejuvenation – as opposed to the abolition – of the CSD. This was the solution eventually to be recommended by the Select Committee and temporarily adopted by Mrs Thatcher in January 1981.[119] The second possibility, Rayner's preferred solution, was a total merger of the CSD with the Treasury. This was immediately rejected by everyone else on the grounds that it would overburden the Chancellor of the Exchequer and almost certainly result in the management of the Service being regarded, as before 1968, as a 'minor excrescence'– and therefore neglected.[120] This would not just offend the unions but also, ironically, Rayner's own principle that management should be regarded as an important policy in its own right. The third solution, which had been strongly favoured by the *Black Book* and again between 1976 and 1979, was the creation of an independent Office of Management and Budget. One of its original attractions especially under Labour, however, had been the consequent opening up for Cabinet discussion of economic issues traditionally internalised within the Treasury. In the new contested world of monetarism this was not an option Mrs Thatcher notably favoured; and to damn it further, it was also the one which the unions supported.[121] The fourth and final solution, and the one which – as will be seen – was ultimately chosen in 1981, was the transfer to the Treasury of responsibility for management and manpower (and more controversially pay) whilst the remaining CSD divisions (principally those dealing with 'human' factors such as appointments and training) formed a separate personnel office, or what Armstrong termed a Public Service Commission. In 1980, however, this option too was instantly rejected on two principal grounds: the management of the Service would remain divided and the 'rump' of the CSD would be too small to justify a separate Minister or Permanent Secretary, let alone one entitled the Head of the Home Civil Service.

Before this set-piece battle in 1980, the CSD's future had already been threatened by a vitriolic attack (led by the MOD) on the perceived heavy-handedness of the manpower freeze in 1979. Its unexpected saviour then had been Rayner. Realising that the Treasury was 'bowed down with work' and the CPRS 'unlikely to get down to brass tacks', he had concluded that the CSD alone had the administrative capacity to help him drive through reform. Moreover, given a strong Prime Ministerial lead, it need not be a broken reed.[122] Mrs Thatcher had accepted his advice; and both Rayner and Bancroft had even envisaged the CSD taking full responsibility for the scrutiny programme in 1980. However, the honeymoon was short-lived. Cabinet on 4 October was insistent that the CSD should be given no such responsibility and Mrs Thatcher's own scepticism was rekindled by her visit to the Department in January which, as she later wrote, was not an 'encouraging experience'. Able young officials appeared to be employed in the inexpert, ineffectual monitoring of other departments, to those departments' open disdain. What they needed, in her opinion, was 'worthwhile jobs'.[123]

The second assault, in March 1980, was the result of a two-pronged attack from Rayner (as part of his lasting reforms programme) and the Treasury and Civil Service Select Committee (in response to Parliamentary criticism of the CSD). Mrs Thatcher requested the 'big four' (Bancroft, Rayner, Armstrong and Wass) to consider the possibility of merger; and when they broadly recommended one, she asked them in July to draft and cost a specific plan. When this plan then revealed how limited both the rationalisation and savings would be, she expressed in November her 'inclination against merger' – an inclination that was fortuitously to be shared by the Select Committee in its delayed report. On 29 January 1981, therefore, the CSD was publicly reprieved.[124]

The CSD's saviour in 1980 had been Bancroft, who had himself become so beleaguered in the Autumn that he had had to deny inspired press rumours that he was about to retire on health grounds.[125] Initially he was heavily outgunned by Rayner and Armstrong, both of whom wanted a 'deep' integration of the Treasury and CSD (in other words, a reversion to the 1962 practice of 'mixed' Treasury divisions combining the oversight of a department's expenditure and manpower). Bancroft resolutely opposed this, not least because 'mixed' divisions had been adjudged ineffective and so disbanded by the Treasury itself in 1962 (during the reorganisation, in which he had made his name).[126] He then expertly deployed a range of spoiling tactics. First, whilst drafting the July report for Mrs Thatcher with the other 'big three', he advocated a reversion to 'shallow' integration as practised in the Treasury between 1962–8, which – as he well knew – would achieve neither the rationalisation nor the economies she was seeking. Then in a covering note to the report, he stressed the danger of disruption. In a thinly veiled attack on Rayner, he wrote:

> My own (as it happens, extensive) experience of machinery of government changes has taught me the costs of re-organisation are usually underestimated and that policies and personalities are more important than

organisational theories. The penalties of disruption . . . are immediate and substantial: the benefits come in the longer term and are inevitably speculative.[127]

Moreover, whilst acknowledging Rayner's commitment to the merger, he conveniently forgot to mention that of Armstrong and Wass.

Bancroft's tactics worked, because at her subsequent meeting with the 'big four', the Prime Minister declared she would not proceed were 'detailed work' to suggest 'much greater costs and dislocation than were presently anticipated'.[128] This gave Bancroft his chance. In an initiative, immediately christened 'operation backtrack' within the CSD, he commissioned two officials from the Treasury and CSD (M.V. Hawtin and J.K. Moore) to make a detailed study of the costs and benefits of merger. Armstrong was wholly and Rayner largely excluded. Simultaneously, Permanent Secretaries were summoned to meet (on 10 September) to record their collective protest; and union opposition was similarly marshalled at a national and departmental level.[129] Both sets of views were then prominently deployed, alongside dire warnings of overload for Treasury Ministers, in the covering note to the Hawtin-Moore report when it was submitted to the Prime Minister on 31 October. Bancroft's trump cards, however, had been his ability to switch attention from Rayner's main aim (greater central direction) to Mrs Thatcher's current concern (immediate administrative savings); and his persuasion of Wass, and through him Treasury Ministers, that 'the present [was] not the most opportune moment to engage in time-consuming reorganisation'.[130] After all, the Treasury was poised to suspend the Service's national pay agreement, replace comparability with cash limits and thereby provoke the national strike. Hence Mrs Thatcher was ready on 14 November to 'abort' the merger. She could, she reckoned, gain all she wanted by giving the Treasury increased control over both pay policy and financial management throughout the Service. In the event, therefore, the report of the Treasury and Civil Service Select Committee (finally published on 11 December) was largely irrelevant to her decision – although it did help her to disarm her backbench critics.[131]

Scarcely drawing breath, however, Mrs Thatcher then launched the third, final assault on the CSD. Like the Select Committee, she had qualified her November reprieve by saying it was only 'for the present'; and, the present ended when she received the first draft of the white paper responding to the Committee's report. Its complacent tone, in her judgement, 'demonstrated everything that is wrong with the CSD' and, as she immediately minuted Rayner, 'we have come to the heart of the matter. In spite of all our efforts and admonitions CSD is not doing the job it was set up to do . . . and intends to carry on as now'. Her attack was somewhat misguided, given that its principal targets were the paper's insufficiently zealous style (arguably the responsibility of Ministers) and a particular passage drafted not by the CSD but, on its later embarrassed admission, by the Treasury (which she was currently seeking to strengthen).[132] Nevertheless, the CSD stood condemned, particularly in conjunction with its response to the outbreak of the strike and successive furores over internal auditing (March 1981), the Wardale report (April) and departmental running costs (May) which confirmed her conviction that it was 'never going to be the McKinseys of the Civil Service'. What, she consequently asked Armstrong on 22 May, could be done? He drafted a plan to be implemented *after* Bancroft's retirement; but, seizing the moment, Rayner (arguably stung by his earlier rebuff) demanded immediate action. Together they then submitted a range of long-familiar recommendations which, in descending order of preference, were: a self-contained Office of Management and Budget within the Treasury; the transfer to the Treasury of the CSD's core responsibilities other than the promotion of efficiency (to be entrusted to the Cabinet Office); and the rejuvenation of the CSD under a dynamic, younger manager.[133]

To their consternation, and to that of others, Mrs Thatcher chose the second option (which, as noted earlier, had been instantly rejected in 1980 by both the 'big four' and the Select Committee).[134] It was regarded as flawed for many reasons. It perpetuated the division of responsibility for managing the Service; gave the Treasury the responsibility which it most dreaded (pay negotiations); was potentially a first step towards a Prime Minister's Department (which Mrs Thatcher favoured but which both Armstrong and Rayner strongly opposed); and, technically, through the transfer to it of executive powers opened up all Cabinet Office business to scrutiny by the Public Accounts Committee and the Ombudsman (see Chapter 10.3).[135] The technical difficulty was soon resolved by establishing the rump of the CSD (the new Management and Personnel Office or MPO) as an independent unit, related to the Cabinet Office solely by its common Permanent Secretary (the Cabinet Secretary, Robert Armstrong – who thus became Head of the Home Civil Service jointly with the Treasury's Permanent Secretary, Sir Douglas Wass). The MPO thus became, in Armstrong's classic phrase, 'of but not in' the Cabinet Office. The more fundamental objections were also resolved, at least in Armstrong's mind, by an examination of similar arrangements in Canada. The MPO, he became convinced, was not a '*pis aller*': the management of manpower and pay would be 'brigaded with the management of resources' in the Treasury, whilst the management of people and organisation would be brigaded with the 'management of policy-making in the Cabinet Office'.[136]

This was the positive message conveyed to the House of Commons in January 1982, when the MPO was presented as having a 'clear, coherent and vitally important responsibility' – the promotion of efficiency through the consideration of 'human factors' and not just the cutting of costs. The Opposition, however, remained unconvinced. It condemned the reorganisation as a lost opportunity finally to implement Fulton and following so swiftly after the strike, was little more than an 'act of petty spite'. The reality, argued Robert Sheldon, was that 'the Prime Minister felt she was dealing with an ill-disciplined body that had to be brought to heel. She could only do this by placing the function of pay in the Treasury, where there are tough people who know how to deal with money'.[137]

The CSD, therefore, remained under constant attack from the 1979 election until November 1981. Outside Government it was seen, on the right, as an 'officials' department' defending Civil Servants' 'privileges' and, on the left, as a symbol of the triumph of a generalist elite over Fulton. Within Government, it was equally dismissed as incapable of driving through reform and thus a superfluous layer of bureaucracy. Such criticisms were not wholly justified because, as has been seen, the CSD's weakness was essentially not administrative but political. As even Rayner admitted, ever since William Armstrong had lost interest in reform,

> the underlying philosophy of CSD and its official heads has been generally quietist, pragmatic and cautious. To a degree this is quite understandable: weak political leadership does not inspire adventurousness among officials.[138]

The advent of strong Prime Ministerial leadership in 1979, however, made no difference. Bancroft, as Head of the Home Civil Service, was granted as little access to the Prime Minister as was William Armstrong to Wilson; and, as the Prime Minister's principal adviser on reform, he was effectively supplanted (again as Armstrong had been by Halls and Hunt) by Rayner. He was unquestionably better suited temperamentally to working with Mrs Thatcher but, after a brief flirtation, he became the CSD's leading critic. Moreover, when both Mrs Thatcher and the Select Committee called in late 1980 for the CSD's revitalisation, action was conspicuous by its absence.

Consequently, the CSD lacked the necessary Prime Ministerial – and Ministerial – leadership essential to overcome the long-standing and long-recognised impediments to reform. These included the refusal of Ministers under Thatcher, as under Heath, to become 'minister-managers'; the rejection by other departments of greater centralisation whilst simultaneously failing to modernise themselves; and the reluctance of unions to embrace those changes which alone could have ensured the rewards and security their members demanded. Above all, there was the duplicity – and resultant obloquy – which officials had to suffer, as Government spokesmen before Parliamentary Select Committees or on the National Whitley Council, defending policies which in private they were simultaneously advising Ministers were indefensible.[139] Weaknesses, therefore, there may have been; but there were also Ministers (such as Heseltine) and officials (such as Sir Frank Cooper) with proven managerial skills. Why were they not appointed?

That, in such circumstances, CSD survived so long was due to a lack of any credible alternative (other than an Office of Management and Budget, which after the 'failures' of the DEA and CSD was regarded as a step too far). Any re-concentration of power in the Treasury had to contend with not just that department's past but also its current failings. As the Select Committee, for instance, was bluntly warned in 1980:

The Treasury has very little experience of large-scale management and practically none of dealing with the unions. Even in its own bailiwick it has not exercised any noticeable influence on the efficiency of the Inland Revenue Department wrestling with an overloaded and very complicated system of direct taxation.[140]

Its policy also veered wildly between the pursuit of its own departmental interests (which turned the Chancellor in 1980 into 'the most vigorous opponent of manpower cuts') and of monetarist goals (which intensified the insensitivity to other departments' needs that had led in 1968 to its being stripped of its managerial responsibilities). The ultimate choice of the Treasury to drive through 'lasting reforms' was taken, therefore, not on administrative criteria but on the *political* grounds that the Chancellor, jointly with the Prime Minister, was the 'guardian' of Government strategy.

What, however, of the 'rump' of the CSD? No immediate solution to this conundrum was found. The management of the Service was divided, as was the post of Head of the Home Civil Service and even Parliamentary representation (with Heyhoe of the Treasury answering for the new MPO in the Commons, whilst Lady Young, the Minister in charge of the MPO, answered for the Treasury in the Lords). The position of the Efficiency Unit also remained ambivalent. In July 1980, one highly experienced official had predicted that

> given clear Ministerial directions about what it wants the central government machine to do, and how it wants it done, there is no reason why the existing structure could not achieve their objectives ... The cost of organisational change would be quite disproportionate to its benefit and would be more likely to conceal deficiencies of policy rather than to remedy them.[141]

Time would tell.

7.6 Conclusion

By 1979, the crisis of consensus was so great and confidence in the economy so low that Sir John Hoskyns (as head of the No. 10 Policy Unit) had reached the somewhat apocalyptic conclusion that Britain was in danger of 'dropping out of the industrialised western world'.[142] This in turn spawned a series of demands for a dramatic reduction in the role of government: for the number of senior officials to be cut to that in 1964; for the style of Treasury control in 1962 to be restored; and, above all, for the Civil Service to revert to its overall size in 1946. There was also, in Britain as elsewhere, a reconsideration of how government could (and should) allocate and manage the reduced resources reserved for the public sector. In this regard, many of the managerial reforms recommended by Fulton remained relevant – as the furtive discussions between Hoskyns and Lord Crowther-Hunt in 1980 demonstrated.

From the start, the Thatcher administration was perceived to have a clear strategy for administrative reform – although there were, at the time, a few dissenting voices. Their dissent proved well-founded.[143] In the first year, given the lack of pre-election planning and the barrenness of Party rhetoric, reliance had to be placed on long-tried and long-discredited expedients. Then once a programme of 'lasting reforms' had been agreed, many – as with so many 'business' initiatives – showed an insufficient awareness of the differing pressures faced by public and private sector management. There was also confusion over the appropriate agency for change. Initially it was to be minister-managers; in the autumn of 1979, the CSD; then Permanent Secretaries, which provided the *raison d'etre* for the May 1980 dinner; and finally, after one very public u-turn and despite its past and current failings, the Treasury. Even more significant was the confusion over the fundamental political and administrative objectives of reform. Was it to reduce the size of Government or to eliminate waste in the delivery of existing policy? Was it to reduce public expenditure (to meet monetary targets) or to cut numbers (to meet Party expectations)? Was it to decentralise (in order to encourage more accountable management) or to centralise (in order to compel compliance)? Each objective was very different and demanded a subtly different approach.

The only constant influence throughout the period was Sir Derek Rayner; but neither his advice nor success was consistent. In his advice, for example, he attacked the use of targets by others (as in the 630,000 manpower target) but then advocated them himself (as in his response to the Wardale report). He also constantly praised the reservoir of ability within the Service, urging Mrs Thatcher 'not to import reluctant heroes from somewhere else'. Yet this is precisely what he advocated in 1981 to make good a perceived lack of financial management expertise.[144] As for success, the results of the scrutiny programme, as has been seen, were arguably less effective in their immediate goal of reducing manpower than the CSD's much-maligned cuts. Moreover, the part-time nature of Rayner's commitment inevitably raised questions over his effectiveness and, above all, the Government's commitment to reform – the more so because Soames, as the Minister in daily charge of the Service, was also part-time and indeed wholly absent for six months in Zimbabwe. This had the somewhat bizarre consequence that the Cabinet debate most crucial to the Government's reform strategy (on 1 May 1980) was led by two individuals without Cabinet status (Rayner and Channon). In addition, despite occasional urges and urgings from Rayner, Mrs Thatcher as Minister for the Civil Service had a thinly veiled contempt – and no time – for her own department. What did this signify about the Government's commitment to administrative reform?

Rayner summarised the objectives of reform under a Thatcher Government as:

> to retrench the large volume of public expenditure; to manage resources, whether large or small, so as to get the maximum value for the taxpayer's pound from them; to speed up the improvement of techniques and

methodology of resource control; and to reform the institutions, attitudes and practices of the Civil Service where necessary so as to provide management adapted to the need of the present and future.[145]

How well, during the trials and many tribulations between May 1979 and November 1981, was the basis laid for the future realisation of these goals? This will be the subject of the next Volume.

Part 4

WIDER ISSUES, 1966–81

8
WHITLEYISM, 1966-81

8.1 Introduction

Whitleyism, as seen in Chapter 2.3.2, was born in 1919 out of union militancy and a brief flirtation by Government with industrial democracy. A remarkably similar set of circumstances recurred between its golden and diamond jubilee. The flirtation with industrial democracy (the 1977 Bullock Report) may have been even briefer.[1] Union militancy, however, was as great. Reflecting the prevailing mood outside the Service, the largest staff association (the Civil and Public Services Association) adopted a policy of strike action in 1969, later supported by a fighting fund. Other associations quickly followed, as did national strikes in 1973, 1977 and 1979. Even the First Division Association, representing the most senior officials, was affiliated to the TUC by 1977.

Whitleyism managed with some difficulty to weather this storm. It could not, however, survive the radicalism of the Conservative Government after 1979. To face that challenge, the federal organisation of staff associations (which had grown out of collaboration on the 'staff side' of the National Whitley Council) was reconstituted as the Council of Civil Service Unions (CCSU). Thereafter, on both National and Departmental Councils the 'staff' side was symbolically re-titled the 'trade union' side.[2] In October 1980, as has been seen, the Government then unilaterally revoked the national pay agreement – the very embodiment of Whitleyism – and it soon became evident that, unlike earlier revocations (as in 1975), it was to be permanent. The five-month strike accordingly ensued in 1981. Whitleyism, as a national force, was never fully to recover.

Why was there this escalation to emasculation? One obvious answer is that, as an embodiment of postwar consensus, Whitleyism could not contain the new political and economic forces of the 1970s. Within the Service, the negotiating freedom of staff associations was constrained both by mutual conflicts and mounting tension between the leadership and an increasingly militant rank-and-file.[3] There were also the predations of other white-collar unions (such as the Association of Scientific, Technical and Managerial Staffs) to combat, as well as the TUC's corporatist ambition to control both pay increases (as in the 'social contract') and industrial action (as during the 'winter of discontent'). Parallel tensions beset the 'official' side. Politically, it became ever more anomalous that Government – as the 'employer' – was represented by senior officials who were not wholly disinterested but had the power to bind Ministers to decisions.[4] Administratively, the tension between the CSD (as the lead department after 1968) and the Treasury, as has been seen, intensified. The CSD was regularly accused of 'appeasement' whenever its negotiators, alert to nuances in the associations' position, supported a claim for improved pay and conditions. Conversely, the Treasury – typically backed by successive No. 10 Policy Units – was condemned for a lack of realism when denying the existence of genuine grievances which, if left unresolved, threatened 'anarchy' and thus administrative paralysis. Outside the Service, moreover, a bigger battle was brewing. Whitleyism's antagonists (militant activists on the one hand and monetarists on the other) were joining in an unholy alliance to promote a return to unfettered free collective bargaining.[5] As on the English Committee, a new 'consensus' – albeit one spuriously based on competing ideologies – was evolving.

To what extent did this new consensus, particularly in its monetarist mode, contain a germ of truth? Rather than being a bulwark against 'anarchy' as its proponents presumed, did Whitleyism perpetuate and even intensify an *existing* state of anarchy? In other words, did its rituals and rhetoric impede modernisation? Fulton certainly feared that it could 'hamper effective management', not least because the structure of staff associations was based on the very class divisions which unified grading was designed to abolish.[6] Increasingly, the economic wisdom was also that, despite their retrospective nature, annual pay awards based on 'comparability' were inflationary. Albeit only correcting lags, they nevertheless increased the PSBR and prevented Government from providing a lead for the private sector on *future* wage restraint. Did Whitleyism, therefore, impede – however unwittingly – the drive for both efficiency and economy? This is the fundamental question which this chapter will address. It will focus principally on the staff associations and their contrasting record of collaboration and conflict with Government. First, however, it is necessary to clarify their individual and collective organisation.

8.2 Organisation

The Civil Service, at some 80 per cent density, was the most unionised sector of white-collar work. It was not, however, united. There were six major and several smaller staff associations. Each had its own vested interest and increasingly acted as a conventional trade union, with varying degrees of aggression towards both each other and Government. 'Anarchy' was prevented by a complex structure of Departmental Whitley Councils (on which one association might be predominant) and, at their head, a National Whitley Council (on which every association was represented, typically by full-time officers). Between 1950 and December 1977 the National Council (NWC) met annually, but only for cocktails. Its formal responsibilities were discharged, on the associations' behalf, by the National Staff Side (NSS) which consisted of their leaders working through a number of committees and coordinated by a very small but influential secretariat. Throughout the period there was a series of mergers and attempted mergers between the associations and even attempts to create (as before 1919) a single union. There were also serious threats of secession, particularly in 1979. These ultimately led to the replacement of the NSS by an enlarged Council of Civil Service Unions (CCSU) which provided the federal framework for strike action in 1981.

8.2.1 The staff associations

By far the largest association, with approximately 200,000 members, was the Clerical and Public Services Association (CPSA) – the buccaneering Civil Service Clerical Association of the interwar years, renamed in acknowledgement of its members who had been 'hived off' when the Post Office became a public corporation in October 1969. Its expansion was maintained with the absorption of the Ministry of Labour Staff Association in 1973 and the County Court Officers' Association in 1975. So too was its reputation for controversy, with a vote-rigging scandal leading to the dismissal of its National Executive Committee in 1978.

The CPSA became, with the Civil Service Union in 1969, the first association to adopt a strike policy backed by a fighting fund. However, particularly as the result of an exodus of senior officers following the publication of the 1962 Radcliffe Report, *Security Procedures in the Public Service* (Cmnd 1681), its leadership was essentially moderate – with the dominant figure, Bill Kendall (General Secretary 1966–76 and Secretary General of the NSS/CCSU thereafter), being a lapsed Communist and devout Catholic.[7] It was the rank-and-file, especially in Newcastle and Scotland, which was increasingly militant. Nevertheless the leadership was willing to use militant tactics in 1970 (in the Post Office), in February 1973 (mounting the first national Civil Service strike with the SCS) and in February 1979 (when, again in alliance with the SCS, it first struck and then pioneered the new tactic of selective action). Following its perceived betrayal by other associations it then threatened to secede from the NSS. The constraints under which it itself functioned, however, were becoming increasingly apparent. Its militant credentials had been tarnished by its failure to join the SCPS strike in November 1977. Then, during the 1981 strike, a deep division developed between the moderate majority on its National Executive and its militant activists who increasingly demanded an all-out strike in order to further the 'class war'. This was the explanation behind the need for Kendall's successor as General Secretary (Ken Thomas) to cloak his essential willingness to negotiate with Government in belligerent rhetoric. His advocacy of an all-out strike in 1981, for example, was not designed for revolutionary ends. Rather it was to disguise divisions within his own union and, above all, to provide a show of strength which would secure favourable 'negotiating circumstances for the next decade'.[8] What, rightly or wrongly, he feared most was a slow drift back to work, which Governments could thereafter exploit as evidence of union weakness.

The second largest association, at half the size of the CPSA, was the Society of Civil Servants (SCS) which – also in recognition of its Post Office members – rebranded itself as the Society of Civil and Public Servants (SCPS) in 1976. It was

Table 8.1 Main staff associations in the late 1970s

Name	Acronym	Size (overall)	Size (Civil Service)	Membership (principal)	General Secretary	[Seats on NSS 1970 + 1979]	Seats on CCSU 1980
Civil and Public Services Association	**CPSA**	224 780	184 684	Clerks, typists, 'machine' operators: old clerical class	Ken Thomas	5/7	20
Society of Civil and Public Servants	**SCPS**	104 847	99 994	Junior/middle management: old executive class	Gerry Gillman	3/4	11
Institution of Professional Civil Servants	**IPCS**	103 342	90 305	Non-generalists, including scientists	Bill McCall	4	11
Inland Revenue Staff Federation	**IRSF**	67 614	67 614		Tony Christopher	2	8
Civil Service Union	**CSU**	46 827	45 732	Lower paid staff: Cleaners/ messengers	Les Moody	2	6
Prison Officers' Association	POA	22 189	22 189		Ken Daniel	1	3
Association of Government Supervisors and Radio Staff	AGSRO	12 043	9682	Supervisors of industrial staff, esp. MOD; radio grade at GCHQ	Percy Avery	1	2
Association of First Division Civil Servants	**FDA**	5706	5706	Senior administrative officials including economists/ statisticians	Norman Ellis	1	2

In addition, there were the Association of HM Inspectors of Taxes (AIT), affiliated to the FDA with some 2500 members; the Northern Ireland Public Services Alliance (NIPSA) with 25000 members; and the Scottish Prison Officers' Association with 5000 members. The 'big six' are in bold.

Principal source: G.K. Fry, *The Changing Civil Service* (1985) p. 123.

the direct descendant of the nineteenth-century Second Division Clerks' Association and continued its expansion with the absorption in 1975 of the Customs and Excise Group and Association of Officers of the Ministry of Labour, both of which largely contained 'executive' officers. It followed the CPSA in adopting a strike policy in 1970 and affiliated to the TUC in 1973, largely to stifle the predatory ambitions of the Association of Scientific, Technical and Managerial Staff. As has been seen, it joined with the CPSA in strike action in 1973 and 1979 and a merger of the two associations was even mooted in 1976. Perhaps to prove its independence thereafter, it made itself a pariah within the NSS by striking unilaterally in November 1977 against the Government's decision not to reintroduce wage settlements based on pay research until 1979. Its General Secretary, Gerry Gillman, was on record earlier as welcoming the Government guarantee that such settlements would be restored in 1979 as 'a great help and encouragement'. Simultaneously he confirmed that 'civil service unions, as bureaucrats, liked the [Whitley] system because it produced orderly settlements'. Nevertheless, his union went on strike, with Gillman even demanding that its picket lines should not be crossed – a demand immediately dismissed by other union leaders as 'preposterous'.[9] To their chagrin, however, such belligerence did the SCPS no harm in the eyes of activists; and it thus prepared the way for greater militancy in 1979. It also strengthened extremists within the SCPS itself and made Gillman – to the concern of many fellow General Secretaries – the captive of conference resolutions.

The Institution of Professional Civil Servants (IPCS), which was equal in size to the SCPS, was – somewhat appropriately – the most professional of the associations, with a 100-strong headquarters staff and the highest paid General Secretary, Bill McCall. It was also the most maverick, being one of the few to register under the Industrial Relations Act in 1971 and amongst the last to affiliate to the TUC (in 1976, following a series of referenda in which its members decisively rejected such a move).[10] As the representative of 'specialists' (somewhat awkwardly straddling those who were professionally qualified, such as engineers, and scientists) its interests diverged from those of 'generalist' associations. This was most apparent between 1970 and 1972 when it provoked something approaching civil war within the NSS. Given that its members had most to gain from a 'horizontal' mobility, it had warmly welcomed Fulton's recommendation of unified grading and opposed, with equal warmth, its emasculation. Organisationally, it also had much to gain from expanding its recruitment into 'administrative' posts (an ambition that did not go unnoticed by the SCPS and FDA). Then between 1976 and 1978, on behalf of its scientists, it almost provoked another civil war by impeding the NSS's attempts to reactivate pay research. Pay research, it had long maintained, was inappropriate for scientists because there were no appropriate analogues: Government was by far the largest single employer and offered a unique career structure. As has been seen in Chapter 6.2.3, however, Callaghan was irked by the suggestion that pay research should be re-activated only when it favoured officials. The CSD were equally angered by McCall's suggestion that a solution to the problem had been sabotaged by the imposition of an incomes policy in 1975. 'Mr McCall's capacity to wriggle out of his undertakings is infinite', bemoaned the CSD's chief negotiator (Gordon Burrett). At the same time, however, it was recognised that such ingenuity was employed solely in his members' interests. 'The IPCS in most respects is a moderate union', Burrett continued, and 'a force for stability and reason in Civil Service industrial relations.'[11] This was particularly apparent during the 1981 strike, during which McCall never despaired of reaching a negotiated settlement, and conformed to the predominantly conservative instincts of his members.

The other major player, despite its relatively small size and – as Fulton would have predicted – its amateurism, was the First Division Association (FDA). It had no full-time staff until 1974 and no representation on Committee 'A' (the key negotiating committee, as will be seen in Chapter 8.2.2) until 1977. This necessitated a working alliance with the SCS after 1970, which was fractured by the SCS's affiliation to the TUC in 1973 and terminated by its failure to support FDA membership of Committee 'A' in 1976.[12] Such influence that it enjoyed depended on those whom it represented (senior 'administrators') and for this reason its honorary secretary (M.G. Jeremiah) was included within the NSS 'inner circle', with which the CSD initiated detailed discussions on implementing Fulton. In the early 1970s, it also provoked two debates of major constitutional importance.[13] The first concerned the degree of enthusiasm with which officials (despite their commitment to political neutrality) should participate in policy-making. This sparked a major debate within the CSD and resulted in William Armstrong's robust defence of the Service's traditional virtues in June 1970. The second, following the damper squib of the FDA's own report, was whether officials should serve a wider 'public interest' than that represented by the current Government. This issue was raised with even greater intensity during the 1971 Vehicle and General affair, in which the Government appeared to abandon the principle of Ministerial responsibility (see above, Chapter 6.4). If officials were expected 'to stand alone . . . unsupported by their superiors', to what extent could – and should – they take public responsibility for, and thus defend, their actions in both formulating and implementing policy? An explicit code, defining the respective responsibilities of Ministers and officials, was demanded.

Such constitutional issues were to dominate the future, but what immediately concerned the FDA – and, if anything, generated more heat – was the defence of its members' living standards. In order to forestall 'impotence' in an increasingly corporatist world, should it join the TUC? Moreover, in 1979 and 1981, should its members strike? As recently as 1973, when it had denounced strike action and membership of the TUC by its affiliates in the SCS, the answer appeared obvious. Yet remarkably an FDA conference and then a ballot (in 1977 and 1981 respectively) endorsed both membership of the TUC and strike action.[14] Both decisions provoked some high-profile defections but in 1977 membership was believed to increase and the losses in 1981 were less than six per cent. This marked the extent to which trust between Ministers (from both Parties) and senior officials had collapsed in the 1970s.

Three other associations were of significance. The largest and, as selective action was to demonstrate in 1979 and 1981 potentially the most powerful, was the Inland Revenue Staff Federation (IRSF). This was because it was able to disrupt and even halt government revenue. Its members, as was seen in Chapter 6.2.3, were not above using such power to blackmail one of its former officials (James Callaghan) but, under the successive leadership of Cyril Plant and Tony Christopher, the Federation was generally consensual. Plant was, according to CSD officials, a 'rumbustious moderate' who ended his career as Chair of the TUC General Council between 1975 and 1976, the year when the national wage agreement and pay research was first suspended. Christopher, his successor as General Secretary in 1976, maintained the tradition of relaying to Ministers details of the NSS's inner thinking; and, in his zeal to get the Labour Government re-elected in 1979, he led the attempts to broker the deal which brought the NSS to the brink of dissolution.[15]

The other union with a seat on Committee 'A' throughout the 1970s was the Association of Government Supervisors and Radio Staff (AGSRO). Its independence was continuously threatened by the IPCS and its long-serving General Secretary (Percy Avery, appointed in 1955) accordingly adopted 'highly individualistic' tactics.[16] The third, and larger, union was the Civil Service Union (CSU) which represented the lowest paid Civil Servants. Initially it was amongst the most militant with its General Secretary (John Vickers, 1963–77) not above using his Cambridge education to heap abuse on Government. A failed 'go slow' in 1970, however, exposed the financial problems for his members in sustaining such action; and since later incomes policies also favoured the low paid, Vickers therefore adopted a more moderate stance which was continued under his successor (Les Moody).[17]

8.2.2 *The NSS and CCSU*

Such tensions between associations (as well as between departments) had traditionally been smoothed over by Whitleyism. At a departmental level, its effectiveness was starting to wither due to constant changes in the machinery of Government, growing alienation within 'giant' departments and, above all, the preference of association activists for direct action. The National Whitley Council (NWC), on which the 27 senior officials and association leaders met formally, was also largely redundant. It was summoned only in December 1977, October 1979 and July 1980, principally in response to the stalled reactivation and then the Conservatives' abandonment of pay research. It was thus, in Douglas Allen's phrase, little more than 'an organ of protest in times of crisis'.[18]

Whitleyism's effectiveness, however, depended less on formal meetings than on day-to-day negotiations between officials and a series of subcommittees of the National Staff Side (NSS). By far the most important of these was Committee A, which was concerned with pay, and consisted of the leading General Secretaries who rotated its chairmanship. So important was this Committee that it was regarded at the time (as it has been regarded earlier in this Volume) as synonymous with the NSS. It was rivalled in importance between 1968 and 1972 by a rather less organic development (although one which had a distinctly similar membership): the Staff Side of the Joint NWC Committee on the Fulton Report. This Committee, as seen in Chapter 5.2, had been designed by William Armstrong to counterbalance his official Steering Committee; and, to encourage informed debate at the associations' annual conferences, it issued a series of progress reports which Armstrong used to concentrate minds on which reforms were, and were not, practical. It was even concertinaed into a five-strong 'inner circle', which confided to Government tensions within the NSS position so that unnecessary antagonisms could be avoided in later and fuller negotiations.[19]

Such committee work had originated during the Second World War in order to expedite decisions; and it had been further developed by two renowned Secretary Generals who headed the very small secretariat servicing the NSS, Sir Albert Day (1939–55) and Sir Richard Hayward (1955–66). Leslie Williams, their successor, was their equal. Despite occasional outbursts of Welsh fire, he was recognised by CSD officials to be wholly trustworthy; and despite such 'collaboration', which reflected his 'passionate' belief in Whitleyism, he fought hard for the associations' cause. He was, however, aware of his own weak power base and so sought greater unity, and even the formation of a single Civil Service Union.[20] Such an eventuality appeared imminent in the wake of Fulton with, as has been seen, a flurry of mergers and accommodations. Hence, in anticipation of more fundamental change, his successor (John Dryden, 1973–6) was a deliberate stopgap appointment.

However, under Dryden and then Bill Kendall (who, as his record at the CPSA suggested, lacked the acumen of earlier Secretary Generals and was additionally hampered by ill-health), circumstances conspired against such a change.[21] It was not unification but secession, and even the collapse of Whitleyism, which became the more likely option. The opposition in 1977 of the IPCS and AGSRO to pay research, the core goal of the other associations, tested unity to the limit.[22] More ominously, activists started increasingly to criticise the concentration of power in Committee A and its apparent 'cosiness' with Government. This, they argued, prevented individual associations from fulfilling conference decisions. This was serious because, whilst the NSS could only move at the pace of the slowest and had neither the resources nor the expertise to mount effective protest campaigns, it was individual associations that bore the brunt of members' dissatisfaction.[23] Hence the unilateral strike by the SCPS in November 1977 and the crisis during the 'winter of discontent', when the General Secretaries of the two largest unions (Thomas and Gillman) resigned from Committee A and Kendall himself felt obliged to offer resignation. This crisis was triggered by the strike in February of the CPSA and SCPS alone and their subsequent programme of selective action. Then, following the Labour Government's loss of a vote of confidence and the effective start of a general election campaign, the remaining General Secretaries on Committee A – without the knowledge of Gillman and Thomas, and in defiance of Kendall – met with Ministers on 29 March in the hope of averting a planned strike by all unions on 2 April. This was widely condemned as both undermining the Secretary General's authority and exploding the myth of NSS unity. The future of Whitleyism appeared in serious jeopardy and activists on the brink of achieving their immediate aim: the replacement of 'orderly settlements' by the chaos of competitive militancy.

Whitleyism survived but not the NSS which – after prolonged bargaining – was replaced in May 1980 by the Council of Civil Service Unions (CCSU). In essence, this was only a cosmetic change because the CCSU played much the same role as the NSS, was serviced by the same secretariat and retained Kendall as Secretary General.[24] It could, however, be less easily portrayed as the creature of Government. Its enlargement from 27 to 63 members was also designed to give activists a greater voice and even to encourage unity through a better understanding of each other's concerns. In addition, power was concentrated less exclusively in a Major Policy Committee (the replacement for Committee A, on which each union was to be represented by a lay member as well as its General Secretary) to which the all-important Negotiating Committee (consisting, for speed of action, solely of representatives of the three biggest unions) was answerable. The smaller unions however, vehemently opposed such changes. Given the less regular meeting of a more cumbersome body, they argued, democracy would be decreased rather than enhanced. Moreover, the balance of power between the unions within the CSSU and its Major Policy Committee would effectively remain unchanged; and the restriction of the Negotiating Committee's membership to the CPSA, SCPS and IPCS was a reversion to pre-1977 practice. This latter charge was openly admitted by the Deputy Secretary of the CPSA, who justified it on the grounds that 'the people who paid substantial monies should comprise such a committee and in the right democratic framework, the minority points of view could be safeguarded'.[25] The smaller unions, nevertheless, stubbornly continued to press for constitutional – rather than moral – safeguards.

Such in-fighting over the constitution, which continued after the CCSU's formal inauguration until January 1981, distracted attention from the Conservative Government's assault on the size of the Service and its other initial reforms. Nevertheless, the CCSU did provide the framework for the highly effective Pay Campaign Coordinating Committee which oversaw the daily conduct of the 1981 strike. It was dominated by the CPSA and SCPS (in the persons of their respective Deputy Secretaries, Alastair Graham and Campbell Christie); but significantly it included representatives of all unions and was chaired by the Secretary of the CCSU (Peter Jones).

8.3 Collaboration

Conflict between associations and with Government attracted the greater attention, but the essence – and achievement – of Whitleyism before 1981 was the minimisation of such conflict. In 1977, Kendall described the NSS as 'a body of consensus and an instrument for negotiation'; and this well reflected the reality that, although it had failed to become a single union, it had developed a distinctive presence which both modified the policy and augmented the bargaining power of even its more powerful constituent associations. Had there been no NSS, as was repeatedly acknowledged, one would have had to be invented.[26] Proof lay in the national pay agreement and a range of other understandings which, as the SCPS was reminded in 1977, were the exclusive 'property' of the NSS. If it disappeared, so too did they. Within Whitehall, Whitleyism had a similar presence. The CSD's initial authority, for example, was largely based on the assurance that agreements with the NSS would be honoured by all associations and, through them, even by militant activists. Hence the fundamental damage sustained by both Whitleyism and the CSD, well before the 1979 election, by the imposition of cash limits and the curtailment of genuine negotiations.

Collaboration was thus the essence of Whitleyism, and, as will be shown, extended beyond wage bargaining to both the modernisation of management and the provision to Civil Servants of a collective political voice. To what extent – as its critics alleged – did such collaboration lead, like interdepartmental committees, to fudged compromises?[27] Alternatively, at a time of increasing militancy, did it not offer the most effective means of optimising efficiency?

8.3.1 Modernising management

The period between 1968 and 1974 came to be seen as a golden age of Whitleyism because of its central involvement in management reform following the Fulton Report. Such a view overlooks the simultaneous adoption by various associations of a strike policy to mollify their increasingly militant members. It also overlooks the conviction of Fulton's proponents that NSS involvement formed part of a conspiracy, orchestrated by William Armstrong, to sabotage the Report. As argued in Chapter 5.2, however, this conviction would appear baseless. The Joint NWC Committee was appointed to *advance* modernisation by both defeating anticipated resistance (from *inter alia* departmental Establishment Officers) and winning the 'vital' support of the rank-and-file. As conceived by Armstrong, it was thus a genuine exercise in industrial democracy (some eight years before the Bullock Report) and accorded both to his readiness to address association conferences and his refinement of the maxim of 'when in doubt, consult' to 'even when in no doubt, still consult'.[28] Armstrong was far from faultless in his attempt to modernise management. An incisive manager could have capitalised more ruthlessly on the apparent readiness of associations to merge and even on Williams' ambition to form a single union – although, given the experience of the TUC's social contract, such centralisation of power might have generated even greater grass-roots militancy. He might have heeded CSD advice that to tie progress to joint reports with the NSS was an abdication of managerial responsibility.[29] Moreover, as Head of the Home Civil Service, he had less excuse than either Wilson or Heath to grow bored with what should have been one of his principal tasks. Such failings, however, did not amount to conspiracy.

For his part, Williams – as Secretary General of the NSS and 'Whitleyism personified' – seized the opportunity that Armstrong offered. Capitalising on his exhaustive knowledge of the Service, he immediately questioned whether unified grading alone could provide the greater flexibility (for which, in his judgement, Fulton had correctly called). Moreover, further investigation was needed to determine the proposal's practicability. Were unified grading to proceed, however, he acknowledged that staff associations would themselves have to make 'painful and difficult' adjustments and was insistent that they should 'approach even the more controversial recommendations with an open mind and with the public interest uppermost'.[30] Such attitudes naturally commended him to Armstrong. Accordingly, both formally through the Joint NWC Committee and informally through a burgeoning range of confidential contacts, the NSS (and thus a core of general secretaries) became major players in management reform. The four progress reports, which the Committee published, between 1969 and 1972 testify to its authority throughout the whole Service. Senior officials (and, in particular, Permanent Secretaries and Establishment Officers) accepted, albeit with some resentment, this infringement of managerial prerogative.[31] Meanwhile, despite their incipient militancy, junior officials were dissuaded from instinctively opposing reform at association conferences.

To what positive purpose, however, was this power put? With regard to structural reform, collaboration blunted the CSD's initial radicalism. It forced, for example, the early concession of interim categories. This, as officials at the time and Norman Hunt later complained, surrendered the initiative to the NSS by giving associations what they wanted (vertical mobility) without obliging them to accept what many opposed (horizontal mobility).[32] Then, over Christmas 1969, the NSS was responsible not just for the effective abandonment of unified grading below the level of Principal (with the CSD's concurrence) but also for its postponement below the level of Under Secretary (against the CSD's wishes). Finally in 1971 irreconcilable disagreement between the associations caused (or became the pretext for) the effective abandonment of any further extension of unified grading. 'IPCS officials', so Heath was informed, 'do not believe they could carry the membership with them if the door was slammed shut on unified grading. The FDA and the SCS will not readily contemplate the possibility of leaving the door ajar'. Hence, on Williams' own admission, to avert a 'civil war' a form of weasel words was incorporated into the final NWC report which, in essence, ended all attempts to implement Fulton's proposals for structural change.[33]

Progress was similarly impeded in the alternative area of reform which the NSS (and arguably Armstrong) had always favoured: improved personnel management. Collectively, associations' anticipated resistance to Fulton's more punitive recommendations (such as the abolition of the concept of 'establishment' in order to end the 'presumption of security until retirement') was so great that the CSD scarcely dared to raise them.[34] Likewise their insistence that all reforms, such as improved training and career management, should apply not just to the elite (as the CSD wanted) but to the whole Service stretched capped resources beyond the limit at which they could be effective. The vested interest of individual associations, in defiance of Williams' initial assurances, also obtruded. Williams himself, for example, complained bitterly in 1971 of the delayed introduction of two initiatives he regarded as vital to ensure greater flexibility in the absence of unified grading: 'lateral movement' and 'opportunity posts'. He conveniently overlooked the fact that the SCS conference had just explicitly denounced them. In short, collaboration (particularly as it became overshadowed by controversy over pay, the Industrial Relations Act and the Conservatives' alternative plans for administrative reform) appeared to confirm its critics' worst fears. As Fulton had warned, staff associations were 'determining and not reflecting' reform priorities and, worse still, past failings were being repeated. 'Success in reaching agreement with the staff side', it observed, had formerly come 'to be treated as an end in itself, and failure to reach agreement as a failure by management; this means that negotiations are sometimes too long drawn out'.[35]

Be that as it may, what became equally transparent was that Whitleyism by itself could make good deficiencies in neither Fulton's reasoning nor the quality of top Civil Service management. One of Fulton's major deficiencies, which was immediately recognised by both association leaders and Armstrong, was its relative neglect of 'ordinary' civil servants.[36] Hence they were equally interested in personnel management and eager to expand it once structural reform had faltered. This eagerness became keener after the CPSA/SCS strike in February 1973 and prompted the initiative which, together with the national pay agreement in December 1974, has come to be identified as the apex of Whitleyism. This was the Wider Issues Review. Commissioned in July 1973 under the general auspices of the NWC, it was completed by an interdepartmental team of officials working to a steering committee (chaired by Ian Bancroft) and an NSS advisory committee (with which its diagnosis was discussed before the final report was published in January 1975).[37] The Review's focus was 'the workaday problems of the middle and lower grades' and its object to look at issues 'wider' than those conventionally handled by Whitleyism. Principal amongst them were workers' psychology and the role of Government as a 'good employer'. Job satisfaction and thereby greater efficiency, it concluded, demanded more humane and imaginative management – such as the introduction of transparent promotion procedures and the redesign of 'specialised, repetitive or grinding' jobs. Only this would sustain the morale of a new and younger workforce, which did not have 'traditional white collar attitudes and do not aspire to them'. To qualify as a 'good employer', Government – and especially Ministers – also needed to demonstrate greater consideration (including the provision of more adequate office accommodation) and fairness (including a better appreciation of the disruption caused by over-frequent changes to organisation and policy, and a readiness to resist discrimination particularly in relation to pay). The Review concluded by recommending the better articulation and achievement of a 'common purpose' through 'fuller and more constructive use of Whitleyism'. This was something of a double-edged sword because it suggested that currently Whitleyism was not working well; and its final report indeed contained some trenchant criticism of the staff associations and, in particular, their increasing pursuit of short-term, sectional interest.[38]

Was 1975, therefore, as commonly portrayed the apex of Whitleyism? Doubts are reinforced by the essential barrenness of the Review itself. In relation to new insights, its rather lame conclusion was that pay and accommodation were the key influences on morale. Like most of its personnel management recommendations, both had already been the subject of protracted negotiation.[39] In relation to results it did demand – in anticipation of Rayner – departmental action plans. The NSS also reorganised itself so that it could better achieve those 'solid' if non-pecuniary reforms which would 'make life a little less intolerable'.[40] The Review's success, however, was ultimately dependent on the prevailing political climate; and, by 1975, this had turned distinctly chilly. For instance, Michael Foot – as Secretary of State for Employment and deeply involved in the drafting of the social contract – responded to its interim report by refusing to guarantee pay comparability, let alone to prevent pay discrimination.[41] The major earlier achievements of the NSS in personnel management and wage bargaining (the 1972 Superannuation Act and the 1973 Pay Board's anomaly ruling) had also consolidated in the public mind the conviction that the Service was 'privileged'. Moreover, even the improved 'facility' arrangements for associations (such as the provision of rooms and time-off for branch meetings), which were intended to 'symbolise the intention of the Staff and Official sides at the national level to take positive steps to restore traditional and staff relations', proved counterproductive.[42] They were increasingly used by militants to undermine national leaders. Most seriously, however, administrative change choked collaboration. As the CSD's authority waned, so the federal nature of the Service reasserted itself and with it the power of departmental Establishment Officers – 'reactionary shellbacks', in the words of the NSS who were 'negative, unimaginative and inextricably wedded to the status quo'. Even before the 1979 election, therefore, practice appeared to be reverting to what it had been before 1969 or, arguably, even 1939.

8.3.2 Political presence

A further advantage of collaboration was that it gave Civil Servants a collective political voice, sufficiently powerful to justify four meetings with the Prime Minister between 1970 and 1974, a further three in 1974 alone and four in 1977. Again, the significance of these meetings should not be exaggerated. Their frequency in 1974 and 1977, for example, may be explained by major industrial relations initiatives within the Civil Service (respectively the signing of the national pay agreement and the reactivation of pay research). Somewhat surprisingly given their mutual dependence, the CSD also discouraged more regular contact. Routine matters, it argued, were more properly dealt with by the Minister with day-to-day responsibility for the Service. Wide-ranging debates should be avoided as 'potentially embarrassing', given that they might raise 'national issues on which the Government normally consults the TUC and other national organisations'.[43]

Nevertheless, particularly before 1974 and in 1976, the meetings did carry some political weight.

The talks with Heath were used to sound out NSS opinion on other unions' reaction to the Industrial Relations Act and led, somewhat ironically, to fulsome praise from the Prime Minister for Whitleyism (as was to recur in 1977 when, in the wake of the Bullock Report, Callaghan commented unfavourably on the lack of industrial democracy in the private sector).[44] They were also used to provide advance notice of important changes, such as the *Reorganisation of Central Government* white paper of 1970 and of the Pay Board's anomalies award of 1973. Such privileged information was not used for political advantage by the NSS. Rather it was appreciated for the status it accorded national leaders which helped to consolidate their authority over their rank-and-file.

Concurrent negotiations at a less rarefied level, however, had even greater political significance. In the wake of Fulton, as has been seen, managerial prerogative over personnel management – albeit with the CSD's collusion – was eroded. This restricted the freedom of Government to implement policy. There was a parallel erosion of Ministerial prerogative in an area of central importance to both Fulton and the Heath Government: structural change. Under Labour, for example, the NSS was given an explicit assurance in relation to hiving off that it would be consulted as soon as any planning proceeded beyond the most preliminary stage; and this was reiterated by Heath in one of his first public statements. 'The interest of the NSS, and therefore the process of consultation with them', he confirmed, 'should extend to the whole structure and functioning of the Service.'[45] Such commitments may not have been honoured as scrupulously as were the ones made by the NSS to confidentiality. Moreover Frank Cooper, the CSD Deputy Secretary most involved in the on-going negotiations, somewhat ruthlessly dismissed any NSS objection as 'ritual noises' to satisfy the rank-and-file.[46] Nevertheless, forcefully expressed concern about officials' employment rights undoubtedly undermined the political commitment to structural change. The NSS's recognised knowledge of, and influence over, the 'temper' of 'the middle and lower grades' also modified policy.

The NSS's political influence arguably reached its peak in 1976 when Callaghan, soon after becoming Prime Minister, broke new ground by discussing manpower policy and even agreed to compromise on the announced target for savings (£95 million as opposed to £145 million). The understanding was that, to reassure overseas financiers, the NSS would present a common front with Government and moderate its militants.[47] He also conceded in May 1976 the appointment of the Armitage Committee on the Political Activities of Civil Servants. A long-standing debate had been re-ignited by Wilson's waiving of the convention of Ministerial collective responsibility during the 1975 EEC referendum and, as seen in Chapter 6.3.1, laxness in applying standard restrictions to special advisers as temporary Civil Servants. If constitutional constraints could be relaxed for others, why not for permanent Civil Servants? Would their active involvement in politics really, as argued in the past, jeopardise the neutrality – or perceived neutrality – of the Service? Did not their current 'political castration' amount to an infringement of civil liberty?

Existing practice was based on the decision taken by the then Conservative Government in 1952 to divide officials into three categories: 'restricted' (which permitted, on request, involvement in local but not national politics); 'intermediate' (which permitted, again on request, involvement in both); and 'free' (which enabled the most junior six per cent of non-industrial Civil Servants to participate without restriction). Unsympathetic management, however, had led to an increase of officials within the 'restricted' category from 14 to 26 per cent. The NSS, at minimum, wanted to reverse this trend by moving all Executive and Clerical Officers to the 'intermediate' category. Ideally, it also sought a fundamental shift in power by freeing all officials, within reason, to participate fully in local and national politics. The onus, it maintained, should be on departments to demonstrate that – given the nature of an individual's work – their impartiality would be impaired.

The Labour Cabinet was divided on the issue, and the Opposition vehemently opposed any change. As Mrs Thatcher wrote to Wilson on 30 March 1976:

> We all feel strongly that the impartiality of the Civil Service must be preserved and we therefore look critically at any suggestion to extend the political activities of civil servants and we are sceptical of any action which might lead to such an extension.[48]

Officials, it was believed, already had too much political power. Despite such opposition, the NSS nevertheless triumphed and the Armitage Committee was appointed. Its report in January 1978 duly recommended that the 'restricted' class should be reduced to the top three per cent of officials and that restrictions on the much enlarged 'intermediate' class be made more transparent. This did not wholly realise the NSS's ideal, not least because – to the particular frustration of the CPSA – restrictions were to remain on officials who dealt directly with the public or who had access to sensitive personal information. Nevertheless, in a highly unsympathetic public climate, the Report represented a considerable achievement for the collective political presence of the NSS.

Parallel changes to employment rights were more elusive. Here the trap was sprung by the 1974 Trade Union and Labour Relations Act which, in order to change the balance of power on the shop floor (as sought by both the TUC and the Labour Party NEC), facilitated the creation of closed shops. As an employer, Government could hardly ignore its own legislation. However, as Permanent Secretaries and then the Opposition pointed out, the sanctioning of closed shops within the Civil Service could seriously impugn its impartiality. Not least, officials could effectively become liable for dismissal were they to defy instructions from either their union or the TUC. Such a prospect so alarmed Mrs Thatcher that she was moved to defend the virtues of Northcote-Trevelyan. Closed shops, she claimed, would 'revive fears that the public service was a source of sinecures and a purveyor of patronage, and could only be detrimental to the quality of government'.[49] The issue consumed an inordinate amount of time at the highest level; but in 1978 it was quietly dropped. This did not necessarily represent a political defeat for the NSS. Despite associations' concern for an estimated loss in annual dues of £1.3 million from 'free riders', the closed shop was always of more concern to the industrial Civil Service (where union membership was far lower). Moreover, there were major internal divisions over matters of principle (such as the potential infringement of human rights and the dual loyalty of officials to democratic government and their union).[50] The CPSA, CSU and IRSF favoured a closed shop; the IPCS was ambivalent; and the SCPS and FDA opposed it.[51]

The political dividend gained from collaboration was, therefore, inherently problematic. Such a dividend certainly existed, as demonstrated by the Armitage Report, but the relationship between the Prime Minister and the NSS was inevitably circumscribed. The former, even in his formal role as the Minister for the Civil Service, had always to be alert to wider political pressures. The latter were ever wary of exceeding constitutional propriety. Their meetings might therefore be described as politically lightweight, designed solely to maintain the confidence – and bolster, within an increasingly militant membership, the status – of moderate leaders. Before 1976, such a depiction would not be wholly accurate. Thereafter it became more so, as the political difficulty of sustaining a minority Government mounted, and attention turned from satisfying demands for greater employee power (from within the Labour movement) to the 'deprivileging' of the public sector (as sought by the electorate at large). In such circumstances Callaghan, as a former IRSF official, was well qualified to exploit the self-denying ordinances under which moderate NSS leaders laboured.[52]

8.3.3 Negotiating pay

However substantial its managerial and political achievements, the true test of collaboration was wage bargaining. Did it, from the very different perspectives of staff association members and the taxpayer, secure better settlements than would have been secured by confrontation? As was seen in Chapter 6.2.3, the period was one of growing confrontation. This was not necessarily inimical to a policy of collaboration. Militancy and, above all, the threat of future militancy could be used to break down Government intransigence. Nevertheless, NSS leaders were personally committed to the maintenance of an 'orderly' system of industrial relations, which in their judgement was their democratic responsibility as well as the optimum way to promote both the welfare of their members and the efficiency of government.[53] As national leaders, increasingly challenged by local militancy, it also served their vested interest.

Collaboration over wage bargaining faced three main tests: the renegotiation of the national pay agreement, finally signed in December 1974; its reactivation after suspension in 1975; and, finally, its defence against the Thatcher Government. The 1974 pay agreement and the subsequent 32.5 per cent pay increase marked a high point in collaborative achievement. Civil Service salaries, as illustrated in Figure 6.1, came as close as they ever did to the mean pay of 'outside staffs employed on broadly comparable work'. Association members had grown increasingly frustrated by the failure to realise this Priestley ideal. First it had been disrupted by the Conservatives' 1962 pay pause (which, like later incomes policies, was perceived to discriminate against the public sector, to which it was applied stringently) and then by Labour's 'staging' of awards in 1968. In addition, biennial awards based on pay research (as recommended by Priestley) had been compromised by inflation. In alternative years, 'central' pay awards based simply on the retail price index had resulted in considerable falls in relative pay rates (particularly affecting those retiring on final-salary pensions at inopportune times). The new pay agreement, by instituting annual research-based awards, removed this major anomaly.

In equal measure, the agreement validated the policy of collaboration and demonstrated the value of confrontation – and the threat of further confrontation – because its negotiation was greatly assisted by the first national strike in February 1973 within the Service and Government's subsequent awareness that it was sitting on a 'powder keg of militancy'.[54] The strike had been provoked by the introduction of the Conservatives' statutory incomes policy – with which William Armstrong was closely identified. The 'standstill' between November 1972 and April 1973 froze a research-based award which was due to a majority of officials in January 1973. Then Stage 2, between April and November 1973, delayed payment of a similar award to the remainder. NSS leaders, however, were less concerned about pay than the restoration of normal negotiating procedures and, in particular, the resumption of pay research. As Williams argued on a delegation to the Prime Minister on 8 January with characteristic 'force, clarity and moderation', the NSS was not 'seeking exclusion from a policy to deal with inflation which applied to the whole community . . . The loyalty of the Civil Service to the Government of the day was not in question . . . This was not a political dispute'.[55] However, were militancy to be contained (particularly in the light of concessions to it in other industries), it was essential that 'orderly' procedures, as represented by Whitleyism, should be – and be seen to be – effective. This argument raged not just with Government, but also within the NSS itself. Uncharacteristic split votes were recorded in April 1973 and Williams (whose own retirement had to be postponed) tried to paper over the cracks by extolling 'the harmonisation of skilled negotiation with genuine militancy'.[56] 'Skilled negotiation' eventually triumphed. The Pay Board's anomalies ruling of November 1973 largely conceded the NSS case and, in addition, recommended the institution of annual research-based awards. Both the Conservatives and the incoming Labour Government (which finally signed the national pay agreement in December 1974) needed little persuasion to agree.

The pay settlement of 1973–4 soon turned to ashes as, rightly or wrongly, it became associated in the political and public mind with an image of a privileged bureaucracy; and the national pay agreement was almost immediately suspended in July 1975 as part of the new voluntary incomes policy.[57] However, as soon as the TUC announced in 1976 a 'planned return to free collective bargaining' in the following year, the NSS insisted that — because of its scientific basis and retrospective nature — research-based pay, and thus the national agreement, should be restored. Circumstances, nevertheless, had changed. Not only had the public mood hardened but, as seen in Chapter 6.2.3, a major battle had been joined within Whitehall between the CSD (which feared anarchy, were collaboration to be abandoned) and the Treasury (which had a greater fear of inflation). Reinvigorated by the introduction of cash limits, the Treasury was seeking awards which achieved not 'comparability' with past wage increases in the private sector but the desired 'tone' of the next overall pay round.[58]

Callaghan initially sided with the CSD, accepting (as did a subsequent Cabinet Committee) that abandonment of the national pay agreement would incite unrest. What other system could guarantee better results? Over time, however, he increasingly sided with the Treasury. Thus, although the pay agreement was ultimately renewed in November 1977, collaboration in the meantime was tested to the limit with the NSS feeling itself to be placed 'under duress' by the imposition of an escalating series of conditions. The moderation of its leaders was also ruthlessly exploited by the Prime Minister. 'Of course', he concluded one particularly confrontational meeting, 'at the end of the day the Civil Service unions might say they wanted another system of agreeing pay. But he doubted it'.[59] Hard bargaining, nevertheless, left unresolved the critical question of how to reconcile retrospective pay research with the 'tone' of future wage rounds; and when, after endless prevarication, the time came in autumn 1978 to negotiate the first settlement under the reactivated agreement, the gulf proved unbridgeable. Pay research suggested an award of 25 per cent, whilst cash limits — mirroring Stage 4 of incomes policy — permitted only five per cent. The subsequent anger at the Government's perceived duplicity fed directly, during the winter of discontent, into the pre-emptive strike by the SCPS and CPSA in February 1979 and the strike by all staff associations in April.[60]

Within the NSS, the attempted reactivation of pay research between 1976 and 1978 was a moment of truth. Reactivation, it had initially been presumed, was assured in 1978 coincidental with the TUC's 'planned return to free collective bargaining'. This presumption was reinforced by the regular reaffirmation by Government of its commitment to 'fair comparisons' and that it had suspended, not abandoned, the pay agreement. Activists at the 1977 SCPS conference were consequently able to bind their leaders to strike action, were reactivation not to occur in April 1978. When protracted negotiations made this impossible, the die was cast; and the SCPS went on strike in November 1977. Nevertheless, it did so alone because the leaders of all the other associations agreed that their paramount objective was to restore an 'orderly' system of industrial relations. Consequently, they were prepared to accept a further year of improvisation.[61] They also persuaded their members to protest peacefully (via a week of demonstrations and a meeting of the full NWC) and excluded Gillman from the delegation to the Prime Minister on 9 November, after which the restoration of research-based awards in 1979 was conceded.

As a consequence, in the 1978 pay round each association exceptionally made separate claims (although a common award was ultimately made at the maximum ten per cent permitted under Stage 3 of incomes policy). Gillman then sought to restore unity through the planning of a common campaign of action in case Government (as he correctly feared) reneged on its promises for 1979. The majority of his fellow leaders, however, were too wedded to collaboration to support such contingency planning. Nor, apart from Ken Thomas of the CPSA, were they prepared during the subsequent winter of discontent to support a pre-emptive strike in February 1979 and a subsequent programme of selective action. In the belief that militancy, or at least the threat of militancy, would make the Government see reason, they pursued collaboration to the last minute – and even beyond. Furtive negotiations on 29 March 1979 to avert a strike by all the unions, as was seen earlier, finally destroyed the NSS. The greater casualty, however, was an unquestioning faith in collaboration. As Lord Peart reported to the Prime Minister following a somewhat tense encounter:

> The hitherto moderate unions . . . accused the Government of deceit in re-activating pay research in 1977. They had not previously thought it right to take industrial action believing that constructive negotiations were possible with Government . . . Those who had held back now felt betrayed.

Moderate leaders then queued up to threaten a 'savage' disruption, with Christopher even predicting disruption of the budget and the Government having to suspend half the Civil Service.[62] The subsequent, and relatively generous, settlement owed less to an 'orderly' system of industrial relations than to the imperative of minimising militancy during an election campaign.

Faith in collaboration was not restored by the election in 1979 of a Conservative Government. Its uncompromising nature soon became apparent. To modernise management, for example, Derek Rayner was immediately seconded from Marks and Spencer. A consensual reformer not unsympathetic towards the Service (see Chapters 5.3.3 and 7.3.3), his 'lasting reforms' were nevertheless dedicated to changing Whitehall's culture, not least through the abolition of the CSD. Politically, in the No. 10 Policy Unit, Hoskyns' determination to 'deprivilege' the Service replaced Donoughue's general antipathy towards it. Moreover, in regard to manpower policy – where Callaghan had been prepared to compromise in 1976 – the Conservatives were adamant that it fell exclusively within the Government's prerogative. This all contributed to Kendall's outburst to Bancroft in April 1980, cited in Chapter 7.4: 'what exactly is going on? . . . The matters in question are crucial to established channels of joint communication in the Civil Service and the Staff Side are not prepared to be bypassed . . . We have a right to put a point of view and to ensure there is a balanced debate'. Even more resignedly Ken Thomas lamented that 'there was now no Government/union dialogue, just naked Party politics which, for non-political trade unions, were not easy to deal with'.[63]

Whether the unions really were 'non-political' is as debatable as the earlier charge against the Civil Service as a whole. What is not debatable, however, is that collaboration over pay ceased after 1979. Driven by Hoskyns' determination to reverse economic decline by using, in direct defiance of the Priestley Commission, the Service as an exemplar to halt wage inflation, Mrs Thatcher in particular was unwilling to brook meaningful negotiations. Earlier attempts by Labour to modify pay research were reinforced by the monetarist Medium Term Financial Strategy; and, following the failure on a technicality to suspend it for the 1980 pay round, the national pay agreement – in a heavily trailed move – was unilaterally abandoned in October 1980. Kendall was irate and refused to meet Soames 'merely to receive a letter the contents of which had already been disclosed to the Press and principal establishment officers'.[64] During the ensuing strike, Soames himself was then – as seen in Chapter 7.4 – frequently embarrassed by the restrictions placed upon him as chief negotiator, not least in June 1981 when a deal (supported not only by the CCSU but also the majority of Cabinet) was vetoed. The Government, or at least a powerful minority within it, was clearly bent on confrontation; and the CSSU, united by so blatant an assault on its 'orderly' system of industrial relations, was ready to respond.

Could the strike, as suggested by some, have been prevented by a fuller use of the Whitley machinery to explain the economic reasoning behind the suspension yet again of the pay agreement? Suspension, after all, had been agreed in 1975 and, throughout the 1981 strike, union leaders were able to contain their more militant members. Moreover, as recognised in the exchange of letters at the end of the strike, the overwhelming priority of the leaders remained the maintenance of an 'orderly' system of negotiation. Moreover, ever mindful of their democratic duty, they had always kept open a channel of communication with Government; and simultaneously stressed that the strike was not political but an 'industrial dispute between a bad employer and aggrieved employees'.[65] Whitleyism, however, no longer offered a magic bullet. Suspension of the pay agreement in 1975 had only been accepted – grudgingly – because it was part of a wider anti-inflation strategy, brokered by the TUC, which did not discriminate against the Service. Had union leaders persevered with a policy of collaboration after 1976, rather than embracing selective industrial action, it is unlikely that they could have contained their more militant members. In addition, exemplars of reasoned rationality though they may have been, it is even more doubtful that they could ever have accepted the very different rationality being promoted by the Conservatives. Similar ideas, when advanced by Labour, had been met with incomprehension and they now had a distinct ideological edge. They were simply inimical to Whitleyism, as currently conceived. Nevertheless, it must be admitted, under the Conservatives collaboration was never afforded a chance.

8.4 Conflict

Conflict thus progressively replaced collaboration throughout the 1970s. The search for consensus by earlier Governments was eroded by escalating economic and political pressure to which was added, after 1979, an ideological edge. Within the staff associations, as throughout British industry, local activists increasingly took the lead and there was a continuing undertow of unofficial disruption.[66] National leaders, albeit wedded to collaboration, consequently adopted 'industrial action', first as a threat and then as reality, to pressurise Government. The result was three set battles.

8.4.1 1973: the first national strike

By the standard of later conflicts, the one-day strike on 27 February 1973 by two staff associations (the SCS and the CPSA) was a modest affair. Moreover, the eventual settlement to the pay dispute – of which it was the intended climax – was secured by more traditional means (reasoned protest via Departmental Whitley Councils, the lobbying of MPs and continuing negotiation by the other associations in Whitehall). Nevertheless, as recognised at the time, it was a defining moment. It was the Service's first national strike and a portent of the pressure under which all associations were to be put by militants. It also sowed the seeds of distrust between junior staff and senior officials and, reciprocally, revived contingency planning in Whitehall.

The underlying cause of the dispute was the imposition of the Conservatives' statutory incomes policy in November 1972. This, as has been seen, disrupted a research-based pay award for the majority of officials, which was due in January 1973. Ideally, the associations wanted this award to be paid as soon as the 'standstill' (Stage 1) ended in April. They also wanted a similar award for the rest of the Service to be paid in full from the start of Stage 2 (which strictly limited increases) rather than in November, at the start of the more liberal Stage 3. At minimum, they wanted an explicit promise that the awards would be paid in full no later than November. The associations' case won the support of the majority of Ministers and MPs by its moderate and reasoned presentation.[67] It also had a strong advocate in Lord Jellicoe, the Minister in daily charge of the Service. In a sequence of prescient letters, he advised Heath that – even if no award could be made until November – there was a need for an early announcement that it would be paid then. In addition, once the Pay Board had been identified as the means to a solution, he demanded that it should be genuinely independent. A real battle was being waged 'between militancy and responsibility', he assured a sceptical Chancellor of the Exchequer and, were the reference to the Board fixed, this would

> turn the whole of the NSS the way of its more militant elements. This is a very real danger; indeed it could well become a reality if we simply and publicly pull the rug from under those who have the courage to call on their members hitherto to avoid militant action and rely instead on arguing their case.[68]

The Chancellor was sceptical not just because he was defending Treasury interests but because, like other Ministers, he was alert to the incipient press attack on the

Service. Just as Government should not discriminate against their 'employees' (by suspending retrospective awards), he argued, so it could not discriminate in their favour (by sanctioning awards higher than those permitted to others). This, however, became the perception of what the Pay Board's anomalies ruling sanctioned.

Militant action in 1973 took two forms: a protest meeting called by the CPSA and SCS during working hours on 10 January and the strike on 27 February. Both were reasonably well supported. The former, which was officially regarded as 'tantamount to a one-hour strike', closed *inter alia* most DHSS offices as well as the DHSS computer centre in Newcastle and the Department of National Savings in Glasgow. The latter involved some 128,000 officials (or 47 per cent of the relevant grades), with Newcastle and Glasgow once again to the fore.[69] Less public, but on the CSD's admission more effective and difficult to counter, was a programme of non-co-operation between January and May, including a work to rule and an overtime ban.

More threatening than all such 'action', however, was the threat by the CPSA to call further one-day strikes or even a one-week strike (supported by £5 strike pay); and the belligerence expressed at all the associations' May conferences (during which the SCS voted to establish a £250,000 strike fund and even the typically moderate IRSF and IPCS called for strike action).[70] Was moderation about to be abandoned, or were such conference resolutions simply gestures to appease activists?

Within the NSS, there had certainly been a heated debate before the strike. Williams defended collaboration on the grounds that Government policy was malleable, but he and other leaders were accused of becoming dangerously remote from the rank-and-file. Moreover, it was asserted, militancy worked. As one of the leading protagonists maintained, the NSS was

> perhaps blessed with too many skilled negotiators . . . and failed to recognise that members had a part to play. Recent actions had clearly shown that members responded to the right kind of leadership . . . Negotiation was the art of the possible . . . and because of pressure that we have been seeing from our members, more was possible than we had originally believed.[71]

Moderation was temporarily saved by the personal affront from the CPSA's precipitate and independent action which other leaders claimed to feel. Such a claim could not be repeated. What could be mobilised, however, were the moderation of most association members and the practical problems of sustaining militant action. Even before the strike, Dryden (of the SCS) had re-affirmed to the CSD officials that he favoured negotiation to militancy and that he could persuade his National Executive to abort the strike were he given 'bankable assurances' about the date of payment. Likewise, well before the May conferences, Kendall reassured William Armstrong that 'strike action could be regarded as over'. The CPSA had run out of money and was seeking to save face through a negotiated settlement and the institution of the *Wider Issues* review.[72] Conference belligerence, in short, was largely rhetoric.

Consequently, in retrospect, the February strike might appear to have been 'more of an irritant than a real problem'. Nevertheless, its symbolic importance was immense. On the 'staff' side, Williams later confessed how concerned he had been about the 'deep divisions' within the NSS. Other moderate leaders railed against the restrictions placed on negotiation by pre-emptive resolutions passed by either the National Executives or conferences of constituent associations. On the 'official' side, William Armstrong also immediately recognised the strike's potential significance and duly warned the NSS that there was 'a crucial distinction between the normally accepted and legitimate forms of protest which staff had hitherto pursued outside their work, and action affecting the work of the Civil Service'.[73]

Ironically, this warning then led directly to an incident which ensured the strike's permanent significance. As Head of the Service, he sent a personal letter to all staff in which he argued that the control of inflation was in everyone's interest and that there was 'nothing at stake which could possibly justify' the risk of alienating the public through strike action. This was bad enough because it failed to acknowledge the validity of the NSS case. It also gave the impression that Armstrong was less concerned about the welfare of his fellow officials than of the Government (in which, of course, he had just been dubbed by Kendall 'deputy Prime Minister'). The most fateful passage of the letter, however, read:

> I know some of our colleagues feel so bitterly . . . that they are looking to militant action to solve their problems. I hope each of them will consider very carefully the likely consequences of such action not only for themselves but also for the Service as a whole.

This was widely interpreted, even by normally equable Williams, as a veiled threat of disciplinary action – which was indeed mandatory under Estacode. Armstrong was adamant that nothing had been further from his mind and documentary evidence supports him.[74] Nevertheless the letter entrenched within junior staff, and especially those working outside London, a sense of alienation which the *Wider Issues* review was intended, but failed, to eradicate.

The strike's historic importance was cemented by a fundamental revision of Government's contingency planning.[75] Because of the latent federalism within the Service, it was less fundamental than many desired. A fine line had to be drawn, for example, between 'central direction' (which might offend departmental sensitivities) and a 'broad strategic framework' (to minimise inconsistencies that might leave the Service open to challenge either in law or on appeal). Another had to be drawn between action which might either provoke militants by its harshness or moderates (and the taxpayer) by its laxity. Nevertheless by September three major advances had been made. A model circular had been drafted by the CSD to standardise departmental practice and a new, albeit non-disciplinary, form of suspension ('relieved from duty' orders) devised, which was to play an important role in the 1981 strike. Second, plans had been finalised both to establish a CSD operations rooms (to act *inter alia* as a source of standardised advice) and to enable the Civil Contingencies Unit to act decisively should the 'soft underbelly' of Government (such as DHSS offices and airport traffic control) be attacked.

Most significant, however, was the consideration given to the role of 'managers'. How could they be differentiated from the rest of the Service? Their defining characteristic, it was agreed, was their 'obligation . . . to undertake whatever work the situation might demand and not solely a limited range claimed to be "proper to their grade"'. All posts at or above the Senior Principal grade were axiomatically covered. The manager of any local office (who might only be an Executive Officer) could also be included, at individual departments' discretion. How then might their 'reliability' be guaranteed? They could not be prohibited from striking (as hardline Establishment Officers wished) because of the long tradition of encouraging all staff – not least in the interests of moderation – to join their appropriate staff association. Greater subtlety was needed. Hence they were to be given 'personal advice' on where their loyalties, and promotion prospects, lay; and there was to be a 'discreet hearts and minds campaign', largely through training programmes, to ensure a 'proper' appreciation of the duties of 'accountable managers'. In turn, however, such a 'hearts and minds' campaign exposed the inherent tensions within management training programmes (which, since Fulton, both the CSD and NSS had been at pains to encourage). Following Armstrong's letter, it also further drove a wedge between senior and junior staff and thus weakened the very sense of common purpose – both between grades and between the 'staff' and 'official' sides – that Whitleyism was designed to foster. This is why the strike was an historic turning point.

8.4.2 1979: the winter of discontent

In popular memory, the winter of discontent marked a similar turning point. It was important for Whitleyism in two respects: it was the occasion for the first national strike by all the associations (on 2 April 1979) and it witnessed the introduction of the new strategy of selective action. However, it did not result – as has sometimes been suggested –in the 'politicisation' of the NSS, in the sense that the constitutional authority of Government was directly challenged. For example, the day of protest organised by other public sector unions on 22 January was ignored; and later, rather than showing solidarity, the NSS expressed anger at both the concessions granted by Government to other unions and the TUC's attempts to orchestrate action.[76] Moreover, the majority of NSS leaders remained wedded to the traditional policy of collaboration, declining to join either the pre-emptive strike organised by the CPSA and SCPS on 23 February or the subsequent selective action. They even, as has been seen, risked unity – and indeed destroyed the NSS – by a last minute attempt to avert their own one-day strike.

Nevertheless, both the one-day strikes and the selective action were deemed a success. An estimated 150,000 joined the CPSA/SCPS strike in February; and a further 288,000 (over half the non-industrial Civil Service) participated in April, including a number of senior managers in the wake of a controversial recommendation by the FDA's Executive Committee (albeit later validated by a delegate conference).[77] For its part, selective action was particularly effective in Scotland where *inter alia* the payment of benefits was disrupted, the Court system effectively closed and Scottish Office computers blacked (leading to some 50 officials being temporarily 'relieved from duty', which in turn sparked an additional one-day strike in Scotland on 21 March and walkouts throughout the rest of the United Kingdom). Elsewhere there was the total shutdown of several computer centres (impeding, for example, the collection of VAT and the payment of EEC subsidies), disruption in certain prisons (such as Walton gaol, Liverpool) and the halting of essential maintenance for RAF aircraft. It was the latter (which compromised NATO obligations as well as operations in Northern Ireland), as well as the threat to escalate 'action' (to disrupt the budget, Easter air travel and even social security payments), that finally convinced Government of the need to settle on NSS terms.[78] The 25 per cent award, as opposed to its 'final' offer of seven per cent prior to the April strike, was a clear victory for conflict over collaboration.

The significance of the winter of discontent, therefore, was that it exposed the atrophy of Whitleyism's traditional methods and validated the new strategy of selective action. Responsibility for atrophy was shared by the Official and Staff Sides. The former was the principal culprit. Increasingly dominated by the Treasury (and cash limits), the Government repeatedly broke both the spirit and the letter of the new national pay agreement (signed as late as November 1977). The Staff Side was not immediately provoked. Despite Callaghan's prevarication and provocation throughout 1977, for example, no other association had participated – as has been seen – in the SCPS's half-day strike.[79] Rather its General Secretary (Gillman) had been ostracised. Then, in 1979, when 'insulted' by both a preliminary offer of seven per cent (despite pay research, which the Official Side confirmed was still operative, indicating 25 per cent) and the Government's promise to other public sector unions of full comparability (despite their lack of any tradition of, let alone mechanism for, pay research), the majority of association leaders still sought to negotiate. Nevertheless the Staff Side was not itself wholly innocent. To prove their worth, traditional methods had to be – and be seen to be – effective; and yet negotiation achieved little and the week of peaceful protest (designed as an alternative to the SCPS strike) was equally ineffective. In July 1978 the NSS then declined, when urged by Gillman, to make contingency plans even for a peaceful protest.[80] In addition, it remained unhealthily insular. Not only was the mood of activists ignored but little was done to dispel suspicion in, and coordinate action with, the wider trade union movement. The Staff Side, in short, was too elite and aloof.

In contrast, selective action (which had been long-championed by activists and practised already in several other industries, including the Post Office) proved its effectiveness by both harnessing members' desire for action and seriously disrupting Government. It was also seen to achieve results. Before the strike in April, for example, Callaghan had been obdurate. 'While he did not want to fight an election with a major Civil Service dispute on', it was recorded, 'he did not think the Government should be trampled on by the Civil Service unions.'[81] Thereafter the escalation, and threatened escalation, of selective action forced him to relent; and a more generous settlement was conceded than was strictly necessary.

In the short term, therefore, the winter of discontent weakened Whitleyism by exposing the impotence of its traditional methods. The NSS was also broken. For the longer term, however, it was potentially offered a new lease of life – and direction – through the creation of the CCSU, which both put it more closely in touch with activists and provided a solid platform for coordinating future selective action. The staff associations of the 1960s had finally, as recognised by the CCSU constitution, become full trade unions. Did this, however, presage their politicisation and, as had long been warned, the supersession of an 'orderly' system of industrial relations by 'anarchy'?

8.4.3 1981: the 21-week strike

Although fears of 'anarchy' and 'politicisation' were to be proved groundless (at least on the part of the unions), the 21-week strike from 9 March to 31 July 1981 was in many ways a natural culmination of past developments. When, for example, the Conservative Government abandoned the national pay agreement in October 1980 (as had Labour effectively in 1978), the CCSU immediately started to coordinate a response (as Gillman had wished in 1978). This response was to commence with a week of mass protest (as in 1977) and conclude with national one-day strikes and a programme of selective action (as in 1979). Admittedly, the Government was less disingenuous than Labour, once it realised that pay research was incompatible with cash limits. It also lacked the opportunity, available to Labour in 1979, to liaise through the TUC. Nevertheless, as was seen in Chapter 7.4, its handling of the strike was equally confused; and the result was once again a settlement far more expensive than earlier ones that union leaders would have accepted. Moreover, on the ground, no clear distinction was established between managers and the managed (as sought in 1973). The depth of resentment amongst senior officials, resulting from the Government's perceived contempt for – and duplicity towards – the Service, was well reflected by the FDA ballot in support of strike action.[82] As in the past, however, a challenge to constitutional government from militant activists was contained by their national leaders.

The CCSU, as intimated earlier, had three overriding objectives in 1981. First, with inflation running at 17 per cent, it submitted a claim for a 15 per cent pay increase (with the objective of gaining nine per cent). It was initially offered six per cent and finally settled for 7.5 per cent. Second, and most importantly, it sought the restoration of an 'orderly' industrial relations system. The *principle* of pay comparability was inviolate. There simply was no alternative, were a sense of justice within the Service to be retained and, more pragmatically, both recruitment maintained and wastage halted. The *practice* of pay research, however, was contestable – particularly if the Government wished to use cash limits to enforce a trade-off between pay rises and redundancy, and to replace national with regional pay rates. The CCSU's final concern was how pay negotiations would be conducted in 1982 whilst the Megaw Committee (the 'independent' inquiry set up in June to devise an alternative pay system) was deliberating. Would any settlement have to be cash limited? Could it, if necessary, be referred to arbitration? Such questions might appear petty, but they were not. They represented, and were seen to represent, a real trial of strength between Government and the unions. Hence Mrs Thatcher's distinct lack of amusement when, having asserted that it would only be permitted 'over her dead body', arbitration was eventually conceded.

Each of these three issues, of course, masked a more fundamental question that had been evaded throughout the 1970s. Was the effective determinant of pay to be retrospective comparability (as enshrined in the Priestley Commission) or a predetermined judgement by Government of what was affordable (be that represented by incomes policy or cash limits)? The principle at stake was so fundamental that it sustained the strike over an unprecedented 21 weeks and eventually brought both parties to the brink of exhaustion. On the union side, such stamina was made possible by the creation of the CCSU which, in October 1980, had established a central Pay Campaign Coordination Committee, supported by some 40 local strike centres, with an initial budget of £2 million. Each constituent union was represented on the central and each local committee. In the short term, a week of peaceful protest was also organised, during which some 53,000 people attended 24 regional meetings. Then, when the Government repeated Labour's mistake in 1979 of offering a derisory initial offer whilst simultaneously making higher awards to other public sector workers, strike action was approved by ballot in each union. It was also endorsed by each General Secretary, including the traditionally hesitant McCall and Christopher. A one-day strike was duly held on 9 March, followed by another on 1 April and a half-day strike on 14 April. The first was particularly impressive with over 60 per cent of union members (or 275,000 people) participating.[83]

Of greater impact, however, was the programme of selective action which was also initiated in March. To minimise expenditure, it rarely involved more than 5000 staff at any one time and had three main targets: the Government's revenue (which came under the general control within the Coordinating Committee of Campbell Christie, Deputy General Secretary of the SCPS), defence (under Miss Platt of the IPCS) and airports (under Alastair Graham, Deputy General Secretary of the CPSA). By July, the attempt to disrupt air traffic – which had the potential to cause the greatest public pressure – had been compromised by a lack of co-operation from other unions (whose members did not qualify for strike pay). Disruption of military installations (including Polaris) was also crumbling because of *inter alia* lack of support by industrial civil servants and fears amongst non-industrials about redundancy following announced defence cuts.[84] In the third area of revenue collection, however, the unions held Government by the jugular. In July alone, the virtual closure of all computer centres deprived it of £1.6 billion; and the additional cost of servicing a cumulative loss since March of some £6 billion had mounted to £0.5 billion. The recovery of the 'lost' revenue, so it was estimated, would take at least another year and thereby incur further charges.[85] In short, the impact of selective action on revenue, and monetary targets, was severe and continuing. This is what forced Mrs Thatcher, at the request of the Chancellor, to override the ideological protests of the No. 10 Policy Unit and to seek a settlement.

By July 1981, therefore, the Government was exhausted. It had not been prepared for so long a battle and, on its own later admission, lacked any defined strategy.[86] Mrs Thatcher's own resolution had also been eroded by wider issues such as the Toxteth riots and her own plummeting popularity; and the Cabinet had become further divided by the 'deflationary' budget. In such circumstances, the escalating loss of revenue made seeking a settlement expedient. 'Victory' as even John Hoskyns (Mrs Thatcher's leading protagonist at the No. 10 Policy Unit) was prepared to concede later, had come at a 'considerable cost'.[87]

Why, given its stranglehold on Government revenue, was the CCSU prepared to respond positively to the offer of peace? The reasons are simultaneously more complex and simple. The CCSU was also unprepared for a long battle, being confident that a united display of militancy would bring swift returns.[88] Nor, arguably, would they have been wrong had not first Mrs Thatcher's resolution caused a peace formula (similar to the one finally accepted in July) to be rejected on 2 April and then Cabinet vetoed on 4 June a deal which initially had majority support (following a clarion call from the No. 10 Policy Unit of 'escalate to win'). Moreover, surprised by the Government's resilience, old jealousies resurfaced and unity started to crack. The Major Policy Committee (MPC), for example, became as dysfunctional as the previous Committee A, with some General Secretaries (such as McCall) unilaterally re-establishing contact with Ministers. Collectively, the MPC also grew jealous of the autonomy enjoyed by the Coordinating Committee. Likewise the National Executive Committees of individual associations resented the independence of local strike centres.[89] Traditional power structures, in other words, were being undermined. So too were union finances – and this is what provided, and has since been accepted as, the pretext for the strike's conclusion. As an early token of the CCSU's greater unity and professionalism, a financial controller (E. Hewlett, a former Deputy General Secretary of the IPCS) had been appointed to oversee a common fund, from which those on selective strike were to be paid.[90] On 14 July he reported that, with weekly outgoings of £555,000, there was insufficient money to support selective action for more than a further one and a half weeks. This conclusion appears unduly alarmist. It discounted the fact that, following an increased levy in June, income over the previous three weeks (at £1.9 million) had exceeded outgoings by some £300,000. It also discounted future income from dues which, according to Gillman, would have been sufficient to finance selective action for at least five more weeks. Nevertheless, the report was music to the ears of Ken Thomas who had announced to the preceding CCSU meeting that the CPSA's strike fund was exhausted and that, in future, its selective strikers would have to be subsidised by the other unions.[91]

Was Thomas' claim genuine? The CPSA, not for the first time, was in some disarray. Its National Executive was seriously split between moderates and militants; and, as enthusiasm for it waned in some quarters, so there was an increasing demand elsewhere for the extension of selective action – if necessary on an unofficial basis – to the local offices of the DHSS and Department of Employment. Thus it was not just the unity of the CCSU but also that of the CPSA that was at stake. Thomas's alternative strategy was to call an all-out strike. Such a show of strength, he maintained, would create the right 'negotiating circumstances' for the next decade.[92] His logic, however, was arguably as suspect as Hewlett's. All unions (bar the CPSA on a very low poll) had just voted by ballot to reject an all-out strike. By definition, there was no money to pay strikers and thus ensure solidarity. No strike could therefore last longer than two weeks, as he himself admitted. How would such a 'show of strength' impress so ideologically committed and resolute a Government? Thomas' real motivation would, therefore, seem to have been his desire to safeguard the unity of the CPSA, his own authority and the strategy of negotiation (to which he ultimately remained loyal even in 1979). There was also a hint of jealousy that it was selective action by the smaller IRSF that had the potential to 'defeat' the Government. Others, exhausted by the unexpected length of the strike, were happy to follow his lead.

If the start and course of the 1981 strike represented a culmination of past trends, then its ending marked the start – or at least a lull before the start – of a new era. Such was the objective of Government and, above all, of Hoskyns. In what might be termed the consummation of the sustained campaign against the Service since the mid-1960s, he sought to politicise the Service.[93] First, it was to be 'de-politicised' by the rejection of the 'cosy' world of Whitleyism, let alone more ambitious experiments in industrial democracy, and its replacement by a culture of 'accountable management'. Then it was to be 're-politicised' by having its pay once again made subject to Ministerial judgement and an exemplar in the battle against inflation. Moreover, the 'model' employer in future was to be the private not the public sector. Such a pre-Priestley vision was anathema to the unions and militant activists were to continue to use the improved 'facility' arrangements (sanctioned by Whitleyism) to sustain selective action, where necessary on an unofficial basis, in order to effect radical change in both national politics and on the shop floor. As for the union leaders, their confusion was epitomised by Thomas' remark on 25 June 1981 that 'we all agree that we've won the strike except that the government does not see it'.[94] Unacknowledged by them, the world both outside and inside Whitehall had moved on. Thus, although the strike in the short term may have had no clear victor and no overtly dramatic repercussions, it marked – like the abolition of the CSD which swiftly followed – an historic parting of the ways.

8.5 Conclusion

The apex of a belief in Whitleyism occurred immediately after its golden jubilee in 1969, under the secretary generalship of Leslie Williams and following Fulton, and its greatest achievements between the Pay Board's anomaly ruling (in 1973) and the appointment of the Armitage Committee (in 1976). Even during this period, however, the seeds of its destruction were being sown. A sustained political and press campaign was launched against the Service (which was to find a logical climax in Conservative Government policy during the 1981 strike). As throughout the rest of the Labour movement, there was a growth in grass-roots militancy (which was again to find its logical climax in the effective use of selective action in 1981). There was also an inherent jealousy between the various staff associations, or at least their General Secretaries, which was to bring it to the brink of destruction in 1979. Its perceived decline was indeed so precipitate that by the late 1970s the question was being widely asked whether, like those whom it represented, should it not be pensioned off at sixty? Certainly staff associations had largely evolved during the 1970s from 'civil service trade unions, able to play a number of clever tricks' to 'true trade unions in the industrial sense', with attitudes to match towards management and a readiness to prioritise private gain over public service.[95]

At its apex, did its rituals and rhetoric impede modernisation? In relation to management, its vested interests undoubtedly impeded the implementation of many post-Fulton reforms and its own reform programme, the *Wider Issues* review, was ineffectual. In relation to the economy, research-based pay awards – although by definition retrospective – also discouraged greater public 'realism' by psychologically fuelling wage inflation. Whitleyism was, however, merely a mechanism. If it 'failed', therefore, it was substantively the fault of others. When efficiency fell victim to fudged compromises, for example, this was more the fault of bad management either at the centre of Whitehall or in individual departments. Similarly, when manifesto pledges went unhonoured, this was more a political failure, with successive Ministers and Prime Ministers unable to resolve (or even sometimes to recognise) the incompatibility of pay research and cash limits. There was also typically as much political resistance to the obligations of 'minister-managers' as there was to reasoned negotiation (as opposed to displays of militancy). Finally, wage inflation was as much the fault of a private sector, not notably over-endowed with either entrepreneurial flair or strong management. In short, Whitleyism – like the Civil Service more generally – was a convenient scapegoat for the failings of others.

As a mechanism, Whitleyism's essential role was to coordinate the disparate view of officials of all grades and to identify practical solutions to practical problems. This was complemented by a willingness of its leadership, even under extreme pressure in 1979 and 1981, to accept constitutional propriety in its dealings with Government and to control militancy amongst its own members. Whitleyism was thus a potent defence against 'anarchy' and a potential force for efficient and effective government. As one initially sceptical CSD official remarked in 1970, it was all too easy

> to forget how fortunate the Government as an employer is in the extent to which once an agreement had been reached the Staff side can and will

make it stick. Given the size, geographical scatter and diversity of the Service, its record in this is no less than astonishing.

This was a sentiment which Jim Callaghan was only too ready to endorse. 'Its worth', he concurred, 'would only become clear if the system broke down and Whitleyism disappeared.'[96] The misfortune was that he was writing as a backbencher in 1953 and not as Prime Minister in the late 1970s.

9
MANAGEMENT CHALLENGES

9.1 Introduction

The pace and nature of administrative reform between 1966 and 1981, as has been seen, was determined by many external and internal forces. Principal amongst the former were the state of the economy; evolving views about the proper role of government; changes in management theory and practice; and escalating militancy within the workforce. Principal amongst the latter were the federal nature of the Service; a weakening of the centre by its division between the Treasury and the CSD; and battles at all levels between policy advisers, managers and the managed. With rising political hostility and an eroding power base, successive Heads of the Civil Service were increasingly impotent to deliver reform. This is not what had been envisaged by modernisers in the 1960s.

In addition to such broad influences, there were particular managerial challenges with which reform was intertwined. Principal among these were the provision of training and pensions; the dispersal of government offices from London; the adaptation of employment practices to new conceptions of gender and race; and the introduction of new technology. It is upon these that this chapter will concentrate. Each was later to assume greater importance but before 1981 they were more than mere harbingers of the future. They were important in their own right. What light does each shine on the attitudes to, and achievements of, reform?

9.2 Training

The continuing battle over the need for, and nature of, training epitomises both the strength and weakness of attempts to reform the Service. Following the Plowden Report, a range of centralised courses had been actively developed within Whitehall to complement the training traditionally provided by departments and external institutions. Consequently the 1960s came to represent for many, both at the time and since, a 'golden age'.[1] The Fulton Committee, however, was not amongst the impressed. It had more ambitious plans to use training as the means to integrate more fully both personnel management (by strengthening the link between recruitment and career management) and personnel (by opening a 'road to the top' for specialists and non-graduates). In addition it envisaged a Civil Service College, with a clear research remit, as the national 'focus for the discussion of . . . the most important problems facing the Civil Service', be they general issues of public administration or the particular needs of individual departments.[2]

Characteristically, Fulton's recommendations contained unresolved tensions on which much high-level time was thereafter spent failing to resolve. As a consequence it was not until the late 1970s, after the ambition of the new courses had been checked (by the 1974 Heaton-Williams Report), the organisation of the College simplified (following the 1975 Management Review) and the initial College Principal replaced (in 1976), that the kind of challenge thrown down by Rayner in 1979 could be answered. To prove the value of the new 'improved' system each department was to be required to pay the full economic cost for its officials' training[3]. In other words, training was a prime example of how Fulton impeded rather than advanced modernisation. Why did its recommendations fail and how well were the Service's training needs ultimately met?

The need for specialist training had first been exposed by the expansion of government prior to the First World War; but, to Parliament's disgust in the Second, only five departments (led by the Ministries of Labour and Health) had thereafter developed coherent induction programmes. The Assheton Committee on the Training of Civil Servants, as noted in Chapter 2.2.2, was duly appointed and reported in 1944 (Cmd 6525). Typical of its time, it proved a 'lost opportunity'. Subscribing to the view, prevalent in some quarters until the late 1960s, that it was a 'crime' to learn from 'books something one just *does*', it recommended continuing adherence to the learning process of 'sitting by Nellie'.[4] Nevertheless, Nellie's virtue was to be guaranteed by the appointment of chaperones within each Ministry in the shape of Department Training Officers (DTOs), answerable to a new Training and Education Division within the Treasury. There was also to be a short, centrally provided induction course on the 'structure of government' for all Administrative Class recruits. The establishment of a Civil Service College was rejected on the grounds that there were neither sufficient academic literature nor qualified staff. However, the contemporary desire (later reiterated by Fulton) for a 'greater understanding between civil servants and the outside world' was satisfied by the establishment in 1946 of an independent Administrative Staff College at Henley. It was designed to cater for those in mid-career within both the public and private sector and thereafter some 24 civil servants typically attended its 2–3 month courses each year. From the late 1950s, such bonding was supplemented more selectively and secretively at The Node.[5]

By the end of the 1950s, dissatisfaction re-surfaced both within and outside the Service about the lack of formal training. This was given an edge by the Plowden Committee's emphasis on better management and, within the Treasury, by the Economic Section's concern about the economic and statistical 'illiteracy' of generalist administrators.[6] Consequently, in 1963, the Centre of Administrative Studies (CAS) was established by the Treasury under a dynamic Assistant

Secretary, Desmond Keeling; and two years later four Training Liaison officers were appointed actively to encourage best practice. The establishment of CAS raised four fundamental questions which were to dog policy thereafter: what should central courses teach, to whom, by whom and where? Should, for example, courses concentrate on applied academic or management skills? Plowden and the Economic Section disagreed markedly on this point, as demonstrated by the rapidly changing nature of the original core course for administrative trainees. By contrast, there was unanimity within Whitehall that there should be no British *Ecole Nationale d'Administration* (ENA) – the ideal of many outside modernisers, based on France's four-year programme of applied and specialist studies combined with postings to both outlying regions and outside organisations. The question remained, however, whether the principal recipients of training should be an elite (as with ENA) or specialists and Executive Officers (as demanded explicitly by staff associations and implicitly by Plowden's call for better management 'down the line')? As for instructors, CAS employed under contract selected academics who could best apply their knowledge to practical problems. This, however, irked academia which – not wholly disinterestedly – wished to use its own less bespoke but ready-made facilities at either old centres of excellence (such as the London School of Economics and Nuffield College, Oxford) or the new business schools (in London and Manchester). Finally, there was the issue of a Civil Service College and its research role. This again aroused considerable animosity because many considered the Royal Institute of Public Administration had been set up in 1922 to discharge just such a role – and was still capable of doing so. All four questions, therefore, were contentious; and, somewhat surprisingly (or perhaps unsurprisingly), they were remitted in November 1965 to the Osmond Working Party on Management Training at the very time that the Fulton's terms of reference, with their stress on training, were being drafted. The Working Party came to act as an effective research committee for Fulton and greatly influenced its Report.[7]

Fulton duly endorsed Osmond's conclusion that there should be no British ENA but added to its proposal to expand centralised courses an ambitious range of additional objectives – without, typically, specifying how they might be prioritised. Confusion was deepened by the appointment of the distinguished demographer, Eugene Grebenik, as the first Principal of the new Civil Service College (CSC). Somewhat incongruously, he was a known supporter of a British ENA. Equally, he was known not to be a team player and to be uninterested in either management or the compromising of academic standards.[8] Thus the inspired improvisation behind CAS's success was placed in jeopardy.

In the event, the CSC provided only a small fraction of training, compared with departments and external institutions. Of this, post-entry training was also a small fraction.[9] Nevertheless, it was by the central courses for administration trainees that the quality of its training came conventionally to be judged. Initial judgements were not favourable. Students' enthusiasm for the majority of courses and their willingness to return (the earlier litmus tests used by CAS) were both noticeable by their absence. The 1974 Heaton-Williams Report explained why. It was, it comprehensively concluded, the result of a 'lack of clarity of the College's objectives, the poor quality of much of its teaching, the over-academic nature of some of its courses, their lack of coherence, the confused lines of responsibility, and the lack of involvement in the life and work of the Civil Service'.[10] One despairing course director had even compared himself to

> the driver of a train of camels across a poorly-charted desert. The beasts have wills of their own, the passengers – some of whom have not wanted to make the journey – see mirages in the form of oases to left and right. The leader . . . has just to keep on smiling, and crying 'Onward'.

As a result of such shortcomings, the College's future remained under constant threat, with as late as 1979 an incoming Principal (Brian Gilmore) being instructed to either 'kill it – or cure it'.[11] Cure it he did, by building on the work of another CSD official (Barbara Sloman, Grebenik's replacement as Principal in 1976) to modify courses and better adapt them to departmental needs. Whereas in the mid-1970s the CSC had seemed condemned to that 'crowded creek where the hulks of failed Whitehall reforms decay on their moorings', therefore, by the early 1980s it had started once again (like CAS) to rule the waves. The timing was opportune. It could duly satisfy the renewed demand for training, driven by Mrs Thatcher's new brand of modernisation.

How – and how well – were the four fundamental issues identified by CAS addressed between 1970 and 1981? Each was subject to three common assumptions. The first was that training should be 'practical'. For example, the majority of post-entry training – unlike in France – should be conducted either within departments or, if provided centrally, mainly in the third year. By then trainees would have been tested against real-world administrative experience and, equally, have the real-world experience against which to test what they were being taught. However, did this not –some critics queried – amount to indoctrination rather than training? Where was there scope to challenge departmental 'common sense' or the opportunity, as demanded by the TUC, to widen social horizons? If Government was to become more interventionist, should not officials be encouraged to shed the assumptions of their 'charmed circle' and gain a better understanding of the world outside Whitehall?[12] A second common assumption was, again unlike in France, training should not be reserved for the elite. This marked a distinct change from the Treasury's view in the 1960s and was a token of the impact of Fulton, or at least the NSS, on policy.[13] Finally, there was the assumption that the budgets and manpower for training should be restricted. This not only compromised the CSC's own development but also denied departments a 'training margin' – let alone the 'training entitlement' for officials, demanded by the NSS. This made departmental Establishment Officers even less willing to release staff.[14]

Within such assumptions, the first two issues (what was taught and to whom) were closely related and the answer somewhat eclectic. It was as though, as Heaton-Williams observed, 'the same institution were expected to combine the roles of All Souls and an adult education centre, with some elements of technical education and teacher training thrown in'.[15] On its 'All Souls' side, the CSC's major task (typically consuming one-quarter of its places and considerably more of its nervous energy) was the post-entry training of potential 'high fliers'. It was designed to provide recruits in their first year and, more critically, in their third year with an understanding of the political, administrative, social and international context in which they were to work as well as specific skills in relation to personnel and resource management. Such conflicting objectives hampered both the integration of the syllabus and the quality of teaching. Insufficient time, it was claimed, was provided for the 'thorough grounding' in the 'administrative specialisms' for which Fulton had called. More fundamentally, 'management training' continued to be considered somewhat vapid. 'I find it a trifle ironic', C.H. Sisson had mused in the 1960s

> that the subject of management training which . . . is designed to instil above all else a sense of cost and the economic consequences of things, should itself have been subjected to so little rigorous enquiry of a kind which would give one a clear idea of the value of the end product.[16]

Grebenik's riposte was that the CSC was providing not job-training (which was a departmental responsibility) but career-training, the value of which would become apparent only in the longer term. In the meantime it should be accepted as a matter of faith. This did not reassure hard-pressed Establishment Officers, who were not noted for being men of faith.

It was, however, the eclecticism not of the teaching but of the taught that most concerned Grebenik himself. Under CAS, post-entry training had been confined to an annual intake of some 75 highly intelligent, and mainly Oxbridge, graduates. The training had consequently, in the restrained language of one participant, been 'shit hot' because 'top-flight' academics had been attracted to teaching 'top-flight' students. After Fulton, however, egalitarianism reigned. 'Post-entry' training had consequently to be provided for some 300 Administration Trainees, one-third of whom were existing Executive Officers with rather less glittering degrees. A fall in the academic standards of those taught was matched by a parallel fall in those by whom they were taught. 'A common course', lamented Grebenik, had to be 'provided for a group with different educational backgrounds, and very different career prospects, who were likely to be employed in very different kinds of work'.[17] Where was the common denominator?

The All Souls' role was not limited to post-entry training. After 1973, there was also the highly successful Senior Professional Administrative Training Scheme (SPATS) provided in advance of 'experience postings', which were designed to determine whether specialists wished to transfer to 'administration'.[18] There were also other courses provided for Principals (either as late entrants or for those needing 'refreshment') and for both Assistant and Under Secretaries ('senior management courses'). What was noticeably lacking from all such courses, however, was an underpinning of original research. For both Fulton and Grebenik, such research was essential and, in retrospect, Norman Hunt bitterly resented the loss of 'this critical spur for better government'. Undeniably there was a need, if not of pure research, then the application of management theory to specific policies and to differentiate between private and the public sector management (thereby modifying the thoughtless domination of the former). Such a need, however, was not met. Exhausted by the demands of repetitive teaching and, unlike other academics, denied both tenure and (under the Official Secrets Act) the freedom to publish, CSC staff in the main lacked the opportunity and incentive – as well as, arguably, the ability – to rise to such a challenge. Training, to Keeling's delight but Gilmore's dismay, was clearly differentiated from education.[19]

Much of this repetitive teaching was provided, moreover, for junior staff – and thus at the academic level of an 'adult education centre'. There were some notable successes here, such as the Specialist Training Wing (inherited from the Treasury and working in conjunction with City University to provide computer skills). However, other courses (such as the four-week Introduction to Management unit, taught to Executive Officers in an attempt to realise Fulton's ideal of an 'open road to the top') were markedly less successful. Establishment Officers came to resent the regular loss of staff to such courses, particularly when their only tangible result appeared to be over-inflated expectations, disillusion and a consequent lowering of morale. Would not, they questioned, such training be better provided by departments (if necessary within a centrally-agreed framework) or external institutions? Such doubts reflected a long-standing conviction that – despite NSS pressure – there was a 'floor' below which central training should not go.[20]

The political battle over training, nevertheless, continued. The English Committee in 1977, for example, sought to sustain Fulton's ideal of equality by recommending the cancellation of the 300-strong Administration Trainee (AT) programme. All graduates, it argued, should henceforth be recruited as Executive Officers and promotion be dependent solely on performance in post. The CSD refused to accept this English patent on the grounds that it would discourage 'high-fliers'. Accordingly, it devised an alternative scheme that would enable first-class graduates to be recruited directly to an HEO (Development) post (in which they would receive a rigorous two-year probation) whilst the most able Executive Officers would be placed on an equally rigorous two-year development programme within their departments before proceeding to the Civil Service Selection Board (which would be bound to pass a significant number).[21] In this way an optimum blend could be attained of academic quality (as favoured by senior officials) and proven administrative ability (as favoured by Fulton). In addition, it would re-establish the principle that central training should be concerned solely with 'developmental' and not routine skills.

The second set of questions (by whom and where courses should be taught) was similarly interrelated. In part this was because, in its early years, the CSC was faced by a number of rivals. It had to contend with not just training within departments but also a range of potential outside providers such as the new business schools, new universities (such as Sussex, of which Fulton was Vice-Chancellor) and technical colleges.[22] What ultimately secured the CSC's future was Whitehall's determination to maintain control. However, as Grebenik soon discovered, this was a double-edged sword. CAS had been run by officials who ultimately controlled the syllabus and contracted out the teaching to visiting lecturers, albeit to the mutual satisfaction of both. Grebenik sought to strengthen the CSC's independence through an academic structure of four specialist directors of studies working within faculties. However, control over the budget remained critically with the CSD; over the timing of courses with a director of programmes (who was a civil servant); and over numbers, and the ultimate impact of training on individual careers, with departmental Establishment Officers. The resulting tensions and organisational confusion were largely resolved by the 1975 Priestley Management Review, after which the Principal was always to be a Civil Servant, albeit at a lower rank than Grebenik (Under Secretary as opposed to Deputy Secretary). Some tension nevertheless lingered, fuelled by Whitehall's latent distrust for academia in general and social science in particular (which CAS had circumvented by concentrating on the 'harder' disciplines of economics and statistics).[23]

Officialdom, therefore, largely triumphed over academia, but where precisely was the CSC to be located? This was no idle question because the choice would both reflect and reinforce prevailing assumptions about the role of training. In 1965 Keeling had ridiculed the concept of the College as a 'stately home in the countryside at which students and peacocks stroll on closely mown lawns, bringing ... "status" on the Civil Service'.[24] Yet, just such a location was chosen for the CSC's principal site. Harold Wilson, who had made its establishment one of his three public commitments to Fulton (see Chapter 5.2), favoured the Royal Naval College at Greenwich. The MOD, however, refused to vacate it. Armstrong was thus able to attain his preferred choice of Sunningdale, a classic Georgian house and estate in Berkshire, which the Civil Defence College was conveniently due to evacuate. The choice, as even the bitterest critic admitted, did not reflect a desire for elitism. Indeed Armstrong's rather ethereal wish was that 'a week at Sunningdale could be the crown of a messenger's career'.[25] To the pleasure of Permanent Secretaries, however, it had the pleasing aura of Oxbridge and of gentility (seemingly an indispensable quality for any attempt to modernise Britain). Moreover, its splendid isolation also encouraged a certain insularity, which had long been the fear of traditional opponents of a 'staff' college.

What the history of training thus reveals about administrative reform is the ability of individual officials to deliver high-quality training between 1963 and 1970 (through CAS) and after 1976 (though the CSC). Equally impressive was the demand for such training both before 1970 (if not from generalists) and after 1979 (increasingly from generalists). Simultaneously, however, there were serious weaknesses – for which the Civil Service alone was not responsible. Fulton's proposals, for example, were typically grandiose and confused, reflecting the plausible speciousness of much of the modernisation movement. Academia was typically self-interested; and neither the social sciences in general nor management studies in particular were sufficiently robust to sustain a rigorous training programme. This was not a problem unique to Britain. The history of training does nevertheless confirm, particularly between 1970 and 1976, a serious managerial weakness at the most senior level of the Service. This was epitomised by Grebenik's appointment. For whatever reason, in the words of one official insider, he was given 'a false bill of sale' which was inexcusable in so critical an appointment.[26] Equally damning was the failure to stand up to departments and the NSS.

Grebenik himself had had a clear vision for the CSC. It was to be an essentially elitist organisation giving all 'high flyers' a rigorous training in their first six months before providing an assessment of their relative ability and aptitude. Like ENA, it would thereby play a significant role in their placement and later promotion. The Head of the Civil Service who appointed Grebenik, had earlier had a similar vision.[27] Every potential 'high flyer', William Armstrong had argued in 1966, should be obliged to take a year-long course in their third year, on which their subsequent career would depend. Apart from instruction in standard subjects such as economics and statistics, there should also be a choice of more specialised subjects. In addition, there was a need for applied research because much academic literature often 'bore little relation to reality'. Such a vision, however, was not driven through once the CSC had been established. Shortage of resources and the Service's federal nature provide some political and administrative explanation for this failure; but the lack of personal leadership at the top was pronounced.

9.3 Dispersal

Even more than training, the dispersal of Civil Service posts from central London represents in microcosm the hopes and frustrations of administrative reform. Building on existing internal initiatives, and untroubled by Fulton, a policy review was announced by the Conservatives in October 1970.[28] Its coordinator was Sir Henry Hardman (a former permanent secretary at the MOD) and his subsequent report, published in June 1973, recommended – from a potential total of 86,000 – the dispersal over ten years of 31,000 jobs in one of three ways, depending on whether priority was to be accorded to operational efficiency, the optimum distribution of national economic resources (the 'regional policy' option) or a balance between the two.

As with all such initiatives during 'modernisation's moment', the review was dogged by continual changes to the machinery of Government and capped manpower. Its implementation was equally ill-fated. Its success, for example, initially depended on support from the NSS and the drive of Jellicoe (as the responsible Minister). In 1973, however, the former became embroiled in its first national strike and, in the very month of the Report's publication, Jellicoe was obliged to resign. Despite this, all vested interests were squared, only for the Conservatives then to lose office in February 1974 and to be replaced by a Labour Government openly committed to a more 'regional' solution. Finally, the major building programme (to facilitate the moves) coincided with the 1976 expenditure cuts whilst the bulk of the moves (always planned for the late 1970s) coincided with the election of Mrs Thatcher. Since her days as Secretary of State for Education, she had opposed dispersal on principle. Now, despite the opportunity it offered to substitute regional for national pay bargaining, its short-term cost and logic were seen respectively to offend monetary targets and the commitment to reduce the size of Government. Consequently the Hardman programme was ended in July 1979, with only 10,000 moves having been completed or agreed.[29]

Why, apart from such contingencies, did so small a mouse emerge from such a mountain of high-level political and administrative effort? Was the logic of the original programme flawed or, given the short-term costs and the number of vested interests involved, had it been politically naive to expect that an agreed programme – however objective – could be sustained over ten years? Alternatively, as was assumed at the time, were London-based officials foremost amongst those vested interests opposing change? Was modernisation, in other words, once again stifled by bureaucratic conspiracy?

The Hardman review was exemplary, delivering on time a clearly defined set of objective recommendations on which Ministers – in so contentious an area – could base necessarily political judgements. Dispersal was contentious because, following the implementation of the 1963 Fleming Report, most self-contained bodies of executive work had already been removed from London. Consequently the review had to focus on more specialised 'policy work' which required regular 'face-to-face' contact with other officials, Ministers or the public. This required acceptance of some loss of operational efficiency and the inability of some local labour markets immediately to satisfy demand. In consequence, the 'human needs' of those to be dispersed had to be examined. Moreover, given the political objective of securing a better geographical balance of service sector jobs to offset industrial decline, what were the most appropriate 'receiving areas'?

To reconcile such conflicting objectives, the review employed the most advanced 'scientific' techniques. The findings of an Operation Research project, initiated by William Armstrong in 1968, were used to establish patterns of communications within and outside departments in order to identify those blocks of work that could be dispersed at least cost to operational efficiency. A computer model was then developed to determine the optimum mix of 'receiving' areas. Simultaneously, a specialist unit at University College, London was employed to identify future developments in communication (such as video links); and the Tavistock Institute of Human Relations contracted to consider the needs of those dispersed. This research placed the CSD in the van of international practice. Its integrity was also defended at the highest level by Jellicoe and William Armstrong whilst, on the ground, the review was organised with exceptional efficiency and sympathy by Rayner's future chief of staff, Clive Priestley.[30] Thus, it was hoped, the review could point a way through the thicket of conflicting political goals to attain the original *administrative* priorities: significant economic savings (through, for example, a reduction in the cost of London rents) and some decrease in existing operational inefficiency (through, for example, an improved quality of recruits and a reduction in the increasing fragmentation of headquarters work in London).

Scientific though its research may have been, the review nevertheless produced two surprising recommendations which made it thereafter vulnerable to attack. First it downplayed the 'multiplier effect' that dispersal might have on local economies. In part this was because local unemployment was predicted to rise rather than fall (as a result of the 'specialist' nature of dispersed jobs and the calculation that a half of spouses would seek waged work); but mainly it was because the numbers involved were adjudged too small to have much impact on what Armstrong termed areas of 'organic employment decay'.[31] Such calculations were seen as unduly pessimistic. Each 'receiving area', for example, was likely to benefit from an immediate increase in purchasing power and, in the longer term, 'psychologically' from a stemming of the exodus of well-qualified school-leavers. The second hostage to fortune was the recommendation that, for the sake of operational efficiency, one-third of the posts should be dispersed within the South East of England – with, by contrast, Scotland receiving little more than 1000. Such a recommendation was impractical. Preference for the South East was distorted, for example, by the allocation of some 11,000 MOD posts to Milton Keynes which, it was quickly conceded, would seriously unbalance the new town. It was also impolitic. As the Labour Party spokesman argued during a major Parliamentary debate in October 1973, it would be 'an insult to our intelligence' to waste so historic an opportunity to redress a national imbalance of white-collar jobs.[32] Ominously the spokesman was Ted Short who, as Lord President of the Council, was soon to assume Ministerial responsibility for the CSD and thus for dispersal policy.

By October 1973, the optimum time for managerial action had passed. Ministers had agreed the dispersal of some 28,000 posts between the receipt by No. 10 of the Report in December 1972 and its publication in June 1973; and discussions had even started over the linking of dispersal with another core 'modernisation' proposal, executive agencies (which similarly required the identification of discrete blocks of work that might be politically, and geographically, separated from close ministerial control).[33] Wary of earlier damage wrought by over-technocratic decisions, however, the advisability of wider considerations was agreed; and, as the Parliamentary debate demonstrated, this opened the floodgates to the special pleading which Hardman's careful research had been designed to prevent. Such lobbying had commenced as early as October 1971 but had been largely resisted. By January 1974, however, a total of 60 formal representations had been made and fourteen deputations received from interested local authorities. In addition, some accommodation had to be reached with the staff associations. Whilst Leslie Williams remained Secretary General of the NSS, a delicate balancing act could be maintained; but following his retirement and the election of a Labour Government committed to 'go one better than Hardman', it grew increasingly difficult.[34]

Labour sought to 'go one better' in two ways – by increasing the number of posts to be dispersed and widening their geographical spread. The first was quickly abandoned but the second – together with the Hardman target of 31,000 dispersals – was successively, and with some courage, re-affirmed by the full Cabinet (and immediately in Parliament) on 26 June 1974, by a key Ministerial Committee in February 1976 and by Callaghan (to a NSS deputation)) in the Summer of 1976.[35] Such re-affirmation, however, masked serious reservations, typified by an extraordinarily acrimonious *ad hoc* Cabinet Committee [MISC 27] in June 1974. In defiance of recent election promises, Ministers offered not the promised increase in posts for dispersal but rather a virtual halving to 16,500. Moreover, two-thirds of these were earmarked for Cardiff and none at all for the targeted triumvirate of Clydeside, Merseyside and Teesside.[36] Harold Wilson was moved to circulate an equally extraordinary handwritten minute. 'Though I am not an emotional man', it started, 'tears almost welled up in my eyes when I read the minutes ... proving the impossibility of dispersal'. His tears, he admitted, were then checked by a 'measure of impatience'. From his personal recollection of the War, when staff had to be evacuated from London and communication systems were more primitive, had not both the CSO and MOD been able to maintain high levels of efficiency?

By such emotive means, it proved possible to maintain Labour's election pledges until the reality of dispersal started seriously to bite in 1977. Then the retreat was sounded, starting with the modification of MOD moves to Glasgow and concluding with the Conservatives' formal abandonment of Hardman in July 1979.[37] All pretence at the scientific evaluation of operational efficiency and the redistribution of national economic resources had by then been long abandoned. What took precedence were the short-term costs to the Exchequer (regardless of potential long-term savings) and political advantage (in relation to which, decreasing nationalism and increasing militancy combined to discourage dispersal to Scotland).[38]

Did such naked politics, however, merely disguise a bureaucratic conspiracy to preserve senior policy-making jobs in London? In 1970, after all, Leslie Williams had welcomed the wide-ranging nature of the Hardman review on the grounds that in the past 'the Administrative Class had been very good at suffering the misfortunes of the Clerical and Executive Classes – as an intellectual exercise'.[39] Moreover, Trend and Allen appeared determined to uphold this tradition by resisting any examination of communication structures within the Cabinet Office or Treasury. As Allen reminded William Armstrong, for example, in August 1971: 'the Treasury is not prone to avoiding work. But I do like to think that the work has some purpose'. At a less rarefied level, the NSS similarly mounted a campaign against an exodus from London, largely on the basis of 'human cost' (such as lost kinship networks, spouse's employment and children's schooling).[40] This was somewhat incongruous given that the majority of its members already worked outside London and that Hardman was committed to enhancing promotion prospects by concentrating work in a few 'receiving areas'. Moreover there was plentiful evidence that, after the initial shock of relocation, staff tended overwhelmingly to appreciate improvements to both their quality of life and working conditions.

Such resistance, however, was far from confined to officials. For example, accountable management – as already noted – provided an ideal context for dispersal; but, once they had assumed a measure of responsibility for the Department of Employment's hived-off agencies, both the CBI and TUC became its implacable opponent. The TUC vehemently protested against the relocation of the Manpower Services Commission to Liverpool and pressurised Michael Foot, as Employment Secretary and guardian of the Social Contract, into a compromise (Sheffield). Likewise the Health and Safety Commission/Executive fought a heroic rearguard action against consignment to the North West of England, before being undone by Mrs Thatcher's seemingly innocent enquiry in 1979: 'surely the TUC won't want to oppose jobs going to Bootle?'[41] Private industry and local authorities were no better. Despite the availability of generous relocation grants, the former was as determined to ignore the Government's lead on dispersal as it was on wage control. Why then, responded the NSS, should officials be singled out to be 'political pawns to meet a national problem'?[42] Equally local authorities, when making their respective pitches, paid scant attention to either operational efficiency (which might favour the South East of England) or the relative advantages of rival bids. Nevertheless, as MISC 27 vividly demonstrated the greatest opponents of dispersal were undoubtedly Ministers. This was not because they had been 'captured' by their officials but for personal and political reasons, such as prestige and their ability to respond speedily to Parliament and the public. Mrs Thatcher herself, as has been seen, had been a leading exponent of such special pleading in 1973.

Dispersal therefore failed; and its failure epitomises the etiolation of modernisation. Initially, scientific research and operational efficiency had been accorded explicit priority over special pleading and regional policy. Yet special pleading, particularly from local authorities and constituency MPs, grew quickly to a crescendo. Priority was then reassigned to regional policy in 1973 and unambiguously to the assisted areas in 1974.[43] Battles over the allocation of 30 or 40 posts became commonplace in Cabinet and Cabinet Committees. The Hardman review team also displayed, as Fulton would have wished, exemplary professionalism. It employed, for example, the latest research and research methods to determine a scientific basis on which necessarily political decisions could be taken. It was also an early exponent of the 'Rayner' techniques of using, in deference to federalism, management teams within departments to draft their own detailed proposals and of mounting audiovisual presentations to maintain Ministers' interest.

Rather than winning praise, however, such expertise attracted obloquy. In his Parliamentary tirade against Hardman's failings in October 1973, for example, Short particularly castigated officials. 'The overwhelming impression left by reading the report', he concluded, 'is that the Civil Service has been the instigator, the witness and the advocate ... The report states the case of the Civil Service.'[44] Arguably nothing could have been further from the truth, as he himself no doubt realised on assuming power in the following March. In any case his error was quickly exposed by the level of debate in MISC 27 and then, more seriously, compounded by his special adviser's attempt to politicise the Service by involving it in a cover-up.[45] In other words, it was not a lack of administrative expertise that caused dispersal – and by inference modernisation – to fail. Rather it was a lack of resolute political leadership. This was initially missing even after 1979, when a blind eye was turned to the opportunities offered by dispersal to attain two key goals of the later, iconic *Next Steps* initiative – executive agencies and regional labour markets.

9.4 Pensions

The element of administrative reform which pension policy best illustrates is the vagary of political support. In the early 1970s there had been widespread consensus that both the value and coverage of public sector pensions were inadequate. Hence the uncontentious passage of both the 1971 Pensions (Increase) Act (which provided for automatic uprating in line with inflation) and the 1972 Superannuation Act (which paved the way for improved benefits under the new Principal Civil Service Pension Scheme). Almost immediately, however, the mood changed. Inflation-proofed pensions became a symbol of administrative 'privilege' and thus a target for politicians and the press alike. Their increasing viciousness was typified by the following contribution of the *Sun* to informed debate prior to the 1981 strike: 'those pensioners living the life of Riley, the former civil servants cannot expect to be loved by those of us who are selling bootlaces on the street corner. Or perhaps they expect us to do little jobs for them like weeding their gardens and licking their boots'.[46] This outburst succeeded some intemperate remarks by Mrs Thatcher and preceded her Government's studied disregard for the Scott inquiry into the Value of Public Pensions (which it had itself commissioned but which had then concluded 'unhelpfully' that, by international standards, it was the private – not public – sector that was out of line). This, in turn, raised the issue of the Government's role as a 'model' employer. Did such a role now require Government to resist or lead the 'race to the bottom', the widely expected response of the market to recession? Pension provision, in short, was caught between two fundamentally different concepts of reform.

The early 1970s were exceptional for not just consensus but also, as with dispersal, the administrative expertise of the CSD. Before the Pensions (Increase) Act, for example, Jellicoe had admitted the situation to be one of 'great confusion with . . . many glaring anomalies'.[47] Confusion arose because of the *ad hoc* way in which Government, in the absence of any automatic mechanism, had to be regularly 'bullied or cajoled' into correcting the erosion of the real value of pensions by inflation. Moreover there was no clear principle for uprating, only a working convention since 1959 that the real value of pensions should decrease during the first twelve years of retirement in order to fund increases for those who, having retired before 1948 or 1958, had either no or a reduced entitlement to the national insurance pension. This convention was generating increased resentment as well as an increased number of anomalies. The remedy appeared simple: the introduction of a biennial review, of which Parliament could take note but need not debate. Its introduction, however, was far from simple and required considerable technical and diplomatic skills. All conventions governing Civil Service and other public service pensions, for example, had to be standardised. This required delicate interdepartmental negotiation. The principles on which to establish uprating and a 'base-line' for each existing group of pensioners (on which future increases might be equitably based) had also to be agreed. As for uprating, officials concluded, the principle should be inflation-proofing (the maintenance of a pension's real value at the time of retirement) and not 'parity' (its increase in line with the pension of someone currently retiring from an equivalent post). As for the establishment of an equitable 'base-line', the only viable solution was a one-off package costing between £25–£30 million (against a total pensions bill of £108 million). This had to be squared with the Treasury.

The 1972 Superannuation Act posed similar technical and diplomatic challenges. The object, once again, was the seemingly simple one of removing pensions from direct Parliamentary control so that, like all other conditions of employment, they might be varied administratively. However, a myriad of statutory controls over other public sector pensions had to be repealed and a degree of standardisation attained. There was also a need to negotiate with the NSS a new pensions package within a strict time-table (set by the passage of the Act), Fulton's demands (such as increased transferability of pensions between the public and private sectors) and a budget agreed with the Treasury. All, to the CSD's credit, was achieved on time and within budget; and the last vestiges of 'Victorian ancestry' were thus swept away and benefits brought into line with rapidly improving private sector practice.[48] Leslie Williams discerned in this yet another 'example of 'Whitleyism at its best', whilst William Armstrong was equally effusive in his praise. The 1972 Act, he concluded somewhat ironically in the light of later developments, was 'a very imaginative and constructive contribution towards the general shaping of the Post-Fulton Civil Service, which will be of great benefit in the future'.[49]

Despite the general consensus, a few adverse comments were made in the press.[50] Two criticisms were standard: that officials had used their influence, in the continental European tradition, to feather their own nest; and that taxpayers were being forced to fund benefits which few themselves could enjoy. The first criticism, at least, was largely unfounded. There had been considerable pressure from special interest groups, such as the Public Service Pensioners Alliance, for a more generous settlement. Citing European practice and the 'dynamism' built into Labour's new superannuation plans, they demanded 'parity' rather than mere inflation-proofing. Such demands, however, were rejected out of hand by the CSD, with the senior responsible official arguing (in contrast to the later Scott Report) that:

> so long as the cost of pensions increase is borne by British taxpayers and ratepayers and what we do compares well with good private sector practice, I doubt whether the Government need to be seriously embarrassed by criticisms that some European public servants do rather better.[51]

In other words, the form of inflation-proofing adopted was the cheapest available. Likewise, the demand for improved benefits from the NSS (which had been stung by rank-and-file criticism of the previous year's deal on premature retirement) was rebuffed – albeit with the collusion of the NSS itself.

Admittedly there is some evidence that, at the margin, private norms were knowingly exceeded and contributions for some benefits underestimated.[52] Nevertheless, were there any policy failure at this time, the most guilty men (and women) were indubitably the very ones who were later to lead the attack on pension 'privileges': the politicians. They were culpable on two principal grounds. First, Ministers of both Parties had acceded since Plowden to a planning system which was 'resource' rather than 'cash' based. Hence, the cost of pension increases could logically be presented as minimal: rising in line with prices, they represented the same percentage of GDP and so consumed no 'real' resources.[53] Second, during the passage of both Acts, there was as little opposition from the backbenches as there was ministerial reservation. In 1970, for example, the Conservative Government replaced without obloquy several manifesto commitments with clauses taken from Labour's draft Pensions (Increase) Bill. In opposition 'we went into all this with the various interested parties with some care', lamented the Financial Secretary to the Treasury (Patrick Jenkin), 'How did we get it all wrong?'[54] Then, during the passage of the Superannuation Act, Party conflict was minimised by Labour's spokesman (Douglas Houghton) being briefed, at his request, by the CSD. During the necessary modernisation of pensions policy in the early 1970s, in other words, CSD officials developed (as Fulton had wished) an unrivalled technical expertise and used it to contain change within rapidly changing market norms. Even a Minister as committed to 'rolling back the state' as David Howell was thereby convinced that Government was doing no more than setting 'a good example as an employer'.

Such perceptions changed rapidly with the escalation of inflation after 1974. With negative real returns on investment, many funded private occupational pensions schemes no longer felt able to guarantee inflation-proofing. The public sector consequently became exceptional in its 'insulation' from market forces – as well as a major cause of the market's problems through its 'crowding out' of private investment.[55] Accordingly, when an inflation-matching rise of 26 per cent in public pensions was announced for December 1975, it was widely condemned; and anger boiled over when it became evident that it would be applicable to all, whereas the new voluntary incomes policy limited pay increases to £6 a week and denied any at all to those on incomes above £8500. Why, it was demanded, should William Armstrong be rewarded for 'failure' of the previous Government's anti-inflation policy by a peerage, a salary of £30,000 as chairman of the Midland Bank and also by a £2000 increase to his public pension – taking it above £10,000?

Armstrong's successor, Douglas Allen, mounted a characteristically robust defence.[56] The British Government, he agued, was doing no more than most Western Governments and, indeed, most leading British employers (including Marks and Spencer and ICI, which had recently increased their pensions in line with inflation). In any case, inflation-proofing was a statutory right and its abandonment would require primary legislation (somewhat embarrassingly, given the recent inflation-proofing of national insurance pensions in the 1975 Social Security Act).[57] More particularly, Allen continued, neither was Armstrong a typical Civil

Servant nor were Civil Servants typical of those who would suffer from 'deprivileging'. The average Civil Service pensioner received only £700 a year; and, in aggregate, they were outnumbered sixfold by other public sector pensioners (such as those retired from teaching or the Armed Forces). Why then was the vitriol focused exclusively on the Civil Service and, in particular, on its most senior officials? Finally, Allen concluded, pensioners were amongst those most vulnerable groups in society whose real income had consistently fallen in relation to wage-earners. Would it not have been unconscionable 'to have penalised them as soon as the boot for once was on the other foot'? In any case there was already a means of resolving 'overprovision', particularly in respect of larger pensions, in a 'fair and even-handed way'. This was the redistributive tax system which, unremarked by the press, already reduced Armstrong's public pension from over £10,000 to under £2000.

Rational though his case was, Allen recognised that the economic crisis of the mid-1970s was no time for rationality. Certainly it did not constrain former members of the Heath Government, which had introduced inflation-proofing, from helping to sustain the press attack by spreading disinformation.[58] Accordingly contingency plans were prepared to suspend the Pensions (Increase) Act, together with the 1975 Social Security Act, for three years. Even on the eve of the IMF's visit, however, Labour Ministers still declined to bite the bullet because of the numbers involved, their spread (including MPs and Ministers themselves) and – despite the rhetoric – the relative paucity of the savings.[59]

The point and intensity of attack was changed by the incoming Thatcher Government after 1979 although, as late as 1981, it was no more prepared to bite the bullet. Treasury Ministers and officials, in defiance of election pledges, persistently sought a 'cut-off' point for inflation-proofing in any one year (at around seven per cent); but their most favoured means of 'deprivileging' the Service (and thereby cutting public expenditure) was to raise pension premiums to their 'full market' level.[60] The Treasury's intended weapon to effect such changes was the Scott inquiry into the Value of Public Pensions, appointed in May 1980 and reporting hurriedly in February 1981 in a vain attempt to avert the 21-week strike. Its essential purpose was evident from the incongruous inclusion in its terms of reference that it should assess officials' relative job security (as a possible bargaining tool for restricting pay rises). This particular task was evaded.[61] So too was consideration of another of the Chancellor's favoured stratagems: the charging of an additional premium for the 'psychological security' which inflation-proofing gave public sector workers. This, Scott argued, required – even more than most actuarial calculations – the quantification of the unquantifiable.

Accordingly the Scott Report, as noted earlier, deeply disappointed its sponsors. It 'erred' in four particular ways. First, like Allen in 1975–6, it highlighted the dangers of making long-term changes in a 'highly-charged atmosphere' and the illogicality of so doing when, on the assumption that monetarism would succeed, the problem was short-term.[62] Second, having stressed the 'highly desirable social objective' of protecting living standards in old age, it described how this was better achieved in continental Europe and, within the UK, by the public as opposed to the private sector. This was not what Howe wished to hear. Third, it exposed the principal myth which Howe himself had done much to encourage since 1974 and little to discourage since 1979: that Civil Servants paid next to nothing for their pensions. 'The effective contribution by civil servants', the Report established, was just under eight per cent of pensionable pay, which was almost 'twice the average direct contribution by employees' in the private sector. Finally, to add insult to injury, the Report then publicly reiterated what Mrs Thatcher had privately been assured by the Government Actuary: far from being unknown, inflation-proofing was rather standard practice (albeit on a discretionary basis) in the private sector. Typically 80 per cent protection was offered against any fall in real value and – even in the worst years – around 55 per cent.[63]

The Report was not wholly uncritical. One-fifth of the analogues used to compare outside pensions were, it concluded, inappropriate and salary deductions (although within an acceptable range) might with prudence be raised.[64] When, however, after the 1981 strike, an Official Committee responded to such criticisms by recommending the simple expedient of raising contributions to ten per cent (mainly to replenish the Exchequer speedily) Cabinet still refused to bite the bullet. Nor did it sanction Howe's continuing demand for some limit to guaranteed inflation-proofing. So blatant a disregard for 'contractual entitlements', it concluded, would be morally – if not strictly legally – indefensible. Instead, by December 1981 it was moving towards an increase in the contribution rate of all public sector workers to 8.5 per cent – an increase which, as has been seen, represented only a marginal increase for Civil Servants if not for others. As under Labour, the principal stumbling block was the tension between orchestrated public demand for change and actual public resistance to it – from the 2.5 million pensioners affected and the further eight million current contributors. Only a minority were Civil Servants, but a majority was thought to vote Conservative.

The battle over public pensions epitomises the change from an elite consensus (in which radical proposals within the Conservatives' 1970 manifesto could be moderated in the light of objective information) to a more popular consensus (in which the moderation of the Conservatives' 1979 election pledges reflected the radicalism of neither earlier rhetoric nor later convictions).[65] What then was an acceptable way forward? Both the CSD in the mid-1970s and the later Scott Report rationally defended the consensual settlement of 1971–2. Arguably, however, both underplayed the adjustments that had to be made to changed political and economic circumstance as well as the psychological impact of the removal by the 1971 and 1972 Acts of direct Parliamentary control over public pensions.[66] A parallel challenge was being mounted to the Government's conventional role as a 'good employer'. In 1972 David Howell, no supporter of 'big government', had openly admitted that, whereas the Civil Service had been a pioneer in pension provision until 1939, many private employers had 'begun to catch up, and not a few have overtaken us'.[67] Market provision was nevertheless patchy; and the 1971 and 1972 Acts were thus tokens of the Government's determination to 'set a good example' for all. Such determination, however, did not last long. By 1979, Conservative Ministers were commonly complaining that public pensions were being measured not against provision in the private sector as a whole, and particularly not for the self-employed, but against 'large firms who had a reputation as good employers'. This was a thinly-veiled invitation to join a 'race to the bottom'. Nor was this an exclusive invitation. When public disquiet over pension 'privilege' had first been widely voiced in 1975, Allen had demanded of the then Labour Government whether its real intention was to reduce public provision to that of the 'financially weakest funded scheme'. There was no more eloquent testimony to the developing consensus that the values of the market should supersede those of public service.

9.5 Gender and race

The other area in which Government was commonly expected to set an example as an employer was the elimination of discrimination on the grounds of gender and race. In relation to gender, under pressure internationally from the United Nations and EEC and domestically from the Women's Liberation Movement, major new legislation was passed: the 1970 Equal Pay Act, the 1975 Sex Discrimination Act (designed to deter discriminatory recruitment, promotion and dismissal practices) and the 1975 Employment Protection Act (which *inter alia* guaranteed the right to maternity pay and a restricted right to reinstatement for mothers). The Civil Service was little affected since it was widely regarded, and regarded itself, as 'a particularly enlightened employer of women'.[68] Since the 1930s, as has been seen, there had been no formal discrimination in relation to recruitment; in 1946 the marriage bar had been lifted; and since 1962 equal pay – denied to some 3 million white-collar workers in the private sector – assured.

That serious gender inequality continued, nevertheless, was made plain by the Halsey Social Survey of the Civil Service in 1969. Commissioned by Fulton and compiled by a leading sociologist, it was not published until September 1969 and so did not trouble the Fulton Committee itself (which failed to include women explicitly amongst the 'potential talent' which the Service was 'seriously mis-using and stultifying'). Nevertheless it did trouble CSD Ministers and top officials by its statistical evidence that women, although tending to be socially and educationally 'superior' to their male colleagues, were concentrated in the lower grades of all classes and that married women were typically denied promotion.[69] Within the Administrative Class, for example, of the 29 Permanent Secretaries none was a woman (following the retirements in 1966 of Evelyn Sharp and Mary Smieton, the first women to be so promoted in 1956 and 1959 respectively). Moreover, of 74 Deputy Secretaries and 274 Under Secretaries, only two and nine respectively were women. The reason for such bias, it was alleged, was 'indirect discrimination' – a concept later classically defined as discrimination occurring when 'the same formal conditions of employment apply to both sexes ... but in practice a considerably smaller proportion of people of one sex or marital status than of another can comply with them'.[70] Just as the Civil Service had been amongst the first to accept the suffragettes' definition of gender equality, so now it was expected to lead the response to this revised definition.

The CSD's swift response was to establish an inquiry into the employment of women within the non-industrial Civil Service, chaired by a senior married woman official (Elizabeth Kemp-Jones). Its report, published in October 1971, was widely hailed as a 'Woman's Lib charter in Whitehall'.[71] More substantively, it was also welcomed in Whitehall and Westminster. In the former, Establishment Officers were immediately requested to implement the majority of its recommendations. In the latter the hope was expressed that it would become a 'landmark in our national attitude towards the employment of women'.[72] Such harmony, however, did not long survive. Progress over the following decade was to be condemned as 'limited and slow' by a major independent inquiry in 1981.[73] Despite a near tripling of posts above the Assistant Principal/ Administration Trainee grade since 1968, so it revealed, women still remained underrepresented in 'top jobs' to 'the point of invisibility' (at 9.6 per cent as compared to the earlier 8.4 per cent, see Table 9.1). Major disincentives also remained for women in mid-career, mainly due to the absence of part-time work – which, by contrast, had rapidly expanded in the private sector (albeit not always for honourable reasons).

A further official inquiry was launched in April 1981 under the auspices of the National Whitley Council and its report, *Equal Opportunities for Women in the Civil Service*, was to provide the basis for a new 'programme for action' in 1984. Its own slow progress was blamed, in part, on its initial coincidence with the 1981 strike. More ominously, however, it was also blamed by union negotiators on officials' intransigence. 'It had been difficult', they reported, to convince officials 'that we are looking at a serious problem and to get across some of the basic concepts e.g. indirect discrimination'.[74] Just as the Service had lost its relative position as a 'good employer' in relation to part-time work, had officials' attitudes also regressed?

Table 9.1 Women in 'top' posts, 1968–81

	1968			1981		
	Total	*Women*	*%*	*%*	*Women*	*Total*
Perm Sec	28	0	0	0	0	42
Deputy Sec	80	2	2.5	2.5	4	158
Under Sec	291	7	2.4	4.4	27	613
Asst Sec	837	51	6.1	5.7	65	1144
Principal	1140	112	9.8	7.9	355	4469
Asst Principal/ Admin Trainee + HEO (A/D)	318.5	54	17	30.4	241	793
TOTAL	2694.5	226	8.4	9.6	692	7219

Sources: M.P. Fogarty et al, *Women in Top Jobs* (1981), p. 36, *Civil Service Statistics, 1982* (1982).

This question is best answered by an examination of the fate of the Kemp-Jones Report. The Committee had been asked to consider the employment of women generally within the Service. In particular, how might it be 'made easier' for married women to combine raising a family with a career or to return to work after a lengthy break raising a family? The Committee made four main recommendations. They were:

> A woman should not be debarred from any job solely on the ground of her sex; secondly, the provisions for leave, and in particular unpaid leave, should be improved to take account of a woman's family responsibilities; third, perhaps the most important and calling for a change of attitude on the part of the Service, opportunities for part time work for women with family responsibilities should be expanded; and, lastly, modifications should be made in the rules governing reinstatement to make it easier for women to return to suitable work when their children are older.[75]

The first recommendation was the easiest to implement and, amid much mirth about the gender requirements of such sinecures as the Purse Holder, the number of restricted posts was reduced to some 15,000 by 1979 (of which the majority were in single-sex prisons). Mirth nevertheless disguised a significant advance. As late as 1964, after all, women had been banned from Administrative Class posts in the defence ministries and a marriage bar still operated in the Northern Ireland Civil Service (as in the private sector there).[76] The second recommendation embraced a range of detailed proposals including improved maternity leave (up to three months paid with a further three months' unpaid leave) and the extension of leave to meet common contingencies (such as 'urgent domestic affairs', child-care during the school holidays and the 'accompanying of husbands to new areas' on a change of job). Most were also implemented, albeit with some misgivings.[77]

It was the final two recommendations which proved the most controversial. This was not just because, as the Report itself admitted, they challenged social norms but because they also exposed a certain confusion about why, and at what level of 'responsibility', reform was being sought. The principal motivation behind senior officials' support for reform was economic (women's high 'wastage' rate representing lost investment as well as resulting in a serious loss of efficiency).[78] This was certainly Armstrong's foremost concern, particularly at the top of the Service. He sensed that, with the rapid expansion of Government, there was a shortfall – in both quantity and quality – of Principals within the Administrative Class and equally that, because of the expansion of higher education, the recruitment of more women was the answer. However, as a result of changing social mores and a better gender balance, they were more likely to marry – and to marry earlier – than women recruited in the interwar period. 'Over the next ten or twenty years much more of the talent and ability in the Civil Service will belong to women', he assured the Women's National Commission in January 1970, and that it was 'increasingly important to us to persuade these women to stay at work, or to return later in life'.[79] Attitudes had to change immediately because several departments were already exhibiting 'customer resistance' to their increased allocation of women as Administration Trainees. Because of the high 'wastage' rate, they were protesting, this did not represent a good investment at a time of stringent manpower control.[80]

However, the Committee – as reflected by its working methods – rejected so exclusive a focus on the Administrative Class. Eschewing further quantitative studies and research outside the Service, it instead collected a random sample of opinion from women who were currently serving or had recently retired from the Service. Of the 830 replies it received, the majority were from Executive and Clerical officers and so their concerns tended to predominate. Admittedly, under pressure from its outside member (Mrs Ward-Jackson), the Committee's Report did make the 'crucial point' that:

> the conditions of employment and career patterns in the Civil Service . . . are based upon a general expectation of unbroken service from entry until retirement. These conditions were designed for and generally are suitable for men and also for women who remain unmarried or childless through their working lives.[81]

This, by current definitions, did not equate to gender discrimination; but it recognised, albeit perhaps unconsciously, the 'indirect discrimination' experienced by women particularly above the level of Administration Trainee. Wholly unacknowledged, however, was another potential source of 'indirect discrimination'. As a concurrent PEP report on *Women in Top Jobs* concluded: 'women who do remain in the Service are steered away from the scenes of important action lessening the likelihood of their being seen as candidates for top posts'.[82] This, so it alleged, was the reason why there were relatively few women in senior positions within major economic ministries and as Private Secretaries, particularly in No. 10.

The notion of the 'natural' gender differences, on which such 'steering' was based at all levels within the Service, was one of the principal 'non-economic' issues Kemp-Jones sought to address. Any change, it realised, was dependent on a revolution in social conventions outside as much as inside Whitehall – as was made apparent by the collective response of junior CSD officials to the Halsey Survey. 'Of course', it had concluded

> women 'compete on less equal terms with men'. Biological difference and the whole social context of our time make this inevitable and it is a little hard to be asked, when the Civil Service is streets ahead of industry and commerce in the practice of non-discrimination, why women are not doing better than they are . . . So long as Western society remains based on the family unit, marriage and child-bearing will always induce a high rate of wastage among young women. It is the same social tradition that

saddles the unmarried woman with the care of aged or infirm relatives . . . The very real physical and mental stresses of the menopause are suffered only by women. In a male-dominated society these inescapable factors help male managers to rationalize their inborn prejudice.[83]

This, of course, begged the question of whether current employment practice did not just reflect but actually reinforced such 'inescapable factors'.

Armstrong did tentatively challenge such gender stereotyping by advocating paternity as well as maternity leave; but his advocacy merely highlighted another complication which dogged the implementation of Kemp-Jones – 'reverse discrimination'.[84] Two of its members had actually teetered on the brink of committing so cardinal a sin. In relation to the right to reinstatement, for example, they had been adamant that any right should be exclusive to women. 'We repudiate', read one of their early drafts of the final report, 'any parallel between the woman who leaves to have children or to look after her children while they are young and the Civil Servant who leaves to engage in an alternative career'.[85] In the event, the final Report itself ducked the issue on the grounds that the Committee's terms of reference covered only women. Ducked also was any discussion of the 'inborn prejudices' which managers were allegedly rationalising.

The majority, therefore, of Kemp-Jones' 25 recommendations were immediately accepted, although their implementation tended to be 'low-key'. This, as has been seen, may be explained in part by a continuing conflict, both within and outside the Committee, over the economic and social purpose as well as the precise focus of reform. There was also an extensive range of other constraints. Outside Whitehall, as Lord Shackleton admitted in the 1971 House of Lords debate, 'the attitude of the general public to "Women's Lib" was hostile or indifferent, as it was to the Suffragettes'. This was well illustrated by many letters to the Committee, even from some who had themselves suffered 'indirect' discrimination.[86] Moreover, both the professions and the unions (with which, as has been seen the Service's management was necessarily intertwined) were bastions of 'traditional values'. For example, the professions – and above all science – were male dominated and the specialist classes (whose role Fulton was seeking to expand) fully reflected this. Staff associations, for all their later claims to virtue, were also vigilant from the start in their monitoring of 'reverse discrimination' – opposing, for example, any increase in part-time work (because its freedom from compulsory overtime might excite jealousy among full-time, predominantly male, staff) and the right to reinstatement (because it would adversely affect the promotion of career staff, who again were predominantly male). Such was their conservatism indeed that, had it not been for a spirited intervention by the Committee's one staff association member (Doris Lancaster), the Report itself would have been rejected by the annual conference of her own union, the Society of Civil Servants, in 1972.[87] A final external constraint was the reality of the labour market. As in the interwar years, rising unemployment in the 1970s reinforced the notion that men, and particularly husbands, should have preference in the job market.[88]

Within Whitehall, the foremost constraint was, as ever, the Service's federal nature. This meant *inter alia* that, when unemployment increased the supply of applicants, the conservative views of many individual departmental Establishment Officers had to be not only respected but reflected. Within the more powerful departments, moreover, unreconstructed views continued to flourish. A commonly held view within the Treasury, for example, was that the Labour Government's 1976 white paper, *Equality for Women* (Cmnd 5724), was a 'transvestite's charter'. This was not a notable advance on its earlier dismissal of the Equal Pay Act as an appeal to 'some primitive notions of inter-personal equity'.[89]

Had such external and internal constraints not existed, however, would CSD officials have been more liberal than union leaders later detected? The evidence suggests not. In her brief to Lord Shackleton on the Halsey Survey, for instance, even the future secretary of the Kemp-Jones Committee (Eileen Conn) had optimistically concluded that its real message was not that 'barriers of discrimination' had to be removed but rather help provided for women to 'return to work, or to continue in work'.[90] After the Report, she reiterated this advice, insisting that many of its recommendations

> are really an attempt to resolve the growing conflict between domestic life and full-time employment rather than to cope with problems unique to women. The majority of the problems caused by this conflict are at present, of course, faced by women. There is, however, no guarantee that this will continue.

Such sentiments were thereafter sustained both by her and her colleagues; and consequently the focus of departmental policy came to be less the promotion of adjustments to the different 'social patterns' of women's lives than the prevention of women becoming a 'new privileged class'.

The extent to which such 'balance' eroded any initial instinct to eliminate 'indirect discrimination' is best illustrated by the fate of three of the Report's critical policy recommendations: the right to reinstatement, the extension of part-time work and the provision of nurseries. The first was designed to compensate for a break from work taken to rear a family, the other two to permit the continuation of a career whilst rearing a family. For fear of reverse discrimination, it was immediately agreed that reinstatement could neither be a right nor exclusive to women.[91] Consequently, there developed a degree of inflexibility in its implementation which led in 1977 to the Service being taken to an Equal Opportunity tribunal, and defeated, by an aggrieved mother (Belinda Price). The age for promotion within the Executive Class, so it was argued, had become 'stereotyped' at 28, so that women returning to work after rearing a family were effectively excluded. This was discriminatory: the age for promotion had to be raised. Likewise, part-time work (which had been actively championed both by Armstrong and the majority of young correspondents to Kemp-Jones) was disparaged. In part this was due to the principle, forcefully defended by J.P. Carswell (the DES Establishment Officer) on the Committee:

'As rank gets higher, there is more need for continuity of actual individuals. Staff have to have leadership. Ministers should be advised at all hours by the same person on the same subject, things are wanted at once ... I don't see how one can have two people in charge of something and if something requires full-time charge, it must have the same person in charge of it'.[92]

In general, however, it was due to a range of technical difficulties (such as the demand, at a time of manpower constraint, on managerial time) which departmental Establishment Officers alleged were insuperable. Nevertheless similar difficulties appeared not to inhibit the private sector – least of all in relation to comparable white-collar work in the banking sector.

However, the real litmus test of official attitudes – as in the immediate postwar years – was the provision of nurseries. As Kemp-Jones maintained, they could be 'socially beneficial' for both the individual and society in general by providing a solution to the dual dilemma of how women might combine a career with a family and, by maintaining their skills, more easily return to work after a break. They were also commonly demanded in the letters to the Committee, especially by junior officials. In consequence their provision, if only as an experiment, was 'pushed hard' at a ministerial level by Jellicoe.[93] At an official level, however, there was little enthusiasm for extending the experiment beyond a minimum period. As explained by W.F. Hartman (the CSD's Chief Welfare Officer to whom the principal administrative responsibility was assigned), this was for two main reasons. First, expert advice was adamant that, in the interest of a child's welfare to the age of five, mothers should stay at home. Second, 'at a time when the justification for all public expenditure is subject to keen scrutiny' so 'controversial' an experiment could be justified by the need neither to make good a recruitment shortage nor to match better private practice.[94] Such reservations were supported by the DHSS (which was equally insistent that any provision should be for child-care not child-minding) and by the Treasury (which was insistent that the full economic cost, including the capital cost, should be recovered).

Under strong pressure from Jellicoe, however, Treasury officials felt obliged to endorse two experimental nurseries.[95] A breach was thus blown in their defences. Had this been zealously exploited – as arguably it would have been by, for example, Edwardian social reformers – a radical departure in policy might have been achieved. Such zeal however, was lacking within the CSD; and at an official level it was duly agreed, between departments, that the nursery programme should be downgraded to 'another embellishment' in the CSD's *Wider Issues* programme for an improved working environment. A highly successful (if highly subsidised) nursery was established in 1973 for the Inland Revenue at Llanishen, near Cardiff, and in 1974 a property was purchased in Croydon for a second experiment.[96] Both initiatives, however, fell early and easy victims to cash limits in 1976.

In the early 1970s, therefore, the Civil Service appeared (under the lead of Armstrong and Jellicoe) in the van of a revolutionary change to eliminate both direct and 'indirect' gender discrimination; and the acceptance of the Kemp-Jones Report was being hailed as 'the most important breakthrough yet achieved in Britain towards adapting employment practices to women's different life cycle' by the three leading independent experts.[97] Within a decade, however, officials were being castigated for their failure to understand the concept of 'indirect' discrimination and the Service in general as being 'an organization run largely by and for men'. Why was there so pronounced a change and what, more generally, did it signify about barriers to modernisation? As has been intimated, there were three principal explanations for changed perceptions. First, as with the Fulton Committee and most administrative reform at this time, attention was almost exclusively focused on the Administrative Class to the neglect of the rest of the Service (which had rather different problems). Second, just as the perceived need for economy and efficiency had temporarily coalesced in the 1850s to prompt the Northcote-Trevelyan Report, but not thereafter to sustain its implementation, so for Armstrong in the 1970s the needs of the Service and women temporarily coalesced. Rising unemployment, however, resolved recruitment problems — especially for Executive and Clerical Officers — and once-desirable reforms, such as the right to reinstatement, began to sit uneasily with both increased threats of redundancy and decreased opportunities for promotion for existing staff. Third, as an internal document, the Kemp-Jones Report betrayed a fatal ambivalence. On issues of principle, for example, it was more alert than an outside single-issue pressure group to potential objections from men and single women. Consequently, it downplayed its 'feminist' ambitions. Likewise, in relation to its practical recommendations, it was more aware of the Service's federal nature and thus of the impossibility of ordering change from above. Its recommendations had to be tempered: nursery provision, for example, could in the first instance only be experimental.

The trouble with such 'reasonableness' was that zeal alone could have changed entrenched attitudes. Moreover, it could provide no answer to the incontrovertible statistical fact that — as was to continue until well into the 1990s — women were clustered at the bottom of each class and never held more than ten per cent of the 'top' administrative posts.[98] Such an imbalance could be, and frequently was, excused as the inevitable consequence of a career service — which the Fulton Committee had explicitly wished to retain.[99] Fulton, however, had equally demanded greater affinity between officials and the public and in this respect, had not women — and particularly those who had experienced all the public and private tribulations of child-care — as much to offer as men seconded (in insufficient numbers) to the private sector? Yet married women continued to be effectively excluded from 'top' administrative posts (by forfeited promotion) and senior executive jobs (by their limited mobility). In other words, to achieve what was arguably not just morally but also administratively right, should not greater risks have been taken? After all, as Doris Lancaster had argued whilst salvaging the Kemp-Jones Report at the 1972 SCS conference: 'if Parliament had waited until public opinion was entirely ready, none of the important legislation we have had in this country in the last hundred years would ever have been enacted'.[100] Such risk-taking had been an earlier feature of the Service but, to the disadvantage of modernisation more generally, it would appear to have fallen victim to the loss of confidence identified in Chapter 6.

In relation to racial discrimination, Government policy and the Service's experience were remarkably similar. Indeed for some the former was rather too similar, with the 1975 Sex Discrimination Act aping many features of the 1965 and 1968 Race Relations Acts and then anticipating the 1976 Act.[101] As for the Service, it again was widely regarded – and regarded itself – as an exemplary employer throughout the period. In the late 1960s, however, it became subject to mounting pressure both from within (given the preponderance of black recruits to clerical positions, particularly in London) and from outside (arising from the demand for improvements in existing race relations as a corollary to the renewed interest in immigration curbs following Enoch Powell's 'rivers of blood' speech in April 1968).[102] The result, as with Kemp-Jones, was a serious policy reappraisal. An internal CSD inquiry was commissioned in May 1972 and reported the following February. Little happened, however, until the publication in 1978 of a semi-independent report from the Tavistock Institute of Human Relations, when another Joint Working Party of the National Whitley Council was established to examine the reasons for slow progress. Progress remained slow until Ministers were propelled by the Brixton riots of April 1981 into conceding, in principle, a long-standing demand (ethnic monitoring) and, in practice, a pilot study of recruitment and promotion in Leeds. As the CCSU commented, it was remarkable what a 'little urban rioting' could achieve.[103]

Similar though the overall trends in anti-discrimination policy were, there were also significant differences. The number of black officials was relatively small (at 16,550 in 1967) and concentrated in the clerical and industrial classes. Allegations of racial discrimination, therefore, were of less immediate interest to William Armstrong and the CSD inquiry was consequently a pale shadow of Kemp-Jones.[104] In contrast, the main pressure for change came from the annual reports of the Race Relations Board and a major report from the CPRS (delivered to Ministers, somewhat infelicitously, during the political crisis of January 1974). The Home Office and Department of Employment, rather than the CSD, also took the lead in defining best practice.[105] In short, racial discrimination within the Service was less a management issue in its own right than an area in which Government was expected to set a good example in order to defuse a far larger social problem, correctly identified within the CSD as 'political dynamite'.

Once anti-discrimination legislation had been controversially extended in 1968 to employment within the Civil Service, there were two particular areas in which a good example was expected to be set.[106] The first, as has been noted, was ethnic monitoring to provide (as had the Halsey Social Survey for gender discrimination) a sound statistical base for the measurement of both social disadvantage and the impact of policies designed to counter it. The second was an improvement to personnel practices to eliminate what was defined for the first time in the 1976 Race Relations Act as 'indirect discrimination'.

With regard to monitoring, the traditional administrative objection was that it served 'no managerial purpose', consumed considerable resources (at a time of budget cuts and more pressing reforms) and could even cause resentment. Thus to the 1969 Select Committee on Race Relations and Immigration, the CSD tendered the standard Treasury response:

> because the Civil Service does not exercise discrimination in recruitment or in other personnel matters, it has not been found necessary, for management purposes, to keep records indicating colour or racial origin of civil servants.[107]

The Select Committee concluded, on the contrary, that statistics were essential; and in time, leading officials acknowledged that it was preferable to defend policy with 'numerate facts' than to remain in 'determined ignorance'. Resistance, nevertheless, continued. Ministers, with good reason, were concerned that any statistical count might excite fears amongst the electorate of enforced repatriation. Officials in turn agonised over the most appropriate means of measurement because, as they correctly concluded, there was no one 'totally satisfactory criterion for colour'.[108] The use of parents' birthplace (as in the census) was flawed because, as a consequence of Empire, many parents of white staff had been born overseas. Moreover it was of declining value because, by the late 1980s, a third generation of migrants (with parents born in Britain) would predominate. The alternative was a subjective assessment of 'colour', be it by self-assessment or management. The latter was the method used both to provide Parliament with rough biennial estimates of 'coloured' staff and by the Department of Employment in 1973 (when it sought to give a lead). It too, however, was flawed. The classification of individuals could not be kept from them and, in so sensitive an area, caused frequent resentment once revealed. As a consequence, the DE census counted as 'coloured' only those of African, Asian or West Indian descent and officials were instructed neither to approach nor include anyone over whom there might be some doubt. This in itself seriously compromised the statistics.

Genuine though this methodological dispute was, there is some evidence that it was deliberately protracted for political reasons. Both Ministers and officials were particularly keen after 1971 to evade the 'positive' policy being urged on them with increasing fervour by the Race Relations Board. Employment practices within the Service, so the Board argued, should not just satisfy the legal minimum but overtly tackle 'indirect discrimination' and thus the social prejudice which nurtured it.[109] Heavily influenced by programmes of 'affirmative action' in the USA, its principal recommendations were the publication of a ringing endorsement of equal opportunity, the involvement of senior management in its circulation, and the appointment of race relations advisers in all departments to monitor progress. In addition, there should be clear statements of the criteria for recruitment and promotion, feedback for failed candidates in both processes, the provision of language classes to counter linguistic disadvantage and explicit targets (to provide management with objective goals, not to guarantee given quotas of 'coloured' staff). Such suggestions offended senior officials on the grounds of equity and practicality. In the first instance, they argued, there could be no divergence from the Northcote-Trevelyan principle of appointment and promotion on merit. Moreover, special language courses hinted at 'reverse discrimination' – as did the introduction of targets. Second, at a time of capped manpower and minimal training margins, would it not be extremely inefficient to employ staff who could not communicate adequately with the public and then withdraw them to enhance their language skills? Moreover, to counsel all applicants who failed to gain either a place or promotion would be extremely costly in terms of manpower – and arouse resentment if reserved solely for 'coloured' candidates.

There were, nevertheless, undoubted instances of 'indirect' discrimination.[110] For example, at a local level (where departments rather than the Civil Service Commission were responsible for recruitment) additional requirements were added to – or retained in – the job specification specifically to exclude 'coloured' applicants. The Commission itself also changed its practice from reliance on paper qualifications (which might be bogus) to interviews (in which language skills could be tested) for clerical officers over 20, of whom some 80 per cent were 'coloured'. Finally, senior officials themselves privately used statistics for 'coloured' staff and those excluded by nationality rules interchangeably (despite their public insistence that such rules were 'colour blind' because everyone born within the Commonwealth was, under the 1948 Nationality Act, a British citizen). Such instances betrayed a distinct lack of concern and of commitment to reform, as was confirmed by the CSD's response to an early draft of the CPRS's 1974 Report. 'The fundamental problem', the CSD concluded, was 'how to deal with people who have arrived in a highly developed urban society and who lack the skills needed for advancement or acceptance in the host society'. By the third generation, this problem would be solved but, in the meantime, race relations policy had to speed the process if only because, when unemployment struck, the 'coloured' workers would blame 'discrimination, either because [they] believe it or because there is special machinery to help'. What was really needed were improvements 'on the shop floor, to help them to integrate into our society and to encourage them to master thoroughly the skills they need to improve their condition. Union opposition also needs to be overcome'. Then came the most telling point. 'Such steps' it concluded

> may well have a useful spin-off for the comparatively small number of large employers whose work force is predominantly or largely white collar, but . . . the problems of organisation and control facing the large white-collar employer are very often markedly different from those of the big industrial employer, and are frequently much more complex.[111]

In short, it was essentially the industrial Civil Service that was involved; and, to the extent that the non-industrial Service was being drawn into controversy, there was rising anger that, at a time when the Service was being pilloried for alleged inefficiency, reforms were being demanded which (however socially and politically justified) could only decrease efficiency.

In relation to both gender and racial discrimination, therefore, the Civil Service continued formally to be an exemplary employer.[112] Just as political consensus was coming under challenge in the mid 1960s, however, so too were the agreed values on which its formal personnel practices were based. The concept, and realisation, of 'indirect' discrimination was becoming increasingly invasive. Particularly in relation to gender, the Service initially reacted with speed and sensitivity; but to combat continually an ingrained popular prejudice required a boldness which neither Ministers nor officials appeared to have. Accordingly the battle against 'indirect' discrimination lacked the heroism of earlier battles; and modernisation was once again thwarted. Public opinion was followed, not led. The Service no longer unreservedly deserved the accolade of a model employer.

9.6 Computerisation

Technological change presented the most direct challenge to the alleged amateurism of the Service (although typically Fulton failed to recognise, let alone address, it). As with gender equality, the Service had long regarded – and regarded itself – as a leading innovator and an internal inquiry (the Atkinson Committee) was likewise appointed in 1969 to maintain this position.[113] Its relative position, however, was steadily eroded by the greater responsiveness to technological change of the private sector and governments abroad. Its own response fell into three phases.[114] Until 1975, the Treasury (through its O&M division) and then the CSD (ultimately through the Central Computer Agency (CCA), established in 1972) exercised a measure of central control. It was during this period that mainframe computers were installed to deliver many labour-intensive tasks, be it concerned with policy-delivery (as with the Police National Computer at Hendon) or purely internal matters (such as departmental payrolls). Then, having commissioned detailed surveys of international practice, the Treasury (as described in Chapter 6.3.2a) started to capitalise on increased computer capacity to modernise management information systems. This immediately restored its authority and ultimately transformed the Service. In the short term, however, it only reinforced financial and manpower constraints through its association with cash limits; and so, during the third phase (the microelectronic revolution of the mid-1970s), there tended to be a lack of flair and flexibility. Technological change instead became a subject of political controversy. This was due in part to changes in work practices but, more significantly, to changes in strike tactics. Computer installations, as illustrated in Chapter 8, provided a natural target for staff associations seeking to inflict maximum damage at minimum cost to themselves. A joint NWC group was appointed in 1980 to improve mutual understanding; but it was even less effectual than those appointed to address gender and racial equality. No new agreement on the acceptance of new technology was ever reached.

Technological change posed two fundamental challenges for management. First, Government – as in all Western countries – was by far the largest user of computers and placed the most complex demands on them. Thus, at a time of rapid change, it was constantly at the cutting edge of innovation. How could potential efficiency gains be maximised (and the strictures of, amongst others, the Public Accounts Committee thereby avoided) without placing too great a reliance on untried technology (which, were it to fail and disrupt the Queen's business, would subject it to even greater criticism)? Second, during the economic and industrial relations turmoil of the mid-1970s, the Service had to replace the original, obsolete mainframe computers without any service disruption. This was a complex enough task but it also coincided with the microelectronic revolution which required, at a time of mounting militancy, the encouragement of staff at all levels to embrace the microprocessor and micro-computer – regardless of increasing, if somewhat premature, predictions of the 'paperless office' and thus of wholesale changes to the nature of clerical work.[115]

To meet this twin challenge, as was acknowledged at the time, management required four essential qualities. The first was a degree of computer literacy amongst senior managers in order to realise the full potential of change, to ensure the clear specification of objectives for each innovation and to counter fear of, as well as unrealistic expectations about, change. For example, as demonstrated by the expensive failure in the USA of Planning, Programming and Budgeting Systems (so beloved by modernisers on both the right and left), senior officials had to realise that technology by itself provided no magic bullet. Rather, as a CSD report later concluded, what was needed was not 'technical revolutions, but an evolution' to enable advantage to be taken of 'technological progress ... at a manageable pace, to make full use of very large investment ... and to use it, where it is effective and economical to do so, beyond the life of a particular machine.'[116] Change, in short, should be solid not spectacular. The second essential managerial requirement was a good organisational structure so that scarce skills could be shared, common lessons learnt and compatibility assured. Third, there was a need for adequate finance. Computerisation was commonly equated to economy because of anticipated manpower savings. However, the machines themselves required routine maintenance and replacement, and once installed, were expected to perform far more complex tasks than the clerical workers they replaced. Costs, in other words, could – and should – escalate to the point at which there were no tangible savings. Finally, there was a need for an adequate cadre of well-trained and well-motivated staff to programme and operate the machines, as well as to win acceptance for further change.

There was one further impediment to good management: procurement policy.[117] As with racial equality, the Service's needs throughout the period were treated as secondary to a broader political goal – in this case the guarantee of a home market to ensure the international competitiveness of the leading British computer manufacturer (ICL). Cabinet had agreed in 1965 that, in the purchase of large machines for central Government, preference should be given to British computers to the extent that they might be 25 per cent more expensive and delivered up to one year later than rival machines. With certain modifications such preference was maintained – albeit not made fully public – until 1980.[118] The potential loss of efficiency was well recognised, for example, by Lord Shackleton (as head of the CSD). There were, he admitted in 1970,

> two different procurement policies in operation: one sought to ensure maximum efficiency and economy in government by the unconditional tender procedure, and the other had the undoubted merit . . . of building up an important national industry by limiting the operation of the tender system.[119]

Cost was not, in fact, unduly inflated by single tenders because, especially in the early days, ICL was price-competitive. What did incur, rather more covertly, substantial additional costs – and cause in-built inefficiency – were ICL's poor delivery and technical record. For example, late delivery together with the (often deliberate) incompatibility of ICL machines with rival hardware and software meant that large numbers of clerical staff had to be employed far longer than planned. Breakdowns and technical shortcomings (particularly in relation to ICL's relative neglect of microelectronics) also limited expected efficiency gains. As noted in Chapter 6.2, the Service was frequently pilloried in the 1970s by politicians and industrialists alike for excessive manpower and expenditure. What was less openly acknowledged was that, in this instance at least, such 'excesses' were frequently the consequence of political decisions taken in the perceived interests of industrialists.

In such circumstances, how well did management – by the four specified criteria – meet the challenge of technological change? For one historian, the attitude of senior management in the early 1960s (following the installation of the first six computers in 1958) was exemplary. 'A program of extensive computerization was under way', he has written, 'and provided a strong link between the upper echelons of the Civil Service (where the attitude of Permanent Secretaries shifted from suspicion to comfort and even enthusiasm) and the technical experts of the government physical laboratories.'[120] In this vision, the driving force was the Treasury's O&M division (headed by a former administrator at Bletchley Park, with a former General Post Office engineer as his deputy) allied to the Treasury's traditional powers of persuasion. Its nemesis was ironically the Fulton Committee which, despite its emphasis on improved management and specialist expertise, diluted the Treasury's power and through its quest for unified grading destroyed O&M as an 'aspirational ideology' for Executive Officers and specialists alike.

Whether so positive an assessment is justified is open to question. The O&M division, as in the interwar period, may have been a model of inspirational leadership at the inception of the computer age; but in the more pluralistic 1960s (when, in particular, technological change was being aggressively exploited in the USA and Treasury control was under political challenge) it was arguably less effective.[121] As the Atkinson Report concluded, for example, the 1960s were characterised by 'the predominance of the individual department, the wide spread of applications and the variety of equipment' and their consequent legacy was a serious incompatibility of systems which jeopardised future developments. Moreover, despite a series of highly effective 'indoctrination' seminars for senior management (anticipating those in the 1980s designed to encourage more professional management), even the most apparently sympathetic of generalists remained ambivalent. For example, one – a future Permanent Secretary of the MinTech – dismissed computerisation for administrative purposes as 'the Treasury equivalent to space fiction'. Another – the initial chair of the key proselytising Steering Committee for Automatic Data Processing – had also effectively to be replaced as Permanent Secretary of the Ministry of Transport, when that department embarked on an ambitious programme of computerisation in the late 1960s.[122]

Such scepticism, it is true, was reinforced by Fulton. Relieved of its dual responsibility for economy and efficiency, the Treasury became more narrowly focused on the former. Consequently, at both a political and administrative level, it constantly questioned the need for increased computer capacity – and, indeed, whether capacity was defining need.[123] The one occasion on which it whole-heartedly embraced computerisation, as seen in Chapter 6.3.2, was when there was an urgent need to strengthen public expenditure control. This shortcoming was not fully made good by the CSD, in which senior 'generalists' were only too happy to admit their technical ignorance.[124] Nevertheless they did speedily delegate detailed responsibility for policy to Reay Atkinson who, despite being a 'generalist' himself, proved himself to be a worthy successor to the O&M specialists. Appointed Director of the CCA, as an Under Secretary, he sought to develop the Agency's technical expertise so that it might lead by example rather than enforce change. The cultural revolution for which he was hoping, however, failed fully to materialise. As he diplomatically commented in one of his final speeches as Director, success was dependent on 'active top management involvement' but 'senior management had not always been willing to identify itself with computer developments and implementation'. This, he then tellingly remarked, was 'not unique to the Civil Service'.[125]

If senior management failed the first test of computer literacy, therefore, what of the second criterion for success: a clear organisational structure? Political direction was confused by a number of conflicting Cabinet committees arising, in large part, from unresolved tensions over procurement policy.[126] Administrative confusion was equally rife. Not only was the centre split between the Treasury and the CSD but, given the Service's federal nature, any central initiative was also bound to be contested. Thus, on its establishment, the CSD essentially became a sixth wheel on a very cumbersome coach. Each department had prime responsibility for its own modernisation programme. MinTech (through its Technical Support Unit (TSU)) could be called upon for detailed advice, whilst the Treasury ensured maximum economy and compliance with procurement policy. Then, once a programme had been agreed, HMSO supplied the computers and Ministry of Public Building and Works (later the PSA) the accommodation – no inconsiderable task in the days of mainframes. To this melee, the CSD (with its overall responsibility for efficiency and staffing) was expected to add a measure of central planning and standardisation. The inevitable result was the frustration both of departments and of progress. Typically it took up to two years to put a project out to tender and a further five before installation was complete.

Just as Atkinson had been appointed to make good computer illiteracy, so the CSD sought to resolve this confusion by the establishment in March 1972 of the Central Computer Agency (CCA). In the previous August it had assumed the Treasury's power to control computer expenditure, and both the Parliamentary Select Committee on Science and Technology and the CPRS had subsequently recommended a stronger 'central competence'.[127] This the CCA aspired to be, by assuming the role of the TSU and HMSO in addition to that of the Treasury. Thereby, it sought to develop with 'user' departments a constructive and consensual programme of innovation, which would maximise compatibility.

This ambition, however, was soon dashed. As one of the first 'departmental agencies', it fell prey to the range of unresolved political and administrative questions identified in Chapter 5.3.3(c). More importantly, it was also denied the requisite money and staff. Financially, it became embroiled in the long-running dispute over whether 'common services' should be paid directly by the 'user' department or from a central 'allied services' fund. Conventionally, the CSD favoured direct repayment and the Treasury the allied services approach. In this instance, however, the roles were reversed. As Douglas Allen pointedly reminded William Armstrong on the establishment of the CCA, the Treasury had only ceded expenditure control in August 1971 on the understanding that there would be a switch to direct 'repayment'.[128] The principal objective of computers, the Treasury contended, was to cut manpower costs and financial discipline (and thus economy) could only be assured if departments were obliged to pay for all initiatives out of anticipated savings. The CSD's counter-argument was that since hardware (for which the 'allied services' budget alone paid) typically amounted to no more than one-fifth of departmental expenditure on a new project, discipline was not in jeopardy. Moreover, in the interest of compatibility (and thus efficiency), CCA officials needed some residual power to persuade departments to follow its technical advice and – under covert political direction – purchase ICL machines. Otherwise they would enter into departmental negotiations naked. The CCA, in short, was caught in the middle of a battle between the Treasury's traditional definition of public expenditure control (that 'economy' demanded that all individual goods should be bought at the lowest possible cost) and the CSD's more relaxed approach (that 'efficiency' permitted the lowest price for a given project to be exceeded were that, for example, to ensure greater interdepartmental compatibility). The victor was ultimately the Treasury because once its budget was cash-limited, the CCA budget was no longer able to finance all initiatives it adjudged 'cost-effective'. Consequently, priority between projects – between, for example, the continuation of an existing service (by replacing an obsolete computer) and the improvement of another (by installing a new one) – had to be determined, often irrationally, on short-term grounds; and so it appeared logical to give departments full economic 'freedom'.

It was, however, shortage of staff which, in the words of the final classic policy overview (1978 *The Longer-Term Review*), gave 'rise to the greatest concern'.[129] At the higher levels this shortage prevented the CCA from giving a clear technical lead. In the mid-1970s, for example, it was so overstretched in fine-tuning ICL's new 2900 series that it was unable to provide informed advice on other innovations (such as those in micro-electronics). Rather than proving invaluable to other departments (and reconciling them to its authority), therefore, it appeared ineffectual and a captive of ICL. Within 'user' departments, there was a similar shortage of technical staff, estimated in 1978 at fifteen per cent rising, in some, to 50 per cent. This was accredited to poor pay and career development. In relation to the former, computing staff fell victim to both the attenuated post-Fulton restructuring of the Service and the crossfire between incomes policy and the National Pay Agreement (see Chapters 5.2.1 and 6.2.3 respectively). Pressure mounted to make them a distinct 'occupational group', so that their pay might be determined by 'fair comparison' with parallel workers in the private sector; but this was resisted on the Fultonian grounds that it would discourage their transfer into management – although, given the lack both of depth in their training and breadth in their experience, such transfers were a remote possibility. The problem was, again, not unique to the Service. There was a national shortage of, and general dissatisfaction amongst, trained computing staff. Nevertheless, it was a problem which – given the new emphasis on personnel management – it should have been uniquely able to solve. That it did not passed a telling verdict on the effectiveness of the post-Fulton reforms.[130]

The 'special case' of technical staff was promoted by staff associations throughout the 1970s; and rising disenchantment made them ready to be the shock troops in industrial disputes. By 1979, however, associations' focus significantly switched from those who were introducing new technology to those who were affected by it; and, given the Conservatives' increased emphasis on cutting expenditure and manpower, the NSS quickly sought to negotiate a formal agreement. 'I have' wrote its Secretary to the CSD

> to emphasise that the Staff Side favour a constructive approach to new technology: it is not our intention to be reactionary. Our aim is to ensure that the new technology will benefit our members, the quality of service to the public and the efficiency of the Civil Service.[131]

The NSS was undoubtedly sincere in the last two aims, but as relations with the Government grew more confrontational, it was the first that inevitably took precedence. The NSS's basic demand, which was accepted as reasonable by most management experts (including Rayner), was that there should be some tangible incentive for staff co-operation over radical changes to their working practices. At minimum, this meant that there would be no compulsory redundancy or reduction in earnings and working conditions. This the Government felt was unavoidable; but what it adjudged unacceptable was a further demand that the working week should be cut to 35 hours. At a stroke, all the financial or manpower savings – which, as the NSS had correctly divined, were its principal objective – would have been lost.

In practice, the stand-off was not so confrontational. In May 1980, for example, DHSS staff (against formal union advice) participated without objection in the introduction of Datalink, which enabled local offices to verify claimants' details overnight with the central Newcastle computer as opposed to over several days by post. The change, it was agreed, would improve the quality of both a service to the public and their own working lives. However, the Prime Minister, was not mollified. 'I should like to make clear in the House', she minuted on hearing the news, 'the very backward attitude the Civil Service takes to the introduction of new technology'.[132] Before the minute was circulated, her Private Secretary judiciously added 'unions' after 'Civil Service' – although, as has been seen, this was not wholly justified.

During the 1970s, therefore, the Service – as with gender and racial equality – lost the lead in technological innovation that it had enjoyed since the 1920s. In part this too was because the nature of the challenge changed, both technologically (with the advance from mainframe to micro-computers) and managerially (with, not least, rising union resistance). The principal cause, however, was again a failure of management. As the NSS had acknowledged, technological change promised increased efficiency, improved services and reduced office drudgery. The post-Fulton Service should have been ideally placed fully to realise this promise. The creation of the CSD had, for example, lifted the narrow emphasis on economy; technical expertise was concentrated in the CCA; and personnel management had been revolutionised. However, it failed to do so. The one mitigating factor was that, as the size of the technological challenge expanded and the Service contracted, greater reliance had to be placed on the private sector. Its record as a contractor was little – if at all – better.

9.7 Conclusion

Below the high politics of administrative reform, there was always the more mundane world of management. How effective, at least in the five areas selected, was management and what light does its record of action (or inaction) shed on attitudes towards, and the achievements of, post-Fulton reform? A principal, albeit rarely acknowledged, precondition for any judgement is an acknowledgement of the exceptional size and complexity of central government. As Plowden had recognised in the early 1960s, this made its professional management all the more important; but at the same time it casts doubt on the validity of comparisons with the private sector, as increasingly favoured after the late 1960s by modernisers of all persuasions. Private sector theories and practice had, after all, been developed for far smaller organisations and were heavily biased towards experience in the USA. Presuming some quantifiable measure of success (such as profit), they also made no allowance for public accountability, be it to Ministers (as *de facto* chief executives) or to Parliament (as the effective representative of shareholders). A clear distinction had been recognised after the First World War between management in the two sectors; and it had then been the public sector which established itself, at least formally, as the model employer and technological innovator.

Such a lead could arguably have been extended into the 1970s had a range of inquiries, initiated by William Armstrong, been fully followed through. These included the Operational Research inquiry into dispersal, the Kemp-Jones Committee on gender discrimination and the Atkinson Committee's 'blue skies' thinking on computers. Moreover, to sustain this lead and as demonstrated by the development of CAS and the consolidation of public pensions, there was an exceptional generation of officials for whom 'everything was achievable'.[133] The profusion of such talent, indeed provided the underlying logic for the employment of a department's own staff in the Rayner scrutinies after 1979.

To be fully effective, however, management requires above all a clear sense of direction and an equally clear organisational structure. Neither was forthcoming. Ministers either dissembled, as in dispersal or computer procurement policy, or, as in pensions policy, bent to the changing public mood. As for organisational structure, Fulton provided no panacea. At the very time a powerful antidote was needed to the Service's ingrained federalism, the centre of government was weakened by the separation of the CSD from the Treasury (and thus the consideration of efficiency from economy). Moreover, despite its emphasis on accountable management which so excited later reformers, Fulton simultaneously discouraged such a reform by advocating the continuation of a career service, bound ever more closely by unified grading. Where was there scope for the greater flexibility over grading and pay that accountable management required? Senior officials themselves, however, were not entirely blameless for the lost lead. William Armstrong, as seen in Chapter 5, was no born manager; and this was further demonstrated by the debacle over the appointment of the first CSC Principal, his partial consideration of gender discrimination, and his failure to act decisively when a measure of Ministerial agreement existed for dispersal in 1973. His successors were equally culpable. They notoriously failed to adapt to rapidly changing outside circumstance, for example, both their attitude towards and their handling of 'indirect' discrimination and technology.

Any final judgement, however, must be relative. Was, for instance, contemporary management in academia, private industry or the trade unions any better? In particular, what was the record of the private sector in relation to dispersal (where re-location grants, to achieve a better balanced economy, were spurned), pensions (where effective cuts were made when need was at its greatest) and gender discrimination (where part-time work was typically embraced as a tax-avoidance measure)? Moreover, had Civil Service management further exceeded private practice (as in the more deferential interwar period) or acted with greater independence (as Fulton seemed to encourage), would not the backlash have been even greater than the one eventually unleashed? In short, incidents of management failure in the 1970s bore as much testimony to the constraints, inside and outside the Service, under which officials had to work as they did to either individual or collective weakness.

10
POLITICAL PRESSURES

10.1 Introduction

The greatest political challenge for the Civil Service between 1966 and 1981, as intimated in Chapter 6, was the collapse of consensus. This threatened both the relative continuity of policy and the respect for 'big government', upon which it had depended since the War. Its core values and character, however, were also threatened by two more specific political pressures: the rising demand for more 'open government' and the onset of what political scientists were later to term the 'hollowing out of the state'.[1] The former reflected decreasing deference and a consequent demand for the lifting of the secrecy under which public policy had traditionally been cloaked. In practice, it meant two potentially contradictory things: greater accountability of the Executive to Parliament and greater public participation in policy-making. Both, in any case, meant an effective transfer of power from Whitehall. The 'hollowing out of the state' involved a similar transfer of power, to either Brussels or Edinburgh. In addition, membership of the EEC (planned at length throughout the 1960s and finally achieved on 1 January 1973) raised fundamental questions about both the Service's national integrity and traditional working methods. So too did Scottish devolution (equally long-planned throughout the 1970s albeit ultimately frustrated by the narrow referendum 'defeat' of March 1979). The impact of each of these challenges will be examined in turn.

10.2 Open government

As with most 'modernisation' proposals, the motivation behind calls for 'open government' – and hence its objectives – were contradictory. At its most basic, motivation reflected the greater prurience and commercialism of the media – to which, significantly, the more able graduates were increasingly being drawn in preference to traditional vocations such as the Service's Administrative Class. Two more high-minded objectives, and thus the media's overt justification, were enhanced decision-making and 'participatory' democracy. On the one hand, outside experts would be better informed about – and thus better able to inform – government policy. On the other, the general public would be more widely consulted and thus become more understanding of both the decisions which affected them and the way in which they had been reached. 'The fuller the information', as the Fulton Report had concluded, 'the closer the links between government (both Ministers and civil servants) and the community; and the smaller the gap of frustration and misunderstanding between "them" and "us"'.[2]

Was such confidence justified? Typically, Fulton's conclusion rested on two false premises: Fabian optimism that there was a 'correct' technocratic solution to each problem and a flawed assessment of practice in Sweden. Equally typically, it acknowledged but then glossed over further complications. For example, were officials to explain policy more fully and consult more widely, would not their traditional anonymity and impartiality be compromised and questions raised about the nature of 'ministerial responsibility'? Moreover, Fulton accepted that a certain 'element of secrecy' was inevitable because 'it was difficult to see how on any other basis there can be mutual trust between colleagues and proper critical discussion of different hypotheses'. Precisely how far, therefore, was it legitimate for Parliament – and the press – to probe? It was such unresolved questions that were to dog attempts throughout the 1970s to make Government more open – primarily through the reform of the Official Secrets Act but also through the sensationalist subplot of the Crossman diaries and, more generally, through the Government's relationship with the press.

Each will be examined; but each raises the same basic question. Whose interest did secrecy predominantly serve? Comforting and convenient though it may have been for officials (as acknowledged, for example, by Weber) were they the principal beneficiaries – or simply the fall guys for those who were? In 1969 Trend identified the key issue with characteristic clarity. 'Much of the enthusiasm for what you might call "more public decision-making"', he wrote to William Armstrong, was based

> on an assumption that decisions are, or should be, taken on merits i.e. on the basis of an objective assessment of the pros and cons in so far as these can be accurately measured ... In fact ... a Government confronted with a difficult decision starts by obtaining the best assessment of this kind that it can but is often compelled thereafter to take into account other factors which are not quantifiable and are not really capable of specific analysis at all – questions of political timing, and of probable reactions of public opinion both at home and abroad, of Parliamentary tactics and so forth. This is not in the least discreditable – indeed, it is only by taking factors of this kind into account that a Parliamentary democracy can work at all. But it is never easy, and it may sometimes be impossible, for a Government to expose them to the public view.[3]

Hence the earlier preference, articulated particularly by Bridges, for describing how Government should – rather than actually did – work. In short, greater openness principally threatened to embarrass Ministers not officials and, more seriously still, to disillusion the public with the 'system'.

10.2.1 Reforming the Official Secrets Act

The origins of the persistent attempts to reform Section 2 of the Official Secrets Act (OSA) throughout the 1970s lay in two disparate concerns. The first, voiced by Fulton, was the need to maximise the *authorised* disclosure of information. It was (as will be seen) finally satisfied, in principle at least, by a 'real change of policy' in July 1977, heralded by the so-called Croham directive. The second, rather more urgent concern was the need to minimise the *unauthorised* disclosure of information. The Official Secrets Act had supposedly performed this function since 1899; but it had so lost public and even judicial support that it proved impossible either to prosecute Peter Jay in 1967 (for his retrospective revelations in *The Times* about the planning of devaluation) or to convict Jonathan Aitken in 1970 (for the disclosure in the *Sunday Telegraph* of a secret report on the Nigerian civil war).[4] A review was duly commissioned under Lord Franks which recommended in 1972 that, to ensure the effective prosecution of any disclosure that might genuinely prejudice national security, the range of 'classified' information covered by the OSA should be greatly reduced. Two decades of agonised debate then followed as successive Governments sought to enact so seemingly simple a recommendation, with the offending Section 2 of the OSA only being reformed in 1989.

The intensity of political agonising throughout the 1970s suggests that something more fundamental than the two overt concerns was at stake. This was true both outside and within Government. Outside, for example, the press and public alike were convinced that secrecy was an artifice employed by officials deliberately to disguise both their inefficiency and influence. 'Modernising' reformers and lawyers in the mid-1960s had been particularly convinced of this; and in the mid-1970s, as will be seen, the role of the then Cabinet Secretary (Sir John Hunt) in the attempted 'suppression' of the Crossman *Diaries* led to much obloquy being heaped on the 'secret' Service.[5] Such attacks, in turn, masked an even more fundamental conflict between the concepts of 'open' and 'closed' government. In a democracy, it was demanded, by what authority did Government have the 'right' to conceal information? Had not the electorate a positive 'right to know'? Freedom of Information Acts in other countries, such as the USA and Sweden, had allegedly resolved this conflict in favour of openness; and, with the commitment in their Party's October 1974 manifesto 'to put the burden on public authorities to justify withholding information', Labour Ministers appeared about to follow suit.[6] Instead there was endless prevarication which, by the late 1970s, raised the conflict to almost theological proportions and FOI campaigners into moral crusaders.

Within Whitehall, unsurprisingly, the demand for 'open government' was viewed somewhat differently. One senior Permanent Secretary (Sir Douglas Haddow) dismissed the professed ambition to enhance policy-making as little more than a 'desire by by-standers to jog the arm of the surgeon engaged in an operation'.[7] Likewise, the media's demand for decreased anonymity was disparaged as a cynical attempt to identify and exploit conflicts between Ministers and officials (and thereby make headlines and money) rather than a serious attempt publicly to debate the policy (and thereby improve decision-making). Such defensiveness masked a fundamental constitutional issue, once again instantly identified by Trend. There were, he argued, 'really only two basic "philosophies" of the conduct of public affairs', with 'no very logical or defensible half-way house' between them. A choice had thus to be made between:

(a) The concept ... that the public service is a self-contained and largely self-sufficient profession in its own right, which, for constitutional reasons, requires its members to remain virtually anonymous, withholds its processes of working from public inspection and leaves wholly to Ministers the defence of its actions, together with such credit or blame as may result from them
(b) The concept of a more 'open' profession, whose members ... would be known to the public in their own persons and would be regarded as eligible to receive praise or to incur blame ... on the basis of a more generous disclosure of the relevant information than is permitted at present.[8]

To endorse the latter would be to swim with the tide, but were modernisers – let alone politicians – ready to accept the consequent reduction in both ministerial accountability to Parliament (and thus Parliamentary democracy) and the perceived impartiality of officials (and thus their ability seamlessly to serve Governments of different political persuasions)? In short, had the campaigners fully seen beyond their own short-term interests? 'Closed' government had its virtues.

Of the two original concerns, the maximisation of authorised disclosure (as sought by Fulton) was the less controversial. Accordingly it enjoyed the most immediate response and ultimately some satisfaction with, as has been noted, the issuing of the Croham directive in 1977. In the past, the then Head of the Civil Service (Sir Douglas Allen) pronounced, it had

> normally been assumed that background material relating to policy studies and reports would not be published unless the responsible Minister or Ministers decided otherwise. Henceforth the working assumption should be that such material will be published unless they decide that they should not be.[9]

Initially Wilson, as Prime Minister, had discouraged William Armstrong from responding instantly to Fulton's recommendation; but his sense of urgency was transformed in January 1969 by Opposition calls for the reform of the OSA. Armstrong duly entered detailed (and highly revealing) consultations with his colleagues, from which emerged the proposal for a public inquiry. The Cabinet, however, rejected this proposal and instead sanctioned the publication of a white paper, *Information and the Public Interest* (Cmnd 4089) which, to reformers' disbelief, lauded the 'increasing liberal attitudes' towards disclosure and deliberately evaded the issue of OSA. It has since been dismissed as 'truly feeble'.[10]

The incoming Conservative Government, with its manifesto pledges to promote 'honest and open' government and eliminate 'unnecessary secrecy', promised much and started well. A major justification, for example, for its radical reorganisation of central government was better government through fuller public consultation.[11] In addition to commissioning the Franks Report, it also oversaw the revision of Estacode to provide officials with clearer guidance through the minefield of competing public, media, judicial and ministerial expectation. Thereafter, however, reform stalled; and progress had to await the succeeding Labour Government in which the junior CSD minister (Robert Sheldon) was not only a former member of the Fulton Committee but also the author of a recent Fabian tract denouncing officials as the principal advocates and beneficiaries of secrecy.[12] One of his foremost demands was greater openness in public appointments; and this, albeit largely on officials' initiative, was immediately met by the establishment within CSD of the Public Appointments Unit (PAU).[13] PAU, together with the Croham directive, was the major formal victory over secretiveness in the 1970s.

Relatively insignificant though this struggle for this restricted concept of 'openness' may have been in itself, it was nevertheless highly significant for two broader reasons. First it revealed senior officials' genuine belief in their 'increasing liberalism' and thus their initial incomprehension of escalating public demands. After all, Armstrong himself had long been a proponent and exponent of openness, and had pioneered the concept of 'green papers' to encourage public discussion of policy decisions before they were taken.[14] He and his colleagues could also point to an explosion in public consultation and information throughout the 1960s. In economic policy, for example, there had not only been the creation of the National Economic Development Council and Office but also extensive publication of economic forecasts and public expenditure projections. The press, public, academia and specialists alike had, so officials believed, therefore been sated with – rather than starved of – information. Such a conviction is revealing because it betrayed an insensitivity to the fundamental issue of power which was increasingly fuelling modernisers' demands: they wanted an active 'right to know', not the passive right to be informed.

Second, the battle over increased authorised disclosure revealed the relative strength of the political and administrative impediments to reform. Despite Sheldon's assumptions, it was patently Wilson and not Armstrong who discouraged a swifter response to Fulton's initial recommendation. It was then the Cabinet which rejected official advice to hold a public inquiry. The situation was similar under the Conservatives, as illustrated in 1971 by a spat between Heath and William Armstrong over the redrafting of Estacode. In it, Armstrong wanted to define 'open government' as 'the publication under *general* or specific Ministerial authority of information about administrative processes and factual or other considerations involved in Government policies'. This was amended and expanded by No. 10 to

> (1) the fullest possible exposition to Parliament and to the public of the reasons for Government policies and decisions *when* those policies and decisions have been formulated and are announced;
> (2) creating a better public understanding about the way in which the processes of government work and about the factual or technical background to Government policies and decisions.[15]

The differences might appear trivial. They were not. Armstrong, in defence of official impartiality, was seeking to establish the principle that anything a Civil Servant might (or might not) say enjoyed the full authority of Ministers. Heath deliberately evaded this constitutional nicety; but otherwise he upheld the doctrine of Ministerial responsibility by denying officials any opportunity to pre-empt Ministerial decisions (which was implicit in the call for increased public consultation and reduced official anonymity). The evolution of PAU told a similar tale of political intransigence. Bernard Donoughue (no admirer, as has been seen, of the Service) was driven to despair in 1978 by the blocking of attempts further to democratise it. The truth, he admitted, was that:

> the Civil Service is actually taking a good and radical line, supported by ... the right and by Tony Benn ... from the left. The opposition is from the soggy middle ... and the conservative right (Shore). Ironically, Peter wrote a book on 'open government'. He doesn't practise it. Any hope of really democratising the patronage system has been torpedoed – by ministers, not by civil servants.[16]

By the mid-1970s, however, the second of the original concerns in relation to openness (the minimisation of unauthorised disclosure) had become predominant. The Official Secrets Act had been regularly extended since 1889 (particularly in 1911 and 1920) so that by the 1960s, in effect, no official could disclose any information acquired whilst on duty and – perhaps more importantly for the press – no-one could receive such information without risking criminal prosecution. As the head of the Security Service, somewhat understating the case, informed the Franks Committee: 'it is an official secret if it is in an official file'. This 'catch all' nature of the Act discredited it amongst the public and, increasingly, among the judiciary so that the Attorney-General became ever more reluctant to prosecute.[17] This had three important consequences. First, there was in effect no legal protection against the disclosure of information, even when it genuinely endangered 'the national interest'. Second, the non-use of the Act brought the law as a whole into disrepute. Finally, there was a mounting sense of injustice because, whilst junior officials continued to be prosecuted, more senior ones were assumed (in Franks' terminology) to have an 'implicit authorisation' to 'leak' and, with increasing abandon under the 1964–70 Labour Government, Ministers did so.[18] Hence the OSA urgently required reform for its own sake, regardless of any 'psychological' predisposition to secrecy it allegedly encouraged in Whitehall.

The Franks Committee, as has been noted, recommended a major reduction in the range of information for which disclosure should be a criminal offence. Other 'sensitive' material, it suggested, could be more lightly and effectively protected by internal disciplinary measures and a new statutory offence of disclosing (and, within reason, receiving) unauthorised material for private gain. It was thus essentially a conservative report, endorsing Government's implicit right to withhold information and denying modernisers' demand for an active 'right to know'. Such a stance was hardly surprising, given the degree of collusion between the Committee and Whitehall. As soon as the Committee was appointed, for example, an official working party had been formed 'to coordinate departmental evidence ... and keep a general oversight of the operation as a whole'.[19] The Committee's secretary (A.D. Gordon-Brown) thereafter maintained regular contact with senior officials, advising them on the nature of their evidence and the Committee's evolving ideas. Finally, Franks himself (with appropriate frankness) discussed the principles on which the report was to be based with senior officials – classically on 15 January 1972 when he met William Armstrong in Oxford for a 'wholly private talk, not as between the Chairman of the Committee and the Head of the Civil Service but between two individuals with an interest in and an experience of the subject'. What was really surprising, therefore, was not how far the Report (finally published in September 1972) mirrored official opinion but how far it diverged from what officials regarded as practical. It was these divergences that laid the basis for a further decade of agonising.

Franks, for instance, sought essentially to restrict the application of criminal sanctions to the disclosure of information in three traditional areas where there was an acknowledged threat to national security: defence and internal security; foreign relations; and currency and the reserves. Even within these three areas, moreover, only information classified as 'secret' or above (some 45 per cent of the total) should be covered. In addition, and regardless of classification, information in three further categories should be protected: that relating to law and order; that given to the Government in confidence; and the records of Cabinet and ministerial Cabinet Committees. The latter mirrored officials' desire to protect not only 'national security' in the traditional sense but also 'good government' (which entailed the confidentiality of discussions between, and official advice to, Ministers). Officials accepted the sincerity behind these recommendations but nevertheless condemned them as being, in practice, both arbitrary and illogical. In economic policy, for example, only currency and the reserves were to be covered. Other policy areas, which the Treasury had asked to be covered by criminal sanction (such as the budget, fiscal changes and bank rate), were to be protected solely by internal discipline and the new law against private gain. 'Much of the Franks Report', exploded Sir Douglas Allen as head of the Treasury, is 'absolute nonsense. I cannot treat seriously a number of recommendations which seem to regard Ambassador's chit chat as requiring the protection of criminal sanctions whereas the budget secrets do not'.[20] Likewise, Trend was concerned at the 'illogical' protection of Ministerial Cabinet Committees but not their shadow Official Committees, which typically drafted Cabinet memoranda and were far more revealing of departmental – and Ministerial – differences.[21] The use of classification to restrict the scope of criminal liability, especially if classification were to be 'overseen' by an outside committee (as Franks suggested), was also regarded as impractical. An internal inquiry, headed by a former Head of the Civil Service (Sir Lawrence Helsby), had sought to clarify classification between 1968 and 1970 but had concluded that it was impossible. Too many issues were interdependent and too many – as well as too many minor foreign dignitaries – had a tendency to leap from obscurity to prominence.

Such administrative reservations (together with the gathering economic and political crisis) halted the enactment of amending legislation under Heath. The baton then passed to Labour first under Wilson in 1974 (when Roy Jenkins was Home Secretary) and then under Callaghan in 1976 (who earlier, as Foreign Secretary had been highly resistant to reform). Jenkins was the one Minister to remain mindful of the dual objectives of reform – a reduction in the scope of the OSA and an active commitment to greater disclosure – and returned from a study visit to the USA determined to be more liberal than Franks. 'Substantially fewer' areas (including foreign affairs, economic policy and Cabinet discussions) should be subject to criminal sanctions, with greater reliance placed on either the civil law or internal Service discipline to ensure any necessary confidentiality. His proposals were remitted to an *ad hoc* Cabinet Committee (MISC 89) but found less than universal support.[22] Then during the first decisive months of Callaghan's premiership, a new Official Information Bill – balancing greater liberalism in some areas (such as economic policy) with increased restriction in others (such as defence and intelligence) – was finally drafted and largely accepted by both the reconstructed Cabinet Committee (GEN 29) and Cabinet itself.[23] Further progress, however, was stalled by the IMF crisis; and all that ultimately materialised was a white paper, *Reform of Section 2 of the Official Secrets Act* (Cmnd 7285), in July 1978, which was even more 'truly feeble' than its 1969 counterpart. Yet again it promised – but made no firm commitment to – greater liberalisation.

Why was the OSA never reformed? In addition to their detailed reservations on Franks, officials had traditionally opposed reform because – in the absence of other effective sanctions – the Act was regarded as the 'psychological anchor' which ensured the integrity of officials at all levels. As Trend somewhat revealingly confided to Armstrong, it acted 'like a cane in the best type of orthodox school – i.e. it is not used very often but the knowledge that it is there has a remarkably stabilising effect'.[24] However, after Franks, this argument was used with decreasing confidence. As one group of Treasury officials, for example, conceded as early as 1973: 'if Ministers decide that we should legislate for no more protection of sensitive economic information than Franks has given us, then we can no doubt manage'. Even more remarkably, in July 1976 Allen (by now Head of the Civil Service) did a complete *volte face*, actively dismissing administrative quibbles from the Home Office, FCO and MOD, and advising Callaghan that Franks 'represented the best compromise available' and so should be accepted in full. Over the next two years 'departmental rats' (in Hunt's inimitable phrase) may have continued 'to nibble away' at the draft Official Information Bill, but clearly the administrative door had been left ajar for its enactment.[25] Did the political will exist to push it fully open? Equally clearly, it did not. When presented with Jenkins' proposals in 1975, for example, Wilson had declared himself 'not in a hurry' and had muddied the water by suggesting a 'press deal' in which greater liberalism in relation not just to the OSA but also contempt and defamation (which had also been the subjects of public inquiries) was to be traded for a stronger law on privacy (itself the subject of the 1972 Younger inquiry).[26] MISC 89 duly took its lead from him and continued, unlike Allen, to seek modifications to Franks. So too did its successor (GEN 29), once it was certain that Callaghan's brief flirtation with liberalism had ended and that he had reverted to type. 'I am a hardliner on this', he responded to Hunt's suggestion in January 1978 that, on so seemingly small an issue as the existence of Cabinet Committees, secrecy might be lifted, 'No official disclosure'.[27] In short, the supposition is wrong that 'until 1979, the mandarins were allowed by the politicians to set the agenda'. The OSA survived because of Ministerial not 'Whitehall obscurantism'.[28]

Administrative and political minds did meet, however, on the final – and arguably most fundamental – issue implicit in the demand for reform: the public's 'right to know'. The issue had first been examined seriously by officials in 1976 and thereafter started to dominate political debate. By July 1978, there were two particular schemes for establishing a statutory 'right of access'. The first was advanced by the Labour Party's NEC (and adopted by the Party conference in October) and the second by the Liberal Party (which informed a private member's bill, introduced to Parliament by Clement Freud in January 1979 and awaiting its third reading in April when Parliament was dissolved).[29] Officials and Ministers, however, favoured a third option advanced by the legal pressure group, Justice (which had initiated the campaign for greater openness in the mid-1960s). It advocated a code of practice (clearly identifying the documents still covered by the OSA) which would be monitored by the ombudsman rather than the courts. This, it was acknowledged, would constitute an 'irreversible shift in power' from Government's right to withhold information to the public's right to attain it. Moreover, were the withholding of a document to be challenged, the ombudsman would effectively be placed in judgement over a ministerial decision (and not just maladministration). This too would set a constitutional precedent (see Chapter 10.3.1). The key point, however, was that the exercise of Ministerial discretion would remain outside the jurisdiction of the courts and thus Ministers would remain ultimately answerable to Parliament. Preserved also would be what Ian Bancroft (Allen's successor as Head of the Civil Service) termed the 'first concern' of officials: the continuing confidentiality of their advice.[30]

Officials also based their case against the public's 'right to know' on practicality. At a time of cash limits and capped manpower, they argued, it would be extremely expensive and labour-intensive to turn 'the government filing system into a public library' and then prepare all documents for release. The contrasting experience of Scandinavia and the USA also demonstrated the advantages of evolution over revolution. In the former, where Government had typically kept ahead of public opinion, both applications for access and litigation were low – in stark contrast to the USA, where Government had suddenly capitulated to public demand. To follow the USA would thus be costly, in terms of money and time, as well as adversely affecting the speed, and thus the efficiency, with which Government could work. Finally, officials argued, even were such concessions made, would public demand abate? Did not the campaigners, regardless of what was typically exempted by corresponding legislation abroad, want 'redder meat' in the shape of internal working papers? 'The Peter Hennessys of this world', as one of Callaghan's Private Secretaries (Nigel Wicks) intemperately noted, 'are particularly interested in knowing about the internal deliberations of Government and Government Departments. It seems that they want Government to operate in a goldfish bowl so that they can peer in, point to differences between Ministers and conflicts between officials and Ministers'.[31] Could their appetites ever be sated?

However determined they were to resist such intrusion, officials nevertheless recognised the seemingly relentless 'political tide running in favour of a statutory right of access'. Accordingly in September 1978, Ken Stowe (Callaghan's Principal Private Secretary,) produced a blueprint for a 'radical, constructive government', which duly inspired an in-depth official reappraisal of constitutional conventions and international precedent. Then John Hunt (as Cabinet Secretary) repeatedly urged Callaghan after Christmas to take the chair of GEN 29, the Cabinet Committee still responsible for policy but which had descended into chaos.[32] This he declined to do, not least because he was preoccupied by the 'winter of discontent'. 'At the moment', Stowe had written in his blueprint, 'the Civil Service is playing for time . . . not out of a sense of obstruction, but simply because it does not see where the Government wants to go'. This lack of political direction prevailed.

Successive attempts to reform the OSA and otherwise to enhance openness in Government, therefore, provided – despite stiff competition – one of the least heroic episodes in the attempt to promote modernisation. By 1978, it was readily admitted, the situation had become 'very soggy'. The Government was

> adopting a defensive posture on the two related fronts of official secrets and openness: on secrets its White Paper offers something less than Franks suggested and rejects the complete reversal of policy which is implicit in a freedom of information act. The current policy on openness, as set out in Sir Douglas Allen's letter of 6 July 1977, is weak in that it embodies no clear-cut principles and lays the present, and all future, governments open to perpetual sniping . . . as to whether or not the policy of disclosure is being honourably fulfilled.[33]

In short, neither Ministers nor senior officials had fully come to terms with the decline in deference, which was fuelling the demand for a public right of access to Government-held material – or at least the right of appeal against non-disclosure. Could swifter action have cauterised such demands? Had, for example, Allen's eventual acceptance of Franks in 1976 and of the 'presumption to disclose' in 1977 been conceded earlier, would the irritation, disillusion and distrust underpinning the escalation of the FOI campaign have been restricted to an implacable minority? The likelihood is not. Such a scenario discounts the international nature of the FOI campaign and the peculiar militancy of Britain in the 1970s. It also discounts the lasting impact of the suspicions of the Service sown by modernisers in the 1960s, the damage wrought to the concept of 'good government' by constant 'leaks' after 1964, and the refusal of the judiciary both to convict under the OSA and to halt publication of Ministerial memoirs. Hence the particular significance of the Crossman *Diaries*.

10.2.2. The Crossman Diaries

The Crossman *Diaries* in themselves are of little intrinsic historical value. Although one of Wilson's more powerful political allies, Richard Crossman neither held any of the major offices of state nor was responsible for any 'landmark' legislation. Moreover, despite his self-professed ambition to write a major book fulfilling 'the functions of Bagehot's *English Constitution* a hundred years ago by disclosing the secret operations of government', he lacked any detailed understanding of how Government – and in particular Whitehall – worked.[34] What was of historical significance, however, was their actual publication in 1975. First, by appearing to document Government failure and the excesses of bureaucratic power, they enhanced the case for modernisation. Second, they irremediably broke the bond of trust between Ministers and officials which had long underpinned the concept of 'good government', so revered by Trend. That bond had assumed an 'obligation of honour' between gentlemen and Crossman, even on his own admission, was no gentleman. Finally, their serialisation in *The Sunday Times* and the later refusal of the Lord Chief Justice to grant an injunction against publication testify to the death of deference, on which prevailing notions of constitutional propriety depended.

The 'obligation of honour', finally destroyed by the *Diaries*, had been under challenge for some time. A succession of Ministerial memoirs since the 1940s (including those of Churchill and Lord Avon) had, for example, breached Cabinet confidentiality; and Conservative Cabinets in 1961 and 1963 had been urged unavailingly to exercise self-restraint. This predated the more widely publicised clash between known diarists and lawyers in the 1967 Labour Cabinet, which frustrated the Lord Chancellor's wish that Ministers should submit manuscripts to the Cabinet Secretary and accept all recommended excisions. By the mid-1960s, however, Whitehall itself was more perturbed by breaches of trust by officials. There was, once again, a long tradition of 'mandarin' memoirs (including those of P.J. Grigg and Tom Jones, published respectively in 1948 and 1954); but in 1965 Attlee had been particularly offended by the memoirs of a former Cabinet Office official (Sir George Mallaby's *From My Level*) of which much play had been made in *The Sunday Times*. It was intolerable, agreed Helsby (then Head of the Civil Service): 'ministers should have full confidence that they can speak their minds plainly in front of their official advisers without any fear that unguarded remarks may be stored up for publication'.[35] Estacode was belatedly revised in 1971; but, by that time, Labour had been defeated and the boot was firmly on the other foot, with many former Ministers (led by Crossman) queuing up to publish accounts of their time in Government.

Crossman himself, when pressed in 1971, expressed a disinclination to defer to the Cabinet Secretary; but, a month after his death in April 1974, the draft first volume of his *Diaries* was submitted for approval. Attempts to prevent its publication were immediately made on the grounds that it would 'corrupt and discredit public life', not least by destroying 'the mutual confidence among ministers and between ministers and civil servants' on which 'the efficacy and the authority of government' depended.[36] There was also the 'subsidiary' issue of the criticism of individual officials who, should they so wish, were now less able to defend themselves because of the revised Estacode. An extra frisson was added by the re-election of a Labour Government in May 1974 and the sale to *The Sunday Times* of serialisation rights by Crossman's executors (who included the Cabinet Minister, Michael Foot). To maximise Government embarrassment and thus sales, *The Sunday Times* initially scheduled the start of serialisation just before the October election. In the event, however, it was delayed until January 1975 when John Hunt (as Cabinet Secretary) went out of his way to interpret as liberally as possible existing conventions and the four 'parameters' agreed with Crossman's executors. As a result, a compromise was reached and a major confrontation avoided. As Hunt consequently informed Wilson, *The Sunday Times* had 'got away with publishing material of a kind which has not been published hitherto, while we have stopped them just short of publishing material which would have forced the Attorney General to apply for an injunction'.[37]

Just such an injunction, however, was taken out in June 1975 to prevent publication in book form of the full manuscript; and then, confounding all legal expectation, the Lord Chief Justice (Lord Widgery) ruled in October that, since no breach of collective responsibility was threatened, publication might proceed. Given the submission for approval of a second volume in December, damage limitation was urgently (and, for some, too urgently) sought. In anticipation of such a need, the Radcliffe Committee on Ministerial Memoirs had been appointed even before the issuing of the injunction; and it duly recommended in January 1976 that, whilst they could not be legally bound, each Minister should sign an undertaking – or at least acknowledge an obligation – not to publish any memoirs for 15 years.[38] Moreover, the Prime Minister's decision should be accepted as final on matters of 'national security and the preservation of international relations', whilst 'careful attention' should be paid to the Cabinet Secretary's views on breaches of confidentiality. Wilson urged all Ministers to sign the relevant undertaking but two (Foot and Benn) refused and later Callaghan (as Wilson's successor) resigned himself to the fact that, given the refusal of Crossman's executors to apply its recommendations to the second volume, Radcliffe was a 'dead letter'. 'Of course', he concluded, 'Crossman had neither sense of obligation nor honour and should never have been in Cabinet. Clem Attlee told me once that he would never include him – and no more would I . . . The literary Executors should have regard to the new rule . . . But it won't do any good for they sniff scandal, character assassination and profit – an irresistible combination'.[39]

What did this furore signify for the Service's reputation? It certainly heaped public obloquy on officials, and especially the Cabinet Secretary. During the stalling of the serialisation after the October 1974 election, for example, even so distinguished a political commentator as Nora Beloff accused officials of being the 'real barrier to publication'; and one local Labour Party went so far as to pass a resolution that:

> The Party is dismayed to hear that Cabinet Civil Servants have been given authority to censor parts of Dick Crossman's diaries . . . A Labour Government should have more confidence in the judgement of the late author, a distinguished party member, than in the judgement of permanent members of the state apparatus.

Its members, like many others, may have been influenced by an inflammatory article in the *New Statesman* by the far from disinterested Anthony Howard (a personal friend and admirer of Crossman and later his authorised biographer). 'The Secretary to the Cabinet', Howard asserted somewhat tendentiously, 'may be the mandarin of mandarins, but under a democratic system that cannot mean that he is entitled to set himself up in business as a self-appointed Platonic Guardian, still less that he should be encouraged to regard the Attorney General as his personal errand boy'.[40] Then, despite his less than convincing performance at the trial in July 1975 (during which he was ridiculed as 'a man in a fog putting up a fence on marshy ground'), Hunt was nevertheless portrayed as a man of menace. He represented, so Bernard Donoughue confided to *his* diary, 'what frightens so many people – the faceless power of bureaucracy, overpaid and unaccountable'.[41] This perceived combination of bureaucratic incompetence and power further confirmed modernisers' stereotypes.

Were such stereotypes, however, justified? The fundamental case against Crossman was based on the same concept of 'good government' that Trend had used to defend the OSA on the grounds that it genuinely served Ministers' and, more importantly, the public interest. 'Ministers', reiterated Hunt in 1975,'will not feel free to discuss matters privately in Cabinet or Cabinet Committee, and to surrender their own preferences to the achievement of a common view, nor can they be expected to abide by a common decision, if they know that the stand they have taken and the points they have surrendered are to become public knowledge prematurely'. Thus the very 'efficacy and authority' of Government was at stake. Confidentiality of official advice was likewise sought for this – and only this – reason. As was explained to Crossman's literary executors, 'the mutual trust which needs to exists between ... Ministers and their senior advisers' was 'an essential feature of the doctrine of collective responsibility which is at the centre of our system of government'.[42] This was because officials had not just to speak truth unto power (albeit, in modernisers' judgement, a somewhat truncated 'truth') but also to tailor arguments to the needs of specific Ministers and circumstances. Were there an ever-present threat of premature disclosure, such deals and compromises – as in the case of Cabinet – would become harder to attain.

Simultaneously, despite much public innuendo, officials were adamant that no general criticism of the Service should ever provide grounds for censorship; and, after an initial flurry of concern, criticism of individual officials was also downgraded to a 'subsidiary' issue. On first sight of the initial *Diary*, Ian Bancroft had exploded, complaining to William Armstrong, that:

> what is in issue here is both a tradition of mutual trust and mere good manners. It seems to me to be importing a new element into our affairs for a Minister to take advantage of a quite special relationship ... to publish subjective opinions about [named officials'] ability, appearance and manner as if he were a buttonholing novelist and they were fictional characters. They exist in real life with families, colleagues and a degree of self esteem to live with. ... A Civil Service which is fraying at the edges would regard the publication of the diary as a huge, perhaps irreparable breach in the compact which governs relations between Ministers and officials. Nothing would be the same again.[43]

Officials, he reminded Armstrong, had 'a long memory, a ready pen and the ability to wound in return' and some, despite the revised Estacode, would undoubtedly retaliate in retirement. Such concerns, however, were never permitted to predominate – not when Lord Goodman (acting rather ambivalently for Crossman's executors) questioned in September 1974 the Attorney-General's ruling that no injunction based solely 'on the ground that the diary was scurrilous or embarrassing or critical of civil servants' would succeed. 'There were', retorted Goodman, 'established disciplinary arrangements for dealing with Civil Servants whose conduct failed to give satisfaction and it would be an unwarrantable extension of those arrangements if a Civil Servant's career could be blighted by adverse comments published in biographies or diaries'. The Attorney-General himself appeared to swing to this view, when considering an appeal against the Widgery judgment; but senior officials remained adamant that 'it would be most undesirable to lodge an appeal which was confined to these points'.[44]

Were such views sincerely held, or did they represent a pragmatic surrender of principle by officials to legal and public opinion? Such a question is critical because, as with the belated acceptance of Franks in 1976 and of the presumption to disclose in 1977, it raises the possibility that Government could have been spared much of the disruption and disrepute it later suffered by earlier and bolder administrative action. For instance, the unenforceability of constraints on

Ministerial memoirs had long been recognised, but could not a formula similar to Radcliffe's have been devised earlier? Moreover, could not Crossman's executors (who included his widow and Michael Foot) have been immediately dissuaded from publication given the damage that both Crossman's own reputation and the Labour Party was likely to sustain? Could not more have been made of Crossman's own, earlier insistence that his diary 'was the basis for a serious book on the inside view of politics, and was not designed as a sensational effort to cash in on topicality'?[45] Finally, would not have speedier legal action in 1974 have prevented the serialisation of extracts, which made it all the harder for the Lord Chief Justice to ban publication of the full text? The Government had a strong case and would appear to have thrown it away.

Were this true, however, did the principal culpability lie with Ministers or officials? There had, after all, been three attempts in the 1960s to persuade Conservative as well as Labour Cabinets legally to constrain Ministers' memoirs. Each had failed. Political prevarication continued into the 1970s, particularly under Wilson (who needed to court the press both during the October 1974 election campaign and to combat inflation thereafter). Personally, he was also in a very awkward position. As an inveterate 'leaker' himself, he had contributed considerably to the erosion of the concept of 'honourable conduct' and 'good government'. His own highly profitable book, *The Labour Government, 1964–70* (published in 1971) had broken many of the conventions and, as Crossman was determined to demonstrate, had on several occasions been somewhat 'economical with the truth'. Moreover, to many within his divided Party and to some in the Cabinet (such as Benn) his powers of patronage as Prime Minister represented a principal impediment to more 'democratic' policy-making and thus more open government.[46] Given such exigencies, the Civil Service as a whole – and the Cabinet Secretary in particular – became a convenient scapegoat for what was in essence political inaction.

There was, however, one issue on which neither the Service nor Hunt could hide behind Ministers. That was the wider relationship between the *Diaries* and open government. When, for instance, both Foot and Benn pleaded in January 1975 for a public debate before a final decision on Radcliffe, Hunt – suspecting a pretext for further delay – advised Wilson to overrule them. This was quite reasonable, but the justification he gave was not. A public debate, he argued, would not be 'helpful' because it 'would all too likely be conducted by vested interests, ill-informed, and directed largely towards the quite separate issue of openness in current government'.[47] At best, this reflected disillusion with the standard of debate during a decade of 'modernisation' and an unwillingness to engage further with it. At worst, it reflected a lack of awareness that deference, and a range of associated assumptions, had died. In what way was publication of the *Diaries* a 'quite separate issue' from 'openness in current government'? If by openness was meant maximum authorised disclosure, then perhaps publication was a distinct issue; but Crossman had always been far more ambitious. His *Diaries*, for better or for worse, were designed 'to dip below the surface, to forget legal fictions and constitutional forms and discover the real basis of our social system'.[48] The electorate, in short, had a positive right to know. In this respect, publication of the *Diaries* did mark a historic watershed after which the Head of the Civil Service (as has been seen) was prepared to concede Franks' revision of the OSA and a presumption, if not yet an obligation, to disclose.

10.2.3 The press

Throughout the period, the Service's leading protagonist – and antagonist – on open government was the media and, in particular, the press. It was actively courted by William Armstrong in the 1960s, and by senior officials thereafter, in order to better inform the public – especially on Whitehall's version of policy and events, which Ministers were often considered to have inadequately or inaccurately explained. Simultaneously, however, increasingly strict (and restrictive) guidance was issued to remind senior administrative staff that – in accordance with concepts of 'good government'– their role was 'to speak for ministers' and that they should therefore avoid 'anything in the nature of political or personal comment'. In particular, they should never place themselves under any obligation, speak unattributably, avoid any reference to contested policy advice and, above all, keep a full record of any meeting.[49] Such caution reflected increasing tension, caused by investigative journalism in its golden age and, in particular, by the OSA – under which reporters could never be certain whether the information they were receiving was authorised (and so publishable with impunity) or unauthorised (for receipt of which alone they might be gaoled). Indeed tension and press criticism of the Service grew so intense that in the mid-1960s and the late 1970s specialist units were established respectively in the Treasury and CSD to combat it.[50]

The tension within this constantly evolving relationship is perhaps best illustrated by the fate of the 'Whitehall correspondent', whom the national press started to appoint in the mid-1960s – largely in response to the Fabian analysis of where real power, and its perceived abuse, lay. The first such correspondent was Anthony Howard of *The Sunday Times* who, as has been seen, became a leading antagonist in relation to both Mallaby and Crossman. As such, he particularly angered Wilson and was denied any special facilities. Rather his editor was unambiguously reminded of prevailing policy. 'If a journalist', he was informed, 'sets out as a "Whitehall correspondent" to "reveal" where power really lies through getting at the personal views of civil servants, he will not get support.' If, on the contrary, 'he sets out as a financial, political, scientific or educational correspondent to seek advice from civil servants on the content, background and meaning of policies, he will find everyone anxious to help'.[51]

The second 'Whitehall correspondent', Peter Hennessy of *The Times*, was a different animal. By 1974, the times were also different. Hennessy's sympathetic reporting of the *Wider Issues* review had won him the confidence of the CSD and, following Franks and Labour's October 1974 manifesto, senior officials (including

Allen and Bancroft) were happy to support a projected series of articles on the post-Fulton Service 'as an example of "openness in government"'. However, Wilson (advised by Joe Haines and Robert Armstrong, respectively his Press Secretary and Principal Private Secretary) reapplied his veto. 'Good old open Government!' was the frustrated response from within the CSD, in which a junior Minister also expressed the fear that 'we might lose a friend and gain an enemy'.[52] A 'friend', however, Hennessy continued to be considered within Whitehall, not least because of the accuracy of his reporting in an era of escalating polemic. Then, in 1978, the tide turned with a vengeance with Bancroft (now Head of the Civil Service) seeking, under strong Prime Ministerial pressure, to reimpose constraints. At the height of the FOI campaign, Hennessy was adjudged to have caused 'considerable embarrassment' by enquiring too deeply into departmental responses (or non-responses) to the Croham directive. He had also, with good reason, exposed government prevarication over such 'liberal' measures as the 'democratisation' of PAU and the extension of Parliamentary Select Committees. Callaghan, with equally good reason, suspected Hennessy's sources. 'The Civil Service', he charged, 'has been very free and easy with the acceptance of hospitality. It should stop ... It is time former standards were restored'.[53] He also launched a series of leak inquiries with predictable results – or rather lack of results. Stalemate ensued, with Bancroft on the Prime Minister's express (but unattributable) instructions decreeing that no official should meet with any journalist except on official premises, with his personal permission and in the presence of a professionally trained Departmental Information Officer. Hence the vituperative nature, as has been seen, of later comments by Callaghan's Private Secretaries and their reversion to the charges initially levelled at Howard. The press, they argued, was at root interested in neither enhanced policy-making nor participatory democracy. Rather, driven by the need to maximise sales, it wished only to be 'privy' to private disputes amongst Ministers and between them and their advisers.[54]

By definition, relations between the Service and the press were ambivalent. They also went largely unrecorded. However, such evidence that does survive suggests that – as so often in relation to open government – a golden opportunity was missed. The appointment of 'Whitehall correspondents' reflected an exceptional public interest in, and concern about, the inner workings of Government. Yet both the mechanics of policy-making and the content of policy remained poorly explained. The fault may have been largely that of the press. It may also have been that of politicians – but given the symbiosis between Ministers and officials, central to the then prevailing concept of 'good government', is any distinction between the political and the administrative sustainable?

10.3 Parliament

An alternative, and more constitutional, route to open government was provided by Parliament. The Service was directly affected by the appointment in 1967 of a

Parliamentary Commissioner for Administration (better known as the ombudsman, after its 'distant Scandinavian relative') to whom MPs might refer alleged instances of maladministration.[55] A more regular means of public redress was thereby assured than the *ad hoc* tribunals appointed to investigate, for instance, the Crichel Down and Vehicle and General 'scandals'. The Service was less directly affected, in theory at least, by a second major reform designed to strengthen the Legislature against the Executive: the restructuring of Select Committees in 1966 and 1979. Nevertheless, since officials were to be the leading witnesses before such Committees, it raised questions about their anonymity and impartiality. Moreover, following the precedent long set by the Public Accounts Committee (PAC), the new Committees tended to be more interested in the administration than the principles of policy;[56] and after 1979 the PAC's staff (headed by the Comptroller and Auditor-General) was used to drive through management reform – a move that was to end with the establishment of the National Audit Office in 1983.

10.3.1 The ombudsman

The appointment of an ombudsman in 1967 was a symbol of declining deference, complementing the 1957 Franks Report on administrative tribunals (which had recommended their greater concentration on 'openness and impartiality' as opposed to administrative convenience) and the increasing animosity of the courts towards Government (epitomised by the 1968 Conway v Rimmer judgment that, in order to ensure a fair trial, it was the courts not Government which should determine whether a document could be withheld). An ombudsman had been first advocated by the legal pressure group, Justice, in 1961 (the Whyatt report), but it only became a practical proposition after its inclusion in Wilson's Stowmarket speech on Parliamentary reform in July 1964. Then it was championed in Labour's October manifesto as a means of 'humanising the whole administration of the state'.[57] Once in office, however, Labour became somewhat less enthusiastic (with Callaghan, amongst others, declining to sponsor even a modified proposal) and it was dismissed as an 'electoral hoax'.[58] Nevertheless the requisite legislation was guided through Parliament eventually by Crossman in 1966; and Sir Edmund Compton (the former Comptroller and Auditor General), who had been the ombudsman-designate since September 1966, finally started work in the following April.

'Few new government agencies', as one commentator has concluded, 'can have begun operations under a darker cloud of adverse publicity' and its reputation never really recovered.[59] This was despite some distinctive strengths (such as a close relationship with the Legislature, replicated in no other country, through a discrete Parliamentary Select Committee, to whose reports Government had to reply) and some notable victories. These included the winning of compensation for wartime servicemen imprisoned in the Sachsenhausen concentration camp (1967), the establishment of the Air Travel Reserve Fund (following the collapse of Court Line in 1974) and the extraction of refunds, with interest, for overpayments of tax from an extremely reluctant Inland Revenue in 1975. Nevertheless, it remained widely ridiculed as an 'ombudsmouse' and Justice's first ten-year review was entitled *Our Fettered Ombudsman*.[60]

It was subject to four main criticisms. First, the initial ombudsmen (Compton until 1971, Sir Alan Marre until 1976 and Sir Idwal Pugh until 1979) were all former Civil Servants, and their largely seconded 60-odd staff remained so. Given that the purpose of the post was to reassure the public about administrative standards within the Service, this – as admitted even in Whitehall – appeared somewhat perverse.[61] The other three criticisms concerned jurisdiction and accessibility. In relation to the former, the ombudsman's powers – in the terminology of the time – were 'advisory rather than decisive'. In other words, he was unable to order a remedy for proven maladministration; and Justice was particularly concerned that he remained supplementary to, rather than integrated with, the other means of redress provided by tribunals and the courts. This lack of 'joined-up' administration seriously weakened the right to redress (although, unlike the active 'right to know', it was never actually denied). In addition, the ombudsman was powerless to question the 'merit', as opposed to the maladminstration, of a particular policy (although a long-running battle was joined in 1968 to remedy this by establishing a right to examine 'bad decisions' and 'bad rules').[62] Finally there was the question of access. All complaints to the ombudsman had to be 'filtered' through MPs and so, unlike in Scandinavia, Australasia and Canada, there was no right of direct public access. This restriction had been introduced in anticipation of a flood of complaints and, more importantly, to maintain the 'dignity' of Parliament. Justice had expected this filter to be removed after five years, but it was not.[63] The second issue of accessibility concerned the ombudsman's investigatory powers. The 'Rolls Royce' nature of his investigations came to be internationally acclaimed. Attendance and the production of documents were compulsory and (unlike in New Zealand, for example) no complaint was simply referred to the relevant department for comment. In almost every case departmental files were examined; in approximately half officials were questioned; and in some 60 per cent, the complainants themselves were interviewed.[64] Owing to the principle of Cabinet confidentiality, however, Cabinet records could not be examined and so it remained impossible to determine whether collective Ministerial decision was the source (or indeed, through misinformation, the victim) of maladministration.

To what extent did these 'fettered ombudsmen' affect the Service and to what extent was it itself responsible for the fetters? Initially there was a fear (ironically expressed most forcefully by Compton) that the initiative might become an 'anti-civil service' body beholden to MPs; and so departments were immediately assured that, as with the investigations of the Comptroller and Auditor General, they would have the right to comment before both an investigation was launched and a report published. Later, individual departments (such as the Inland Revenue) were undoubtedly inconvenienced; and by 1974 sufficient 'concern' was being expressed over the ombudsman's apparent determination to 'substitute his decisions for those of government' to warrant discussion by Permanent Secretaries at Sunningdale.[65] Officials within the central departments, however, were relaxed – arguably because, with few executive responsibilities, they had little to fear. Admittedly they initially agreed that the ombudsman should be a current civil servant; but this was largely because, like the Comptroller and Auditor General, it was a 'supernumerary' post, which provided an ideal solution to problems of 'succession planning' when senior posts within the 'regular' Service were either unavailable or deemed inappropriate. For example, when considering Compton's successor in 1970, William Armstrong expressed a reluctance 'to deprive the Executive of the services of one of our better Permanent Secretaries', but then pressed the claims of Sir Alan Marre (the Second Permanent Secretary at the DHSS) on the grounds that his relative attention to detail (which arguably disqualified him from more 'regular' promotion) would ideally suit him for the post.

However, such deals – which allegedly fettered the post – were not, exclusively administrative. Compton's own transfer from Comptroller and Auditor General had, after all, been engineered by Wilson (who knew him well as a past Chairman of the PAC) to provide a post for Sir Bruce Fraser, whom Crossman had refused to accept as his new Permanent Secretary – hence Compton's long period in waiting and the determination with which Wilson and Crossman ultimately pushed the bill through a reluctant Labour Cabinet.[66] In addition, there were many other instances in which officials appeared more liberal than politicians. It was, for example, the Labour Cabinet in 1966 which deliberately restricted the ombudsman's jurisdiction and access to him through MPs; and these were restrictions which neither MPs themselves nor even the Select Committee as late as 1978 appeared overanxious to reverse. Over time officials also encouraged further relaxations of the rules, albeit with mixed success. In 1976, for example, they warned the Prime Minister that the 'institution's credibility' would be endangered were the next ombudsman to be a civil servant. In consequence, the shortlist contained none and a QC, Sir Cecil Clothier, was appointed. A 'persuasive case' was also made in 1978 by the Cabinet Secretary for the opening to scrutiny – under certain restrictions – of Cabinet papers. This was, however, unambiguously vetoed by the Prime Minister.[67]

Despite such liberalism, the Service continued nevertheless to be held directly responsible for the ombudsman's perceived weakness. One respected legal commentator, for example, condemned the original Act as an 'infamous victory' for Civil Servants; and more generally the reform's essential conservatism was blamed on the 'cautious and consensual' advice of officials, which overloaded Ministers had necessarily to follow on less urgent matters (which typically included constitutional reform).[68] Such criticism, as has been seen, was not wholly justified; and in any case, caution soon came to be viewed as being advantageous. 'One does not have to seek for sinister reasons', one early critic later admitted, to explain the nature of the first three appointments: Civil Servants over time had 'simply proven [themselves] to be very careful, thorough, and unbiased investigators with considerable knowledge of administrative practices and behaviour'. Consequently, it would have been 'difficult to find outsiders with better qualifications'.[69] Indeed, when an outsider was finally appointed in 1979 he proved to be less innovative than his immediate predecessor.

Moreover, the imprecision of the original legislation permitted policy to evolve with changing needs, just as suasion (as opposed to the judicial powers demanded by reformers) reassured departments and thereby encouraged their co-operation in the righting of wrongs.[70] Typically for the time, modernisers also used inaccurate international comparisons to denigrate the Service. For instance, the British ombudsman – as claimed – was not unique in lacking judicial powers. So too did all other ombudsmen, even in the most 'advanced' nations of Sweden and New Zealand. Access in France was also solely through MPs. Leading modernisers, after all, were not disinterested. As lawyers, they had as political an agenda as their predecessors in the 1920s and as professional an interest in 'open government' as contemporary journalists.

The creation of an ombudsman, therefore, was not the great advance its original advocates anticipated. In conjunction with a revitalised system of tribunals and courts, no bold tripartite assault was launched on bureaucracy; and by itself it tackled relatively few important cases. 'The average complaint', as one contemporary ombudsman admitted, was 'not of the most earth-shattering importance'.[71] Senior officials naturally welcomed such domestication, but they were not exclusively responsible for it. Ministers and Parliament alike offered no alternative or a more positive lead. Indeed, it could be argued that, the Service was – somewhat ironically – a principal victim of reform. Just as senior officials continued to be publicly pilloried for their 'infamous victories', so more junior officials suffered continuing defeats as a result of the ombudsman's statutory inability to investigate 'public personnel complaints'. It was consequently such complaints – and especially those lodged by the Civil Service Pensioners Alliance – which were among the most frequently disqualified.[72]

10.3.2 Select Committees

The more conventional way to enhance open government lay in the strengthening of the investigatory powers of Parliament. This was attempted by incoming 'radical' Governments in 1966 and 1979. Labour, as part of a package of Parliamentary reform (which included a failed attempt to televise the Commons), established on an experimental basis six new 'specialist' Select Committees covering either discrete departments (such as Education and Science) or policy areas (such as race and immigration). The evaluation of this experiment prompted a major policy review by both the outgoing Wilson and the incoming Heath Governments during 'modernisation's moment' in 1970. Then in 1979, the Conservatives established twelve new Committees to shadow individual departments (including the Treasury and Civil Service Committee which, as was seen in Chapter 7.5, became heavily involved in the demise of the CSD). Such Committees had been long demanded. The 1917 Haldane Committee, for example, had concluded that 'the continuous and well-informed interest of a Parliamentary body' in each department would significantly improve 'the efficiency of the public service', whilst Fulton had urged MPs to become 'more purposefully associated' with policy implementation.[73] Strong precedents also existed in both the well-respected PAC (established in 1862) and the Expenditure Committee (established as the Estimates Committee in 1912 but renamed, following the 1970 review, on the extension of its remit – which, as seen in Chapter 6.2.4 (a), permitted its English subcommittee to scrutinise the development of the post-Fulton Service).

There had, however, been equally strong long-standing political, operational and constitutional reservations about such Committees. Politically, it was argued, Parliamentary reality and ideological differences would always stifle the backbench unity required effectively to redress the balance between the Legislature and an ever more powerful Executive. Committee membership, for example, had to mirror differing Party strengths in the Commons and so Opposition spokesmen (although they might seize the opportunity to gain more information and publicity) would always be in a minority. Meanwhile the ruling Party's representatives, chosen by the whips, would be fully aware – or, at least, soon made fully aware – that preferment did not lie through the embarrassment of Ministers.[74] Even if there were a will, however, was there a way? Only the PAC had a dedicated team of investigators (the staff of the Comptroller and Auditor General). All the other Committees had to rely on the support of a few generalist Parliamentary clerks, temporary specialist advisers and the 'native wit' of members, whose attendance was often less than meticulous. Finally, what of the Committees' constitutional power? They had the right to summon officials to give evidence and officials were formally instructed to be as 'helpful' as possible. What, however, did 'helpful' mean? All was revealed in May 1980 with the release of the so-called Osmotherly rules, updating the wide range of issues which officials had traditionally been discouraged from discussing. These included the substance of official advice to Ministers, the manner of Ministerial decisions and, even more damningly, any policy 'in the field of political controversy'.[75] In short, at the very time when regular appearances before Committees were progressively denying officials the 'thrill of non-recognition', the convention of official anonymity (as a corollary of Ministerial responsibility) was being reaffirmed. Simultaneously, another paradox (which unfailingly transformed radical Oppositions into conservative Governments) was exposed. In principle Ministers were, and openly proclaimed themselves to be, answerable to Parliament. In practice, however, they refused to appear before the very Parliamentary bodies best able to hold them to account.[76]

Such paradoxes, which could only be resolved politically, placed officials in a potentially embarrassing position and set them up as convenient scapegoats for the 'failure' of open government. To what extent, however, did they collude in their own fate? The attempted reforms of 1970 and 1978–9 are particularly instructive. In 1970, officials recognised that the issue was essentially political and – even on the ominously named Official Committee on Parliamentary Procedure – were genuinely reticent in tendering advice. Nevertheless, they were alive to the nature and scale of the political and constitutional challenge. Labour's experiment had stemmed from Wilson's promise to backbenchers that their 'collective wisdom' would be used to enhance policy-making. Initially, therefore, backbenchers were to be empowered to discuss the formulation of current policy and to summon Ministers to provide evidence. There was to be an implicit understanding, however, that such concessions were designed only to educate Parliament and that, were policy to be enhanced, it should only be at the margin. In no way was the Government's authority to be challenged. This was wholly consistent with the contemporary policy on openness (the 'controlled' disclosure of information); but just as reformers were dissatisfied with that 'passive' right as opposed to a positive 'right to know', so backbenchers wanted the right not just to moderate policy at the margin but actively to influence its implementation. Such an ambition had indeed been encouraged, on the experiment's initiation, by Crossman's high-flown rhetoric (designed ironically to disguise the paucity of the reforms following fierce Cabinet battles). The new specialist Committees, he had suggested, could be used to ensure 'a continuous and detailed check on the work of the Executive and an effective defence of the individual against bureaucratic injustice and incompetence'.[77]

As officials immediately realised, this combination of backbench pressure and political rhetoric posed a major challenge to the authority of the Executive (in the guise of both the Cabinet and the Civil Service). They, therefore, no longer had the option of acting like 'a collection of academics' and had to recommend hard choices to determine 'how little we can get away with'.[78] Their advice to Ministers started with the lauding of the 'praiseworthy attempt by Parliament to bring its own procedure for the consideration of long-term expenditure into line with the Government's own improved procedure'.[79] The latter included, in particular, the compilation of long-term expenditure surveys (following the Plowden Report) and expansion of accountable management (following Fulton). Both had undoubtedly enhanced efficiency; but, as backbenchers noted, they had also raised the danger of real bureaucracy by potentially weakening Ministerial control over officials. Emboldened by both Crossman's rhetoric and an increased flow of information (not least from PESC), backbenchers now wished formally to exert control not just over policy formulation but also its delivery. All this, officials agreed, was 'splendid' for democracy; but was it practicable? The new balance between the Legislature and the Executive would only work if 'the Government of the day' were prepared to 'pay regard' to Parliament. If, on the contrary,

> when it comes to acting on the reports, the Government (as it invariably will when faced with a report which it doesn't like) puts the Whips on and ensures inaction, then all one is doing is building up a head of resentment and frustration in the House, and making it all look very silly in the eyes of the public . . . In short . . . under our constitution, any Government is going to retain control over legislation and parliamentary time by means of the Whips; that being so, the activities of select committees, if they are going to exert any effect . . . must operate within certain constraints.[80]

Likewise, Parliament's attempts further to control the Service were likely to be counterproductive. Rather than ensuring efficiency and economy, 'the constant monitoring of departmental performance' would simply impede administration and consume additional resources.

Such premonitions proved prescient. Just before the fall of the Wilson Government, for instance, a Ministerial Committee vetoed any concession of power to the Legislature. 'The whole notion of control over the Executive should be viewed with suspicion by a Labour Government', it concluded seemingly without irony, 'since the existence of a strong executive was essential to the carrying out of socialist policies.' A change of Government brought no change of policy – despite, or perhaps because of, the appointment of a leading reformer (David Howell) to the CSD. In September 1970, Howell's immediate superior (Jellicoe) explicitly vetoed any 'shift of power from ministers' and Heath (backed by Whitelaw as Lord President) likewise vetoed increased Parliamentary control over the Service on the grounds that 'elaborate machinery of inquisition could but impair the efficiency of government'.[81] Neither Government felt, however, that they could 'get away' with as little as officials advised; and so in 1971 the Expenditure Committee was established and assumed (albeit not precisely in the way reformers had hoped) the role of both the old Estimates Committee and Labour's experimental 'specialist' committees.

What, however, of the 'constraints' within which – as officials had warned – Select Committees had necessarily to work? Foremost among them were the 'rules of engagement' for officials providing evidence, first codified by Brook in May 1958 but since having undergone several revisions – and attempted revisions – before the Osmotherly memorandum.[82] Among the more radical attempts at revision was that mounted after December 1971 by Howell (this time supported by Jellicoe). Officials, he argued, should be 'more forthcoming' about 'the main advantages and disadvantages' of the various policy options presented to Ministers and the 'policy reasons' for the eventual decision. Given the greater delegation of administrative responsibility (particularly in relation to the creation of departmental agencies) a wider range of officials should also be available as witnesses; and, to demonstrate the effectiveness of policy coordination, the structure of Cabinet Committees should be revealed. This latter suggestion immediately attracted the attention of Trend, who duly warned Heath that any revelation of the method of decision-making would whet the media's appetite for exposing divisions within the Executive. On any specific policy, for example, there would be incessant questions such as:

> When was it first examined? By what Committee or Committees? Was their advice unanimous; or was there disagreement among their members? What was their recommendation to the Cabinet? Did the Cabinet endorse it? If not, why not?[83]

This would enhance neither policy-making nor 'participatory democracy'. Heath agreed and rejected any relaxation of the rules.

Despite Trend's intervention, however, this outcome was not unanimously welcomed in Whitehall. Those responsible for policy in the CSD, for example, had initially been condemned as conservative by Howell; but their advice had been based on their perception of Cabinet policy. 'If the Parliamentary Secretary wants to fight', minuted one official (Peter Mountfield) early in the confrontation, 'he must reopen it with colleagues'. When Howell did just that, he received his officials' whole-hearted support. As the responsible Assistant Secretary (Tom Caulcott) recalled, in his final recommendations to William Armstrong, Howell 'did not like' the initial revision of the rules by the CSD's Machinery of Government Division because he regarded it as a

> very anti-open government document. I am bound to say that in MG we all agreed with him but had felt constrained by the existing rules . . . I would recommend that it is worth making another . . . attempt, despite the political difficulties, to get these changes which would favour open government.[84]

Armstrong duly lent his support, but to no avail. The political impediments to increased openness were too great.

This issue was revisited, albeit at the more rarefied level of the Permanent Secretaries' Sunningdale conference, in 1978.[85] Again it was accepted that, in order to avoid the impression – and danger – of bureaucracy, officials should be more answerable (but not accountable) to Select Committees and that the Committees themselves should be more adequately staffed. Three caveats, however, were made. First, the confidentiality of officials' advice to Ministers should be protected. Second, to increase their effectiveness, Committees should be less adversarial and not prejudge policy options. Third, and more controversially, officials should be able to deflect 'improper' questions (to which Committees were becoming prone) to Ministers. Otherwise the Government should consider the replacement of career officials by, as in the USA, political nominees. No such suggestion was ever seriously considered by Callaghan, despite the Cabinet Secretary's urgings – not least because the relevant Parliamentary debate was held in February 1979, at the height of the winter of discontent.

Once in office, the Conservatives (who had actively championed the strengthening of the Legislature whilst in opposition) duly established – albeit with some misgivings – twelve departmental Select Committees. This may have broadened the scrutiny of the Executive. Did it, however, deepen it? The crunch came with two critical reports in the spring of 1981. The first for the PAC, by the Comptroller and Auditor General, condemned the low quality of internal audit within central Government and squarely placed the blame on the Service's lack of professionalism stemming from indifference at the top. This confirmed the prognosis in Rayner's programme of 'lasting reforms'. 'It is extraordinary', minuted his chief of staff (Clive Priestley), 'that – despite all the emphasis the Service lays on accountability to and the Accounting Officer's special relationship with Parliament – the audit arrangements should be so bad'. The report was consequently seized upon by Mrs Thatcher; and the CSD's perceived tardiness in responding to its recommendations (albeit in the middle of the Civil Service strike) was another nail in its coffin.[86]

The second report, which elicited a rather different Government response, was that issued by the PAC itself in February 1981 on the more traditional subject of the Legislature's independence and power. Its core concern was no longer the confidentiality of Ministerial discussions and official advice because, whatever they may have advocated in opposition, the Conservatives in office had vigorously defended such confidentiality (especially during early altercations over council house sales). What the PAC principally wanted was total independence from the Executive of its investigatory staff (under the Comptroller and Auditor-General) and the right to 'follow public money wherever it goes' (which included nationalised industries and private contractors, and thus threatened another of the Government's seminal policies – privatisation).[87] This the Government clearly did not welcome. A formal response to the report was delayed first by the strike and then by the Falklands War; but its hand was ultimately forced – as had been Labour's over open government in 1979 – by a private member's bill. This was the 1983 Parliamentary Control of Expenditure (Reform) Bill; and it was particularly embarrassing for the Government because it was sponsored by Norman St John Stevas (the Minister who had established departmental Select Committees in 1979, but who had since been dismissed) and had the support of the chairmen of the two leading Select Committees as well as the majority of backbenchers. Ministers' instinctive reaction was to concede nothing. Mrs Thatcher, for example, dismissed the bill as a 'snooper's charter' and Geoffrey Howe forewarned that a more independent Comptroller's office would become 'a Department of the Opposition, with full access to Government papers'.[88] Nevertheless, it was recognised that some concessions had to be made; and ultimately the Comptroller was granted greater independence and his staff renamed the National Audit Office. Both were to be solely responsible to Parliament – although, to protect the Executive, the PAC was denied two further powers which it regarded as preconditions for effective reform (the power of Parliament to order the Comptroller to undertake particular inquiries and to second NAO staff to other committees).

Just as the redefinition of the Chief Press Secretary role in 1983 marked a truce in the demand for open government, so St John Stevas' bill (eventually entitled the National Audit Act) marked the culmination of a battle between the Legislature and the Executive which had been waged continually since 1964. Neither represented a major victory for openness or Parliamentary democracy; but, although there may have been considerable collusion within Whitehall, the ultimate reason for the relative lack of success was patently political.

10.4 Constitutional change

The final challenge to the Service arose from the two major constitutional changes, or potential changes, in the 1970s: accession to the EEC in January 1973 and devolution. Both had an instant impact on the balance of power between the central departments (and thus between the three 'top posts' which, as was seen in Chapter 3.3.2, had been a matter for concern since the Plowden Report). Two new coordinating bodies, the European Interdepartmental Unit and the Constitution Unit, were established within the Cabinet Office thereby boosting its trajectory towards, in effect, a Prime Minister's Office at the expense of the Treasury and (more significantly in the short term) the CSD. The impact of the changes was otherwise relatively muted. In the case of devolution this was understandable, given that the adverse referendum result of 1979 suspended the implementation of detailed plans for a further twenty years. In the case of the EEC, it was less so – given that accession was at the time (and has long since been) identified as a major 'turning point in British administrative history'.[89] Accession, for example, required a transformation of culture – and career profiles – within departments. It redressed the relationship between departments (with the Diplomatic Service, for instance, trespassing into the traditional preserve of the Home Civil Service and previously unfashionable departments, such as MAFF, gaining a new prominence). Moreover, the very context within which the Service worked was revolutionised with, given the primacy of EEC law, the courts enjoying ever greater power to challenge not only Government (as with the OSA) but also Parliament itself. In short, accession to the EEC had far greater potential to reform the Service than any of Fulton's recommendations. Why was this potential so little realised before 1981?

10.4.1 Europe

The administrative impact of accession to the EEC depended ultimately on the degree of political commitment to membership; and, as is well recognised, this – apart from the period between the opening of negotiations (in June 1970) and accession – was limited under both Labour and Conservative Governments.[90] Political scepticism bred, or at least sustained, administrative scepticism and thus discouraged change. Of necessity, however, membership demanded some administrative adjustment. An early decision had been taken that there should be no central dictation of policy from a Ministry of Europe. Accordingly, each department was required to 'think' and act 'European', in the formulation not only of domestic but also Community policy. This meant regular communication with, and visits to, Brussels as well as permanent postings there.[91]

William Armstrong in 1962 and Howell a decade later (due respectively to a misunderstanding of French practice and a characteristic attempt to ensure full control by the 'chief executive') had flirted with the idea of a central Ministry of Europe; but both during the negotiations and the preparations for accession, such an innovation was rejected as a 'certain way to guarantee ineffectiveness'.[92] Policy could not be imposed from above. Rather each department had to be 'tuned' to the working of the Commission. However, what positive action should be taken to prevent progress being stalled by 'interdepartmental wrangles' or strategic coherence being lost by departments going 'their own way'? The answer was the establishment, in May 1972, of a new five-man coordinating committee (the European

Interdepartmental Unit or EIU) within the Cabinet Office under the traditional tier of an Official and Ministerial Committee. Its remit was:

> to provide direction and management of our policies as members of the European Community and to generate and sustain the continuing impetus which will be necessary to achieve them. It will be responsible both for establishing our priorities and for ensuring that action taken is consistent with them.

Coordination was familiar territory to the Cabinet Office. Such a potentially interventionist role, encroaching upon departmental autonomy, was not. The chair of the Unit had, therefore, not only to be the master of an array of highly complex detail but also to possess exceptional political sensitivity. Unsurprisingly, the post quickly became a testing ground for those destined for higher office.[93]

Given the federal nature of Whitehall, such 'controlled' decentralisation was undoubtedly well advised. However, it also reflected the Home Civil Service's determination to restrict the power of the FCO (which might otherwise have monopolised relations with the Commission) as well as entrenched scepticism amongst senior officials (which prevailing political and popular attitudes towards Europe did little to allay).[94] Such scepticism was particularly pronounced in the two officials upon whom a constructive administrative response immediately depended: Trend as Cabinet Secretary (who was politically fearful of compromising links with the Commonwealth and the special relationship with the USA) and William Armstrong (who was administratively fearful of compromising standards of public service).[95] Consequently, a 'cold hostility' was encouraged which, in turn, discouraged innovation. Before accession, Heath had called for each department to adapt its 'organisational arrangements' and to familiarise itself with the Community's 'techniques'. In particular, this meant the adoption of a new 'mind-set' (in which the needs and experience of other member states were to be borne constantly in mind); and a readiness, in the words of Patrick Nairne (as chair of the EIU), to 'play the Community game' by acting as 'entrepreneurs as much as administrators' and thus engaging in open 'horse trading'. It would not, as he warned his fellow Permanent Secretaries, 'be enough to be Church of England, doing our duty in church from time to time: we need to be practising Christians as well'. Such advice, however, was largely ignored and so, from the start, involvement with Europe was too often assigned to 'mavericks', deemed unlikely to reach the top but known to dine well, play hard, speak freely and enjoy decision-taking.[96] In short, by revelling in greater openness and the freedom to base policy advice on compromise rather than principle, they offended all that Trend and Armstrong considered essential to 'good government' and good administrative practice.

Political, public and administrative scepticism thereby caused the loss of another seminal opportunity for reform, equivalent to that in the 1940s. Significant changes occurred only in those departments most closely involved with the Commission – essentially those represented on the EIU, with the singular exception of the

Treasury. Elsewhere, few tended to play the 'Community game' with the result that 'strategic coherence' was harder to attain in Whitehall than during 'negotiations in Brussels because people tended to come with absolutely firm departmental positions: that was the British position that had to prevail in Brussels'.[97] It was in this respect that the post-Fulton Service might with some justice have been condemned as 'amateurish'. The major adjustment to membership of the EEC had to wait until later.

10.4.2 Devolution

The constitutional change which was explicitly addressed – but, unlike accession to the EEC, never fulfilled – was devolution. This was, at root, a European-wide issue, with the widespread growth of 'sub-nationalism' leading to the concept of a 'Europe of the regions'. However, in the UK, it acquired particular political potency when the Scottish National Party (SNP) won 22 per cent and then 30 per cent of the Scottish vote in the two general elections of 1974. More importantly, it won seven seats in February and eleven in October, thereby threatening one of Labour's traditional heartlands and the Party's prospects of ever again winning a sizable Parliamentary majority.[98] Accordingly, it became a live issue within Whitehall from the autumn of 1974 (when Permanent Secretaries exceptionally discussed it twice, first at Sunningdale and then at a special conference) until the Summer of 1978 (when the Scotland and Wales Acts received the Royal assent). It was also a source of much tension, particularly in relation to the necessary degree of administrative restructuring and the maintenance of a 'unified' Civil Service.

The degree of structural administrative change was, by definition, dependent on the degree of political commitment. Labour's ambitions for devolution have been described as 'minimalist', with the granting to devolved executives of only specified powers (with the rest reserved for the UK Government) and limited financial freedom (with the bulk of the executives' income coming from the UK exchequer in a block grant). Nevertheless, fundamental disagreements arose which were only resolved by a meeting of senior officials in May 1978.[99] The Wilson and Callaghan Governments – against the advice of officials – had decided that, to resolve any political difficulties and to prevent the UK from disintegrating, Joint Councils should be established of UK Ministers and members of the devolved executives; and that, for administrative simplicity, communication between governments should be mainly through the Scottish and Welsh Offices (the 'territorial departments'). For officials, however, the creation of Joint Councils threatened to over-formalise discussion and thus hamper political compromise; and the territorial departments patently lacked both the requisite capacity and impartiality (particularly given that their Ministers would have constituencies, and so have to seek re-election, in the relevant 'territory'). As one senior CSD official (inevitably born in Scotland) remarked resignedly, we shall 'have to rely on the staff of the Scottish and Welsh Offices to behave like good Englishmen'.[100] The Cabinet Office's preferred alternative was to strengthen the central UK Government through the appointment of a high-powered Ministerial committee, supported by a re-styled Constitution Unit to 'provide for consultation with, and for the monitoring of, the devolved administrations'. To yet others, however, this smacked of 'back-seat driving'. As Bancroft (as Head of the Civil Service) warned: 'the underlying assumption behind devolution is that the devolved authorities will want to do things differently and the English Departments will have to learn to live with the differences'.[101] In addition, CSD officials feared that increased 'monitoring' would lead to an explosion of bureaucracy. More economical, they suggested, would be the augmentation of the 'territorial departments' (as Ministers wished) and the entrusting of day-to-day coordination to the functional departments (whose staff would continue to exceed those of the devolved administrations even in the relevant 'territories').

The Cabinet Office lost the battle in May 1978 but won the war. Devolution, it was agreed, should be a 'reality' with no strengthening of the centre 'derogating' from that. Rather, officials should unite to 'strenuously discourage' UK Ministers 'from interference in wholly devolved matters'. The 'territorial departments' should also be augmented and daily coordination left to the 'functional' ones, as the CSD wished. Significantly, however, augmentation was to amount largely to an injection of Treasury expertise (particularly in relation to the block grant); and a small central Constitution Unit was to be retained to resolve 'borderline questions' (arising especially from the need to implement international, and above all EEC, obligations). Parallels were even drawn to the joining of the EEC. As one of Callaghan's Private Secretaries observed:

> The ministerial Committee on Europe and the Cabinet Office European Unit . . . is necessary because Europe is too important to be left to the FCO. It involves the interests of many departments and coordination is needed, even though individual Ministers retain their own responsibilities. The same arguments apply to devolution, with at least the same force.

The Principal Private Secretary (Ken Stowe) agreed and added the embellishment that 'a central capacity would (as with the FCO and Europe) still leave the Scottish Office acting in a "front" capacity, i.e. it is not a threat to them'.[102] Few, however, would have failed to appreciate the very considerable threat that such a strengthening of Treasury influence and the retention of a 'central capacity' posed to the 'reality' of devolution.

What of the second major administrative challenge, the maintenance of a 'unified Civil Service'? This was not a narrow issue because, as a national institution, the Civil Service was a quintessential symbol of the United Kingdom. Initially a unified service was not expected to survive since both the majority and minority reports of the Kilbrandon Report on the Constitution (published in 1973) agreed that each devolved territory should have its own Service. This, with the creation in 1922 of a separate Northern Ireland Civil Service, had, after all been the outcome of the UK's one previous act of devolution. Moreover, officials at the Northern

Ireland Office were amongst the most pessimistic about the practicality of retaining a 'unified Service', given the inevitable 'desire of the new political authorities . . . to demonstrate the separateness of their Administrations'.[103] Given the federal nature of the existing Service, the administrative reality was also that departments diverged and the majority of careers were local (or, at best, regional). Greater decentralisation, as has been seen, was even being promoted as a precondition for efficiency.

Nevertheless, a political decision was taken in 1975 to retain a 'unified Service' and, to this end, an administrative 'framework' was drafted in November 1976, refined in May 1978 and translated into an action plan in January 1979.[104] No principles were advanced to justify the decision, but the hope was expressed that a unified Service would help 'to cement the United Kingdom'. Pragmatic considerations were, therefore, all-powerful. For example, Welsh Office officials fought to retain uniform standards of recruitment 'having some regard to some things that go on in local government'. The NSS was fearful of a likely reduction in career opportunities for its members and the adoption of 'parochial' attitudes by devolved administrations. More immediately, it warned of serious disruption: existing Civil Servants might refuse to be co-opted into the new services, senior officials object to the different 'styles' of government, and specialists jib at restrictions on both their professional freedom and prospects.[105] More generally, the CSD expressed concern that, given a less than 'optimal deployment of resources', administrative standards might fall. The principal purpose of the administrative 'framework' was, therefore, to maximise transferability through the ensuring of the common recruitment standards, grading, and pay. The 'second best' solution, if separate services were to materialise, was that there should be 'common elements' and 'shared facilities'. However, the 'best permanent solution' (which gained increasing support over time) was the maintenance of a fully unified service. Central control through a UK Prime Minister, as the Minister for the Civil Service, might be politically impossible but the advice of the Head of the Service on senior appointments would, it was hoped, be accepted by the leaders of devolved authorities, as well as both the CSD being permitted to regulate other promotions and discipline over numbers or pay being retained (if only surreptitiously through the block grant). In any case, officials reassured themselves in 1979, a unified Service had to survive in the short term, because there was no time to establish an alternative and, even had there been, it would have been impolitic to prejudge the wishes of the new authorities.

Many, particularly within the CSD, were fully aware of the 'precariousness' of this 'framework' and the assumptions on which it was based. 'In seeking to maintain a unified Civil Service to serve what will in effect be three separate governments', remarked one official early in the planning process, 'we are attempting to square a circle (a not uncommon feature of the devolution package as a whole).'[106] Consequently there remained, right up to 1979, serious reservations about preserving a unified Service 'for any length of time' after devolution and embarrassment over the subterfuge involved. 'The general policy', wrote Bancroft in one of his last circulars on the subject, 'is not to carry matters so far that the freedom of the devolved executives to take their own decisions would be pre-empted *or would seem to be pre-empted.*' The real embarrassment was, of course, that the creation of what came later to be known as a 'unified but not uniform' Service had already been planned in the early 1970s with the creation of departmental agencies. Totally divorced from devolution, it was also to be effected after 1988 with the creation of *Next Steps* agencies.

10.5 Conclusion

The momentum of administrative reform cannot be divorced from the political pressure on the Service; and, in the years following Fulton, exceptional pressure was certainly exerted by both Parliament and the public for more open government (in all its guises), by Ministers against 'big government' (in two very different guises, epitomised by Crossman's *Diaries* and Thatcherite rhetoric) and by the EEC and devolution upon the UK's unwritten constitution. What, above all, the Service demonstrated in response was that it was no monolith. Central departments tended to be more liberal than their 'functional' counterparts (arguably because of their relative proximity to the political battle and distance from policy-delivery); but even their officials were torn between a greater accommodation of public demand and the optimisation of managerial efficiency (as illustrated by the planning of devolution). At root, of course, what such administrative tension reflected was the lack of both political consensus and leadership.

How, ideally, should the Service have responded? The Fabian presumption was that, as the experts, officials should lead. However, constitutional convention – and increasingly the Conservatives – suggested otherwise. Initially the instinct of senior officials, as personified by Trend, was to adhere to the concept of 'good government', whereby 'discreditable' but necessary political (and administrative) deals should be concealed and the risk of public disillusion minimised; but this instinct was undercut by both general trends (such as declining deference) and particular ones (such as 'dishonourable' ministerial leaks and, above all, the publication of the Crossman *Diaries*). What was the principled alternative? As Armstrong, in the immediate aftermath of Fulton, and Trend later emphasised, the modernisers had none.[107] The press was concerned principally with profit and was relatively unconcerned that its revelations would enhance neither decision-making nor 'participatory democracy' but would rather – as they duly did – trivialise politics and cause public disillusion. Parliamentary reformers, in seeking to strengthen the Legislature against the Executive, were equally blind to both the adversarial nature of politics and the power of the Whips. Likewise, Ministers typically 'sleepwalked' into the major challenges to sovereignty posed by the EEC and devolution.[108] 'Open government' and the 'hollowing out' of the state were, in short, little more than acts of faith and promised, at least in the short term, little more than chaos.

The efficacy and efficiency of 'big government' in the 1970s were subject to universal doubts; and the political and administrative vacuum which greeted such doubts in both Westminster and Whitehall seriously damaged the international standing of both. The failing was essentially political, not administrative. The basic understandings on which the Service served had been invalidated; and until new understandings were agreed, the nature of any necessary administrative reform remained – by definition – unclear. This was a subject that Fulton had been forbidden and, for all its alleged radicalism, had dutifully failed to address. However, until there was greater clarification of its working relations with Parliament, the public and Ministers and constitutional relations with sub-national and supranational bodies, the principal role which the Service could – and would – play, was the role of scapegoat.

Part 5

CONCLUSION

11

RINGING OUT THE OLD, RINGING IN THE NEW

11.1 The challenge

As the interventionist role, and thus size, of central Government grew in Britain – as in the rest of the Western world – from the late nineteenth century, so it faced three specific challenges. How, given market failure, was it to acquire the expertise to inform its intervention? Second, how was such expertise to be translated into policies that were compatible, practicable and democratically acceptable (the challenge of 'administration')? Finally, how were those policies to be delivered cost-effectively by an ever larger and more diverse bureaucracy (the challenge of 'management')? The 1854 Northcote-Trevelyan Report was widely perceived to have definitively answered the second question, albeit for a 'night-watchman' state. Then, during the interwar period, a bowdlerised version had underpinned the first era of sustained intervention – arguably a 'golden age' of public administration, in which the British Civil Service consolidated its reputation as the 'best in the world'. Unlike many of its international counterparts, it remained financially and politically incorrupt. Despite much obloquy (both at the time and since), it also delivered cost-effective mass programmes of social relief whilst simultaneously providing an example of a 'model employer' to the private sector. The Second World War, as for so much else in Britain, was its finest hour.

However, in the best traditions of Greek tragedy (as, given their education, many senior officials may have well appreciated) the War was a moment of hubris. With the establishment of the welfare state and the adoption of Keynesian demand management, the role and size of Government fundamentally changed. However, its organisation – and, more importantly, the constitutional context within which it worked – did not. This made it all the more urgent to resolve the two challenges upon which Northcote-Trevelyan had remained largely silent (the acquisition of specialist expertise and managerial skills); but this, in turn, was made increasingly difficult by rapid political and social change – particularly the decline in deference, the transformation by affluence of citizens into more demanding 'consumers' of state services and the ultimate resurgence in market values. Three belated attempts were made in the 1960s to 'modernise'. Of these, the Fulton Report was the most famous and the least effective. Designed to remedy a perceived 'skills gap' at the top of an expanding Service, its actual legacy was to popularise the need for better management within a contracting one. Fulton had been preceded in 1961 by the Plowden Report which more effectively, if covertly, had confronted all three challenges and prompted an internal reform programme which addressed each (largely through greater planning and a reorganisation of the 'centre'). Fulton also coincided with a bout of prescient rethinking by the Conservatives in opposition, which anticipated the national and international decline of faith in 'big' government and a corresponding rise in the conviction that 'business is best' (especially when supported by private sector, and preferably North American, management techniques). Once the Conservatives were in power, however, its impact was limited.

Modernisation's moment, therefore, failed; and the Service was thereafter subjected to a decade of vilification. Perceived as a principal cause of Britain's relative 'decline' and 'ungovernability', both major political Parties (albeit for contradictory reasons) made its reform a priority; and in this, they were abetted – as a dividend of decreased deference – by an 'investigative' press reluctant to pursue any further its search for scapegoats. This vilification, in turn, heavily influenced (or at least reinforced the convictions of) Mrs Thatcher – the one Prime Minister in the twentieth century with the drive and determination to stamp, like Gladstone in the nineteenth, her personality on administrative reform. Urged by her political advisers to treat it (in comparison to economic recovery or trade union reform) as a second-level issue to be tackled later, she nevertheless immediately appointed the managing director of Marks and Spencer as a personal adviser on 'the promotion of efficiency and the elimination of waste'. This testified to her determination to modernise the Service's management; but the other two challenges (the acquisition of expertise and enhanced administration) were left unanswered. Two seminal events in 1981, however, cleared the way for them to be addressed in Mrs Thatcher's second term. First, the Civil Service strike and then the abolition of the CSD removed two impediments to reform, commonly associated with national decline: the power of the unions to resist, and an unwillingness (or inability) of management to seek anything but consensus.

11.2 The response

The end of the old order had long been predicted, although its actual occurrence was perhaps – even in 1981 – less widely expected. Within the Service, there had always been a dedicated core of reformers (upon whom, for example, Plowden and Rayner successively relied). Accordingly the election in 1964 of a Labour Government, committed to institutional reform, had been eagerly welcomed; and disillusion was all the greater when not only was a unique opportunity to honour the commitment wasted but also contemporary concepts of 'good government' were betrayed by Ministers through 'dishonourable' leaks and disclosures (culminating in the publication of the Crossman *Diaries*). As vilification mounted thereafter, so demoralisation replaced disillusion – especially as senior officials were constantly reminded, and reminded themselves, of both their culpability for and their complicity in earlier failures to reform. They nevertheless remained largely loyal to the principles of 'good government' even when, by their own criteria, Government policy was irrational. As Sir Douglas Wass, for example, reminded them in his valedictory address as joint Head of the Home Civil Service in 1983:

> The civil service's innate preference for ... the way public administration functions must ... not be allowed to take precedence over what society wants.... The civil service must above all be responsive to the needs of government and the wishes of Parliament.... Institutional values are not ends in themselves ... the public services are the instrument of the general will.[1]

One 'institutional value' did, however, continue to raise concern – not least to Wass himself: the Service's political impartiality (an issue which Northcote-Trevelyan was believed permanently to have resolved). Senior officials remained convinced that an essential 'check and balance' within Britain's unwritten constitution was their ability to 'speak truth unto power'; but over time they felt their status had remorselessly declined from gentleman (in the nineteenth century) to gentlemen's gentleman (in the interwar period) to courtier or, even less flatteringly, prostitute (by the 1970s).[2] How could a 'department's collective and historical knowledge' continue to be injected into policy decisions to ensure that 'objectivity that sometimes escapes the political enthusiast'? To maintain objectivity in a period of adversarial politics, moreover, how personally – as opposed to professionally – committed should a permanent official be to a particular policy? Answering the latter question in the wrong way or at the wrong time was known to have blighted several careers. 'Conviction politicians, certainly: conviction civil servants no', was the unambiguous answer of Ian Bancroft – after his forcible retirement as Head of the Home Civil Service.[3]

Such niceties and so broad a focus tended to elude those brought in from outside to reform Whitehall. Labour's initial advisers had concentrated, in true Fabian fashion, upon the provision of expertise and then Conservative businessmen upon management. Indeed Rayner, in his own valedictory address in 1984, characterised his work as 'the first coherent, sustained attempt to assess the operation of the state from a management perspective'.[4] Given his past experience, he was fully appreciative of the pool of talent within Whitehall and the 'uneconomic' pressures to which the Service was subjected by Ministers, Parliament and the public alike. Nevertheless, he was damning of its managerial deficiencies and of the leadership that had caused, and continued to condone, them. John Hoskyns, when he in turn resigned as head of the Policy Unit in 1983, was surprisingly more sympathetic. The Service, he admitted, had 'a real problem'. It could not 'by definition, provide its own objectives, strategy or leadership for the country because that is not its job'; but if Ministers did 'not provide these things' to halt Britain's spiralling decline (which only Government could achieve) what could it do? Left to itself, it inevitably became 'increasingly inward looking, with its own self-serving objectives and ethos'. This was a telling critique of both earlier Fabian reformers and administrative culture following the creation, on Fulton's recommendation, of a dedicated Civil Service Department. In the early 1980s, it was also a telling description of the Catch-22 situation in which

> a deeply pessimistic Civil Service looks for political leadership . . . to a tiny handful of exhausted ministers [whilst] those same ministers look in vain to their officials to provide policy options which, to be of any use, would have to be too 'politically controversial' for the officials to think of.

Hoskyns' solution for this dilemma was rather more ruthless, building – somewhat ironically – on the old Fabian premise that there could be no 'radical government without radically-minded officials'. 'Difficult problems', he maintained, could only be 'solved by people who desperately want to solve them' and so the whole political establishment had to be changed. Ministers should be recruited from business as well as from Parliament and, above all, the top tier of officials replaced from either within or outside the Service.[5] This would, as was well recognised at the time, effectively politicise the Service; and, as a result, it wholly overlooked the continuing need for good 'administration' (the assurance of the compatibility, practicality and acceptability of each policy). So too did Rayner's exclusive focus on management.

11.3 The future

Such a burst of valedictory addresses signified not just a rapid turnover of senior personnel within Whitehall during Mrs Thatcher's first years in power, but also an awareness of the passing – scarcely a decade after Fulton – of the old order on which the Service's reputation as the 'best in the world' had been based. This did not mean that the three challenges, which had long faced modern Government, had been resolved either individually or collectively. On the contrary, the prospect of resolving each had seemingly receded. In making good gaps in expertise, for example, one traditional expedient (the appointment of expert 'special' advisers) had been crowded out by the constitutional innovation of which modernisers were most proud (the more regular appointment of generalist 'political' advisers). In relation to good 'administration', the gaping hole at the centre of Britain's unwritten constitution had also – if anything – widened. The constitutional convention of 'ministerial responsibility' was the vital hinge between pure bureaucracy (which no-one and, in particular, no senior officials wanted) and democratic, or at least Parliamentary, accountability; and, since at least the First World War, it had been recognised to be a myth. The engorgement of departments and the increased aggressiveness of questioning by the new Select Committees in the 1970s made it even more untenable for Ministers to claim responsibility for all – and officials to deny responsibility for any – departmental activity. Yet, to the detriment of good government and democratic accountability, this is precisely what happened. Good management was also cramped by the same convention since it underpinned the 'constitutional independence' of each 'federal' department and consequently their ability ultimately to ignore central directives. In addition, management was impaired by a continuing inability to define the key goal of 'efficiency'. Did it mean the 'elimination of waste' (as in Rayner's job title), cost-effectiveness (the business manager's preferred option) or the optimum allocation of national resources (as sought by Plowden)? Clearly, new management techniques, which might (or might not) work in private industry, were not as instantly transferable to the public sector as some believed.

By the early 1980s, therefore, the three challenges were no nearer to – and arguably further from – being resolved. The political context had also, if anything, deteriorated. The ending of the old order, it was accepted, required a fundamental 'culture' change; but, although senior officials slowly attuned themselves to the needs of management, outside advisers remained as insensitive as ever to the needs of 'administration'. The Treasury's resumption of responsibility for industrial relations also threatened once again to desensitise central policy advisers, and thus Ministers, to the very different needs of officials at every level in every part of the country. Given that, at best, Government could only be rolled back at the margin, and that it had to continue, these unresolved issues meant that the brave new world after 1981 had to be both brave and new.

CHRONOLOGY

For the more detailed entries between 1968 and 1981, events have been grouped into four broad categories: general context; institutional change (as chapters 5–7); managerial, political and constitutional issues (as chapters 9–10); and industrial relations and pay (as chapter 8). To differentiate the latter further, it has been italicised.

1854 **Northcote-Trevelyan Report** published
1855 Civil Service Commission established
1859 Superannuation Act
1866 Exchequer and Audit Act
1870 Order in Council establishing open competition
1875 **Report of the Civil Service Inquiry Commission (Playfair**, C 1113, C 1226); Treasury minute on official secrecy
1876 Order in Council establishing Service-wide lower division
1884 Treasury minute on political impartiality
1885 Treasury minute on financial probity
1889 First Official Secrets Act
1890 **Report of the Royal Commission on Civil Establishments (Ridley**, C 5545); Order in Council regulating pay and conditions for Second Division
1904 Committee of Imperial Defence, with secretariat, permanently established
1910 Order in Council consolidating 'Civil Service code of regulation' and Treasury's powers of inspection
1912 **Royal Commission on the Civil Service (MacDonnell)**: six reports to 1915
1916 War Cabinet Secretariat established; Conciliation and Arbitration Board established (abolished 1922–5)
1917 Haldane Report on the Machinery of Government (Cd 9230); Final Report of the Committee on Relations between employers and employed (Whitley, Cd 9153)
1918 *Association of First Division Civil Servants (FDA) founded*
1919 **National Whitley Council formed**. Treasury reorganisation: Establishment Division (Feb); 3 Departments with Permanent Secretary as

Head of the Civil Service (Sept); **Fisher appointed** (Oct); *Institute of Professional Civil Servants* (IPCS) founded

1920 **Interim Report of NWC Joint Committee on Organization of the Civil Service** (final report, 1921). Treasury circulars: Prime Minister's consent required for appointments to top four departmental positions (March); Treasury control over departmental expenditure and staff (July). Committee on the salary of heads of departments

1921 *Civil Service Confederation* founded

1922 **Committee on National Expenditure (Geddes, Cmd 1581)**; *Civil Service Clerical Association* founded

1923 Treasury circular: Treasury as 'central department' to be given prior notice of all proposals to Cabinet incurring expenditure (minimum notice of 5 days, 1924)

1925 *Ministry of Labour Staff Association* founded

1926 Treasury circular: all Permanent Secretaries to be departmental accounting officers; Civil Service reaches lowest interwar size

1927 Trade Disputes and Trade Unions Act

1928 Francs report (Cmd 3037): definitive statement on personal conduct

1930 *Society of Civil Servants* founded (amalgamating executive class unions)

1931 **Report of the Royal Commission on the Civil Service (Tomlin, Cmd 3909)**. Committee on National Expenditure (May, Cmd 3920)

1932 Committee on the Post Office (Bridgeman, Cmd 4149); Committee on Minister's Powers (Donoughmore, Cmd 4060). *National Association of Women Civil Servants* founded

1935 Superannuation Act

1936 *Inland Revenue Staff Association* founded

1938 Bridges replaces Hankey as Cabinet Secretary

1939 Wilson replaces Fisher as Head of the Civil Service (succeeded by Hopkins in 1942); *Civil Service Alliance* founded

1942 Machinery of Government Committee established (Anderson/Morrison to 1949)

1943 Committee on Scientific Man-Power (Barlow, Report 1946, Cmd 6824). *Proposals for the Reform of the Foreign Service* (Cmd 6420) recommends division of Foreign from Home Civil Service

1944 Committee on the Training of Civil Servants (Assheton, Cmd 6525)

1945 **Bridges Head of the Civil Service; replaced as Cabinet Secretary by Brook in 1947**

1946 Marriage bar ends

1948 Committee on the Political Activities of Civil Servants (Masterman, Cmd 7718). CSSB introduced

1954 Crichel Down: Maxwell Fyfe definition of ministerial responsibility; commitment to equal pay, implemented 1955–1961

CHRONOLOGY

1955 **Report of the Royal Commission on the Civil Service (Priestley, Cmd 9613)**

1956 **Brook** replaces Bridges as **Head of the Home Civil Service**; Pay Research Unit set up

1958 Estimates Committee, *Treasury Control of Expenditure* (July)

1959 H. Thomas, *The Establishment*. Plowden Committee commissioned (July). First 'Sunningdale' meeting of senior Permanent Secretaries (Dec)

1960 Frank Lee, Joint Permanent Secretary to the Treasury. Second Plowden Report (June) leading to the Ministerial Group on Public Expenditure (Dec–Dec 1962)

1961 Public Expenditure Survey Committee (**PESC**) established permanently (March). Final **Plowden Report on Control of Public Expenditure** (Cmnd 1432) and letter to Chancellor on senior posts (June). NEDC announced (July, first meets March 1962). Chief Secretary to the Treasury appointed (Oct). Treasury Organisation Committee (**TOC**) established (Dec, reports June, implemented Nov)

1962 Agreement on need for 3 top posts (March). A. Sampson, *Anatomy of Britain*; first meeting of the Fabian Group on Civil Service reform; dismissal of one-third Cabinet on 'night of long knives' (July). W. Armstrong replaces Lee as Treasury Permanent Secretary (October). Macmillan 'modernisation' speech to Cabinet (October)

1963 Brook replaced as Head of the Civil Service by **Helsby** and as Cabinet Secretary by **Trend** (Jan). NEDC announce 4% growth rate (Feb). Centre of Administrative Studies opened (Oct)

1964 Estimates Committee, *Treasury Control of Establishments* (May). Fabian Society, *The Administrators* (June). S. Brittan, *The Treasury under the Tories* (Aug). **Election of Labour Government** (Oct, maj 4). Department of Economic Affairs and Ministry of Technology established. Conservative Party Machinery of Government Study Group established (Dec)

1965 Estimates Committee, *Recruitment to the Civil Service* (Aug). Cabinet agrees preference for UK computers (Aug). Race Relations Board established (Dec)

1966 **Fulton Committee appointed** (Feb); first meeting (March); Management Consultancy Group starts work (Sept). **General Election: Labour re-elected** (March, maj 98). Crossman reform of Select Committees announced (Dec)

1967 Ombudsman takes up post (April); application to join EEC (May, vetoed Nov); devaluation (Nov). First draft of Fulton's first chapter (Sept); Management Consultant Group report (Dec)

1968 George Brown resigns (March). **William Armstrong** Head of Home Civil Service (May). **Fulton Report:** Cabinet discussion (20, 25 June); published (26 June); Steering Committee first meets (July); **Civil Service Dept established** (Nov); House of Commons debate (21 Nov); preference for relevance rejected by Wilson (Dec)

CHRONOLOGY

1969   *In Place of Strife* (Jan); *CPSA, CSU adopt strike policy* (May). **Fulton:** Halsey's Social Survey of the Civil Service submitted, *Whitley Bulletin* announces 'abolition of classes' (Sept); Steering Committee rejects unified grading below Principal (Dec). **Conservative Reform: PSRU Sundridge** meeting; formation of business team (Sept). *10 Years Ahead* (Atkinson report on computers completed, published Jan 1971). *Information and the Public Interest* (Cmnd 4089, June)

1970   Michael Halls dies (April); **General Election: Heath succeeds Wilson (18 June**, maj 37); Iain Macleod dies (July); application to EEC (Oct). **Fulton:** Civil Service College opened (June). **Conservatives:** Howell, *A New Style of Government* (May); PSRU *Black Book* (3 June); Meyjes head of Business Team (June); *Reorganization of Central Government* published (Cmnd 4506, Oct); DoE and DTI established; Rothschild to head **CPRS** (from 1 Feb). Equal Pay Act (May).

1971   Industrial Relations Act (Aug); Armstrong's 'Cockaigne' taskforce formed (Nov). **Fulton:** General Category and Administrative Group (Jan) and Science Group formed (Sept); Armstrong 'draws the line under Fulton' (Jan); last meeting of Fulton Steering Committee (Oct); Heath suspends further unified grading (22 Nov); 'moment of truth' for personnel management (Dec). **Conservatives:** PAR starts (Jan); Rayner heads new Procurement Agency (May); CAA hived off (Sept); Employment Service Agency formed (Dec). Pensions (Increase) Act (May). *Women in the Civil Service* (**Kemp Jones** Report) published (June). Expenditure replaces Estimates Committee (Feb). *SCS adopts strike policy; FDA allies with SCS (May)*

1972   *Economy*: miners' strike and unemployment to over 1m (Jan); reflationary budget (March); Industry Act (May); £ floated (June); PIP pay standstill (Nov).*N. Ireland*: Bloody Sunday (30 Jan); direct rule (March). *European Communities Bill*: 3rd reading (July). **Fulton:** Senior Policy and Management Group, Prof and Technology Category + Works Group formed; formal letter on the Post-Fulton programme sent to NSS and Fulton sub-committees wound up (Dec). **Conservatives:** Howell replaced by Baker at CSD (March); PSA (May), Training Services Agency (June), Central Computer Agency (Aug) established; Business Team disbanded (Sept). **Superannuation Act** (March); Principal CS pension scheme (June). **Franks Report on Official Secrets Act** (Cmnd 5014, Sept). European Interdepartmental Ctte (Cab O, May)

1973   UK joins EEC (Jan); **Hunt** Cabinet Secretary (Sept);Yom Kippur war (6–22 Oct); miners' overtime ban (Nov); 3 day week (31 December–7 March). **Fulton:** last meeting Joint Fulton Committee (Feb); Heaton-Williams inquiry into training (July, reports April 74). **Conservatives:** Jellicoe resigns (May); Rothschild's Letcombe speech discredits CPRS (Sept); *Dispersal of Government from London* (**Hardman Report**, Cmnd 5332, June). Kilbrandon Report on the Constitution (Cmnd 5460, Oct).

PIP stage 2, with Armstrong dubbed 'deputy Prime Minister' (Jan); **One-day strike** *(SCPS, CPSA, 27 Feb); SCS affiliates to TUC (May); anomalies ruling (Nov)*; **Wider Issues inquiry launched** *(July, reports March 1974, Feb 1975); Dryden replaces Williams as Sec Gen, NSS (Oct)*

1974 Miners' strike called (for 9 Feb); **General Election** (28 Feb) **and Labour Government** (4 March, min 33); TUC agree social contract (Sept); second **General Election** (10 Oct, Labour re-elected, maj 3). *Institutions established*: MSC, Dept of Energy (Jan); Cash Flow Group (Feb); **No 10 Policy Unit** (March); ACAS (Sept); Health and Safety Exec, Constitution Unit at Cab O (Oct). *Institutions abolished or taken out of CS*: DTI, Training Services Agency (April); Employment Service Agency (Oct). W. Armstrong ill (1–27 Feb), replaced by **Allen** as **Head of Home Civil Service** (June); Berrill replaces Rothschild as head of CPRS (Sept). 'Memo of agreement' on special advisers circulated (Dec). *New pay agreement signed (Dec)*

1975 Mrs Thatcher leader of Conservatives (Feb); EEC referendum; first North Sea oil (June); unemployment 1m (Dec). Cash Control Group's report, advocating **cash limits** (May); *Attack on Inflation* (Cmnd 6151), FIS report (July); Treasury reorganised (Oct); cash limits for 1976/7 announced, FIS implementation team appointed (Nov). Cabinet agree to cut cost of CS by **£140m** by 1978/9 (11 Dec). Priestley Management Review of CS College. Sex Discrimination Act (establishing Equal Opportunities Commission) and Employment Protection Act (Nov). Accounting Officer minutes furore with Benn (Jan). **Crossman Diaries**: serialised by *Sunday Times* (26 Jan–March); trial (July); Widgery judgment (Oct). *32.5% pay award (April). Incomes Policy: stage 1 (£6) (July)*; **pay research suspended** *(to July 1977)*

1976 *Public Expenditure* white paper (Cmnd 6393, Feb) – £3.4b cuts by 1978/9; HC defeat and vote of confidence (10/11 March); **Cash Limits on Public Expenditure (Cmnd 6440)**, FIS 1 implemented (April). **Callaghan Prime Minister** (5 April); *New Society* leak on child benefit (June). Callaghan rejects Keynes at Party Conference (26 Sept); IMF arrive (2 Nov); Labour loses overall majority (4 Nov); Cabinet discusses IMF package (23 Nov–2 Dec); letter of intent (15 Dec). **Peart** replaces Shepherd as LPS, Dept of Transport established (Sept). Radcliffe Report on Ministerial Memoirs (Cmnd 6386, Jan). *IPCS affiliates to TUC (May);* **Kendall** *becomes Sec Gen, NSS (July); Official Working Party on Pay (July, reports Jan); Incomes policy: stage 2 (5% to max £4) (Aug)*

1977 Lib-Lab Pact (March). **English Report** published (Sept, reply March 1978). FIS 2 implemented (April). Edinburgh Centre of CSC closed. Commission for Racial Equality (March). Croham directive on openness (July). *Industrial Policy (Bullock, Cmnd 6706); FDA last association to affiliate with TUC (May). GEN 64 on pay (Jan – June); Incomes policy: stage 3 (10%) (Aug);* **½-day strike by SCPS** *(8 Nov); new pay agreement; week of protest (28 Nov–2 Dec); Pay Research Board appointed (Nov); full meeting of NWC (1 Dec)*

CHRONOLOGY

1978   Devolution Acts (July). Armitage Report on Political Activities of Civil Servants (Cmnd 7057, Jan). **Bancroft** replaces Allen as **Head of Home Civil Service** (Jan). *Longer Term Review of Administrative Computing* (April). *Reform of Section 2 of OSA* (Cmnd 7285, July). *CPSA vote rigging scandal (May); Incomes policy: stage 4 (5%) (Aug), rejected by Lab Conference (Oct)*

1979   **Winter of discontent**: public employees' strike (22 Jan). **CPSA/SCPS one-day strike** (23 Feb) and **selective action** (from 26 Feb); one-day strike, Scotland (21 March); NSS split (29 March); full **one-day strike (2 April)**. Settlement (with Admin Gp, 12 April; P&T Gp, Oct); Ctte A suspended and Kendall's resignation rejected (5–26 April). Tavistock Report on Race Relations in the Civil Service (Feb). **General Election** (3 May, **Mrs Thatcher** maj 43). **Short-term measures:** recruitment freeze, 3% cut, 'options' exercise (May), cash limits on manpower costs agreed (July); Cabinet agrees 10% cut in Civil Service costs by 1982 (Sept); Pliatzky inquiry into quangos commissioned (Aug, reports Jan). **Rayner** appointed **head Efficiency Unit** (8 May); departmental projects' launched (June); presentation of projects to Cabinet and transformed into annual **scrutiny** programme (4 Oct); charging for CSC training encouraged (partial 1983; full 1986). NWC meets (23 Oct). **Robert Armstrong** replaces Hunt as **Cabinet Secretary** (1 Nov); Soames absent from CSD in Rhodesia (Dec to April 1980)

1980   Start of 3 month steel strike (Jan); Bristol riots (April); inflation at 22% (April); unemployment over 2m (Oct). Reagan President of USA (4 Nov); Foot Labour leader (10 Nov). Cabinet agrees 14% cash limit on CS costs leading to 2.5% manpower cuts (28 Feb). Permanent Secretary's dinner (6 May). Mrs Thatcher conditionally agrees to CSD-Treasury merger (July), then rejected by Hawtin-Moore (Oct), Mrs Thatcher (Nov) and Treasury Select Committee (Dec). Mrs Thatcher first considers PM Department (Dec). **Rayner:** first version of **Lasting Reforms** submitted and annual scrutiny of departmental running costs launched (Jan); Cabinet meeting on Lasting reforms and 630,000 manpower target by 1984; MINIS circulated to Ministers (1 May). Joint NWC Groups appointed on equal opps (reports 1982) and new technology (no report) (July). CCSU replaces NSS (first meeting 10 July); NWC meets (30 July); **National Pay Agreement suspended** (Oct); week of protest (24 Nov–1 Dec)

1981   SDP formed (March); Mrs Thatcher's approval rating falls to 25% (July); Brixton riots (10–12 April); Toxteth riots (8 July); Scarman report (Nov). Hayhoe Parliamentary Secretary, CSD (Jan); Cassells to Efficiency Unit (July). Walters appointed Economic Adviser (Jan); 6% cash limit announced (Feb); Ministers' revolt over manpower targets (Feb); **'non-reflationary' budget** (10 March); Financial Management Coordination Group first meets (April); Treasury paper *Control of Expenditure* foreshadows FMI (June). C&AG criticizes internal audit (March). Mrs Thatcher agrees closure of CSD with Armstrong (May); decides to act (7 Sept); Lady Young

393

replaces Soames (14 Sept); Bancroft interview (24 Sept); formal **closure of CSD (12 Nov)**. Govt accepts ethnic monitoring in CS (Dec). Scott Report on the value of public pensions (Cmnd 8417, Feb). ***Civil Service Strike (9 March–31 July)***, *one-day walk-out (1 April), ½-day walk-out (14 April); Megaw Ctte appointed (29 June)*

NOTES

INTRODUCTION

1 K. Dowding, 'The Civil Service' in J. Hollowell, *Britain Since 1945* (2003), p. 188. The phrase was that of the then Cabinet Secretary, Sir Robin Butler, in a lecture to the Association of First Division Civil Servants in February 1991, see *FDA News*, November 1991.
2 See, in particular, the ninth report of the Committee on Standards in Public Life (2003) entitled 'Defining the boundaries within the executive: ministers, special advisers and the permanent Civil Service'. The quotation is taken from the first paragraph of the initial Civil Service Code published in 1996.
3 V. Bogdanor and R. Wilson, *Civil Service Reform: a Policy Management and Policy Association Report* (2001) pp. 24–7.
4 The National Archives, Kew (hereafter TNA): CAB103/562, N. Brook to heads of departments, 5 December 1957. See P. Beck, *Using History, Making British Policy* (2006) ch 2 for a full discussion of this initiative and, more generally, of the use of historical evidence within Government. The revival of Brook's initiative was widely debated in 1969 (see BA17/978) and the jewel in its crown, the Treasury's Historical Section, sacrificed to economy in December 1975 (see T371/92 and below, Chapter 6.3.2a).
5 Quoted in J. Harris, 'If Britain had been defeated by the Nazis' in Wm. R. Louis, *Still More Adventures with Britannia* (2002), pp. 211 and 226. This article, together with R.A. Chapman, *Ethics in the British Civil Service* (1988), best describes the early years of the Civil Series of Official History.
6 TNA: CAB103/598, M. Cary to B. Trend, 11 December 1962.
7 For a good summary of the objectives of 'historical institutionalism' (albeit, given its emphasis on the comparative, one surprisingly focused on the USA), see the entry by E. Sanders in R.A.W. Rhodes *et al* (eds), *The Oxford Handbook of Political Institutions* (2006).
8 Sir Edward Bridges in TNA: CAB 134/304. The later quotation is from TNA: CAB193/562, K. Hancock, 'Report on the Official History of the War Civil Series', January 1957, p. 8.
9 The Intelligence Agencies are well covered in C. Andrew, *The Defence of the Realm: the authorised history of M15* (2009) and K. Jeffery, *The History of the Secret Intelligence Service, 1909–1949* (2010). Omitted also are two subjects to which an introduction was first provided in P. Hennessy, *The Secret State* (2002): transition-to-war planning and the vetting of officials. Both clearly affected the Home Civil Service, not least because of the time and nervous energy consumed amongst senior officials – albeit to incalculable effect. Thankfully there was no transition to a Third World War and the net number of careers overtly blighted by the reinforcement of negative vetting in 1948 and the

introduction of positive vetting after 1950 would appear, up to the early 1980s, to have amounted to as few as 105 (*Secret State*, p. 97). However, where Attlee led, this book has followed. He decreed with typical bluntness that scarce resources should not be devoted to civil defence were this to impede economic recovery (quoted, ibid, p. 120). Likewise, for this book, it was decided not to devote scarce time and space to the undeniable but indeterminable impact of the Cold War were that to impede a better understanding of administrative reform in all its other complexities. The 'Industrial Civil Service' consisted of manual workers employed predominantly by the Ministry of Defence in the Royal Ordnance Factories and Dockyards. Equally densely unionised, they were members of conventional trade unions affiliated to the TUC (rather than staff associations) and their management was kept largely separate from that of the non-industrial Civil Service (see, in particular, ch 8).

10 A more positive defence for self-denial is provided by Sir Douglas Wass in *Decline to Fall* (2008) p. xvii. 'In general', he professed, 'I have tried to depersonalise the narrative . . . One reason for doing this is that the opinions and advice expressed, although usually signed by one individual, were really those of the Sector of the Treasury he worked in. A personalized account would, in my view, have given the impression of personal differences, whereas the differences, when they occurred, were usually of a functional kind.' Others may argue this was simply a necessary defence mechanism for dealing with a period when many exceptionally strong personalities stalked the Treasury's corridors (see ch 6.3.2).

11 See, for example, R. Bacon and W. Eltis, *Britain's Economic Problem: too few producers* (1976) and below, chs 6.1 and 6.2.2.

12 Treasury Occasional Paper 1, *Civil Service Staffing* (1994).

13 Smaller, but arguably of more central importance to the Home Civil Service, was the DHSS (see table 1, col e); the Inland Revenue, employing some 82,000 in 1976, one of the new super ministries, the Department of the Environment which employed some 73,000 in 1976 (see ch 5.3.2c); and a Department at the forefront of the earliest experiments in accountable management, Employment, which through its range of agencies employed some 58,000 by 1981 (see ch 5.3.3c).

14 Inner London conventionally referred not just to Whitehall but any area within a 4-mile radius of Charing Cross. Outer London was any area beyond but within a 16-mile radius of Charing Cross.

15 See Cmd 3909, 1931, paras 8 and 9. The same definition was adopted by the Priestley Commission on the Civil Service (Cmd 9613, 1955, para 11); but the issue was typically evaded by the 1968 Fulton Report, although it did favour a more explicit employment contract (Cmnd 3638, para 143).

16 TNA: BA17/852, A.R. Smith to T.H. Caulcott, 27 February 1970. The master copy of the 1974 CSD memorandum, entitled 'What is a Civil Servant?' and written by J.B. Pearce is preserved in BA17/976. The 'specified contexts' included, for individuals, coverage of superannuation (recently revised in 1972, see ch 9.4), Estacode and Whitleyism and, for institutions, lists of departments attached to the 1958 Public Records Act and the 1967 Parliamentary Commissioner Act. Each, however, contained differences of omission and commission.

17 Hence the consternation in 1968 when it was suggested the Race Relations Act be applied to the Civil Service (see chapter 9.5). Civil Servants' lack of an individual contract could arguably be interpreted as an example of what Harold Macmillan termed, when reforming private sector practice through the 1963 Contracts of Employment Act, 'a remnant of a medieval system and shameful to a modern society' (TNA: PREM11/3930).

18 In the 1970s, many resigned from staff associations, and especially the FDA, on the grounds later specified in R. Wilding, *Civil Servant* (2006) p. 36: 'If civil servants went on strike, whom exactly were they striking against? It was ministers who . . . were

ultimately responsible for fixing all the conditions of civil service employment. But they were not themselves the employers of civil servants, who were servants of the Crown. Could you remain loyal to the Crown while going on strike against your employer?' Later concerns led in 1986 to the specification in the 'Armstrong' memorandum, *The Duties and Responsibilities of Civil Servants* (Cm 2627) that 'Civil servants are servants of the Crown. For all practical purposes the Crown in this context means and is represented by the Government of the day ... The Civil Service as such has no constitutional personality or responsibility separate from the duly constituted Government of the day' (p. 3).

19 F. W. Maitland, *A Constitutional History of England* (1926) p. 418.
20 TNA: BA17/976, J.B. Pearce, 'What is a Civil Servant?', August 1974, pp.10–12. English case law was based on a ruling by Lord Denning, which was later challenged by the Scottish courts and set aside by the Treasury solicitor when recognising the Forestry Commission to be a 'Crown body'. The Forestry Commission (whose staff in certain circumstances might, in addition, be paid from grants-in-aid) was thus, concluded Pearce, 'a good example of the extent to which the boundaries of "the Crown" are in places indeterminate'.
21 See, for instance, Harris, 'If Britain had been defeated', pp. 219, 224–6.
22 For a powerful defence of both the 'public service ethos' and the 'golden age', see B. O'Toole, *The Ideal of Public Service* (2006). On the constitutional duty of Civil Servants, he concludes: 'public officials, elected and non-elected, share the responsibilities of office and thus share the responsibility of determining the public interest. Democracy implies pluralism, and although the primary source of legitimacy in a democracy is election, it is not the only source, nor is it over-riding' (p. 99). On the 'golden age', he likewise concludes that there never was one in the 'sense of a pure concern with acting out of public duty. Human nature is deeply flawed in this sense, as in all others. Nevertheless, there was an *ideal* of public service; and however imperfect from the perspective of the actual world, this acted as a *guide* to public servants' (p. 2).
23 For an example of a characteristically robust but partial use of the Report to defend more recent reforms, see the valedictory speech by Sir Andrew Turnbull as Cabinet Secretary in 2005 at http://politics.guardian.co.uk/whitehall/story/0,9061,1537060,00.html (accessed January 2007).
24 Such 'bias', it might be argued, accorded fully with social norms at the time. This, however, underestimates the potential for radical change after the First World War as typified by, for example, the 1919 Sex Disqualification (Removal) Act (see Chapter 2.3.3). In any case, it underlines the fact – as with the later disadvantaging of non-Keynesians – that 'merit' is not a 'value-free' concept.
25 TNA: T275/190, R. Armstrong to C. Whitmore, 1 August 1980. As Chapters 6 and 8 will demonstrate, deep disillusion with the prevarication of the 1974–9 Labour Governments affected the Service at all levels .
26 On the chimera of value-free judgements by officials and academics alike, see in particular M. Bevir and R.A.W. Rhodes, 'Searching for civil society: changing patterns of governance in Britain', *Public Administration* 81 (2003) 41–62.
27 A. Booth and S. Glynn, 'The public records and recent economic historiography', *Economic History Review*, 32 (1979) 314.
28 Investigative journalism into the Civil Service was pioneered in the 1970s by Peter Hennessy. See TNA: PREM16/762 for a record of his initial impact as a 'Whitehall correspondent' of the national press, repairing the damage earlier wrought by Anthony Howard; other PREM files for regular testimony to his effectiveness; and *Whitehall*, first published in 1989, for the fruits of these labours. Social scientists were granted exceptional access to Government under the ESRC *Whitehall* programme in the 1990s. For the fruits of their labours, see R.A.W. Rhodes (ed), *Transforming British Government*

(2 vols, 2000). The importance of posterity was also acknowledged in K. Hancock and M. Gowing, *British War Economy* (1949): 'the official historians of this generation have consciously submitted their work to the professional verdict of the future' (p. xii).

1 THE NORTHCOTE-TREVELYAN REPORT AND THE EVOLUTION OF THE CIVIL SERVICE, 1854–1916

1. Cmnd 3638 (1968).
2. R. Jenkins, *Gladstone* (1995) p. 165; K.C. Wheare, *The Civil Service in the Constitution* (1954); G. Drewry and T. Butcher, *The Civil Service Today* (1988), p. 46.
3. Cmnd 3638, para 15. The Northcote-Trevelyan Report is reproduced as Appendix B in this volume of the Fulton Report, and all later references are to this source. The quotations above are from pp. 108–9. The original Report may be found in P.P. (1854) xxvi. The authors later apologised for their 'error' in not expressing 'more distinctively' their admiration of the Service's merits. See their letter of 10 April 1854 in *Papers on the Reorganisation of the Civil Service*, P.P. (1854–5) xx (hereafter *Papers on Reorganisation*).
4. Ibid, p.111.
5. Cmnd 3683, pp. 112–15. The italics are added.
6. M. Wright, *Treasury Control of the Civil Service, 1854–1874* (1969), p. 75.
7. P. Hennessy, *Whitehall* (1989), p. 47. Hennessy even describes 4 June 1870 as the 'day the Northcote-Trevelyan report was implemented' (p. 48).
8. *Seventeenth Report of Her Majesty's Civil Service Commissioners*, P.P. (1872) xix, pp. vi-vii. There were so few Class 1 vacancies because most work was classified as 'mechanical' and there was accordingly a large number of redundancies.
9. Cd 7338, *Fourth Report* (1914), ch 2, para 6. See also the observation in ch 1, para 54: 'uncontrolled patronage continues to fill some of the highest of Departmental offices as well as some of the lowest situations'.
10. H. J. Hanham, 'Political patronage at the Treasury, 1870–1912', *Historical Journal* 3 (1960) 75–84. This article also provides details of the late use of patronage by Northcote and Gladstone.
11. See, for instance, Cmnd 3683, p. 110: 'there are a *few* situations in which such varied talent and such an amount of experience are required, that it is probable that under any circumstances it will *occasionally* be found necessary to fill them with persons who have distinguished themselves elsewhere than in the Civil Service'. Italics added.
12. Order in Council, 1910, clause 7. The dispensations were consolidated into clause 7 and 11 of this Order.
13. For details about these appointments, and of labour exchange managers, as well as a comparison with practices in other social policy departments, see R. Davidson and R. Lowe, 'Bureaucracy and innovation in British welfare policy 1870–1945' in W. J. Mommsen, *The Emergence of the Welfare State in Britain and Germany* (1981), pp. 264–77.
14. For Beveridge's own account, see Lord Beveridge, *Power and Influence* (1953), pp. 68–9 and J. Harris, *William Beveridge* (Oxford, 1997), p. 165. His position was not made pensionable ('established') until the following year.
15. Beveridge, *op. cit.*, pp. 76–7; Sir Harold Emmerson, unpublished autobiography; F. A. Norman, *From Whitehall to West Indies* (1952), p. 29. This use of competitive interview so impressed the First Commissioner, Sir Stanley Leathes, that he successfully championed its permanent incorporation into the Class I selection process.
16. For a biography of, and a full summary of the literature on, Trevelyan, see K. Theakston, *Leadership in Whitehall* (1999), ch 2. For comprehensive contemporary criticism, see *Papers on Reorganisation*; and for a powerful individual denunciation, see A. Trollope, *The Three Clerks* (1858), ch 28. This polemical chapter is sometimes omitted from editions of the novel.
17. Quoted in Theakston, *Leadership*, p. 32. Northcote's patronage was driven by the need to find financial support for seven sons, whilst Gladstone's was justified more by the

NOTES FOR CHAPTER 1

    promotion of efficiency. The classic historical defence of patronage is J. M. Bourne, *Patronage and Society in Nineteenth-Century England* (1986).
18 R. A. Chapman and J. R. Greenaway, *The Dynamics of Administrative Reform* (1980), p. 47.
19 This and successive quotations are from *Papers on Reorganisation*, pp. 133, 76 and 165–6. See also Chapman and Greenaway, *Dynamics*, p. 27. Examinations were, of course, a novelty in the 1850s and of suspect oriental origin. The considered view of *The Times* on 22 September 1855, for example, was that they were a 'Chinese scheme for filling the civil service of this country with pedants and book-worms'.
20 Both the Playfair and the Ridley Commissions sought to moderate the potentially adverse affects of reform. Playfair suggested that a modicum of patronage could be maintained by passing more examination candidates than required and then allowing departments to select their favoured one. Ridley recommended a two-year probation to ensure recruits had aptitudes other than that of 'being able to succeed in a literary examination'. See the excellent summary provided by J.B. Bourn, 'The main reports on the British Civil Service since the Northcote-Trevelyan Report', Fulton Report, vol 3 (2), memo 10, paras 38 and 51.
21 Cd 6535, q. 13110. For criticism of the Home Office, see Davidson and Lowe, 'Bureaucracy and innovation', p. 269.
22 Cd 6535, qs 13359 and 13164. Llewellyn Smith was pressed particularly on the status of statisticians. Directors of statistics qualified through their expertise for First Division salaries but, as specialists who were expected neither to undertake nor apply for generalist work, they held 'staff posts' within the Second Division. Llewellyn Smith approved of this anomaly. The Treasury did not. It liked even less the fact that statistics were starting to be collected not just for administrative but also 'speculative' purposes (and so had policy implications). Both salaries and work, in its opinion, should be at a 'mechanical' level.
23 There was a precedent in that such a division had been successfully introduced by Sir James Stephen into the Colonial Office in the 1830s. The subsequent history of attempts to distinguish between the 'intellectual' and the 'mechanical' is well summarised in Chapman and Greenaway, *Dynamics*, pp. 22–36.
24 The 1910 Order in Council, for example, regulated their hours of attendance and required the signing of an attendance book as well as confirming a maximum of 48 days' annual leave.
25 Trevelyan's deputy at the Treasury, Arbuthnot, wrote a strong critique of the proposed division arguing that 'to fulfil the superior offices satisfactorily a previous apprenticeship in the inferior classes is essential'. See *Papers on Reorganisation*, letter of 6 March 1854.
26 Cmnd 3638, pp. 112, 115; *Papers on Reorganisation*, p. 422. 'Supplementary' clerks was the early name for 'lower' or 'second division' clerks.
27 Downgrading was even formalised by the creation of new grades. Intermediate and supplementary clerks were appointed in some departments wholly to replace the First Division; and women and boy clerks were appointed as well as assistant clerks to undertake work formerly assigned to the Second Division.
28 Cd 7338, ch 3, para 6.
29 Cmnd 6368, p. 118.
30 Between 1855 and 1894 only 129 recruits failed probation. The majority failed because of ill-health and only 31 through 'inefficiency'. See R.A. Chapman, *Civil Service Commission*, p. 29.
31 Cmnd 6368, p. 118. These views were later modified when Northcote and Trevelyan were obliged to concede that 'specialist' knowledge was an 'essential condition' for the 'usefulness' of permanent officials to generalist Ministers. They therefore accepted that 'the regular course of promotion should be within each department'. See *Papers on Reorganisation*, p. 421.
32 Cd 6210, *First Report of the Royal Commission on the Civil Service* (1912–13), appendix, pp. 129–30.

NOTES FOR CHAPTER 1

33 Quoted in J. Pellew, *The Home Office, 1848–1914* (1982), pp. 98–9. This book is the most effective study of the impact of reform on a particular, albeit conservative, department. See also Trollope, *Three Clerks*.
34 Cmnd 3638, pp. 110 and 118. These views, as has been seen, were later modified when both authors accepted that promotion within departments should be the norm. They even downgraded unification to a secondary objective behind the introduction of competitive examinations and promotion by merit. See *Papers on Reorganization*, p. 422.
35 Chapman, *Civil Service Commission*, p. 11. The number of transfers is also taken from this source (p. 28).
36 See, for example, Trollope, *Three Clerks*, p. 314. Trollope actually proposed that up to twelve parliamentary seats be reserved *ex officio* for Ministers, so that the ablest of 'permanent' officials could join the Cabinet. See also D.N. Chester, *The English Administrative System* (1981), pp. 298–9. Parliament first recognised the common needs of 'permanent' civil servants in the 1810 Pensions Act and the term was first used statutorily in the 1859 Superannuation Act.
37 This was Sir Henry Primrose, one of the private secretaries who owed his elevation to Gladstone's patronage, quoted in Chapman and Greenaway, *Dynamics*, p. 17. Hence the conventional wisdom that before 1919 the Civil Service was 'more a conglomeration of departments than a unified service', see V. Bogdanor (ed), *The British Constitution in the Twentieth Century* (2003), p. 241.
38 *Treasury Minute of 12 April 1853*, P.P. (1854–5) xxx; Wright, *Treasury Control*, appendix II. This assertion inspired the whole debate over whether the Permanent Secretary of the Treasury was Head of the Civil Service before 1919. The general consensus is that officially he was not, but *de facto* he was. See Wright. *op cit*, and H. Roseveare, *The Treasury* (1969), pp. 249–52.
39 Wright, *Treasury Control*, pp. 359–60.
40 Quoted, but not referenced, in Roseveare, *Treasury*, p. 251. This quotation does illustrate the very real political and administrative barriers to reform at this, and indeed any, time. There is, however, little evidence that Treasury officials actively sought to breach them or favoured disunity to facilitate greater departmental specialism. That would have threatened greater public expenditure.
41 See, in particular, Wright, *Treasury Control*, ch 8. The 1910 Order in Council reaffirmed the Treasury's competence to examine the pay and staffing of individual departments every five years (clause 12).
42 Quoted in Wright, *Treasury Control*, pp. 357–9 on which much of this paragraph is based. After the creation of the Service-wide division, and despite the establishment of the Second Division Clerks Association in 1890, the bargaining strength of permanent officials at this level was nevertheless sapped by Treasury insistence that negotiations should be conducted at departmental level. In translating Service-wide unity into effective action, they were overtaken by temporary staff particularly after the founding of the Assistant Clerks Association in 1903. See B. V. Humphreys, *Clerical Unions in the Civil Service* (1958), p. 57.
43 Gladstone pressurised Northcote and Trevelyan into being more radical than they had intended. They had shown greater awareness of potential political hostility by originally suggesting that seven-eighths of patronage, including all appointments to the Treasury's sub-departments, be retained. By 1869 Gladstone, as Prime Minister, was more ready to compromise – perhaps because his fear of social revolution, and thus his commitment to administrative reform, had diminished. Lowe's intransigence forced him to be more radical than he then intended and arguably advanced the introduction of open competition by a decade. See J. Winter, *Robert Lowe* (1976), p. 262.
44 H. C. G. Matthew, *Gladstone 1809–1874* (1986), p. 85.
45 Quoted in A. Briggs, *Victorian People* (1965), p. 117. The following quotations are from Theakston, *Leadership*, pp. 27–8 and Winter, *Lowe*, p. 262. The former cites Trevelyan's

expression of confidence that the Report's outcome would be 'decidedly aristocratic, but it will be so in a good sense by securing for the public Service those who are, in a true sense, worthy'. The latter records Lowe's fear that a non-graduate might 'not pronounce his "Rs" or commit some similar solecism, which might be a most serious damage to a department in the course of negotiations'. Consequently government would suffer 'if we allow everybody to rise up to everything' (p. 266). Such a fear is less gratuitous when account is taken of the prevailing conviction that officials should not directly enforce, but persuade independent outside bodies to observe, the law.

46 Both quotations are from Benjamin Jowett's letter to Trevelyan in January 1854, which accompanied the submission of the Report (see P. P. (1854) xxvii). Jowett, a Fellow of Balliol College, was in the forefront of educational reform particularly in relation to Oxford University (for which Gladstone was the MP). Jowett in Hennessy's classic phrase represented a 'potent mixture of lofty idealism and hard-headed job creation' which was to serve Oxford graduates well over the following century (Hennessy, *Whitehall*, p. 42). There had also been concern about attracting students to Oxford were job prospects to be limited to the law, the church and to university fellowships (for which, as ever, celibacy was required).

47 Cmnd 3638, p. 114; Winter, *Lowe*, pp. 183, 264. Macaulay predicted that the effect of his similar recommendations for entry examinations for the Indian Civil Service would 'be felt in every seat of learning throughout the realm'. See his report, reproduced in Cmnd 3638, p. 120.

48 O. MacDonagh, 'The nineteenth-century revolution in government: a reappraisal', *Historical Journal* 1 (1958) 52–67. The state of this long-running debate was constantly reviewed, see R. Macleod, *Government and Expertise* (1988).

49 Classically Sir John Simon, having replaced Chadwick and tried to encourage (rather than compel) local authorities to improve public health, was forced to admit that 'local self-government . . . meant . . . no government at all' (see R. Lambert, 'Central and local relations in mid-Victorian England', *Victorian Studies* 6 (1962) 121–50).

50 C. Wood to Russell, 27 December 1850, quoted in H. Parris, *Constitutional Bureaucracy* (1969), pp. 208–9. Dickens caricatured this attitude in *Our Mutual Friend* in the exclamation of Mr Podsnap: 'Centralization. No. Never with my consent. Not English'.

51 For a brief comparative overview, see E. Barker, *The Development of Pubic Services in Western Europe, 1660–1930* (1944).

52 J. Harris, 'Society and state in twentieth-century Britain' in F. M. L. Thompson (ed), *The Cambridge Social History of Britain* (1990), vol 3, pp. 67–8.

53 For this and Dicey's defence of the common law, see J. Jowell, 'Administrative law' in Bogdanor, *British Constitution* ch 10 and H.W. Arthurs, *Without the Law: administrative justice and legal pluralism in nineteenth-century England* (1985).

54 Parris, *Constitutional Bureaucracy*, p. 212. Reference to the royal prerogative could also be helpful in cases of excess.

55 Earl Grey, *Parliamentary Government* (1858), pp. 190–1.

56 Parris, *Constitutional Bureaucracy*, pp. 29–33.

57 Ibid, pp. 42–8; and see ch 1.2.4 above.

58 Pellew, *Home Office*, pp. 6, 19, 181. The reasons why the Report had so little impact were the continuation of patronage until the 1880s, the partial implementation of open competition and its acceptance of the need to appoint some 'strangers' to senior posts which left a way open for late entrants and specialists whose career commitments lay elsewhere.

59 G. Kitson Clark, '"Statesmen in disguise"', *Historical Journal* 2 (1959) 35.

60 Ibid, pp. 22–3. Trevelyan himself was one in a long line of senior officials who refused to vote in elections for fear of jeopardising his neutrality. Sir Edward Hamilton, the Permanent Secretary of the Edwardian Treasury was another. The irony was that, within Whitehall, both acted with extreme partisanship. See Parris, *Constitutional Bureaucracy*, p. 94 and Roseveare, *Treasury*, pp. 220–2.

NOTES FOR CHAPTER 1

61 Stephen himself had been pilloried in the 1840s as 'Mr Mother Country' and 'Mr Over-Secretary' because of his hidden influence as Permanent Under-Secretary at the Colonial Office. The dispute, according to Kitson Clark, represented the classic attack against 'the habitual triumph of the all-pervasive self-deprecatory power of the permanent official over the inexperience of his successive political masters'. '"Statesmen in disguise"', p. 26.

62 G. Roth and C. Willich, *Max Weber. Economy and Society* (1968), vol 3, pp. 973–94. The late Victorian and Edwardian Treasury was, of course, one of the most partisan departments being, in the words of its own historian, 'permeated with the prejudices of one political party'. This was neither the protectionist Conservative nor the nascent Labour Party. See Roseveare, *Treasury*, p. 215.

63 Specialists tended to come from a more exclusive social and educational background than 'generalists'; and although they also tended to appreciate better the problems of an increasingly pluralistic society, this did lead to a deep wartime rift between, for example, the trade unions and the Board of Trade – and in particular the charge that 'you govern labour for the good of labour on behalf of labour, but keep labour at a distance' (Parl Deb (Commons) 95, col 596, 28 June 1917). For their part, 'generalists' certainly had less exclusive backgrounds than many other professional workers. Given that they were funded by the taxpayer, that was perhaps right.

64 For this, and a defence of Chadwick and other zealots including Trevelyan, see Kitson Clark, '"Statesman in disguise"', pp. 24 and 30–3. See also Parris, *Constitutional Bureaucracy*, pp. 93–9.

65 Pellew, *Home Office*, pp. 195–9. Askwith provides a prime example of an Edwardian official seeking to defend both the 'public' interest and the impartiality of the state against narrow vested interests, including those of political parties. This principled stance was somewhat marred by his formation of a Middle Class Union on his enforced resignation in 1919. See R. Lowe, *Adjusting to Democracy* (Oxford, 1986), p. 67. The 'impartiality' of Board of Trade officials has been most thoroughly examined by Roger Davidson, particularly in 'The Board of Trade and industrial relations, 1896–1914', *Historical Journal* 21 (1978) 571–91 and *Whitehall and the Labour Problem in Late-Victorian and Edwardian Britain* (1985).

66 Bourne, *Patronage and Society*, p. 166; Theakston, *Leadership*, p. 32.

67 Parris, *Constitutional Bureaucracy*, ch 3. The quotation is on p. 104. The term 'vicarious accountability' and the political nature of ministerial responsibility, developed in the next paragraph, is taken from the chapter by D. Woodhouse, 'Ministerial responsibility' in Bogdanor, *British Constitution*, pp. 281–332.

68 Chapman, *Civil Service Commission*, p. 154. For the start of the process see Wright, *Treasury Control*, ch 4.

69 Roseveare, *Treasury*, p. 215.

70 Between 1870 and 1908, the number of its Class I posts increased by one to 26 whilst the size of the Civil Service trebled.

71 Roseveare, *Treasury*, p. 200. Wright has attempted a defence of the Treasury by arguing that of necessity the 'manner in which it discharged its responsibilities resembled an elaborate game, the rules of which were well known to both contestants but never openly discussed between them' (*Treasury Control*, p. 173). Opaqueness would seem to have few benefits as a long-term strategy. The playing field also appeared distinctly unlevel.

72 See, for example, this description of the Home Office's reaction to proposals for a more logical division of its work in the 1870s: 'such a change would have meant a Home Office largely staffed by supplementary clerks and writers. *In terms of work this would have been feasible*, but no minister – certainly not the Home Secretary – was likely to want apparently to downgrade his department to such an extent'. Pellew, *Home Office*, p. 26. Italics added.

73 R.M. Macleod, *Treasury Control and Public Administration* (1968), pp. 41–5.

NOTES FOR CHAPTER 2

74 Theakston, *Leadership*, p. 23. This reflected the sentiment in Gladstone's minute setting up the Report: 'the gain in point of economy will probably be important. But the gain in point of efficiency will be far greater' (P.P. (1854–5) xxx). The wider tension anticipated key issues within administrative reform after 1945. Trevelyan's ideal of mutual co-operation, for example, foreshadowed the Plowden Committee's call for 'joint working in a common enterprise' (Cmnd 1432, para 34) and his attitude towards economy Sir Derek Rayner's policy of 'spend to save' (see ch 7.3.2).

75 The Treasury assumed control over the nature and balance of entry examinations from the Civil Service Commission in 1870. It also dismissed all notion of specialist post-entry training – although even Trollope was calling for a 'college for the civil service', see *Three Clerks*, p. 320. Haileybury had, of course, provided just such a function for the Indian Civil Service until 1854.

76 Cmnd 3638, pp. 114, 111. The quotation from Jowett's letter of January 1854 is in P.P. (1854) xxvii, p.27.

77 Macaulay's report is reprinted in Appendix B to the Fulton Report, which makes even more inexcusable its assertion that 'the Macaulay Report extolled the merits of the young men from Oxford and Cambridge who had read nothing but subjects unrelated to their future careers' (para 3). The quotation from Macaulay is taken from p. 120. The argument in this and the preceding paragraph is supported by Parris, *Constitutional Bureaucracy*, pp. 288–94.

2 WAR AND PEACE: THE FISHER-BRIDGES SETTLEMENT 1916–56

1 This was an unlikely legacy of the then Prime Minister, Lloyd George, who was antipathetic both to 'business' (as opposed to certain businessmen's) methods and Victorian perceptions of order and morality.

2 Fabian Society, *The Reform of the Higher Civil Service* (1947) p. 5. The report did, however, qualify its praise by suggesting that 'the Civil Service has been saved from disaster by two wars'.

3 P. Hennessy, *Whitehall* (1986), pp. 188–9 (plate 7). Bridges, nevertheless, was somewhat dismissive of the continuing relevance of the Northcote-Trevelyan Report. As he wrote in an article to celebrate its centenary, it 'did not set out to be a bible for the Civil Service administration of all time . . . It is a matter-of-fact, closely argued document directed to proving a limited number of propositions and securing their acceptance'. See 'The reforms of 1854 in retrospect' in W.A. Robson (ed), *The Civil Service in Britain and France* (1954), p.34.

4 See T.A. Critchley, *The Civil Service Today* (1951), p.13. The attacks were thus somewhat optimistically explained away in the classic contemporary account of the interwar Service: 'there is no real malice . . . The assailants know that the Civil Service will suffer no harm and bear no resentment. Even at such moments it finds defenders, and always there is an underlying conviction that in general "the Civil Service is all right"'. See H.E. Dale, *The Higher Civil Service of Great Britain* (1941), p. 65.

5 *New Statesman*, 28 January 1939. The classic polemic against the negative role of the Civil Service in both domestic and foreign policy was Cato, *Guilty Men* (1940).

6 Sir Edward Bridges, *Treasury Control* (1950) and *Portrait of a Profession* (1950), p. 5; Estimates Committee, Sixth Report (1957–8), HC 254, para 94.

7 G.K.Fry, *Statesmen in Disguise* (1969), p. 58; Hennessy, *Whitehall*, p. 120.

8 Bridges himself typically 'only thought of the top 1% when he spoke or wrote about the Civil Service'. This undoubtedly coloured his judgement. See Chapman, *Ethics*, p. 310.

9 Roth and Willich, *Weber*, vol 3, pp. 983–5; see also M. Albrow, *Bureaucracy* (1970), ch 2–3.

10 Cmd 7046, para 8. For a fuller discussion of the historic tension, see R. Lowe and N. Rollings, 'Modernizing Britain' in Rhodes (ed), *Transforming British Government* (2000),

vol 1, pp. 100–108; and of the evolution of social and economic policy, R. Lowe, *The Welfare State in Britain since 1945* (3rd ed, 2005) especially chs.5.1 and 6.1. In the interwar period, official self-effacement was demonstrated in social policy, for example, by the channelling of money to the voluntary sector through the National Council of Social Services; and in economic policy by the covert programme of 'industrial diplomacy' to prompt a 'private enterprise' recovery. See R. Lowe and R. Roberts, 'Sir Horace Wilson', *Historical Journal* 30 (1987) 641–62.

11   There is an interim review of the extensive literature on interwar economic policy in G.C. Peden, *Keynes, the Treasury and British Economic Policy* (1988). The historical revision of the state's social role was commenced in G. Finlayson, 'A moving frontier' *Twentieth Century British History* 1 (1990) 183–206. A pioneering summary and expose of the literature on 'decline' is J. Tomlinson, *The Politics of Decline* (2000).

12   Cabinet decisions had previously been recorded only in confidential letters by the Prime Minister to the Monarch, to which Ministers were not always privy. This impaired collective memory let alone collective responsibility and could have serious administrative consequences, as illustrated by Beveridge. In relation to a key wages decision during the First World War, he recalled that the only way to discover the Cabinet's ruling was 'to ask the Prime Minister or another member of the Cabinet. To make sure, we asked three separate Ministers . . . and received three different answers', *Power and Influence* (1953), pp. 134–5.

13   See A. Baker, *Prime Ministers and the Rule Book* (2000), ch 1.

14   *The Times* of 27 October 1922, for example, attacked the Office as a 'Prime Ministerial Department for the conduct of important international affairs apart from, or even in subversion of, well-tried constitutional practices and safeguards'. For a full account, see S. Roskill, *Hankey: Man of Secrets*, vol 2 (1972), pp.310–20.

15   The interwar Cabinet Office was in a better position than the Treasury to unite the Service because, by servicing the Committee of Civil Defence, its officials could relate military and civilian issues. It also had an overview of intelligence and diplomatic issues, areas where the remit of the Head of the Civil Service was hotly disputed.

16   Quoted in K.Middlemas (ed), *Thomas Jones: Whitehall Diary*, vol 2 (1969), pp. 167–8. For a fuller analysis of his influence and that of other Cabinet Office officials, see the relevant entries in the *Oxford Dictionary of National Biography* (2004). The early history of the Secretariat, its origins in the Committee of Imperial Defence (CID) and its relationship with Lloyd George's 'garden suburb' of political advisers is well covered in J. Turner, 'Cabinet committees and secretariats' in K.Burk (ed), *War and State* (1982) and *Lloyd George's Secretariat* (1980). His conclusion is that initially the Cabinet Secretariat, like the CID, rather than creating unity merely disguised disunity.

17   The phrase is John Anderson's in 'The machinery of government', *Public Administration* 24 (1946) 153. Anderson epitomised the ambivalence of the time by arguing that 'while I emphasize the departmental responsibilities of Ministers as a necessary and vital principle, I at the same time stress the importance, as a practical matter, of adequate machinery for making a reality of collective responsibility'. As the former chairman of the wartime Ministerial Machinery of Government Committee, he ultimately recommended a strengthening of the Cabinet Office whereas the Official Committee in June 1945 did not (see TNA: CAB87/75, MGO74, para 15, which also contains Bridges' historical survey of the Secretariat in Appendix 2). The phrase 'making a reality of collective responsibility' was significantly used by the Treasury during the drafting of the Plowden Report to justify the introduction of PESC (see T291/14, CPE(SC1)10, para 13).

18   This radical reorganisation was no more successful than the one in 1961–2. In 1927 the Controllerships of Supply and Establishment were merged; and in 1932 responsibility for Finance and Supply reverted to conventional Second Secretaries, whilst Establishments were entrusted to an Under Secretary. In each move the status of establishment work was significantly lowered.

19 This is discussed more fully in ch 2.3. The intention to reinforce Treasury control over staff had been signalled by the creation in February 1919 of a dedicated Establishment Division, as recommended by the MacDonnell Commission. The sanctioning of departmental classes once again blurred the distinction between 'intellectual' and 'mechanical' work; but in 1939 they contained only 17,000 officials, compared to 124,000 by the time of Fulton.

20 The appointment of PEOs in all departments had been recommended by the 1918–19 Bradbury Committee on the Organization and Staffing of Government Offices, of which Fisher was a member. The appointment and special status of PFOs were the proposals of the Baldwin Council of Finance Officers working to the Cabinet Finance Committee in late 1919. See Cmd 62 (1919) and E. O'Halpin, *Head of the Civil Service* (1989), pp. 47–9.

21 E.E. Bridges, *The Treasury* (1964), p.173.

22 TNA: CAB87/75, MGO 74 (June 1945) Appendix 2, para 26. Although written in the Treasury, this appendix had been widely circulated in draft and was acknowledged to represent 'the agreed view of the whole of Whitehall'. Ibid, main report, para 3. The title had been changed from 'permanent' to the less provocative 'official' head after a hostile Parliamentary debate in 1926; and to Head of the *Home* Civil Service in 1943 following the belated triumph of the guerilla warfare waged by the Foreign Office against the original decision that Fisher's remit should extend over that department, but not the diplomatic service. Earlier, in 1928, Fisher was thought to have secured a significant victory by having Foreign Office officials formally described as 'Civil Servants' in the report on the Francs case (Cmd 3037).

23 In 1947, for example, Bridges stirred Attlee into action by arguing that if attacks on officials as 'parasites' continued unanswered, there would be a 'highly adverse effect on morale, and this in itself decreases efficiency and increases numbers'. Moreover 'new entrants on whom the building up of a more efficient Service largely depends will disappoint us if the heart is taken out of them by an unanswered campaign of unjust criticism'. There were arguably lessons here for the 1970s. See Chapman, *Ethics*, p. 279. For a similar outburst by Fisher in 1921, see O'Halpin, *Head*, p. 58.

24 The intervening heads were Sir Horace Wilson (1938–42) and Sir Richard Hopkins (1942–5). Bridges was the only one to have spent his entire career in the Treasury.

25 Bridges, *Portrait*, p. 32. Fisher and Bridges both enjoyed a classic 'Northcote-Trevelyan' background in that their fathers (respectively a Cumberland landowner and the Poet Laureate) had independent means. This may partly explain their commitment to high moral standards – as an antidote to a perceived decline in political morality. This was not simply a reaction to corruption under Lloyd George (whom Fisher idolised). In 1937, for example, Fisher reportedly argued: 'we shall need men who will have the guts to stand up to their Ministers. As English politics gets increasingly Americanised, we shall find Ministers more disposed to do shady things . . . and the Civil Servants of the day will have to possess the courage to say to their political chiefs "That's a damned swindle, sir, and you can't do it'. Quoted in R.A. Chapman, *Leadership in the British Civil Service* (1984), p. 170.

26 Quoted in Chapman, *Ethics*, pp. 175–6. The succeeding quote is on p. 304. The Francs case concerned financial speculation by Foreign Office officials, for which they were disciplined although charges of corruption and the misuse of official information were dismissed. It was dramatised by the wife of one of those disciplined in a book which revealed both Fisher's idiosyncratic behaviour and the social snobbery to which he was subjected: A. Bridge, *Permission to Resign* (1971). The principal victim of the moral 'code' was Sir Christopher Bullock, who was dismissed as Permanent Secretary of the Air Ministry in 1936 for seeking both a place on the board, and an honour for the chairman of Imperial Airlines with which he was in negotiation. It was agreed retrospectively that he was treated unfairly by Fisher and Bridges unavailingly sought some redress. See Chapman, *Ethics*, ch 4.

27 See Parl Deb (Commons), 194, cols 289–234,14 August 1926; 208, cols 57–110, 17 June 1927; and (Lords) 125, cols 223–325, 25–6 November 1942. Curzon, as Foreign Secretary in 1920, well summarised the main Ministerial grudge: 'if a man is fit to be appointed . . . head of any . . . department of state, he must be considered competent to decide who shall fill the higher posts in the office for which he was responsible' (TNA: T1/12564/20935). There was also a justified fear of a reversion to patronage with so much influence concentrated in one man. For an official defence of the post, see TNA: CAB87/75, MOG 74, Appendix 2, para 29.

28 See Roskill, *Hankey*, vol 2, pp. 310–20; and TNA: T199/50C, Fisher's evidence to the Treasury Organisation Committee, 2 November 1936. Greater standardisation and Treasury control *was* achieved by the exclusive staffing of the Prime Minister's Private Office with Civil Servants after 1928; and by the eventual appointment in 1938 of a Treasury official as Cabinet Secretary (Bridges).

29 Bridges, *Treasury*, p. 171. It is now established that, as with Fisher's 'quasi-theological' constitutional defence for the headship of the Civil Service being sited in the Treasury, there is little substance in the charge that Fisher manufactured the position for himself. It was the political creation of the Cabinet's Finance Committee in 1919, acting on an original suggestion by Sir John Bradbury – a Treasury Joint Permanent Secretary, with perhaps a personal interest in the position himself. See O'Halpin, *Head*, pp. 31–7, 150–3.

30 P.Barberis, *Elite of Elites* (1996), p. 14; Sir William Murrie, quoted in Chapman, *Ethics*, p. 22; W. Bagehot, *The English Constitution* (1878 ed), pp. 192–201. Promotion policy under Bridges prompted questions about whether the principle of promotion by merit was being compromised. The most able individual did not always gain immediate promotion because 'like placing the members of a cricket eleven in the field' an eye had to be kept on how to secure 'the strongest results for the team as a whole'. See Bridges, *Treasury*, p. 177.

31 See TNA: CAB87/75, Appendix 2, esp. paras 14–18, 31. Amongst others, MacDonnell in 1914 personally favoured an independent agency as did Tom Jones in 1944. See J.R. Greenaway, 'Warren Fisher and the transformation of the British Treasury, 1919–1939' *Journal of British Studies* 23 (1985) 128 (which provides the most succinct analysis of the wartime challenge to Civil Service unity and thus the size of Fisher's actual achievement) and *The Observer*, 21 May 1944. 'Agreement' to reject a Civil Service Department in 1945 was secured in Whitehall only by a classic piece of draftsmanship. The Treasury had alternately denied and admitted the existence of a working relationship between its two sides in order to ward off, respectively, criticisms of financial constraints on staffing and proposals for a separate department. The form of wording finally agreed was: 'there is a certain area in which financial control and control of establishments overlap: because of this overlap it is as difficult to separate them entirely as it is wrong to identify them too closely'.

32 Quoted in Theakston, *Leadership*, p. 47. Hennessy has called the Committee 'one of the true benchmarks in the history of the modern Civil Service and a *locus classicus* for those who delight in tracing the imprint of the alleged dead-hand of Treasury orthodoxy', *Whitehall*, p. 69.

33 Quoted in O'Halpin, *Head*, p. 35; *The Times*, 27 September 1948. Fisher, who was a member of the Bradbury Committee, had twice been rejected by the Treasury and been treated contemptuously by its officials whilst at the Inland Revenue. His admission was in the *Manchester Guardian*, 11 December 1942.

34 TNA: CAB 87/75, MOG 74, main report, para 11 and Appendix 2, para 18. For examples of disunity see Lowe, *Adjusting to Democracy*, especially ch 3, and G.C. Peden, *British Rearmament and the Treasury* (1979). It has also been argued that 'despite the overall homogeneity of the upper levels of the home Civil Service . . . the interwar social service ministries differed materially, both in their methods of recruitment and in their patterns of promotion' at a junior level – leading directly to different professional identities and

NOTES FOR CHAPTER 2

departmental views towards state intervention. See G. Savage, *The Social Construction of Expertise* (1996), p. 9. Fisher himself was partly responsible for the exceptionalism of social service departments because his formalisation of a departmental hierarchy in 1920 confirmed the prewar practice that – despite changed electoral priorities – their senior posts should have the lowest salaries.

35 Louis Petch, quoted in J.M.Lee, *Reviewing the Machinery of Government* (1977), p. 52.
36 For a comprehensive review of relevant primary and secondary literature up to the Fulton Report, see Fry, *Statesman in Disguise* and for a particular line of attack on the Administrative Class, see K. Theakston, *The Labour Party and Whitehall* (1992), ch 5.
37 R.K. Kelsall, *Higher Civil Servants in Britain* (1955). See in particular tables 15, 22 and 25. A proportion of these posts, rising from 18 to 24%, were held by officials who had not attended university. They had largely been promoted or transferred from other classes. There was, of course, a lagged effect with those holding interwar posts, for example, having been educated before 1914.
38 See *Public Administration* 33 (1955) 383–8 and 34 (1956) 169–74 for a classic exchange of views between Kelsall and Kenneth Robinson (a fellow of Nuffield College who had served twelve years in the Administrative Class). A traditional defence of 'biased' recruitment since the MacDonnell Commission had been that an Oxbridge education was in reach of a state scholarship boy. This was largely a delusion. The cost (and foregone income) alone would have been prohibitive for any but the most exceptional of parents. Recruitment into the Higher Civil Service required, at minimum, three extra years of schooling, four years for a typical Greats degree at Oxford, further months spent cramming for 'additional' subjects and finally a week's unsubsidised accommodation in London during the examination itself.
39 Chapman, *Civil Service Commission*, pp. 63 and 227. The Commission's failure to adhere to Northcote-Trevelyan's aspiration that the subjects for examination should be 'as numerous as may be found practical, so as to secure the greatest and most varied amount of talent for the public service' (Cmnd 3638, p. 113) was well illustrated by the battle between 1936 and 1961 to win acceptance for sociology. Ibid, p. 231.
40 Typically 60% of the interwar Administrative Class was recruited through open competition. For those in 1939 at the rank of Assistant Secretary or above, there had been three other means of access: promotion from a lower class (20%), transfer from specialist classes (10%) and direct recruitment principally by special postwar competition between 1919 and 1925 (12%). Further reconstruction competitions were held between 1946–9 and were condemned by Kelsall (pp. 94–5) as well as by a future Assistant Commissioner, C.P. Snow, in *Homecomings* (1956), ch 44. Snow's fictional depiction of an interview ends with an outburst that the process favoured the second-rate and that 'any society which deliberately made safe appointments was on the way out'. The Second World War also so facilitated promotion 'from below' that by 1950 36% of Assistant Secretaries and above had been appointed via that route. This was equally condemned by Balogh in his classic 1959 diatribe (reprinted as 'The apotheosis of the dilettante' in H. Thomas, *Crisis in the Civil Service* (1968), p.16): 'promoted warrant officers and privates' were depicted as seeking, to outdo each other in imitating 'the worst characteristics of the public school educated graduates of the old universities'. No doubt he had in mind the example of Sir Horace Wilson, who had risen from the lowest grade of boy clerk in the Patent Office in 1898 to Head of the Civil Service in 1938.
41 See Kelsall, *Higher Civil Servants*, table 23, pp. 93 and 95–6. See also Chapman, *Civil Service Commission*, p. 53.
42 Kelsall, *Higher Civil Servants*, pp. 84–5 and Chapman, *Civil Service Commission*, p. 225. Robinson, in his spat with Kelsall (see footnote 38) waspishly counter-attacked those who suggested that Oxbridge graduates were favoured by the exams being set and marked by their tutors: 'criticisms of Oxford and Cambridge predominance in the open competition for the Civil Service still continues. Is this possibly due to most of the

NOTES FOR CHAPTER 2

critics continuing to be, as they seem to have been in the past, professionally connected with another university?' Kelsall was, of course, based at the London School of Economics.

43 This paragraph is largely based on Chapman, *Civil Service Commission*, ch 11, with the final quotation coming from p. 242. The most relevant TNA files are CSC5/281 (for the 1930s) and CSC5/502 (for the 1950s). Chapman seeks to explain the Commission's apparent failings by concluding that it 'saw particular schools and universities as customers in a business relationship' whilst simultaneously expressing genuine 'surprise about expressed criticism of bias in recruitment' (p. 259). Chapman's criticisms are all the more damning given his explicit sympathy for the Commission.

44 This paragraph is based on TNA: T273/209. Fisher's letter is dated 2 July 1936 and Bridges' memorandum 8 July 1954.

45 See above, ch 2.1.1; and also ch 1.4.1 for the early rather chequered history of the concept of ministerial responsibility. The fullest historical account of Crichel Down is I.F. Nicolson, *The Mystery of Crichel Down* (1986). There is an interesting retraction by J.A.G. Griffiths (who had largely been responsible for perpetuating the myth about the classic nature of Dugdale's resignation) in *Contemporary Record* 1 (1987) 35–40. The claim that officials were mere extensions of their Minister with no powers of their own had been given legal force by the Carltona Ltd v Commissioner of Works and Others in 1943; but it started to be challenged by the 1957 Franks Report on administrative tribunals and inquiries (set up in the wake of Crichel Down) which recommended that planning inquiries, numbering some 6000 a year, should be published since it was idle to pretend that each decision was the Minister's. As David Vincent has argued, 'deploying the convention of ministerial responsibility as an argument against rather than for official secrecy' marked a significant departure. See *The Culture of Secrecy* (1998), p. 218.

46 On the Official Secrets Act, see D. Hooper *Official Secrets* (1987) and Vincent, *Culture of Secrecy*, ch 4. On Fisher, see O'Halpin, *Head*, pp. 219–20 and Chapman, *Ethics*, p. 277. On Bridges and Brook, see D. Reynolds, *In Command of History: Churchill Fighting and Writing the Second World War* (2004).

47 Chapman, *Ethics*, pp. 237–8 and more broadly, ch 6 and *Civil Service Commission*, ch 8. The Commission, for example, never discussed Kelsall's findings with him and swiftly lost its one copy of his book.

48 TNA: T273/18. For a fuller account of relations between the government and the Institute, which received its royal charter in 1954, see R. Nottage and F. Stack, 'The RIPA 1922–1939' *Public Administration* 50 (1972) 281–302 and Chapman, *Ethics*, pp. 244–58. Fisher's ambivalence was epitomised by his becoming vice president without becoming a member, that of Bridges by his sanctioning of major grants to the British Institute of Management (to improve management in industry) whilst denying much smaller grants to the better-run Institute. The 1922 letter made the somewhat surprising assertion that 'for the most part Civil Servants have no concern with administration'. This demonstrated how far management was divorced from the contemporary definition of public administration.

49 For Fisher, see Fry, *Statesmen*, p. 57. For Bridges, see *Portrait*, p. 16 and *Treasury Control*, p. 28.

50 For Northcote and Trevelyan, see ch 1, fn 31. The fullest contemporary summary of the debate is Dale, *Higher Civil Service*, Appendix D. He too concluded that promotion should normally be within departments. The dispute, in any case, was a storm in a teacup. Beneath the high-flown rhetoric there was in fact no 'Fisher effect'. After 1900 there was an actual increase, not a decrease, in the proportion of Permanent Secretaries who – on their first appointment – had previously worked in the department to which they were appointed head. See K. Theakston and G.K. Fry, 'Britain's administrative elite', *Public Administration* 67 (1989) 129–47. A contributory reason for this was that fewer appointments were made from outside the Service.

NOTES FOR CHAPTER 2

51 See Sir F. Floud, 'The sphere of the specialist in public administration', *Public Administration* 1 (1923) 126. The succeeding quotation is from the evidence of Sir Evelyn Murray, cited in Fry, *Statesmen*, p. 203.
52 On the defence ministries, see D. Edgerton, *The Warfare State* (2006), chs 3–4; Balogh also favoured 'a committee of equal officials' advising the Minister, see *Apotheosis*, p. 46. On the Bridgeman Report and its impact, see Cmd 4149 and Kelsall, *Higher Civil Servants*, pp. 114–16.
53 The seven postwar specialist classes, with the date and chairman of the relevant inquiry, were: scientific (Barlow, 1943), works (Gardiner, 1952), legal (Barlow, 1944), medical officer (Howitt, 1951), accountant (Gardiner, 1952), statistician and economic. Before the War, many such specialists had been recruited into separate departmental classes. The creation of a Scientific Civil Service following a white paper based on the 1943 Barlow Report (Cmd 6679) blazed the trail for service-wide classes.
54 *Report of the Machinery of Government Committee* (Cd 9230), para 12. See also ch 1, fn 22 and Agar, *Government Machine*, ch 3. For a critique of the low quality of statistics at the interwar Ministry of Health, see C. Webster, 'Hungry or healthy Thirties?', *History Workshop Journal* (Spring 1982) 110–29; and for the demise of the Board of Trade's influential labour statistics department, Lowe, *Adjusting to Democracy*, pp. 55–6.
55 See G.C. Peden, 'The Treasury as the central department of government' *Public Administration* 61 (1983) 383; S. Brittan, *Steering the Economy* (1971), p. 38; and, more generally, A. Cairncross and N. Watts, *The Economic Section* (1989).
56 A. Bertrand, 'The recruitment and training of higher Civil Servants 'in Robson (ed.), *Civil Service*, p. 175. The Assheton Report was published in 1945 as Cmd 6525.
57 Vincent, *Culture of Secrecy*, p. 169.
58 Dale, *Higher Civil Service*, p. 215; Brook, quoted in Fry, *Statesmen*, pp. 172–4. For an evocation of administration as the 'awareness of Ministerial responsibility', see C.H. Sisson, *The Spirit of British Administration* (1959), ch 1.
59 M. Beloff, 'The Whitehall factor' in G. Peele and C. Cook (eds) *The Politics of Reappraisal* (1975), p. 210. For an earlier sighting of 'secret dictators' in Edwardian Whitehall, see E. Halevy, *The Rule of Democracy* (1961 ed), p. 265; and for Stephen's warning, ch 1.4.1 above.
60 Two other officials who became Ministers were Hankey (Chancellor of the Duchy of Lancaster and Paymaster General, 1940–2) and Admiral Chatfield (Minister for the Coordination of Defence, 1939–40). Both had entered their administrative careers through the Navy not open competition. In the cull of prewar specialists were many exceptional Board of Trade officials. For example, Beveridge felt obliged to retire and Askwith was dismissed in 1919, whilst a year later Llewelyn-Smith was translated to the largely honorific post of the Government's Chief Economic Adviser.
61 As Dale admitted, 'a high official outside the Treasury, unless he is by nature devoid of personal ambition or is near the end of his career, is rather reluctant to press to the utmost a difference of opinion with the Treasury'. In a reference to past practices, which Northcote-Trevelyan had tried to stamp out, he then quoted Fisher as asserting that 'the secret to efficiency is favouritism'. See *Higher Civil Service*, pp. 168, 226. For Fisher's impact on defence policy, see G.C. Peden, 'Sir Warren Fisher and British rearmament against Germany' *English Historical Review* 94 (1979) 29–45.
62 W.J. Brown, *So Far* (1943), p. 220. He was also a principal target in Cato, *Guilty Men* (1940), ch 15. For a more balanced view, see his entry in the *Oxford Dictionary of National Biography* (2004). Wilson had earlier raised the Labour movement's ire by persuading successive governments not to compromise in the General Strike or to adopt 'Keynesian' measures to combat unemployment – although he worked tirelessly behind the scenes to encourage industry to improve its industrial relations and productivity. See Lowe and Roberts 'Horace Wilson'.
63 TNA: T273/74; Balogh, *Apotheosis*, p. 45.

NOTES FOR CHAPTER 2

64 Chapman, *Ethics*, pp. 284 and 307. Although Bridges urged officials to display integrity and the 'ardour of the chase', he nevertheless encouraged them to be 'slightly detached and withdrawn' ('The reforms of 1854' in Robson, *Civil Service*, p. 31). The planning and implementation of radical programmes arguably required rather greater commitment – a point forcefully made later by Mrs Thatcher. For a catalogue of Bridges' conservative instincts, see Theakston, *Leadership*, pp. 77–85. Devaluation in 1949, for instance, was codenamed 'Caliban' because it was adjudged dishonest and unsavoury; and in 1951 Gaitskell's defeat of Bevan over the introduction of charges in the NHS was heralded as 'the best day we have had inside the Treasury for ten years'. Likewise Brook, Bridges' successor, bemoaned the absence of a 'Geddes axe, which ought to have been allowed to swing freely through Whitehall immediately after the end of the war'. Ibid, p. 110.
65 Bridges, *Portrait*, pp. 16–19.
66 Dale, *Higher Civil Service*, pp. 51–2; Savage, *Social Construction*, p. 11. Savage's analysis is somewhat flawed because *inter alia* it was unable to establish the social background of typically one third of officials or, inevitably, the 'departmental view' of every responsibility of each ministry.
67 On Britain's failure to build a 'developmental state', and officials' complicity in it, see in particular D. Marquand, *The Unprincipled Society* (1988).
68 Armstrong wrote: 'The biggest and most pervasive influence is in setting the framework within which questions of policy are raised ... We set the questions which we asked Ministers to decide arising out of that framework and it would have been enormously difficult for any Minister to change the framework, so to that extent we had great power ... We were very ready to explain it ... but most Ministers were not interested, were just prepared to take the questions offered to them, which came out of that framework without going back into the preconceptions of them', *The Times*, 15 November 1976. This accorded with the experience of Sidney Webb (who should have known better). Having heard that the National Government had taken Britain off gold in 1931, he complained that the outgoing Labour Government had never been advised that such a thing was possible. For the extensive literature on the Treasury view, see Peden, *Keynes*.
69 TNA: T215/96, W. Robson's evidence to the 1948 Masterman Committee; Hennessy, *Whitehall*, p. 78. Leo Amery, as a proactive Colonies Secretary in the 1920s, was famously dismissed by officials as the 'mad mullah Minister' (see Beloff, 'Whitehall factor', p. 218).
70 Balogh, *Apotheosis*, p. 29.
71 TNA: T273/232. The statement was a response to an article in *Tribune* in 1949.
72 Dale, *Higher Civil Service*, pp. 75, 133, 139.
73 H.E. Dale, *The Personnel and Problems of the Higher Civil Service* (1946), p. 6. G.M. Young articulated officials' case even more colourfully in the *Observer* on 17 May 1942: 'You ask us to take responsibility, to be constructive, imaginative and all the rest of it. What happens if we do? As likely as not, we shall be grilled by the Public Accounts Committee and pilloried in the newspapers. Disgusted taxpayer will take up his pen and demand business methods in Government Offices, and the Member for Buckwash will wake from his slumbers bawling "Sack the lot!" – every single fault alleged against Whitehall could be shown to be the necessary outcome of some restriction or some injunction originating from Westminster.' He concluded: 'You cannot expect us to do twentieth-century work under nineteenth-century restraints.'
74 For Fisher's early aspirations, see O'Halpin, *Head*, ch 1; and for Wilson's, Lowe, *Adjusting to Democracy*, pp. 106–7. 'Stoical realism' is Dale's phrase in *Higher Civil Service*, p. 84.
75 Fabian Society, *The Administrators* (1964), p.3. Agreement on the need for unemployment relief in the 1930s did not extend to the means, and it was duly 'taken out of politics' with the creation in 1934 of a prototype executive agency: the Unemployment

NOTES FOR CHAPTER 2

Assistance Board. In another premonition, 'politics' were swiftly reintroduced: following street protests, the Board's initial relief scales were suspended. This was strictly unconstitutional but, as its chairman reasoned, the Board 'were in effect officials of the Government and cannot act in the last resort contrary to the policy of the Government', see Lowe, *Adjusting to Democracy*, p. 176.

76 On Tomlin, see Bourn, 'Main reports', in Fulton Report, vol 3(2), memo 10, p. 130; and on Priestley, TNA: T215/297 and W.J.M. Mackenzie, 'The Royal Commission on the Civil Service' *Political Quarterly* 27 (1956) 129. Both Tomlin and Priestley (like their predecessors in 1875, 1890 and 1912) were appointed because of unrest among Civil Service unions.

77 Chapman and Greenaway, *Dynamics*, p. 73. The quotations from the Report (Cd 9230) are from Part I paras 14, 33 and 56(d). PFOs were called for in Part I, para 29 and PEOs in Part II, para 20(a). The Report is placed in its fullest historical and theoretical context by R. Thomas, *The British Philosophy of Administration* (1978). For the Report's influence on Fisher, see O'Halpin, *Head*, p. 129 and on Bridges, see 'Haldane and the machinery of government', *Public Administration* 35 (1957) 254–63. This influence, as will be seen, was more conceptual than practical.

78 R.B. Haldane, 'An organized Civil Service' *Public Administration* 1 (1923) 16.

79 Cd. 9230, pp. 13, 20 and 11. Rejected also were later attempts by Haldane to improve post-entry training and to emulate Trevelyan by using Civil Service recruitment as a lever to improve the education system (albeit by encouraging greater equality of opportunity). See Thomas, *British Philosophy*, p. 158. A central research capability was established in the shape of the Committee of Civil Research (1925–30) and then the Economic Advisory Council (1930–9). However, both bodies were divorced from the policy-making departments and in consequence largely ineffectual.

80 Ministerial responsibility was endorsed at the Committee's second meeting, see p. 82 of Chapman and Greenaway, *Dynamics*, which provides a succinct summary of its workings. The Committee contained four politicians but in addition to Haldane himself, the leading participants were two officials (Sir George Murray and Sir Robert Morant) and Beatrice Webb. These four have been described as standing 'aloof from the hurly burly of politics, viewing its practitioners with disdain and even contempt' (ibid, p. 79). The illusion of Ministerial responsibility was particularly attacked by Beveridge in the 1920s, as was the convention of anonymity by the Webbs and Laski. On this and comparisons with the USA, see Thomas, *British Philosophy*, pp. 41–54 and ch 6.

81 The Anderson Committee papers are at TNA: CAB 87/71–75 and those of the GOC at TNA: CAB134/307–10. A Ministerial Machinery of Government Committee existed fitfully after 1945; and the GOC was the product of one of five committees of departmental heads on business efficiency set up in 1946. For a full history of these committees, see Lee, *Reviewing*, and for a guide to the confusion of committees related to economic policy, see B.W.E. Alford, R. Lowe and N. Rollings, *Economic Planning, 1943–1951* (1992). At its peak in 1949 the Treasury's O&M division and MG section were staffed respectively by 86 and 7 officials.

82 Bridges' appointment of a Steering Committee for Economic Organization Enquiry in December 1949 was an implicit acknowledgement that the GOC was incapable of doing anything which offended any departmental vested interest. See Lee, *Reviewing*, pp. 52 and 111.

83 TNA: T273/202, Bridges' evidence to the Treasury Organisation Committee.

84 Lee, *Reviewing*, p. 6.

85 There was therefore no administrative or constitutional 'revolution' in wartime comparable to the Beveridge and Keynesian 'revolution' in welfare policy. Both those 'revolutions', however, appeared more complete in retrospect than they did at the time. The Beveridge Report was fiercely contested (and disowned by Churchill) and the 1944 *Employment Policy* white paper was a hasty, and contradictory, amalgam of Treasury and

Keynesian policies. See R. Lowe, 'The Second World War, consensus and the foundation of the welfare state', *Twentieth Century British History* 1 (1990) 152–82. For the failings of the Attlee Government, including Cripps, see Theakston, *Labour Party* (1992), ch 3.

86 CAB134/308, GOC(49)10, para 37. Treasury officials, for reasons of their own, incorrectly classified the Haldane Committee as an 'outside' committee. It had, of course, a classic mix of insiders and outsiders. There were some mavericks, like Evelyn Sharp, who did want a public commission so that 'parliamentary and public opinion would compel acceptance of its conclusions'. See Chapman and Greenaway, *Dynamics*, p. 134.

87 B. Fraser, quoted in Lee, *Reviewing*, p. 2; TNA: T222/71, Anderson to Cripps, 9 July 1942; Bridges, quoted in Lee, *Reviewing*, p. 113. Bridges expounded his philosophy more fully in a message to the Institute of Public Administration in 1947: 'The lessons taught by practical experience have always stood high in the ways of thought and methods of work traditional in this country. Many changes, which elsewhere would have meant a break in continuity have, with us, been brought about by adapting what already existed, to meet fresh needs or novel purposes' (TNA: T273/18).

88 Chapman, *Ethics*, p. 194; Lee, *Reviewing*, p. 151. Bridges' comment was to Brook (TNA: CAB21/1998).

89 Lee, *Reviewing*, pp. 83, 139; Anderson, 'Machinery of government', 150. Lee, relating the work of the O&M Division to the interdepartmental committees, has written despairingly of the 'vacillations in juxtaposing young, keen and ambitious "intelligence" staff' against the tactical mind of the Head of the Civil Service, constrained by the collective wisdom of the permanent secretaries in the GOC and occasionally harried by sudden flurries of Ministerial anxiety' (ibid, p. 47). A further impediment to incisive action, as the Civil Service Department was later to discover, was that central departments had no power without the Prime Minister's express consent to compel other departments to act.

90 TNA: T/134/1308, GOC(49)10, para. 36.

91 Fulton Committee, vol 4, pp. 271–2. The figures exclude the Post Office. The principal employment of these officials was the raising of revenue (where the Inland Revenue and Customs and Excise employed some 66,500 by 1956), the administration of the social services (where the Ministry of Labour, despite being shorn of the major responsibility for national insurance, still employed some 22,300 staff in 1956) and defence.

92 A further manifestation was the growth of central government's administrative powers, particularly in relation to local government. The 1929 and 1948 Local Government Acts, for example, required the district auditor to declare a local authority in default if, in his judgement, its expenditure was excessive and unreasonable. In short, an official could override, without any right to appeal, the decisions of democratically elected councillors. The 1944 Education Act also permitted government to 'control and direct' local education authorities – a form of words last used in 1834 to empower the Poor Law Commission, which was expressly not accountable to Parliament. See W.A. Robson, 'Administrative law in England' in G. Campion *et al*, *British Government since 1918* (1950), pp. 130–7.

93 Cmd 4060, p. 7; W.A. Robson, *Justice and Administrative Law* (1947), p. 374. For the Committee, see D.G.T. Williams, 'The Donoughmore Report in retrospect', *Public Administration* 60 (1982) 273–92. Its non-official members might have been less sanguine had they realised the care with which 'reliable' tribunal members were chosen and the persistent hostility of the Treasury towards tribunals. Their awards set precedents which tended to weaken its control over public expenditure. See Lowe, *Adjusting to Democracy*, pp. 163 and 182.

94 J.A.G. Griffiths, cited in J. Jowell, 'Administrative law' in Bogdanor, *British Constitution*, p. 385.

95 L.M. Friedman. Quoted in ibid, p. 395.

96 Cmd 4060, p. 23.

97 Ibid, pp. 110–12 and Campion, *British Government*, pp. 87 and 154–5. For the final quotation, see Jowell, 'Administrative law', p. 389.

NOTES FOR CHAPTER 2

98 Other major amalgamations were the formation of the Union of Post Office Workers in 1919 (which remained the largest Civil Service 'union' up to 1956); the grouping of 'departmental class' officials (who fell outside, and were generally employed on less favourable terms than, the four Whitley classes) into the Ministry of Labour Staff Association in 1925 and the Inland Revenue Staff Association in 1936; the founding of the National Association of Women Civil Servants in 1932; and finally the formation of the National Guild of Civil Servants in 1954 to represent ex-service personnel. The Civil Service Confederation, which never included the Post Office unions, dissolved in 1939 when the CSCA joined with the Ministry of Labour and Inland Revenue staff associations in a new Civil Service Alliance (thereby reintroducing a division between clerical and 'manipulative' workers that had existed before 1921). The principal institutional histories are B.V. Humphreys, *Clerical Unions in the Civil Service* (1958), J.E. Mortimer and V.A. Ellis, *A Professional Union: the evolution of the IPCS* (1980) and B.J. O'Toole, *Private Gain and Public Service: The Association of First Division Civil Servants* (1989).

99 Such an ideal was generally acknowledged to be impracticable by 1925. This was confirmed in 1928 when an 'all-service' programme launched by the Staff Side of the National Whitley Council (embracing *inter alia* equal pay and a minimum wage) found little active support.

100 A full history of these events is provided in H. Parris, *Staff Relations in the Civil Service: fifty years of Whitleyism* (1973), upon which much of the following analysis is based. It records, *inter alia*, Treasury ambivalence about Ministerial responsibility. 'The government has bound itself by a declared intention to make the fullest use of Whitleyism', wrote a senior official, but 'this pledge cannot be held to relieve Ministers of their primary responsibility for taking whatever action may be deemed necessary to be right in the public interest' (quoted on p. 33). Whitleyism had only a very limited impact on the private sector.

101 Ibid, pp. 53–72. Much of the credit for constructive collaboration has been given to Sir Alan Day, the chair of the NSS from 1939 to 1955.

102 Ibid, p. 48

103 Humphreys, *Clerical Unions*, p. 207. By her calculations, between 1914 and 1920 real wages for clerical officers rose by 23% while those for the Administrative Class fell by twice that amount. Between 1920 and 1932, the rise for clerical officers was below whereas that for the Administrative Class was double the national average. Between 1932 and 1950, the average real wages of the clerical and administrative officials fell respectively by 21% and 43%. Ibid, ch 10.

104 See Humphreys, *Clerical Unions*, pp. 176–80 and O'Halpin, *Head*, pp. 154–6. Many of the Act's more draconian measures were never implemented and Fisher was scrupulous in discouraging victimisation. He was appalled, however, when the Labour Government in 1929 restored forfeited pension rights to strikers, although this did not prevent him from dining privately with Brown.

105 See Chapman, *Ethics*, pp. 107–34. The full text of the ultimate agreement is reprinted in the Fulton Committee Report, vol 4, pp. 402–5. In a classic piece of drafting departments were 'urged to give permission to the maximum extent consistent with the maintenance of the reputation of the Civil Service for political impartiality' in relation to both the intermediate class and the participation of the 'restricted' class in local politics (para 6).

106 Parris, *Staff Relations*, pp. 35–6; *Red Tape*, November 1917, p. 10.

107 The quotations are all from the Fulton Report, vol 1 (Cmnd 3638), para 271.

108 The fullest history of mechanisation is provided by J. Agar, *The Government Machine* (2003). He claims convincingly that, despite its virtual absence from 'the voluminous literature on the history of the Civil Service', knowledge of technological change is essential to an understanding of the 'capacities and action of government' (p. 414). However, his simultaneous claim that 'if there has been a distaste for the machine it has been amongst the writers on government rather than in government itself' – and

particularly his claim that the Treasury over time was a 'technophilic' body – appears more tenuous. On his own evidence, the Treasury's interwar Investigating Division (responsible for technological change) had a staff of only four; and, after 1945, Administrative Class officials tended to regard mechanisation as a 'grubby' process beneath their notice and of interest only because of potential economies (pp. 165, 170). With the possible exception of the mid-1950s, mechanisation was pioneered very much 'from below' by Executive Officers (p. 10).

109 Typewriters were initially provided free on trial by Remington. Their use, however, posed serious moral dilemmas. One department insisted that their female operators be approached and fed only through a hatch in the wall (H. Martindale, *Women Servants of the State* (1938), p. 67). To maintain propriety, the Civil Service Commission placed its telephone before 1914 in a closed box to which messengers had to summon administrative staff. Ever keen thereafter to raise its public profile, it also remained ex-directory until 1934. See Chapman, *Civil Service Commission*, p. 32.

110 Agar, *Government Machine*, p. 412. Post Office mechanisation was overseen by Myra Curtis, one of only four women who were temporary officials during the First World War and then permanently appointed to the Administrative Class in the reconstruction examinations. She was the daughter of a telegraphist in the Post Office. Initially some 16 million and 2.25 million people were covered respectively by health and unemployment insurance. The mechanisation of the former was contracted out to the Prudential. For a year, a losing battle was fought to handle unemployment insurance records manually. They were then mechanised by the Government at Kew.

111 Ibid, pp. 305–15. The lead within the Treasury was provided by Sir Edward Playfair, who recognized that a secure home market was essential, were the export potential of the British computer industry to be realised. He duly followed Desborough into the private sector, as chairman of a leading computer firm, ICL. The technical lead was provided by James Merriman, a Post Office engineer, transferred to O&M in 1955 by its then head P.S. Milner-Barry, who himself had been a prominent figure at Bletchley Park. O&M was actively hostile to 'operational research', the application of quantitative reasoning to organisation favoured by many wartime scientists such as Sir Patrick Blackett. For its history, see M.W. Kirby, *Operational Research in Peace and War* (2003).

112 These jobs were not preordained to be female preserves. After its invention in the 1830s shorthand was perceived by male clerks to be a useful skill which could advance promotion. Many men also trained as typists but, once it was perceived not to advance promotion, it was abandoned. Changes mirrored those in the private sector where, as Gregory Anderson has remarked, 'no other occupation . . . changed its sex label so completely or so quickly' (*The White-Blouse Revolution* (1988), p. 2).

113 Cd 9230, p. 14. The War did not wholly dispel the belief that women were unequal to men. See, for instance, Ministry of Reconstruction, *The Business of Government* (Reconstruction Problems 38, part 3, 1919) pp. 26–7.

114 For the evolution of feminist aspirations from the demand for formal equality ('fair field and no favour'), see J. Lewis, *Women in England 1870–1950* (1984) particularly pp. 102–6.

115 As Meta Zimmeck has written, 'minimal acceptance of qualified ex-servicemen by the usual channels' was swiftly supplanted by 'maximum acceptance of unqualified ex-servicemen by unusual channels'. See 'Strategies and stratagems for the employment of women in the Civil Service, 1919–1939', *Historical Journal* 27 (1984) 910–17. See also the same author's chapter in Anderson, *White-Blouse Revolution*, on which the statistics in this paragraph are based. Women additionally suffered from the NWC's postwar assimilation of classes (during which their jobs were typically downgraded) and from separate 'establishment lists' and promotion boards which limited opportunity.

116 G. Savage, 'Entering the corridors of power' in J. Burton (ed), *Essays in European History* (1988) and Kelsall, *Higher Civil Servants*, ch 9. As a result of the Second World War, the number of (greatly increased) administrative posts filled by women rose from 3% to 7%; and of posts at Assistant Secretary level and above from 3% to 29%. The majority of the latter were Oxbridge graduates. The percentage of posts filled by postwar reconstruction and open examinations, and by promotion up to 1951 never exceeded 11%.

117 Zimmeck, 'Strategies', p. 909. The CSCA, which represented the greatest number of women, supported abolition but the majority of unions representing Post Office workers and departmental classes opposed it. See Parris, *Staff Relations*, p. 152. The bar significantly remained in the Post Office until 1963 and in the Foreign Office until 1972. The first woman to gain exemption from the bar was Alice Reisner (nee Jennings) of the Ministry of Labour in 1938.

118 Cmd 6937, part 2. The Commission also noted that equal pay for equal work in the Civil Service was the norm in the USA and France, albeit not Australia. Fear of offending public opinion was the explanation provided by the self-proclaimed 'feminist', Fisher, for failing to achieve more whilst Head of the Service. His 'reverence' for women clearly extended in practice no further than his 'reverence' for the Haldane Report. See, O'Halpin, *Head*, pp. 180–1. On the Conservative budget, see P. Catterall (ed), *The Macmillan Diaries: the Cabinet years* (2003), pp. 301–3.

119 The tight interwar labour market was also a factor here. Postwar full employment presented major recruitment problems.

120 TNA: T222/678, memorandum by J.H. Woods, 29 July 1954. The quotation was attributed to Douglas Jay.

3 MODERNISATION BEFORE FULTON, 1956–66

1 The term was coined by A.J.P. Taylor in the *New Statesman*, 29 August 1953, popularised by H. Fairlie in the *Spectator*, 23 September 1955 and then refined by Anthony Sampson in *Anatomy of Britain*, first published in July 1962. Sampson rejected the concept of a monolithic establishment in favour of a 'cluster of interlocking circles' (pp. 624, 632). He did number Permanent Secretaries, however, amongst the 'real rulers' (p. 624). In relation to Suez, only two senior officials, in the Foreign Office, appear to have resigned in protest. Others only went so far as to pen a round robin or, like William Armstrong, wear a black tie. See Hennessy, *Whitehall*, pp. 164–8.

2 It was not until 1956 that the 'fortnight rule' (that no subject could be discussed on radio or television a fortnight before its discussion in Parliament) was withdrawn. For the satire boom and its essential conservatism in attacking not authority but rather the perceived misuse of authority, see H. Carpenter, *That Was Satire That Was* (2000). *That Was The Week That Was* was spontaneously withdrawn by the BBC for fear of causing public, not Party political, offence during an election year.

3 This and the following paragraph rely heavily on J. Tomlinson, *The Politics of Decline* (2000). It demonstrates how the concept of decline, partly because of its elusiveness, appealed over time to all who advocated radical change (from Marxists to neo-liberals). In the early 1960s the principal focus was on redeemable differences with Europe. After the mid-1970s Britain's problems were seen to be more chronic and, as European growth rates slowed, comparisons were made with other 'successful' economies such as Japan and Korea (until their own period of 'catch up and convergence' ended). Polemics from this time, such as C. Barnett, *The Audit of War* (1986), with their lack of analytical precision and systematic international comparisons let alone empirical accuracy, have – in Tomlinson's judgement – seriously distorted an understanding of the post-Suez period.

4 Sampson, *Anatomy*, p. 630.

5 Increased competitiveness was not wholly abandoned as a spur to growth. It was a motive behind the initial application to join the EEC and also the removal of Resale Price Maintenance in 1964 (which, by disaffecting small shopkeepers, who were the stalwarts of constituency parties, may ironically have cost the Conservatives the 1964 election). For a summary of Robot and its historiography, see Peden, *The Treasury*, pp. 458–62; and for Thorneycroft's resignation, R. Lowe, 'Resignation at the Treasury', *Journal of Social Policy*, 18 (1989) 505–26 and E.E.H. Green, *The Ideologies of Conservatism* (2002), ch 7.
6 TNA: PRO, PREM11/4520, note by H. Macmillan for Cabinet, 25 October 1962.
7 TNA: CAB129/105, C(61)94, 10 July 1961. This Report itself received less consideration than it deserved because its completion coincided *inter alia* with a major economic crisis, the announcement of Britain's application to the EEC and the creation of the NEDC, and the serious illness of Sir Frank Lee. Likewise the impact of the final Plowden Report in 1961 was muted by its coincidence with Macmillan's serious illness and that of the Prime Minister's own modernisation initiative with the Cuban missile crisis. Such were the pressures of the real world.
8 TNA: PREM11/2244, N. Brook to Churchill, 23 March 1953; PREM11/688, N. Brook to Churchill, 4 February 1953; PREM11/4778, note by B. Trend, 21 January 1964. 'The great reappraisal' was a phrase coined by S. Brittan in *The Treasury under the Tories* (1964), ch 7.
9 H. Heclo and A. Wildavsky, *The Private Expenditure of Public Money* (1974), p. xvii.
10 For a copy of the letter, written on 9 June 1961, see TNA: T199/733 and Churchill College, Cambridge: PLDN 6/5/2/2.
11 A. Sampson, *Anatomy of Britain Today* (1965), p. 674.
12 Ferranti was alleged by the PAC (under Harold Wilson's chairmanship) to have made £4m in excess profits from a missile contract, which it was then obliged partially to repay.
13 Sixth Report (1957–8), H.C.254, para 95; Fifth Report (1963–4) H.C. 228, para 49; Sixth Report (1964–5), H.C. 308, para 112. The Estimates Committee was the new name given to the Select Committee on Estimates on the strengthening of its terms of reference in 1960. In both Wars, the Select Committee had merged with the Public Accounts Committee to form a National Expenditure Committee which, as has been seen, made powerful demands for reform.
14 Sixth Report (1957–8), H.C. 254, para 94; R. Lowe, 'Milestone or millstone? The 1959–1961 Plowden Committee and its impact on British welfare policy' *Historical Journal* 40 (1997) 468–9.
15 N. Johnson, *Parliament and Administration* (1966), p. 155. This book provides the fullest analysis of the postwar Estimates Committee and is damning of contemporary attempts at reform. 'The idea that more members want to take part in this kind of work, and that they still more want to make use of the fruits of their labours in preparation for debates, is', so it concluded, 'part of the mythology of those who would reform the procedures of the House without regard to the kind of members who inhabit it' (p. 145). For the views of a leading participant, see Sir R. Clarke, 'Parliament and public expenditure', *Political Quarterly* 44 (1973) 137–53; and see also TNA: T320/688 for a history of the Treasury's fluctuating relationship with the Committee.
16 Other popular analyses of relative economic decline, such as A. Shonfield, *British Economic Policy since the War* (1958) and M. Shanks, *The Stagnant Society* (1961) only contained passing references to the Service. Later critiques included M. Nicholson, *The System: the mismanagement of modern Britain* and H. Thomas (ed.), *Crisis in the Civil Service* (1968). Chapman's comparison was only with Europe, despite President Kennedy's attempts to rejuvenate government in the USA between 1960 and 1963.
17 Thomas, *Crisis* p. 45. Balogh never criticised officials for lack of management skills. On the contrary, he insisted that they were 'often superb' in policy implementation. Perhaps this was because he knew nothing about management himself.

18 Balogh's principal concern was the use of economic and statistical expertise. The Economic Section of the Treasury, he argued, should be directly responsible to the Chancellor; and economists integrated into the Administrative Class so they could reach the highest posts (ibid, p. 48). On patronage, he urged *inter alia* that all appointments to nationalised industries should be vetted by Parliament.
19 Sampson, *Anatomy*, p. 227.
20 B. Chapman, *British Government Observed* (1963), pp. 33, 61.
21 Chapman, *British Government*, p. 27.
22 Chapman's book was the subject of a devastating attack in *Public Administration* 41 (1963) 375–84. 'Angry young men may be good as novelists and playwrights', wrote D.N. Chester, the doyen of public administration and Chapman's former tutor, 'but an angry middle-aged professor writing about comparative administration is tiresome, particularly if one wants to learn something.' A charge Chapman was lucky to escape was misogynism. To him, Private Office staff were 'unwise virgins', senior officials 'sheltered spinsters' and Parliament 'a weak old lady' (pp. 24–7). For a devastating criticism of Snow, see Edgerton, *Warfare State*, ch 5.
23 S. Brittan, *Capitalism with a Human Face* (1996), p. 7; Sampson, *Anatomy*, p. 631.
24 The idea for the book was provided by Sir William Armstrong soon after he became the Treasury's Permanent Secretary. Typically he talked to the author 'freely at home in the evenings' before warning him 'the following morning not to delve too deeply ... into Treasury advice'. See Brittan, *Capitalism*, p. 11.
25 Brittan, *Treasury*, pp. 303–4.
26 Ibid, pp. 30, 77, 314. Brittan especially welcomed the opening up of debate represented by the encouragement of outside bodies, such as the NIESR, to act as 'licensed rebels' (pp. 36–7, 70).
27 Fabian Group, *The Administrators* (1964), p.43. The same officials collaborated in the drafting of the Labour Party's submission to Fulton.
28 Ibid, pp. 1, 15, 17. The first draft of the report was rather less acerbic. It read: 'it is a good civil service by international standards, but these are often low. The question is whether it is the best service we could have to meet the needs of the day' (London School of Economics (LSE): Fabian papers, K66/1, draft by R. Neild, October 1963).
29 Ibid, p.15. Warming to this theme, the Treasury was to be deprived of its management role because its officials appeared like 'lugubrious characters in a medieval morality play rather than [members of] a department anxious to secure value for money through enlightened personnel procedures' (LSE: Fabian papers, K 65/3, draft report on Treasury control of policy, n.d.).
30 Ibid, pp. 2, 41. The weakness of the Administrative Class was pithily summarised as the taking of more pride in effecting change than in the effectiveness of change. The Report's objectives were self-consciously similar to those of Northcote-Trevelyan – to 'hold out to the liveliest-minded young men and women the prospect of a really challenging and worthwhile career in the Civil Service, with first rate training and the early prospect of doing interesting things – or moving elsewhere' (p. 26).
31 Ibid, p. 33. The following assessment of the Treasury was by an Assistant Secretary in the Post Office, R.J.S. Baker, who was a regular contributor to *Public Administration* (LSE: Fabian papers, K 65/2, letters of 6 July and 13 October 1963). It was comments such as these which qualified the enthusiasm for the Treasury's further reorganisation initially expressed by non-officials.
32 For the Report's historical reputation, see Hennessy, *Whitehall*, pp. 172–5. The Group's Fabian members were largely economists. Robert Neild (who became a special adviser in the Treasury in 1964) took the lead, supported by Frank Blackaby (NIESR), David Henderson (then an expert at the Ministry of Aviation) and John Grieve Smith. They were supported by James Ogilvy-Webb, Honorary Secretary to the First Division

NOTES FOR CHAPTER 3

Association and responsible for the writing of the Treasury's historical memoranda (a responsibility he was given, somewhat ironically, because of his perceived unsuitability for normal administrative work, see TNA: T235/82, report by R. Clarke, 27 April 1962). The co-opted officials who are recorded as making a sustained contribution were R.J.S. Baker (Post Office), Maurice Kogan (Education), D. Simms (DSIR) and Tina Constantine (Housing). They consistently urged their colleagues not to confuse the Treasury with the Civil Service as a whole.

33 LSE: Fabian papers, K67/3, A.J. Ogilvy-Webb, n.d. The original purpose behind the enquiry, as proposed by Balogh and Neild, is recorded in a letter by S. Williams to D. Henderson, 2 July 1962 (ibid, K65/1). Good management practice is acknowledged in a memorandum on the 'control of the Civil Service' in July 1963 (ibid, K65/3).

34 Ibid, pp. 17, 18–19. The latter-day defence of the Administrative Class was mounted by Maurice Kogan, stirred in part by a reawakening of the nineteenth-century fear that, as experts, HM Inspectors of Schools might assume a policy-making role in the Ministry of Education. He was also stirred by an ambitious young official's resentment of special advisers. 'Do you want administrators to be expert in their own sphere?', he asked, 'if so what are relations to be to the (overrated and overpaid) Christopher Foster?' (ibid, K, 67/4). Foster was then advising the Ministry of Transport and the DEA on regional and urban problems.

35 K. Theakston, 'Whitehall reform' in P. Dorey (ed), *The Labour Governments, 1964–1970* (2006). K. Theakston, *The Labour Party and Whitehall* (1992) chronicles the relationship from its origin.

36 Fulton, vol 5 (3), memo 97, paras 9, 11, 60, 63 and G(1). The initial draft of this memorandum contained a far more bitter attack, which relied heavily on Chapman – in contrast to the final document which approvingly quoted articles by serving officials in *Public Administration* (LSE: Fabian papers, K67/4). The draft thus revealed the atavistic hostility of many activists, which was later to erupt in the 1970s.

37 Ibid, paras 22, 47, 54. For Wilson's renunciation, see Theakston, *Labour Party*, p. 126. He had already pre-empted such a charge before the election (see, N. Hunt (ed), *Whitehall and Beyond* (1964) p. 11: 'the idea ... that a change of government means sabotage from the Civil Service is ... nonsense'). He was also profuse in his early praise. 'I am not unaware', he wrote to the Head of the Civil Service on 21 October 1964, 'that the changes ... involved fundamental changes in Government machinery such as we have not seen in peacetime in the past generation. They would not have been possible without the fullest degree of administrative know-how and equally of imagination such as you and your principal colleagues have shown. As a somewhat junior civil servant and as a Minister I have seen some of the great names of our generation in action ... But never in the days of Bridges, John Henry Woods and the rest have I seen anything so impressive as you have done in the past few days' (TNA: T235/119).

38 See Theakston, *Labour Party,* which concludes: 'Labour has never had a clear blueprint for civil service reform, different critics pointing to different "problems" and sometimes making contrary proposals for change' (p. 11). In relation to the social background of officials, the Fabian Society (mindful perhaps of its own members' class background) long argued that positive discrimination might be incompatible with executive efficiency.

39 A summary of the key developments in the first two Wilson administrations is provided in A. Blick, *People who Live in the Dark* (2004), chs 3 and 4.

40 There was a particular tension between Brittan (himself a special adviser at DEA) and the Fabians. Brittan favoured only experts and their employment as a ministerial 'brains trust' (*Steering the Economy* (1970), pp. 55–60). The Fabians had always advocated the additional employment of personal advisers and opposed experts being segregated in *cabinets* (see Fulton, vol 5(2), memo 78, para. 28).

41 Some aides were appointed. John Allen (briefly) and John Harris were, for example, employed for their public relations skills by Wilson and Jenkins respectively. For the

battle over the Economic Section, see A. Cairncross, *The Wilson Years* (1997), ch. 1, and for a summary of the debacle over devaluation, Blick, *People*, pp. 78–84. Neild had long argued that so politically sensitive a post as Chief Economic Adviser should change with governments; and his appointment effectively displaced Alec Cairncross, the then permanent Economic Adviser to the Government, whose dismissal was announced in the press. Cairncross vigorously opposed the making answerable of non-partisan economists within the Section to a political appointee (and hence their 'politicisation'). Cairncross triumphed. He became head of the non-partisan Government Economic Service (responsible for all economists employed within Government) whilst Neild acted as a personal adviser to the Chancellor. This compromise could be reached because of the personal trust between the protagonists. Trust was not a quality normally associated with the other high-profile special advisers.

42 Fulton, vol 5 (2), memo 78, para 10.
43 For the sea-change in political interest in 'machinery of government' questions, see C. Pollitt, *Manipulating the Machine* (1984), ch 4, which also chronicles the various manifestations of DEA and MinTech. Both offered distinct 'political' advantages. The former provided a prestigious role for Labour's Deputy Prime Minister, George Brown, whilst the latter enticed into government Frank Cousins from the TUC (in a possible attempt to emulate Bevin's role in the 1940s) and also C.P. Snow (in what Wilson later confessed was largely a public relations exercise, see D. Cannadine, 'C.P. Snow' in Wm. R. Louis (ed), *Yet More Adventures with Britannia* (2004), p.110).
44 See R. Clarke, *New Trends in Government* (1971), ch. 1. The creation of a 'giant' department such as MinTech did provide an opportunity for managerial reforms, for which modernisers had been calling and with which Fulton was concerned. These included the breaking down of barriers between administrators and professionals, and better career planning.
45 Conservative Party Archives (CPA): CRD3/4/10. The phrase was David Howell's. Heath might have expressed himself differently. Backbench Conservatives, under Airey Neave, even made a contribution to the modernisation debate in *Change or Decay* (1962); but some doubts remained over the Party's commitment. There had been an indeterminate 'brain-storming' meeting at Chequers on government reorganisation in April 1963, chaired by Heath, which concluded that Parliamentary reform should take precedence (TNA: PREM11/4406). Moreover had the Conservatives won the 1964 election, Enoch Powell was reputed to have been asked to 'reform Whitehall' (see P. Hennessy, *Cabinet* (1986), p. 168). What, if anything, would have resulted, is a moot point given Powell's vehement assertion to Fulton that 'what is needed is more of the best type of old style civil servant'. Professionals should be excluded from top jobs, he maintained, as should businessmen ('fishes out of water'). As became a former professor of Greek, he also advocated arts-based generalists advising lay Ministers in the necessarily 'crude' process of political decision-making. Reform, if required, best lay in a reduction of government's responsibilities and the streamlining of Cabinet decision-making (see TNA: BA1/4, CCS(66)20th, 26 July 1966 and Hunt, *Whitehall and Beyond*, passim). For a general summary of evolving Party attitudes, see Pollitt, *Manipulating*, pp. 82–8.
46 See F.W.S. Craig, *British General Election Manifestos, 1959–1987* (1990), p. 74. The pledges were reported to have been made 'in the heat' of the 1966 election on the suggestion of Ernest Marples and Mark Schreiber, who were to be key figures in PSRU, and without consultation with the Shadow Cabinet (CPA: CRD3/14/7, B. Sewill to M. Fraser, 24 November 1967).
47 TNA: BA1/38, CCS(67)197, report of meeting, 19 June 1967.
48 CPA: CRD3/14/2 and ACP(66)32. After March 1965, it was chaired by Sir Edward Boyle, a future member of the Fulton Committee.
49 CPA: CRD/3/14/4–5. The new group became active in May 1968 and represented the apex of collaboration with Civil Servants, who included Sir Eric Roll, Sir Henry

Hardman and Freddie Bishop. Conservative contacts with the Service, compared to Labour's, tended to be with more senior and retired officials. They included Sir Norman Brook and Tim Bligh in 1964 and Sir Thomas Padmore and Sir William Strath in 1968. Both Bligh and Bishop had been Macmillan's Private Secretary and their involvement thus gave some substance to Wilson's charges about the politicisation of the Service at this level (P. Ziegler, *Wilson* (1993), p. 214).

50 TNA: BA1/38, CCS(67)197 (meeting 19 June 1967) and article by Heath in *The Times*, 20 January 1967.

51 One of the earliest and most 'sensational' of the lectures was by a future member of the Fulton Committee, Sir James Dunnett, urging Whitehall in 1961 to adjust to its new interventionist role, see 'The Civil Service administrator and the expert', *Public Administration* 39 (1961) 223–37. Like Select Committee reports and Otto Clarke's later lectures, however, it went – according to Anthony Sampson – 'largely unnoticed' (*Anatomy*, p. 241).

52 W.W. Morton, 'The Plowden Report III. The management function of the Treasury', *Public Administration*, 41 (1963) 29. The collective wisdom of Establishment Officers throughout Whitehall in 1963 was also that 'the Executive Class was the one class to which recruitment was good and the quality of recruits high' (see TNA: T199/784, EOM(63)8th). For the views of Brook and Padmore see CPA: CRD3/14/3 and CRD3/14/10; and of Sharp, CRD3/14/5.

53 CPA: CRD3/14/10. For Sharp's Report, see CRD3/14/4–5. Sharp was so angered by the 'amount of tripe' which was referred up to interdepartmental committees, thereby clouding strategic decisions that the phrase, coined in 1959, was recycled in her 1966 evidence to Fulton – thereby suggesting that there had been little progress (see TNA: T249/216, Sharp to Brook, 7 October 1959 and BA1/4, CCS(66)22nd).

54 TNA: T249/216, particularly letters from E. Sharp to N. Brook, 8 July, 7 October and 14 December 1959. The first 'Sunningdale' was held, rather confusingly, at the ICI conference centre in Kingston-upon-Thames, after Sharp had discussed the need for the Civil Service to follow best practice in the private sector with its chairman, Lord Heyworth. The topics chosen by the Treasury for discussion were recruitment, training at a staff college, promotion and retirement, to which the systematic identification of 'fliers' was added at Sharp's request. Ironically, Sharp was not considered to be a good departmental manager herself. For example, she tended to intimidate her juniors and insist that all policy advice to Ministers be routed through her – which notably upset one of her more notorious Ministers, Richard Crossman. See Theakston, *Leadership*, pp. 142–5.

55 Churchill College, Cambridge: Plowden papers, PLDN 5/2/2–3, Plowden's meeting with Sharp and Brook, 16 December 1960; E. Sharp to Plowden, n.d. and 3 February 1961. In the later letters Sharp was vitriolic about Treasury attempts to draft the remit of the Plowden Committee so as 'to draw the hunt off' itself. In conjunction with others, she also expounded her duty and credentials for expressing a 'Service point of view'. Who else in Whitehall would be willing to criticise the Treasury to such a body as Plowden, which included 'people outside the Service and also senior representatives of the Treasury'? She also considered 'harder things' should have been said when Plowden finally wrote to Brook about the need for Treasury reorganisation (PLDN 5/2/2, Sharp to Plowden, 7 June 1961).

56 Ibid: PLDN5/2/2, Plowden to Brook, 9 June 1961. Clarke's lectures were published as *The Management of the Public Sector of the National Economy* (the Stamp Memorial lecture for 1964), 'The formulation of economic policy' and 'Machinery for economic planning: the public sector', *Public Administration* 41 (1963) 17–29 and 44 (1966) 61–72. Like most such informed comment, they were largely overlooked by outsiders. Clarke's retrospective views, debated before an audience of senior insiders and outsiders at the new Civil Service College, were published as *New Trends in Government* (1971); and he

also wrote two postwar administrative histories, most notably *Public Expenditure Management and Control* (1978) which were published posthumously. The latter reproduces the Stamp lecture, from which the succeeding quotations are taken, pp. 170, 174.
57 Theakston, *Leadership*, esp pp. 164–9. For the report on economic growth, see ch 3.1 above.
58 TNA: T199/734, paras 1 and 22. Significantly, in the light of the offence caused by the opening sentence of the Fulton Report, this memorandum explicitly attacked the 'amateurism' (as well as the 'in-breeding' and 'defensiveness') of the current Treasury and asserted that there could 'be no place for dilettantism in administration'.
59 Fulton, vol 5, memo 128 by 'a Group of members of the Association of First Division Civil Servants', para 8 This paragraph is based on written evidence to Fulton printed in this volume and also includes the views of two serving officials (memos 144 and 149) and four who had recently resigned – including, most notably, Peter Jay (memos 132, 139). The succeeding quotes are from memo 128, para 45 and memo 132, para 19.
60 Such units had already been set up experimentally. For example, one was established in the National Assistance Board in 1960 from which, at the start of a distinguished career, Kenneth Stowe challenged *from within* the quality of policy which was being simultaneously being praised *from without* by critics such as Chapman (see J. Veit-Wilson, 'The National Assistance Board and the "rediscovery" of poverty' in H. Fawcett and R. Lowe (eds), *Welfare Policy in Britain* (1999), pp.116–57).
61 For a summary of the primary evidence and secondary literature on which the succeeding analysis is based, see R. Lowe, 'Milestone', 463–491 and 'The core executive, modernisation and the creation of PESC, 1960–64', *Public Administration* 75 (1997) 601–15. Lord Plowden was, on appointment, chairman of the Atomic Energy Commission and had ended his official career as Chief Economic Planner between 1947 and 1953. The other outside members were Sir Jeremy Raisman (deputy chairman of Lloyds Bank), Sir John Wall (a director of EMI) and Sir Sam Brown (a partner in a firm of London solicitors). The officials were Sir Thomas Padmore and Bruce Fraser (replaced in February 1960 by Richard Clarke) from the Treasury and Evelyn Sharp, Sir Richard Way (Deputy Secretary at the Ministry of Supply) and Henry Hardman (Deputy Secretary at the Ministry of Agriculture). It was with Way and Hardman that Sharp wrote her letter of 3 February 1961 to Plowden criticising the Treasury.
62 G.K. Fry, *The Administrative 'Revolution' in Whitehall* (1981), p. 35; Cmnd 1432, para 7.
63 TNA: T291/7, CPE(Report)2; L. Pliatzky, *Getting and Spending* (1982), p. 49.
64 S. Brittan, *Steering*, p. 119.
65 PREM 11/4779, Trend to A. D-Home, 22 January and 8 April 1964. Trend had been the Treasury official chosen 'to steer the Plowden Committee in its work on "Establishments"'. Consequently he was a member of subcommittee 8 and the only one to attend all its meetings (TNA: T291/84, T. Padmore to Trend, 22 November 1960, and T291/39). For the MGPE, see Lowe, 'Core executive', 610 and T329/320, 330–2 and 423. The Group was made a standing Cabinet Committee in the autumn of 1965 but stopped meeting early in 1966. The political alternative was the appointment of a Chief Secretary to the Treasury to oversee public expenditure but, before 1979, its holder was only intermittently in Cabinet (1961–4, 1968–70 and 1977–9).
66 Cmnd 1432, paras 105–6. Treasury officials, as earlier noted by Robson, were typically sceptical of Parliament. The Estimates Committee, for example, was dismissed as a 'time-wasting nuisance' because of its 'irremediable amateurism'; and 'any attempt to make the estimates more meaningful to Parliament' was resisted because it 'might result in Parliament taking upon itself more responsibility for controlling expenditure'. Plowden had himself at times to amend draft Treasury reports because they were 'too critical and patronising'. See Lowe, 'Millstone', 485 and TNA: T291/63, TIP(M)2, 25 April 1960. Officials in general resented the fact that MPs, responding to electoral

pressure, typically demanded increased expenditure whilst simultaneously, on Select Committees, demanding stricter expenditure controls. See, for instance, the Treasury's first submission to the Committee, T291/1, GFC – M2, para 11.

67 TNA: T320/41, N. Brook to H. Macmillan, 8 May 1962; Heclo and Wildavsky, *Private Government*, p. 202. Public expenditure white papers were published annually after 1969. The Report's opposition to them was in para 17, although Plowden himself soon recanted (Churchill College, Cambridge: PLDN5/2/2).

68 TNA: T320/41, Ministerial Group on Public Expenditure, minutes of second meeting, 22 Dec 1960. For Clarke's covert attack on the social services, see R. Lowe, 'Resignation', 505–26. He had actually started the first draft of the critical second interim Report; 'the first and central problem to which the Committee has applied itself is that of how to stop – or at least to contain – the growth of public expenditure' (T235/64, April 1961). There had been earlier surveys, for instance, of public investment (since the 1940s), defence (since 1955), technical education (in 1956) and Plowden's own Atomic Energy Authority (in 1959).

69 TNA: T291/7, Vinter to Peck, 26 October 1960; Cmnd 1432, para 17. Paragraph 13 admitted that the surveys were 'at an experimental stage, which is full of technical and administrative pitfalls'; and that, were policy to be based on them 'before the underlying ideas had been thoroughly digested . . . their use might do more harm than good'. Such a patent contradiction, albeit sanctioned by the Committee, arguably reflected what a colleague identified as a character flaw in the Report's chief drafter (Clarke): a 'strong Napoleonic streak combined with a contempt for facts and a pleasure for experimental novelties' (A. Cairncross (ed), *The Robert Hall Diaries* (1991), p. 170). William Armstrong was particularly damning about the surveys' feasibility (T235/64, January 1960).

70 TNA: T291/14, CPE (SC1), 10, para 13; CAB128/36, CC(62)75, 20 December 1962; T298/115, letter by Powell, 16 September 1961; Cairncross, *Hall Diaries*, p. xviii.

71 Cmnd 1432, para 33. For Plowden's concurrence with this conclusion, see TNA: T291/39, CPE (SC8)1st, 19 October 1960.

72 TNA: T291/44, CPE(4) and T291/79, 7 March 1960. See also TNA: T291/11, *Eighth Interim Report* for evidence of other Permanent Secretaries' grievances. On expenditure control, Treasury officials privately admitted *inter alia* 'enormous and absurd variation' in the control of supply (T291/84, P. H. Davies to T. Padmore, 9 February 1960); and 'a system of control' over social services expenditure which was '"phoney" . . . pretending that control exists . . . where . . . there is no effective control in fact' (T291/84, report by J.A.C. Robertson, 13 October 1959). In relation to establishment policy, they also admitted that senior appointments were only intermittently referred to the Prime Minister 'because we do not have sufficient knowledge of the potential candidates or because those . . . who do have such knowledge are not consulted' (T291/69, memo by Widdup, 25 March 1960); and Trend later confessed to Plowden that 'if we have succeeded in letting a little fresh air into the murky and overcast world of establishments, we shan't have toiled in vain' (Churchill College, Cambridge, PLDN 5/2/2, 13 June 1961).

73 T291/44, CPE(4); Cmnd 1432, para 34. The following quotes are from paras 39, 48, 50 and 55–6.

74 W.J.M. Mackenzie, *The Guardian*, 25 May 1963, reprinted as 'The Plowden Report: a translation' in R. Rose (ed) *Policy-Making in Britain* (1969), pp. 273–82.

75 The full remit is in TNA: CAB129/97, C(59)77, 'The control of public expenditure', 30 April 1959. The confessions are in TNA: T291/85, Ninth Interim Report, para 41 and Eighth Interim Report, Appendix 1, paras 1 and 4.

76 Plowden was appointed the vice-chairman of British Aluminium in January 1960, and both he and Raisman were reported to have insufficient time to read memoranda at the Committee's most critical time (T291/5, MacPherson minute of 5 July 1960). Wall's chairmanship of the management services subcommittee, where private sector influence could arguably have been at its greatest, was – to say the least – relaxed.

NOTES FOR CHAPTER 3

It left the Treasury (and in particular Clarke) to select the membership, write the remit, submit the evidence and draft the report (see correspondence in T291/37–8, *passim*). Clarke's own summary of the Committee was that it 'proved troublesome to run . . . three outside members made no effective contribution. And the fourth was promoted in the course of the work and could do little afterwards. The physical job of getting the committees and subcommittees to meet, and of providing material for discussion was therefore arduous and often frustrating' (T235/82, letter to E. Abbot, 28 July 1961).

77 TNA: T291/9, R. Clarke to T. Padmore, 2 February 1961; T291/65, Clarke to Padmore, 29 March 1960; Padmore in T291/63, TIP(M)1, 12 April 1960. Omitted altogether was any reference to areas where Treasury competence was most challenged, such as the social services (uninvestigated by the Committee) and defence (the subject of the Third Interim Report).
78 TNA: T291/11, CPE (Report) 8, paras 6, 14, 16.
79 Cmnd 1432, para 53. In drafting the Eighth Interim Report, Clarke made some criticisms of the Treasury as well as departments in order to appease the outside members. He then omitted the former but not the latter from the Final Report.
80 Plowden, 'Introduction' to the symposium on the Report, *Public Administration* 41 (1963) 1. Treasury reorganisation was trailed in Cmnd 1432, para 59.
81 Plowden's recommendation to be 'ruthless' was applied in the Treasury itself, with the transfer of the Second Secretary (Sir Thomas Padmore), who might have expected one of the top posts, to the Ministry of Transport. This was not Padmore's only disappointment. In 1951 his appointment as Cabinet Secretary had been announced but was then vetoed by the incoming Churchill on the grounds that he wished to keep Brook in post. Later, Barbara Castle unavailingly sought to remove him from Transport and then circumnavigated him. See Theakston, *Leadership*, p. 101 and B. Castle, *Fighting All the Way* (1993) pp. 367–8.
82 Both the MacDonnell Commission and the Machinery of Government committees in the 1940s addressed such issues and they were regularly aired by outside commentators. Up to 1962, the Treasury significantly described the Cabinet Office as one of its 'sub-departments' (see, for example, TNA: T199/796).
83 For Plowden's letter (a draft of which was discussed with all the Committee members and with Brook), and the subsequent internal debates, see TNA: T199/733. For Plowden's further views, see Churchill College: PLDN5/2/2–3, especially his letter to D.N. Chester, 9 November 1962.
84 TNA: T199/733, Brook to Selwyn Lloyd, 6 September 1961. In the covering note, Brook noted that Macmillan's mind was 'moving in the same direction', and Lloyd noted his own agreement. Joint Secretaries had first been appointed in 1956, when Brook became Head of the Home Civil Service and Cabinet Secretary (an expedient temporarily employed with Bridges between 1945 and 1947). Since 1919, the 'deputy' responsible for economic and financial policy had had the status, but not the rank, of an 'ordinary' Permanent Secretary.
85 Ibid, Plowden's letter of 9 June 1961, Brook's of 6 September 1961 and Padmore's of 22 March 1962 (which included Lee's description, which he later denied). For Lee's incontrovertible views, expressed in a letter of 6 June 1961 to Brook poignantly written in Hertford Hospital following his first heart attack, see Churchill College, Cambridge: PLDN 5/2/2. Bridges strongly opposed Lee's suggestion arguing, like later opponents of the Civil Service Department, that 'you cannot have two centres' (Bridges, *Treasury*, p. 203).
86 Ibid, Padmore letter of 13 February 1962 and 'note for the record' by Brook following the final meeting of the 'big four' on 22 March.
87 Ibid, Brook's letter of 6 September 1961, and Helsby to Fulton, 23 May 1967. Helsby waspishly noted of Brook that he was 'very strongly attached to the Cabinet Office job, and by contrast had relatively small affection for the Treasury generally (where he had never worked) and for Civil Service management in particular'. As a result, 'he never

fully accepted or perhaps understood the importance of the Civil service job'. Initially Helsby, as a former Permanent Secretary of the Ministry of Labour, oversaw incomes policy which, because it was relevant to both economic policy and Civil Service pay, straddled both sides of the Treasury; but responsibility was later transferred to the DEA.

88 A major battle ensued over the integrity of economic advice. To whom should economists be responsible – their new generalist head or the head of the Economic Section (Sir Alec Cairncross) who had previously represented all Treasury economists? The dispute highlighted the fact that the integration of specialists and generalists, as demanded by modernisers, could result in professional losses as well as administrative gains. The ultimate, and somewhat empty, compromise was that economists should remain responsible to Cairncross for 'professional matters' (such as the techniques of economic analysis). A second battle concerned lines of command. It was ultimately decided that the Third Secretary responsible for the National Economy divisions should report directly to the Permanent Secretary and not through the Public Sector Group (which would have further weakened Cairncross and further strengthened Clarke's empire). The Third Secretary was D.A.V. Allen, who had an economics and statistics degree and was later to be Head of the Civil Service. See TNA: T199/930–2, particularly the letter by Sir F. Lee to N. Brook, 22 March 1962.

89 The divisions grouped together expenditure on defence (DM), the social services (SS), nationalised industries (PE) and environmental planning (AT, a combination of agriculture, housing and local government and transport). The final division (AS), covering expenditure and manpower in the Arts and Science, was a traditional 'mixed' division; but such a mix was eschewed elsewhere because both sets of responsibilities required specialised skills and because, so it was believed, it trapped Treasury thinking on departmental 'tramlines'.

90 Cmnd 1432, para 36d; TNA: T199/932, I.P. Bancroft to N. Brook, 29 March 1962.

91 The phrase was Burke Trend's, see TNA: T199/931, TOC(62)18. Although Trend was a powerful presence on the Committee, its main driving force was the Treasury's Deputy Establishment Officer and future Head of the Civil Service, Ian Bancroft. Aping Clarke on the Plowden Committee, he provided many of the ideas, drafted the Report and then oversaw, with consummate skill, its implementation.

92 TNA: T199/733, Plowden to Selwyn Lloyd, 9 June 1961; Churchill College, Cambridge, CLRK 1/3/3/1, 1/3/2/2, Clarke to W. Armstrong, 16 October 1962; TNA: T320/330, F.R.P. Vinter, 21 May 1965.

93 For the growing enlightenment of Clarke, for example in relation to social returns on investment, see Churchill College, Cambridge: CLRK 1/3/4/5, memo to R.R. Neild on 'A Social Report', 14 February 1966 and valedictory report on the Public Service Group, March 1966.

94 TNA: T199/930, B. Trend to N. Brook 30 November 1961, p. 18. Lack of staff was admitted by Helsby to the Chancellor of the Exchequer on 13 May 1963 (TNA: T199/947) and confirmed in T199/816. The Estimates Committee was particularly damning of the Management Services (General) Division, leading to Helsby's bid for extra resources in December 1965, to which the Chancellor eventually acceded (T199/1004). Callaghan was perhaps convinced by the argument that 'we must be in the forefront in considering all management techniques, and their application to Government activities. This is essentially a way of saving money and of getting the best value for money, among the most potent that we command'. This was a premonition of Lord Rayner's mantra in the 1980s: 'spend to save'.

95 TNA: T199/941, B. Trend to N. Brook, 7 May 1962 and W.W. Morton to B. Trend, 26 April 1962. Training was another area where great deficiencies were admitted; but, to remedy this defect, the Centre of Administrative Studies was established in October 1963 (see ch 9.2).

NOTES FOR CHAPTER 4

96 For a review of the comparative studies programme, see TNA: T325/117, P.R. Baldwin to J. Archer, 10 November 1965. The same file contains a record of the meeting, chaired by Helsby on 28 October, which led to his bid for extra resources.
97 TNA: T199/992, Clarke's report on the Public Sector Group, March 1966; T119/941, TPEC(62)13, 7 June 1962; T199/936, TOC(65)5, November 1965. For Clarke's earlier ruminations, see T325/117, *passim*. His 1966 report included the admission that 'satisfactory working arrangements are yet in sight'.
98 TNA: T199/937, TOC Report, June 1962, paras 8, 53. The Treasury's internal committee that shadowed PESC (TPEC) was initially the forum for collaboration (see T199/941, minute by Clarke, 4 May 1962). For Operation Vigilant see T320/313, T325/117 and T325/119. It was chaired by Sir Philip Allen, the new head of the Management Side and a future member of the Fulton Committee. For the planning of the Management Accounting Unit, see T325/117, *passim* and T199/1004, L. Helsby to the Chancellor, 2 December 1965.
99 T325/117, R. Clarke to L. Helsby, 21 October 1965, para 9; T199/992, Clarke's report on the Public Sector Group, March 1966, para 25; T199/941, minutes of meeting, 23 May 1962. For a summary of the Management Group's philosophy, see W.W. Morton, 'The management function of the Treasury', *Public Administration* 41(1963) 34: 'If central management reaches out too far, the individual officer may come to feel that beyond his department is an authority, out of reach, controlling his career ... This leads to an apprehension of a "They" beyond the departmental "they" to no great contentment for anyone.' He concluded that more 'central management leads to more coordination, more effort ... more staff, possibly even to more callousness and less human sympathy'.
100 Churchill College, Cambridge: CLRK1/3/3/1. Clarke did float the idea in July 1963 that 'one Second Secretary [ideally himself] could look after both the P.S. group and most (perhaps all) of the management group'. By February1966, however, his remedy for the two sides 'drifting further apart' was to 'forge inter-departmental instead of intra-departmental links, especially as [spending departments] would have to come to us for money'. The division he was anticipating here, somewhat in contradiction to his later published and oft-cited views, was between a 'Ministry of Finance and a Ministry of Civil Service' (see TNA: T325/119 and Clarke, *Public Expenditure Control*, p. 105).
101 For the preparations of this submission to Fulton, and Armstrong's address to staff on becoming Permanent Secretary, see TNA: T199/992–3. A working party was set up in May 1966 and its report discussed first with six selected Permanent Secretaries and then by all Permanent Secretaries (including those on Fulton) on 23 September. Whilst accepting its substance, they had reservations about its 'tone' of complacency and self-satisfaction.
102 Churchill College, Cambridge: PLDN 5/2/3. The Estimates Committee in 1964 also commented on the remarkable extent and speed of reorganisation (see ch 3.2.1 above).
103 C. Booker, *The Neophiliacs* (1970), p. 91.
104 Nevil Johnson in his submission to Fulton (vol 5, p. 959).
105 Crossman, *Diaries*, vol 1, p. 616; CPA: CRD3/14/10, letter by Mark Schreiber, 19 February 1969.

4 THE FULTON COMMITTEE, 1966–8

1 For evidence of a potential coup (to be led by the new Chancellor, Roy Jenkins, had he sufficient resolve) see, for example, G. Radice, *Friends and Rivals* (2002) pp. 167–9. June 1968 was seen to be the optimal time.

2 For the Fabian Society and the Estimates Committee, see above ch 3.2.1 and the concluding paragraph of ch 3.2.2. The evidence to the latter by Mackenzie and Chester as well as Helsby and Armstrong is in its *Sixth Report,* PP (1964–5) 6 (see especially questions 788 and 1083–4, and paras 107–11of the Report).

3 See, for instance, the letter drafted by Helsby but sent by Callaghan (as Chancellor) to Wilson which argued that, whilst 'there has a been a good deal of criticism of the Service', much was 'misguided' and 'so needs to be answered with authority'. Admittedly it was then acknowledged that, were any criticism found to be justified,'radical remedies' might be needed. This was perhaps added to placate Wilson, who provoked by Balogh, had become particularly concerned about the social background of the Administrative Class (see TNA: PREM13/1757 and T216/865). The Fulton Report itself later admitted that 'the lack of knowledge and understanding of the outside world for which we have criticised the Service has its mirror-image in the outside world. The public interest requires that active steps should be taken to reduce it' (Cmnd 3638, Appendix G, para 10).

4 See Cmnd 3638, paras 1, 15. The full text of the opening paragraph is: 'The Home Civil Service today is still fundamentally the product of the nineteenth-century philosophy of the Northcote-Trevelyan Report. The tasks it faces are those of the second half of the twentieth century. This is what we have found; it is what we seek to remedy'. For Wilding's remark, see G. K. Fry, *Reforming the Civil Service* (1993), p.257. Fry's book is an exemplary history of Fulton, and contains a quarry of information from the press, oral testimony and the Committee's records – albeit not from official files, to which he was denied access. This chapter relies heavily upon it, together with the transcript of a symposium on 'Fulton: 20 years on' published in *Contemporary Record* 2 (1988) 44–55.

5 The potential international damage was considered to be so great that the FCO immediately issued a communiqué stressing *inter alia* that perceived weaknesses in the Service were due not to laziness but insufficient training. The recognition of a need to reform, it also argued, was a sign of strength not weakness (see TNA: PREM13/1971, June 1968).

6 Wilson himself alluded to Northcote-Trevelyan when both announcing the Committee's appointment and its report in Parliament (Parl Deb (Commons), 724, col 209, 8 February 1966; 767, cols 454–9, 26 June 1968). So too throughout the Committee did the Chairman and those members seeking radical change (such as Robert Neild, who circulated copies to the Committee *pour encourager les autres*). Treasury officials were less enthusiastic. 'The difference', wrote Helsby on 7 February 1966, 'is that the Northcote-Trevelyan inquiry is associated in the minds of those in the Civil Service, and also in the minds of those outside who know about the Report, with the curing of a vice – the selection of recruits by patronage; and we do not want to suggest that the present inquiry also stems from similar need' (TNA: PREM13/1757).

7 See Fry, *Reforming* (pp. 241–59) for the majority of quotations in this and the succeeding paragraph. For the comment by Rayner, see PREM19/250, 16 July 1980; by Fry, see 'More than "counting manhole covers"', *Public Administration* 77 (1999) 536; by Hennessy, *Whitehall*, p.190; by Barberis, *The Whitehall Reader* (1996), p. 1; by Armstrong, 'Taking stock of our achievements' in *The Future Shape of Reform in Whitehall* (1988) p. 13; and by the author of *Next Steps*, K. Jenkins, *Politicians and Public Service* (2008), pp. 29 and 86.

8 Cmnd 3638, paras 292, 54 and 12 (in order of citation). One of the few contemporaries to challenge the Report's bias towards big government was David Howell in the House of Commons debate on the Report (Parl Deb (Commons) 773, col 1635, 21 November 1968).

9 See Cmnd 3638, para 177. Sir Robin Butler, as Cabinet Secretary and Head of the Civil Service, coined the phrase 'unified not uniform' after the agreement that *Next Steps*

agencies should recruit staff independently (see Introduction, opening para); and one of his successors, Sir Andrew Turnbull advocated that there should be 'a permanent civil service but not permanent civil servants' (see P. Riddell, *The Times*, 16 June 2005). Fulton specifically considered the question of whether departments should recruit independently and rejected it 'on the grounds that it would encourage wasteful competition, place the less glamorous departments at too great an advantage and break up a Service which, in our view, should remain unified' (para 67).

10 Ibid, para 134. The Committee's attitude towards a career profession was very similar to that of Northcote-Trevelyan (see para 196 and Appendix B, p. 111) although it condemned its limited perception: 'civil servants do not normally think in terms of a career in the Service – they have a career in a class' (para 203).
11 Ibid, paras 275, 32, 54.
12 Ibid, paras 38, 45–8. On the encouragement of mobility, which some commentators have suggested Fulton opposed, see paras 49–51.
13 Ibid, paras 101–106. The College was to have some responsibility for specialists and executive officers (see paras 108–9); but, as with Northcote-Trevelyan, the emphasis was, and was to be, on the 'administrator'.
14 Ibid, paras 76–7, 80. The Report explicitly expressed the hope that the 'curricula in schools and universities will gradually be modified' in response to the Service's need for greater numeracy and 'familiarity with major modern languages' (para 81). For the views of Northcote-Trevelyan and Macaulay on training, see above ch 1.4.2.
15 Ibid, paras 62, 117, 121–2. The Report was particularly damning of Establishment Departments in paras 164–7. Even Bridges had admitted that 'some Departments used to put their old fossils as Principal Establishment Officer' (TNA: BA1/8).
16 Ibid, paras 188–91,147, 214–25, 213.
17 Ibid, paras 91–6, 238(d), 197
18 Ibid, paras 209(d), 238, 229, 138–43.
19 Ibid, paras 288, 19.
20 Ibid, paras 124–8, 156–62. Accountability was also to be increased by shortening 'the chain of command'. As Sir Alexander Johnston (Chairman of the Board of Inland Revenue) admitted to the Committee with typical frankness: 'there were perhaps too many grades in the Administrative Class. Departments often seemed to work best in the holiday season when some layers in the hierarchy were removed' (TNA: BA1/3).
21 Ibid, paras 175, 181. The average age, it was noted, of French *directeurs du cabinet* was 46 and of Swedish under-secretaries 45 whilst that of Permanent Secretaries in Britain was 56 (para 182). More importantly, at the time when Barbara Castle – like several other Ministers – was seeking to remove her Permanent Secretaries (see ch 3.2.2, fn 81), the Committee recommended that such dismissals should be exceptional because 'Ministers change often, whereas the running of the department requires continuity'. Removal of a Senior Policy Adviser should be less exceptional and of a Private Secretary even less so (see para 286).
22 Ibid, paras 163, 186, 285.
23 Ibid, para 252.
24 Ibid, paras 248, 245, 271, 274.
25 The members were Robert Neild and Sir Phillip Allen. See 'Fulton: 20 years on', *Contemporary Record*, 45, 50.
26 Tomlin reported within 21 months and Priestley within 2 years. Fulton took 28 months, which was only marginally shorter than the contemporary Donovan and Redcliffe-Maud Royal Commissions on industrial relations and local government respectively. That five Royal Commissions sat concurrently with Fulton, made its status all the stranger. All the Labour Government perhaps wished was a validation of the Fabian Society's proposals, for which no elaborate inquiry was needed (see Fry, *Reforming*, pp. 23–7).

NOTES FOR CHAPTER 4

27 Parl Deb (Commons), 724, cols 209–10, 8 February 1966. The Committee itself stated that the 'terms of reference excluded the machinery of government' which 'imposed limits on our work' (Cmnd 3638, Appendix A, para 6).
28 P. Kellner and Lord Crowther-Hunt, *The Civil Servants* (1980), p. 27. Hunt's innate suspicion and somewhat cavalier attitude towards inconvenient 'facts' are illustrated by his claim that, by being made a departmental committee, it was 'downgraded' and that officials were given 'for the first time . . . such a substantial role in an inquiry into themselves' in order to ensure a 'safe' report (see p. 26). This overlooked the Northcote-Trevelyan (given that Trevelyan was a serving official), Playfair (on which six out of eight members were serving officials) and Haldane Committees (two out of seven), let alone Plowden. In Hunt's defence, however, Helsby did boast to other Permanent Secretaries in September 1965 that 'the real advantage of this type of committee was the way in which its deliberations could be guided . . . In the case of a Royal Commission, civil service witnesses would have to take a publicly defined stand with the possibility of having no greater influence on the findings of the committee than other people who have appeared before it' (TNA: T216/865).
29 Hennessy, *Whitehall*, pp. 190–1. For Beveridge's sense of adventure, see J. Harris, *William Beveridge* (1997), esp pp. 374–6. Similar adventurism was encouraged, amongst others, by William Ryrie of the Treasury (see Fulton, vol 5, memo 144).
30 The specific critics were Michael Halls (TNA: PREM 13/1970, Halls to Wilson, 9 March 1968) and Lord Shackleton (the first Minister for the Civil Service), in 'Fulton', *Contemporary Record*, 48. See, more generally, J. Davis, *Prime Ministers and Whitehall, 1960–1974* (2007), ch. 3.
31 The Secretary was Richard Wilding of the Treasury, of whom Simey commented in October 1967: 'what is missing from our work is not so much skill in drafting, as agreement about the substance of the reports themselves. It is virtually impossible to draft a report without really clear agreement as to what is to go into it, and there has never been any common agreement about this. Wilding is now, I fear, a defeated and much disappointed man' (quoted in Fry, *Reforming*, p. 235).
32 Fry, *Reforming*, p. 19. Despite their strong backing, Callaghan eventually vetoed Mackenzie ('not at any price' – perhaps because he had been championed as chairman by Balogh) and Helsby vetoed Chester on the incredible grounds that he was 'too light weight' (TNA: T216/865, additional note by I.P. Bancroft, 18 October 1965).
33 See Davis, *Prime Ministers*, pp. 59–61 and TNA: PREM 13/1970, M. Halls to H. Wilson, 9 March 1968. The ill temper reputedly surfaced with particular venom at evening meetings of the 'inner group' (Fulton, Kipping, Neild, Hunt and Dunnett).
34 See Fry, *Reforming*, pp. 231–41. As an outside academic warned Fulton: 'you cannot really have a latter-day Macaulay or Northcote-Trevelyan statement; the issues and the organisation your committee has to deal with are much more complex than anything the investigations of the 1850s looked into; nor are people today as sure of having found the key as those men were' (ibid, p. 235). Helsby, had his own retrospective, and somewhat complacent, explanation for the Report's tone. 'At bottom', he argued, it was not a radical report and so it was perhaps 'natural that the Committee should have been tempted to divert attention from the relative modesty of its proposals by presenting its criticisms in a somewhat ferocious way that was bound to make headlines. Old fashioned doctors used to believe that the potency of quite ordinary drugs could be increased by speaking severely to the patient and making the medicine look horrible. A patient who was fundamentally healthy usually did very well' (*The Listener*, 18 July 1968, pp. 66–7).
35 Fry, *Reforming*, pp. 236–7. Simey's reservation, which was reputedly drafted with the knowledge of William Armstrong, disputed the historical accuracy of the analysis, but more particularly objected that it was 'unfair to the Civil Service' and gave a 'misleading impression of its future potentials' (Cmnd 3638, pp. 101–3, esp para 2).

NOTES FOR CHAPTER 4

36 'Fulton', *Contemporary Record*, 46–7. Marcia Williams, Wilson's Political Secretary, who was as committed as any in the Labour Party to breaking the power of the 'permanent politicians' in Whitehall, spoke darkly of the prospects of 'Fulton plus' (see Fry, *Reforming*, p. 262).
37 Parl Deb (Lords) 295, col 1105, 24 July 1968.
38 As William Armstrong, for example, immediately minuted the Prime Minister's Principal Private Secretary on seeing a draft: 'from the point of view of getting the positive recommendations accepted' it would have been far better for the Committee to have 'recognized more fully both the improvements that have been made in recent years, and the difficulties under which the Service has been labouring' (TNA: PREM 13/1970, W. Armstrong to M. Halls, 9 May 1968).
39 Fulton (vol 2) para 8. The MCG praised officials' sense of vocation and intellectual capacity, which it adjudged 'comparable with the best at equivalent levels in industry'. At a lower level, there was 'much more training than is general in industry'; the Service was 'a particularly enlightened employer of women'; service deliverers were 'scrupulously fair' and provided a 'personal service beyond that officially required'; and industrial relations were 'largely trouble free . . . compared with some situations in industry and commerce' (paras 8–19). The radical signatories of Fulton compounded their error. Northcote and Trevelyan had almost immediately recanted (see above, ch 1 fn 31). They never did.
40 Quoted in Fry, *Reforming*, p. 3. As Fry remarks, some testimony to earlier inquiries (such as that of W.J. Brown to MacDonnell, and of Fisher to Tomlin) had been of considerable contemporary and historical importance. Written evidence was also collected rather randomly and was often submitted well after the deadline of December 1966 (ibid, pp. 30–7). A further failing was that the views of the actual consumers of state services were ignored.
41 Fry, *Reforming*, pp. 38–44, and also pp. 55–6. Such a cavalier attitude to evidence was typical. 'I have never heard', claimed its Secretary later, 'of a committee which paid less attention to evidence that was put up to it'. Neild concurred in relation to the Social Survey: 'there was just a core of us and we were anxious about the main stuff, which did not rest on that kind of research material' ('Fulton', *Contemporary Record*, 45). The Committee's historical understanding was equally flawed (see ch 1.4.2 above, Simey's reservation and R. Thomas, *The British Philosophy of Administration* (1978), pp. 69–70). This was not wholly the Committee's fault: when approached to assist, academic historians took flight (TNA: BA1/4).
42 TNA: BA1/11, 17th meeting, 6 June 1968. See also Fry, *Reforming*, pp. 47–9. The principal concerns of the Social Survey were officials' social and educational background; the relative impact of educational qualifications on promotion; officials' relationships with those outside the Service; and the position of women (which, as will be seen in chapter 9.5, had a particular long-term impact).
43 For the MCG in general, see Fry, *Reforming*, ch 3. Walker's accolade is cited on p. 62. Management consultants had, contrary to some claims, been used in government before 1966. McKinseys had investigated the Post Office, for example, and Ivor Young (from the leading firm of Urwick, Young and Partners) had been seconded to the DEA.
44 The MCG's reticence was in many ways justified. Glassco was later criticised for overlooking the issue of democratic accountability and for failing to square the circle of central control and greater decentralisation. Indeed, in contrast to contemporary calls in Britain for an independent CSD, Glassco recommended – in apparent contradiction of its professed desire to 'let managers manage' – the integration of financial and manpower control within a Treasury Board. See D.C. Rowat, 'Canada's Royal Commission on Government Organisation' *Public Administration* 41 (1963) 193–205.
45 The superior status of these Commissions was assured by the choice of chairmen: the Hoover Commissions (1947–9 and 1953–5) had a former President whilst the Coombs Commission (1974–6) had the leading public servant of the day, who had masterminded

postwar reconstruction and was later Governor of the Reserve Bank. The chairman of the Glassco Commission (1960–2) was a leading businessman. Their assumptions about the proper role of 'modern' government were somewhat different but their methods were similar. Both Glassco and Coombs followed Hoover's example by employing a large number of researchers and management consultants in dedicated task forces to study particular issues. Glassco, for instance, employed some 210 specialists and spent some $2m on consultants. Coombs employed some 60 research staff and 50 consultants in a carefully structured research programme. Whether such expenditure secured more practical results is, admittedly, debatable. Glassco's shortcomings have already been noted. Coombs has also been described as a 'text-book case in non-implementation'. Nevertheless, it was simultaneously described as a 'watershed' document because, like the other enquiries, it amassed evidence which revolutionised the understanding of government and helped to direct later reform. See, in particular, P. Wilenski, *Public Power and Public Administration* (1986), pp. 184–5 and D. Saint-Martin, *Building the New Managerialist State* (2000).

46 'Fulton', *Contemporary Record*, 45.
47 Cmnd 3638, paras 75–84, 228. The record of the 'radical' members on these issues was somewhat perverse. They were in the majority which supported 'preference for relevance', were divided over Method I (the traditional method of recruitment, introduced after Northcote-Trevelyan, based purely on written examinations) and were in the majority that *opposed* job evaluation and performance pay. There were three other notes of reservation in the Report. Hunt favoured the presence of junior ministers on promotion boards (to prevent too much 'in-breeding') and on official interdepartmental committees (to provide some urgency and political direction). The 'radicals' were also in the majority which demanded formal monitoring of the Report's implementation over the first five years. Ibid, paras 120, 285 and 302.
48 Fulton (vol 2) para 98. For the dispute over unified grading, see Fry, *Reforming*, pp. 180–93.
49 Cmnd 3638, para 248. See also paras 45, 103, 106. Of other unresolved issues, the conflict between unified grading and occupational groups was left to the CSD, whilst the issue of officials' anonymity was assigned to the Civil Service College (which was expected to provide a forum for public debate on administrative reform).
50 Sir Phillip Allen quoted in Fry, *Reforming*, p. 13; J.L. Garrett, *The Management of Government* (1972), p. 54. The Committee's terms of reference did formally preclude discussion on 'machinery of government' topics, but it was recommended that four other such issues should become the subject of immediate inquiries: 'hiving off', official secrecy, Whitleyism and the speed of recruitment. Garrett also complained later that many of the changes, such as job evaluation, which the 'Consultancy Group suggested should be the subject of research programmes ... were promulgated by the committee as full-blown principles of management without any further evidence or deeper discussion' (*Managing the Civil Service* (1980), p. 22).
51 Marcia Williams quoted in Fry, *Reforming*, p. 263. Halls had been appointed against the wishes of senior Civil Servants and understandably resented what he perceived to be their 'class snobbery' (see, for instance, TNA: PREM13/1970, Halls to Wilson, 25 February 1968 and P. Ziegler, *Wilson* (1993), pp. 213–4). On the anodyne nature of the meetings, see Neild's comment that Wilson was a 'great lover of busy-body meetings, at which nothing whatever would happen' ('Fulton', *Contemporary Record*, 46).
52 Hennessy, *Whitehall*, p. 201, and pp. 199–202 for the political manoeuvres. See also R. Crossman, *Diaries of a Cabinet Minister* (vol 1, 1977), pp. 98, 103 and 107; and B. Castle, *The Castle Diaries* (1984), p. 464 ff. Needless to say, Balogh was prominent in the intrigues.
53 *Economist*, 21 June 1968. 'A page out of a fashion magazine' was C. H. Sissons' terse description (*Spectator*, 5 December 1970).

5 MODERNISATION'S MOMENT, 1968-72

1. TNA: PREM13/1971, record of a meeting between Wilson, the National Staff Side of the Whitley Council and senior Treasury officials, 1 July 1968. Armstrong had succeeded Helsby as Head of the Civil Service in May 1968 in anticipation of the Fulton Report and the creation of CSD. Fisher had, of course, served on the Bradbury Committee which in turn had recommended the Treasury's radical overhaul. Had history repeated itself, Sir James Dunnett might have been plucked from the Fulton Committee to drive through reform.
2. TNA: BA16/80, note by N.M. Hale, 19 July 1972 and the earlier note by Hale to J. Chilcot, 24 May 1972.
3. See Kellner and Crowther-Hunt, *Civil Servants*, pp. 63, 75 and 66 (in order of citation). These suspicions had earlier been aired before the House of Commons' Expenditure Committee, when it investigated Fulton's fate in 1976. The temper of Hunt's account – which quoted from restricted memoranda – may be measured by his claim that the 'feline' Armstrong 'had seen off the one man capable of challenging their actions' (namely himself) and by its attack on a serving official, Richard Wilding, on grounds which surviving records show to be unfounded (pp. 77 and 68). John Garrett was more circumspect in his contemporary judgements (see *Managing the Civil Service*, ch. 2). Howell reiterated many of Hunt's complaints in T*he Edge of Now* (2000), Appendix 1, as well as providing a classic description of the 'official embrace' in S. Ball and A. Seldon (eds) *The Heath Government* (1996), p. 69: 'Armstrong and Trend moved in on me', he recounted of his first days in office, 'lunch at the Athenaeum . . . they said these were interesting ideas and they had also prepared a number of papers on how Whitehall could be run more effectively. And, hey presto, it was all in their hands, not mine'.
4. *Eleventh Report of the Expenditure Committee, 1976–7*, 'The Civil Service', vol 2, pt 2, p. 788. On Heath's declining interest, see Hennessy, *Whitehall*, p. 242. At the CSD, Howell was Parliamentary Secretary and Sheldon later Minister of State (with Garrett as his Parliamentary Private Secretary). Sheldon had, of course, been a member of the Fulton Committee and Garrett of its MCG.
5. On 22 September 1970, the Cabinet agreed to cut the number of non-industrial officials by 5% by April 1973 and again, in August 1972, by 1% a year for 3 years (see TNA: CAB128/47, CM(70)21.4; CAB128/50, CM(72)40.8).
6. TNA: BA19/220, EOM(68)7th, 18 July 1968.
7. In August 1971 the *Whitley Bulletin*, the official publication of the NSS, summarised the 'incipient insecurity' within the Service in an atypically strident editorial. 'To the more pessimistic civil servant', it read, 'even if he avoids redundancy or willy-nilly transfer to another employer, he fears that he may well find himself transported to a depressed area in another part of the country, with reduced career prospects and considerable disturbance to family life . . . One would not wish to give the impression that the Civil Service is on the verge of an outbreak of mass anxiety-neurosis. Nevertheless there is a groundswell of apprehension' which had to be allayed were morale not to be permanently damaged. Fulton had earlier expressed concern about both potential obstruction of reform by staff associations and working conditions (Cmnd 3638, paras 271–2 and Appendix I).
8. TNA: PREM13/3100, W. Armstrong to N. Hunt, 19 January 1970. Hunt's quotation from this letter in *Civil Servants* (pp. 75–6) infringed, without penalty, the Official Secrets Act. The verdict of a later Head of the Civil Service, Sir Douglas Wass, on Hunt's allegations was telling: 'whether it is right to regard the opposition of the Civil Service to ill-thought ideas as a conspiracy . . . is a matter of terminology' (University of Leeds: Fry papers, Wass to G.K. Fry, 7 November 1988).
9. The complexity would have delighted Bridges, to whom Armstrong had been Private Secretary during the War. The Steering Committee was restructured several times but typically consisted of some 14 Permanent Secretaries and was attended by the relevant

CSD specialists. Its five specialist subcommittees covered structure; management and training; recruitment; the organisation of work; and pay and grading. The Joint Whitley Committee had ten representatives of both the official and staff sides. Armstrong chaired both committees. The joint reports were successively *Developments on Fulton* (1969), *Fulton – a Framework for the Future* (1970), *Fulton – the Reshaping of the Civil Service: Developments during 1970* (1971) and *The Shape of the Post-Fulton Civil Service* (1972).

10 This was the long-held private view of Leslie Williams as Secretary General, which was expressed openly in his lecture on 'Industrial relations in the Civil Service' to the Civil Service College on 14 May 1974, soon after his retirement. For Fulton's recommendation, see Cmnd 3638, para 248.

11 Wilson and Heath were supported respectively by Lord Shackleton and Lord Jellicoe, both of whom combined day-to-day responsibility for the Service with leadership of the House of Lords. Both were personally sympathetic to reform but arguably lacked that combination of political weight and personal ambition which characterised Robert Lowe in the 1870s and was again to be displayed in Australia in the early 1980s. There, in circumstances similar to the UK a decade earlier, including the division of an all-powerful Treasury, the Minister of Finance (John Dawkins) who enjoyed the additional title of 'Minister assisting the Prime Minister for public service matters' drove through a reform programme for personal as well as party political reasons.

12 University of Leeds: Fry papers: Sir Frank Cooper to G.K. Fry, 28 March 1989. Cooper's testimony was all the more powerful for his having been an advocate of reform within CSD in the early 1970s, frustrated – like so many of his colleagues – by an inability to instruct (rather than just advise) other departments. He later became Permanent Secretary of MOD and was seriously considered as Head of the Service in 1978 and of the Efficiency Unit, in succession to Rayner, in 1983. Leslie Williams concurred. 'This was an organisation and management challenge', he recalled, 'for which by experience [Armstrong] was not well equipped'. From their frequent meetings 'he learnt more from me than I did from him' (ibid, 26 October 1988).

13 Wilson's unilateralism possibly illustrated how seriously he took his formal role as First Lord of the Treasury. It certainly illustrated how seriously Chancellors had taken, and been taken in, their role as managers of the Service.

14 TNA: PREM13/3100, N. Hunt to W. Armstrong, 12 February 1970.

15 As he argued in his address to the whole Service on 26 June 1968: 'the Report sets the stage for what can be a great effort to improve the Service, introducing changes that many of us have long desired' (TNA: PREM13/1971). Armstrong, like Lee in 1962, had expected the Head of the Civil Service to be in regular contact with the Prime Minister, but – although he never became a 'pale unhappy ghost' – he never achieved such contact with Wilson. As early as January 1969, there was a despairing request for a 'leisurely meeting' but access, not to mention the subject of administrative reform, was policed by Halls as Wilson's Principal Private Secretary (see PREM13/2528, M. Halls to H. Wilson, 23 January 1969). Armstrong certainly had more rapport with Heath, especially after he had reverted to his role as 'chief policy adviser' in 1971 (see ch 5.1).

16 See successively Armstrong's evidence to Fulton (TNA: BA1/3), his somewhat desperate advice to Wilson before Cabinet on 20 June 1968 (PREM13/1970), his address to Establishment Officers on 18 July 1968 (BA19/220, EOM(68)7th) and his lecture to the British Academy on 'The role and character of the Civil Service' on 24 June 1970 (a copy of which is in BA16/59).

17 See *Whitley Bulletin*, 48 (July and August 1968) pp. 104 and 118. Establishment Officers' reservations had been forcefully expressed at their first meeting with Armstrong after the Report's publication (TNA: BA19/220, EOM(68)7th, 18 July 1968).

18 See Cmnd 3638, para 252. In February 1968, Halls had reported to Wilson that, in relation to unified grading, 'the present Civil Service establishment (Helsby, Petch, Osmond, Rogers) neither see its advantages nor think it workable in practice . . . Unless

someone is brought in from the outside to do this it is unlikely that the implementation will have the dynamic behind it which is needed' (TNA: PREM13/1970). Helsby retired in 1968 but Sir Louis Petch became the CSD's Second Permanent Secretary whilst Osmond and Rogers became Deputy Secretaries. The third Deputy Secretary was John Hunt who, as First Civil Service Commissioner, strongly opposed the Report's recommendations on recruitment. Each was significantly to chair a specialist subcommittee of the Fulton Steering Committee. A copy of the concordat is in T224/2973.

19 TNA: BA17/34, W. Armstrong to M. Halls, 14 November 1968. Armstrong had initially requested 100 additional staff immediately, given the 'need to keep the Civil Service going while the brave new world is being fashioned' (TNA: PREM13/1970, 9 May 1968). In the light of manpower constraints, an addition of a mere 20 was gingerly suggested at an internal meeting on 8 July, although it was readily admitted that 'staff expansion on this scale was hardly ideal and barely even satisfactory' (BA16/76).

20 TNA: PREM13/2692, W. Armstrong to M. Halls, 7 October 1968. This file also records the MOD's rearguard action (led by Dennis Healey) against permitting the CSD a toehold in Whitehall. Hunt would, of course, have been aware of these political impediments.

21 Amongst others, Cooper Brothers (the management consultants) were contracted to advise on the streamlining of the recruitment and the job evaluation programme to facilitate unified grading, whilst J.E.B. Drake was seconded from BP in 1970 to advise on personnel management. One of Armstrong's managerial failings was arguably the successive appointment as his deputy of two senior Treasury officials (Sir Louis Petch and Sir David Pitblado) rather than someone of the calibre of Otto Clarke (who had helped to drive through his plans for reorganising the Treasury in 1962).

22 For this and the earlier quote, see Kellner and Crowther-Hunt, *Civil Servants*, pp. 89, 94; and for outside resistance to the College's research role, TNA: BA17/34, K. Couzens to R. Wilding, 14 October 1968.

23 TNA: PREM13/1970, W. Armstrong to H. Wilson, 9 May 1968.

24 Kellner and Crowther-Hunt, *Civil Servants*, p. 64. As early as 25 February 1968, Halls had urged Wilson to endorse unified grading on the grounds that it would 'establish a Service with opportunities for all, eliminating the defects of what is in fact, at present, class snobbery' (TNA: PREM13/1970). In his memoirs, Wilson clouded the issue. He claimed, in direct contradiction to Hunt and Halls, that both classlessness and unified grading were achieved by the merger of the administrative, executive and clerical classes in January 1971. As a variant, Marcia Williams in her memoirs attacked the social exclusiveness of the administrative elite without mentioning unified grading. See H. Wilson, *The Labour Government, 1964–70* (1971), p. 682 and M. Williams, *Inside Number 10* (1975) ch 14.

25 Halls minuted Wilson on 8 June 1968: 'we are really turning our backs on Northcote-Trevellyn [sic]'. This was countered by Armstrong's warning about the dangers of a return to the 'plodding mediocrity' of pre-Northcote-Trevelyan days (TNA: PREM13/1970). For the rationale behind Northcote-Trevelyan's 'division of labour', see ch 1.2.2.

26 See TNA: BA16/58. The speech was part of a far-reaching internal debate on the professional standards and ethos of the Service, the highlights of which were a paper by Richard Wilding, on 'The character of the Civil Service' on 9 July 1969 (ibid) and a First Division Association report on professional standards in November 1970 (BA16/82). The debate centred on Fulton's technocratic concentration on skills and organisation to the neglect of ethical standards; and was, in effect, a defence of the old Administrative Class's role as an agent for unity and as a custodian of both the public service ethos and the constitution. Foremost amongst the issues raised was one that was to become increasingly controversial: should officials' loyalty be exclusively to the

Government of the day or as, 'servants of the Crown', should they be trustees of a wider public interest?
27 For coverage of training and superannuation, see chs 9.2 and 9.4.
28 Cmnd 3638, paras 217, 193.
29 The figures are taken from the paper, 'Structure Policy', which formed the basis of a major discussion on future policy within the CSD, chaired by Armstrong on 21 November 1972. It claimed that 639 out of a total of 678 main classes had yet to be assimilated into the new structure, and listed them in full. The variance with Fulton's figure of 1400 departmental classes can be explained in part by the *unknown* number of minor departmental classes, some of which contained only one official (TNA: BA19/284).
30 Unified grading was to be based on the three main grades in the Administrative Class (Under Secretary, Assistant Secretary and Principal) with the responsibilities of all other officials within the Executive, Scientific and Professional Classes being defined in relation to them. The main equivalents of Assistant Secretary were respectively the Principal Executive Officer, Chief Scientific Officer and Directing Grade B grades. The main equivalents of Principal were Chief Executive Officer, Principal Scientific Officer and Senior Grade posts.
31 Parl Deb (Commons), 767, col 456, 26 June 1968.
32 TNA: BA16/6, FS(S)(69) 26, 17 October 1969.
33 An annotation on a memorandum by Halls of 27 December 1969 made clear Wilson had little time to spare, although the barrage of memoranda from Hunt and Halls convinced CSD officials that 'the Prime Minister scrutinizes everything we say on Fulton with some care' (see respectively TNA: PREM 13/3100 and BA16/42, R. Wilding to C. Gilbraith, 14 January 1970).
34 TNA: PREM13/3100, Shackleton to H. Wilson, 16 January 1970. Armstrong warned Halls even more bluntly in a letter of the same date that it would be 'unwise either to set a date for the extension of unified grading to cover the whole Service or to state categorically that this is our fixed objective before we have satisfied ourselves that it is practical'. This checkmated Halls who, without prior consultation, had drafted Wilson's letter of 14 January demanding the explicit commitments so that the 'interim' programme would not be taken as a 'green light to pursue the implementation of Fulton up to but well short of the unified grading structure' (ibid, memo to H. Wilson, 10 January 1970).
35 Cmnd 3638, para 226. Shackleton's actual words were: 'the key issue (perhaps in the last analysis the only one) is pay. Some skills are scarce and command a higher rate in the market than others even where the level of responsibility is equal . . . There is, as Sir William says, a dilemma. Is the pay of the common grade to be high enough to attract the scarce skill – at the cost of paying the others too much? Or fair to the others – at the cost of failing to attract the scarce?' (TNA: PREM13/3100).
36 TNA: PREM13/1970, memoranda of 9 May and 14 June 1968 (para 5). Armstrong was fortified in his views by a series of meetings with his fellow Permanent Secretaries and professional Civil Servants between 8 and 15 June.
37 The findings were published in an annex to a major report, 'The study of structure', which launched the CSD's job evaluation programme, and was submitted to the Structure Subcommittee of the Fulton Steering Committee. The Subcommittee received three reports on international practice. Two, on Canada and the USA were the principal outcome of Armstrong's delegation (see TNA: BA16/ 1, FS(S)(69) 3, 9 and 10). An earlier paper, on Australia by D.N. Chester, had tellingly commented that it 'was unfortunate that the Fulton Committee did not study the experience of the Commonwealth Public Service . . . They would have discovered that they were very thankfully extricating themselves from the serious problems associated with a simple classification in which every job and level of work are related to every other, just at a

NOTES FOR CHAPTER 5

time when Fulton was making it a basic recommendation . . . The experience would have been far more rewarding than the two or three days spent in Sweden, or in the US for that matter' (FS(S)(68) 17, 16 October 1968). Even more damningly, it was later established that the percentage of Civil Servants in the USA covered by unified grading had been decreasing since the early 1960s. Moreover, approximately half of all officials were employed in agencies, which were exempt from it (BA19/286, H. Collings to D.J. Gerhard, 22 June 1973). The BBC had also abandoned unified grading in 1968 because of the problem of maintaining pay comparability (PREM13/3100, W. Armstrong to M. Halls, 16 January 1970).

38 Norman Hunt spelt out the MCG's thinking in a letter to Halls on 21 November 1969 (TNA: PREM13/3099). For the official estimates, see A.J. Wyatt to A. Bailey, 10 June 1968 (BA16/97) and R. Wilding to E.H. Simpson, 13 March 1969 (BA16/36). Both, it was admitted, were highly tentative but the latter was consistent with the National Prices and Incomes Board's estimate that private sector wage costs typically rose by between 2 and 12%. For the PESC confrontation between Shackleton and the Chancellor over the 'cost of Fulton', see BA16/36 and PREM13/3096.

39 The strategy of 'top slicing' is described in *Fulton: A Framework for the Future*, para 26 and justified most fully in memoranda, drafted at Armstrong's request, by J.B. Pearce and N.G. Morrison on 1 and 2 January 1970. The feasibility of unified grading at Assistant Secretary level depended on the acceptability of taking an average of pay rates from the widest possible range of comparable jobs. Wilson recalled that he and Fulton had agreed that 'scarcity factor' supplements could resolve most difficulties, but Morrison and later Armstrong underlined the limited applicability to the UK of this US expedient, given the nature of free collective bargaining (see, respectively, TNA: BA16/42 and PREM 13/3100, W. Armstrong to M. Halls, 9 February 1970).

40 'Categories' were first conceived by the Investigating Team, see TNA: BA16/6, FS(S) (69) 28, 21 October 1969.

41 TNA: PREM13/1971, W. Armstrong to M. Halls, 19 June 1968. Establishment Officers similarly reported a month later that 'professionals were doubtful about the classless structure and particularly disliked the idea of losing their identity or becoming 'civil servants grade x''' (BA19/220, EOM(68)7th). A year later, P.L. Gregson succinctly summarised the resulting dilemma. There were, he argued, three overall considerations: '(1) as a matter of social justice we ought to try and provide, so far as is practicable, equal opportunities for those employed within the Civil Service, irrespective of their background and type of education. (2) The Civil Service needs, in the national interest, to make the best use of the human resources within the Service. (3) Again in the national interest, the Civil Service needs to get an adequate share of able people . . . The Fulton Committee did not really produce an answer to the problem of how to reconcile these different considerations' (PREM13/3099, Gregson to M. Halls, 7 November 1969).

42 Permanent Secretaries particularly expressed their displeasure at the Steering Committee on 9 December 1969 (TNA: BA16/12, FS (69) 6th). Another issue dear to Fulton's heart, administrative specialism, was raised in the course of this battle and resulted in Armstrong informing Hunt that the original concept of two broad specialisms (economic and social) had foundered 'on the rock of practical management: the 2 broad armies could not be made into workable management units across our federal organisation'. Instead sub-fields and functional specialisms (such as personnel management) were being developed to deepen the expertise of 'generalists' without impairing their interdepartmental mobility (TNA: PREM13/3100, W. Armstrong to N. Hunt, 19 January 1970).

43 The classification of 'administrative specialists' led to a further 2000 questionnaires, whilst a planned restructuring of clerical work resulted in 1400 clerical jobs being examined in 13 different departments (see *Fulton: a Framework for the Future*, paras 15–16, 21, 50 and 55). Each questionnaire and interview took on average four and two hours respectively to complete (TNA: BA29/2, letter from P. Rogers, 6 April 1969).

NOTES FOR CHAPTER 5

44 TNA: PREM13/3100, W. Armstrong to M. Halls, 16 January 1970. For Fulton's estimate, see Cmnd 3638, para 243.

45 Armstrong originally had greater ambitions for these committees. Fulton, he advised Wilson, 'covers some areas of policy in a patchy way and is silent on others. I propose . . . to use these bodies . . . to raise, and to encourage others to raise, topics which are not covered by Fulton' (TNA: PREM 13/1972, 4 October 1968). These hopes evaporated in line with the broader vision of his role as Head of the Home Civil Service.

46 See in particular TNA: PREM13/3099, W. Armstrong to M. Halls, 16 January 1970. The same file contains Halls' complaint to Wilson on 27 December 1969 that 'William is giving way to Staff Side pressure'. For a record of 'inner circle' meetings on 22 December 1969 and 6 January 1970, and evidence of other informal dealings, see BA16/9 and 42. Negotiations with the NSS in general and the inner circle were vital as a means of forestalling a debilitating battle between the various associations. The First Division Association and the SCS, for example, opposed the dilution of the 'generalist' classes whilst the IPCS wanted maximum sideways movement for its members. The CSU wanted the emphasis less on top and more on the clerical grades – hence the ultimately abortive Clerical Work Review. See ch 8.3.1.

47 TNA: PREM13/1970, 8 May 1968 and PREM13/3099, M. Halls to H. Wilson, 27 December 1969.

48 Hunt's objections were summarised and then expanded in memoranda to Halls on 22 December 1969 and 2 January 1970 (TNA: PREM13/3099). Halls dismissed the reasons given by Shackleton and Armstrong for their refusal to comply with Wilson's request as 'gratuitously inconsistent' with the Prime Minister's original commitment to Parliament (PREM13/3100, M. Halls to W. Armstrong, 24 February 1970).

49 TNA: BA29/1, note of a meeting on 11 February 1969. Armstrong's response to Shackleton is worth quoting more fully: 'although in strict logic structure was a secondary issue, its political importance was fully recognised. The statement made by the Prime Minister . . . had been worded with great care. There was total agreement on the basic objective of removing classes, but the Prime Minister had accepted the need for a study to work out a practicable system. *The implication was that it might be found impracticable to have a simple all-embracing unified grading system*' (italics added). This, despite Hunt's insinuations in *Civil Servants*, did not align Armstrong with traditional Treasury obstructiveness. The circular informing Establishment Officers of the CSD's role on 30 October 1968, for example, cited a 'comprehensive review of the grading system' as a priority for the new department (BA16/112, appendix B) and Armstrong was prepared to face down opposition from Permanent Secretaries on the Steering Committee.

50 TNA: BA29/1, report of CSD Directorate meeting, 18 April 1969. The other reasons given were 'grass roots pressure for more vertical movement within classes . . . the fear of the SCPS that the territory of the Executive Class would be eroded and a general fear that pay determination would be more difficult'. For corroboration of the CSD's greater radicalism, see also BA16/27, P. Rogers to Shackleton, 18 April 1969 and BA29/2, P. Rogers to Walker, 29 April 1969. Where Armstrong was arguably less radical but was obliged to make similar concessions to the NSS was in his 'defence' of the Administrative Class. The battle centred on the preservation of a 'fast stream' of graduate entrants, guaranteed early training and promotion, so that 'fliers' would still be encouraged to apply. He wanted an 'outside' system, whereby the graduates were not assimilated into any existing grade. The NSS wanted, and secured, an 'inside' solution by which they were assimilated into Executive Officer grades on condition that they could still receive rapid promotion or 'grade skip'. See, chapter 9.2 and more particularly BA16/9, note on a meeting with the NSS on 15 December and brief for a meeting of the Steering Committee on 19 November 1969.

51 TNA: PREM13/3099, W. Armstrong to Shackleton, 11 July 1969; and PREM13/1972, Progress Report, 4 October 1968, para 28. CSD officials had also opposed the

NOTES FOR CHAPTER 5

concept of a 'category' when it was first proposed by the Investigation Team because of the vertical rigidities it could potentially introduce (see BA16/6, FS(S)(69)28, 21 October 1969).

52 Wilding was responding on 4 December 1969 to doubts raised explicitly for the first time by D.R.J. Stephen, see TNA: BA16/9. Armstrong's forewarning that Fulton had failed to examine 'less fundamental and risky methods of achieving the same ends' was in a memorandum of 14 June 1968 (PREM13/1970, para 13). Before December, there were innumerable expressions of support by the CSD for the further extension of unified grading (see, for example, an explicit commitment to the Structure Subcommittee on 23 October 1969 in BA16/6, FS(S)(69)27). Afterwards, the issue of cost was not allowed to cloud commitment. At the height of confrontation in January 1970, for example, one official warned: 'we must be extremely careful in view of the pay implications... to emphasise that a favourable decision on the feasibility of unified grading at whatever level, and agreement on a scheme... do not commit anyone to its actual introduction'. The Deputy Secretary in charge of the restructuring programme (Philip Rogers) insisted that it did (see BA16/42, correspondence on 1 January 1970).

53 TNA: PREM13/3099, N. Hunt to M. Halls, 2 January 1970. This was not the limit of Hunt's disingenuousness (see above fns 3 and 8). His further claim that two of its members (Alex Jarratt and John Heath) fought for Fulton's principles on the Structure Subcommittee (*Civil Servants*, pp. 68–9) is also not borne out by the records. On the contrary, Heath wrote a series of papers condemning what he regarded as the Report's inanities (see, for example, BA16/2, FS(S)(68) 22 and BA16/5, FS(S)(69) in November 1968 and February 1969).

54 TNA: PREM13/3097 and 3100, P. Shore to Shackleton, 2 March 1971. For signs of Hunt's approval, see his description to Halls of the CSD's first annual report as 'good and impressive' (PREM13/3100, 2 April 1970).

55 R. Wilding, *Civil Servant* (2006), p. 53. He did admit, however, that it might have been at a cost which would have proved unacceptable.

56 On the relative size of the Investigating Team, see TNA: PREM13/1972, Progress Report, 4 October 1968, para 27. For the battle on the Steering Committee, see in particular the minutes of its second and third meetings in 1969 (BA16/12); and for the comments of S. Mullally of BP on 25 March (BA16/42). Significantly the Investigation Team was headed, as Fulton would have wished, by a secondee from the Ministry of Transport (R.H. Bird), a management consultant (A. Skae) and a representative of the NSS (R.G. Brown, a Principal at the Ministry of Housing and Local Government). Of equal significance was the scepticism of the staff associations: 'job evaluation was a gimmick invented by management consultants for their own benefit... No doubt management consultants in general would welcome the massive job and fees... but it was by no means clear that the results would be of benefit to anyone else' (TNA: PREM13/1971, meeting with Prime Minister, 1 July 1968).

57 TNA: BA16/27. The bemused official was the Deputy Secretary, S.P. Osmond. For Wilding's warning, see his letter to L. Petch on 10 January 1969 (BA16/7); and for Cooper's later observation, see above fn 12. Agreement on a joint report was very much at the request of the Secretary General of the NSS, to strengthen that body's authority over its constituent parts (see BA29/14, briefing by R. Wilding for the 11 February 1969 meeting of the NWC Joint Committee).

58 For Heath's final decision, see TNA: PREM15/1341, note of a meeting on 22 November 1971 by P.L. Gregson to B. Gilmore: and for the Joint Whitley Committee, BA16/77, F(JC)(71)1st, 23 October 1971. Armstrong's urgency perhaps reflected his re-engagement with policy advice as head of a task force to combat growing unemployment (which was to lead to the Government's notorious economic u-turn). The briefing note for Armstrong for the Joint Whitley Council made explicit that the CSD would have advised Ministers to veto unified grading 'at this stage' had the staff associations suddenly united

in its support (see D.L. Pearson to N.M. Hale, 18 November 1971, para 5 [BA 16] PLN26/01/E), although the finality of the decision was not made explicit by Lord Jellicoe, the Minister in daily charge of the CSD, to key Fulton sympathisers (see, for instance his letter to Sheldon in March 1972, in BA16/78). On the possibility of later implementation, the final NWC progress report (*The Shape of the Post-Fulton Civil Service*) ended with some classic drafting: 'if in the longer term and taking due account of any marked reduction . . . in the obstacles, it should appear on balance that the extension of unified grading would be the best contribution to the objective, it is accepted that there should be no bar to either the Official Side or the Staff Side raising the issue afresh'.

59 'The moment of truth' was a phrase coined in December 1971 when the CSD was awaiting decisions from other departments about what resources they would commit to the improvement of personnel management. Cooper responded with characteristic bluntness: 'this is the moment of truth. The truth is for management as a whole and not simply for personnel management' (TNA: BA16/75, F. Cooper to N.G. Morrison, 13 December 1971).

60 Armstrong's initial desire to draw a line and its first serious collective discussion within the CSD on 6 April 1971 are recorded in TNA: BA 16/67. For his 1968 warning, see PREM13/1970, memorandum of 14 June, para 5.

61 Williams' perception was expressed in a letter to D. Houghton on 17 March 1972, see TNA: BA 16/ 93. Jellicoe recommended abortion to Heath (PREM 15/1341, letter of 19 November 1971). See also ch 8.3.1 below.

62 TNA: BA16/77, F(JC)(71) 1st, 23 November 1971. For the concurrence of Shackleton and Houghton, see BA16/93, note of a meeting on 21 March 1972. Shackleton and Houghton (a former head of the Inland Revenue Staff Federation) may not have been wholly disinterested; and fearing a backlash, Jellicoe wrote to key Fulton members to argue the case. He wrote to Sheldon, for instance, in March 1972: 'my initial personal preference had been to opt for unified grading at least down to and including the Assistant Secretary . . . level. However, the more I thought about all this, the more I came to the conclusion that it was the objectives rather than the means . . . that were the most important. I have therefore come to the firm conclusion that we must by one means and another lend our energies to securing the freest possible deployment in the Service so as to ensure the optimum use of talent to the benefit of both government and of individual civil servants. In view of this and in view of the limitation of resources, I believe that our immediate aim must be to concentrate on improving personnel management' (BA16/78).

63 Progress Report of March 1971 taken at the top management 'Tuesday' meeting, chaired by Armstrong on 6 April 1971, and based on an initial memorandum by D.L. Pearson (see respectively TNA: BA16/67 and BA19/280). The Report contained the first comprehensive checklist of Fulton recommendations so far implemented; and the meeting marked the first collective departmental discussion of abandoning of unified grading. Following a Prime Ministerial request for downsizing, however, Permanent Secretaries at Sunningdale in October 1971 had collectively expressed the hope that it 'would not proceed below Under Secretary' (see BA16/71, PERSEC(71), p. 3).

64 TNA: BA16/112, EOM(70)3rd, 12 March 1970.

65 Rogers (chair of the Steering Committee's Structure Subcommittee and recently appointed Deputy Secretary) was transferred to the DHSS in July 1970 as was Wilding (head of the Development Division with direct responsibility for overseeing Fulton's implementation) in September 1970.

66 The Bird Report was presented to the staff associations in F(JC)(71)3. For an evaluation, see a summary for the Steering Committee (TNA: BA16/68, FS(71)8, 8 October 1971); the briefing for the critical meeting of the Joint NWC Committee on 23 November 1971 (ibid, PLN26/61E, annex C, D.L. Pearson to J.J.S. Shaw, 19 November 1971); and a retrospective review of structure policy (BA19/286, H. Collings to D.J. Gerhard,

NOTES FOR CHAPTER 5

22 June 1973). For increasing scepticism, see BA25/224, A.A. Creamer to B. Thimont, 8 June 1971.The Report was also seen to threaten 'proliferation' by recommending three grades between Under Secretary and Principal: Assistant Secretary +; Assistant Secretary; and Senior Principal (to incorporate the former post of Senior Chief Executive Officer, whose immediate responsibilities were thus acknowledged to be greater than those of most Principals in the old Administrative Class).

67 For this and the other quotations in this paragraph (together with further disingenuousness), see TNA: BA16/68, FS(71)8, 8 October 1971.
68 The fundamental problem was how – especially in the Ministries of Defence and Technology – to assimilate some 40 Chief Scientific Officers 'B' in the Science Category and 70 Directors 'A' in the Professional and Technology Category. Each had 'direct management' rather than 'policy' responsibilities. A similar dilemma had arisen above the level of Under Secretary. Management consultants had suggested a 'twin structure', with two intermediate grades of Under Secretary (Directing) and Assistant Secretary (Directing or +) being made available for 'direct managers'. To conform to the principle of *unified* grading, job descriptions should be drafted for generalists in these grades; but to prevent proliferation, no generalist should be permitted to fill them. This was recognised to be a nonsense (see TNA: BA16/68, FS(71)9, 8 October 1971 and BA16/73, Report on the Structure of the Higher Civil Service, 23 October 1970).
69 TNA:BA16/74, December 1971, Report of the Project Team on Communications between the CSD and Departments, para 46. It was discussed by Establishment Officers in February 1972 (BA16/86, EOM(72) 3rd).
70 See, for instance, TNA: BA16/74, EOM(71) 10th, 7 October 1971.
71 TNA: BA16/77, F(JC)(71)1st, 23 November 1971. On Fulton's political objectives, Armstrong reverted in May 1972 to praising the classic ability of the old Administrative Class to 'draw out the best' from professionals. The occasion was, of all things, his address to the annual conference of the IPCS. For the reaction and evidence of the limited impact so far on the rank-and-file of either reform or Armstrong's bridge building, see BA16/83. CSD concerns about the 'political' limits of its alternative programme were admitted to the Steering Committee in BA16/68, FS(71)8, 8 October 1971.
72 For the letter on 29 December 1972 from J. Moore to J.L. Williams and the minutes of the Joint Whitley Committee for 6 February 1973, see respectively TNA: BA16/121 and PREM15/1341, F(JC)(73)1st.
73 The most substantial attacks on categories were in memoranda by D.L. Pearson on 24 February 1972 (TNA: BA16/84) and by D.J. Gerhard on 7 June, which referred to 'wasted effort' (BA19/282). The latter drew the response from two 'planners', R. Wilding and N. Hale, that categories were 'meaningless' and 'dead' (ibid, letters of 4 and 31 July). The first file also illustrates the extent of the political retreat from Fulton. An increasingly prevalent belief of junior officials was that there was ' no intrinsic merit in destroying the class system as it now operates' although managerially there were 'too many classes' (14 March). This led some to predict the class system rising 'phoenix-like from the post-Fulton ashes' (D.J. Gerhard to C. Tuck, 18 September 1972).
74 TNA: BA19/284, notes of a meeting in Sir William Armstrong's room, 21 November 1972; BA19/286, memorandum for the Permanent Secretary's Management Group, 3 July 1973. The eight new categories amalgamated typists and personal secretaries, prison officers, messengers, machine operators, instructional officers, departmental police and photoprinters as well as lawyers. The first two groups, it was hoped, could ultimately be incorporated into the Administration Group and the next two into the General Category; but a reduction in the number of CSD restructuring staff in 1973 slowed progress towards even these modest objectives.
75 See TNA: BA16/51, memorandum by B. Strong, 3 December 1969; PREM15/270, Jellicoe to Heath 10 December 1970. Drake's intervention was at the height of a search for manpower savings, but also at time when businessmen were still favoured.

76 See TNA: BA16/113, EOM(71)16, especially paras 3,13, 17. The Civil Service, Drake concluded, had to change from an organisation which directed 'its main effort towards excellence at the top into an organisation which is required more and more to demonstrate publicly its excellence at middle and lower levels where it comes into contact with the public'. A nucleus of professional personnel managers, supporting proactive line managers, was required to ensure job satisfaction since 'reliance on fear, discipline and tradition' was no longer sufficient, as before the War, to guarantee efficiency.

77 The NSS particularly stressed the need to improve personnel management to counter 'the troublesome mood at the bottom of the Service', which was soon to erupt into strike action (see TNA: PREM15/1341, F(JC)(73)1st, 6 February 1973, paras 15 and 24; and ch 8.4.1). Armstrong's proclamation may not have been totally unwilling since, on reading its draft, he had criticised Fulton for wilfully ignoring the plentiful research on the 'psychology of office workers' (PREM13/1970, memorandum of 9 May 1968). He later tentatively set up a Behavioural Science Research Division in the CSD.

78 NWC, *The Shape of the Post-Fulton Civil Service* (1972), para 43; TNA: PREM15/1341, F(JC) (73)1st, 6 February 1973, para 22. These two documents provide a summary of the personnel management programme and its shortcomings, on which this and the following paragraphs are based. Additional detail is taken from the CSD's working papers in BA16/88-9 and 121, especially the Programme as discussed by Establishment Officers in June (EOM(72) 21) and the final version as sent to J.L. Williams by J. Moore on 29 December 1972.

79 The career development of specialists was to be overseen by management committees for each specialism. One of the main grievances of the IPCS was that, within the Professional and Technology Category, these arrangements were still in embryo as late as 1973. For a review, see TNA: BA19/284, brief for the Permanent Secretary's Management Group, 3 July 1983.

80 Both policies were fully explained in the 1971 NWC Report, *Fulton – the Reshaping of the Civil Service*, pp. 11–13. Lateral movement enhanced equity by maximising the number of 'sideways' movements through 'vertical' class barriers. It was first mooted in June 1969. Opportunity posts had been first discussed in the preceding October and were managerial posts for which 'specialists' might apply, thereby providing them with a taste of 'generalist' management (see TNA: BA16/12, FS(69)3rd, 5 June 1969 and BA16/1, FS(S) 3rd, 8 October 1968). As Armstrong stressed at the final meeting of the Steering Committee, the primary purpose of both was to advance the 'parity of status' of scientists and to overcome their 'very real problems . . . in competing with administrators for management posts' (BA16/68, FS(71)1st, 21 October 1971).

81 For these delays, see TNA: PREM15/1341, F(JC)(73)1st, 6 February 1973, and the briefing notes for this meeting in BA16/121. Something as simple as the standardisation of the traditional annual review was not to be accomplished until mid-1973 and even then, to the detriment of interdepartmental transfers, its data was not to be entered onto the new computerised personnel system (**PRISM**) until 1975.

82 TNA: BA16/89, I.P. Bancroft to J. Herbecq, 27 October 1972. The response of Herbecq, who was the Under Secretary in charge of personnel management, was not to allow Bancroft to 'get away' with putting personnel management, as so many Establishment Officers wished, into 'the bottom of the in-tray'. This file contains an even more robust complaint from the Inland Revenue about JARs, with which Richard Wilding retrospectively agreed in *Civil Servant*, pp. 73–4. After a detailed exercise, the CSD had agreed with departments that an extra 1000 personnel officers were needed over two years, but the renewed manpower cuts threatened an actual reduction (ibid, N. Morrison to W. Armstrong, 5 July 1972).

83 Ibid, meeting with the 'inner circle', 15 September 1972. The SCS conference actually passed a resolution opposing lateral movement and opportunity posts. Another outside

NOTES FOR CHAPTER 5

expert, Keith Robertson, had been appointed in April 1971 to lead the job satisfaction programme.

84 Ibid, meeting with the 'inner circle', 15 September 1972. The NSS was as obsessive about the quantity as Fulton had been about its quality of personnel management work. In response, the CSD calculated that between 1968 and 1972 the number of personnel officers had risen from some 6000 to 8700, and those above the level of Assistant Secretary by 20% (ibid, report by S. Barraclough, 23 October 1972).

85 Ibid, EOM(72)21, 17 May 1972, para 7 and EOM(72)8th, 1 June 1972, p. 3.

86 For a good, but indeterminate, discussion of these issues, see TNA: BA16/86, EOM(72)5, January 1972. The CSD's commitment might also be questioned on the grounds that the Under Secretary in charge of personnel management between 1970 and 1973 was for most of the time fully engaged on the complexities of the Superannuation Act and professed no interest in 'trendy management theory'. (private information).

87 TNA: PREM13/1970, memorandum of 9 May 1968, para 12.

88 TNA: BA16/71.

89 TNA: BA19/282, J. Drake to C. Tuck, 2 June 1972 and R. Wilding to C. Tuck, 27 June 1972. Drake disparaged Fulton's claim to originality. 'A number of the Committee's recommendations were already in train before the Report e.g. Reorganisation of the Civil Service Commission, management training, spread of accountable management, interchanges with industry', he wrote, 'others were probably inevitable developments for reasons unconnected with Fulton e.g. revision of superannuation (in conformity with national pension trends) leading to a redefinition of "establishment".'

90 For this and the earlier quotation from Fulton, see Cmnd 3638, paras 248 and 274.

91 Efficiency Unit, *Improving Management in Government: the Next Steps* (1988) para 10.

92 The pamphlet was published by the Conservative Party Centre. The quotations in this paragraph are taken successively from pp. 5, 39, 7 and 14. The term 'privatisation' was coined on p. 8 and an apology offered for the ugliness of the term.

93 D. Howell, *A New Style of Government* (1970), pp. 37 and 22. Howell dismissed Fulton's charge of amateurism against the Civil Service as 'unfair' although elsewhere he stressed that Conservative plans 'in no way' contradicted Fulton; and he even praised its recommendations of accountable management and planning units, so long as the former acknowledged the possibility of privatisation and the latter the need to analyse current, as well as future, policy (see pp. 5, 13, 22).

94 Although based in the CSD with a remit to 'concern' himself with 'methods of decision-making in Government and of the management of Government activities', Schreiber always enjoyed direct access to the Prime Minister. He was one of three special advisers paid from public funds (the others being Brendon Sewill at the Treasury and D. Howe briefly at the Northern Ireland Office). The other six were paid by the Party or, in one case, by William Whitelaw (TNA: BA6/54, B.M. Thimont to R.I. McConnachie, 27 February 1974). The PSRU had initially been created to harness Ernest Marples' energies on his demotion from the Opposition front bench.

95 These broader issues formed the remit of Action Group 1, on the Central Capability, in which Schreiber supplanted Meyjes as the dominant presence. Sundridge was significantly organised by PA Management Consultants, and two other such firms became heavily involved in planning: RTZ (which developed the concept of projects and executive agencies, to be discussed later) and Booz, Allen and Hamilton (a US firm which advocated the early involvement of selected businessmen). On the etiolation of, and disharmony within, the action groups, see a report by Meyjes in June 1970 in TNA: BA17/208.

96 The *Black Book* (a copy of which is preserved in TNA: BA17/232) was in fact two hastily assembled and poorly integrated documents: the report of Action Group 1 and an 'urgent action dossier'. The quotations are taken from paras 1.2 and 3.4 of the former and section 5 of the latter. The latter also includes a tentative list of some 7 'major' and 8 'lesser' areas where significant savings could be made.

NOTES FOR CHAPTER 5

97 The meetings at the CSD were held on 29 June and 1 July 1970 and the Cabinet Committee on Analytical Capability and the Use of Businessmen on 3 July, under Heath's chairmanship (see TNA: BA17/232 and BA17/305). For the Cabinet paper and its discussion in Cabinet on 16 July, see CAB129/150, CP(70)11 and CAB128/47, CM(70)5th.6

98 See TNA: CAB128/47, CM(70) 21.4, 22 September 1970 for the Cabinet commitment; BA 17/211, for Heath's directive excluding Ministers, and CSD Ministers' complaints (for example at meetings of 16 and 20 July); and PREM15/71, Jellicoe to E. Heath, 8 September 1970 and the minutes GEN12(70)1st (preserved in BA17/213). Lord Jellicoe (as Lord Privy Seal) had day-to-day control of the CSD but had not been involved in the pre-election plans. Under pressure from backbenchers, his priority until November 1971was to achieve a 'Plimsoll line' of 500,000 non-industrial Civil Servants. Armstrong resisted this on the grounds that 'much of our central planning is directed to improving the basis of the government's decision-taking. To base our manpower planning on an arbitrary cut across the board would be a bad start' (PREM15/270, Armstrong brief, 15 September 1970). Armstrong equally tried to persuade Howell that the review of departmental functions was political because Permanent Secretaries were 'mandated spokesmen of their Ministers'.

99 For the various drafts of the white paper, which was largely written by officials within the CSD, see TNA: BA17/218–21; for the quotations from the published version Cmnd 4506, paras 5, 45 and 51; and for Howell's alternative title, his letter to Jellicoe on 14 September in BA17/213. The paper's lack of coherence was readily admitted. It was, wrote one CSD official, 'a gallant attempt to put together several lines of thought and conclusions which are not altogether compatible' (R.R. Pittam to J. N. Archer, 23 September 1970 in BA17/218). Howell claimed later that, given his appointment, he had quite reasonably expected to be the author (*The Edge of Now*, p. 349).

100 In the words of the Cabinet Secretary, Burke Trend (a man not given to hyperbole), the review was completed with 'a thoroughness and competence which I have never seen approached let alone equalled' (see TNA: BA17/225, B. Trend to W. Armstrong, 21 May 1970). Its origin lay in the emasculation of a previous exercise by a Cabinet reshuffle which *inter alia* had established Anthony Crosland as Secretary of State for Local Government and Regional Planning with a mandate to merge a range of ministries into what later became the Department of the Environment. Armstrong's response to Wilson had been forthright. 'The Civil Service would accept the changes', he minuted, 'if they felt convinced that they were of a somewhat permanent nature ... Some of your colleagues did not accept the rationale of the proposals and feared that after this upheaval it would all be unscrambled again' (TNA: PREM13/2680, note by M. Halls, 13 September 1969). This contempt for 'gimmickry' was explicitly vented in the 1970 Conservative manifesto, *A Better Tomorrow*, pp. 1–2. Crosland's appointment, like that earlier of Richard Crossman as Secretary of State for Social Services, essentially amounted to the creation of an 'overlord' to satisfy a big political personality. Both somewhat anomalously were given small planning staffs within the Cabinet Office.

101 For Heath's approval, see TNA: BA17/212, R.T. Armstrong to W. Armstrong, 7 September 1970; and for the minutes of the Cabinet Committee, BA17/305. A key paper on 'the organisation of government functions', first drafted by J.A. Chilcot in May 1970 (BA17/225), was submitted and noted by Heath on 19 June (PREM15/70) and then provided a basis for Chilcot's first draft of the white paper (BA17/218).

102 For this draft and later versions, see TNA: BA17/230–1. A Conservative victory was so little predicted that no final brief had been prepared for Heath and one was produced on time only because his audience with the Queen on 19 June was delayed by her absence at Ascot. 'Talk about Ethelred the Unready' was the caustic reaction of a later CSD official (see BA17/420, 'History of the machinery of government', section J, and BA17/431).

NOTES FOR CHAPTER 5

103 TNA: BA17/225, B. Trend to W. Armstrong, 21 May 1970 (elaborating on a letter of 26 March, in BA17/230). Trend's view had been crystallised by a debate on the Fulton Steering Committee between January and April 1970, which led to a decision not to publish a draft white paper on planning (see BA16/44, FS(70)1); and by the incremental development of specialist teams in the Cabinet Office concerned with the social services, environmental pollution, scientific policy and population as well as the assessment of intelligence. His hopes that such staff could remain 'objective' and 'neutral' as between departmental interests appeared rather unrealistic. Armstrong was steeled by this debate to oppose the concept of a Prime Minister's Office at his meeting with Heath on 7 June (BA17/231). For Plowden's ideals, see above, ch 3.3.1.

104 B. Sewill, quoted in G.K. Fry, *Policy and Management in the Civil Service* (1995), p. 24; D. Howell, 'Notes on Dinner with the Shadow Cabinet', PSRU papers, quoted by J. Davis in *Prime Ministers*, p. 92. Later Howell somewhat disingenuously admitted this resistance whilst in opposition, but not in government (*Edge of Now*, pp. 335–6).

105 TNA: BA17/231, 'Note for the record', 8 June 1970. After a meeting with Heath on 25 June 1970, Armstrong recorded an even more emphatic rejection of a Ministry of Programmes: 'the Prime Minister had shown little interest . . . and the Lord Privy Seal had indicated that he doubted whether he should trouble to go deeply into the pros and cons: he assumed that the Chancellor of the Exchequer would not even consider the matter' (BA17/210, 'Note for the record'). Heath's broader political ambivalence has been dissected most forensically by Fry: his 'supposed "strategy" embraced both sides of Conservatism at one and the same time, meaning statism on the one hand, to which Heath subscribed by personal preference, and economic liberalism on the other hand, to which Heath had made public commitments . . . There could be public administration solutions and there could be market solutions' (*Policy and Management*, p. 28). Such ambivalence and uncertainty over how far, if at all, the Prime Minister would consult his colleagues constantly bemused CSD officials (see, in particular, BA17/211, F. Cooper to C. Gilbraith, 30 July 1970).

106 TNA: BA17/232, 'Urgent action dossier', p. 53; BA17/208, Meyjes report, June 1970. At the first meeting between Jellicoe and the members of Action Group 1 on 29 June 1970 to discuss the implementation of the *Black Book* proposals, it was noted: 'Mr Meyjes said the rush with which it was prepared and the impossibility of detailed consultation with Whitehall meant that the Black Book was only a "chopping block": he would not wish to die in the ditch for its detail' (BA17/232). Howell later concurred before adding that 'our instincts were absolutely in the right direction and a more open-minded bureaucracy would have seen that and helped us' (*Edge of Now*, p. 353).

107 TNA: BA17/208, D.O. Henley to S. Goldman, 2 June 1970. For the CSD's corroboration, see successive comments by B. Sewill between 1967 and 1969 in Conservative Party Archives: CRD 3/14/ 8 and 10.

108 Meyjes was highly critical of Schreiber's 'abrasiveness', as a director of PSRU and later as the CSD's political adviser, which he claimed *inter alia* lay behind the unnecessary 'vehemence' of the *Black Book* (TNA: BA17/282, 'Note of a meeting to discuss businessmen in Whitehall', 25 June 1970; and BA17/232, 'Note of a meeting to discuss . . . the Black Book', 29 June 1970, para 14). He did not want the Business Team constrained by a working group containing Howell and Schreiber.

109 TNA: BA17/296, J.F. Mayne to N. Forward, 7 September 1970 and Jellicoe's complaint of 13 October 1970. See also BA17/302 for the warning by the Chief Secretary of the Treasury (M. Macmillan) to Howell on 3 September 1970. The entry of Schreiber and Howell into the CSD allegedly formed the basis of the episode of *Yes Minister* in which the threat to officials' power was successfully neutralised by the separation of the special adviser from his Minister and the overloading of the Minister with files.

110 TNA: BA17/232, 'Proposals from Action Group 1', para 4.8.

NOTES FOR CHAPTER 5

111 Canada had long had a vestigial PMO but its political role was greatly extended in the 1970s. A Department of Prime Minister and Cabinet was likewise established in Australia in 1977. Samuel Brittan first resurrected the idea in Britain in the *Financial Times*, 23 August 1972: for Armstrong's brief (in which he also opposed a Ministry of Programmes and a Cabinet and Public Services Department, somewhat anticipating the MPO in 1981 by reserving some personnel management functions for the centre) and for Heath's reaction, see TNA: PREM15/1603, W. Armstrong to R.T. Armstrong, 12 September 1972.

112 Theakston, *Civil Service since 1945*, p. 108; Hennessy, *Whitehall*, p. 238.

113 TNA: BA17/231, W. Armstrong, 'Note for the record', 8 June 1970. For the post-Plowden debate, see above ch 3.3.2.

114 For Armstrong's increasing influence, see TNA: PREM15/611 and 841 (the latter providing details of the task force, 'operation Cockaigne', carried out without the knowledge of junior DTI Ministers, such as the laissez-faire Nicholas Ridley). Trend's penchant for neutrality (which persuaded him not to vote in elections) was well illustrated by his refusal throughout 1970 to meet Heath's request to match projected reforms against manifesto commitments. This, he adjudged, was too political (PREM15/421).

115 In 1975, when the Conservatives were again in opposition, reports of Armstrong's behaviour bolstered the conspiracy theories on their 'Authority of Government' inquiry, which cemented Party hostility towards the Civil Service. Armstrong, it was said, became a 'Head of the Civil Service in a way that was very different to previous practice, being involved in a far more political way than usual and . . . able to effectively initiate policy on somewhat tenuous directives arising from GEN [ad hoc Ministerial] meetings' (see Conservative Party Archives: CRD4/13/2). The speaker was Maurice Macmillan who had been Chief Secretary to the Treasury until 1972 and then Secretary of State for Employment. It was Bill Kendall, the leader of the CPSA, who first dubbed Armstrong 'deputy Prime Minister'. For a full range of evidence about his breakdown, see Davis *Prime Ministers*, p. 150.

116 The minutes and papers of the successive working groups are in TNA: BA17/296–8; BA17/512–14; and BA17/727–8. The original terms of reference were set by Heath on 31 July 1970 (BA17/296) and apart from Howell, membership was wholly official, bolstered by two special advisers: Schreiber and (after December 1970) Brian Reading, Heath's economic adviser. The minutes and papers of the MPC are in CAB134/3008, and the reference to its 'somewhat desultory' discussion in BA17/983, 'History of the Business Team', p. 24. The MPC (the description of which by Howell on p. 347 of *Edge of Now* is at some variance with the records) was merged with the Ministerial Committee on the Central Capability (MCA) in July 1971. The CSD encouraged Howell, particularly at the peak of his influence between September 1970 and February 1971, to work through other Ministers but, according to the secretary of his working group, he regarded this as 'an old fashioned convention' and believed 'the Prime Minister is looking to him for material to improve the way in which he governs his senior Ministerial colleagues'. The minute continued: 'perhaps he is right, but if so it is requiring of his colleagues a change in human nature of the same order as that required in general by extreme forms of socialism' (BA17/302, N.S. Forward to F. Cooper, 8 September 1970).

117 TNA: BA17/211, M. Schreiber to M.J. Elliot-Binns, 21 July 1970; PREM15/79, Schreiber to C.R. Walker, 15 July 1970 (which contains the fateful phrase); BA17/575, D. Howell to R.T. Armstrong, 12 February 1971; and BA17/516 for the exchange of view between Howell and Armstrong on 15 April 1971.

118 For Armstrong's views, see TNA: PREM15/270, brief of 15 September 1970; BA16/59, 'The role and character of the Civil Service', p. 9; and BA17/517, D.O. Henley to N.S. Forward, 17 December 1970. The last statement was admittedly by a Treasury official; but it illustrates concurrence throughout Whitehall with Armstrong's

NOTES FOR CHAPTER 5

view, which was directly expressed to Howell on 31 March 1971 when he first sought to end the working group. It had 'provided an independent cross-check on the department's reaction to the Prime Minister's original minute', he admitted, and 'no doubt in some cases the action we know to be going on in departments would not have taken place – or at least not so speedily'. There was, however, 'a limit to what can be achieved by direct application of pressure on departments and Ministers on subjects for which they themselves are responsible to Parliament' (BA17/516).

119 TNA: BA17/515, N.S. Forward to T.H. Caulcott, February 1971; BA17/728, minute by Caulcott, 11 February 1972. CSD officials were not alone in their recalcitrance. For evidence from the Cabinet Office and the Treasury, for instance, see BA17/296, J.F. Mayne to N.S. Forward, 7 September 1970, BA17/515, Forward to T.H. Caulcott, 13 January 1971.

120 TNA: BA17/516, R.T. Armstrong to D. Howell, 30 April 1970; CAB134/2985, MCA(71)2nd, 17 November 1971; and BA17/515, T.H. Caulcott to F. Cooper, 11 March 1971. Heath's reply to Howell's letter after two and a half months largely brushed aside its proposals and, in particular, dismissed the renewed suggestion that a Ministry of Programmes should be established (originally designed, it may be assumed, to provide Howell with a stronger power base).

121 References to chaos are frequent and the written record certainly bears out the charge, see for instance TNA: BA17/727, D.G. Hoskins to T.H. Caulcott, 9 November 1971. It might be argued that it was officials' duty to anticipate and prevent such problems. This they sought to do. The Prime Minister's two personal minutes were, for example, official initiatives (designed to ensure that suggestions for reform came from departments rather than from on high) as was a second white paper (to provide the exercise with a focus and end date). Much other advice was tendered, but it tended to fall on deaf ears.

122 TNA: BA17/230, I.P. Bancroft to C. Gilbraith, 21 May 1970.

123 See C. Pollitt, *Manipulating the Machine* (1984), p. 100 and J. Campbell, *Edward Heath* (1993), p. 319. For Rothschild's disgrace, see T. Blackstone and W. Plowden, *Inside the Think Tank* (1988), pp. 54–5 and TNA: PREM15/1342. It was caused by an unvetted speech at Wantage (concerning Britain's economic decline) which not only contradicted but, more culpably, received greater publicity than a speech given by Heath on the same day. The CPRS's fortunes might, however, have already been waning. Rothschild on his own admission was seeing Heath only every five to seven weeks (*The Listener*, 28 December 1972) and in September he had lost as his deputy, Peter Carey, who was a master of internal Whitehall politics. On the change of name to CPRS from the 'Central Capability' or 'think tank' (which Heath resisted into January 1971), see Hennessy, *Whitehall*, pp. 221–2.

124 The phrase was Sir John Hunt's, see Blackstone and Plowden, *Think Tank*, p. 17. For the rest of this paragraph, see especially TNA: BA17/225, B. Trend to W. Armstrong, 21 May 1970 and PREM15/70, brief on the 'machinery of government –central departments', 19 June 1970. The projected planning brief was, of course, consistent with the 1918 Haldane Committee's plea for 'investigation and thought as a preliminary to action' and, more consciously, with the Fulton Committee's advocacy of planning units (see Cd 9230, para 12 and Cmnd 3638, paras 172–7).

125 See TNA: BA17/232, the *Black Book*, in particular 'Proposals from Action Group 1', para 1.9. Howell later defined his ideal as a unit directly responsible to the Prime Minister and having 'the power and authority to bully departments. We wanted our kind of bullying to be as persistent as that of the Treasury, but coming at issues from a different angle . . . We believed the unit could do what the Treasury by its narrower and cruder approach to departmental spending had notably failed to do for decades past – namely to get to the very heart of the process which somehow led to the unending expansion of government' (*Edge of Now*, pp. 336–7).

NOTES FOR CHAPTER 5

126 TNA: CAB129/150, CP(70)11, 'Analysis and the decision making process', 14 July 1970. For Armstrong's circumscription of an earlier CSD draft, see BA17/233, W. Armstrong to C.R. Walker, 9 July 1970. It had, as Howell wished, closely linked the second unit (significantly entitled the Programme Evaluation and Review Unit) with the Business Team's direction of output budgeting within the Treasury. Earlier, at the meeting on 29 July Carr and Carrington on behalf of Action Group 1 had confirmed that their primary object had been to give the Prime Minister 'an independent source of advice'; and Howell had emphasised his political ambitions for the 'capability' (in which Meyjes disowned interest), see BA17/232.

127 TNA: PREM15/406, 8 August 1970. The minutes of the preceding *ad hoc* Cabinet Committee on Management Projects and the Central Capability on 31 July 1970 are in BA17/305. Trend was at pains to emphasise this was not the first meeting of the MPC because he wanted to maintain a clear distinction between the managerial thrust of businessmen's projects and the political tasks of resource allocation and strategy (to be entrusted to another Cabinet Committee, dedicated to the Central Capability). The memoranda battle may be tracked through BA17/233 and BA17/984. It was actually circulated to Cabinet (CAB129/151,CP(70)37) on 17 August but was never discussed.

128 Ibid, D. Howell to Jellicoe and thence E. Heath, 20 August 1970, who minuted that Howell's objections were 'very important'. These objections, if inconsistent with Howell's compliance on 31 July, were consistent with alternative, but unused, drafts of Jellicoe's original submission to the *ad hoc* Committee submitted by him and Schreiber. In them, Howell had stressed the need for the unit both to 'expose ongoing policies to systematic investigation' and to act more boldly as a 'think tank' on the Californian model. Schreiber had stressed more its 'staff' role for the Prime Minister, enabling him independently to evaluate policy and develop a strategic framework: 'although the main inspiration and direction of the new capability will come mainly from the Prime Minister, in practice, by identifying and clarifying the issues and options within the decisions which are taken by Ministers collectively, it will be serving the whole Cabinet and helping Ministers individually' (BA17/984, M.J. Elliot-Binns to C.R. Walker, 28 July 1970).

129 For details of the search, see TNA: PREM15/406 *passim* and BA17/301, F. Cooper to W. Armstrong, 19 August 1970. The CSD's favoured candidate was C.R. Ross, an economics professor at the University of East Anglia currently at the OECD. He became the CPRS's long-standing deputy director and from the start took charge of the PAR programme. Ford's name had been raised by Heath in his pre-election meeting with Armstrong on 7 June. Armstrong's response belied his alleged outward-looking interest and exposed his fascination with Hollywood. Heath, he somewhat disdainfully reported, 'mentioned the name of a Mr John Ford who, I gather, is a professor of engineering, or some such discipline, in one of the universities. I remarked that people with an engineering background were often extremely good at this kind of thing' (BA17/231, 'Note for the record', 8 June 1970).

130 See Campbell, *Heath*, p. 317 and Howell, *Edge of Now*, pp. 337, 348. Rothschild had enjoyed a sufficiently distinguished career as an MI5 bomb disposal officer to have been awarded the George Cross and as a research scientist to have been elected to the Royal Society. At the age of 60, he was about to be compulsorily retired as Research Coordinator of the Royal Dutch Shell Group. Heath's Political Secretary drew the classic portrait of his roaming 'like a condottiere through Whitehall, laying an ambush here, there breaching some crumbling fortress. . . . He wrote in short, sharp sentences; he made jokes; he respected persons occasionally but rarely policies. He had the independence of position and personality which was needed to make the CPRS a success from the start' (D. Hurd, *An End to Promises* (1979), p. 38. Howell, perhaps unwittingly, confirmed Rothschild's charm. His views, he later admitted, 'on the role of CPRS

NOTES FOR CHAPTER 5

were very different from mine and he knew nothing about business or wealth creation, nor was he much interested in privatisation . . . But he was excitingly conspiratorial and anxious to . . . counterbalance the enormous and ever-growing influence of Burke Trend and Sir William Armstrong . . . So on the basis that "enemies of my enemies are my friends" I found myself working extremely close to him' (*Edge of Now*, p. 351).

131 V. Rothschild, *Random Variables* (1984), p. 69; TNA:CAB134/2985, MCA(71)1, 1 March 1971. The CPRS's official terms of reference were approved by Cabinet on 3 February 1971 (CAB129/155,CP(71)17). The Ministerial Committee on the Central Capability, which formally oversaw it, met only once before being merged with the Management Projects Committee in July 1971, and only twice thereafter (in November 1971 and February 1972) – although a subcommittee met regularly to oversee the PAR programme. Mayne had been detailed in July 1970 to take charge, within the Cabinet Office, of the planning of CPRS (which may be tracked through CAB/184,1, 3–4, 80 and 142). Howell was deliberately excluded from this planning although, with Jellicoe, he demanded in January 1971 that the CPRS adopt a far more political role (see, respectively, CAB184/1, J.F. Mayne to Lloyd Jones, 16 October 1970 and CAB184/4, 'Notes of a meeting, 13 January 1971'). This was not evidence of a bureaucratic conspiracy because Heath was constantly consulted, as were other Ministers (see, for example, CAB184/142, 'Note of a meeting with the Prime Minister, 2 December 1970'). Howell's proposals for the CPRS, and particularly its use of PAR, were considered by Rothschild and deliberately rejected (see CAB184/80, note of 8 December 1970 and CAB184/4, note of 13 January 1971).

132 These shortcomings were admitted in Blackstone and Plowden, *Think Tank*, pp. 48 and 31. See also Campbell, *Heath*, p. 319. Howell was not enamoured, writing later that as a 'rather absurd fifth wheel on the coach of policy, chasing after will-o'-the-wisp fashions and notions, a less helpful piece of tinkering it is hard to imagine' (*Edge of Now*, p. 337). Another sin to which Blackstone and Plowden pointed was that its staff was largely recruited through acts of 'personal patronage which it had been the explicit aim of the Northcote-Trevelyan Report to eliminate' (p. 28) – William Waldegrave, for example, profiteering from a family, and Robin Butler from an Harrovian, connection. On the other hand, as a pale reflection of PSRU aims, it did include some who would later serve the Conservative Party in a political capacity (such as Waldegrave and Adam Ridley) and others from business (such as Anthony Fish) who helped to establish the CPRS's long-standing expertise in energy issues. Intriguingly, in January 1971 Alan Walters was strongly promoted as a candidate for inclusion by Jellicoe (to counteract a perceived 'left wing bias') and Nigel Lawson was persistent in promoting his own candidature. Both had been on the original list of potential members given to Rothschild by Armstrong on his appointment (see TNA: CAB184/4, 'Notes of a meeting on 13 January 1971'; CAB184/142, note by P. Carey, 10 May 1971; CAB184/3).

133 Hurd, *End to Promises*, p. 39; Pollitt, *Manipulating*, p. 101. Macmillan had of course called a strategy meeting at Chequers in April 1963 during his own modernisation drive, albeit within the benefit of a collective brief (TNA: PREM11/4406).

134 Blackstone and Plowden, *Think Tank*, pp. 44 and 60. The low opinion of the policy process had been well expressed in an early version of the Cabinet Office brief for the Barbados meeting: 'by exercising an "uninformed" choice between conflicting proposals from different Ministers on the basis of papers drafted more with an eye to winning the battle than to making an unbiased presentation of the facts', it read, 'in practice such a "political" choice is little more than an agreed leap in the dark'. Departments should end this 'shoddy work' and justify 'their value judgements in an honest and convincing way' (TNA: BA17/984, memorandum by J.F. Mayne, 26 August 1970). The CPRS's success on this score was discussed by Permanent Secretaries in May 1972 and their general conclusion (expressed most forcefully by Douglas Allen) was that it concentrated too much on the short term, was antagonistic

to departments and complicated rather than expedited policy-making. Rothschild's typically robust reply was that Ministers wanted opinions 'uncontaminated by years of experience' (CAB184/142).

135 Quoted in Hennessy, *Whitehall*, p. 221. Mayne's memorandum, cited in the previous footnote, tried to square the political circle. The CPRS, it warned, must be 'extremely careful not to act as a party-political instrument . . . but it will have the perfectly legitimate official function of drawing to Minister's attention those areas of policy in which new political choices can be exercised in the realisation of the Government's known political aspirations; and in analysing for Ministerial consideration what the political choices are'.

136 See Pollitt, *Manipulating*, pp. 93–6; and for a summary of all the organisational changes, TNA: BA17/415, 'History of the Machinery of Government, June-November 1970'. Most controversial was the reintegration of the Ministry of Overseas Development in the FCO.

137 Cmnd 4506, paras 11–14. For the brief submitted to Heath ('Machinery of government 1970 – the Cabinet'), see TNA: PREM15/70. A section on the strengthening of Cabinet Committees was an addition to the parallel brief prepared for Wilson. The brief was based on a longer paper, initially drafted by J.A. Chilcot ('Machinery of government 1970 – organisation of government functions'), preserved in the same file, which also provided the basis for the *Reorganisation of Central Government* white paper.

138 TNA: PREM15/70, 'Machinery of Government 1970 – organisation of government functions', para 39 and *passim*. This paper considered the full gamut of ways by which the responsibilities of departments and Secretaries of State might be reduced, but found each wanting. Administrative devolution, for example, would destroy 'common standards and control points'. Likewise, 'federal' departments (in which junior Ministers held particular statutory powers) would increase the potential for disagreement and rigidity. On the other hand in 'super' ministries (where the Secretary of State retained the final authority) work could be delegated as appropriate.

139 See Pollitt, *Manipulating*, p. 97. The Department of Environment, planned by CSD for Labour (see TNA: BA17/208, J.A. Chilcot to T.H. Caulcott, 28 May 1970), was nevertheless very different from Howell's original conception. Howell opposed 'super' ministries which represented competing interests (such as industrial efficiency and consumer protection) and so he favoured a Regional Development Department supported by a number of separate agencies (such as an Environmental Pollution Unit) under the control of the Lord Chancellor. For Walker's prayer meetings and evidence of the controlled freedom allowed to junior Ministers, see M. Heseltine, *Life in the Jungle* (2000), ch 9. See also P. Draper, *The Creation of the DoE* (1977). Draper was the former PEO at the Ministry of Transport.

140 The reincarnation of a Ministry of Transport was a personal initiative by Callaghan when he succeeded Wilson as Prime Minister. It was taken largely for political reasons (to avoid the creation of an over-powerful Secretary of State and to balance the new Cabinet with the appointment of the 'moderate' William Rodgers), see Pollitt, *Manipulating*, pp. 116–17.

141 For the recommendations of RTZ consultants, see TNA: BA17/207, R.T. Renton, 'Memorandum summarizing recommendations' March 1970; and for a summary of the subsequent Whitehall battle, BA17/415, 'History of machinery of government'.

142 The disruption to 'Administrative Class' officials (and especially, in defiance of Fulton, the speed of change between jobs) was the subject of an appendix to the memorandum on the 'Organisation of government functions' submitted to Heath (TNA: PREM15/70). The disruption lower down was the subject of frequent NSS complaints (see, for example, BA17/642, meeting with F. Cooper, 21 June 1971). The IPCS tended to look more favourably on super ministries than other staff associations, since they were perceived to offer specialists greater opportunity for promotion. More

NOTES FOR CHAPTER 5

generally the stability, which *The Reorganisation of Central Government* had made one of its principal goals, was not achieved. Even the size of the Cabinet reverted to 21 from its initial size of 18.

143 Conservative Party Archive: CRD4/13/1, D. Howell to K. Joseph, April 1975. On the Cabinet, he revealingly remarked: 'the real strategic work can be handled by a smaller inner group informally, as it always has been. Sir William Armstrong taught me this'.

144 Of Meyjes' original team, the two management consultants left first: Alan Fogg (of PA Consultants) in November 1970 having completed the planning of PAR, and Kenneth Lane (of RTZ Consultants) in April 1971 on his appointment as a part-time special adviser in the Department of Employment. Ronald East (from GKN) similarly became a special adviser ('director of the PAR project') in the Treasury in July 1971. The fifth member of the team, Robin Hutton (from the bankers, Hambros), was the only one, other than Meyjes, to serve out his full two-year contract. He advised on nationalised industries, chaired the inquiry into the Public Trustee Office and subsequently became a special adviser in the Ministry of Posts and Telecommunications. The final member of the team Rayner (from Marks and Spencer) was given a new two-year contract as chief executive of the PE in May 1971, but left early in October 1972. Cruickshank and Sainsbury were appointed on one-year contracts in March and June 1971 respectively to examine the Government's construction and property management responsibilities. They both left in May 1972 when, as a result of their work, the Property Services Agency was established with another businessman, John Cuckney (of the Anglo-Eastern Bank and a former chairman of the Mersey Docks and Harbour Board) as its chief executive.

145 TNA: BA17/211, M. Schreiber to Jellicoe, 3 July 1970. For Meyjes' views, see BA17/232, 'Notes of a meeting to discuss businessmen in Whitehall, 25 June 1970' and 'Notes of a meeting to discuss the *Black Book*, 29 June 1970'. He was particularly resistant to any involvement in the post-election programme of crash cuts which, in his opinion, would 'only muddy the water'. For the subsequent tension, see above ch 5.3.2 (a) and (b).

146 Armstrong had been active since 1962, when Norman Brook had first expressed concern about the weakening of wartime contacts between Whitehall and business. Contacts had since been strengthened in a variety of ways: joint training schemes (see ch 9.2); the meeting of 30 top businessmen and officials at Spring 'Sunningdales'; joint membership of bodies such as the British Institute of Management; and secondments and direct recruitment (amounting respectively by 1972 to an annual intake of some 30 to 40 'businessmen'). The DEA had also appointed industrial advisers (of whom 5 remained in MinTech by 1970). The eight-man Bellinger Committee, drawn from leading firms such as Marks and Spencer, ICI and Unilever, worked part-time and unpaid. It mounted action groups in 13 departments to identify means of simplifying administrative procedures and its final report in December 1970 (before which it had been rather embarrassingly superceded by Meyjes' Business Team) revealed equally embarrassingly that, over 2 years, it had saved only 1000 staff. Its main recommendations were the strengthening of internal audit (to reduce excessive checking of payments) and the charging of realistic fees – panaceas to be regularly reiterated by business experts in the 1970s and 1980s. For the final report and its discussion with Heath, see TNA: PREM15/274.

147 For the CSD welcome, see TNA: BA26/62, F. Cooper to C. Gilbraith, 25 June 1970; and for his acceptance letter to Heath on 20 June 1970, BA17/982.

148 For Meyjes' views, see TNA: BA17/982, Meyjes to Heath, 20 June 1970 and BA17/212, Meyjes to Jellicoe, 1 July 1970.

149 Armstrong's views were first spelt out to Douglas Hurd (as Heath's Political Secretary) in September 1969 and fought out with Meyjes and Howell at the two meetings to

discuss the *Black Book* on 29 June and 1 July 1970 (see TNA: BA17/982 and BA17/232).

150 TNA: BA17/983, Report by the Business Team, 1 March 1971. Significantly in the light of later events, it recommended that 'a Business Team should not be a permanent feature of the scene once the current range of major projects are completed' (section 6). Under pressure from Hurd, who was close to Schreiber, Meyjes had nevertheless identified four new major projects by autumn 1971 and favoured the retention of businessmen as 'franc-tireurs ... mobile individuals moving from one area to another, stirring up new ideas and challenging old ones' (PREM15/523, D. Hurd note for the file, 1 December 1971). In the meantime officials suggested that Meyjes and Hutton should see out their contracts as, respectively, a management and a policy adviser to Cabinet Ministers.

151 For their respective views, see TNA: BA17/691, Howell to Jellicoe, 6 March 1972; and PREM15/923, Meyjes to Heath, 27 March 1972 as well as Jellicoe to Heath, 19 April 1972. These views were expressed in anticipation of a meeting with Heath, which was cancelled in part because Rothschild had intervened to suggest that businessmen would be best employed either in Ministerial *cabinets* or as Principal Finance Officers. Armstrong reacted to the suggestion of a single business adviser on the strong, if somewhat politically incorrect, grounds that 'with the increasing numbers of such people and the wide disparity of jobs they do, I do not see how anyone could take on the "father figure" role even if he were an Arab sheik' (BA17/876, W. Armstrong to Rothschild, 7 June 1972). He nevertheless flirted with the idea that a market retailer might be appointed to improve 'the interface' between Government and the public.

152 TNA: PREM15/923, W. Armstrong to Jellicoe, 9 May 1972. Heath's final decision is alluded to in BA17/983, which also contains plans for the creation of a second business team after the next election.

153 TNA: BA17/983, Report by the Business Team, 1 March 1971, p. 6 and T.H. Caulcott to F. Cooper, 26 January 1971. The extent and nature of resentment was well captured in a memorandum of 29 June 1970 on 'Lessons of the Bellinger Panel' (BA26/62). 'There was in some departments', it acknowledged, 'a tendency to take the attitude that the Panel were an efficiency unit imposed from outside, and that the first duty of the department was to defend its existing policies and practices.'

154 TNA: BA17/982, 'Note for the record', 24 June 1970. The post was actually offered to Duncan, who declined. He recommended Marcus Sieff (of Marks and Spencer) and Peter Cadbury (of the Keith Prowse Group). Raymond Brookes (of GKN) and James Gulliver (of Fine Fare) were also considered. Heath was equally secretive when he courted Sieff (whom Rothschild had engaged as a consultant on the creation of CPRS) as a potential replacement for Meyjes in 1972.

155 TNA: BA17/983, Report by the Business Team, 1 March 1971, pp. 4–6. For evidence of the continuing lack of appreciation, see PREM15/983, unsigned discussion paper, December 1971.

156 TNA: BA17/983, notes by N.S. Forward, 4 March 1971; BA17/690, M. Macmillan to Jellicoe, 12 July 1971 and F. Cooper to B. Gilmore, 10 December 1971. Howell also admitted to Ernest Marples that the chosen businessmen were not 'as good as he had wished', to which Marples characteristically replied that Howell had set them a wholly inappropriate task (BA17/233, E. Marples to Jellicoe, 16 July 1970). When approached, Jim Slater had also warned Heath that he would never get 'top class people'(see CAB184/37: V. Rothschild to R.T. Armstrong, 17 May 1972).

157 TNA: BA17/876, D. Rayner to Jellicoe, 25 September 1972. Rayner's admission that he had been unable fully to exploit the wealth of talent in Whitehall and his advocacy of a businessman as deputy CEO 'to drive through an established programme' perhaps hinted at some of the frustrations that led to his early retirement (see BA26/62, Rayner to W. Armstrong, 2 February 1973).

NOTES FOR CHAPTER 5

158 PAR was described as 'Whitehall's major and perhaps only effort at institutionalising rational policy analysis' by A. Gray and B. Jenkins in 'Policy analysis in British central government' *Public Administration* 60 (1982) 429. This article, together with Heclo and Wildavsky, *Private Government of Public Money* (ch 6) provides the best analysis of its early years.
159 For the final version of the report, 'Improved Expenditure Decisions by Government' by East, Fogg and Meyjes, see the annex to Jellicoe's submission to Cabinet. PAR was the pre-election brainchild of East who, contrary to some received opinion, insisted that no review should be too wide, accountancy-based or secret (see Pollitt, *Manipulating*, pp. 86, 99).
160 TNA: CAB128/47, CM(70)38th, 17 November 1970.
161 Even then the themes remained somewhat broad and vague: facilitating industrial and technological change and meeting its human consequences; enhancing the quality of urban and rural life; resources deployed in preparation for employment and community life; relief of poverty, hardship and illness; law and order; and European and overseas commitments (see TNA: PREM15/1587, P. Jenkin to E. Heath, 26 January 1973 and CAB134/2985, MCA(73)1, 31 January 1973).
162 TNA: CAB129/154, CP(70)101, 2 November 1970, para 7.2. For Meyjes' reassurance of Jellicoe on 27 October 1970, see BA17/481.
163 Gray and Jenkins, 'Policy analysis', p. 442. The authors continued: 'as a result of failing to satisfy ... technical conditions, PAR lacked the appropriate instruments and information for effective analysis. Disaggregating objectives (and *ipso facto* the means to reach them) was too difficult; finding a path through competing claims of quantitative and qualitative factors too hazardous; and designing output measures remained unresolved ... PAR was an approach and not a technique' (p. 445). For similar observations, see Heclo and Wildavsky, *Private Government*, p. 289.
164 TNA: BA17/487, 'Introducing PAR', 16 October 1970. This was the fullest statement of Treasury policy and coincided with a letter from Douglas Allen to William Armstrong, stating the terms on which it would accept the Business Team's report (BA17/304). Treasury's fears were justified. The greatest impact of PAR on policy was the planned 50% increase in expenditure over ten years announced in the 1972 white paper, *Education: a framework for expansion* (Cmnd 5174). The then Secretary of State for Education was Mrs Thatcher. Despite – or possibly because of – this, she abolished PAR in 1979.
165 TNA: CAB129/154, CP(70)101, Annex, para 7.1. Throughout 1971, Howell sought to prioritise PAR's strategic role. In April he was reported as wishing PAR to replace 'the whole of the PESC operation' and, in July, as seeking belatedly to transform the MCA subcommittee on PAR into a Central Capability 'processing all major policy decisions' (see CAB 184/142, note of 23 April and CAB184/30, J.F. Mayne to B. Norbury, 22 July 1971).
166 TNA: BA17/292, 'Improved decision making' by the Treasury's Management Accountancy Unit, 7 September 1970, para 19. PAR also created organisational tensions within departments. The Treasury, for example, feared that the increased power of 'planners' would undermine the authority of PFOs, on whom it relied for departmental self-restraint. Likewise Permanent Secretaries feared that – like the senior policy advisers recommended by Fulton – they would undermine their own authority. Arguably, however, PARs were precisely what the Permanent Secretaries, particularly in the new super ministries, needed to rationalise their expenditure; and certain departments, such as the MOD and significantly the DES under Sir William Pile, had already adopted such reviews. Thus the claim in the Business Team's report and by Heclo and Wildavsky (*Private Government*, p. 265) that PAR represented organic change was correct.
167 Heclo and Wildavsky, *Private Government*, p. 279. See TNA: BA17/487 for the hostile reception of the Business Team's report by Permanent Secretaries on 9 October and the

inauguration of PAR by a temporary co-ordinating committee based at the CSD under Armstrong's chairmanship; and CAB134/3413, for the records of the MCA subcommittee (chaired by the Chief Secretary to the Treasury) which thereafter co-ordinated policy. The Treasury also chaired the official committee overseeing the operation of the reviews (PARC), which has been condemned as a 'passive rather than an active body' (Gray and Jenkins, 'Policy analysis', 436). Widespread cynicism within Whitehall was reflected in March 1971 by a glossary compiled within the MOD which included: 'PARable, skilled at telling the PAR tale; PARboil, cook the books in preparation for PAR; and PARrot, an in-depth study which satisfies no requirements' (PREM15/419). For the continuing battle between the CPRS and the Treasury, particularly over the choice of PARs for 1972, see *passim* CAB184/29, 30, 32 and 134.

168   Howell and Schreiber were the most vociferous advocates of junior Ministers' participation (see, for instance, TNA: PREM15/1587, Schreiber to R.T. Armstrong, 8 December 1970). Armstrong agreed the issue was 'terribly important' but countered that it was not for Cabinet to 'decide for an individual Minister how he is to run his own department'. Heath nevertheless leant his weight to the proposal (CAB134/2985, MCA(71)2nd, 17 November 1971) as, after some initial resistance, did Jellicoe and the Treasury in July 1972 (PREM15/1587; see also PREM15/419, note of 11 August 1971).

169   TNA: PREM15/1588, P. Walker to M. Macmillan, 16 December 1971. John Hunt, the Treasury's chief protagonist on PAR and soon to become Cabinet Secretary, later conceded Walker's point. In January 1972, for instance, he admitted: 'some Ministers feel their departmental prerogative is being intruded upon. The short point is that it is' (TNA: CAB184/134).

170   TNA: PREM 15/419, W. Armstrong to R.T. Armstrong, 4 January 1971. Trend's earlier reservation was noted in ch 5.3.1. The issue was 'reportedly' raised at Cabinet on 17 November because, although the published minutes provide a comprehensive list of objections, the Cabinet Secretary's notebook records only one brief Ministerial interjection. On 4 November 1970 Trend had significantly minuted Heath that, because of unresolved operational issues, 'it might be premature and counterproductive to allow the Cabinet to discuss the report itself in any detail or to ask Ministers to endorse it formally' (see CAB128/47,CM (70)38th, 17 November 1970; Trend's notebook 12; and PREM15/419). Might the listed objections have been his alone – although at the hostile meeting of Permanent Secretaries on 9 October, he had denied there was a constitutional problem and insisted that 'no derogation from Ministers' individual responsibilities' would occur (BA17/487)? Nevertheless, his caution was further illustrated by his opposition to the publication of PARs (which the Business Team from the start and both the CSD and Treasury later supported) on the grounds that disclosing the *way* in which particular decisions were reached might create an embarrassing precedent for Ministers (see, most fully, PREM15/419, B. Trend to E. Heath, 31 March 1971; CAB134/2985, MCA(71)6, 15 November 1971; and MCA(73)1, 31 January 1973).

171   Gray and Jenkins, 'Policy analysis', 446; TNA: BNA17/487, R.A. Meyjes to Jellicoe, 27 October 1970; Heclo and Wildavsky, *Private Government*, pp. 296–9.

172   Hennessy, *Whitehall*, pp. 235–6.

173   Rothschild was allergic, temperamentally and technically, to PAR and delegated responsibility for it within the CPRS to his deputy, C.R. Ross. Before assuming his post he had expressed 'very strong' doubts about its viability and in the autumn of 1971 critically opposed, on evidence from Washington, Howell's continuing vision of 'total' (strategic) rather than 'selective' (expenditure cutting) PARs. Shortage of manpower was a further reason why a programme of 'total' PARs had always been regarded as unrealistic (see TNA: CAB184/4, Rothschild to J.F. Mayne, 13 January 1971; CAB184/32, D. Howell to Rothschild, 17 August 1971; CAB184/30, W. Plowden to C.R. Ross, 25 August 1971 and correspondence between Howell and Rothschild, 7 September 1971).

174 Ronald East, who had masterminded the idea of PAR before the election, was a joint author of the October report and subsequently Director of the PAR project initially in the CSD and then, after June 1971, in the Treasury. His attention to detail, tactical appraisal and ability to work with others, was each deemed wanting. Likewise Meyjes was considered as chairman of the co-ordinating committee prior to the creation of CPRS but was considered to lack the mental toughness to 'preside over the resolution of any really serious problems' (see respectively TNA: BA17/983, note by N.S. Forward, 4 March 1971; BA17/690, F. Cooper to B. Gilmore, 10 December 1971; BA17/303, F. Cooper to W. Armstrong, 7 October 1970).

175 D. Hurd, *An End to Promises*(1979), p. 30 and Pliatzky, *Getting and Spending*, p. 99. The leading advocate of rationality within Government (and the creator of PESC) actively supported PAR in the hope that it would bring together at the centre a large number of Ministers and officials who would then 'understand the programmes of all departments and relate them to each other', see Clarke, *New Trends in Government*, p. 43.

176 See Conservative Party Archives: CRD3/14/5, Third Report of the Machinery of Government Group; Cmnd 3638, paras 188–91; and TNA: PREM15/70, 'Machinery of government 1970 – the Cabinet'. Sharp, like CSD officials later, warned that hiving off could reduce as well as increase efficiency. 'We think it very important to resist any tendency towards indiscriminate hiving off, which could only increase the administrative chaos of Whitehall', her report concluded, 'no agency should be set up unless it is quite clear that its task could not be done equally well by an existing organisation'.

177 The paper including these definitions was presented to and approved first by Permanent Secretaries at Sunningdale in October 1971 and then by Cabinet in December (TNA: BA16/71, PERSEC(71)5 and CAB 129/160, CP(71)148). It had been gestating for a year within the CSD under the title 'executive agencies and hiving off'; and the term 'departmental agency' was adopted in July 1971 when it was suggested that 'executive agency' might 'appear to describe a particular type of activity [i.e. management not policy advice] and . . . calls to mind Executive grade type operations' (BA17/439, note by J.N. Archer).

178 Cmnd 3638, para 153. For the belated introduction of joint appraisal reviews (JARs), see above ch 5.2.2.

179 See TNA: PREM13/1571, W. Armstrong to H. Wilson, 19 June 1968. In the Swedish model (to which Fulton was attracted) small policy departments with fewer than 1000 staff were supplemented by large executive bodies, employing some 200,000. Individual rights were protected by administrative law. Howell's vision was similar, particularly in relation to labour (where he advocated agencies responsible for placement, training and conciliation) and the environmental and individual rights (where he proposed *inter alia* agencies responsible for anti-pollution measures and consumer rights). See *A New Style of Government*, section 4.

180 TNA: PREM15/70, 'Machinery of government 1970 – the Cabinet'; Cmnd 4506, para 14. For the papers of the Organisation Subcommittee, see BA16/18–20 and 48–9; and of the Hiving Off Steering Committee, BA17/78 and 173. A number of 'external' inquiries into hiving off had also been set up under Labour. These included the Edwards Committee (Cmnd 4018) which led to the hiving off of the Civil Aviation Authority in September 1971, the Dainton Committee (Cmnd 4028) which led to the establishment of the British Library in July 1973 and, most significantly, the Mallabar Committee on Government Industrial Establishments which, despite its initial instincts, recommended in July 1971 that the Royal Ordnance Factories and Dockyards should not be hived off (Cmnd 4713). See Pollitt, *Manipulating*, pp. 102–3.

181 TNA: BA17/78, circular of 15 August 1969. Opposition to hiving off and even accountable management was particularly expressed at the fifth and tenth meeting of the Fulton Steering Committee on 27 November 1968 and 27 October 1969 (see BA16/11–12).

NOTES FOR CHAPTER 5

182 For these impediments, see respectively TNA: BA17/147, FS(O)(70)1st, 6 May 1970; BA17/160, 'Thinking session paper on accountable management' by J.N. Archer, 4 September 1969; BA17/78, response to the Comptroller and Auditor's letter, 23 September 1969; and BA17/146, T.H. Caulcott to I.B. Bancroft, 25 March 1970. A useful distinction was later drawn between 'internal' accountability –answerability to senior managers for the exercise of delegated authority – and 'external' accountability to Parliament. Emotions ran particularly strong at the Ministry of Public Building and Works where, preceding the formation of the PSA, a merger was planned with HMSO.

183 TNA: BA17/70, Armstrong circular of 15 August 1969. See also the admission on 3 April 1970 that the CSD had 'long contemplated . . . a situation in which hiving off discarded itself as a banner, in favour of accountable management' (BA17/147, I.B. Bancroft to T.H. Caulcott). 'Management by objective' required a regular review of the responsibilities and achievements of each level of management and only in its final stages required a critical evaluation of the whole unit's objectives and output.

184 The minutes of the strategy meeting and the two memoranda are in TNA: BA17/306. The assumption behind 'common services' was that the consuming department would pay for services (such as the supply of equipment and paper by HMSO) whereas with the more traditional 'allied services' the cost was covered by the supplying department's budget. The strategy meeting also agreed that there could be no department 'philosophy' on so 'political' an issue as hiving off, although this did not stop CSD officials from categorising initiatives under two heads ('resource saving' and 'political management'). The former included savings in public expenditure and manpower. The latter included the easing of Ministers' burdens, depoliticisation (the reduction of constraints on individual rights and freedoms as well as on entrepreneurial management) and the honouring of the Government's pledge to cap manpower (see BA17/550, chart by J.A. Chilcot).

185 For the failure of the review of departmental functions, see above ch 5.3.2(a); for NSS protest (particularly at the meeting of 21 June 1971) see TNA: BA17/361; and for the Treasury Steering Group, T227/2615–6. The Treasury was also concerned, with good reason, that agencies should be of a certain size, accounting officers of sufficient seniority and that 'efficiency' should be judged in relation to the overall, not just an agency's, use of resources. A measurable index of performance would also have to be agreed before any relaxation of central controls could be contemplated (see also BA17/439, note of a meeting at the CSD, 8 July 1971).

186 TNA: BA17/440, W. Armstrong to A. Creamer, 18 August 1971. The change to a more proactive policy, noted in the next paragraph, was led by T.H. Caulcott, with major memoranda to F. Cooper on 12 and 20 May (BA17/307).

187 TNA: BA17/440, annex to the final Sunningdale submission. For a similar list of restrictions provided by Meyjes, see Pollitt, *Manipulating*, p. 102. The debate was confused by the simultaneous granting to the hived-off CAA in September 1971 of the regulation of air traffic licences (which, since it involved discretion, was opposed by the CSD) and the Vehicle and General scandal, concerning the crash of the country's second largest motor insurer (for full details, see ch 6.4). Kept ignorant of the basic facts, Conservative backbenchers argued that a hived-off agency could have averted the V & G scandal (because it would have developed the requisite expertise and clarified individual officials' responsibilities). In response, the CSD successfully argued that the regulation of the private sector required political judgement and so could never be divorced from Ministerial responsibility (see BA17/736 and 851).

188 TNA: BA17/441, J.N. Archer to T.H. Caulcott, 14 December 1971. Frank Cooper, as Deputy Secretary, was even prevented from visiting other departments to make them offers they could not refuse in relation to the creation of departmental agencies.

189 TNA: BA16/99, minutes of the Permanent Secretaries' Conference, 6–7 October 1971. For the CSD's promotion on management by objectives, see Garrett, *Managing*

NOTES FOR CHAPTER 5

the Civil Service, pp. 134–6; and for the 'moment of truth' in personnel management, see above, ch 5.2.2.

190 See, for example, TNA: BA17/513, PS(WG)(RF), 8th, 25 March 1971; PREM15/404, D. Howell to R.T. Armstrong, 7 April 1971; and BA17/455, meeting at the Treasury, 21 June 1971. State pubs in the former munitions areas of Cumbria and south-east Scotland, formally termed 'state management districts', were finally privatised in January 1971.

191 TNA: CAB134/2985, MCA(71), 2nd, 17 November 1971. This dispute prompted a classic defence of an official's duty to 'speak truth unto power'. As T.H. Caulcott chided a colleague on 19 May 1971: 'it is basic to our approach as central departments that we do not give advice to Ministers which confuses shadow and substance. It was a charge often levied against the old Treasury. I do not regard it as part of our job as civil servants to encourage [Ministers] in what we all know to be folly' (BA17/307). Howell's successor as Parliamentary Secretary, Kenneth Baker, had a personal, as well as an expedient, interest in management. He was particularly interested in 'management by objectives' and was 'for once knocked off his perch', on a fact-finding trip to Washington in 1973, by a reply to his enquiry about how it was proceeding there: 'Oh', came the response, 'we scrapped it' (private information). Such incidents confirmed for many CSD officials the essential transience of management techniques, particularly those imported from the US private sector.

192 See TNA: BA17/301, D.G. Rayner to R. Meyjes, 14 August 1970 and BA17/483, meeting with the Business Team, 24 November 1970. For the rest of the paragraph, see BA17/439, R. Meyjes to F. Cooper, 22 July 1971; BA17/983, R. Meyjes to Jellicoe, 8 September 1972; and BA17/876, D.G. Rayner to Jellicoe, 25 September 1972.

193 Rayner's report, *Government Organisation for Defence Procurement and Civil Aerospace* (Cmnd 4041) was published in April 1971. It was the first stage in meeting the promise in *Reorganisation of Central Government* that fall-out from the closure of the Ministry of Technology would be resolved by April 1972. The Chief Executive was to be directly answerable to the Secretary of State for Defence but was to advise on, and co-ordinate procurement, for civil aviation through a Ministerial Aerospace Board on which the DTI was represented as well as the MOD.

194 The PSA emerged from two reports, on construction and property management, drafted by two specially commissioned business men (Herbert Cruikshank and Timothy Sainsbury) and assumed responsibility for all 'common services' provided to departments (other than the HMSO's former printing and computing responsibilities).

195 For unified hierarchies, see Cmnd 3638, para 162; for Rayner's report, TNA:BA17/545, background brief I(b); and for Rayner's resignation letter, BA17/876.

196 For Chapman, see below, esp. ch 7.2.3. See TNA: BA17/532 and 718–9 for the fullest record of the internal debate in the papers of a Common Services Working Subgroup of a Permanent Secretaries' Steering Committee, chaired by Frank Cooper, which ran concurrently with the Cruikshank and Sainsbury enquiries between July 1971 and February 1972; and BA17/724 for Armstrong's final advice to Heath, 15 March 1972. Sainsbury pressed for the continuing valuation of all Government property so that each department or agency might know its true cost. Would not, however, the cost of such an exercise exceed any efficiency savings? Treasury officials duly accepted that 'there was a role for financial inducements' before adding the classic rider that 'it was probably a very small role' (BA17/696, minutes of a meeting with Sainsbury, 17 April 1972).

197 TNA: BA17/723, P. Walker to E. Heath, 3 May 1972. For a defence of administrative resistance to any loss of hard-won departmental unity, and evidence of the damage incurred by such wild rumours as the imminent establishment of a 'state buying authority' that would purchase everything 'from paper clips to power stations', see Draper, *Creation of DoE*, pp. 69–79 and 83–91.

198 See D. Price, *Office of Hope* (2000), ch 9; and for an early and full rejection of the concept of an MSC, TNA: BA17/307, T.H. Caulcott to G.A. Brand, 14 May 1971. Its eventual acceptance was arguably political: it provided a means for the Government to rebuild bridges with the TUC following the furore over the Industrial Relations Act and the introduction of a statutory incomes policy. Several other agencies were also established by the Conservatives (such as the Industrial Development Executive in 1972, and the Pay Board and Prices Commission in 1973) but they were far smaller and, covering new areas of intervention, removed no old ones from Parliamentary accountability.

199 TNA: BA17/307, T.H. Caulcott to F. Cooper, 12 May 1971. For the later confession, see BA16/98, R.W.L. Wilding to J.A. Chilcot, 18 August 1972. On the CSD's managerial deficiencies, see also Garrett, *Managing the Civil Service*, chs 4 and 7.

200 See, for example, Cmnd 3638, para 58 and Howell, *New Style of Government*, p. 13. Howell committed another hostage to fortune. 'The lesson for the next Conservative government', he had written in 1968, 'is that without a powerful impulse from politicians, administrative reform will not take place on the scale required . . . Politicians have no one to blame, no one to whom to pass the buck' (*Whose Government Works*, pp. 15, 24). The sentiment was repeated in *New Style of Government*. Fulton, he claimed, had been grossly unfair in its charge of amateurism: 'if blame is to be allotted then it can be fairly placed on the shoulders of those political leaders who have so far done so little' (p. 10).

201 This made Howell, contrary to received opinion inside and outside Whitehall, the better harbinger of future reform.

6 THE CRISIS OF CONSENSUS, 1973–9

1 For the English Committee, see in particular P.P. (1976–7), *Eleventh Report of the Expenditure Committee* (HC 535) and ch 6.2.4(a) below.

2 Conservative Party Archives: CRD4/13/2, report submitted to Mrs Thatcher on 6 January 1978. For the academic version of Armageddon, see S. Brittan, 'The economic contradictions of democracy', *British Journal of Political Science* 5 (1975) 129–59. During the 1960s, as has been seen, Brittan had both participated in the modernisation debate and worked as an 'irregular' in Whitehall.

3 For tensions and paralysis in No.10 under Wilson, see B. Donoughue, *Downing Street Diary*, vol 1 (2006) *passim*. Party conferences also defeated government policy on the EEC in 1975 and, rather more significantly, on incomes policy in 1978. Following the collapse of the power-sharing executive in May 1974, Northern Ireland posed additional constitutional as well as security questions.

4 For Crossman, see ch 10.2.2. In Britain the most popular exposition of 'public choice' theory, which was heavily dependent on very different constitutional arrangements in the USA, was W.A. Niskanen, *Bureaucracy: servant or master?* (1973).

5 Anger at the Civil Service was often a proxy for hostility towards an explosion in the size of the public sector as a whole, largely caused by the reform of local government and the NHS under the Heath Government. Keith Joseph had been one of its leading proponents, although this did not prevent him later from becoming its leading critic.

6 In September and October 1978, for example, the Cabinet reviewed its record in order to take a bold 'forward look' at a co-ordinated set of policies which would 'reaffirm and update the traditional values of the Labour movement, demonstrate that only bold interventionist policies of the kind we have adopted can provide for a stronger economy and a fairer and more just society, and seek to strengthen the sense of public participation and responsibility'. The Civil Service was implicated in the last objective because, 'the old bases of authority' having broken down, there was a need for the 'machinery of the modern state' to be less distant and remote. See the Cabinet discussion on 14 September 1978 (TNA: CAB128/64/11) and Callaghan's memorandum of 19 October 1978 (CAB129/204/6).

NOTES FOR CHAPTER 6

7 B. Donoughue, *Prime Minister* (1987), p. 191.
8 L.A.Windmill, *A British Achilles* (2006), ch 13. As noted earlier, a member of the Fulton Committee (Robert Sheldon) was a Minister at the CSD between the two elections in 1974. His swift transfer to the Treasury was significant, as was his replacement as Minister of State by Charles Morris. This appointment surprised most people, not least Morris himself. Short exceptionally held the post whilst Lord President because, after one day, Wilson was persuaded from within No.10 that his original choice of Harold Lever was inappropriate (Donoughue, *Diary*, vol 1, p. 67). For a less than flattering portrait of Peart, see R. Denman, *The Mandarin's Tale* (2002), pp. 161–2.
9 Wilson wanted little to do with Heath's 'deputy Prime Minister' and therefore worked through Hunt rather than Armstrong. This marked a significant step in the rise of the Cabinet Office and decline of the CSD (Donoughue, *Diary*, vol 1, p. 526). Armstrong's transfer aroused considerable public controversy (because of the convention that officials should not accept appointments relevant to their work for two years) and within his family (as a surrender to Mammon). The move had, however, been planned and approved in 1972 (see the unpublished manuscript of P. Connelly, *Portrait of a Mandarin*, ch 9).
10 Allen's lack of interest in management was confirmed by the Treasury's management review in 1974–5, which noted a 'lack of involvement of senior staff in management matters' arising from a very un-Fultonian concentration of their training on 'policy work'. He was renowned, however, for the 'humanity' with which he treated personal problems, a virtue confirmed by his handling of the legal case brought against Government by the widow of Michael Halls (TNA: T277/3091, TMR(75)9th; for the settlement of the Halls case, see BA7/40–42). In general he was, as a close colleague has recalled, a strange mixture of 'intellectual arrogance and personal humility' (see also Hennessy, *Whitehall*, p. 237). The former enabled him quickly to identify key issues but discouraged him from suffering fools – and most politicians – gladly. The latter generated a shyness which prevented him from developing a close relationship with staff at No.10 and, in particular, with Hunt as Cabinet Secretary. This was damaging because, as William Armstrong emphasised in 1975, there had to be 'agreement between the three at the top . . . Friction could only create trouble as in the days when Sir M. Hankey had done battle with Sir W. Fisher'. Hence his own 'private compact' with Trend 'never to cross each other' (BA7/22, C. Priestley to J. Hobson, 23 August 1976, annex F).
11 Significantly neither of the other 'big two', the Cabinet Secretary (Hunt) and the head of the Treasury (Wass), wished to succeed Allen at the CSD. The effective choice was thus between Bancroft and Sir Frank Cooper who, Allen noted, 'had the virtue of great toughness' (TNA: PREM16/1658, Allen to Callaghan, 'Succession as Head of the Civil Service', 22 September 1977, note (b)). Bancroft had the advantage of having served as Callaghan's Private Secretary at the Treasury and of appealing to the Prime Minister's innate sense of 'safety first'. As he was reputedly advised, Bancroft could 'keep you out of trouble' whilst Cooper would 'get you out of trouble'. Both Callaghan and the Civil Service were arguably in trouble.
12 DHSS staff, for example, demanded substantial bonuses to implement the immediate uprating of pensions and social security benefits which the Labour Government sought to introduce between the two 1974 elections. Overtime and the employment of casual staff were simultaneously banned. Armstrong and the CSD fought hard, particularly against Ministers, to ensure that such 'blackmail' did not succeed. Civil servants, they argued, were employed to serve Government and such 'peak loads' were common to many departments. Concessions would make militancy 'a chronic rather than a crisis feature of Civil Service staff relations' (see TNA: PREM16/314, particularly W. Armstrong to R.T. Armstrong, 1 May 1974).
13 See TNA: PREM16/313 for the main Prime-Ministerial file on the *Wider Issues* review, which fully involved the NSS and visits to over forty outstations; and CAB164/1249

for its discussion by Permanent Secretaries at Sunningdale in 1974. Wilson's Parliamentary statement was on 30 April 1974.
14 For the minutes of the meeting on 21 January 1976, see TNA: PREM16/764, which also includes the supportive memoranda by Donoughue and Joe Haines. Both were disparaging, particularly of senior officials, in their published diaries and the latter even referred elsewhere to the CSD 'crying all the way to the bank in the Securicor convoy guarding their monthly pay cheques'. Amongst their suggestions were a reduction in the number of honours awarded, more open consideration of pay awards and manpower increases (the latter even to be overseen by the Public Accounts Committee) and a clear statement on what parts of Fulton had, for good reason, not been implemented. For Wilson's lack of reaction, see Donoughue, *Diary*, vol 1, p. 639.
15 J. Barnett, *Inside the Treasury* (1982), p. 82. That the cut was an unexpected initiative from Wilson is confirmed by T. Benn, *Against the Tide* (1990), p. 439 and in Hunt, Cabinet Secretary's Notebook 4. For the Cabinet meetings, see TNA: CAB129/57 CC(75) 39th and 55th; and for the papers of the Cost of Central Government Steering Committee, T227/3108 and PREM16/992. The work of the Committee is further discussed below in ch 6.2.2.
16 TNA: CAB164/1324, PERSEC (75)3, 'The Civil Service in the changing economic, social and political scene'.
17 This paragraph is based on the records in TNA: CAB164/1249 and 1324 concerning Sunningdale debates on devolution in 1974 and 1975, and the special conference of Permanent Secretaries in October 1974. The quotations are taken from the minutes of the September 1974 meeting (p. 8) and Allen's summary of the 1975 conference (p. 3). The discovery of North Sea oil was identified as a major cause of increased 'divisiveness and self-seeking' in Scotland. For the administrative impact of devolution planning, see below ch 10.4.2.
18 This paragraph is based on documents in Cabinet Office, 35/3 parts 7 and 8. The quotations from 1976 are taken from PERSEC(76)2, 'The institutional character of government' by Sir J. Garlick (p. 7) and PERSEC(76)1, 'The government and the governed' by P. Baldwin (para 7). The association of the CBI and TUC with the MSC was identified by Baldwin in Hayekian terms as the 'innocent forerunner of a more sinister development'. Allen's farewell address in 1977 was entitled 'Civil Servants, Ministers and Parliament' (PERSEC(77)2) and was succeeded in 1978 by Sir P. Nairne's paper, 'The Civil Service and accountability to Parliament' (PERSEC(78)3). For changing administrative attitudes to Parliament in general and to select committees in particular, see also ch 10.3.2 below.
19 Ibid. Allen's views in this paragraph are taken from his farewell address (p. 1) and his letters of 14 December 1976 and 11 November 1977 summarising successive Sunningdales. The 1976 letter underlined the perceived impotence of the Civil Service: 'we felt that there was not a great deal that civil servants could do to help, except perhaps to exert what influence they can in the direction of deliberation, simplicity and of costing policy options'. The one 'distinct ray of hope', rather cynically, was that shortage of money would 'slow down activity'. For a further example of internal sympathy with the 'crowding out' thesis, see TNA: CAB164/1249, 'Civil Service manning constraints' (para 4), the CSD submission to the 1974 Sunningdale conference.
20 In effect the Treasury had ceded to the CSD responsibility for detailed negotiations over staff numbers and grading as well as for the internal and external 'efficiency' controls.
21 See TNA: T331/1044, J.E. Pestell, 'Review of central control of Civil Service manpower', January 1975.
22 TNA: T371/125, E. Dell to M. Shepherd, 24 February 1976. An earlier example of outmoded attitudes was the attack by a Treasury official on the CSD's 'Jekyll and Hyde' character because it controlled pay and numbers as rigorously 'as the old Treasury ever did', whilst promoting expenditure on, for example, improved working conditions. Given the strike and the *Wider Issues* inquiry, such expenditure might more reasonably

NOTES FOR CHAPTER 6

have been seen as essential to efficiency (see T331/1044, marked significantly 'Treasury eyes only', C.W. France to R.L. Workman, March 1973).

23 See TNA: PREM16/1170, 1974 meeting: 'The Staff Side hoped they could be assured that the Civil Service would be staffed as the workload required, without arbitrary cuts in numbers. The Prime Minister said that he entirely accepted that staffing must follow from policy decisions.'

24 Manpower numbers are infinitely adaptable depending on whether, for example, they are a crude head count or refer to full-time equivalents, and whether (and when) they are measures of staff in post, staff estimates or PESC forecasts. The cited figures, which differ marginally from those commonly used, are taken from definite analyses provided to F.E.R. Butler by the CSD on 25 July 1974 and 19 March 1975 in TNA: PREM16/767. See also Table 6.1. For all the Conservatives' efforts, hiving off only reduced the net number of staff by some 2000.

25 The epithets were those of Sir John Hunt in TNA: PREM16/768, memorandum to the Prime Minister, 12 May 1976 and of Dennis Healey in the Cabinet of 8 July 1976 (Hunt, Cabinet Secretary's notebook, 4). The projected cut was made explicit in February 1976, *Public Expenditure* (Cmnd 6393), p. 14, table 1.4; and the three Cabinets to discuss the programme were on May 13, July 8 and July 29.

26 Hunt described Wilson's calculation as ' back of the envelope'. It also assumed a representative range of posts would be lost (TNA: PREM16/768, memo to Callaghan, 7 July 1976). The MOD had agreed to cuts of 30,000 by 1978/9 and of a further 3000 headquarters staff by 1983.

27 One of the attractions of the initiative to Wilson was that it involved future rather than immediate economies or redundancies and was thus 'painless'. Nevertheless, the proposed across-the-board cut led to some radical suggestions, such as the reductions of juries from 12 to 10. The annual saving of £700,000 in expenses may have been meaningless in relation to total public expenditure but was highly meaningful in the context of the Lord Chancellor's budget. This exposed the full absurdity of the 'numbers game'. See TNA: CAB129/190/14, 1 July 1976.

28 The fullest statement of the official Treasury view, particularly in relation to VED, is in TNA: T371/826, P. Cousins to G. Downey, 12 May 1976. Majority Cabinet support for the abolition of VED (which Healey inaccurately recalls supporting in *The Time of My Life* (1989), p. 408) is recorded in CAB128/59, CM(76)14th, 8 July 1976. Most of the additional posts were ironically a consequence of a decision not to raise tax allowances in line with inflation. Fiscal drag may have increased revenue but it also increased the number of taxpayers whose returns had to be processed. In all, the number of staff employed by Inland Revenue and Customs and Excise rose from 93,400 to 113,900 between January 1973 and 1979 – not an example '*pour encourager les autres*'.

29 TNA:T371/3168, draft report of the Steering Committee, para 7. The Committee accepted that certain concessions to the staff associations (such as the formula for increasing social security staff in line with unemployment) inflated the number of lower paid jobs. It was adamant, however, that annual efficiency savings from improved management (and particularly staff inspection) could not exceed 1% despite the Chief Secretary to the Treasury's claim, without supporting evidence, that up to 4% was possible – albeit not in the Treasury (T371/126, P. Cousins to G. Downey, 12 May 1976). The economies suggested, such as 'rougher justice' for the public (which was to feature again in Rayner's 'lasting reforms' programme under Mrs Thatcher) was dismissed in Cabinet as impractical, given the prevailing public demand for 'finer' justice. Cabinet on 13 May 1976 specifically recorded that efficiency was no worse in the public than the private sector, whilst simultaneously launching an inquiry into the more economical administration of tax and social security. After a year, the inquiry concluded that 'large staff savings' could only be achieved by the introduction of tax credits although an 'inexorable increase' in tax officials might be staunched by further computerisation and simplification and,

NOTES FOR CHAPTER 6

above all, a moratorium of political fine-tuning (see CAB128/59, CM(76)4th.3 and PREM16/1283).

30 PREM16/1959: N.L. Wicks to Callaghan, 19 June 1978. In 1976 alone, numbers were kept 15,000 below the projections (see TNA: PREM16/795, correspondence between J. Herbecq and L. Pliatzky in which Treasury officials, despite the imminence of the IMF's arrival, resisted the reopening of the £140m cuts campaign and derided the idea of a recruitment ban).

31 The NSS at a particularly confrontational first meeting with Callaghan on 27 July 1976 (TNA: PREM16/1170) expressed anger at the lack of consultation, the implied addition to unemployment and the threat to personnel management inherent in a 13% cut in CSD manpower. It was insistent that there should be no compulsory redundancy. Its aggression encouraged Callaghan to end the search for further economies. On DVLA, the Welsh Office clearly favoured the retention of VED. Devolution as a whole, however, was estimated to require 3000 additional posts – which, at a time of job losses elsewhere, also displeased the NSS.

32 TNA: PREM16/767, M. Shepherd to J. Callaghan, 14 April 1976. The final presentation of the CSD's recommendations for cuts is at CAB129/ 190/14, 1 July 1976. For the Treasury's less flattering assessment, see T371/126, P. Cousins to J. Anson, 6 April 1976.

33 The memoranda of 13 October and 19 November, respectively entitled Public Expenditure Cuts and PSBR Cuts, are in TNA: PREM16/794.

34 Lack of honesty about political constraints was not new. As William Armstrong recalled for the Prime Minister in 1977: 'manpower control . . . depends ultimately on Ministers . . . It was hell's delight to do it since every Cabinet Minister would agree on a ceiling . . . so long as it did not affect him. And of course there was cheating, not least by the Treasury itself' (see TNA: PREM16/1658, transcript of meeting 20 October 1977). Significantly, manpower issues were mentioned neither by the NSS in their regular meetings with the Prime Minister after January 1977 nor in the PREM files after June 1978 – except in relation to wastage rates and 'sluggish recruitment'.

35 For further details of staff associations and 'industrial action', see ch. 8.

36 Cmd 9613, para 769 (2). Pay research drew comparisons with over 100 establishments in the public and private sector.

37 A summary of pay research and incomes policy is provided in Annex 5 of the final Report of the Working Group on the Re-entry Problems of Pay Research submitted to the Prime Minister in January 1977 (TNA: PREM16/1172). All awards excluded the Professional and Technical Group (which, as will be seen, had its own bargaining procedures) and posts above Assistant Secretary (which were covered by a Standing Advisory Council until 1971 and thereafter the Top Salaries Review Board). The original intention had been to make research-based pay awards every five years but, due to inflation, the period was narrowed to four (1964), three (1967), two (1971) and finally one year (December 1974). The 1968 award had been 'staged' or, in other words, not paid in full until January 1969.

38 For details of the negotiations and later developments, see TNA: PREM16/770, especially M. Shepherd to M. Foot, 7 March and Hunt's brief for the Prime Minister prior to Cabinet, 13 March 1975. The Government had feared that pay research would recommend a rise of over 40% but it recommended only 34%. Staff associations could thus have bargained for more. For their leaders' warnings, see the transcript of a meeting with Shepherd on 19 March, and for Wilson's retrospective regret, see B. Donoughue, *Diary*, p. 645. Donoughue, as seen earlier, was a foremost critic of research-based pay and opposed its revival on the grounds that it had created a 'depth of feeling in the productive sector of the economy that the <u>overall</u> rewards for public service employment are provocatively generous'.

39 This and the succeeding paragraph are based on correspondence in TNA: PREM16/1172. See respectively Peart to J. Callaghan, 12 January 1977, enclosing

NOTES FOR CHAPTER 6

the final report of the Official Working Group; B. Donoughue to Callaghan, 17 November 1976; J. Hunt to Callaghan, 14 January 1977; and N.L. Wicks to Callaghan, 19 January 1977, on which Callaghan minuted his response.

40 For the Ministerial Committee's final report, see Ibid, GEN64(77)14, 27 June 1977. In the negotiations preceding the reactivation, several subtle changes were made to the Committee's recommendations. For example, the new PRU Board (which was established in November 1977) did not replace the Steering Committee and could only offer general guidance. Plans to ensure greater openness were also compromised.

41 See the correspondence in TNA: PREM16/1172 and 1546, particularly D. Allen's report on the NWC meeting to the Prime Minister on 7 December 1977, which summarised association leaders' concerns thus: 'the first two stages of incomes policy had been loyally accepted but now they feared discrimination in 1978. There was also resentment of the effects of expenditure cuts and the imposition of cash limits as well as of the considerable and unjustifiable criticism from outside. They would not wish the strength of feeling of their members to be underestimated'. See also transcripts of the meetings between the Prime Minister and the NSS on 14 July, 27 October and 9 November 1977 in PREM16/1170.

42 TNA: PREM16/1546: manuscript notes on letters from J. Barnett and Peart on 27 and 31 October 1977 respectively.

43 Ibid, Callaghan note, 4 September 1978.

44 This paragraph is based on PREM16/1962–1965. 'Costly disorder' was part of Bancroft's post mortem to K. Stowe on 1 May 1979. He was particularly scathing about negotiations being taken from the CSD (and especially its industrial relations experts, such as G. Burrett and K. Lawrance, who appreciated every nuance of the NSS position, and whose professionalism was proven by their later settlement of the award). Instead they were handled by Roy Hattersley (who, as Minister for Prices and Consumer Protection, had little expert official support) and Len Murray, the General Secretary of the TUC (an institution for which the NSS had scant respect, hence its disregard of both the Social Contract and the intended 'compact' of 14 February 1979).

45 Ibid. The key meeting of the Subcommittee on Pay Negotiations of the Ministerial Committee on Economic Strategy was EY(P)17th, 14 March 1979 and Le Cheminant reported to K. Stowe on the following day. Its arguments were relayed to Cabinet on 20 March 1979 (CP(79)25) and augmented by B. Donoughue, who asserted that it was the Civil Service 1975 pay award – not the failings of private employers – which 'was a critical factor in encouraging the pay explosion'. 'Many of our economic difficulties', he concluded, 'have stemmed directly from that pay round'. In homage to the crowding-out thesis, he then begged the question: 'who can blame the best graduates for entering the public sector when the salary differentials (notwithstanding the PRU) appear . . . so great?' The PRU indeed was subject to continuing criticism in No.10 on the grounds *inter alia* that comparisons were made only with 'good' employers. So much for the tradition of Government as a model employer. Even the chair of the new Board (which included Derek Rayner) belatedly voiced private doubts about its integrity (Shepherd to J. Callagan, 9 April 1979).

46 Ibid. For the reaction of the NSS at a meeting with Peart on 26 March, see Peart's immediate report to the Prime Minister; for the reaction of the Principal Private Secretary to the 'high price' of concessions, see Stowe's note of 12 April and his letter to S. Hampson, 19 April; and for Hunt's advice, see his note to Callaghan on 28 March 1979. Callaghan agreed that 'we must keep Ministers as far as possible out of the negotiations' and between January and 26 March, plans to rationalise negotiations matured into the Clegg Commission on Comparability – whose recommendations Mrs Thatcher, to her lasting embarrassment, promised during the 1979 election campaign to honour. In the defence of 'costly disorder', it should be noted that the

initial down payment was less than the 12.5% predicted as a minimum from within the NSS at the start of negotiations (A. Christopher to J. Callaghan, 31 January 1979).

47 TNA: PREM16/1172, para 35 (iii); *Financial Times*, 15 July 1982.

48 The Bullock Report on Industrial Democracy (Cmnd 6706) was published and hastily buried by Ministers in April 1977.

49 Of the super ministries, the DTI was immediately divided into three by Wilson in 1974 and a separate Department of Transport carved out of the DoE in 1976. They gained further notoriety in 1977 with the death, reputedly from overwork, of Anthony Crosland. He had been head successively of two 'super ministries', Environment and the FCO. Hiving off was reversed in 1976 when the MSC was reintegrated into the Civil Service – to the satisfaction of many CSD officials, who had earlier engaged in a typically agonised debate over the status and definition of a Civil Servant (see TNA: BA17/852 and 975–6). The disappearance of a dedicated Business Team, which might have appeared somewhat misplaced given Labour's Social Contract with the TUC, did not mean the loss of all contact with business. It was maintained *inter alia* by formal meetings (including regular Spring conferences at Sunningdale), the continued use of management consultants and staff interchange. The latter was the subject of a report by senior Permanent Secretaries in 1977, albeit geared to improving industry's understanding of Government rather than Whitehall's working methods (see PREM16/1286).

50 The initial Report was published as the *Eleventh Report of the Expenditure Committee for 1976–7* (HC535) and the second as the *Twelfth Report ... for 1977–8* (HC576). The latter also includes transcripts of the further evidence.

51 See B. Sedgemore, *The Secret Constitution* (1980) for his alternative chapter (which the Committee rejected) and a general summary of his views; and Garrett, *Managing the Civil Service*, ch 3. For the views of Ridley and Lawson, see Conservative Party Archives (especially CSD4/13/9 and 12) and Question 81 to Sir Douglas Allen on 3 May 1976 (*Eleventh Report*, volume 3). English's agenda, of 2 February 1976, is in PREM16/Civil Service, A suggestion by John Garrett. Lawson resigned from the Committee before it completed its work.

52 The record of the CSD was summarised in the memorandum, 'The Response to the Fulton Report' of 10 October 1975 (*Eleventh Report*, vol 2) and defended by Douglas Allen to both Wilson on 23 December 1975 (see PREM16/Civil Service, A suggestion by John Garrett) and the Committee on 3 May 1976 (vol 2, transcript). The dispute over training was most heated during the cross-questioning of Lord Peart on 18 April 1978, from which the quotations are taken (*Twelfth Report*, transcript, qq 5–7). Allen also sought in vain to rebut charges of elitism by pointing out that there were more Oxbridge graduates on the Committee than in his Permanent Secretary Management Group at the CSD. He himself had graduated from LSE and his deputy (Sir John Herbecq) had not gone to university, entering the prewar Colonial Office as a Clerical Officer.

53 PREM16/ Civil Service, A suggestion by John Garrett: D. Allen to K. Stowe 23 December 1975. In the face of Garrett's relentless attack, the CSD took delight in quoting Fulton's own dictum that 'the Service must avoid a static view of a new ideal man and structure which in its turn could become as much of an obstacle to change as the present inheritance' (Cmd 3638, para 24).

54 *Eleventh Report*, para 74. Convinced that Fulton had not been frustrated by its own flawed logic, Labour members targeted the CSD as the epitome of bureaucratic conservatism, rather than a vehicle for breaking such conservatism. Sedgemore identified the tipping point as Armstrong's assumption of the role of 'deputy Prime Minister' (*Twelfth Report*, transcript of evidence, 18 April 1978, qq 54–64).

55 See above, ch 6.2.2.

56 The principal supporter of the CSD was the NSS which recognised that, given that the Service was 'a federal collection of semi-autonomous departments', its effective 'power' amounted to little more than 'the art of persuasion' (see TNA: PREM16/1658,

W.L. Kendall to Callaghan, 24 October 1977). Earlier it had advised English that 'the essence of an improved working relationship lies in an acceptance by departments that the CSD have the authority to lay down central rules and guidance to provide a mandatory framework within which departments and line managers would work'. Then when, in an exceptional burst of industrial democracy, the Prime Minister consulted its Secretary General in October 1977 on the future of CSD, Kendall advocated its strengthening rather than its abolition. Consulted simultaneously on the choice of the next Head of the Civil Service, he declared a preference for neither Bancroft nor Cooper (PREM 16/1170; see also ch 8.3.2).

57 For the origins of the debate and Hunt's explanation for acting without prior consultation, see TNA: BA7/22, J. Hunt to D. Allen, 22 December 1976. 'My sole objective', he wrote somewhat sheepishly, 'was to put down a marker that, in considering the Healey replacement problem ... the PM did not necessarily have to think of someone who could cover the whole range of existing responsibilities'. Hunt temporarily disagreed with Allen over whether personnel policy should be assigned to a non-ministerial Public Service Commission but, once the highly political issue of pay was raised, quickly withdrew the suggestion. For the full exchange of views, see PREM 16/1662, correspondence of Hunt and Allen with K. Stowe between 16 December 1976 and 10 January 1977. See also Clarke, *New Trends in Government* p. 66 and, for the *Black Book*, ch 5.3.1 above.

58 TNA: PREM 16/1662, D. Healey to J. Callaghan, February 1977 and annex 3 (ii).

59 TNA: PREM 16/1658, K. Stowe to J. Callaghan, 11 October 1977. Stowe's advice was strongly influenced by Hunt's conviction that the CSD had compromised departmental efficiency by becoming 'a Department for the Civil Service rather than a Department of the Civil Service i.e. it settles for a quiet life with the Civil Service unions' (ibid, Hunt to K. Stowe, 28 September 1977). Allen denied such charges, particularly when they were used – after his transfer to the Treasury – by Robert Sheldon to justify the use of cash limits to reimpose Treasury control on pay 'leaving the CSD to use its understanding with the Civil Service unions to reach the actual settlements'. Such a proposal suggests that, as a Treasury Minister, he had gone fully native. Fulton (of which he had been a signatory) had, after all, insisted that the CSD 'should be in a position to fight, and to be seen fighting, the Treasury' (ibid, Sheldon to Callaghan, 7 October 1977; Cmnd 3638, para 252 (c)).

60 Ibid, note of a meeting between the Prime Minister, Allen, Hunt and Wass, and attended by Stowe, 31 October 1977. For the drafting of the pre-election briefs, see BA17/MG39/386/05 A-D, Preparatory work for the general election 1979. The Ministerial nominees were Stowe's inspired suggestions, see note for the record by J. Hobson, 17 April 1978 (ibid, file A).

61 On Healey's might, see TNA: PREM 16/1658, N.L. Wicks to K. Stowe, 4 November 1977. For the fullest demolition of English, see ibid, D. Allen to K. Stowe, 'Alternative ways of organising the central departments of government'. Allen concluded that reducing CSD to a 'rump' made no sense 'as all the effective management functions would be in the Treasury, which would then in most respects have assumed a pre-Fulton shape except that the subordination of Civil Service management questions to financial priorities, which the Fulton Committee criticised in 1968, would be substantially reinforced'. The greatest advocate of enhanced co-operation was Douglas Wass, for fear of the cost of further disruption. 'The Civil Service', he pleaded, 'has been subjected to a series of institutional changes since 1964 most of which were subsequently abandoned as failures. Ministers should think three times before inflicting any more' (see BA7/22, Wass to Allen, 21 January 1977 and PREM 16/1662, Healey to Callaghan, February 1977, Annex).

62 BA17/MG39/386/05C, the 'Red Centre' brief forwarded by I. Bancroft to K. Stowe, 19 March 1979, para 5. For Wass's desperation, see TNA: PREM 16/1658, record of

the 'council of state', 31 October 1977. Advice, for the first time, was heavily influenced by the experience of Canada and Australia where, within similar 'Westminster' constitutions, Public Service Boards dealt with pay and personnel issues. Australia had also just established a Ministry of Finance, separate from the Treasury, to deal with public expenditure. It was to become a powerhouse for administrative change but to ensure co-operation, however, its officials had initially to report to the Treasurer. Hunt favoured a similar 'hybrid' solution (with the Chief Secretary to the Treasury taking political responsibility for the new Bureau of the Budget). This was opposed by Allen and others in the CSD because, given that officials would have to refer expenditure to Treasury Ministers and Civil Service issues to the Prime Minister, it involved 'double lines of reporting'. They favoured instead 'common citizenship' (or the sharing of certain 'backroom' services and regular staff interchange). See, in particular BA17/MG39/386/05A, 'Reorganisation of the Centre', forwarded by J.B. Pearce to Rivlin, 31 May 1978.

63 The phrase '*status quo* with knobs on' was coined by J.B. Pearce in a memorandum to A.W. Russell on 24 July 1978 (BA17/MG39/386/05B). For the initial blueprint of an Efficiency Unit, see TNA: PREM16/1658, Allen to Stowe, 12 October 1977; and for Callaghan's response, PREM16/1659, Stowe to J. Hunt, 7 March 1978.

64 For Allen's views, see the note and annexes sent by C. Priestley to J. Hobson on 23 August 1976, which were then forwarded to Bancroft in December 1977 (TNA: BA7/22); and for Fulton's assignation, see Cmnd 3638, para 267 (a). Allen enjoyed 'seniority' because he was the longest serving Permanent Secretary and both Hunt and Wass had served under him.

65 For the 1961–2 post-Plowden debate, see ch 3.3.1 above. Hunt's ambition to chair the Senior Appointments Selection Committee was well-known, as was Allen's distaste for other selection duties (such as honours) which he dismissed as 'gilt-edged slush'. A wide range of opinion was collected during the CSD's management review (TNA: BA7/22, C. Priestley to J. Hobson, 23 August 1976, Annex I); and, on forwarding them to Bancroft, Priestley's typically forthright advice was that he should not seek to be the chief adviser (a role which Warren Fisher had never enjoyed) but to make the CSD 'more muscular'.

66 For Hunt's predatory instincts, see Hennessy, *Whitehall*, pp. 254 –7. See also B. Donoughue, *Diary*, vol 1, pp. 526–7 for the fears generated in 1975 by 'Hunt's empire building' and other tensions between the 'top three'.

67 See TNA: PREM16/1658 for Allen's advice to Callaghan on the role of Head of the Civil Service and his successor (22 September 1977), his retirement letter (16 December 1977), Callaghan's reply (29 December 1977) and Callaghan's interview with William Armstrong (20 October 1977).

68 For this and the rest of the paragraph, see TNA: PREM16/1658, record of the 'council of state', 31 October 1977. For the first of Hunt's regular denials (prompted by a somewhat mischievous suggestion from Allen) see PREM16/1662, Hunt to K. Stowe, 6 January 1977. 'I suspect', backtracked Hunt, ' that at some time in the more or less distant future this will materialise: but its constitutional significance should not be minimised'. At the 'council of state', he then somewhat disingenuously argued that 'the Cabinet Office . . . would eventually become the department of the Chief Executive and the Prime Minister but he was anxious not to run down this road and had indeed tried to repel' most tasks thrust at it.

69 For PAR's earlier history, see above ch 5.3.3 (b) and for English's recommendations, ch 7 of its first report. A *cause celebre* exploited by English was the quotation by the OECD from a 1972 Department of Education and Science PAR, which the Committee itself was forbidden to see. The decision to withhold the document was political, but it was persistently used as a stick with which to beat officials. Ironically, officials typically wanted PARs reclassified as 'official working papers' rather than 'policy-forming documents' so

NOTES FOR CHAPTER 6

that they might be made public or at least their factual analysis remain available after a change of government (see TNA: T371/61–62).

70 See the transcript of the 1978 Sunningdale meeting of Permanent Secretaries in TNA: CAB164/ Cabinet Office 35/3, part 8, p. 7. For the 1974 tussle, see PREM16/39 and T353/79. For internecine warfare in 1976, see T371/59–60 and PREM16/794. According to Tony Benn, Cabinet in May 'more or less killed' PAR, but it later rose from the dead at the Treasury's behest (see CAB128/59, CM(76)6th.4 and Benn, *Against the Tide*, p. 569; CAB128/60, CM(76) 26th.3 and CAB129/192/7). Before the crunch meeting on 13 October 1976, even the No.10 Policy Unit was moved to advise: 'the PAR system is still desirable in principle. It has not failed' (B. Donoughue to J. Callaghan, PREM16/794).

71 Hennessy, *Whitehall*, p. 235; TNA: PREM16/794, J. Hunt to J. Callaghan, 13 October 1976. The rest of this and the succeeding paragraph is largely based on PERSEC(78) meeting, in Cabinet Office 35/3, part 8.

72 TNA: CAB184/134, J. Hunt to J.B. Unwin, January 1972. Secrecy was advocated *inter alia* by two *ad hoc* Ministerial Committees in 1976: MISC 89 and GEN 29 (see T371/62 and PREM16/374).

73 TNA: T371/41, D. Wass to D. Allen, 23 June 1975; Wilding, *Civil Servant*, p. 74. Both, however, were contradicted by a management consultant working within the Treasury who argued: 'since the war the Treasury has preached the virtues of financial control but there have been very few positive steps to implement the pious hopes . . . The CSD has exercised rather more leadership and particularly the Management Services division has had a valuable missionary role' (T371/41, V. Watts to P. M. Hills, 13 May 1976).

74 For Armstong's account of Heath's blind spot, see his discussion with Callaghan on 20 October 1977, recorded in TNA: PREM16/1658.

75 TNA: PREM16/431. This section of the speech was drafted by Bernard Donoughue, the head of the new No.10 Policy Unit and, to their annoyance, was cleared with neither the Cabinet Office nor the CSD (see BA17/994). For the historical precedents, see Blick, *People Who Live In The Dark*, which identifies 1974 as the 'breakthrough' in the regularisation of special advisers, whilst agreeing with Lord Croham that John Harris, Roy Jenkins' public relations adviser between 1965 and 1970, was the 'first true special adviser' in the modern sense (pp. 74, 113). See above chs 3.2.4 and 5.3.2(b) for earlier recognition within Whitehall of the need for special advisers and also Hurd, *End to Promises*, p. 37 for Conservative support for a No.10 Policy Unit. Fulton alluded to the appointment of advisers but, as a Fabian document, its emphasis was on experts rather than non-experts (Cmnd 3638, paras 129, 285). This was confirmed, despite Wilson's denials, by Norman Hunt in a letter to William Armstrong on 29 March 1974, in which Hunt was scathing about 'political assistants' as opposed to 'senior professional experts' – amongst whom he naturally included himself (BA17/989).

76 TNA: PREM16/1282 and 1660, K. Stowe to Callaghan, 25 February 1977 and Callaghan's note on another letter from Stowe, 14 March 1977. For the broad welcome by senior officials, see two papers (PERSEC(73)6 and (74)1) for Sunningdale in 1973 and 1974, and the reports of the subsequent debates, in CAB164/1249. The first debate was heavily influenced by Barbara Castle's article on 'Mandarin Power' in the *Sunday Times* of 19 June 1973, which started somewhat disarmingly by asserting that 'the danger of the British Civil Service lies in its excellence' before emphasising the 'crying need' for it to be 'trained, re-trained and re-re-trained' in the two key issues: 'the supremacy of the political function in a democracy over the administrative function and . . . getting into the mind of a Minister'.

77 The role of the Policy Unit has been progressively revealed by Bernard Donoughue in *Prime Minister* (1987); *The Heat of the Kitchen* (2002) which contains a devastating critique of Marcia Williams; and two volumes of *Downing Street Diary* (2005 and 2008). On the

NOTES FOR CHAPTER 6

Unit's establishment, see in particular *Heat*, pp. 124 –135 and the letter from Robert Armstrong to I. Bancroft on 6 September 1974 describing how the Private Office and Policy Unit did 'not just coexist but positively . . . complement each other' (TNA: PREM16/105). Donoughue was a Gaitskellite and, apart from a few weeks as a pollster, had had no contact with Wilson before his appointment. The Prime Minister then became immediately embroiled in the 'slagheap' scandal involving Marcia Williams' brother and was thus even less able to define what he wanted. The quotations are from pp. 132–3. Early bonding on the Unit's side is illustrated by a diary entry by Donoughue on 9 April 1974: 'I find, grudgingly, that some . . . civil servants are refreshingly sane and helpful. Thinking of the situation in No.10, if I had to choose between the Bureaucratic and the Neurotic, I know which way I would go', *Diary*, vol 1, p. 95. On his furtive examination of Hunt's briefs, see *Prime Minister*, p. 23.

78 Donoughue, *Prime Minister*, p. 70. For a fuller account of the incident and a vignette of Wilson's dysfunctional style of government, see *Diary*, vol 1, p. 468: 'Am flabbergasted and a bit amused about . . . HW trying to exclude . . . me from the White Paper discussions . . . In the end he was coming up to chat to me appreciatively in committees from which he had banned me. He had ordered me not to get the papers, yet we were *drafting* much of the bloody papers, and he praised them. Crazy.'

79 On the relationship between Donoughue and Callaghan, see *Heat* (ch 13) and K.O. Morgan, *Callaghan* (1997), pp. 492–6, which suggests a rather more constructive relationship. An authoritative 'insider' account of the IMF crisis is D. Wass, *Decline to Fall* (2008).

80 The Unit was never more than eight strong and two of its heavyweights returned to academia on Wilson's retirement: Andrew Graham (although he was replaced by the equally impressive Gavyn Davies) and David Piachaud (although he returned part-time). For a full list, see *Heat*, pp. 130–1 and for Donoughue's disappointments ch 14–15. Amongst his tactical suggestions, which Callaghan considered impractical, were the rejuvenation of the Cabinet in 1978 and a tougher stance against the unions in 1979; amongst the strategic, the sale of council houses. The Unit was concerned solely with domestic policy.

81 Donoughue, *Diary*, vol 1, p. 462. Donoughue then described Berrill as 'very much the Treasury's man' but two months later noted his compliance with Hunt's promotion of the CPRS 'while "regularising" it and fully integrating it into the Cabinet Office'. This, he concluded, reduced the CPRS to 'an extra wheel on the Civil Service coach, and not the grit in the oyster which was originally intended' (pp. 500–1). In *Inside the Think Tank*, Blackstone and Plowden acknowledge the CPRS's growing reputation as a 'tool of the mandarins' but describe Berrill's relationship with Hunt as one of 'mutual dependence' not subservience (pp. 63–4). Nevertheless they note a subtle reordering of the heading on CPRS notepaper. Under Rothschild, Central Policy Review Staff preceded Cabinet Office. Under Berrill it followed.

82 On the contrasting influence of the Policy Unit and the CPRS, see Morgan, *Callaghan*, p. 492; and on the continuing decline of the CPRS, see Donoughue, *Diaries* (vol 2), esp pp. 123 and 205. On the *Review of Overseas Representation* (which was ironically commissioned by Callaghan whilst Foreign Secretary) see Blackstone and Plowden, *Think Tank* (ch 8) and for its reception, Hennessy, *Whitehall*, p. 270. Another initiative which was not a 'great success story' was Hunt's attempt to realise Whitehall's long-standing ambition to rationalise welfare policy via the Joint Approach to Social Policies, see *Think Tank* (ch 6).

83 TNA: PREM16/907, 21 September. McNally had himself previously held Lipsey's post at the FCO (at a far higher salary) and was awarded a 'responsibility' bonus on his transfer to No.10. Donoughue himself claimed he left No.10 'seriously broke' (*Heat*, p.282). However he had always been paid on the Under Secretary scale and thus enjoyed a salary of over £8500 which, under the incomes policy he himself had drafted,

disqualified him from receiving any increment. What perhaps particularly angered him was that permanent officials had received their 15 month 'comparability' award of 32.5% in 1975 whilst, on Wilson's orders, special advisers only received an annual increase of 21.2%, based on the Retail Price Index (PREM16/431, note by K. Stowe, 10 July 1975).

84 The House of Commons was not only highly suspicious of patronage but seeking, through its select committees (see ch 10.3.2), to track the expenditure of public money more closely. For anger within the CSD and William Armstrong's protests, see TNA: BA17/990 (K. Lawrance to J. Colman, 3 June 1974) and PREM16/104 (note to R. Armstrong, June 1974).

85 For the admission of a shambles, see TNA: PREM16/907, K. Stowe to J. Hobson, 11 July 1976; and for Wilson's rejection of advice that an age-scale was needed to 'establish some consistent principle, defensible in terms of relativities between advisers, and between them and other civil servants, and hence also defensible in the event of any public criticism of particular rates', see PREM16/431, E. Shepherd to H. Wilson, 12 June 1975. Special advisers themselves were consulted but each tended to argue that they should be made an exception to any general rule (see BA17/994, especially B. Gilmore to K. Lawrance, 23 January 1975).

86 TNA: PREM16/1660, D. Allen to M. Palliser, 27 July 1977. For Callaghan's initial judgement and then its reversal, see PREM16/907 and 1282, note on Stowe's minutes of 23 July 1976 and of February 1977.

87 This paragraph is based on TNA: PREM16/104–5 and BA17/989–94 (which contains the MISC 34 records). The relevant meetings of Cabinet were on 16 and 23 May (CAB128/54, CC(74)16 and 17) and of the Commons on 27 June (Parl Deb, 875, cols 1744-5). The best insight into Conservative Party thinking is provided in the evidence of Brendon Sewill (the former director of the Conservative Research Department and publicly funded adviser in the Treasury between 1971 and 1974) to the 1976–8 Armitage Committee on Political Activities of Civil Servants (see BA3/16).

88 A copy of the original memorandum is in TNA: PREM16/430. The italics are added. As temporary civil servants, advisers were bound by administrative convention, as enshrined in Estacode. Parliamentary candidacy alone was formally subject to an Order in Council – which could be amended without legislation. Financial support for opposition Parties was approved by Parliament in March 1975.

89 See TNA: BA17/988 for the various drafts of the pre-election brief; and PREM16/105, Allen to Hunt, 16 October 1974 for the fullest statement of Allen's views.

90 See TNA: PREM16/906: K. Stowe to D. Allen, 28 January 1976, and to the Prime Minister, 5 March 1976. In a letter to Stowe on 4 March, which precipitated the crisis, Allen had come close to mutiny. 'If the measure of freedom proposed is given to special advisers', he wrote, 'it would seem impossible to continue to take the line publicly that these Advisers are civil servants'.

91 See TNA: PREM16/907, note of a meeting 30 April 1976; D. Allen to K. Stowe, 18 May; R.J. Meadway to K. Stowe, 14 June covering a much revised memorandum; and T. McNally to K. Stowe, 21 September 1976. For Callaghan's approval on 14 March 1977 of a yet further revised memorandum, see PREM16/1660. The particular source of friction was Callaghan's agreement in October 1976 that David Hill, on appointment to the Department of Prices, should remain an officer in his local constituency Party. In 1972, the Labour Party had successfully demanded that Conservative advisers in a similar position (such as Sewill and Schreiber) should resign. Special advisers themselves emphasised to the Armitage Committee (details below) that they did not want 'total' political freedom, only freedom from official control. They would use their 'proper discretion' to prevent conflicts of interest and embarrassment to the Government (BA3/16). Given the track record, it was unsurprising that Armitage did not agree.

NOTES FOR CHAPTER 6

92 This paragraph is based on voluminous papers in PREM 16/1660. The PCC issue was summarised for Callaghan by R.J. Meadway on 4 July 1977, but not before McNally had asserted that the Parliamentary uproar on 27 June 1974 could be safely disregarded (note to K. Stowe, 10 June 1977). On the 'five year rule' see I. Bancroft to Stowe, 27 June 1978 and the latter's note on a memorandum from Donoughue to Callaghan on 7 July 1978. The issue had led Peter Hennessy in *The Times* of 31 May 1978 to warn of the impending politicisation of the Service.

93 See TNA: PREM 16/1660, esp R.J. Meadway to Callaghan, 4 July 1977. The crisis was precipitated by the nomination of Jack Straw (Peter Shore's adviser at DoE) as Prospective Parliamentary Candidate for Blackburn. He eventually agreed to switch to private funding, but only after threatening to go to an industrial tribunal to gain severance pay (regardless of the convention that Civil Servants did not qualify for it if they resigned 'voluntarily'). This was the third time Straw had tested the limits of what was possible. On appointment in 1974 as Barbara Castle's adviser at DHSS he had been permitted, after considerable prevarication by Wilson and William Armstrong, to stand for re-election to Islington Borough Council (TNA: PREM 16/104; BA17/988). Somewhat incongruously, he then ruled himself out of 'participation in virtually any important aspect of the Council's work' (PREM 16/907, Straw to T.M. Heiser, 15 April 1976). In 1975 he aroused further controversy by advising the Labour Party in Blackburn on electoral boundary changes (see PREM 16/431).

94 See TNA: PREM 16/105, Hunt to Allen, 25 October 1974; PREM 16/430, R. Armstrong to Wilson, 25 November 1974; and more generally, CAB 164/1249, conference of Permanent Secretaries at Sunningdale, 1974.

95 After June 1974, the NSS was particularly insistent that, as temporary Civil Servants, special advisers should enjoy no political privileges denied to permanent officials. The Armitage Committee on Political Activities of Civil Servants reported in January 1978 (Cmnd 7057). It recommended a reduction from 26% to 3% of Civil Servants within the 'politically restricted' category (which prevented them from participating in national politics). They were to be transferred to the 'intermediate' category where the nature of their work rather than their grade would determine whether they could participate in both local and national politics. Were special advisers to remain Civil Servants, they would have to remain within the 'restricted' category and so required, as the CSD had long advocated, 'separate and distinct' rules (para 136).

96 For the initial conflict with Benn, see TNA: PREM 16/437, in which Wilson minuted: 'the rule should be that special advisers should do what a sane Minister would authorise them to do – but their names should be kept out of the press. In this case the main fault was that of the Minister' (note to Stowe, 5 May 1975). He then invented the rule that Ministers could only have two non-expert advisers in order to prevent Benn, on his transfer to the Department of Energy, appointing Tony Banks (PREM 16/431). As Benn's *Diaries* confirm, both Cripps and Morrell had an active role in developing policies which challenged Cabinet orthodoxy, although no direct action was taken against them until the 1979 election when Morrell participated in the 'Labour Activists' campaign. She then resigned from the campaign rather than forfeit her publicly funded salary (PREM 16/2073).

97 See the correspondence between Allen and Hunt between 16 and 25 October 1974 in TNA: PREM 16/105; and for the 1974 Australian report, which caused many junior CSD officials to doubt the wisdom of a 'special regime', BA17/992. The Australian parallel was not wholly convincing. The Labour Party there had been out of power far longer and the federal Civil Service was more independent than in Britain. The geography was also different. Ministers had their offices in Parliament, where they could be surrounded by their advisers, rather than in their departments, where they would be surrounded by officials.

NOTES FOR CHAPTER 6

98 A *cause celebre*, which further stiffened Allen's determination to clarify the rules, was an expose in *New Society* on 17 June 1976 (based on leaked Cabinet papers) of the Government's intention to renege on a commitment to introduce child benefit. A police investigation led to Ministers being questioned and fingerprinted. The prime suspects, however, remained certain special advisers – particularly after they admitted exchanging confidential information amongst themselves for political purposes and being 'economical with the truth' during an earlier internal enquiry headed by Allen (TNA: BA7/25–8). Such incidents further impeded the adoption of a 'special regime' because, as Stowe advised Callaghan on 14 March 1977, the change would 'draw attention on the fact that special advisers have been operating outside the spirit, if not the letter, of Civil Service rules for some time' (PREM16/1660).

99 For an overview, see Blick, *People who Live in the Dark*, ch 6 (and p. 161 for DoE distress); and for initial CSD hopes, TNA: BA17/989, meeting with R. Sheldon, 4 April 1974.

100 On marginality, see Sir John Hunt's lecture to the Royal College of Defence Studies in 1978. Earlier, after strong hints from Short and Wilson, both Allen and Bancroft had assured CSD colleagues in January 1975 that non-expert 'special advisers were the gimmick of 1974' and were already 'somewhat passé' (TNA: BA17/994). On Donoughue's critical mass, see the record of the meeting on 30 April 1976 (PREM16/907). On networking, see the CSD brief for the February 1974 election in BA17/988.

101 Incompatibility was exemplified during the 1975 EEC referendum, when the special advisers attached to Castle and Benn formed the 'dissenting minister's secretariat' (Castle, *Diaries*, vol 2, p. 367). There were also personal animosities with Donoughue, for example, dismissing Morrell as 'one of those large aggressive women who gravitate naturally into politics where they can exercise their frustrations' (*Diary*, vol 1, p. 265).

102 See Hennessy, *Whitehall*, p. 51; for the Godley problem, L. Pliatzky, *Getting and Spending*; and for the inaccuracy of forecasts, Healey, *Time of My Life* esp p. 381. For a critique of Treasury in December 1976, see TNA: PREM16/1662 particularly the testimony of a former and a serving Treasury official (K. Berrill and N.L. Wicks, currently one of the Prime Minister's Private Secretaries). The Treasury was deemed inward-looking because 'creative effort' was sacrificed on the 'treadmill' of computerised forecasts; and to lack authority because its frequent attempts to 'bounce' others were interpreted within Whitehall as unwillingness to respect even Cabinet decisions. Such contempt was frequently noted by Donoughue, with a Cabinet Committee being described by one official to much mirth as an interruption to 'serious business' (*Diary*, vol 1, p. 447).

103 In this respect, officials were not well served by the Chancellor who, as an 'eclectic pragmatist', provided no strong or consistent lead. He did, however, retrospectively defend his officials by acknowledging that parallel forecasts both at home and abroad were equally fallible (Healey, *Time of My Life*, esp p. 381–3).

104 For evidence, see TNA: T277/3093, TMR(75)37, Sir D. Wass address to senior Treasury staff, 22 July 1975. He admitted that, before becoming Permanent Secretary, he had acquired a 'tremendous admiration for the quality of the people in the Treasury' but had 'less than complete admiration for the way we use that quality'. It was inexcusable that so small a department as the Treasury should be 'so indifferent to staff management'.

105 TNA: PREM16/1662.

106 Management Reviews were an initiative, introduced in 1972 and coordinated by the CSD, to encourage each major department at five-yearly intervals to modernise its management. The papers of the 1974–5 Treasury Review are in TNA: T227/2965–6 and 3091–3. The Review sought to end the dislocation of policy advice resulting from William Armstrong's allocation of separate policy areas to watertight compartments, which Wass had already started to remedy through the creation of a high-powered Policy Coordinating Committee (PCC). The Review recommended *inter alia* that it should be reinforced, but this created two new problems. First, partially in reaction to

Tony Benn, industrial policy was concentrated within a new Domestic Economy Sector under its own Second Permanent Secretary (the astringent Alan Lord). This clashed with the simultaneous centralisation of control over all public expenditure in a new Public Services Sector (under the equally astringent Leo Pliatzky). Second, reinforcement of the PCC exaggerated what Wicks (see footnote 102) called the 'All Souls Common Room syndrome': the exhaustive discussion by senior officials of major policies and a subsequent reluctance, given their strong characters, to compromise thereafter even should the Chancellor or Cabinet so wish. Consequently the Treasury's rehabilitation was incomplete until 1977 when, in an unprecedented 'bout of musical chairs', the three most combative Second Permanent Secretaries were removed (Lord to industry, Mitchell to the City and Pliatzky to the Department of Trade). Even then Callaghan insisted that economic and financial policy should continue to be debated in a powerful 'Cabinet' Committee with the deceptively anodyne name of the Economic Seminar. It met 14 times in 1977–8 (Pliatzky, *Getting and Spending*, p. 165; Morgan, *Callaghan*, pp. 508–9).

107 The papers of the Cash Flow Group are in TNA: T277/2878 and 2983; and those of the subsequent FIS Study Group in T227/2901 and 3004–5. Underspending on departmental votes doubled between 1971/2 and 1972/3 and was even greater as measured by PESC planning totals (in 1972/3 over £1b out of a total of £27b). The initiative owed something to Fulton, although the Treasury was reluctant openly to admit it. 'Treasury Ministers', as one admitted, 'have not been much involved in the thinking which Mr Sheldon and Mr Garrett have done about modernising and reforming the financial intelligence system' (T353/1117, H. Copeman to P. Baldwin, 28 March 1974). Officials did then extensively research practice abroad, in France and Italy as well as the USA and Germany (see T353/117–9 and 147–54).

108 TNA: T353/148, H. Copeman to P. Baldwin, 17 March 1975 and to D. Henley, 21 March 1975. For the late awakening of interest in May 1975 amongst senior officials, see T353/149.

109 For the initial policy-neutral nature of FIS, see the letter by Sir Douglas Henley to all Permanent Secretaries on 26 August 1975 admitting that it was 'unfortunate that this exercise has to be carried out at the same time as the introduction of cash limits' because improved departmental and central monitoring of expenditure flows was desirable in its own right (TNA: T374/37). A year later T.P. Turner (the Operational Research expert who initiated FIS) confirmed that it was only a 'starting point for investigation and decision'. It told a PFO 'that he has a problem; it does not tell him how to solve it' (letter to F.E.R. Butler, 6 July 1976).

110 So complex, for example, was the relationship between cash limit 'blocks' and the estimates 'subheads' that, despite the scrupulousness with which the relationship was recorded in Appendix 2 of the white paper introducing cash limits (Cmnd 6440), 37 errors had sheepishly to be admitted in June 1976 (see TNA: T371/36). For a critique of the preceding chaos, see TNA: T353/151, H. Copeman to F. Jones, 7 July 1975 and Copeman's covering note to the final FIS Report.

111 Standardisation was complicated by several contingent factors. They included the urgency with which agreement had to be reached before the PGO, for its own needs, updated its own system (to be renamed APEX – 'the analysis of public expenditure') and the continuing requirement, for industrial reasons, to purchase British ICL machines (although American IBM machines were increasingly acknowledged to have greater capacity). For the major battle with ICL over the PGO upgrade, which eventually resulted in the free provision of higher powered machines, see T374/GEA588/100/01 and TNA: T374/46. The Treasury idiosyncratically had little-known American UNIVAC machines, which caused innumerable problems throughout 1976 in relation to the writing of programmes to process the material generated by APEX.

NOTES FOR CHAPTER 6

112 For a summary of their resistance, see TNA: T353/152, H. Copeman to F. Jones, 5 August 1975.
113 See for example, F.E.R. Butler to I. Beesley in GEA577/100/1, 16 March 1977, just before the introduction of Proposal 2: ' there is an argument, which I have never considered negligible, that it is positively detrimental to Treasury and CSD control if they know how expenditure is going in the course of the year. The argument is that this obscures the constitutional position that it is the Departmental Accounting Officer who is responsible and knowledge shared by the Treasury dilutes the responsibility of the departments'. On balance, he countered, PFOs would be strengthened – particularly against ministerial pressure for higher spending – by the knowledge that the Treasury was regularly monitoring expenditure.
114 As the two officials most directly responsible for the implementation of FIS retrospectively admitted, 'there was no better time to introduce a project for the close monitoring of departments' expenditure than when cash limits were being introduced!' See F.E.R. Butler and K. Aldred, 'The Financial Information Systems Project', *Management Services in Government*, 32 (1977) 24–30.
115 The magnitude of the FIS Study Group's achievement was well summarised in the covering note to its final report by H.A. Copeman: 'It is not an easy subject; it cuts across a number of disciplines, each of which have a professional language – Departmental accounting, Vote control, PESC planning and control, policy decision-making, economic forecasting, financial forecasting, the management of the Consolidated Fund, as well as data processing, systems analysis and Departmental organisation and staff management' (TNA: T353/151, 18 July 1975).
116 See, for example, TNA: T374/37, D.O. Henley to Permanent Secretaries, 24 March and 26 August 1975 and to the Chief Secretary to the Treasury, 15 August 1975.
117 For Brown's maxim, see T374/GEA577/56/02, M. P. Brown to D.O. Henley, 15 January 1976. The implementation team reported to a Steering Committee, on which three of the more recalcitrant departments (DHSS, DES and DI) were deliberately represented. The team itself was divided into a 'Treasury team' of consultants (responsible for writing the necessary programmes) and a 'Departmental team' (which helped departments with their particular problems). A major concession during the planning of Proposal 2 was a *de minimis* limit of £5m for programmes which required monitoring. This cut the paperwork by over 75% whilst only removing some 4% of expenditure from scrutiny.
118 For Brown's praise of PGO staff, led by Ray Heavens, see T374/GEA588/100/01G, letter to F. Clay, 12 October 1977; and for Butler's appreciation of the management consultants, led by Vincent Watts, see section two of his 'last will and testament' of 27 April 1977 in T374/GEA500/148/01. Butler himself won universal praise for his leadership and diplomacy (see, for example, the appreciation by F. Clay in T374/GEA588/100/01F).
119 T374/GEA577/273/01, K. Burgess (of Arthur Andersen) to M.P. Brown, 31 January 1978. Brown had been warned almost immediately about the inflexibility of the system, see a letter by K. Aldred on 17 June 1977 in T374/GEA500/148/01. For her summary of the broader ambitions of FIS, see her letter to all PFOs on 17 November 1977 (TNA: T277/3122).
120 GEA531/332/01, 'Short Term Study of Departmental Financial Information Systems', March 1980. For further details of FMI, see vol 2.
121 See briefing note to Callaghan on 20 October 1976 (TNA: PREM16/794); and for Healey's announcement, see Parl Deb (Commons) 894, cols 1189–90 and below.
122 *Cash Limits on Public Expenditure* (Cmnd 6440). See paras 18 and 19 for the later quotes. Cash limits only covered about half total public expenditure since local government (through rates) and nationalised industries (as trading companies) could raise money independently. Exempt also was expenditure on the 'demand-determined' services of

NOTES FOR CHAPTER 6

central government including, in addition to benefits, expenditure on GPs and support for both agriculture and industry. These services accounted for some 35% of the expenditure sanctioned by Parliamentary estimates.

123 On the first political change, which Harold Wilson famously said 'gave the Treasury 51% of the votes' in Cabinet, see Pliatzky, *Getting and Spending*, pp. 135–6. In relation to the Estimates Committee, its Conservative members were particularly keen to curb public sector wages immediately through cash limits and, after a hostile grilling of Treasury officials in 1975, published a highly critical *Twelfth Report* (see TNA: T331/1086, F. Jones to the Chief Secretary, 25 July 1975). In contrast, in 1976, the Committee lionised Pliatzky for bringing expenditure under control although, as he admitted, he had played little part in either the design or introduction of cash limits.

124 The report by J.A. Marshall, a long-serving Under Secretary in the Public Sector Group, is in TNA: T353/145. The inquiry had started languidly in May 1974 but was hastily concluded in time for a discussion on public expenditure control at Sunningdale (see TNA: CAB164/1249, PERSEC(74)3, from which the first quote is taken). The eventuality of the Conservatives winning the October election also loomed large. Sir Kenneth Berrill, as head of the CPRS, equally condemned cash limits as a 'considerable step back from Plowden' as did Sir Douglas Henley, as head of the Treasury's Public Sector Group (see T353/145, J.A. Marshall to D.O. Henley, 15 August and P. Baldwin to H. Copeman, 27 November 1974). Nevertheless, they had long been used in the NHS in relation to staff costs and had been introduced in relation to construction in 1973 when tenders escalated by 80% in cost.

125 Parl Deb (Commons) 894, cols 1181–90, 1 July 1975 (italics added). The minutes and papers of the Cash Control Group are in TNA: T331/1075–8 and its impact can be tracked in T353/145. For Barnett's concern about the size of the supplementary estimates, which preceded that of Healey with wages, see his meeting with senior officials on 3 December 1974 (T331/1075). The estimates amounted to £3,500m.

126 This paragraph is largely based on the final report of the Cash Control Group, as eventually forwarded by D.O. Henley to the Chief Secretary on 13 May 1975 (TNA: T353/149). Other quotations are taken from a letter to Henley from D. Wass on 11 December 1974 (T331/943); a memorandum by P. Baldwin on 9 December 1974, which was the first seriously to champion cash limits (T353/145); and a riposte from Henley to Wass on 25 February 1975 (T331/1074). As with FIS, practice in West Germany impressed. Medium-term planning as well as current year accounting was in cash not by volume. In France planning was by volume but, unlike in the United Kingdom, it was not binding – whilst annual cash budgets were. For further comparisons, see a note by J. Anson on 3 March 1975 (T331/1082).

127 TNA: T331/1073, K. Couzens to Henley, 3 February 1975. Such ambitions help to explain Couzens' commitment to a statutory incomes policy, to which Donoughue took such exception, see *Diary*, vol 1, p. 447. The alternative to 'economical' was 'economic' – or the containment of cost through efficient management, as advocated by the CSD.

128 For the papers of the Interdepartmental Committee, see TNA: T277/2881–2 and 3106–7; and for the transcripts of the Permanent Secretaries' meetings, the first of which was amicable and the second less so, see T331/1083 and T374/36. Treasury diplomacy was best illustrated by F. Jones' letter to all PFOs in April 1976 thanking them for launching a comprehensive system of cash limits in eight months 'with cooperation and good humour' and J. Anson's suggestion that they report back regularly on the need for any central back-up (see T371/91).

129 The assurance was given most explicitly in the 1976 white paper on public expenditure (Cmnd 6393) and had been exposed as hollow as early as 25 February 1975 by Sir Douglas Henley in a devastating critique to Sir Douglas Wass (TNA: T331/1076). These reservations were regularly repeated by both himself and others.

NOTES FOR CHAPTER 6

130 TNA: T374/36, transcript of meeting on 8 January 1976, p. 2. For a full list of the revaluation factors (which for 1976/7 varied from −12% for land prices to + 84% for postal charges) see the press briefing for Cmnd 6440 in T371/65. Other operating rules, for which departments asked, included the freedom to vire expenditure between blocks and to carry surpluses into the next financial year. To departments, both would have assisted managerial efficiency; but to certain Treasury officials, they represented a threat to managerial discipline. Both were denied on the grounds that they would affect Estimates and that Parliament would not permit such latitude (see T277/3107, IGCC(76)13).

131 TNA: T374/47, statement to the NSS on cash limits; and T371/90 D. Allen to D.O. Henley, 30 May 1975. Ian Bancroft was the CSD'S leading protagonist, initially protesting to Henley on 24 March (T331/1076) and finally on 28 August 1975 (T353/146). Even in West Germany, it was noted, future staff costs were calculated according to a low Government target (because to do otherwise might prejudice the outcome of negotiations). Then the cash limit was surreptitiously raised.

132 TNA: T 371/79. The protagonists in the Treasury were respectively J. Anson (in a minute to F. Jones of 18 September 1975) and P. Baldwin (in a minute to D.O.Henley on 2 September 1975). For the administrative convenience of the centre, there were separate blocks for 'pay and general administrative expenses' and for other expenditure. The former was monitored by the CSD, the latter by the Treasury. However, it made little sense to departments which − for reasons of greater efficiency − wanted the option of viring expenditure between staff and non-staff costs. Cash limits thus provided a further reason for reintegrating the CSD and the Treasury.

133 As late as April 1976, for example, the Interdepartmental Group was still being assured, in relation to specific enquiries, that 'if general rules are needed, they can be formulated when more experience has been gained' (see TNA: T277/3017, IGCC(76)13). However, the Treasury's aversion to firm rules may also have reflected its fear, as later confirmed, that in the last resort it was powerless to impose its will on other departments and that 'too frequent references to Cabinet' would be counterproductive as the 'odds' there were stacked against it (T374/76, I. Beesley to J. Anson on 7 January 1977). An additional reason for earlier improvisation was a staff shortage caused by manpower economies. To release resources for FIS, the Treasury's Historical Section was closed in December 1975 and thus gained the distinction of being the first casualty of cash limits (T371/92).

134 See TNA: T237/47, I. Beesley to F. Jones, 29 July 1976 and T371/69, memorandum by R.H. Wilson, 21 September 1976. The allusion to 'biting' was frequent although it was temporarily replaced in May 1977 by a reference to the 'ultimate flood barrier qualities for which cash limits were in large part devised' (T371/ GEP20/01, PERWG(77)1). Even this memorandum warned, however, that − desirable though it was 'to impart something of the cash limit discipline lower down the chain of formal command' − the imposition of detailed control on departments could be counterproductive in the long run.

135 For the debate within No.10, see TNA: PREM16/794; the Parliamentary statement, Parl Deb (Commons) 918, written answers, col 561, 2 November 1976; and Barnett's triumphant report of 29 November on the winter supplementaries, PREM16/795. On the potential obduracy of PFOs and their ultimate compliance, see I. Beesley to the Chief Secretary, 15 November 1976 (T371/69) and to J. Anson, 4 May 1978 (T374/GEA577/44/01). The underspend in 1976/7 had been 2.6% (or £670m) and in both years was higher in the CSD blocks than the Treasury's (approximately 5% compared to 2%). This reflects in part the CSD's success in achieving the £140m manpower cut. As predicted earlier, there was typically a major 'surge' in the final month of each financial year, with expenditure some 47% above the monthly average.

136 See TNA: PREM16/788, J. Hunt to H. Wilson, 17 March 1976 and a comment by Callaghan on 20 October 1976. Henley had admitted to the Chief Secretary on 15 August 1975, when submitting the key report of the Interdepartmental Group, that it represented 'something of a revolution in our whole attitude and systems' (T331/1083).

137 In 1972 there had been a further retreat from Fisher's 'semi-theological' convention of ministerial responsibility (see above ch 2.2.2 for its last restatement in 1954; and also ch 5.3.3(c)). In 1971, despite its regulation by the DTI, the second largest motor insurance company in Britain (the Vehicle and General) crashed. The resultant tribunal found four officials guilty: an Under Secretary of negligence; two Assistant Secretaries of overcaution; and the whistleblower (a photoprinter) of misconduct. Given that Government had known since the early 1960s that V & G had been flirting with insolvency, the unanswered question was why Ministers (not to mention the industry's regulatory body, the BIA) were not equally castigated. In Parliament it was asserted that the officials could, and should, have publicly defended themselves. This was questionable as, before Parliamentary select committees, they were expressly forbidden so to act (see ch 10.3.2). Officials thus became openly 'responsible' for policy without either the right to defend themselves or the traditional reassurance that their Minister would ultimately provide cover. See especially, R.A. Chapman, 'The Vehicle and General affair', *Public Administration* 51 (1973) 273–90 and TNA: BA17/ 736 and 851.

7 MRS THATCHER AND THE DEMISE OF THE CIVIL SERVICE DEPARTMENT, 1979–81

1 Craig, *British Election Manifestos, 1959–1987*, pp. 269–72.
2 For the importance accorded industrial relations and monetary policy, to the exclusion of administrative reform, see in particular J. Hoskyns, *Just in Time* (2000) and G. Howe, *Conflict of Loyalty* (1994). John Campbell's biography, *Margaret Thatcher* (2 vols, 2000 and 2003) provides a peerless introduction.
3 For Howe's intervention, see BA17/:MG39/386/05D: Preparatory work for the 1979 General Election, J.B. Pearce to Miss Badham, 'Reorganisation of central departments', 2 May 1979, with manuscript note by Sir John Herbecq. For Mrs Thatcher, see the testimony of the first head of her No. 10 Policy Unit (Sir John Hoskyns): 'She had something of a blind spot about organisation because she really did not have it in her experience. I remember her saying to me when she was still in Opposition that there was no problem that could not be settled without two or three motivated intelligent people sitting down for an afternoon and deciding what to do. I thought then how there were problems that would take weeks to define, before people can start to think who is to do what. She came to office with tremendous burning energy and determination, but a simplistic idea. She was always saying that she wanted the people who would fight for what she believed in. That was pretty important. Organisations bored her.' (http://www.ccbh.ac.uk/witness_civilservicereforms_index.php session 2, p. 88; last accessed June 2010).
4 TNA: CAB 128/66, CC(79)1, 10 May 1979. The Cabinet Secretary's notebook for this meeting only records the ratification of the earlier informal decisions and Mrs Thatcher's insistence that bureaucracy had to be diminished.
5 When Rayner was seeking to persuade a meeting of Permanent Secretaries to accept his proposals for long-term reform in May 1980, for example, he stressed the interest of the Conservative Opposition in 1968 in management and the subsequent creation of the Business Team, of which he had been a member (see ch 5.3.3(a)). He then continued that his experience as Chief Executive of the Defence Procurement Agency had 'convinced him that the Service had the talent and capacity to bring about necessary changes. The lead could and indeed must come from the Service'. Earlier the same gathering had

NOTES FOR CHAPTER 7

unanimously accepted that Rayner was 'generally well inclined towards the Civil Service' (see Cabinet Office 35/40, part 7: minutes of the Wednesday morning meeting of Permanent Secretaries, 28 May and 27 February 1980). The Efficiency Unit was initially called 'the Rayner Unit', but its later title has been used a-historically from the start for the sake of consistency. For Rayner's earlier exploits, see above ch 5.3.3 (a) and (c).

6 See Churchill College, Cambridge, MISC 84: Herbecq papers, 'Brief note on events leading to retirement. November 1981', p. 7. Lady Young, on replacing Lord Soames as head of the CSD in September, was not told of her department's imminent closure (pp. 3–4).

7 See Hoskyns, *Just in Time*, p. 309; Churchill College, Cambridge, MISC 84: Herbecq paper, Memoirs, pp. 319–20 (and Soames papers, SOAM/20 for a range of similar appreciations); and Howe, *Conflict*, p. 252. That Soames was 'exactly the type of bluff grandee' the Prime Minister most disliked is confirmed in Campbell, *Thatcher*, vol 2, p. 104, whilst in relation to his discomfiture Howe described him as 'a very big fish if not exactly out of the water then at least in the wrong sized pool of the wrong sort of water' (p. 221). Channon was no better placed, having in 1974 somewhat injudiciously selected Mrs Thatcher as one of three MPs least likely to become Prime Minister – to which she instantly, albeit incorrectly, retorted: 'there will be no room in my government for that millionaire' (*Daily Telegraph* obituary, 20 January 2007).

8 PREM19/245 7 December 1979. The *Report* rejected the term 'quango' (or quasi-autonomous non-governmental organisation) because, rather than being non-governmental, these bodies were deemed to conceal a growth in government. A working definition finally agreed was 'a body which has a role in the process of national government, is not a government department, but is accountable to a minister' (ibid, part 4: R. Luce to N. Ridley, 13 August 1986).

9 PREM19/245: record of a meeting, 28 August 1979. The meeting was also attended by Bancroft, Rayner, Wolfson (the Prime Minister's Chief of Staff) and Pattison (one of her Private Secretaries) and entered Whitehall folklore as a 'shout in'; but the Prime Minister later warmed to Pliatzky for his speedy production of so authoritative a report despite the serious illness of his wife and the need to care for a handicapped son.

10 See TNA: CAB128/66, CC(79)14th.4 and PREM19/245: L. Pliatzky circular, 4 October 1979. The departmental answers were published in Part 2 of the *Report*, while Part 3 contained the categorised list of public bodies.

11 *Report on NDPBs*, para 47.

12 Ibid. Mrs Thatcher herself was guilty of defending certain bodies for which, by her own criteria, there was no *prima facie* case. For example, the Women's National Commission (of which she had been co-chair in the early 1970s) was adjudged to be 'an ineffective body which does not satisfy most of the criteria'. Yet she not only endorsed it but also secured it increased administrative support. See PREM19/245: M.A. Pattison to M. Thatcher, 'Cutting back government', 26 October 1979.

13 *Report on NDPBs*, para 69. Another contentious area was the levy-raising powers of some NDPBs. A major battle was joined, for example, between the Prime Minister and MAFF over the Egg Board, because Mrs Thatcher was incredulous that small producers supported a compulsory levy to finance television advertising. It was finally abolished in 1985 – demonstrating the extent high-level power was expended to achieve such minor economies. See, in particular PREM19/245: L. Pliatzky to M.A. Pattison, 29 November 1979.

14 *Report on NDPBs*, paras 63–84. PREM19/Government Machinery, The future of quangos, part 3: B. Heyhoe to M. Thatcher, 22 April 1981.

NOTES FOR CHAPTER 7

15 PREM19/Government Machinery, The future of quangos, part 3: A. Cockfield to M. Thatcher, 12 July 1983.
16 PREM19/5: J. Hunt memorandum, 16 May 1979.
17 Ibid. For Mrs Thatcher's views, see her comments on CSD's draft paper for Cabinet, 11 May 1979. For opposing views, see Hunt's brief to M. Thatcher on C(79)7 and Ministerial replies to the suggestion of raising the ban on 17 July as well as TNA: CAB128/66, CC(79)2nd.6, 17 May 1979.
18 Ibid: Lord Soames to all Secretaries of State, 5 June 1979. For his later incredulity and Prime-Ministerial support, see 'Note for the record' of a meeting of 10 September attended also by Channon and Wolfson.
19 M. Heseltine, *Where's There a Will* (1987), p. 17.
20 As summarised by R. Armstrong in his brief to the Prime Minister on 31 October 1979 in PREM19/6.
21 Cabinet Secretary's notebook for Cabinet of 1 November 1979; Parl Deb (Commons) 975, col 630, 6 December 1979. Soames had earlier written: 'where it costs more it largely loses its point where the government is concerned, will look like dogma from outside, and will arouse resentment amongst staff' (C(79)38, 'Further action to reduce the size of the Civil Service', 7 September 1979). The assurance that no task would be contracted out, were costs thereby increased, was confirmed in Treasury and Civil Service Committee, Fourth Report (1979–80), *Civil Service Manpower Reductions*, vol 1, para 8.
22 TNA: CAB128/66, CC(79)19th.8, 1 November 1979.
23 See PREM19/6: P. Channon to W. Whitelaw, 24 January 1980; MISC 38; and C(80)15, P. Channon, 'Civil Service cash limits', 26 February 1980, para 10. The commitment to 2.5% was agreed in CC(80)8th.4, 28 February 1980. The calculation of savings is from the Fourth Report of the Treasury and Civil Service Committee (1979–80), vol 1, para 5.
24 C(80)15, para. 17. Rayner's views were summarised by M.A. Pattison to M. Thatcher on 29 February and best expressed in a memorandum on the previous day (see PREM19/153).
25 Mrs Thatcher's Principal Private Secretary admitted to being 'taken aback' by the decision. 'It makes no sense to me', he reasoned, 'to have Rayner assigned to No. 10. Since he wants to proceed by helping all Cabinet Ministers, and needs their collective backing, his proper location is in the Cabinet Office – whence he can still report to the PM as he wishes' (see PREM19/60: K. Stowe to D. Laughrin, 11 May 1979).
26 PREM19/150: M.A. Pattison, 14 June 1980. This admission was in response to a letter from Rayner on 2 May urging the Prime Minister to stay permanently interested in Civil Service reform.
27 PREM19/61: C. Ponting to T. Lankaster, 11 September 1979; *The Guardian* 24 September 1979. Chapman had written in *Your Disobedient Servant*: 'arbitrary percentage cuts in staff and money may sound impressive but they do not work in practice, and worse still they discredit the opportunities for genuine economies'(p. 54). As late as July 1980, however, Mrs Thatcher used the threat of employing Chapman as a goad for recalcitrant ministers, see CC(80)30th.6.
28 PREM19/60: J. Hunt to M. Thatcher, 7 May 1979.
29 In response to Party rhetoric, Rayner was also asked to mount an 'eye-catching' exhibition to illustrate the excessive range of forms which overburdened the public and business. It was eventually mounted by Marks and Spencer's staff in August 1980; but Rayner did subsequently oversee a multi-departmental scrutiny of administrative forms before drafting a less than 'eye-catching' white paper: *Administrative Forms in Government* (Cmnd 8504, 1982).
30 See PREM19/60 for the record of the meetings and the submissions on which they were based (especially D. Rayner to M. Thatcher, 24 May and 3 July 1979). The 'sick lamb' epithet is in a 'Note for the record' by C. Priestley on 26 June 1979. Rayner's

initial views were well summarised in BA17/94/421/02A, Public expenditure cuts, J.B. Pearce to J. Buckley, 21 May 1979.
31 Ibid: 'Note of a meeting' at 10 Downing Street, 16 July 1979. It was at this meeting that, exasperated by the 'turgid' response of Ministers and the feeling that 'pressing ideas into the Civil Service machine was like feeding into a feather bed', she threatened once again 'to let Mr Leslie Chapman loose on departments'.
32 Ibid, part 3: 'Note of a meeting' at No. 10 Downing Street, 2 October 1979. The Cabinet record of the presentations is at TNA: CAB128/66, CC(79)16th.5, 4 October 1979.
33 Ibid, part 4: D. Rayner to M. Thatcher, 'Efficiency and waste in central government: the "Rayner projects"', 30 November 1979, p. 3. This page also refers to the DHSS project as the bedrock of the programme. For the revision of the figures, see Treasury and Civil Service Committee, Fourth Report (1979–80) vol 1, para 10.
34 This paragraph is based on PREM19/365 and Social Services, Rayner study on arrangements for paying social security benefits, part 2. A consultative white paper (Cmnd 8106) was issued in December 1980 and the compromise announced in the House of Commons on 12 May 1981. Rayner was infuriated by the Post Office, which earlier had tried to cancel certain services on the grounds that it should be treated like a business not a charity, and because of the exploitation of the taxpayer by vested interests (see PREM19/Government Machinery, The Rayner programme, part 6: D. Rayner to M. Thatcher, 19 December 1980).
35 PREM19/243: P. Channon to M. Thatcher, 25 March 1980.
36 The original purpose of Cabinet on 1 May, according to M.A. Pattison's brief to Mrs Thatcher on 18 April, was to 'show Sir Derek, Mr Heseltine and Mr Channon between them can offer specific ideas to help Ministers become managers'.
37 PREM19/153: D. Rayner to M. Thatcher, 26 February 1980; and PREM19/154 4: Rayner to P. Channon, 13 March 1980.
38 PREM19/148: T. Lankaster to G. Green, 10 April 1980. On the return to London Channon had admitted to Clive Priestley, who had also attended the meeting, that he was unclear about its outcome. Priestley himself was also uncertain because Mrs Thatcher, as well as hinting that she might take unilateral action as Minister for the Civil Service, had also talked of reducing 'fundamental blocks of work' by one-third. Ibid, part 1: Priestley to T. Lankaster, 10 April 1980.
39 The memorandum was C(80)24, 'Civil Service numbers and cost', 25 April 1980 and the Cabinet minute CC(80)18th.4, 1 May 1980. The note of the meeting on 22 April by M.A. Pattison is in PREM19/148. Earlier drafts had *inter alia* accepted Rayner's call for an independent inspector general so long as the post was attached to the CSD not No. 10; and the first reference to a target figure of 630000 was made in the 11 April draft. It emanated most likely from the Policy Unit but the CSD also claimed paternity (see Churchill College, Cambridge, MISC 84: Herbecq papers, Memoirs, pp. 275–6).
40 PREM19/149: P. Channon to M. Thatcher, 25 April 1980.
41 H. Young, *One of Us* (1989), p. 230.
42 Parl Deb (Commons) 984, cols 1050–61, 13 May 1980. Flatulence was detected by John Garrett, who went on to ask 'why does she give so much support to the clumsy forays of Sir Derek Rayner instead of opting for the systematic method proposed by the Fulton committee' (col 1057). If nothing else, this showed how Rayner's reputation had been tarnished by association with the 'crude cuts' programmes.
43 The full sequence of Cabinet memoranda and minutes is: C(80)43 discussed in CC(80)30th.6, 24 July; C(80)56 discussed in CC(80)36th.7, 23 October; and C(80)74 discussed in CC(80)74, 5 December and CC(80)45th.5, 18 December 1980.
44 PREM19/152 and Civil Service, Long-term management and manpower policy, part 7: R. Armstrong to M. Thatcher, 17 December 1980.

45 Treasury and Civil Service Committee, Fourth Report (1979–80), vol. 1, para 14. The Committee particularly pilloried Sir John Herbecq, who had direct responsibility for the cuts – thereby epitomising the inequity of expecting officials to defend before select committees Ministerial policies against which they had earlier fought (see ch 10.3.2). Herbecq had forcefully opposed the setting of a manpower target 'in advance of any clear conception of how it [was] to be attained' as well as contracting out at any cost. 'What will cause trouble', he argued, 'are cuts which mean that work is transferred outside the Service at greater cost and with less efficiency with the sole aim of reducing Civil Service numbers – as if work were acceptable anywhere and at whatever cost... so long as it is not done by Civil Servants.' See Cabinet Office 35/3. Part 9 annex, Conference of Permanent Secretaries at Sunningdale, PERSEC(80)2, 24/5 October 1980.

46 PREM19/149: F. Pym to M. Thatcher, 30 April 1980. See also ibid, part 7: K. Joseph to C. Soames, 18 May 1981.

47 PREM19/149: R. Armstrong to M. Thatcher, 30 April 1980. The following quotes are from J. Nott to P. Channon, 8 September 1980 (part 5); P. Walker to P. Channon, 3 November 1980 (part 6); and Lord Hailsham to C. Soames, 7 January 1980 (part 7).

48 Ibid, part 7: P. Jenkin to C. Soames, 12 January 1980 and J. Prior to C. Soames, 14 January 1981. Howe's rebuff was in a letter to Soames, 12 February 1981.

49 Ibid, part 4 covers the whole dispute. See especially the exchange of letters between Rayner and Bancroft on the 15 and 16 May; C. Priestley to C. Whitmore on 5 May; and Priestley's annotation on the suggestion in a letter to M.A. Pattison on 21 May that Permanent Secretaries might find it useful at an early stage to consult the CSD – 'like blazes'.

50 TNA: CAB128/66, CC(79)16th; L. Metcalfe and S. Richards, *Improving Public Management* (1990) p. 10.

51 PREM19/62: D. Rayner to M. Thatcher, undated (1 October 1979?) and 30 August 1979. Mrs Thatcher long contested the term 'scrutiny' before accepting that it meant exactly what Rayner intended: 'close investigation, examination into detail'. Ibid: memoranda, 26 October–16 November 1979. For a sympathetic and perceptive account of 'Raynerism' by a former scrutineer, see A.J.M. Bray, *The Clandestine Reformer* (1988).

52 Ibid: Rayner's speaking notes for Cabinet, 4 October 1979.

53 The quotation is from PREM19/Manpower, DE/DHSS study into payment of unemployment benefit: D. Rayner to M. Heseltine, 8 April 1981.

54 PREM19/62 and Government Machinery, Promotion of efficiency and elimination of waste, part 8. The guide was circulated in November 1979 and February 1981. The italics signify an addition in the revised version.

55 Lord Rayner, *The Unfinished Agenda* (1984), p. 10.

56 See PREM19/Government Machinery, Rayner programme, part 10, 'Report on the efficiency of central government', 29 November 1981, para 8; and BA17/MG94/421/02B, Public expenditure cuts: T.P. Turner to B.W. Smith, 29 November 1979 and B.W. Smith to R. Wilson, 10 December 1979.

57 Hunt, as Cabinet Secretary, was fully alive to Ministers' sensitivity. Before Cabinet on 4 October 1979, he stressed to Mrs Thatcher that the programme was 'not a question of the centre arrogating the responsibilities of Departments. The role of central Departments will be limited to giving the thing a push, reviewing progress periodically, and ensuring that lessons are read-across from one area to another'. The hostility towards the CSD displayed in Cabinet fully justified his warning. See TNA: CAB128/66, CC(79)16th.5; Hunt, Cabinet Secretary's notebook 9; and PREM19/62: J.Hunt to M. Thatcher, 3 October 1979.

58 See Efficiency Unit, *Making Things Happen* (1985) and National Audit Office, *The Rayner Scrutiny Programmes, 1981–1983* (1986). These reports covered the projects and three rounds of scrutinies. The 1980 calculations are in PREM19/Government

Machinery, Rayner programme, part 9: D. Rayner progress report to M. Thatcher, 26 June 1981.
59 Centralisation became more intrusive because requests for proposals in each annual round of scrutinies were issued exceptionally from the Prime Minister's, not the Cabinet Office. The terms of reference for each were examined by Rayner, who typically returned a fifth to departments for reconsideration. He then took a close interest in the more important scrutinies and in the drafting of all reports and 'action plans'. A collegiate spirit was also consistently nurtured amongst scrutineers with, in February 1980, a reception even being held in No. 10 for all those involved in the original 'projects'. All this greatly strained conventions of departmental loyalty.
60 PREM19/244: D. Rayner progress report to M. Thatcher, 19 December 1980, paras 34–5. The 1981 round was adjudged particularly disappointing because the total number of jobs covered was only 8000 – less than the potential savings from the 1980 round (ibid: D. Rayner to M. Thatcher, 30 January 1981). In October 1980, Rayner had complained to Mrs Thatcher that some scrutineers were becoming 'dispirited by the lack of support from the top' of their departments and that he was 'minded to disengage' from such departments. See PREM19/152: M.A. Pattison to C. Priestley, 15 October 1980.
61 For the above quotations, see PREM19/244: D. Rayner progress report to M. Thatcher, 19 December 1979, para 11; and PREM19/Manpower, DE/DHSS study into the payment of unemployment benefit, part 1: D. Rayner to F. Pym, 17 March 1981 and Pym's reply, 23 March 1981. See also Metcalfe and Richards, *Improving Public Management*, p. 14.
62 The unemployed frequently had to register for work at a jobcentre, claim benefit from an Unemployment Benefit Office and then have it topped up with supplementary benefit at a DHSS office.
63 Metcalfe and Richards, *Improving Public Management*, p. 110. The following examples are taken from letters written to W. Whitelaw, as chair of the Home Affairs Committee, by M. Heseltine (27 February 1981) and G. Howe (3 March). See also PREM19/Manpower, DE/DHSS study into the payment of unemployment benefit, part 1: M.A. Pattison to M. Thatcher, 5 March 1981.
64 Ibid, parts 1 and 2: annotations on letters from G. Howe to M. Thatcher, 23 January 1981 and N. Fowler to M. Thatcher, 16 February 1983. The dispute saw a rare defeat for Alan Walters, the Prime Minister's economic adviser, who endorsed Rayner's original suggestion that checks on fraud should initially be limited, but that after three months all claimants should be obliged to accept any work in their relevant area. Fowler successfully opposed this in a letter to Thatcher on 27 May 1982. Even Norman Tebbit had supported the holiday dispensation, on family grounds.
65 See Metcalfe and Richards, *Improving Public Management*, ch 6. Decreasing integrity was reflected by the 31 changes to the criteria for unemployment statistics between 1981 and 1997.
66 Rayner, perhaps unwisely, issued detailed instructions to Ministers for the pilot scrutiny (see PREM19/Civil Service, Annual scrutiny of departmental running costs, part 1: D. Rayner to W. Whitelaw, 22 February 1980. To authenticate the scrutiny, Channon had to reissue the instructions on 22 April.
67 The returns were summarised in C(81)5 and discussed in Cabinet on 29 January 1981, see CC(81)4th. The increase in costs was later revised down to 19% which, given the impact of the large pay award sanctioned by the outgoing Labour Government, suggests costs may not have been so out of control and the anger rather synthetic.
68 PREM19/Civil Service, Annual Scrutiny of departmental running costs, part 1: Soames to M. Thatcher, 11 May 1981; D. Rayner to Thatcher, 18 May 1981, para 10; C. Whitmore to Thatcher, 22 May 1981. Mrs Thatcher agreed that 'the worst fears of the CSD are confirmed'.

69 BA17/:MG94/421/02A, Public expenditure cuts: note of conversation between Bancroft and Rayner, 7 November 1979; and PREM19/Government Machinery, Rayner programme, part 7: note by M.A. Pattison, 18 December 1980. As will be described in the next volume, presentations on MINIS were given to the Prime Minister in September and, after the demise of the CSD, to Ministers and their Permanent Secretaries in February 1982. The February meeting was not a success, as the Chief Whip had predicted (see PREM19/Civil Service, Annual scrutiny of running costs, part 2: M. Jopling to C. Whitmore, 5 February 1982 and M. Heseltine, *A Life in the Jungle* (2000), p. 193.
70 Rayner, *Unfinished Agenda*, pp.12–15.
71 PREM19/Civil Service, Annual scrutiny of departmental running costs, part 1: M.A. Pattison to C.Whitmore, 13 January 1981.
72 The Policy Unit criticism was reported to the Prime Minister by Pattison on 20 January 1981 and the Chancellor of the Exchequer on 28 May agreed later that the scrutiny was in danger of being 'overelaborate and expensive'. Nott's letter of 26 September 1980 and its annotations are in PREM19/152.
73 PREM19/Civil Service, Annual scrutiny of running costs, part 1: D. Rayner to P. Channon, 18 December 1980 and to M. Thatcher, 23 December 1980.
74 See above, ch 7.2.3. The fuller wording was drafted by K. Stowe in the amended minute to Ministers of 31 May 1979 (PREM19/62). A preliminary draft of the lasting reforms programme was submitted to Mrs Thatcher on 4 January 1980 and the final one on 26 March 1980, when it was approved at a meeting with Channon, Rayner, Bancroft, Armstrong and Priestley. Mrs Thatcher informed the Chancellor of the Exchequer of her decision on 3 April and a duly amended version became the memorandum C(80)25 discussed at Cabinet on 1 May (see PREM19/147).
75 Hence the title of his 1984 Stamp Memorial lecture, *The Unfinished Agenda*, and the comment therein that 'things did not really get going until 1982' (p. 14). There was a simultaneous battle within the No. 10 Policy Unit between Hoskyns and Norman Strauss over whether Civil Service reform should be a task for a first, second or third term in office.
76 PREM19/149: invitation by C. Whitmore, 1 May 1980. Bancroft's suggestions were submitted to Whitmore on 2 May, Priestley's on 5 and 6 May. A meeting to encourage mutual trust had been suggested by both Rayner and Whitelaw. Bancroft proposed a dinner. It was intended to be an annual event.
77 M. Thatcher, *The Downing Street Years* (1993), p. 48. Officials' recollections informed the accounts in H. Young, *One of Us* (1989), pp. 230–1 and Hennessy, *Whitehall*, p. 629.
78 PREM19/149: I. Bancroft to C. Whitmore, 2 May 1980. The Permanent Secretaries' letters of thanks to the Prime Minister are in the same file, except for Cooper's and Bancroft's which are in PREM19/150. Rampton (Energy), Garlick (Environment), Baldwin (Transport) and Clucas (Trade) were, with Nairne, the greatest enthusiasts.
79 Hennessy, *Whitehall*, p. 592. Earlier Hennessy records Bancroft's lament that 'ritual words of praise, forced out through clenched teeth in public, deceive no one if they are accompanied by noisy and obvious cuffs round the ears in semi-private' (p. 150).
80 PREM19/147: D. Rayner to M. Thatcher, 'The efficiency of central government: lasting reforms' paras 22–3.
81 Initially the programme had seven targets. These were a factual summary of *all* departmental resources; a theoretical exercise on their management and the development of a plan to clarify departmental responsibilities; and critical examinations of the role of central departments, the management of people, work management and of the responsibilities of Ministers and officials alike. The latter was the most controversial, raising questions about effectiveness of Parliamentary, Ministerial and official control, and was replaced in the final programme by a greater emphasis on 'the scale of government' (see PREM19/242: C. Priestley to M.A. Pattison, 4 January 1980).

82 PREM19/Civil Service, Long-term management and manpower policy, part 7: interview with P. Hennessy, 26 February 1981. Surprisingly technology was never identified as a means of reducing the scale of government.
83 Ibid, part 1: D. Rayner to M. Thatcher, 18 April 1980. The general aim, as expressed in *The Reorganisation of Central Government*, was 'less government, and better government carried out by fewer people' (see above ch 5.3.1). Rayner's specific objectives were based on lessons learnt from the 1979 projects and the subject of a powerful letter to the Prime Minister on administrative reform by John Nott on 12 March 1980 (ibid).
84 Ibid, part 8: Rayner to B. Heyhoe, 22 April 1981. Rayner's initial aims had been expressed to Mrs Thatcher on 26 February 1980 (PREM19/153). Wardale was a former Second Permanent Secretary of the Department of Environment.
85 Ibid: letters to M. Thatcher by Soames, 16 July, W. Whitelaw, 17 September and Hailsham, 21 September 1981. For officials' attack on the 35% target as impractical and, more generally, Rayner's response as 'superficial and wedded to prejudices that a grade should be abolished regardless of the evidence', see BA8/5/2 (2): S. Taylor to C.W. Hopkinson, 5 May 1981; and 5/2(1) G. Wardale to I. Bancroft, 31 March 1981. Rayner's condemnation of the 'amiable coterie' was in the same lecture as his praise for the 20% cut in senior posts achieved after Wardale, see *Unfinished Agenda*, pp. 9, 12 and 16.
86 Ibid, part 1: the first draft submitted by D. Rayner to M. Thatcher, 26 March 1980, para 14a. The excised passage is from para 18.
87 Ibid, para 17a. The terminology came from the USA where progress chasers called inspector generals had been appointed in 1978; but they worked within federal departments and reported direct to their departmental head as well as to Congress.
88 Ibid, Bancroft to Rayner, 18 July 1980. Rayner replied that the post would be accountable to a central Minister – Mrs Thatcher as First Lord of the Treasury and Minister for the Civil Service (ibid, parts 4 and 5). The other opposition had come from Hoskyns in the Policy Unit, Wass and even from Whitmore, as the Prime Minister's Principal Private Secretary. It replicated Stowe's initial reaction to the siting of the Efficiency Unit outside the Cabinet Office in 1979.
89 A copy of the report, and the response to it, is in PREM19/Government Machinery, Review of the Exchequer and Audit Acts, part 1.
90 Ironically, the CSD welcomed the creation of a 'single body of accounting expertise' at the centre, while the Treasury resisted the transfer to it of the Head of the Accountancy Service because it would involve it in such detailed work (see BA8/Organisation of the Centre, 6/3 (6): R.W.L. Wilding to I. Bancroft, 8 December 1980 and 19 February 1981). The dispute also raised doubts about the leadership qualities of the Head of the Government Accountancy Service, K. Sharp, and the downgrading of the position from Second Permanent Secretary to Under Secretary on transfer to the Treasury was agreed. This flew in the face of Rayner's instincts concerning professionalism; but accountants, it was pointed out, should simply advise and not be financial managers.
91 C(81)26, 2 June 1981, para 7. Rayner had earlier informed the Prime Minister that 'the Chancellor of the Exchequer, the Lord President and I take the view that central departments should drop a good deal of the "consultancy" flavour from their role and become much more prescriptive' (PREM19/Civil Service, Long-term management and manpower policy, part 7: D. Rayner to M. Thatcher, 'The Management Review Programme', 30 January 1981). The Chancellor and his policy advisers had wanted, as in 1919, PFOs to be 'outposts' of the Treasury but were defeated by Rayner and senior Treasury officials. Instead Rayner favoured plain speaking and action, such as the rejection of departmental estimates, denial of honours and the dismissal of Permanent Secretaries (see BA8/Organisation of the Centre 6/3 (4): D. Rayner to G. Howe, 27 August 1980, paras 4–7 and 24–26).

NOTES FOR CHAPTER 7

92 PREM19/Government Machinery, Rayner programme, part 8: C. Priestley to W. Rickett, 15 May 1981 and 'Record of the main points made in discussion at presentation on financial management', 8 September 1981 (ibid, part 9). Wolfson's objection was noted by W. Rickett on the submission to M. Thatcher of the draft Cabinet paper on 15 May 1981. Mrs Thatcher 's own conclusion was: 'it is a beautifully written narrative . . . but it will not make any difference whatsoever . . . we just haven't the expertise to do what we ought' (ibid, part 8). Rayner replied on 8 July 1981 (ibid, part 9).

93 PREM19/62: D. Rayner to P. Channon, 28 November 1979; and D. Rayner to M. Thatcher, 23 January 1981 (ibid, part 7). For the row with Heseltine, see M. Heseltine to M. Thatcher, 6 February 1981 (ibid, part 8). The means of increasing the PSA's efficiency was also a flashpoint between Rayner and Chapman (who had long advocated an army of outside auditors).

94 The compromise was originally suggested by Rayner in his letter to Channon of 28 November 1979 (ibid) and finally acted upon on 10 August 1981, see B. Heyhoe to W. Whitelaw (PREM19/Civil Service, Long-term management and manpower policy, part 8). Repayment for training and accommodation had both been the subject of Rayner projects in 1979, the latter leading to the 1980 interdepartmental Kemp report, *Repayment for PSA Services*, which recommended full cash repayment and sparked a major political row (ibid, part 8: M. Heseltine to M. Thatcher, 6 February 1981). Another technical issue, which Rayner strove to reform, was 'annuality', the prevention of departments carrying unused resources over into the following financial year. Little progress was made because, as has been seen, it was regarded as essential to Parliamentary control.

95 PREM19/148: R.T. Armstrong to M. Thatcher, 21 April 1980. The section excised from the original draft of 26 March 1980 was paragraph 10b (PREM19/147). Rayner did send to Geoffrey Howe, who typically opposed reform, some 'principles of good management' on 28 April 1980 (PREM19/149). 'Machiavelli is not dead', he wrote, and to retain independence of thought and action he recommended various techniques, such as planning by Ministers of their own diaries and first-hand contact with those who 'actually do the job (Knowledge is power)'.

96 PREM19/148: opposition came from a wide range of people, including A. Cockfield as Minister of State in the Treasury (21 April 1980) and R. Ibbs as head of CPRS (24 April 1980). Rayner modified his views during an interview with the *Daily Mail* on 21 April 1981 (question 14), but Mrs Thatcher did not in her comments to B. Heyhoe on 4 August 1981 (ibid, part 8).

97 PREM19/147: D. Rayner to M. Thatcher, 'The efficiency of central government: lasting reforms', March 1980, para 2d. The principal excisions were from paras 41–2.

98 See ibid, part 7: Soames to W. Whitelaw, 24 February 1981 for the preparation of the scheme. An alternative strategy, favoured by Rayner, was direct outside recruitment (as with PFOs) but this was surprisingly vetoed by Mrs Thatcher. Until the recruitment ban of 1979, 25 outside appointments had typically been made each year to senior administrative posts; and in 1981, the CSD wanted to revive the practice. The Prime Minister, however, was persuaded by colleagues that able young officials would be demoralised by a further shrinkage of promotion prospects (see B. Heyhoe to W. Whitelaw, 6 February 1981,with an annotation by Mrs Thatcher which led to the proposal's withdrawal in April).

99 The exercise was agreed by Cabinet in CC(80)20.4 and, given deteriorating relations with Parliament, was abruptly abandoned in April 1981 (see below ch 10.3 and ibid, part 8: F. Pym to B. Heyhoe, 25 March 1981). 'Alibi consciousness' was a phrase coined by Rayner (para 43 of the original March draft of the lasting reforms programme); and Hunt and Armstrong expressed their respective support on 7 May 1979 and 21 April 1980 (see PREM19/60; and PREM19/148: annex, para 15). Thoms' protest is amongst others recorded in BA17/MG94/421/02A, Public expenditure cuts, 9 November 1979.

NOTES FOR CHAPTER 7

100 Rayner recommended fewer automatic honours for senior officials and more for junior officials in recognition of specific achievements. See paras 25–6 in the original programme which were later excised (PREM19/147: D. Rayner to M. Thatcher, 26 March 1980).

101 PREM19/152: R.T. Armstrong to C. Whitmore, 3 November 1980. For Whitelaw's and Hailsham's objections, see their letters to Soames on 2 and 6 November, and 4 December. Soames' revised proposal (C(81)2) was rejected by Cabinet on 15 January 1981 (CC(81)2nd.6)., but not before a major row between Soames and Howe over the Treasury's suggestion that increased increments should be funded by reductions in basic pay. This, it was pointed out, would break legally enforceable contracts and was based on the misapprehension that officials were overpaid in relation to the private sector (Soames to G. Howe, 14 November and 1 December, ibid, PREM 19/Civil Service and Long term management & manpower policy, part 7).

102 PREM19/148: Rayner's admission to Mrs Thatcher on 18 April 1980 that the programme 'would crown much useful thinking that had been going on slowly over the past ten years or so'. For the extent of this 'useful thinking', see BA17/MG94/421/02A-B, Public expenditure cuts. Support within the Service was also stifled by the nature of Rayner's appointment and the way he was lauded by both Ministers and the media. During the negotiations over lasting reforms, for example, the CCSU attacked his 'presidential appointment' and the impression that all the problems of a 'swollen and growing bureaucracy' could be solved by 'one man and a boy' (TNA: T275/196, W.L. Kendall to I. Bancroft, 7 July 1980).

103 Howe, *Conflict*, p. 221. The final offer was 7.5% (as compared to the original union demand of 15%) and was compatible with the 6% cash limit because of an acceleration in the reduction in manpower – thereby helping to attain the 630,000 target.

104 For example, Armstrong, Cabinet Secretary's notebook 7: notes for the CC(81)20th.4, 21 May 1980.

105 See Hoskyns, *Just in Time*, p. 196; PREM19/Civil Service, Pay and pensions, parts 3 and 4: J. Hoskyns to M. Thatcher, 8 April and 18 May 1981; I. Gilmour, *Dancing with Dogma* (1992) p. 51 and J. Prior, *A Balance of Power* (1986).

106 Gilmore, *Dancing*, p. 51. Treasury officials also privately admitted a better deal could have been struck in June, see PREM19/Civil Service, Pay and pensions, part 6: meeting in the Chancellor's room, 30 July 1981, para 4. Taking a broader view, it could be argued (as it has been, for example, by Sir John Hoskyns in private correspondence) that 'Gilmour got it exactly wrong... At just £500m and a lot of ruffled feathers, it was a snip; the first real stepping-stone to economic stability'.

107 This and the following paragraph are based on papers by W. Ryrie (of the Treasury) and Sir J. Herbecq (of the CSD) and the transcript of the Sunningdale debate in CAB164/Cabinet Office 35/3, part 9: Annex. Herbecq characterised Treasury policy as 'investment in failure'.

108 TNA: CAB134/4335, E(79)15, Chancellor of the Exchequer, 'Cash limits for 1980–81 and public sector pay', 3 July 1979, para 2.

109 Before the strike, decentralisation had been deemed dangerous, and therefore rejected, until local management had been strengthened (see PREM19/181: R.T. Armstrong to M. Thatcher, 12 February 1980).

110 See, for example, PREM19/Civil Service, Pay and pensions, part 6: meeting in the Chancellor's room, 3 July 1981.

111 PREM19/147: D. Rayner to M. Thatcher, 26 March 1980, para 39. Rayner's assertion that 'some advances had been blocked by Luddism' was later amended to 'staff associations'; but in his draft speech for Mrs Thatcher at the Permanent Secretaries' dinner in May 1980, Priestley still alluded to the fact that 'since the Fulton Report there has been a somewhat tiring tension between the developing accountability of

NOTES FOR CHAPTER 7

staff and the staff association's insistence on rights and interests' (PREM 19/149, 6 May 1980). One of the objectives of the dinner was, of course, to pool ideas on how to minimise union resistance.

112 PREM19/148: W.L. Kendall to I. Bancroft, 17 April 1980. The General Secretary was Ken Thomas of the CPSA at the 71st meeting of the National Whitley Council on 31 July 1980.

113 See in particular the Chancellor of the Exchequer's memoranda on public sector pay at CAB134/E(80)46, 2 June 1980 and E(80)118, 13 October 1980.

114 PREM19/Civil Service, Pay and pensions, parts 3 and 5: J. Hoskyns to M. Thatcher, 8 April and 8 June 1981. These views are more fully and forcefully expressed in Hoskyns, *Just in Time*, esp pp. 193, 293 and 304.

115 Whitmore had informed Bancroft of the decision on 22 September and reported back to Mrs Thatcher that it had come 'as a great surprise: he clearly had no inkling of the way your mind was moving'. For this, the transcript of the 24 September meeting and Robert Armstrong's use of the epithet 'unhappy' in a minute to C. Whitmore on 30 September 1981, see PREM19/Government Machinery, Future of the CSD, part 4. In the face of hostile leaks, CSD officials continued to display exceptional integrity by keeping the decision secret for two months. Bancroft, however, permitted himself one last protest to the Prime Minister on 9 October. 'I believe', he wrote, 'the re-organisation will make the Service a less efficient instrument to serve the Government of the day. It splits a number of closely inter-related functions and is fundamentally unstable . . . . It will be ill-received within the Service. To many, it will be seen as further evidence of the low esteem with which this Administration regards its employees . . . You have made your decision, and I will now hold my peace' (ibid).

116 Another passage excised from an early draft of the 'lasting reforms' programme had given a full explanation, asserting that the separation 'gave credence to a fundamental misconception, namely treating manpower, organisation, personnel and indeed "management" as different in kind from the policies, programmes and operations which in fact dictate the use of resources. This tended to suppress the importance of money as the critical factor in management' (see PREM19/147: D. Rayner to M. Thatcher, 26 March 1980, para 15). More succinctly Rayner later confided to the *Sunday Telegraph*: 'I've never known a business organisation with two headquarters at opposite ends of the street. It's crazy' (1 February 1981). Lord Plowden, when asked in 1979 to reflect on the changes he had earlier inspired, took a broader view. The CSD 'undoubtedly' knew and had done much good personnel work but had signally failed to 'establish itself as an authority on major questions of how government actually does, and should, work; of the structure and style of central government as a whole' and of its optimal relationship with outside bodies (see Churchill College, Cambridge: Plowden papers, PLDN 2/3/6, memo of 22 November 1979).

117 Treasury and Civil Service Committee, *The Future of the Civil Service Department* (HC 54, 1980–1), para 12. Rayner was cited in the same paragraph as asking why, given the combined responsibilities of Permanent Secretaries as accounting officers within departments, control over money and men could not also be united at the centre.

118 For Rayner's comments and Priestley's gender-related observation, see PREM19/250: D. Rayner to M. Thatcher, 22 July 1980 and Priestley's insistence to Rayner, 16 July 1980 on the need for a powerful centre to stop departmental management being regarded largely as a 'private matter, settled by the action or inaction of top people'. See also PREM19/Prime Minister, Visits to government departments, part 3: D. Rayner to M. Thatcher, 9 January 1980, para 13; PREM19/149: C. Priestley to C. Whitmore, 5 May 1980; and ibid, part 8: M.A. Pattison to M. Thatcher, 9 March 1981. These files regularly allude to private dinners and meetings at which Rayner discussed Ministerial and official personalities with the Prime Minister.

NOTES FOR CHAPTER 7

119 The white paper responding to the Committee's report (*The Future of the Civil Service Department*) concurred that 'the right course at the present time [was] to strengthen and improve the existing organisation rather than change the machinery of Government' and that the CSD was an 'essential instrument' for 'the good management of central administration and the achievement of a smaller and more efficient Civil Service' (paras 2 and 9). Later, to expedite reform, Armstrong suggested the replacement of Bancroft – on his retirement – by a dynamic young 'progress chaser', with the title of Head of the Civil Service either being scrapped or transferred elsewhere (see PREM19/Government Machinery, Future of the CSD, part 4: R.T. Armstrong to C. Whitmore, 20 May 1981).

120 Letter by Lord Armstrong, *The Times*, 8 July 1980. Later, it was admitted that such dangers could be averted were CSD personnel to be transferred to the Treasury's public expenditure divisions to create an effective Office of Management and Budget within the Treasury with its own Cabinet minister (the Chief Secretary) and Permanent Secretary (who might be designated Head of the Service). Before 1968, after all, the Treasury had had joint Permanent Secretaries.

121 BA8/Organisation of the Centre, 6/3 (5), W.L. Kendall to I. Bancroft, 7 October 1980.

122 PREM19/5: J. Hunt to M. Thatcher, 14 June 1979. Rayner went so far as to advise Mrs Thatcher that the CSD was her 'department and it seems odd to suggest to the Prime Minister, qua Minister for the Civil Service, that she should be denied the ability to use it' (PREM19/62: D. Rayner to M. Thatcher, 24 September 1979, para 7e). CSD officials concurred. Recognising that the Department's establishment might have been a mistake, for example, Herbecq identified the need 'either to wind it up or, with the authority of the Prime Minister ... put some weight behind it and use it effectively' (Churchill College, Cambridge, MISC 84: Herbecq papers, Memoirs, p. 274).

123 Hunt, Cabinet Secretary's notebook 9. For Mrs Thatcher's views, see *Downing Street Years*, p. 48 and PREM19/250: record of a meeting on 23 July 1980.

124 PREM19/250: note for the record of a meeting on 14 November. This file and the preceding one in the sequence document Bancroft's battles and can be supplemented by his personal files: BA8/Organisation of the Centre, 6/3 (1–7). Individual references from these files will be provided later, when apposite.

125 Bancroft rebuffed Peter Kellner's allegation (after an interview with Rayner) in the *Sunday Times*, 31 August 1980.

126 The history of Treasury control was debated by the 'big four' at their meeting on 18 June 1980 (BA8/Organisation of the Centre, 6/3(2)). Bancroft also argued that 'deep' integration was inappropriate because all areas of management had become more specialised since 1962; and he was supported in this by the then head of the CPRS and Rayner's ultimate successor (Robin Ibbs), who argued that all large organisations should have discrete personnel departments divorced from all economic responsibility (see PREM19/250: Ibbs to R.T. Armstrong, 31 October 1980).

127 The report and covering letter were sent to the Prime Minister on 30 June (PREM19/249). The report, despite Rayner's best efforts, won unusual praise for Bancroft from the Prime Minister.

128 PREM19/250: record of a meeting on 23 July 1980, which was attended by Howe, Soames and Wolfson as well as the 'big four'. Bancroft's cause may have been helped from an unlikely source: the No. 10 Policy Unit. Hoskyns had minuted the Prime Minister in June (n.d.) that abolition of the CSD would be a 'strategic error' because, although he was no friend, he saw it – like Rayner in 1979 – as a possible nucleus for a 'ministry of change' to dynamise the Service as a whole. Simultaneously, Hoskyns and Strauss of the Policy Unit held an indiscreet meeting with Lord Crowther-Hunt and Kellner, following the publication of *The Civil Servants* (with its savage attack on

officialdom) and reportedly compounded their indiscretion by offering Kellner a job in the Unit, despite his being an active Labour Party member.
129 See BA8/Organisation of the Centre, 6/3 (3) for the epithet, recorded immediately after the 23 June meeting; 6/3 (4) for the transcript of the Permanent Secretaries' meeting; and 6/3 (4 and 5) for correspondence with the unions. Some Permanent Secretaries, especially Nairne and Cooper, favoured central action to enforce best practice on management systems in the belief that this would maximise devolution of detailed decision-making to departments.
130 Bancroft's covering note (which included Wass' admission of a change of heart) is in PREM19/250. See also BA8/Organisation of the Centre 6/3 (6), G. Howe to Prime Minister, 13 November 1980. Wass additionally feared Ministerial overload and a dilution of the Treasury's financial expertise, whilst Howe foresaw his department becoming 'schizophrenic over public expenditure and public sector pay as well as increasing militancy among his staff'. Soames, ironically, continued to support a merger (ibid, meeting with Prime Minister, 15 October 1980).
131 *The Future of the Civil Service Department*. The report advocated the revitalisation of the CSD over a merger 'at the present time' because of the potential disruption. The Committee had also been swayed by the growing specialism of personnel policy; the Treasury's lack of expertise and time to develop it; and suspicions about Rayner's analogy of the Civil Service with business. Evidence from Sir Anthony Part, Sir Samuel Goldman, William Plowden and Lord Croham had been particularly persuasive on these points. The Committee had also been deeply divided between Conservative (who favoured a merger) and opposition MPs (who championed either a revitalised CSD or a Public Service Commission).
132 PREM19/Government Machinery, Future of the CSD, part 3: minutes by Mrs Thatcher, 18 and 22 January 1981; Rayner's reply, 22 January; and, for the admission of Treasury guilt, Howe to Mrs Thatcher, 27 January. Wass also apologised to Bancroft on 23 January for 'your exposure to Prime Ministerial displeasure on our account' (BA8/Organisation of the Centre, 6/3 (7)).
133 PREM19/Government Machinery, Future of the CSD, part 4: R.T. Armstrong to C. Whitmore, 20 May 1981 for the first plan; Whitmore to Armstrong, 22 May 1981 for Mrs Thatcher's conclusion; and D. Rayner to M. Thatcher, 29 June 1981 for the revised assault.
134 Ibid: C. Whitmore to R.T. Armstrong, record of a meeting with Armstrong and Rayner on 7 September.
135 The debate over creation of a Prime Minister's Department became particularly heated in September 1981 (see for example PREM19/Government Machinery, Future of the CSD, part 4: R.T. Armstrong to C. Whitmore, 21 September 1981 and Prime Ministerial annotations). The proposal to create an Inspector General (which was interpreted as an attempt by Rayner, in anticipation of his retirement, to institutionalise his own role) had earlier prompted an attempt to resolve the long-running battle over the accountability of the Efficiency Unit. Eventually, in July 1981, an additional Second Secretary was appointed to the CSD (J.S. Cassells), with all officials working in the Efficiency Unit instructed to report to him. However, the appointment was not a success (Cassells' managerial achievements at the MSC having been largely dependent on an effective partnership with his deputy, Geoffrey Holland); and, in any case, Rayner retained the right to report direct to the Prime Minister. The Efficiency Unit (particularly if linked to the MPO), therefore, remained a potential nucleus for a Prime Minister's Department – whatever the personal hostility of Rayner and his staff to such a development.
136 Ibid: R.T. Armstrong to M. Thatcher, 16 October 1981.
137 Parl Deb (Commons) 16, cols 368, 374, 20 January 1982.
138 PREM19/Government Machinery, Future of the CSD, part 4: D. Rayner to M. Thatcher, 29 June 1981, para. 3. For a perceptive contemporary account of the

historic forces behind the CSD's downfall see J.M. Lee, 'Epitaph for the CSD', *Public Administration* 60 (1982) 3–9.
139 Sir John Herbecq, as noted in ch 7.3.1, was particularly pilloried by the Treasury Select Committee for failing to expand on the political, economic and social consequences of the 'arbitrary' 630,000 manpower target – whilst at a Sunningdale conference of Permanent Secretaries he deplored the arbitrariness of the *Ministerial* decision. Likewise Bancroft had to support Ministers by denying the target was arbitrary at the National Whitley Council in July 1980. Herbecq's embarrassment was taken in No. 10 as further proof of the CSD's inadequacies (see CAB164/Cabinet Office 35/3, part 9, Annex).
140 Sir Anthony Part's evidence to the Committee, para 14, printed as appendix 1 in its report (*Future of the CSD*). The Chancellor's antics particularly angered Channon, see his letter to Soames on 21 July 1980 (BA8/Machinery of Government at the centre).
141 Ibid, K. Stowe to I. Bancroft, 25 July 1980.
142 J. Hoskyns, 'Westminster and Whitehall: an outsider's view', *Fiscal Studies* 3 (1982) 163.
143 See, for example, G.K. Fry, 'The British career Civil Service under challenge', *Political Studies*, 34, 1986, pp. 533–55.
144 PREM19/Government Machinery, Future of the CSD, part 3: D. Rayner to M. Thatcher, 15 December 1980.
145 Ibid, part 3: D. Rayner to M. Thatcher, 22 January 1981.

8 WHITLEYISM, 1966–81

1 The Bullock Committee had been appointed at the instigation of the then most powerful trade union leader and architect of the social contract, Jack Jones, who also became one of its members. The majority report recommended an equal number of trade unionists and shareholder representatives on the boards of larger private companies; but a minority report (written by employers' representatives) vehemently opposed such a suggestion. This made it impracticable. As Callaghan confided to the NSS before the report's publication: 'there was a risk that industrial democracy could be the CBI's Industrial Relations Bill. He was not interested in enacting legislation that the Conservatives would repeal' (TNA: PREM16/1170, transcript of meeting on 20 January 1977). See also Morgan, *Callaghan*, pp. 560–2. In the Civil Service it led to a formal, and largely ineffectual, review of Whitleyism in 1979.
2 There was a continuing debate in the 1970s, and in subsequent union histories, over when staff associations should properly be called trade unions. By December 1974 even Leslie Williams and the *Whitley Bulletin* were objecting to the term 'staff association' (vol 54, no 10, p. 160). 1976, with the affiliation of all but the FDA to the TUC, is conventionally seen as the watershed. In this chapter, however, the formal change of name in 1979 will be taken as decisive. This is because attitudes differed so much between each organisation, and between leaders and activists. Activists within the SCPS, for example, would certainly have regarded themselves as trade unionists by 1976, whereas the General Secretary of the CPSA was still ambivalent in 1981 (see the extract from his diary in ch 8.5). The smaller unions were particularly reluctant to make the change; and none, unlike most unions affiliated to the TUC, had a political levy.
3 The reasons for escalating militancy were fully examined in *Civil Servants and Change* (1975), the final report of the *Wider Issues* review (see ch 8.3.1). Foremost amongst them was the postwar predominance of officials based in the traditional heartlands of labour militancy, as opposed to their prewar concentration in the more docile South East of England. Hence the particular effectiveness of selective action during the 1979 and 1981 strikes in Scotland and the North East of England. Ironically the planned dispersal of further jobs to these regions, to combat unemployment and cut costs, was discouraged by such militancy.

NOTES FOR CHAPTER 8

4 The anomaly became ever more glaring under the perceived attack on the Service by the Conservative Government after 1979. 'The Trade Union side', it was stated at the 1980 National Whitley Council, 'recognised the constitutional limits imposed on the Official Side but the Official Side cannot be above the battle'. Even more provocatively the SCPS representative at the meeting in 1979 claimed Whitleyism was being 'destroyed because the Official Side was becoming an instrument of Government' (see the transcripts of the respective meetings in TNA: T275/195–6).

5 The danger of anarchy and the need to maintain Whitleyism in order to prevent it was a common refrain of both the staff and official sides in public and in private. See for example BA22/ P(1)334/523/03L, memorandum by W.L. Kendall, 19 August 1977.

6 Cmnd 3638, paras 269–274.

7 As General Secretary since 1967, Kendall was described by CSD negotiators as a 'quiet and somewhat mixed-up character' whose advocacy of militancy and strike action was designed to advance his members' interests rather than wider political ends. He was therefore designated a moderate (which was borne out by his later confession that 'unions are not revolutionary or particularly radical . . . but are conservative and essentially reactive', see Churchill College, Cambridge, SOAM/20, Kendall to Lord Soames, 15 September 1981). Personal information, as for all union leaders in this subsection, is based on a mix of CSD briefs in TNA: PREM15/776 and 1346; the records of the CCSU at the Modern Records Centre, University of Warwick (MSS 296/1995); and private information (including the 1981 strike diary of Ken Thomas).

8 MRC, Warwick: CCSU minutes, vol 22, 7th meeting (2 July 1981). Thomas, an articulate Welshman, had worked within CPSA headquarters since 1955 and, with Kendall, first conceived the idea of selective action. This made his early disillusion with it in 1981 the more surprising, although it is perhaps explained by the fragility of selective action at the MOD (where his members had been angered by a Conference decision, engineered by militants, to affiliate to CND) and the militants' wish to extend it to DHSS and DE offices, regardless of the likely adverse impact on claimants and thus CPSA. Such tensions later led Thomas' then deputy, Alastair Graham, to describe the CPSA at this time as the 'Beirut of the trade union movement' (http://www.icbh/witness/civilservicereform/index.html, seminar 1). The decision not to strike with the SCPS in 1977 was purely tactical. Thomas fought hard for 'tangible' results both to satisfy his moderates and disarm his militants in negotiations, from which the SCPS – because of its strike action – was to be excluded (see, for example, TNA: PREM16/1172, transcript of meeting with Lord Privy Seal, 5 July 1977).

9 For Gillman's confessions, see TNA: PREM16/1170, transcript of meeting on 20 January 1977 and for his reprimand BA22/P(1)334/523/03Q, W. McCall to G. Gillman, 3 November 1977. McCall wrote further that 'it is the unanimous opinion that your action is contrary to the strategy and tactics which the NSS has been pursuing with some success and that it will harm rather than help negotiations'. Gillman had succeeded John Dryden, whom CSD officials described as 'the intellectual of the NSS both in appearance and approach', in 1973. Earlier, as Dryden's deputy, Gillman had acted as the part-time General Secretary of the FDA during its temporary affiliation with the SCS between 1970 and 1973; and during the 1973 strike he had masterminded the press campaign. The CSD seemed obsessed with the fact that he collected Chinese porcelain (although he actually collected snuff boxes).

10 The resources of the IPCS meant that it could gain kudos by hosting meetings of the NSS and CCSU when it was deemed inappropriate to use the normal room in Whitehall; and its greater internal discipline meant that McCall could regularly use these meetings to lecture fellow leaders, especially of the CPSA and SCPS, about not 'hiding behind' militant members, executive councils and conference decisions (see, for example, MRC, Warwick: NSS minutes, vol 19, meeting 685, 27 April 1973). On

NOTES FOR CHAPTER 8

its joining the TUC, see J.E. Mortimer and V.A. Ellis, *A Professional Union* (1980) pp. 306–7, 371–4. Given the TUC's influence over incomes policy, affiliation was ultimately seen to be the only alternative to 'impotence' in wage bargaining.

11 BA22/P(1)334/523/03Q, G. Burrett to K. Stowe, 27 October 1977 and to J.K. Moore, 19 October 1977. The previous part of this file (/03P) contains a major report to the Lord Privy Seal, prior to his meeting with the NSS on 13 October, which details both sides to the dispute over scientists' pay (Appendix 3 and 4). CSD officials, nevertheless, grudgingly admired McCall as a 'lively if sometimes excitable Scot' who, since his appointment as General Secretary in 1963, had used dark arts to maximise – despite attacks from major private employers and the blandishments of NSS colleagues – the pay of his disparate membership. This, they admitted, was the one instance where public criticism of overpaid civil servants had some justification.

12 B. O'Toole, *Private Gain and Public Service* (1989) pp. 131–43. Formally, in acknowledgement of the need to rationalise in line with post-Fulton reorganisation, a Joint National Committee linked the FDA with the IPCS and SCS between 1970 and 1976. Its formal relationship with the former, however, was never strong and that with the latter effectively ended in 1973 when the FDA appointed its first full-time General Secretary, Norman Ellis (a former research fellow in industrial relations at Nuffield College, Oxford) to replace Gillman.

13 For the first debate, which was sparked by an intervention by D.H. Morrell at its 1969 conference, see TNA: BA16/58, 59 (which includes the text of Armstrong's speech to the British Academy on 20 July 1970) and 82 (which includes the CSD's less than enthusiastic response to the FDA report). For the second, see in particular B. O'Toole *The Ideal of Public Service* (2006) pp. 118–24.

14 For the details and individual explanations of defection, see O'Toole, *Private Gain*, pp. 162–80. With a response rate of just under 80%, the majority in the ballot for affiliation was 57% and for strike action in 1981 52%. The results may have been affected by the FDA's working alliance with the 2500-strong Association of HM Inspectors of Taxes (AIT) after 1976. An attempt to reconcile the irreconcilable was made by a classic piece of drafting: affiliation to the TUC was agreed only 'on the strict understanding that . . . our neutrality will not thereby be affected'. Nevertheless in 1981, the classic conflict occurred. As FDA chairman, Mike Fogden, actively helped to coordinate strike action whilst, as deputy controller of the DHSS's Newcastle Central Office, he was equally active in minimising its impact on social security claimants (see Hennessy, *Whitehall*, p. 535).

15 See, for example, Christopher's regular communications with the Prime Minister in PREM16/1962 and 1964, *passim*. He also maintained contact with Ministers throughout the 1981 strike although, because of the suspension of its members, the IRSF became more militant and was in fact the only union to reject the final settlement. Christopher did not dispute this decision because, on his own admission, he knew the CCSU had the necessary two-thirds majority for its acceptance (MRC, Warwick: CCSU minutes, vol 22, meeting 8, 30 July 1981). The reward for his and his members' efforts during the strike was allegedly the earmarking of a £2m surplus in the CCSU's strike fund for the construction of its new headquarters.

16 Avery, as chairman of Committee 'A' during the reactivation of pay research in 1977–8 was occasionally regarded by CSD officials as 'gratuitously offensive', not least because he wanted to exclude his members (BA22/P(1)334/523/03 T). He received equal opprobrium from the leaders of CPSA and SCPS for leading the fateful delegation to Ministers on 29 March 1979.

17 Vickers was initially seen by CSD officials as a militant and a 'stubborn and often tedious negotiator'. In the end, however, he prevented the CSU from 'going down the wrong road' and after his chairmanship of Committee A became a 'highly effective, but at the same time basically reasonable, union leader with good control of a well-managed

and on the whole happy union' (BA22/P(1)11/04K, G. Burrett to N. Gurney, 22 February 1977). Moody was the most articulate defender of smaller unions' interests during the metamorphosis of the NSS into the CCSU.

18 The 1977 NWC was requested by the NSS when negotiations over the reactivation appeared to falter and Kendall sought to cancel it once reactivation had been agreed, but was overruled by his colleagues (see BA22/P(1)334/523/03R and S, G. Burrett to Hobson, 12 November and W.E. Wightman to B.S. Smith, 24 November 1977). The transcripts of each meeting (and a photograph for 1977) are preserved in TNA: T275/194–6. For the 1977 and 1980 meetings, see also *Whitley Bulletin*, vol 58, nos 2 and 3(1978) 33 and 48–50 (which includes Allen's comment) and vol 60, no 9 (1980) 134–6. The 1979 meeting, designed as a protest against the Conservatives' manpower cuts and political attacks on the Service, was regarded of insufficient importance to be recorded in the *Bulletin*. Ian Bancroft even sought a fourth meeting, in April 1979 'to avert a breakdown of the Whitley system' (T275/191, Bancroft to Callaghan, 3 April 1979).

19 At the peak of its influence in December 1969, the 'inner circle' comprised of Leslie Williams and Peter Jones (representing the NSS), McCall, Dryden and Jeremiah. Jones was the Secretary of the NSS from 1963 to 1980 and then of the CCSU until 1992. He was also editor of the *Whitley Bulletin* which, with its normally restrained editorials and reproduction of correspondence between the NSS and Government, is an exemplary 'journal of record' for the period.

20 See, in particular, pen portraits by CSD officials in TNA: PREM15/776 and 1346 and his reported speech in *Civil Service Opinion* (August 1972). On his retirement, he was described by Gillman as 'Whitleyism personified' (MRC, Warwick: NSS minutes, vol 19, meeting 691, 1 November 1973). The desire for unity stemmed from the greater sense of cohesion following the departure of the Post Office unions in 1969 and was further expressed in the *Whitley Bulletin*, vol 55, no 1 (1975) 2. For an overview of Whitleyism since 1945, see H. Parris, *Staff Relations in the Civil Service* (1973), ch 3.

21 The difference between Dryden and Kendall as Secretary General was anticipated by a brief submitted to Heath during the January 1973 crisis by B. Gilmore: 'Mr Dryden is a moderate by conviction and has adopted militancy only under severe pressure from part of his membership and Executive Committee . . . Mr Kendall, on the other hand, believes basically in militancy as such although his enthusiasm for adopting it within the Civil Service fluctuates markedly.' Thus Dryden, like Williams, was trusted with confidential information in 1973 whereas Kendall was not (see TNA: PREM15/1334 and BA19/262).

22 During the 1977 struggle, however, Kendall successfully parried a particularly insidious attempt by Callaghan to use the NSS to blackmail the IPCS into submission. The Prime Minister, he countered, 'failed to recognise the basis on which the NSS was constructed'. He then gave a classic description of it as 'the custodian of all the interests of the staff but . . . constructed as a collection of independent units [with] no power to direct any one of its component parts to agree a particular line'(see TNA: PREM16/1170, transcript of meeting on 9 November 1977).

23 Power had accumulated in Committee A because TUC involvement in incomes policy had centralised wage bargaining; but, particularly after its expansion in 1977, the Committee lacked cohesiveness. Thomas, for example, complained in 1979 that recent meetings had 'revealed decisions and attitudes not conducive to consensus opinion. There may have been clashes of personality but one of the fundamental changes of recent times was the different speeds at which unions moved. The NSS had for too long been papering over cracks' (MRC, Warwick: NSS minutes, vol 21, meeting 752, April 1979). Its disunity was ruthlessly exploited by Callaghan throughout 1977 to the particular frustration of the SCPS, whose May conference had mandated Gillman to secure the immediate reactivation of pay research. It was further frustrated by the

NOTES FOR CHAPTER 8

NSS's ineffective protest rally on 29 November. For Kendall's version of later events, see *Whitley Bulletin*, vol 59, no 5 (1979) 67–8.

24 The transformation accordingly raised no serious qualms in the CSD (as confirmed by the correspondence in *Whitley Bulletin*, vol 60, no 6 (1980) 89–90). The full constitution, which did at least give the CCSU the legal entity the NSS had lacked, is recorded in no 3 (1980) 35–6.

25 MRC, Warwick: NSS minutes, vol 21, meeting 759, 16 January 1980; similar points were made at meeting 761 on 3 March 1980, when the smaller unions forced a number of decisions to the vote. The NSS was financed by a 'call' on each seat (which by the late 1970s was approximately £7700 pa). The big three managed to maintain their two-thirds majority vote on the CCSU, but were unsuccessful in reducing the power of the secretariat (which smaller unions regarded as genuinely neutral). Battles were waged until January 1981 over the membership of other policy committees, on which each union was finally granted a vote although each chair had to have the support of one of the big three unions.

26 Kendall's remarks are recorded in MRC, Warwick: NSS minutes, vol 21, meeting 736, 17 November 1977. A typical appreciation of the NSS was ironically provided by Gillman at its 765th and final meeting on 24 April 1980. He concluded: 'in more recent years there had been increasing difficulty in reconciling the various views of unions . . . there had been the traumas of differing if not opposing views. However, if there had been no NSS at these times, it would have been necessary to invent one'. This was not an empty eulogy.

27 Fulton was typically confused on this subject. It asserted that Whitleyism inhibited good management and yet simultaneously stated that it was 'very much in the public interest' that the current 'atmosphere of agreement and of co-operation should be preserved' – apparently overlooking the fact that, were private sector management practices introduced on the 'employer's side', the culture of private sector trade unions was likely to be adopted by staff associations (see Cmnd 3638, paras 270–1). Some justification of Fulton's reservations, however, is provided by the Joint NWC Committee on Efficiency, set up in 1965 and remarkably barren of results (see TNA: T216/810).

28 *Whitley Bulletin*, vol 49, no 10 (1969) 154. Armstrong's prescience, it could be argued, was matched by a certain blindness towards the consequences of his proposed actions. His conference addresses also frequently courted controversy. He was strongly warned, for example, not to address the 1972 IPCS conference because of the jealousy it would arouse of other associations. He was rewarded by being denounced by both Conference and McCall for both abandoning Fulton and, rather rashly, reasserting the virtue of generalists in being able to 'draw out the best from professionals' (see TNA: BA16/83 and *State Service*, July 1972).

29 The author of the 1969 Report, and former secretary of the Fulton Committee, initially opposed its becoming a joint report. 'This is a management programme with which we intend to associate the staff as fully as we can', R. Wilding wrote to L. Petch on 10 January 1969, 'not a joint programme, with the implication of action limited to the higher common factor of agreement'. Later, he openly admitted that 'management paid a price' for such collaboration although by then he had accepted Armstrong's argument that it was 'self-evidently right' (see, TNA: BA16/7 and R.W.L. Wilding, 'The post-Fulton programme', *Public Administration*, 48 (1970) 398).

30 *Whitley Bulletin*, vol 48, no 7 (1968) 104–7. He expressed similar views at a meeting between the NSS and Harold Wilson on 1 July 1968, although some of his colleagues were more outspoken. Dryden, for example, alleged that 'job evaluation was a gimmick invented by management consultants for their own benefit'. No doubt they 'would welcome the massive job, and fees, . . . but it was by no means clear that the results would be of benefit to anyone else'. McCall, equally significantly, claimed restructuring

would take twenty years and should initially be restricted to the grades above Principal (see TNA: PREM13/1971).

31 Williams had insisted that the reports should be joint publications because he wanted to reassure association members that, as part of 'Joint Committee', the NSS was 'in control of the whole Fulton operation'. Initially he wanted their publication as special editions of the *Whitley Bulletin* but even Armstrong baulked at this (see TNA: BA29/14, Wilding to C. Gilbraith, 6 February 1969). The introduction of categories, nevertheless, was exclusively revealed in its September 1969 edition.

32 See, for example, Kellner and Crowther-Hunt, *Civil Servants*, p. 65. For detailed evidence to support the analysis in this and the following paragraph, see above ch 5.2.1.

33 TNA: PREM15/1341, Jellicoe to Heath, 17 November 1971 and BA16/93, L. Williams to D. Houghton, 17 March 1972.

34 Cmnd 3638, para 142. By November 1971, after 'one of the most protracted and difficult negotiating marathons', agreement was reached on early retirement; but it was not to apply to anyone below the level of Principal and managerial freedom was to be constrained by an independent appeals board (see *Whitley Bulletin*, vol 51, no 11 (1971) 153).

35 Cmnd 3638, paras 274 and 271 (d).

36 See TNA: PREM13/1991, Kendall's intervention during the NSS meeting with Wilson, 1 July 1968 and PREM13/1970, Armstrong's criticism of the draft Report on 9 May 1968 for ignoring the burgeoning research on the 'psychology of office workers'. At the final meeting of the Joint NWC Committee in February 1973, Armstrong reiterated the criticism that Fulton had ignored 'junior staff' (PREM15/1341, F (JC)(73) 1st). In the meantime, new personnel management initiatives had been launched in 1971 under John Drake at the CSD, for the same reasons as those advanced by the Wider Issues Review: 70% of civil servants worked outside London and had been almost wholly ignored by Fulton (see above, ch 5.2.2). For an insight into the contemporary mood, see C. Painter, 'The post-Fulton malaise', *Public Administration* 53 (1975), which praises as 'exemplary' Armstrong's awareness of 'poor morale in the lower grades' (p. 429).

37 The final report was published as *Civil Servants and Change* and the succeeding quotations are taken from paras 5, 26 and 12. Its most forceful comment was that 'civil servants feel they have been mucked about a lot in the last five to ten years. So there is an atmosphere of sourness in many parts of the service, and we have found it at every level' (para 14). For the Interim Report, with a foreword by the NWC and significantly less critical of staff associations, see TNA: PREM16/313; and for a discussion of Government's role as a good, but not a model, employer P.B. Beaumont 'The obligation of the government as employer', *Public Administration* 56 (1978) 13–24. The final quotation in the paragraph is taken from the CSD report to the 1974 Sunningdale meeting of Permanent Secretaries (CAB164/1249).

38 *Civil Servants and Change*, paras 51–2.

39 Ibid, paras 24 and 39. Even Fulton, for example, had noted in relation to accommodation that 'too much of virtue' was made out of 'austerity' (Cmnd 3638, appendix I). This was hardly surprising as poor working conditions had been under almost constant discussion since at least 1964; and indeed a Joint Committee with the NSS on accommodation was established in March 1971.

40 *Whitley Bulletin*, vol 54, no 9 (1974) 138. The NSS expanded its specialist committee structure in 1976 and the *Bulletin* thereafter regularly reported its work. Committees A and B (dealing respectively with major policy and secondary conditions of service) had been formed as joint NWC committees during the Second World War. They became exclusively NSS in 1945, joining an existing Superannuation Committee (founded in the 1920s) and new Welfare and Training Committees. After Fulton, Personnel Management and Management Services Subcommittees were formed which were given full status by 1974. A joint Welfare and Accommodation Committee was also

NOTES FOR CHAPTER 8

established in 1976. Each worked to a similarly named Joint NWC Committee (with the PM and MS Committees additionally working to Joint Committees on dispersal and computers).

41 TNA: PREM16/313, response to Wilson's letter of 18 March 1974.
42 *Whitley Bulletin*, vol 55, no 10 (1975) 150. The succeeding quotation is taken from vol 58, no 3 (1978) 41. The occasion for this outburst was the latest rejection of a proposal for open reporting, negotiations for which had commenced in 1963. On 24 October 1977, Kendall had complained to the Prime Minister on behalf of the NSS about the relative powerlessness of the CSD, which could 'only seek to persuade a federal collection of semi-autonomous departments to accept its view'. The answer was that it, rather than departments, should become the direct 'employer ' of officials so that it could better ensure their management (PREM16/1658).
43 TNA: PREM16/1170, briefing notes, 16 July 1976. The NSS consistently asked for regular biannual meetings in 1976 and 1977 but this, CSD officials argued, would 'debase what should remain a rare and valuable currency'. It certainly felt its power to be diminished by the TUC's increasingly corporatist role – hence the perceived need of all its constituent associations to affiliate. The TUC was coming increasingly to be dominated by white-collar unions (of which the CPSA was amongst the largest) but they felt their influence did not match their numerical strength.
44 See TNA: PREM15/776 and PREM16/1170, transcripts of meetings on 3 July 1972 and 20 January 1977. The Bullock Report had little to offer the NSS and merely led to some inconclusive meetings on issues such as the earlier and fuller release of information on cash limits. Transcripts of other meetings with Heath are in PREM15/1346.
45 See TNA: BA17/642. I. Bancroft to L. Williams, 14 April 1970 and PREM15/1346 for a copy of Heath's speech at the opening of the Civil Service College. Reputedly, the commitment was sprung on him by CSD officials, some of whom later regretted it. 'I hope they don't remember this,' T.H. Caulcott, for instance, minuted to F. Cooper of NSS leaders on 17 February 1971, 'it went a bit far' (BA17/642). Bancroft simultaneously promised that there would be no automatic assumption that the private was more efficient than the public sector and that, to protect their status, national leaders would always be informed of planned changes in advance of Departmental Whitley Councils.
46 TNA: BA17/361, F. Cooper to D. Howell, 5 July 1971. There are transcripts of six such meetings between February 1971 and 1972, at which details of manpower and hiving off policy were divulged. However, in January 1971 the Home Office gave only 24 hours notice of the sale of state pubs and the Department of Employment gave no advance warning of the creation of the Employment Services Agency. The CSD also had two 'hiving off' lists, only one of which the NSS was made aware.
47 TNA: PREM16/1170, transcript of meeting on 27 July 1976. This deal preceded the compromise's endorsement by Cabinet and arguably was simply a device used by Callaghan to break deadlock there. During 1976, the CSD significantly, and to the later annoyance of the NSS, revealed neither its planned manpower cuts nor the existence of the Official or Ministerial Committee on the reactivation of pay research.
48 See, PREM16/769, on which most of this paragraph is based. The NSS enjoyed an effective veto over the choice of members for the Armitage Committee, one of whom was Barbara Castle who, together with Short and Benn, had been the only Ministers fully to support the NSS in Cabinet. Greater transparency over restrictions was mainly to be achieved by more simplified rules, *en bloc* exemptions and an appeals system (*Political Activities of Civil Servants*, Cmnd 7057, para 161). On the 1948 Masterman Report, which Armitage superseded, see above ch 2.3.2.

NOTES FOR CHAPTER 8

49 TNA: PREM16/1547: Thatcher to Callaghan, 12 May 1977. The views of Permanent Secretaries are summarised by K. Stowe in a note to Wilson on 10 December 1975 (ibid) and expressed individually in TNA: BA7/21. The majority were concerned about the Service's impartiality and the difficulty of dismissing non-union members. To some CSD officials, their objections epitomised an attitude that 'we are not only out of sympathy with what the Labour movement wants but that we simply do not understand it' (K. Clucas to I. Bancroft, 19 September 1975). The CSD's alternative view was that Government legislation had to be implemented and that the NSS was sufficiently responsible to accept adequate safeguards (such as ballots and 'conscience' clauses) to prevent abuse. In any case, a closed shop was a corollary of the current active encouragement of voluntary membership and would strengthen, rather than weaken, forces for moderation.

50 Douglas Allen, as Head of the Civil Service, was characteristically robust on the subject of 'free riders'. The unions, he claimed, had 'few legitimate grievances'. Pay research was wholly financed by the taxpayer and the cost of union 'facilities' far exceeded membership dues. Hence it was 'almost indecent for them to argue that non-members are free riders when the whole movement is a cheap fare rider' (TNA: BA7/21, memo of 1 December 1975). He also feared that any increase in industrial democracy would be 'unpalatable and expensive' with 'monumentally adverse' effects on efficiency and ultimately would involve unions in 'the determination of policy' (see CAB 164/Conferences of Permanent Secretaries at Sunningdale, part 7, correspondence with J. Hunt, 1976).

51 As NSS Secretary General, Kendall embodied the generally accepted collective view, which mirrored Allen's, that industrial democracy was a 'nonsense'. He was, R. Wilding reported to N. Gurney in September 1976, 'utterly opposed to littering management bodies with "neuters" whom their unions would repudiate at the drop of a hat. As a taxpayer, he attached importance to the elective principle and thought that the proper pursuit of sectional interest should be kept quite separate from governmental policy-making' (BA22/P(1)11/334/05B).

52 The consultation (noted in ch 6.4.2(a)) of Kendall on 27 October 1977 over the structure of central Government, and the choice of the next Head of the Civil Service, was thus more likely to have been a diversionary tactic to minimise discussion on the more controversial issue of pay rather than a peak of NSS political influence. Kendall had requested the meeting following the English Committee's suggestion that the CSD should be abolished and expressed the strong hope that the CSD would instead be strengthened. 'We want', he claimed, 'to deal with people who can deliver'. He was reportedly too 'non-plussed' at being asked about the Headship of the Civil Service to offer an opinion. See, PREM16/1658.

53 'Good staff relations', the *Whitley Bulletin* for December 1969 (vol 49, no 11, p. 166) acknowledged, were 'neither sacrosanct nor imperishable': the continuing success of Whitleyism depended both on the compliance of existing staff and whether it 'brought home the bacon'. Government concessions to militant action were thus not helpful. A later edition (vol 55, 1975, no 6, p. 81) admitted that the whole Whitley process was 'time-consuming and laborious . . . But this is what democracy is all about – and it does work'.

54 TNA: PREM16/770, John Dryden in transcript of NSS meeting with the Lord Privy Seal, 19 March 1975. The threat was taken sufficiently seriously in Cabinet to rebuff Michael Foot's concern that the subsequent pay award would undermine his understanding with the TUC over the social contract. The Civil Service, it was feared, might be transformed into an 'organisation dominated by militancy, a development which would in the long run be more damaging even than the miners' strike' (CAB128/56,12th. 6 (confidential annex), 13 March 1975).

55 TNA: BA21/915, transcript of meeting between the Prime Minister and NSS, 8 January 1973. To offset the call for strike action by the SCS (which was driven by its

NOTES FOR CHAPTER 8

militant National Executive), Williams arranged the lobbying of Parliament, a wide range of meetings with Ministers and controlled protests by departmental Whitley Councils. This created the political sympathy which permitted the Pay Board to make an independent judgement (see, in particular, BA22/526, K. Lawrance to J. Chilcot, 30 January 1973).

56 MRC, Warwick:, NSS minutes, vol 19, meetings 681–2 (17 January and 15 February 1973) and 690 (4 October 1973). The *Whitley Bulletin* went so far as to claim that the only groups of workers to benefit from the Conservative pay policy were the 'miners and –wait for it! – the non-industrial Civil Service' (vol 54, 1974, no 8, p. 122). Less commendably, there was a further split vote in February (with the SCS and FDA subsequently 'reserving their position to protect their members' interests') over acceptance of a Stage 2 pay deal because of the implicit redistribution of income to lower-paid workers. This, fulminated one union leader, was tantamount to asking young men with mortgages to surrender their pay to 'married women earning pin money or the young living at home'.

57 The TUC brokerage of the incomes policy increased long-standing tension between it and the NSS. Before the majority of staff associations affiliated, Heath was advised that the NSS had 'never regarded the TUC as being in any position to speak for their interests' (TNA: BA21/915, CSD brief, 8 January 1973): and even after the affiliation of all, it was angered by its blue-collar bias and suspicion of comparability. Mutual suspicion led to a later dispute over the virtues of a permanent, research-based incomes policy for the whole public sector to be overseen by the TUC (*Whitley Bulletin*, vol 59, no 2 (1978)). The NSS opposed this, presumably because it threatened its autonomy.

58 The main battle between F.G. Burrett (for the CSD) and K. Couzens (for the Treasury) is recorded in BA22/P(1)334/523/031. For the Working Group on the Re-entry of Problems of Pay Research and GEN 64, see above ch 6.2.3.

59 TNA: PREM16/1170, transcript of meeting on 14 July 1977. At this time, Callaghan reputedly commented at a training session in the Treasury: 'if you kick officials hard enough, they'll do anything' (private information).

60 Kendall was particularly bitter and suggested the following addition to the Queen's speech: 'My Government will behave with more than usual hypocrisy and will continue to preach the priceless virtues of conciliation and arbitration but at the same time will dismantle conciliation and arbitration machinery when it thinks fit. In so doing it will support those elements in society which have a preference for confrontation rather than the civilised methods of resolving disputes.' See *Whitley Bulletin*, vol 58, no 11 (1978) p. 169. As Head of the Home Civil Service, Allen was equally concerned about duplicity behind the assumption that pay policy, and thus cash limits, could be made compatible with pay research (see TNA: PREM16/1170, transcript of meeting on 9 November 1977). He was later thanked by the NSS for his 'decisive' action in getting the pay agreement reactivated (*Whitley Bulletin*, vol 58 no 1 (1978) p. 2).

61 MRC, Warwick: NSS minute, vol 21 *passim* but especially meeting 735 (3 November 1977) for the repudiation of the SCPS and 744–7 (July-November 1978) for the repudiation of its later contingency plans. See also ch 8.4.2. The timing of the protest action is explained by the need to assemble pay-research information over two years. Government intentions could therefore be identified well in advance. The SCPS strike in November 1977 was prompted by lack of any formal commitment to restore the pay agreement by the time the collection of information should have commenced for the 1978 settlement. The strike possibly coerced Government into making such a commitment.

62 PREM16/1964: Peart to Callaghan, 26 March 1979. Peart was reporting the last formal meeting, from which the NSS walked out, not the inopportune informal one with Roy Hattersley on 29 March.

NOTES FOR CHAPTER 8

63 MRC, Warwick: CCSU minutes, vol 22, meeting 1, 10 July 1980. Earlier Soames' refusal, and the calling of a full NWC, to discuss manpower policy were recorded in the minutes of the NSS for October and November 1979 (ibid, vol 21). The NSS in desperation used the 1975 Employment Protection Act (a remnant of Labour's attempt to alter the power balance on the shop floor) to force the disclosure of information.

64 Kendall's letter is reproduced in *Whitley Bulletin*, vol 60 no 11(1980) p. 175. For Priestley's principles, see Cmd 9613 (1955) para 99. One of the *Bulletin's* favourite analogies was that, just as Henry Ford allowed his customers any colour so long as it was black, so Government allowed free pay bargaining so long as awards did not exceed predetermined cash limits (see, for example, vol 60, no 4, p. 49).

65 *The Bulletin*, vol 1, no 3 (1981) p. 37. The exchange of letters between F.G. Burrett and Kendall on 27 July is recorded in the same volume, no 7, pp. 106–7. The contacts varied in their degrees of formality. Kendall, for example, would often meet CSD officials 'by chance' whilst walking in St James Park.

66 Unofficial disruption included a go-slow by the CSU in 1970, attempts to disrupt pension and social security uprating in 1972 and 1974, the disruption of Department of Employment statistical work by the CPSA in 1976 and the attempted blackmail of the Treasury by the IRSF in 1977.

67 Sympathetic Parliamentary statements were made on 4 January, and 5 and 12 February, coinciding with a letter to all MPs from Williams on 6 February. For equally sympathetic Ministerial responses to delegations between December 1972 and January 1973, see TNA: BA22/526. Typically Keith Joseph was amongst the most sympathetic, once he became aware that many of his officials paying out family income supplement (targeted on the poorest wage-earners) qualified for the benefit themselves. The basic NSS assertion went unchallenged that since 1971 officials had suffered a 20% fall in relative wages.

68 TNA: BA22/527, Jellicoe to A. Barber, 20 March 1973. This advice might have been heeded by Government in 1979. Jellicoe's even more prescient memorandum to Heath on 30 November 1972 rehearsed the arguments that were to recur throughout the 1970s. Inconvenient though it might be at times, he argued, the pay system had 'nurtured one of the best and most trouble-free systems of industrial relations in this country'. Consequently it could not be 'too strongly emphasised that, whatever criticisms are made of it, no other system is likely on balance to be anything like as satisfactory'. In the short term, Jellicoe accepted that inflation was too severe to permit research-based awards. This might be accepted by the NSS as an 'unfortunate necessity' and contained with 'comparatively small scale industrial action'. Suspension after Stage 2, however, would be regarded as a 'repudiation of the existing pay system' and forfeit the 'basic goodwill' of all associations. Heath generally followed this advice. See BA 21/915 for Jellicoe's letter and the transcript of an emergency meeting between Heath and the NSS on 8 January 1973.

69 TNA: BA22/915, Jellicoe to Heath, 21 December 1972. The figures are Government figures taken from BA22/915, C.N. Groves to A. Duke and Duke to J. Herbecq, 11 January 1973; and from BA16/115, EOM(73)13, 9 April 1973. The CPSA also employed traditional protest methods such as advertisements in (and letters to) the press, regional rallies, and a postal ballot of MPs. Ironically, persistent unrest in the traditional heartlands of labour militancy, such as Scotland and the North East of England, discouraged the dispersal of jobs there (which the Treasury in particular was championing to reduce costs). This angered union leaders there, but not the NSS in general, which sought to relieve existing members of the threat of dispersal (see ch 9.3).

70 For the CSD admission and details of the May conferences, see TNA: BA16/116, EOM(73) unnumbered, 18 July 1973. The CPSA favoured the dramatic strike,

the SCS more subtle disruption. Arguably, this was perhaps because the CPSA had a long experience in overtime bans during which it had been unable to contain unofficial action (for example by DHSS officials in Manchester on 16 February 1973).

71 MRC, Warwick: NSS minutes, vol 19, meeting 682, 15 February 1973. The speaker was J.E. Morrish of the Customs and Excise Group, which was currently merging with the SCS and seeking to maximise the opportunities for disruption offered by the switch to VAT on Britain's accession to the EEC. He was supported by Kendall who refused to play down his members' anger, arguing that whilst the CPSA might appear to some as 'anarchistic . . . to others it did not go far enough'. Williams was particularly angered by the Government's reaction. It was, he claimed in a lecture to the Civil Service College in May 1974, 'ironic that it takes a dose of militancy to force attention on problems which the NSS have stressed over many years'.

72 See TNA: BA22/527, K.C. Lawrance, 'Note for the record', 16 February 1973 and J.A. Chilcot to J. Moore, 8 April 1973 for the respective confessions of Dryden and Kendall. Chilcot noted that Kendall had been identified by his members as a 'bad general who lost the battle, now that the CPSA have run out of money and have produced no tangible results for their efforts'.

73 See respectively TNA: BA16/1176, EOM(73) unnumbered, 18 July 173; MRC, Warwick:, NSS minutes, vol 19, meeting 691, 1 November 1973; TNA: BA22/526, summary of meeting between Armstrong and the NSS on 1 February 1973.

74 For a copy of the letter and Williams' reply of 1 March 1973, see TNA: BA22/527. Estacode Na10 stated: 'there is no law forbidding Civil Servants as such to strike. Striking would, however, be treated as a disciplinary offence'. Thus the final advice to Armstrong was that it would be within his right to warn that 'disciplinary action would or could follow' but that Establishment Officers as a whole would discourage this because, particularly in relation to junior staff, it would be 'wrong to penalise strike action, when workers in other more essential jobs (e.g. power stations) are not thus liable.' Their preferred tactic was 'to say nothing on the disciplinary question, but to make sure the drafting included some reference to the inevitable loss of pay' (TNA: BA19/144: J. Moore to Armstrong, 2 February 1973). That such advice was followed is apparent from the papers in BA22/527, not least a second letter drafted for Armstrong to send all officials in March confirming that 'Those who strike lose their pay and pension entitlement for the days in question. This is an automatic consequence of unauthorised absence from duty, and is in no sense a punishment'. Both Heath and Jellicoe had approved the first letter.

75 The key administrative forum for these debates was the monthly meeting of Establishment Officers; and the key documents by the CSD, preserved in TNA: BA16/115–6 and all classified as EOM(73) unnumbered are: 'Report of the Working Group on industrial action in the Civil Service', 24 May 1973 (which first floated the concept of 'relief from duty'); 'Participation in industrial action by staff in management', 1 June 1973; 'Industrial action in the Civil Service: a forward look', 18 July 1973 (which was discussed at the 2 August meeting); and, 'Draft paper for the CCU', 4 September 1973. The CSD from the start was aware that management's response had been 'feeble' and that displays of 'passive resistance' could demoralise the mass of moderate officials. 'We must not lose the propaganda battle', minuted a future Second Permanent Secretary (actively supported by the official who was to be the chief negotiator during the 1981 strike), 'middle management will have a vital role to play and we must do everything practicable to keep them up to the mark'. The strike on 27 February was thus viewed as the final one which 'we can pretend has not happened' through the maintenance of a low profile (see BA19/262, minutes by J.E. Herbecq and G. Burrett, 20 and 21 February 1973).

76 Antipathy between the NSS and the TUC was mutual. In April Len Murray, the TUC's General Secretary, was entrusted with brokering a deal. He accused Kendall of

NOTES FOR CHAPTER 8

'cowardice in the face of the enemy' and, of the two main protagonists, would talk only to Thomas. He could bear 'to do no more' than have a brief conversation with Gillman whom, he considered, was 'enjoying it all too much'. See PREM16/1964, R. Hattersley to J. Callaghan, 2 April 1979.

77 For details of the strikes and selective action, see the regular CSD reports in PREM16/1964 as well as chs 6.2.3 and 8.3.3. For the FDA's reaction, see O'Toole, *Private Gain*, p. 174.

78 Fears about social security payments may have been exaggerated. They were voiced by Len Murray (PREM16/1964: T. Lankester, 'Note for the record', 9 April 1979) and were arguably an example of the unwisdom of overriding the professional expertise of CSD negotiators, for which Callaghan later expressed regret. CSD negotiators, he acknowledged, might well 'if left alone have achieved a more economic result for the Government' (ibid, exchange of correspondence between K. Stowe and I. Bancroft, 25 April-1 May).

79 There was an estimated response rate of 30–35% from the SCPS's 100,000 members, and little sympathy action from other unions except in the DHSS. The public impact was adjudged 'negligible', although over half of DHSS local offices were closed and immigration, especially at Heathrow, delayed for up to one hour (see CSD report in BA22/P(1)334/523/03Q).

80 The 1977 week of protest started with an ill-attended meeting at Central Hall, Westminster on 29 November and ended with the equally vapid meeting of the full National Whitley Council on 1 December. For Gillman's later suggestion, see MRC, University of Warwick: NSS minutes, vol 21, meeting 744, 6 July 1978. Kendall, supported by McCall and Christopher, countered that 'a blue print in July for action the following April' was precipitate but later (meeting 747, 2 November) admitted that associations' constitutions and policies were too diffuse to permit anything other than a strategy of 'parallelism'.

81 PREM16/1964, 'Note for the record', 27 March 1979.

82 This anger was epitomised by a letter which Robert Armstrong persuaded a dissident Under Secretary, Jack Hibbert, to write instead of going on strike. It was forwarded to Mrs Thatcher. Apart from the 'sustained denigration of civil servants and the work that they do', he expressed particular anger at Ministers' 'gross misrepresentation' of pay increases; the 50% cut in the recommendations of the Top Salaries Review Board in a futile attempt to set the private sector an example; and the Government's apparent readiness to respond to militant action but not to reasoned argument. Cumulatively they had resulted in a total collapse of trust in Government (see PREM19/Civil Service, Pay and pensions, part 3, J. Hibbert to R. Armstrong, 6 March 1981). In relation to 'gross misinterpretation', Mrs Thatcher claimed in Parliament on 7 April that the current 7% offer would add 11% to the wages bill. Her Private Secretary, with some trepidation, asked her to name her source since the true figure was between 8–9%. She declined, saying 'it has come up in discussion and I think has been in the press' (ibid, M.J. Scholar to M. Thatcher 7 April 1981).

83 The figures for the peaceful protest are the CCSU's (*The Bulletin*, vol 1, no 1 (1981) p. 3) and for the strike the Government's (PREM19/Civil service, Pay and pensions, part 3). Participation in the latter was numerically lower than in April 1979 but neared 90% in the Inland Revenue and two previous focal points of militancy, the Department of National Savings and the Scottish courts. Customs and Excise, the DHSS and the Scottish Office recorded rates of over 70%, while the lowest participation was at the Home Office and CSD.

84 On the travails of selective action see MRC, Warwick: CCSU minutes, vol 22, meeting 7, 2 July 1981. Details of the CCSU's plan of action are best provided in *The Bulletin*, vol 1, no 3 (1981) pp. 44–5. In defence, the closure of the GCHQ communication centre on 9 March and planned action at its various outstations was designed to be

NOTES FOR CHAPTER 8

no more than 'token' action to underline solidarity throughout the Service. There was, however, a dramatic long-term consequence: the banning of trade unions from GCHQ.
85 See in particular PREM19/Civil service, Pay and pensions, part 8, P.S. Jenkins to M. Scholar, 18 November 1981. The Treasury's apologia continued: 'it might be argued by some critics that the interest cost, amounting to roughly 10 per cent of the total Civil Service bill, is greater than it might have cost to settle the dispute earlier; but to have conceded a larger pay settlement would have entailed permanent additional costs, and would probably have had repercussions on pay in the rest of the public and private sectors'. A wide range of computer centres was targeted, of which those of the Inland Revenue (at Shipley and Cumbernauld) and of Customs and Excise (at Southend) were the most important. Lost revenue from the former and from national insurance amounted to £1.4b in July alone, while the net loss from Customs and Excise was only £300m (because repayments as well as receipts were halted).
86 For a fuller analysis of Government policy, see above ch 7.3.
87 PREM19/Civil Service, Pay and pensions, part 8, J. Hoskyns to M. Thatcher, 13 November 1981.
88 Union leaders, for example, reacted with incredulity when the Coordinating Committee drafted contingency plans for as long as four weeks (private information).
89 Ken Thomas, 'Strike diary' and other private information.
90 The fund was financed (for equity) by 'calls' on the varying number of seats held by unions on the CCSU and (for fraternity) by a levy on individual members. There were two calls of £500 and one of £1000 before the strike. Weekly strike dues initially amounted to £2 for Executive Officers and above; £1 for Clerical Officers; and 50p for Clerical Assistants and below. This was doubled in June and a one-off levy charged at £10 for EOs and above; £5 for COs; and £2.50 for CAs and below. Selective strikers, in return, received 85% of their normal pay (see *The Bulletin*, vol 1, nos 1 and 3 (1981)).
91 MRC, Warwick: CCSU minutes, vol 2, meeting 7 and 8, 2 July and 14 July (for the comments by Thomas and Hewlett respectively). There is a retrospective consensus that shortage of money ended the strike (see the transcript of a witness seminar in 2006 on the strike at http://www.icbh.ac.uk/icbh/witness/civilservicereform/index.html) but this is questionable given the sizable surplus in the strike fund which later helped to fund the new IRSF headquarters (private information)
92 Ibid, CCSU minutes for 2 July. Thomas' 'strike diary' (dictated daily) confirms that he was concerned about finance and advocating an all-out strike from the start of April. It also confirms divisions within the CPSA, not least to the detriment of selective action in defence (where, as has been seen, MOD delegates were less than impressed by the passing of a Conference motion supporting CND). The June ballot had recorded 45,000 in favour of an all-out strike, 33,000 for an immediate settlement and 23,000 for selective action. On a 50% turnout, therefore, less than a half (and less than a quarter of CPSA members) voted for an all-out strike.
93 See ch 7.4 above and Hoskyns, *Just in Time, passim*. Hoskyns was acutely aware that if the Government did not act now, in mid-term, both the opportunity and its reputation for robust action would be lost.
94 K. Thomas 'Strike diary'.
95 Ibid, p. 65. A further change in attitude, occasioned by Cabinet's veto of a deal proposed by Soames and its support for an imposed settlement, is recorded in the entry for 5 June 1981. It was, Thomas wrote, the 'worse thing that had happened for 35 years . . . I had attempted always to do deals with governments in power, regardless of their political complexion . . . If they impose this on us now and the strike came to an end in a degree of bitterness . . . I don't want to see a Minister again under this Government and I certainly was not prepared to ask my members to cooperate in any endeavour whatsoever'.
96 Wilding, 'The post-Fulton programme' 397; L.J. Callaghan, *Whitleyism* (Fabian Society, 1953).

NOTES FOR CHAPTER 9

9 MANAGEMENT CHALLENGES

1 See, for example, G.K. Fry, *Policy and Management in the British Civil Service* (1995), p. 92 although it contains a characteristic caveat: 'if centrally provided post-entry training in the Civil Service ever had a golden age in Britain, and it was debatable if it ever did, then ... the era of 1963–70 was it'. This echoes the reservations of the academic management expert, Trevor Smith, in his evidence to Fulton. The newly created Centre of Administrative Studies represented, he admitted, 'a revolution in attitudes' but in 'the still pond of civil service training there is, not unnaturally, a tendency to mistake a ripple for a tidal wave' (vol 5, para 34). For an excellent overview of training since the 1940s, see D.L. Bird, *The Civil Service College 1970–1995* (1995).
2 Cmnd 3638, para 103. Fulton did admit that, due to recent improvements 'the total training effort is ... impressive – particularly vocational training' (para 97). In other words, departmental but not central training was praised.
3 See above, ch 7.3.3. Departments long resisted payment and then only agreed to pay for 'job-specific' training, with all other costs of the 'common service' being met centrally. Rayner's challenge was fully taken up only in 1986.
4 C.H. Sisson, *The Spirit of British Administration* (1959) p. 28. Sisson, the Establishment Officer of the Ministry of Labour (which had a tradition of employing poets in such posts), wrote this classic defence of traditional practice whilst, somewhat ironically, on a sabbatical at Manchester University and ten years before applying unsuccessfully to become the first Principal of the Civil Service College. Sisson described how 'the British administrator travelling abroad is shocked to discover that many countries are administered by men who read books about public administration'; and concluded that 'such people are committing the crime of learning from books something that one just *does*. It is rather like venturing into matrimony only after a course of Havelock Ellis which, for a healthy nature, should not strictly be necessary' (p. 28).
5 Cmnd 3638, para 111. The Node was a meeting once a year over some 10 days of 24 'high-flying' officials and businessmen in their 40s, selected by a Steering Committee (of which William Armstrong later became joint chair). It was held in a country house in Hertfordshire owned by BP and Shell. Its seriousness was marked by the absence of trade unionists and academics (other than as director of the course, frequently in the shape of Asa Briggs). The object was, through group work and responses to short talks from the Great and Good, to develop mutual understanding and thereby new insights into national problems. At Henley, by contrast, the emphasis was on personal development. See, in particular, memoranda by J.B. Bourn, W.C. Knox and P.D. Nairne in TNA: BA21/42. Bonding with business was also strengthened by the inauguration of meetings between Permanent Secretaries and leading industrialists at 'Spring Sunningdales', initiated in the 1960s.
6 See A. Cairncross, *Living with the Century* (1998) pp. 238–9. For an excellent insider account of the subsequent development of CAS, see D. Keeling, 'The development of central training in the Civil Service, 1963–70', *Public Administration* 49 (1971) 51–71.
7 See G.K. Fry, *Reforming the Civil Service* (1993), pp. 224–5. For the Working Party's somewhat hasty appointment (on the recommendation of CAS's independent advisory committee but without the express knowledge of either the Chancellor or the Prime Minister), see TNA: T249/241. Wilson in particular suspected a pre-emptive plot against Fulton.
8 The mystery of Grebenik's appointment has long been explained by a desire in Whitehall to prevent Norman Hunt gaining the post. More positively it guaranteed the College academic status and, as a Ukrainian immigrant who had graduated – with Douglas Allen – with a BSc (Econ) from LSE, Grebenik met the Fultonian ideal in triplicate by being numerate, classless and non-Oxbridge. He had even been a wartime civil servant. For his part, he was becoming increasingly unhappy with the University,

NOTES FOR CHAPTER 9

and his wife with the City, of Leeds (See University of Leeds: correspondence between G.K. Fry and Grebenik, Lord Croham, Barbara Sloman and John Bourn).

9 In the 1970s, less than 10% of training was provided centrally. In 1971–2, of 1900 student weeks of training, little more than 2000 were consumed by Administration Trainees. Short introductory courses for Executive Officers accounted for double that amount.

10 R.N. Heaton and L. Williams, *Civil Service Training* (1974) para 5.5. The succeeding quotation is from the Principal's *Third Annual Report* (1972–3), p. 15. The College's early development was made all the harder by a major building programme at its main residential site at Sunningdale, the disruption caused by the Northern Ireland constitutional conference held there in December 1973, and a 20% budget cut in 1976 (which necessitated the closure of its Edinburgh site). The new buildings at Sunningdale were significantly all named after hallowed officials from the past ranging from Pepys to Norman Brook.

11 Bird, *Civil Service College*, p. 85. For the later quotation, see Peter Hennessy, *The Times*, 11 November 1980.

12 See the TUC evidence to Fulton, reprinted in vol 5(2) pp. 799–801.

13 The influence of the NSS was exerted through the NWC Joint Committee on Training. In 1964, it had produced a major report stressing the need for training throughout the Service (see TNA: T199/285) and thereafter the SCPS was insistent on the provision of centralised training for Executive Officers (although the CPSA and IPCS tended to favour day release). The Heaton-Williams Report was a NWC initiative designed, in part, to divert attention from differences within the NSS (TNA: BA21/46).

14 For a summary of Establishment Officers' initial objections, see TNA: BA16/44, FS(70)13. From the start, modular training had been suggested as a means of reducing the blocks of time for which trainees had to be absent from their departments (see, for example, BA16/208, memo on 'the scale of training', February 1971). It was finally introduced in September 1981.

15 Heaton and Williams, *Civil Service Training*, para 5.3.

16 For Fulton, see Cmnd 3638, paras 44–9 and Kellner and Crowther-Hunt, *Civil Servants*, p. 89; for Sisson's views, see TNA: T 249/242, letter to P. Osmond, 11 August 1966. Parallel misgivings were expressed about management studies in the USA, despite their longer academic pedigree. They merely generated mutual incomprehension, one contemporary account concluded, giving the young (and long-haired) 'an opportunity very much like that of taking a long, analytical look at one's prospective mother-in-law' whilst giving the practitioner (and short-haired) further 'inducements for family planning' (R. Egger, 'Civil servants in mid-career', *Public Administration* 54 (1976) 96).

17 The appreciation of CAS is recorded in Kellner and Crowther-Hunt, *Civil Servants*, p. 141, whilst Grebenik's lament is contained within his account of the CSC's first year in *Public Administration* 50(1972) 131.

18 The number of participants in such postings was small and typically only one-tenth transferred. However, by effectively breaking down the perceived barrier between specialists and generalists, they more than satisfied Fulton's wishes, IPCS demands and CSD plans for 'lateral movement' (see ch 5.2.2).

19 For Keeling's views and Gilmore's apostasy, see respectively 'Central training in the Civil Service', *Public Administration*, 50 (1972) 1–18 and Bird, *Civil Service College*, pp. 91–2. Hunt's bitterness boiled over in Kellner and Crowther-Hunt, *Civil Servants*, p. 94.

20 TNA: T249/241, D. Keeling to P. Osmond, 30 September 1965.

21 *Report of the Administration Trainee Review Committee* (1978), chaired by the CSD's able Director of Establishments, J.M. Moore. Executive Officers, it established, were applying in insufficient numbers for the current AT programme, because *inter alia* of the disruption involved (in moving themselves and frequently their families to London)

NOTES FOR CHAPTER 9

without any guarantee of faster promotion. Problems with the AT programme were exacerbated by a continuing battle (in defiance of Fulton) over whether– as originally envisaged by the Treasury – there should be a fast-stream whose members would gain promotion to Principal in their late 20s, some ten years before the main-stream.

22 For a summary of the planning of the CSC, and the search for a suitable location, see P.D. Lindley, *A Short Account of the Administrative Processes which Led to the Setting Up of the Civil Service College* (1973).

23 One of the few political scientists to be seconded to the Treasury (and who became secretary to the working party selecting course material for CAS and the nascent CSC) was surprised by the attitudes of those responsible for general policy, if not directly responsible for its implementation. Scorn for 'any application of social theory' and a 'deep prejudice against the academic study of public administration' was matched only by an equally damning 'ignorance of provincial universities' (personal correspondence with J.M. Lee). An Advisory Committee to the CSC, initially chaired by William Armstrong, was meant to bridge the gap, but rarely met.

24 TNA: T249/241, D. Keeling to M. Tennant, 25 May 1965.

25 Quoted in Kellner and Crowther-Hunt, *Civil Servants*, p. 93. Apart from Sunningdale, the CSC also had non-residential premises in central London and residential ones (until 1976) in Edinburgh.

26 J. Moore quoted in Bird, *Civil Service College*, p. 80. Management failure was the less excusable since the Army provided a template for training, with a hierarchy of staff colleges culminating in the Royal College of Defence Studies. First, majors were trained for specialist work, then colonels for wider responsibilities and finally brigadiers for the widest. Many other public officials had their own dedicated staff colleges, such as the police and the prison service.

27 TNA: T249/242, evidence to the Osmond Working Party, June 1966.

28 The review was announced in the *Reorganisation of Central Government* white paper (Cmnd 4506, paras 56–7). Its Report was entitled *The Dispersal of Work from London* (Cmnd 5322); and its original recommendation (submitted on 18 December 1972) had been for the dispersal of 33,000 posts. Hardman himself was the fifth choice of coordinator behind two military men (Admiral LeFanu and Sir John Hackett) and two former Permanent Secretaries (Sir Michael Stevenson and Sir Malcolm Dean); but having overseen Covent Garden's relocation, he was well qualified and proved highly effective in driving the review forward. The Report was preceded by the 1963 Fleming enquiry, which had led to the dispersal of some 30,000 posts and the location of a further 20,000 new posts outside London – with *inter alia* the Royal Mint moving to South Wales, HMSO to Norwich, the Civil Service Commission to Basingstoke and, more controversially, the Department of National Savings to Glasgow. A businessman, Sir Ronald German, had also been contracted in 1967 to make a further study but his report, discouraging further dispersal, was deemed too superficial to submit to Ministers. See respectively TNA: BA17/201, W. Armstrong to Jellicoe, 23 October 1970 and BA17/383, Jellicoe to E. Heath, 18 February 1971; PREM15/1339; and BA17/204, note by W. Armstrong 25 November 1968.

29 The decision was taken by Cabinet on 26 July 1979 (TNA: CAB128/66,12th.4) and immediately announced to Parliament (Parl Deb (Commons) 971, col 902–22, 26 July 1979). In 1973, Mrs Thatcher had been in a distinct minority at the critical Cabinet Committee meeting of 29 November in arguing that agreement to disperse 21,000 posts was sufficient. She had then added that 'she saw no reason why her staff should be divided into "blocks of work" and treated like a pack of cards'; and thereafter successfully resisted any dispersal of DES headquarters staff. Simultaneously, Derek Rayner opposed any further dispersal of his Defence Procurement Executive (see TNA: BA17/781, verbatim report of the MCA(L) meeting).

30 It was Jellicoe who initially suggested that dispersal should be included in the *Reorganisation of Central Government* white paper because it 'represented an important feature of our work on the rationalisation of government and constitutes a significant contribution to greater efficiency and economy'. Thereafter he resolutely defended the need for operational efficiency over regional policy. Armstrong also dissuaded Heath *inter alia* from demanding quicker action to relieve unemployment on the grounds that it would 'destroy the whole basis of the Government's systematic review' (see TNA: PREM15/777, Jellicoe to E. Heath, 23 September 1970 and W. Armstrong to R.T. Armstrong, 31 December 1971).

31 TNA: PREM15/777, W. Armstrong to R.T. Armstrong, 31 December 1971. For the original draft of the report, see PREM15/1339, esp para 9.

32 Parl Deb (Commons) 861, col 70, 16 October 1973. Rejection of Milton Keynes led to an interminable battle (complicated, sometimes deliberately, by a coterminous Defence Review) over the dispersal in two tranches of MOD staff to Cardiff (which was acceptable to MOD staff at all levels) and Glasgow (which was not). In the end, the Cardiff development was aborted and fewer than 2000 officials were sentenced by Mrs Thatcher to Scotland.

33 TNA: PREM15/1339, Jellicoe to E. Heath, 16 March 1973 and record of an ad hoc Prime Ministerial meeting on 18 April 1973. For earlier discussions of the link, see BA17/204, notes of W. Armstrong meeting with Permanent Secretaries, 1 August 1968 and PREM15/777, Jellicoe to E. Heath, 22 September 1970.

34 The CSD Minister who made this commitment was ironically a former member of the Fulton Committee, Robert Sheldon. He was firmly discouraged by the Hardman team which argued that 'as officials' they were 'firmly convinced' that attempts to implement the commitment would be 'very costly in terms of time and our relations with staff and departmental management . . . vexatious for the expectant regions and might yield only lemons' (see TNA: BA17/932, memo by C. Priestley 14 March 1974). Relations with the NSS were particularly sensitive because of the need to honour the promise of genuine consultation without proscribing Ministers' right to decide between the various options; and the need to expedite Establishment Officers' negotiations with their respective departmental Whitley Councils whilst not undermining the standing of national leaders. Earlier Williams, and Committee A, had frequently been given privileged information and both formal and informal briefings (see BA17/400 and 615, *passim*). No confidences were breached.

35 See TNA: CAB 128/55/4, 26 July 1974 and Parl Deb (Commons) 878, cols 482–94, 30 July 1974; CAB 134/3982, Ministerial Committee on Government Accommodation, 26 February 1976; and PREM16/771, NSS meetings with the Lord Privy Seal and the Prime Minister, 14 May and 27 July 1976. The abandonment of the electoral pledge to increase numbers is documented in BA17/932, Robert Sheldon minute, 20 March 1974.

36 TNA: CAB 130/744, Ministerial Committee on the Dispersal of Government Work from London, 17 June 1974. Wilson's minute of 25 June is in PREM16/14. The *ad hoc* Committee, which almost ended before it started because of Short's late arrival and from which four Ministers left early to attend other business, concluded with an extraordinary series of threats: from Roy Mason that the MOD would disperse no more jobs, from Short that it would have to and from the Secretary of State for Scotland that the SNP would triumph were the jobs not relocated to Glasgow. 'I must give you serious warning' Mason had concluded theatrically. 'Your serious warning is reciprocated' responded Short. See the partial transcript in BA17/934.

37 For Labour's retreat, see TNA: CAB 128/62/6, 28th.4, 28 July 1977 based on CAB 129/197/15, 25 July 1977 and PREM16/1958. For the Conservatives', see PREM19/4, particularly CAB134/4336, E(79)26, and CAB128/66,CC(79)12th.4,

26 July 1979. Abandonment was accompanied by the token allocation of 4000 posts to Glasgow and Merseyside (Bootle).
38 Militancy had long been an implicit and, after the 1981 strike, became an explicit reason for rejecting dispersal on 'regional policy' grounds. For example, in January 1982, Patrick Jenkin opposed the relocation of some 650 posts in the Hayes branch of the Passport Office to Scotland on the grounds that it would be 'poor reward' for the current staff's refusal – unlike all other Passport Office staff – to strike in 1981 especially when 'their replacements in East Kilbride would almost certainly be more militant'. 'I agree' wrote Mrs Thatcher emphatically on the memorandum (PREM19/Civil Service, Dispersal policy, part 2).
39 For Williams' observation, see TNA: BA17/400, meeting with F. Cooper, 3 December 1970; for Allen's later ones, see BA17/384, 3 August 1971.
40 The fullest statement of the NSS case was made to the Lord Privy Seal on 14 May 1976 (see TNA: PREM16/771). The NSS was particularly anxious to increase transfer allowances, and the Treasury particularly anxious to refuse the request *inter alia* because it would postpone from the mid-1970s to the late 1980s the 'break even' date (on which the 'costs' of dispersal would have ended and savings started to accrue). On location, the NSS had admitted in 1971 that 'Glasgow and Clydeside were particularly unpopular, South Lancashire and Tyneside less so'. There was also some sympathy for Teesside following an earlier debacle over the relocation of the Department of National Savings. Staff had voted for Durham, been prepared to compromise on Teesside and then been dispatched to Glasgow.
41 For the dislike of Liverpool, see the transcript of the Cabinet Committee (MCA(L)) on 29 November 1973 in TNA: BA17/781; and of Bootle, PREM19/Civil Service, Dispersal policy, part 2, note on minute by M. Pattison, 26 October 1979. The same file records the Foreign Office's great escape, abetted by Lord Carrington's protest that 'you can't post a man from Bogota to Bootle'.
42 TNA: PREM16/771, opening statement by John Dryden at the NSS meeting with the Lord Privy Seal, 14 May 1976.
43 For the subtle change, see the priority accorded 'operational efficiency' by Jellicoe to Heath on 23 September 1970 (TNA: PREM 15/777); the opening remark at the critical Conservative Cabinet Committee meeting on 29 November 1973 that dispersal was 'very much part of regional policy' (BA17/781, transcript by C. Priestley); and the conclusion of a meeting of the Home Affairs Committee (H(75)10th) under Labour on 1 August 1975: 'the Government's policy was for a strong bias in favour of the dispersal of work to Assisted Areas.' Heath had initially been impervious to special pleading. 'Scotland will bellyache whatever we do', for example, was his considered view in October 1971 (PREM 15/777).
44 Parl Deb (Commons) 861, col 61, 16 October 1973.
45 See TNA: BA17/934, C. Priestley to J.E. Herbecq, 15 July 1974; and PREM 16/14 for the note by the special adviser, Vicky Kidd, to Short on 3 June 1974 that to improve presentation of the backtracking 'the ideal solution . . . would be to have an "official" in charge of co-ordination, but obviously a politically committed official, not a career civil servant.'
46 *Sun*, 9 February 1981. Mrs Thatcher's comments, *inter alia* encouraging the Scott inquiry to exceed its terms of reference to condemn inflation-proofing in principle, were reported in the *Sunday Times*, 7 December 1980.
47 TNA: PREM15/265, Jellicoe to Heath, July 1970. For the fullest analysis of the confusion and its possible resolution, see BA27/196, J.E. Herbecq to M. Johnston, 5 January 1970.
48 TNA: BA27/269, J.E. Herbecq to B. Gilmore, 20 October 1970, which contains an overview of the Act's benefits. For Fulton, see Cmnd 3638, paras 135–44 and appendix H; for negotiations with the Treasury, see especially BA27/208; and with the

NSS (through the Whitley Council's Joint Superannuation Review Committee), BA27/315–6, 325 and 551. In the private sector, occupational pensions had been rapidly extended to half the workforce and their quality improved following the 1959 National Insurance Act (which had encouraged the 'contracting out' of employees from a vestigial state earnings-related pensions scheme). In order to satisfy Fulton, improvements were made to the preservation and transferability of pensions for those leaving the Service; and, to match best private practice, *inter alia* widows' pensions were increased from a third to a half of that of the deceased husband; the size of pension based on final salary (not average earnings over the past three years) and the number of days worked (not completed years); and all temporary work since 1949 made fully 'reckonable'.

49 For the comments by Williams and Armstrong in February 1972, see TNA: BA27/551. See also the memoirs of Sir John Herbecq in Churchill College, Cambridge, pp. 166–83. From 1966 to 1972 Herbecq was the official directly responsible for pension reform and its perceived success earned him both praise and promotion. In many ways this vindicated Fulton's call for greater 'administrative specialism' and the longer retention of 'key men' in key posts. It also vindicated its call for an 'open road to top' – albeit revealing that one already existed. As seen earlier, Herbecq had joined the prewar Colonial Office as a Clerical Officer, without a university degree, and ultimately rose to be the Second Permanent Secretary at the CSD – taking early retirement at the same time as Bancroft in 1981.

50 The lead was taken by the *Financial Times* on 30 November 1971, to be swiftly followed by the *Daily Telegraph*. For officials' reaction, see TNA: BA27/290.

51 TNA: BA27/373, J.E. Herbecq to Owen, 27 February 1970. 'Parity' was also rejected because its estimated cost was £75m and would have placed the Service 'an embarrassingly long way ahead of other occupational schemes' (BA27/196, P. Osmond's review of future policy for E. Shackleton, 20 January 1970). For the negotiations with the NSS and the moderation of its leading negotiator (Ken Thomas of the CPSA), see particularly BA27/316. The rank-and-file had been disconcerted by the proposals to meet Fulton recommendations concerning early retirement on the grounds of 'limited efficiency' and 'structural' needs (i.e. redundancy). They were, however, mainly designed for those at or above the level of Principal and, culminating in an independent Appeals Board, were both exhaustive and exhausting.

52 See particularly TNA: BA27/380. Actuarial forecasts were notoriously imprecise, but the Government Actuary did express concern at the low contribution for the widows' improved pension (at 1.5% of salary, whereas a more realistic 2% had originally been agreed with the NSS). Significantly for later developments, he also expressed concern about the limited deductions to pay *in lieu* of pension contributions that were agreed during wage negotiations (K.C. Lawrance to B. Gilmore, 23 August 1972).

53 By PESC logic, all that inflation-proof pensions 'cost' the Treasury was a windfall of which it had been oblivious. As Herbecq later explained; 'all we were asking the Treasury was that they should give up a saving (through the erosion by inflation of the real value of the pension) that they had not even realised they were making' (see Churchill College, Cambridge: Herbecq memoirs, p. 175).

54 Ibid, pp.176–7 and TNA: PREM15/265. Houghton originally asked the NSS for a brief, the NSS then asked the CSD to provide one and regular contact followed thereafter (BA27/289, A.W. Wyatt to E. Conn, 12 November 1971). See also Parl Deb (Commons) 826, col 824, 19 November 1971 for Howell's conviction. Political consensus was all the more remarkable, or comprehensible, because of the bitter battle after 1959 over the degree of inflation-proofing, redistribution and contracting out to be permitted in what ultimately became the State Earnings Related Pensions Scheme (SERPS) in 1975.

NOTES FOR CHAPTER 9

55 A typical attack on public pensions, together with a refutation of both it and public choice theory, may be found in TNA: BA27/577, G. Burrett to Shackleton, 18 September 1975. Shackleton had, of course, been the Minister in charge of the CSD before 1970 and was thereafter employed by Rio Tinto Zinc, whose chairman (Sir Val Duncan, Heath's most favoured businessman) was the author of the attack.

56 This paragraph is largely based on two letters by Allen, on 30 September 1975 to all Permanent Secretaries (TNA: BA 27/578) and to Harold Wilson on 19 December (PREM16/763). He also argued that, in equity, the pensions of those moving into, as well as out of, the public service would have to be capped. Legislation would thus have to be introduced to break contractual agreements with, amongst others, the chairmen of BNOC and British Airways (Lord Kearton and Sir Frank McFadzean) whose public salaries – let alone private pensions – far outstripped any Permanent Secretary's income. They would not, he assured Wilson, appreciate such 'confiscation'. For inflation-proofing in the private sector, see BA27/577.

57 The full irony of the Treasury's demands for statutory control over public pensions in 1975 was exposed by Ian Bancroft: 'the only statutory part of a declared voluntary policy would be the limitation of occupational pensions – something which has not even formed part of a statutory policy accompanied by a total freeze in the past' (TNA: BA27/575, memo to N. Gurney, 17 July 1975).

58 Geoffrey Howe was singled out by Allen for his 'misleading and nonsensical' assertion that the capital value of all public service pensions was £410,000. He had, Allen explained to Wilson, 'assumed the highest possible pension (paid only to a handful of people) and the continuation indefinitely of current levels of inflation, which, if it actually happened, would bring about the collapse of inflation-proofing along with pretty nearly everything else' (TNA: PREM16/763, 19 December 1975). Government communication with *The Economist* was almost severed in September 1975 because of a deliberately misleading article by the CSD's former special adviser, Mark Schreiber, 'Gilding the golden bowler' (see BA27/577).

59 Even Leo Pliatzky, at the height of his powers implementing cash limits, blanched at the prospect of temporary suspension because the political cost was so disproportionate to the budgetary gain (see TNA: PREM16/795, memo to K. Stowe, 18 November 1976 and Churchill College, Cambridge: Herbecq memoirs, pp. 178–9). While Ministers dissembled, retired officials – including Gilbert Fleming, Evelyn Sharp, Mary Smieton and Philip Rogers – acted by refusing to accept their increased pension. Their altruism, however, was a little tarnished by the speed with which they informed the press (see BA27/577–8).

60 The main battle over pensions, principally between the Treasury and the CSD, was fought in the Ministerial Committee on Economic Strategy (principally at E(80)1st and 7th, 15 January and 20 February 1980) and at Cabinet. After the first E Committee, the Scott Committee was commissioned; and at the second, Paul Channon (as Minister of State at the CSD) made a powerful political case against 'breaking the link' with the actual rate of inflation. The most important Cabinet meetings were on 15 January and 10 December 1981 (CC(81) 2 and 40), at which reports from the Official Committee 'following up' Scott were received (C(81)3 and 58). At the first, it was decided somewhat weakly to delay comment on Scott until the public's reaction was known. At the second it was recorded, apparently without irony, that Parliamentary debate should be encouraged 'to explain the complexity of the subject and to bring home the fact that, contrary to public opinion, civil servants already make a substantial contribution to their pensions'. The following paragraphs are largely based on these records.

61 For Scott's evasions, see its report (Cmnd 8141): General considerations, paras 34 and 39. 'Psychological security' was a phrase used by Robert Armstrong in his briefing of the Prime Minister on 29 October 1979 (PREM19/144).

NOTES FOR CHAPTER 9

62 For the offending passages, see respectively Cmnd 8141, General considerations, paras 36, 6–7 and 13–14. The members of the Committee had been selected for their presumed sympathy to the Government's case. Sir Bernard Scott was an engineer, who had been chair of Lucas Industries since 1974 and was currently a director of Lloyds Bank. Of the other four members, one was Alex Jarrat (who had famously left Whitehall to become chair of Reid International) and another Professor Harold Rose (an economist at the London Business School, with strong links to the Institute of Economic Affairs).

63 See PREM19/144 for the Government Actuary's report to Mrs Thatcher as early as May 1979. A breakdown of contributions was then presented by Soames to the Ministerial Committee on Economic Strategy in October 1979 (TNA: CAB134/4337, E(79)60). They could, it was admitted, be easily overlooked because payment was through salary deduction, with the only overt contribution being a deduction of 2.6% (raised to 3.8% in 1980) designed to cover the *additional benefits* of public over private pensions and not, as widely reported, the full cost of inflation-proofing. Despite such contributions, the overall cost of pensions to the taxpayer, and its consequences for the PSBR, were huge. For Civil Servants alone, it rose from £92m to £755m in the ten years to 1980/1 and stood at £3.27b for the public sector as a whole. £1.3b was the estimated cost of matching inflation since 1971. As for the proposed remedies, an extra 1% levy on salaries would have realised £30m from Civil Servants and £300m from the whole public sector in 1980.

64 Cmnd 8141, General considerations, para 17. For the later Cabinet discussion and the Attorney-General's disquiet at any interference with earned entitlements, see CC(81) 40th, 10 December 1981. One of Howe's other favoured ploys was to make public service pensions 'formally contributory'. This was doubly ironic because it had also been the objective of the NSS in 1971 on the grounds, previously endorsed in the 1942 Beveridge Report, that this would make benefits a right and not discretionary. The CSD had opposed contributions on the equally classic grounds that it would add to administrative costs – and possibly Exchequer costs, because greater transparency might have fuelled NSS demands for compensatory pay increases (see TNA: BA27/315, especially B.F. Hudson to J.E. Herbecq, 31 March 1971). When Cabinet discussion of Scott was resumed after the strike, Howe's policies were singularly unchanged.

65 The election pledges were collected in an annex to the first report of the Official Committee on the Value of Pensions, circulated to the Ministerial Committee on Economic Strategy in July 1981 as E(81)78. All candidates had been recommended, if pressed, to state that 'we are not proposing to change the index-linking provision for public sector pensions' although an independent inquiry would be undertaken to ensure that contributions were 'realistic'. Howe repeated this specific pledge on radio on 22 April 1979.

66 Both were arguably even more culpable for not examining more closely how actuarially based salary deduction was modified during the annual pay negotiations with the NSS. Frustration at formal pay restrictions could be, and not infrequently were, assuaged by 'adjustments' to this deduction.

67 For the following commentary on Government as a good employer, see respectively Parl Deb (Commons) 826, cols 824–7, 19 November 1971; the minutes of the Ministerial Committee on Economic Strategy on 30 November 1979 (TNA: CAB134/4335, E(79)14th); and D. Allen to K. Stowe, 11 February 1976 (PREM16/763). For a contemporary commentary on Government's historic role as a 'good' but not 'model' employer (in other words following, not determining, best practice), see P.B. Beaumont, 'The obligation of the British Government as an employer', *Public Administration* 56 (1978) 13–24.

68 Fulton (vol 3, part 1), Halsey Social Survey of the Civil Service, p. 418; and for some internal evidence TNA: BA19/107, N.G. Morrison to C. Gilbraith, 17 June 1971, but

also see ch 2.3.3 above for the reality below the earlier rhetoric. The United Nations had established a 'status of women' commission in 1946, which produced innumerable reports. It also designated 1975 International Women's Year, which Barbara Castle as chair of the Women's National Commission (appointed in 1969 to ensure the 'informed opinion of women' was always given 'due weight' in Government policy and public debate) exploited to the full. The political demand for equal opportunities was such in the late 1960s that the Conservatives in opposition produced two blueprints: the Cripps Report, *Fair Share for the Fair Sex*, designed to eliminate legal inequalities, and more pertinently the Bow Group pamphlet, *Less Equal than Others* (1969), recommending that Government should mount a 'campaign to break down job segregation, starting with its own employees'. For their later influence on policy, see PREM15/1614.

69 Halsey Report, esp p. 417. For Fulton's own indiscretion, see Cmnd 3638, para 91. It also continued to talk blithely of 'a man's career' (see, for example, para 115). William Armstrong's initiative in seeking reform was praised by successive heads of the CSD (Lords Shackleton and Jellicoe) during the House of Lords debate on the Kemp-Jones Report in December 1971 (Parl Deb (Lords) 326, cols 800, 826, 8 December 1971). See also TNA: BA19/82 (2 October 1969) and BA19/107 (22 June 1971) for further evidence of their support. Armstrong had ensured the Committee's appointment by his address to the Women's National Commission in January 1970 (BA19/82).

70 M.P. Fogarty, I. Allen and P. Walters, *Women in Top Jobs, 1968–1979* (1981), p. 16. For the sake of simplicity, the term 'gender' has been used throughout this subsection although – as illustrated by the 1975 Act, and suggestive of a rather less radical form of feminism – the term 'sex' was more commonly used until the late 1970s.

71 *Daily Mirror*, 14 October 1971. Kemp-Jones was the Chief Insurance Officer at the DHSS and, after much agonising by Armstrong, was preferred to the 'senior woman member of the Service', Miss Riddelsdell (Deputy Secretary, and soon to be Joint Permanent Secretary, at the DHSS). This was because, as a married woman, she had first-hand experience of the problems to be investigated. She had been twice married, had returned to the Service as a widow and had twice taken maternity leave. The other members of the Committee were three CSD officials (including Barbara Sloman, who was married with children, and John Drake, the adviser on personnel management recently transferred from BP); two Establishment Officers (from the DES and MOD); Doris Lancaster (representing staff associations); and Muriel Ward-Jackson (the personnel director of John Lewis, the pioneer of maternity provision in the private sector). For the selection process, see TNA: BA19/82.

72 For the welcome in Whitehall, see TNA: BA19/131; for the 'Dear Establishment Officers' letters of 13 March 1972, BA19/206; and for Jellicoe's welcome in the House of Lords, Parl Deb (Lords) 326, col 827, 8 December 1971.

73 M.P. Fogarty *et al*, *Women in Top Jobs* (1981) esp pp. 3, 9, 27 and 36–7; and E. Brimelow, 'Women in the Civil Service', *Public Administration* 59 (1981) 313–36. The former was a Policy Studies Institute report and a follow-up to a similarly titled PEP report in 1971, during which Patricia Walters as research assistant had received extensive help from the CSD (see TNA: BA19/82). The author of the latter was a member of Women in the Civil Service, a pressure group founded in 1978 to fight discrimination at the top of the Service. Part-time work expanded in the private sector to meet not just the needs of many women but also of many employers (who wished to minimise their social security contributions).

74 *CCSU Bulletin*, vol 1, no 6 (1981) 99. This number also includes details of the joint negotiations, which culminated in the 1983 report, summarised in vol 3, no 1 (1983) 8–16.

75 TNA: BA19/107: Kemp-Jones Report, 14 June 1971, ch 1, para 4. The Committee's terms of reference are on p. ii.

NOTES FOR CHAPTER 9

76 The marriage bar in the Diplomatic Service was also only fully lifted in 1972.
77 There were two principal misgivings. First, why should such benefits be targeted solely at women? Did not some men also require leave to meet, for example, 'urgent domestic affairs'? Second, how should the delicate balance be struck between departmental efficiency (in the public interest) and compassion (in an individual's interest)? A tendency to favour the former resulted in the Service in 1979 being taken to tribunal by a claimant (Linda Coyne) with the support of the Equal Opportunities Commission and defeated on its over-rigid interpretation of the right to maternity leave. One 'benefit' which women did lose was the marriage gratuity, an anachronism from the days when women had to resign on marriage and thereby forfeit their pensions rights. With those rights preserved under the 1972 Superannuation Act, such compensation was no longer required.
78 The waste of educational as well as departmental investment was also emphasised in many letters to the Committee written by younger women. For example, Mrs J. Holmes from the Ministry of Public Building and Works wrote in exasperation: 'the present rigid system seems a complete waste of expensive training and intellectual ability . . . It is surely ridiculous to welcome girls into responsible jobs while making it impossible for many of them to carry on with their chosen career' (TNA: BA19/84, WCS (70)16, annex D, 26 October 1970).
79 TNA: BA19/82, press release, 9 January 1970. It was this speech which prompted the appointment of the Kemp-Jones Committee. One conventional explanation for the decline in the number of women in top posts was the artificially high number of single career women previously in the Service, who had been unable to marry because so many men had been killed in the First World War.
80 TNA: BA19/84, WCS(70) 3rd, 6 August 1970, testimony of J. Hunt; and BA16/113, EOM(71)4, note to Establishment Officers by the Civil Service Commission, 27 January 1971. The percentage of women as Assistant Principals/Administration Trainees rose from 8% in 1959 to 31% in 1970. Wastage was accredited not just to marriage but also to some women's preference for careers, such as the probation service, in which they dealt with people directly rather than 'through files'; and later because they were 'poached' for jobs outside Whitehall, mainly in academia or teaching (see the list provided on 5 January 1970 by Miss T. Oliver in BA19/82).
81 BA19/107, Kemp-Jones Report, ch 1, para 1. For Mrs Ward-Jackson's insistence, see her letter to E. Conn in March 1971 (TNA: BA19/105).
82 M.P. Fogarty, *Women in Top Jobs* (1971), pp. 279–81, 303. The CSD deflected this criticism by insisting that there was no 'evidence to prove or disprove' it (undated comment on the Report in TNA: BA19/104); but for evidence at a political level, see Donoughue, *Downing Street Diary* (vol 2), p. 244: Callaghan as Prime Minister 'said he is an old fashioned male chauvinist. He would not want a woman private secretary in Private Office (not that there is any danger!)'. A fuller list of gender stereotyping is provided in Fogarty *et al*, *Women in Top Jobs, 1968–1979* (1981), p. 55 and its persistence confirmed by the confession of John Drake, the 'progressive' personnel manager from BP, that all women were temperamentally averse to 'bureaucratic management' (TNA: BA19/82, Drake to D.R.J. Stephen, 27 January 1970). Such sweeping statements were particularly well countered in a letter to the Committee from a Mrs James in the MinTech. Of women, she wrote, 'there have been discernible some sub-conscious, and conflicting assumptions. Women under thirty are flighty, over forty getting to the "difficult" age. Unmarried, they are over intense: married they put their families before their job. (If they didn't they ought to!) They are over logical. Their judgement is biased and emotional. They lack stamina. They are super thyroid . . . The same reflections can be made about men, and are. But with differing implications: not as sins, afflicting a group, but as misfortunes happening to befall an individual' (TNA: BA19/84, WCS(70)12, 20 August 1970).
83 TNA: BA19/82: D.J. Chapman to J.F. Gwynn, 14 October 1969.

NOTES FOR CHAPTER 9

84 At his meeting with the Women's National Commission in January 1970, for example, Armstrong argued that 'it should become usual for men to have maternity leave in order to share domestic burdens' so that all 'disabilities in relation to a career would not all fall on the wife' (see TNA: BA19/82, transcript). 'Reverse discrimination' was to be explicitly banned by the 1975 Sex Discrimination Act.

85 TNA: BA19/105, M. Ward-Jackson to E. Conn, March 1971. She was strongly supported on the Committee by the DES Establishment Officer, J.P. Carswell (ibid, Carswell to E.M. Kemp-Jones, 15 March 1971).

86 Parl Deb (Lords) 326, col 799, 8 December 1971. See also, for instance, the protest by Mrs E.H. Boothroyd (a Treasury Under Secretary) to E. Conn, 5 August 1970: 'married women, like other people, tend to want the best of all worlds. They want an interesting job, time to see their children and promotion in line with their male colleagues. They must, however, decide which to put first. If they wish to opt for part-time working over a longish period, they must accept some of the consequences'. This protest was made despite her awareness that, whilst working part-time herself, she had been given 'rather unsatisfactory work' and 'debarred from normal promotion' (TNA: BA19/84).

87 For the initial cautious (and confidential) reaction of the NSS to Kemp-Jones, see TNA: BA19/107, L. Williams to N.G. Morrison, 20 July 1971; and for the SCS's misbehaviour, BA19/132. Throughout the 1970s there were also formal arrangements in departments, such as the DES and the Inland Revenue, to ban reinstatement other than with the express agreement of Departmental Whitley Councils; and it was an explosion of 'anger and frustration' at 'blatant sexism' during the 1978 CPSA's annual conference that led to the formation of the Civil Service Women's Rights Group, to fight for greater equality in the Executive and Clerical Classes, see Fogarty *et al, Women in Top Jobs* (1981), p. 86.

88 Another reality of the labour market was that certain careers, such as teaching and academia, were more conducive to family life (and in particular child-care during school holidays) and so would always be more favoured by married women than the Civil Service. Some 'wastage', in short, was inevitable.

89 See respectively TNA: T353/83, note by R.H. Seebohm, 26 July 1976 and T342/234, N.G. Walsh to S. Goldman, 3 September 1969. Seebohm was a Principal in the Home Finance Division, Walsh an Economic Adviser. Such conservatism was, of course, matched by liberalism in other departments – such as the Department of Employment where, to the extent that discrimination existed, it tended to favour rather than penalise women.

90 TNA: BA19/82, 30 October 1969. For the succeeding quotation see Conn to Lord Windlesham, March 1972 in BA19/131. Confident predictions of more 'companionate' marriages had been made since at least 1918. For male echoes of such complacency, see BA 19/107, note on CSD reactions to the Kemp-Jones Committee, June 1971 and BA 23/9, note of a meeting on 27 August 1971 to discuss its implementation. 'New privileged class' was a phrase coined by the DTI's Establishment Officer in August 1971 (BA20/52).

91 BA19/107, note on CSD reactions, June 1971. For the Equal Opportunity Commission ruling, see Fogarty *et al, Women in Top Jobs* (1981), p. 80. There is no evidence that the CSD was using this incident as a 'test case' to clarify the legal position, possibly to the advantage of women.

92 TNA: BA19/84, Carswell to E.M. Kemp-Jones, 13 August 1970. For an imaginative list of technical objections, see BA16/74, EOM(71)30, annex. The French Civil Service was reported at this time to permit part-time work for both men and women for up to nine years. In the UK labour market as a whole, the percentage of women working part-time expanded between 1971 and 1981 from 35% to 42% (see J. Lewis, *Women in Britain since 1945* (1992), ch. 3). At the same time, in a workforce of some

500,000, the number of part-time non-industrial Civil Servants rose by a mere 2000 to 17,000.
93 For Jellicoe's commitment, see in particular his note to E. Conn on 23 January 1972 (TNA: BA 23/9). For the suggestion in the Kemp-Jones Report that nurseries should initially be experimental, arising from an awareness that the private sector, including John Lewis, had baulked at the cost of provision, see para 45. It thus implicitly accepted the Treasury proviso that not just women but also employers should benefit. Hartman had been promoted from an Executive Officer to Senior Principal; but his 'administrative' superiors were similarly lukewarm, perhaps because it was assumed that women at this level could – as, on occasion, they did – employ private nannies.
94 TNA: BA23/9, W.F. Hartman to H.G. Ardley, 2 June 1971. DHSS opposition is recorded in the same file and the fullest expression of Treasury opposition is in T341/845, B. Fox to Allman, 19 October 1972. For a summary of the revolution in public attitudes towards married women working, see Lewis, *Women in Britain*, p. 76. Total opposition to married women's work had fallen to 11% by 1980, but 60% of survey respondents still believed that women with pre-school children should stay at home.
95 TNA: T341/845, B. Fox to W.F. Hartman, 25 October 1972. The downgrading was agreed at a meeting of Treasury, CSD, PSA and Inland Revenue officials on 29 September 1972, recorded in the same file.
96 Ibid, including the Inland Revenue's first annual report on Llanishen (1974). The initial charge for mothers of the 32 children at Llanishen (£5 a week) was higher than comparable local charges, but fell well below the full economic cost (calculated 'generously' by the Treasury at £16). The disparity was caused in part by the Welsh Office's veto on a private scheme and its insistence that the nursery be run by Cardiff's Social Services Department – which in turn insisted on a high level of child-care (some 13 staff for 32 children). To provide a comparison, the Croydon experiment was both to be private and serve a range of departments. A lack of official zeal was demonstrated by the failure to establish mothers' demand for places either at Croydon (where only 3 'customers' were identified) or at Nottingham (where an earlier experiment had been mooted, with the support of the Corporation but apparently only 14 mothers).
97 M.P. Fogarty, R. and R. Rapoport, *Women and Top Jobs: the next move* (1972), p. 67. For the later criticism, see in particular Brimelow, 'Women', 332. In relation to the industrial Civil Service, there was never any pretence of combating discrimination, with the *Guardian* on 19 October 1972 reporting that it was 'dotted with Martello towers literally manned with trade unionists . . . on their guard against any advance by women invaders'.
98 A. Hede, 'Women managers in the Civil Service', *International Review of Administrative Sciences* 61 (1995) 587–600.
99 For Fulton's contradictory wishes, see Cmnd 3638, paras 134 and 287–91.
100 See transcript in TNA: BA19/132.
101 On the Sex Discrimination Act, for example, the Women's National Commission deprecated 'the linking of this legislation with the Race Relations Act which was designed to deal with a minority situation. Women are not a minority and should not be treated as such' (TNA: CAB134/3817, bulletin for 6 December 1974). The 1965 Act had set up the Race Relations Board to receive and investigate complaints about discrimination; the 1968 Act *inter alia* had extended its remit to employment; and the 1975 Act was to establish a system of industrial tribunals to which cases of alleged discrimination might be brought with or without the assistance of the new Commission for Racial Equality. The WNC particularly objected to a parallel tribunal system and the Equal Opportunities Commission's proactive role.

NOTES FOR CHAPTER 9

102 See TNA: T216/920, EOM(67)37, 28 November 1967 for the rising sense of panic within the Inland Revenue, the Ministry of Social Security and the General Post Office. 32% of all recruits to the GPO in London during the first half of 1967, for instance, were 'coloured' (T216/966, S. Burrow to L.M. Alessi, 31 August 1967). The insouciant response of the head of the Treasury's Management Services Division (P. Osmond) was that 'the extent to which the Civil Service employs coloured staff is already exemplary, indeed to a degree which in some ways creates a lot of managerial problems' (ibid).

103 *CCSU Bulletin*, vol 2, no 9 (1982) 202. The unions' evolving reactions following the publication of the Tavistock Institute's *Race Relations Policy in the Civil Service* (which had been commissioned by the CSD) may be traced through the annual report of its Personnel Management Committee in the December editions of the *Bulletin* and the preceding *Whitley Bulletin*. The Tavistock Institute was a charitable foundation, founded in 1947, which applied social scientific research to organisational change. It was regularly employed by Government on a consultancy basis throughout the 1970s.

104 For Armstrong's relative lack of engagement, see his meeting with Permanent Secretaries on 18 May 1972 and with the head of the Race Relations Board, Sir Geoffrey Wilson, on 15 February (TNA: BA19/276). The working party for the inquiry was headed by G. Watson, not the most assiduous of Assistant Secretaries, who on being transferred to another post found his four page interim report at the bottom of a cupboard and forwarded it to Armstrong on 9 February 1973 (ibid).

105 For the CPRS report, see Blackstone and Plowden, *Think Tank*, pp. 118–20 and a critique by Watson's successor, the appropriately named W.E. Wightman, in July 1973, TNA: BA19/277. The Race Relations Board's 1971–2 Annual Report, supported by the Department of Employment's Code of Industrial Practice, first laid down a 'positive' policy for all employers and its 1973 report, *Race Relations Legislation in Britain*, first broached the topic of 'unconscious' or 'indirect' discrimination. In addition, the House of Commons Select Committee on Race Relations and Immigration was active throughout the period, publishing a major report (*The Organisation of Race Relations Administration*) in 1975. For the dynamic nature of the subject, and particularly the issue of ethnic monitoring, see Wightman's critique, p. 2.

106 For the anguished dispute between the Home Office and Treasury over whether the 'Crown' could and should be included in the legislation (which was only really resolved after Roy Jenkins switched departments in November 1967), see especially TNA: T216/920-4 and T216/965-6. The major point of principle was whether, for the first time, the employment practices of the Government's own employees should be determined by law or, as in the past, by Orders in Council and statements by Ministers accountable to Parliament. The Civil Service Commission argued that its political independence would be jeopardised by the change, whereas the Home Office argued (and, in committee, the House of Commons agreed) that 'privileged exemption' for the Service would set a bad example and delay necessary changes in social attitudes. Some exemptions had to be agreed, particularly on security grounds (where every effort was made to keep secret the existence of negative vetting). The Race Relations Board was also debarred from bringing civil proceedings against the Crown. If found guilty of discrimination, departments had to make appropriate *ex gratia* payments.

107 TNA: BA19/276, 'A Civil Service adviser on race relations', Appendix A, transcript of evidence, June 1972.

108 For the most succinct summary of the arguments, see the CSD memorandum to Establishment Officers on 22 August 1973 (TNA: BA16/116, EOM (73) 30). The enlightened CSD official cited earlier was its Establishment Officer, J.K. Moore, in a letter to J. Chilcot, 14 February 1973.

NOTES FOR CHAPTER 9

109 Foremost examples of this pressure are the meetings of Sir Geoffrey Wilson, as chair of the Race Relations Board with the CSD's Parliamentary Secretary on 28 November 1972 and with William Armstrong on 15 February 1973 (see TNA: BA19/276); and a meeting of the Board with representatives of five Government departments on 18 May 1973 (transcript in BA19/277). With regard to protraction, the Leeds pilot was completed in 1982 without the anticipated trouble, but the Government's reaction was to plan further pilot studies rather than take appropriate policy initiatives.

110 For the admission of additional job specification, see TNA: BA19/277, transcript of meeting between the Race Relations Board with departmental representatives, 18 May 1983; for the CSC's misdemeanours, T216/921, note by P.S. Ross, 22 January 1968; and for the interchangeability of statistics, T216/966, particularly P. Osmond to Skinner, 19 September 1967. For Establishment Officers' evidence of local practices, see BA19/78, especially G. Moseley to C. Barclay, 21 July 1969.

111 TNA: BA19/277, W.E. Wightman to A. Duke, 18 July 1983.

112 There was one other area of potential discrimination: male homosexuality. In 1972 the Campaign for Homosexual Equality wrote to each department querying the position. The CSD, in co-ordinating a reply, recognised that there had been many homosexuals within the Service over time and that they had caused no noticeable 'moral problems'. Accordingly CHE was assured that there was no formal discrimination in relation to either appointment or promotion. Some reservations, however, remained in relation to promotion (because of the reaction of junior staff), relations with public (because of popular prejudice) and security (because of the danger of blackmail, given that illegality – but not social stigma – had been ended by the 1967 Sexual Offences Act). These reservations, so it was argued, were not blanket bans but simply accorded to the long-tried practice that any official, who displayed personal traits which might lead to the less than efficient discharge of a given responsibility, should not be given that responsibility. More explicit forms of 'indirect' discrimination did exist, however, such as the compulsory salary deduction of 1.5% (introduced in 1972) to pay for a widow's pension.

113 For the Service's early technological lead, see ch 2.3.3. The 1961 Plowden Committee noted that the Civil Service remained 'in the forefront of national progress' (Cmnd 1432, para 51); in March 1965 Callaghan (as Chancellor of the Exchequer) assured the Prime Minister that 'the Government Service has been in the van of progress in this country in the use of computers and the record so far is a good one' (TNA: PREM13/1781); and as late as 1980 the Head of the Civil Service was lauding its 'high reputation' and citing, for instance, the computerisation of the Land Charges Index in 1974 (which had won the British Computer Society award for the project most beneficial to society) and of the National Savings Bank in Glasgow (which had cut staff by half since 1968 – thereby perhaps sowing the seed for its exceptional militancy). See I. Bancroft, 'The Civil Service in the 1980s', *Public Administration* 59 (1981) 146. The internal Atkinson Report, which was published by the CSD in 1971, was entitled *The Future of Computing in Central Government: 10 Years Ahead* (for a copy, see CAB 151/52). This report succeeded Merriman's initial ten-year programme of February 1957 (in T222/1304) and was itself succeeded by the CSD's *Longer-Term Review of Administrative Computing in Central Government* (1978). Together with two of Atkinson's public speeches, as head of the CCA, in 1975 (T374/42) and 1977 (*Whitley Bulletin*, vol 58, no 1 (1978)), these reports provide the backbone of this subsection.

114 The following discussion is concerned only with the use of computers for administrative purposes. The procurement and use of large computers for military purposes and scientific research have a different history.

115 W.R. Atkinson, 'Future developments in Government computing', *Whitley Bulletin*, vol 58, no 1 (1978) 16–17.

116 CSD, *Longer-Term Review*, para 21. For the support, particularly by Conservative Party modernisers, of PPBS see ch 5.3.1. In the USA, it employed over 1000 staff over 7 years but still failed.
117 Another constraint on efficiency was the issue of privacy which generated particularly strong emotions after 1967 and led ultimately to data protection legislation. Had a unique personal identification number for each British resident been politically acceptable administrative systems could have been greatly streamlined. Preference in procurement was extended by the Heath Government from hardware to software. Development of in-house expertise was discouraged, in part to reduce Civil Service manpower, but mainly to strengthen private industry through direct purchases and the subsequent employment of consultants.
118 For a summary of procurement policy see TNA: CAB164/435, April 1970 and PREM16/1953. The original Cabinet decision is recorded in CAB 128/39/2, 44.3, 3 August 1965. ICL was actually formed in 1968 through a merger of ICT (for whom the initial decision was taken) with English Electric, and designed to provide large mainframe computers for Government – although the first two prototypes (Project 51 and 1908A) had to be abandoned. The UK was hardly unique – the USA, for instance, supported IBM with defence contracts and France favoured CII-Honeywell in its public sector contracts. The EEC discouraged such preference after 1980.
119 TNA: CAB134/2843, GC(70), 1st, 17 April 1970. Reliance on one manufacturer had potentially one major administrative, and economic, advantage: compatibility between systems.
120 J. Agar, *The Government Machine* (2003), p. 339. See also pp. 340–2, 366–9. The director was P.S. Milner-Barry and his deputy, James Merriman, whose unpublished autobiography is held by the BT Archives.
121 TNA: CAB159/52, paras 8.2–8.4.
122 The two culprits were Otto Clarke and Sir Thomas Padmore. For this and further exploits in 'the year of indoctrination and implementation', see Agar, *Government Machine*, pp. 314, 329–33, 340. Sir Douglas Wass, later Permanent Secretary at the Treasury and joint Head of the Civil Service, was amongst the most appreciative participants in the seminars (which used amateur dramatics to ensure the impact later achieved by visual aids).
123 See, for example, TNA: T224/2068 and T338/135 for the reservations expressed, amongst others, by the Chief Secretary, Patricia Brown and Brian Hopkin. FIS, whilst fulfilling the role required of it by cash limits, of course failed in its broader objectives to improve departmental management information systems and increase the compatibility of all departmental returns to the Treasury (including those covering Estimates and PES).
124 For the confessions of CSD officials, see TNA: BA17/44, A. Creamer to J.S. Whyte, 29 March 1968 (whilst Creamer was still at the Treasury); and Churchill College, Cambridge: J. Herbecq, *Autobiography*, p. 224. Herbecq, as the responsible Under Secretary, delegated responsibility to Atkinson because of his own 'virtual complete lack of any technical understanding which I was not much minded to attempt to rectify'. Atkinson had joined the Service as a tax inspector in 1950, before becoming a Principal in 1958.
125 *Whitley Bulletin*, vol 58, no 1 (1978) 15. Ministers, as well as private sector management, were equally at fault. Typical of their neglect was the handling of the original Atkinson Report, submitted in September 1969 but not published until January 1971 despite Shackleton's early advice to Wilson that this was 'an area where Ministers themselves must really get "stuck into it"' (TNA: CAB 164/435, January 1970). Then the new Ministerial Committee on Computers in Central Government, which he had demanded, concerned itself solely with procurement (CAB134/2843).

NOTES FOR CHAPTER 10

126 To wrest power from the Treasury (which controlled the Ministerial and Official Committees on Public Sector Purchasing and, more importantly, the Procurement Policy Committee) Shackleton had demanded in January 1970 the establishment of new Ministerial and Official Committees on Computers in Central Government. The former was disbanded by the Conservatives, but the latter was retained – although the Treasury added 'and economic' to the original terms of reference: 'to promote the efficient use of computers in support of the processes of government' (TNA: CAB165/872).

127 For the views of the Treasury, the Select Committee and the CPRS, as well as the Conservatives' Business Team (which naturally favoured a hived-off agency), see TNA: T319/1371. For the creation of the CCA and its objectives, as conceived by its first short-lived director (S.W. Spain), see BA18/20.

128 The somewhat tart exchange is in TNA: T338/175, and the fullest exposition of the rival attractions of repayment and 'allied services' in T224/3223, R. Jones to L. Pliatzky, 14 January 1975 and in CSD, *Longer-Term Review*, ch 6. The Treasury initially conceded control, for an experimental period, because it lacked the expertise (which the CSD allegedly had) to vet departmental expenditure plans. Moreover, computers only performed tasks which were not 'normally of a controversial nature' and were designed to 'produce savings in manpower' for which the CSD was responsible (see T319/1371, P. E. Lazarus to A. Creamer, 22 February 1971). A leading later advocate of repayment was the future project manager of *Next Steps*, E.P. Kemp (see T224/2973, memo to D. McKean, 29 March 1974 and T341/802, memo to R. Jones, 10 October 1974). Allied Services annual expenditure by 1977/8 was just under £60m.

129 This paragraph is largely based on CSD, *Longer-Term Review*, esp paras 5, 52–61 and section 10. Appendix C contains a summary of the more exhaustive 1976–7 Howard Report on Computing Staff.

130 Instead of a solution, the 'absurd situation' arose whereby the Service, having played its part to reduce a national skills shortage, then lost its trained staff to the private sector and had to hire them back at great expense.

131 P.D. Jones to G.W. Moseley, 2 November 1978, reprinted in *CSSU Bulletin*, vol 1, no 6 (1981) 96 (which provides the fullest published account of the dispute). Union conferences were duly asked to, and did, endorse a resolution in 1981 for a 'positive programme of non-cooperation', amounting to a 'refusal to participate or assist in the trial stage or in pilot running, no acceptance of training obligations, and a refusal to co-operate in the implementation of new applications which are ... "blacked"'. Atkinson had earlier reflected the managerial consensus that 'the human aspects' of new technology were 'all-important' and that it was imperative to negotiate change through the relevant trade union. See *Whitley Bulletin*, vol 58, no 1 (1978) 17.

132 For the dispute over Datalink, see PREM19/Civil Service, Long-term management and manpower policy, pt 7. Mrs Thatcher's amended minute was on 10 December 1980. For an explicit admission that a major purpose for computerisation was to reduce the Service's size, see ibid, Soames to G. Howe, 23 September 1980.

133 Ian Bancroft, quoted in Hennessy, *Whitehall*, p. 131.

10 POLITICAL PRESSURES

1 See, for instance, R.A.W. Rhodes, Understanding Governance (1997) pp. 17–18.
2 Cmnd 3638, para 280. The quotation in the next paragraph comes from para 279. Sweden was held as an exemplar because, in addition to widespread public inquiries prior to major policy decisions, a constitutional right of access was believed to have existed to 'all files of any administrative office' since 1766 – subject to certain

exemptions, such as national security. What Fulton (and others) failed to appreciate, however, were the institutional separation of policy formulation and implementation; the effective exemption of policy 'working papers' by various administrative expedients; and the inviolability of a Minister's decision on what should remain closed (see, for instance, TNA: BA19/86, testimony of W. Armstrong to the Franks Committee and Cmnd 7285, Reform of Section 2 of the Official Secrets Act (1978) para 45).

3 TNA: CAB 164/640, B. Trend to W. Armstrong, 6 February 1969. For Weber's views on the 'natural' tendency for all bureaucracies to invent the concept 'official secrecy' in order to sustain their 'superiority' and protect them from criticism, see H.A. Gerth and C. Wright Mills, From Max Weber (1970 ed) pp. 233–4.

4 See D. Hooper, Official Secrets (1987) esp ch 9.

5 Maladminstration was, for instance, the charge levelled by Justice (the campaigning name of the British Section of the International Commission of Jurists) in their 1965 pamphlet, The Law and the Press. The pamphlet inspired a House of Lords debate on 25 May 1966 and later Reginald Eyre's private member's bill (The Freedom of Publication (Protection) Bill) which further concentrated Wilson's mind in 1969.

6 Craig, Manifestos 1959–1987, p. 252. In the USA, Freedom of Information legislation was notoriously difficult to activate and so initially realised little of its overt purpose. By contrast, in the UK, the 1967 Public Records Act effectively ensured the release after 30 years of virtually all relevant Government files and thereby provided historians with an exceptional service.

7 TNA: BA19/49, D. Haddow to W. Armstrong, 6 February 1969. Sir Douglas Allen, later the author of the Croham directive, was equally cynical. 'Those who call for a reduction in anonymity', he wrote, 'are not really interested in knowing the names of civil servants but are mainly interested in the genesis of policy and therefore in the views and attitudes of civil servants. When they get their name and not their views, the press sometimes go so far as to invent the views in order to produce an interesting story' (CAB 164/640, D. Allen to W. Armstrong, 31 January 1969).

8 TNA: CAB 164/640, B. Trend to W. Armstrong, 21 May 1968.

9 A copy of the directive is in PREM19/Home Affairs, Open Government, part 1. On his retirement at the end of 1977, Allen was ennobled as Lord Croham.

10 Armstrong's initiatives, including an early Permanent Secretaries' meeting on 7 June 1968, are recorded in TNA: CAB164/640 and BA19/49; Wilson's varying responses are in PREM13/1970 and 2528. The latter records Cabinet's referral of the inquiry to the Parliamentary Committee and its eventual rejection on March 21 (CAB134/3032, P(69)6th.1). 'Truly feeble' was the judgement of Peter Hennessy in 'Open government, Whitehall and the press since 1945' in H. Stephenson (ed) Media Voices (2001) p. 318. Whitehall's increasingly liberality was asserted in para 2.

11 As Heath pronounced to Permanent Secretaries collectively on 3 October 1970: 'in an open society ... there must be an informed dialogue between Government and the public. This did not mean that there would be a return to the past practice of inspired leaks ... this would be an abdication of Government responsibility. What it did mean was that in each situation of choice, there should be a skilful analysis within Government of all the possible options, and a presentation of the options for public consideration with either a statement of the Government's choice (or decisions) and the reasons ... or an indication that the Government would make its choice in the light of informed public debate' (TNA: CAB184/3).

12 See J. Garrett and R. Sheldon, Administrative Reform: the next step (1973): 'we believe that the main requirement of secrecy comes from within the Civil Service itself. As a result of it, they are better able to control events, outside influences matter less and decisions can be unhurried ... To control the information is to control the argument

NOTES FOR CHAPTER 10

and so to control the decision'. Sheldon's tenure prompted a discussion of openness by Permanent Secretaries at Sunningdale in 1974. It concentrated on three topics (the availability of information, the process of consultation and the anonymity of civil servants) but reached no startling conclusions.

13 For a history of PAU and the search by its head, John Charkham, for 'chaps of both sexes' to fill posts, see Hennessy, Whitehall, pp. 553–6. Charkham was a late recruit from industry and later decamped to the Bank of England.

14 See, for example, Brittan, Capitalism with a Human Face, p. 11 and also TNA: CAB164/640, for Armstrong's address to Permanent Secretaries on 20 January 1969.

15 TNA: BA19/91. Emphases added.

16 Donoughue, Diary, vol 2, p. 321, recalling the first meeting of GEN 119(78) on 3 May 1978. The CSD had recommended a procedure for nominating potential appointees by third parties outside Whitehall, whilst Benn wanted all posts to be advertised and all candidates interviewed by a selection board. The CSD won a partial victory in March 1979.

17 Between 1945 and 1970, there were only 36 prosecutions under section 2 of the OSA. 20 of these arose from espionage or the disclosure of weapon systems (see TNA: CAB164/922, Home Office, 'OSA: consideration of the case for a review', June 1970). A full list of prosecutions is in HO292/34.

18 For the doctrine of self-authorisation, see Vincent, The Culture of Secrecy (1998), p. 248–50.

19 For evidence of collusion, see respectively TNA: CAB164/922, B. Trend to N. Cairncross, 20 April 1971; CAB 165/943, meeting of officials with A.D. Gordon-Brown, 20 April 1972; CAB164/1134, J.A. Chilcot, 'Note for the record', 18 January 1972.

20 TNA: T199/1225, D. Allen to W. Armstrong, 12 October 1972. For a full Treasury critique of the 'cavalier' way Franks went against 'the weight of official advice', see T199/1270, R.L. Sharp to D. Allen, 30 November 1972; and for later advice to the Ministerial Committee considering legislation (GEN 149) T199/1345, Sharp to Allen, 13 June 1973 and Sharp to the Principal Private Secretary, Chancellor of the Exchequer, 15 November 1973.

21 See TNA: PREM15/1737, B. Trend to E. Heath, 18 June 1973 prior to the first meeting of GEN 149. For a summary of the Helsby Committee, and the attempts by William Armstrong to keep it secret from Franks until let slip – for his own reasons – by the MOD's Permanent Secretary, see BA19/87. It was the Committee's working rule that 20% of material was 'top secret', 25% 'secret', 45% 'confidential' and 10% 'restricted'.

22 For a running account of Jenkins' battle with MISC 89, see TNA: PREM16/668–9 and 1854–5. For Jenkins' proposals, see his letters to Wilson on 27 February and 18 June 1975 (PREM16/668). Having studied FOI in the USA, he concluded it was 'cumbersome, very expensive and of [too] little value' to be copied. For the 'strong, indeed almost universal opposition' to him, see PREM16/1854: Wilson to the Lord Chancellor, 22 December 1975.

23 For a parallel running account on Callaghan's battles, see TNA: PREM16/1855–8. The Cabinet decision was on 22 November 1976 and was in part inspired by Donoughue's widely quoted advice that a blunderbuss should be replaced by an Armalite rifle (see Donoughue, Diary, vol 2, p. 61).

24 TNA: CAB184/640, B. Trend to W. Armstrong, 21 May 1968 and, for the anchor, CAB164/1134, Trend evidence to Franks, p. 7. Of the other deterrents identified by Franks, CSD officials dismissed both as ineffectual: civil law (as was proved in the Crossman case) and internal discipline (because *inter alia* it would neither cover the retired nor concern those on short-term contacts, such as special advisers,

NOTES FOR CHAPTER 10

who might feel it to be a 'public duty' to leak – as in the 1976 child benefit case, see ch 6.3.1).

25 For the Treasury view, see TNA: T199/1345, R.L. Sharp to D. Allen, 13 June 1973; for Allen's *volte face*, PREM16/1855, Allen to K. Stowe, 21 July 1976; and for Hunt's rodents, PREM16/1856, Hunt to Callaghan, 3 August 1977. Allen may have been reacting to defeat over the Crossman diaries (which blew apart Trend's justification for the OSA, that it protected Cabinet confidentiality and thus 'good government'). Similarly, Callaghan's renewed hardness may have been a response to the apparent leaking of Cabinet documents on child benefit to *New Society* in June 1976, which led to the interviewing and fingerprinting of Cabinet Ministers by the police (see BA7/25–8).

26 For Wilson's lassitude despite Hunt's pleas, see TNA: PREM16/668, 5 March 1975. The first meeting of MISC 89 was then repeatedly delayed until October. The Younger Committee on privacy (which reported in 1972, Cmnd 5012), the Phillimore Committee on contempt (1974, Cmnd 5794) and the Faulks Committee on defamation (1975, Cmnd 5909) had each been appointed by the Heath Government in an attempt to clarify the law.

27 TNA: PREM16/1857, Callaghan to J. Hunt, 30 January 1978. Later, and regardless of both the legal defeat over the Crossman diaries and his own Ministers' constant 'leaking', Callaghan mounted a defence of 'good government' that would have warmed Trend's heart. 'Ministers conducting the affairs of government', he noted in November 1978, 'are entitled to exchange views privately and frankly with each other; and they should not be required to make public all their discussions and exchanges about their responsibilities as Ministers. It would change the very nature of Cabinet government as we know it if Ministers were not able to conduct their affairs in this way; and breaking this mutual trust, whether it be by Ministers or civil servants, has nothing whatever to do with open government' (PREM16/1858).

28 J. Vincent, *Culture of Secrecy*, p. 258. Kellner and Crowther-Hunt, *Civil Servants*, would appear to be the source of this misjudgement.

29 For a summary, see TNA: CAB130/876, GEN29(78)3, 'Open Government' by Lord Peart, 9 October 1978. Benn became involved in early 1978, typically seeking to extend Government policy to the disclosure of all external and internal advice before Ministerial decisions were taken (see PREM16/1875, for Callaghan's rebuff on 19 April 1978). Open government had become an issue of such political and public concern that it was the subject of the first *Yes Minister* programme in 1980.

30 For the fullest exposition of official views in 1978 and 1979, on which this and the following paragraph are based, see TNA: PREM16/1858, I. Bancroft to K.R. Stowe, 23 October 1978, covering a note by the chairman of GEN 146; PREM16/2242, Bancroft to Stowe, 19 January 1979; and PREM19/Home Affairs, Open government, part 1, election brief, May 1979. The latter file confirms that, having given little thought to the subject whilst in opposition, the Conservatives reaffirmed Labour's formal objection to a Freedom of Information Act in their first policy statement on 20 June 1979. On the grounds that there was 'little difference between a Code of Practice and a statutory scheme', they sought to disassociate themselves even from the Justice proposals – arguing (as will be seen in ch 10.3.2) that open government was better served by a strengthening of Parliamentary Select Committees. In October 1981, after the CSD's demise, the Prime Minister rejected a suggestion that the Croham directive should be replaced by a more explicit 'presumption to disclose'.

31 TNA: PREM16/1858, N.L. Wicks to K.R. Stowe, 25 September 1978. Such defensiveness illustrated the collapse of confidence in Whitehall since the 1960s, when Ministers had been considered the principal potential losers from such intrusion. 'It does not matter to us' Peter Le Cheminant of the Cabinet Office had written in May 1968 'whether we advise on policy in a goldfish bowl or a bunker' (PREM13/1930).

NOTES FOR CHAPTER 10

For the fullest summary of international practice, see GEN 29(79)6, 1 February 1979, Conclusion of Overseas Study.

32 See TNA: PREM19/1858 for Stowe's blueprint; and PREM16/2243 for Hunt's urging. How far they represented the view of the whole Service may be judged from a comparison with Bancroft's memoranda and a personal plea from Robert Armstrong at the Home Office that 'the counterpart' to a Government's duty to disclose information was 'not a right to the citizens to have access to Government documents: it is a right to the citizens to receive that information' (ibid).

33 TNA: PREM16/1858, K.R. Stowe to Callaghan, 25 September 1978. The effectiveness of the Croham directive was monitored by yet another Cabinet Committee (MISC 106) which found it wanting because of the lack, not just of an appeal mechanism but also of adequate funding (anticipated by Allen and, in itself, reflecting a lack of political will) and of consistency in departmental practice. Typically, when the Parliamentary All-Party FOI Campaign asked for a copy of the directive, the CSD's instinct was to send an abridged copy before being overruled by the Prime Minister (PREM 16/1856, September 1977).

34 On his ambition, see *Diaries of a Cabinet Minister*, vol 1, p. 11; on his conduct, vol 3, pp. 898–9. His command of detail was well known to be imperfect (although, as Roy Jenkins maintained in *Gallery of Twentieth Century Portraits* (1988) p. 60, he tended to be 'remarkably accurate in essentials') and his political trustworthiness earned him the sobriquet, 'Double-Crossman'. See also K. Theakston 'Richard Crossman', *Public Policy and Administration* 18 (2003) 20–40 and, for a more partisan account, H. Young, *The Crossman Affair* (1976).

35 TNA: BA19/58, L. Helsby to S. Garner, 21 October 1965 and B. Trend to Helsby, 5 March 1965. Ironically Crossman's much-vilified 'Dame', Evelyn Sharp, was amongst the first to assure Helsby that she would not publish, despite allegedly having received some half dozen offers from publishers.

36 TNA: PREM16/465, Robert Armstrong to Wilson, 7 June 1974 and the Parliamentary answer to Tam Dalyell on 14 November 1974, also largely drafted by Robert Armstrong (which was the definitive public statement of Government policy prior to serialisation). 'Subsidiary' was the term employed by William Armstrong in his memorandum of 10 June 1974 in the same file. As Head of the Civil Service, he took responsibility for policy concerning criticism of individual officials, whilst the Cabinet Secretary led on collective responsibility

37 TNA: CAB164/288, Hunt to H. Evans, 23 January 1975; PREM16/466, Hunt to Wilson, 27 February 1975. The four parameters were '(a) no blow-by-blow accounts of Cabinet discussions or the revelation of differences between members of the Cabinet or detailed discussion of other Minister's policies; (b) no breach of the confidentiality of the advice given by civil servants to Ministers; (c) preservation of the confidentiality surrounding senior civil service appointments; (d) no details of discussions between Ministers on policy matters which one of the parties must have regarded as private'(CAB164/1256, note of meeting 10 July 1974).

38 For the Government's handling of the Radcliffe Report (Cmnd 6386), see TNA: PREM16/440, 904 and 1293. Wilson tried to bounce its acceptance through MISC 89 on 13 January and Cabinet on 15 and 21 January 1976, leading to several complaints about the accuracy of each meeting's minutes (see, for example, PREM16/1293, minute by B. Donoughue, 17 February 1976).

39 TNA: PREM16/1293 and CAB164/1364/1, annotation on K.R. Stowe to J. Hunt, 14 June 1976. A principal bone of contention for many Ministers, and especially Roy Jenkins, was that their freedom to publish was seemingly to be determined by an official – although it was often repeatedly stated, not least in the Parliamentary statement of 14 November 1974, that the Cabinet Secretary was working expressly to the Prime Minister and had no independent powers.

40 TNA: PREM16/465, N. Beloff to J. Hunt, 20 November 1974. The local Party was Battersea, and the *New Statesman* article was on 15 November 1974. Earlier Howard had demanded, even more tendentiously, why 'an Establishment clique should be allowed to interfere with the publication of a book written by one of the great socialist teachers of our time' (*New Statesman*, 27 September 1974). As the records demonstrate, Hunt always felt bound by the Attorney-General's rulings and so the 'errand boy' image was simply the consequence of constant legal prevarication.

41 *Observer*, 27 July 1974; Donoughue, *Diary*, vol 1, p. 523.

42 TNA: PREM16/440, Hunt memorandum, annex B, March 1975; CAB164/1256, Hunt letter, 22 June 1974. A brief foray into 'ethics' (the morality of keeping confidences secret) and into normal standards of behaviour (the necessary keeping of confidences, for example, in commerce) was mounted in 1975 for fear that both Radcliffe and Widgery might adjudge that the abundance of 'authorised' leaks had already destroyed the 'mystique' of Government (see TNA: CAB164/1292, note for counsel, 11 July 1975). As seen earlier in ch 10.2.1, Callaghan strongly reaffirmed the views of Trend and Hunt in 1978.

43 TNA: CAB164/1256, I. Bancroft to W. Armstrong, 7 June 1974. See also Hunt's memorandum of March 1975 in PREM16/440 for the assertion that 'I have repeatedly made it clear that I am not concerned about criticism of the Civil Service as a whole' and Armstrong's memorandum of 10 June 1974 in PREM16/465.

44 TNA: PREM16/466, D. Allen to J. Hunt, 2 October 1975. For the earlier conflicting legal advice, see PREM16/465, Hunt's note of a meeting, 14 June 1975 and CAB164/1256, R.T. Armstrong to Hunt, 11 September 1974. It was in this letter that Armstrong admitted to a 'scintilla of doubt' about Goodman's integrity. Both the executors and *The Sunday Times* could afford to be more single-minded and, when necessary, unscrupulous than publicly accountable officials.

45 Quoted in TNA: CAB164/1256, memorandum by G. Child, 18 June 1974. Foot felt morally bound by a promise to the dying Crossman to ensure publication; but the succeeding furore did contribute to the suicide of one of Crossman's sons.

46 A test case of Wilson's veracity was the prosecution of oil sanctions against Rhodesia, which became subject to a public inquiry chaired by Lord Bingham at the height of the FOI campaign in 1978. For the fullest contemporary summary of Benn's views, see TNA: PREM16/904, T. Benn to H. Wilson, 20 January 1976. He was especially critical of officials. 'Just as Ministers', he wrote 'in recent years have become much more involved in administration, so have officials become much more involved in policy matters, submit departmental views and are even involved in the public presentation of them. At one extreme we have the Common Market Commissioners who are paid and appointed officials enjoying full Ministerial rights ... We have also the public interrogation of officials on policy matters by Parliamentary Committees and the publication of Reports by officials – as for example CPRS reports which are almost policy statements'. Officials, as has been seen, had earlier warned that all these problems were inherent in Fabian modernisation proposals (as replicated in Fulton).

47 TNA: CAB130/187, MISC89(76)2, Ministerial Memoirs, 6 January 1976, drafted by Hunt.

48 R. Crossman, *Plato Today* (1959) p. 98.

49 Instructions on relations with the press had been first issued by Helsby in November 1967. They were tightened by Armstrong on 13 September 1971 (TNA: BA18/91), reissued by Allen in January 1976 and further strengthened by Bancroft in 1978 (see his circular in PREM16/1540, from which the quotations are taken). Simultaneously there was a rapid increase in the numbers of the Departmental Information Officers within the Government Information Service although – partly as the result of staff association pressure – they remained almost exclusively career civil servants even after

the 1979 election. Policy was fully explained to, and approved by, Mrs Thatcher in December 1981, when *The Times* planned a further detailed expose of Whitehall (PREM19/Civil Service, Interview with *The Times*). Particular trouble was taken to ensure the press did not see the instructions.

50 See TNA: T245/41 and 48; PREM16/1858 and *The Times*, 31 August 1978.
51 CSD: MP3/63/01G, C. Raphael to W. Rees-Mogg, 26 June 1969. Wilson's disapproval was confirmed by Robert Armstrong to D. Allen on 18 February 1975 (TNA: PREM16/762).
52 See TNA: PREM16/762; and BA17/1020 for both the CSD's initial support (especially A. Duke to J.K. Moore, 28 August 1974) and the reaction from J. Herbecq on 14 November.
53 TNA: PREM16/1858, annotation on K.R. Stowe memorandum, 4 July 1978. This file not only contains the vituperative minutes by Stowe and Wicks but also covers the official response to the full range of Hennessy's 'errors' in 1978, including J. Woodrow to T. McCaffrey, 16 June 1978. Woodrow had unavailingly sought to identify Hennessy's sources over time; and he concluded that there was no evidence either that 'having a highly articulate correspondent working in Whitehall for an influential newspaper like *The Times* has been of much positive benefit to the Government' or that 'the public's understanding of how Government works' had been enhanced.
54 Relations deteriorated further after 1979 with the Prime Minister's Principal Private Secretary (Robin Butler) advocating a 'really serious effort to catch and punish leakers' and her Chief Press Secretary (Bernard Ingham) ever more dismissive of the media's 'arrogant and inflated view of its role in democracy' (see PREM19/Information and Publicity, Media relations, B. Ingham to F.E.R. Butler (with annotations), 1 September 1983). The role of the Chief Press Secretary changed dramatically in 1981 when it was agreed that he should play an 'integral part of policy making rather than [be] simply a means of announcing it' (Mrs Thatcher to M. Heseltine, 4 March 1981, letter annexed to EOM(81)8, 21 April 1981). Hence the ending of the experiment of 'Whitehall correspondents' in 1982. See also B. Ingham, *Kill the Messenger . . . Again* (1991) chs 11–12.
55 The lineage is explained in J. Jowell, 'Administrative law' in Bogdanor, *British Constitution*, p. 385.
56 As departmental accounting officers, Permanent Secretaries could themselves use their relationship to the PAC to challenge Ministerial policy – on the grounds of either financial impropriety (as laid out in the standard circular issued to them after 1937) or financial imprudence (as specified in an additional covering note by the Treasury after 1964). Notoriously Benn (as Secretary of State for Industry) was issued in 1974 with four accounting officers' warnings because projected loans to two workers, co-operatives (in Kirkby and Meriden) and the *Scottish Daily News* were adjudged financially unwise and, in addition, a grant to the Welsh TUC was deemed to impair 'efficient and economical administration'. Benn avoided censure by arguing that officials had not followed the correct procedures and, more importantly, were motivated by a political 'unwillingness to welcome innovation' rather than genuine financial concern. Allen, as Head of the Civil Service, was asked by Wilson to defuse the situation and duly did so. The issuing of an accounting officer note, he reported, should not be equated to 'a major political crisis'. Rather it was an indication that a 'Minister has perfectly properly used his political judgement to override in exceptional circumstances the financial or other disadvantages, and that the Accounting Officer wishes his position before the PAC to be defensible' (TNA: PREM16/444, Allen report to R.T. Armstrong, 21 March 1975, para 40). For the full history of this stand-off, see PREM16/444, BA7/11–14 and T. Benn, *Against the Tide* (1989), *passim*.
57 *Let's Go with Labour*, conclusion. Full histories are provided by A. Gregory and P. Giddings, *The Ombudsman, the Citizen and Parliament* (2002) and on the website of the Parliamentary and Health Service Ombudsman (www.ombudsman.org.uk) which, in

NOTES FOR CHAPTER 10

March 2009, contained the Fourth Report for 2006–7: R. Kirkham, *The Parliamentary Ombudsman: standing the test of time*.

58 Cited in W.B. Gwyn, 'The ombudsman in Britain: a qualified success in government reform' *Public Administration* 60 (1982) 177. For Callaghan's reticence, see TNA: CAB21/5803.

59 Gwyn, 'Ombudsman', 177. Other relative strengths included the power to compel attendance and the production of documents; the absence of charges (unlike in New Zealand); and its right to investigate the administrative actions of Ministers (unlike in New Zealand and Scandinavia).

60 W. Gwyn, 'The British PCA: ombudsman or ombudsmouse?' *Journal of Politics* 35 (1973) 45–69. *Our Fettered Ombudsman* was published in 1977.

61 Equally perverse were the reasons for consulting neither Parliament nor even the Select Committee on successive appointments to the post. They included the limiting of 'the discretion of the sovereign', (even more unbelievably) the prejudicing of 'the independent nature of the appointment' and (rather more rationally) the invidiousness of candidates' 'merits' being openly debated in Parliament (PREM16/2067: D. Allen to K.R.Stowe, 20 October 1976). Allen did successfully recommend that the Select Committee chair should be both consulted about possible candidates and informed of the shortlist.

62 By demanding the right to investigate alleged maladministration stemming from either a 'bad' policy decision or the inappropriateness of general rules to implement it ('bad rules'), the ombudsman – or more correctly the Select Committee – was deemed to be surreptitiously encroaching upon the 'merit' of government policy (see TNA: BA17/968, brief by C.D. Stevens for the 1974 Sunningdale conference). Another common complaint was the narrowness of the ombudsman's jurisdiction. It was extended to the NHS in 1973 and a separate system was established for local government a year later.

63 Trend summarised the issue with characteristic clarity. Was the ombudsman to be a 'public' or a 'Parliamentary' institution, 'an *alternative* means of securing the redress of a grievance' or 'an *additional* means whereby Members of Parliament discharged their responsibilities'? In line with an earlier Official Committee, he advised Wilson against restricting public access (TNA: CAB21/1802, January 1965; CAB 21/5803, 5 April 1965); but the Labour Cabinet decided differently (CAB128/39). This was perhaps because it was chaired not by Wilson but by George Brown, whose sense of constitutional propriety was such that, in the Sachsenhausen affair, he used the convention of Ministerial responsibility for the last time to deflect criticism from officials.

64 Gwyn, 'Ombudsman' 181. The disadvantage of such thoroughness was the opportunity cost. In Sweden, for example, there was the time to investigate six times as many complaints. The advantage was that it generated trust and encouraged departments to amend practices in anticipation of, as well as in response to, investigations.

65 TNA: BA17/28, Compton to L. Helsby, 13 July 1964; BA17/968, C.D. Stevens brief, 10 April 1974.

66 PREM16/2067: D.J. Mitchell, 'Note for the record', 20 January 1966 and W. Armstrong to R.T. Armstrong, undated. See also Crossman, *Diaries*, entry for 7 April 1966. Crossman on 18 October 1966, whilst guiding the Act through Parliament, also noted 'the enormous investigatory powers' the ombudsman would enjoy and, more characteristically, that Compton had slipped into the officials' gallery at the very point in his peroration when he was assuring MPs that the appointee would be no Government stooge. Compton nevertheless repaid Crossman's faith, by vigorously pursuing the Select Committee suggestion that his powers be extended to cover 'bad decisions' and 'bad rules'.

67 For the Labour Cabinet meeting of 6 April 1965, see TNA: CAB128/39; and for the non-appointment of a Civil Servant and access to Cabinet papers, PREM16/2067,

K.R. Stowe to J. Callaghan, 23 November 1976 and J. Hunt to Stowe, 6 December 1978.
68 G. Marshall, 'The British PCA', *The Annals* 377 (1968) 91–6; Gwyn, 'Ombudsman', 194.
69 Gwyn, 'Ombudsman',180.
70 I. Pugh, 'The ombudsman – jurisdiction, powers and practice', *Public Administration* 56 (1978) esp 133; Kirkham, 'Ombudsman', p. 6.
71 Pugh, 'Ombudsman', 136. Pugh emphasised the anti-democratic nature of reformers' demands. 'It would', he argued, 'be a major constitutional departure in this country if an appointed person like myself had the power to overthrow a decision taken either by or in the name of or on behalf of a minister who is elected and in the end answerable to Parliament' (ibid, 134). He nevertheless introduced significant changes, such as the seeking of independent legal advice and the recruitment of staff from outside the Service.
72 Gwyn, 'Ombudsman', 192.
73 Cd 9230, para 52; Cmnd 3638, para 281. Between the two reports there had been mounting support for more specialist committees from backbenchers (particularly in relation to colonial and defence policy) and academics (such as Bernard Crick in his widely-read 1964 book, *The Reform of Parliament*). The televising of Parliament, like the reform of Section 2 of OSA, finally occurred in 1989.
74 This was another source of imbalance on the Committees. Government supporters were often 'mavericks', with no – and little chance of gaining – Ministerial experience, whilst the Opposition members were often former Ministers. For instance, the Select Committee on Procedure (which prompted the 1970 review by recommending the strengthening of the Estimates Committee) included John Macintosh and David Marquand, as 'moderns' pressing for change, and Selwyn Lloyd, as an 'ancient' advocating caution. Traditionalists particularly opposed any decrease in adversarial politics or committees restricting debate on the floor of the House.
75 See Hennessy, *Whitehall*, pp. 361–3 and D. Woodhouse in Bogdanor, *British Constitution*, p. 287. The formal title of the rules was *Memorandum of Guidance for Officials appearing before Select Committees*.
76 Quoted in Vincent, *Culture of Secrecy*, p. 269. 'Schizophrenia' rather than paradox is the preferred term of Seaward and Silk in Bogdanor, *British Constitution*, p. 171.
77 The contrasting speeches by Wilson and Crossman are in Parl Deb (Commons), 727, col 78, 21 April 1966 and 738, col 480, 14 December 1966.
78 TNA: BA17/190, P. Osmond to R.S.Allison, 25 February 1970 and E.J.G. Smith to I. Bancroft, 24 February 1970.
79 TNA: BA17/96, note of a discussion between P. Osmond and Lord Shackleton, 8 August 1969 (following officials receipt from the Select Committee on Procedure of its draft September report, demanding radical change). The initial reaction of both CSD and Treasury officials to better informed MPs was equally enthusiastic – provided the information given was 'controlled'. See, for example, minutes of a meeting, 1 August 1969: 'Mr Rogers agreed that a small number of informed and adequately staffed committees, at which officials gave evidence on the execution of policy without being obliged to refer frequently to Ministers, would be helpful'. Modernisers' attempts to draw parallels with Congressional hearings in the US were dismissed on the grounds that, unlike the President and his staff, British Ministers could already be questioned in Parliament.
80 TNA: BA17/190: I. Bancroft to R.S. Allison, 25 February 1970.
81 For the Labour Government, see TNA: BA17/191,SC(70)1st, 6 May 1970, minutes of the Ministerial Committee on Select Committees; for the Conservatives, BA17/763, notes for 23 and 30 September 1970. Labour's Ministerial Committee highlighted the opposition of Parliamentary traditionalists to any transfer of power from the floor of the House, especially to 'small groups of unrepresentative MPs' in committees.
82 A copy of Brook's letter of 27 May 1958 is in TNA: BA17/595. It encouraged officials to 'give all the information they can' but then discouraged them from voicing

personal opinions, revealing interdepartmental disputes or entering into subjects 'of political controversy'. The rules were revised in 1967, 1969 and 1972, but not again until 1980.

83 See TNA: BA17/595 for Howell's altercation with officials (including Mountfield's comment of 2 December 1971) and BA17/596 for Jellicoe's letter to Heath of 24 March 1972, Trend's interjection on 15 April, and Heath's final decision on 25 April. Heath argued that policy options, which might be identified in white papers, should not be orally discussed by officials when 'under the pressures of examination' they might be unable to 'withhold an indication of the advice they have given or the action they have recommended'. Revelations of the structure of Cabinet Committees might also lead to their chairs or secretaries being required to give evidence (a consideration which, as seen in ch 10.2.1, still bore heavily on Callaghan in 1978).

84 TNA: BA17/595, Mountfield note of 2 December 1971; BA17/596; T.H. Caulcott to W. Armstrong, 10 February 1972. For Donoughue's insinuation that the Service was 'always' hostile to Parliamentary accountability, see *Diaries*, vol 2, p. 189. The CSD's views may, admittedly, have been atypical.

85 See Cabinet Office 35/3, part 8 for Sir Patrick Nairne, 'the Civil Service and Accountability to Parliament' and resulting discussion. The paper was prompted by the highly critical second English Report (HC 576, 1977–8) and the report by the Select Committee on Procedure (HC 588–1, 1977–8), which first recommended the creation of 12 departmental committees. Earlier, there had been an economists' revolt over the giving of evidence, which was only resolved when Healey (as Chancellor) agreed that they should not be 'obliged to seek to justify their views on economic policy as if they themselves held them when in fact they do not' (TNA: T331/1051, Healey annotation on memorandum by P. Baldwin to D. Henley, 4 February 1975).

86 PREM19/Government Machinery, Review of Exchequer and Audit Act, part 1, C. Priestley to M. Pattison, 12 March 1981. This file also contains a copy of the Comptroller's report and plentiful evidence of Mrs Thatcher's disdain for Bancroft's response to it. A Government Accountancy Service and an Audit Commission for local government were established in 1982.

87 Ibid, part 1 and 2, passim. The PAC recommendation for scrutinising subsidies to industry produced this telling remark from the Secretary of State for Industry (Patrick Jenkin), which was somewhat at variance with the insistence that – to maximise efficiency – the Service should ape business methods: 'in order to cover themselves against scrutiny by Parliamentary Committees . . . they would have to document every decision and maintain detailed and meticulous records of every transaction . . . In other words they would have to behave like Government Departments and not like commercial companies'(11 March 1982).

88 Ibid, part 2, note of a meeting between Mrs Thatcher and G. Howe, 15 December 1982; G. Howe to M. Thatcher, 24 December 1982. The two other chairmen were Joel Barnett (PAC) and Edward Du Cann (the Treasury and Civil Service Committee), and 300 backbenchers initially indicated their support.

89 TNA: BA17/632, transcript of a speech ('Whitehall into Europe') drafted by the CSD for Sir Christopher Soames and published, amended, in *Public Administration* 59 (1972) 271–9. For contemporary Whitehall's appreciation of 'the biggest revolution in the government of Britain since Cromwell', see R. Denman, *The Mandarin's Tale* (2002), p. 141; and for a more recent appreciation see, amongst others, Hennessy, *Whitehall*, p. 253 and A. King, *The British Constitution* (2007), p. 92. In relation to the central departments, Treasury officials had since the 1940s chaired coordinating committees on Europe (although, somewhat bizarrely, in a 'non-departmental and independent' capacity) and the CSD's Machinery of Government Division was a natural home for planning the administrative response to devolution.

NOTES FOR CHAPTER 10

90 Following Labour's renegotiating of entry terms in 1974–5, a referendum (which itself broke constitutional convention by suspending Cabinet's collective responsibility) endorsed membership by a margin of 2:1. Rather than marking a political turning point, however, this marked 'the start of almost nothing' and the 'line of least collaboration' continued (see H. Young, *This Blessed Plot* (1998), p.299).
91 Jobs in Brussels might be either permanent appointments to the Commission (which, exceptionally after accession, could be made at a senior level) or secondments to UKREP (the body supporting Britain's Permanent Representative – or ambassador – to the EEC and, more generally, British interests and personnel in Brussels).
92 TNA: BA17/410, J.A. Chilcot to T.H. Caulcott, 29 April 1971; BA17/632, D. Howell memorandum, 13 March 1972. The FCO may also have viewed such a Ministry as a derogation of its power – hence the ultimate compromise between a Home Civil Servant chairing the EIU and the FCO coordinating UKREP.
93 For Heath's original remit for the Unit, see TNA: PREM15/940, Heath to R.T. Armstrong, 30 April 1972; for Trend's response on 9 May, CAB165/946; and for the final office note of 12 May, BA17/632. The five original members were John Hunt (as chairman,) and four senior officials from the Treasury, FCO, MAFF and DTI. Hunt succeeded Trend as Cabinet Secretary and, of his first three successors, Sir Patrick Nairne became head of the DHSS, Sir Roy Denham Director General for External Affairs at the European Commission (and later EEC ambassador in Washington) whilst Sir Michael Franklin became head first of the Department of Trade and then of MAFF.
94 On hostility towards the FCO, see TNA: BA17/632, T.H. Caulcott to F. Cooper, 10 April 1972. One of the major opportunities to remedy this was the still-born 1975–7 CPRS Review of Overseas Representation, which recommended the creation of a Foreign Service Group within a united Civil Service, or at least greater interchange with 'home' officials in order to increase expertise in overseas negotiations. Discredited for other reasons, the Review arguably underestimated the resistance of 'home' officials to postings abroad ('posting someone from the DHSS to serve in Mogadishu'). See Blackstone and Plowden, *Inside the Think Tank*, ch. 8 and TNA: BA7/34–7. On the continuing popular identification with the Commonwealth rather than Europe, see the anecdote in Denman, *Mandarin's Tale* (p. 170) concerning Lord Soames' return to London after two years as Vice President of the European Commission: 'Haven't seen you for some time, Christopher', he was greeted, 'You been in Kenya?'
95 On Trend, see Hennessy, *Whitehall*, p. 215; on Armstrong and the 'cold hostility', Denman, *Mandarin's Tale*, pp.140–1, 266.
96 For Heath's personal minute of 9 November 1972, see TNA: PREM15/884; for Nairne's warning, CAB164/1249; and for Hunt's views on the need for mavericks, Young, *Blessed Plot*, pp. 224–5. For the confessions of one particularly colourful 'maverick', see Denman, *Mandarin's Tale*, which provides the following commentary on the culture clash: '"You mean," an incredulous voice from one Ministry asked one afternoon, "that we have to change what we've been doing for several hundred years because of some bloody foreigners in Brussels?" "Yes," I replied crisply. "Look," he said, "there is a dividing line between lunacy and common sense." "Since 1973," I said, "you've been on the wrong side of it."' (p. 152).
97 Sir Stephen Wall, quoted in King, Constitution, p.109. The EIU's typical success in removing such departmental road blocks prior to negotiations in Brussels, however, meant that the UK quickly gained a reputation there for greater strategic coherence than Germany and even France.
98 Although the devolution debate was dominated by Scotland, it involved also Northern Ireland (where government had been devolved for fifty years before the reimposition of direct rule in 1972) and Wales (where Plaid Cymru's victory at Carmarthen in July 1966 preceded by over a year the SNP's first by-election victory). The political importance of the SNP was matched economically by the discovery of North Sea Oil.

NOTES FOR CHAPTER 11

For the broader, and more volatile, reaction of Permanent Secretaries to devolution, see ch 6.2.1.
99 PREM16/1661, K.R. Stowe note, 2 May 1978. Labour's lack of ambition is noted in V. Bogdanor, *Devolution in the United Kingdom* (1999), p. 179.
100 BA8/Permanent Secretary's Office 6/5(5), J. Herbecq to J. Hobson, 28 March 1978. Early official views may be gleaned from the two Sunningdale meetings in 1974 and a third in 1975 (see TNA: CAB 164/1249 and 1324).
101 PREM16/1661, I. Bancroft to J. Hunt, April 1978. For the preliminary correspondence in this 'tussle' between Bancroft and Hunt, see BA8/Permanent Secretary's Office 6/5 (5). For its resolution, see note of a meeting on 9 May 1978 and the subsequent letter from Hunt to the Prime Minister on 6 June in the PREM16 file.
102 PREM16/1661 The general quotations are taken from the note of the meeting on 9 May 1978 and Hunt's subsequent letter to Callaghan on 6 June; those on Europe from Philip Wood to K.R. Stowe and Stowe to J. Hunt on 8 May.
103 The speaker on 16 May 1978 was J.D.W. Janes, but his views mirrored those of his Permanent Secretary (Brian Cubbon, see BA8/Permanent Secretary's Office 6/5(5), Cubbon to I. Bancroft, April 1978). Norman Hunt (as Lord Crowther-Hunt) was a signatory of the minority Kilbrandon Report (Cmnd 5460) and maintained his Fultonian disdain for the Service. It was not, he maintained 'a viable proposition for the Scottish and Welsh assemblies to be served by officials whose basic loyalties and promotion prospects will be with Whitehall' (TNA: BA17/1002 Hunt to E. Short, 21 April 1975).
104 For a copy of the revised 1978 framework and the action plan of 11 January 1979, together with related papers, see BA8/Permanent Secretary's Office 6/5(5). The following analysis is based on, and quotations extracted from, this file unless otherwise stated.
105 TNA: BA17/1000, H. Evans (Permanent Secretary, Welsh Office) to I. Bancroft, 17 December 1974; and PREM16/1170, transcript of meeting on July 1976. The NSS used devolution as a pretext for seeking the end of dispersal; but with 45,000 and 24,000 officials already serving in functional departments (such as the MOD) within Scotland and Wales respectively, increased dispersal was defended as logical and a further means of 'cementing the United Kingdom'. At the time the Scottish departments and the Welsh Office each employed some 1000 officials.
106 TNA: BA17/1005, W.F. Mumford to J. Hobson, 24 October 1975. Fear at the 'precariousness of the position' was best expressed by J. Herbecq to R. Wilding, 11 January 1979 (BA8/Permanent Secretary's Office 6/5(5)). Bancroft's embarrassment is recorded in a circular of the same date in the same file.
107 See above, ch 5.2 for Armstrong's warning to Wilson on Fulton that although 'some move in this direction is desirable ... the move would be much more marked than Ministers collectively or the public would want if we accept the report as it stood'; and ch 10.2.1 for Trend's explicit warning.
108 King, *Constitution*, p. 96.

11 RINGING OUT THE OLD, RINGING IN THE NEW

1 Sir Douglas Wass, 'The public service in modern society', *Public Administration* 61 (1983) 19–20. Earlier, Sir Patrick Nairne (who was later to applaud Mrs Thatcher at the May 1981 dinner) had reminded his fellow Permanent Secretaries in 1978 that, despite its common likening to a Rolls-Royce, Whitehall had seen 'the horse' succeeded not by 'the internal combustion engine' but by an 'elephant – slow and ponderous in movement; inclined to trample people under its feet; given to trumpeting its own success; and with a long memory when its files are properly kept' (Cabinet Office 35/3, Conferences of Permanent Secretaries ... at Sunningdale, part 8). Wass' lecture provides some refutation of the claims that Mrs Thatcher 'politicised' the Service. Asked

NOTES FOR CHAPTER 11

whether she wished to censor any part of it, she replied: 'Sir Douglas is free to say whatever he wishes. I shouldn't dream of trying to stop him' (PREM19/Civil Service, Lecture by Sir D. Wass).

2 In a premonition of the furore aroused by the Rayner scrutiny of statistics, the alleged response of a future Head of the Home Civil Service (Robin Butler) to the refusal by Treasury forecasters to massage figures at the Chancellor's request was: 'we are all prostitutes here; if they want to be pure they should go elsewhere'. The reaction of the Head of Callaghan's Policy Unit was equally revealing. Butler was, he concluded, 'an immensely impressive administrator and ought to be made boss of the Treasury now'. For the whole episode, see B. Donoughue, *Diary*, vol 2, p. 452.

3 Wass, 'Public service', 13–14; Bancroft, 'Whitehall: some personal reflections', Suntory-Toyota lecture, London School of Economics, 1983, 10. Prominent amongst those whose careers were blighted were Donald Derx (see Campbell, *Thatcher*, vol 2, pp. 42–3) and Richard Wilding (who had the misfortune to have published in April 1979 a Civil Service College paper, 'The professional ethic of the administrator' which, whilst stressing the 'absolute necessity to pursue today's policy with energy', also emphasised the need 'in order to survive, to withhold from it the last ounce of commitment').

4 Rayner, *Unfinished Agenda*, p. 2.

5 Hoskyns delivered two valedictory lectures: 'Westminster and Whitehall: an outsider's view' to the Institute of Fiscal Studies in October 1982 (later published in *Fiscal Studies* 3 (1982) 162–72) and 'Conservatism is not enough' to the Institute of Directors in September 1983 (*Political Quarterly* 55(1984) 3–16), from which these quotations are taken. The former caused a certain panic in No. 10 because it was followed by a call for a cull of all senior officials over 50. Rayner agreed that, up to a point, such officials formed 'a state within a state' (a phrase borrowed from Tony Benn) and should be moved if they did not implement government policy promptly; but the recalcitrant, he maintained, were only a minority and a cull was therefore unnecessary and 'too idealistic a solution'. Mrs Thatcher hastily reassured the Cabinet Secretary that she did not favour a cull (see PREM19/Civil Service, Sir John Hoskyns' lecture).

REFERENCES

This history has been largely written from a mix of released and unreleased government files. Where the file has been released, the location is given (TNA – The National Archives, Kew) followed by the full TNA reference (for example TNA: PREM13/1757). Where a file was read whilst still closed, but has since been released, every effort has been made to provide the new TNA reference. Where files are still retained, their future TNA class reference (where known) is given, followed by their broad subject category and file title, which should make them readily identifiable in the TNA catalogue once they have been released (for example, for Mrs Thatcher's papers: PREM19/Government Machinery/The future of quangos, part 3). The one exception is Cabinet records. Cabinet minutes (conclusions) will be located in CAB128, memoranda in CAB129 and the Cabinet Secretary's notebooks in CAB195.

Where a footnote contains multiple TNA references, location at TNA is only cited once. Where the footnote contains a mix of references to released and unreleased papers, some unavoidable confusion may occur. Released documents should be distinguishable by having two simple numbers (the class and piece numbers, for example PREM13/1757, where PREM 13 relates to the 'class' of Prime Minister's papers between 1964 and 1970, and 1757 to the individual file or 'piece').

SOURCES AND SELECT BIBLIOGRAPHY

Interviews and private correspondence

The main structured collection of oral testimony was at three 'witness seminars', attended by some 50 senior officials, held at Churchill College Cambridge in November 2006 on Civil Service reform in the 1980s. I am particularly grateful to Lord Wilson of Dinton for helping to facilitate this event and for the chairmen of the three seminars, Peter Riddell, William Plowden ('the demise of the CSD') and Brian Gilmore ('the 1981 Strike'). A transcript, and list of contributing participants, is permanently available at http://www.ccbh.ac.uk/witness_civilservicereforms_index.php

Brian Gilmore subsequently invited me to a meeting of OWLS (the Old Whitley Lags Society) at the Athenaeum, to meet CSD officials and leading staff association leaders from the 1970s (some of whom, I must confess, I believed to have been in an even more illustrious place). Others who have given me invaluable advice and insights include:

Sir Christopher Audland
Jenny Bacon
Ian Beesley
Lord Butler of Brockwell
Sir John Chilcot
Lord Christopher
Lord Donoughue
Jo Durning
Sir Michael Franklin
Professor Geoffrey Fry
Professor Peter Hennessy
Sir John Herbecq
Sir John Hoskyns
Sir Robin Ibbs
Rosemary Jefferys
Kate Jenkins
Peter Jones
Sir Peter Kemp
Keith Lawrance
Professor Michael Lee
Helen Leiser
Lord McNally
John Nethercote

Michael Pattison
Clive Priestley
John Rimmington
Sandy Russell
Professor Kevin Theakston
Ken Thomas
Lord Turnbull
Sir Stephen Wall
Professor Patrick Weller
Richard Wilding

Unpublished sources

Official

The National Archives (TNA)

CABINET

CAB 21	Registered files (1916–1973)
CAB 23	Cabinet minutes (1916–1939)
CAB 24	Cabinet memoranda (1916–1939)
CAB 128	Cabinet minutes (1945–)
CAB 129	Cabinet memoranda (1945–)
CAB 130	Ad hoc Committees (1945–)
CAB 134	Standing Committees (1945–)
CAB 164	Subject (Theme Series) files (1966–)
CAB 165	Committees (C) (1965–)
CAB 184	Central Policy Review Staff (CPRS)(1970–1983)

PRIME MINISTER

PREM 11	1951–1964
PREM 13	Wilson (1964–1970)
PREM 15	Heath (1970–1974)
PREM 16	Wilson/Callaghan 1974–1979
PREM 19	Mrs Thatcher (1979–1990)

TREASURY

T 199	Establishment Officer's Branch (1821–1985)
T 215	Establishment, General Division (1914–1967)
T 216	Establishment, Manning Division (1920–1976)
T 222	Organisation and Methods Division (1953–1978)
T 249	Training and Education Division (1925–1971)
T 275	National Whitley Council (1917–1982)
T 277	Committee Section (1948–)

SOURCES AND SELECT BIBLIOGRAPHY

T 316   Management Accounting Unit (1961–1974)
T 320   Public Income/Outlay Division (1958–1974)
T 321   Civil Pay Division (1960–1969)
T 325   Sir Richard (Otto) Clarke (1940–1977)
T 326   Finance, Home and General Division (1953–1974)
T 330   Management Services Division (1959–1969)
T 331   General Expenditure Division (1960–1975)
T 341   Environment and Purchasing Division (1960–1975)
T 353   Public Sector Group (1960–)
T 371   General Expenditure Policy (1975–)
T 372   Public Services Sector, Accounts and Purchasing (1974–8)
T 374   General expenditure Analysis (1974–)

CIVIL SERVICE DEPARTMENT

BA 1   Fulton Committee papers (1966–1969)
BA 3   Armitage Committee papers (1976–1978)
BA 6   William Armstrong papers (1968–1974)
BA 7   Douglas Allen papers (1974–1997)
BA 8   Ian Bancroft papers (1978–1981)
BA 16   Machinery of Government and Development Group (1955–1979)
BA 17   Machinery of Government (1956–)
BA 18   Personnel Services (1964–)
BA 19   Personnel Management (1960–)
BA 21   Training (1963–)
BA 22   Pay (1965–)
BA 25   Manpower and Complementing (1960–)
BA 26   Organisation and Methods (1966–)
BA 29   Structure Review (1968–1972)

HOME OFFICE

HO 287   Police files (1917–1983)
HO 291   Criminal files (1902–1983)
HO 292   Departmental Committee on the Official Secrets Act (1971–1972)

TREASURY SOLICITOR

TS 49   Registered files (Department of Energy) (1928–1987)

Private

British Library of Political and Economic Science, London School of Economics

Fabian Society
Robert Sheldon

SOURCES AND SELECT BIBLIOGRAPHY

Brotherton Library, University of Leeds

Lord Boyle papers (MS 660)
Geoffrey Fry papers

Churchill Archives Centre, Churchill College, Cambridge

Sir Richard (Otto) Clarke
Sir Michael Franklin
Sir John Herbecq
Lord Plowden
Dame Enid Russell-Smith
Baron Soames

Conservative Party Archives, Bodleian Library, Oxford

Conservative Research Department (CRD)

Modern Records Centre, University of Warwick

Council of Civil Service Unions, 1918–1994 (GB 0152 MSS 296)

Official publications

Cd 6210 *Royal Commission on the Civil Service, First Report* (MacDonnell, 1912)
Cd 6535 *Royal Commission on the Civil Service, Appendix to the Second Report, Evidence* (MacDonnell, 1912)
Cd 7338 *Royal Commission on the Civil Service, Fourth Report* (MacDonnell, 1914)
Cd 9153 *Committee on Relations between Employers and Employed, Final Report* (Whitley, 1917)
Cd 9230 *Machinery of Government Committee, Report* (Haldane, 1918)
Cmd 62 *Committee on the Organization and Staffing of Government Offices, Report* (Bradbury, 1919)
Cmd 1581 *Committee on National Expenditure, Report* (Geddes, 1922)
Cmd 3037 *Board of Inquiry . . . to Investigate Certain Statements Affecting Civil Servants, Report* ('Francs' Report, 1928)
Cmd 3909 *Royal Commission on the Civil Service, Report* (Tomlin, 1931)
Cmd 4060 *Committee on Ministers' Powers, Report* (Donoughmore, 1932)
Cmd 4149 *Committee of Inquiry into the Post Office, Report* (Bridgeman, 1932)
Cmd 6525 *Committee on the Training of Civil Servants, Report* (Assheton, 1944)
Cmd 6679 *Scientific Civil Service* (Barlow, 1943)
Cmd 6937 *Royal Commission on Equal Pay, Reports* (1946)
Cmd 7718 *Committee on the Political Activities of Civil Servants, Report* (Masterman, 1949)
Cmd 9613 *Royal Commission on the Civil Service, Report* (Priestley, 1955)
Cmnd 1432 *The Control of Public Expenditure* (Plowden Report, 1961)
Cmnd 3638 *The Civil Service* (Fulton Report, 1968) with *Report of the Management Consultancy Group* (vol 2), *Surveys and Investigations* (vol 3), *Factual, Statistical and Explanatory Papers* (vol 4) and *Proposals and Opinions* (vol 5) (HMSO 1968–70)
Cmnd 4089 *Information and the Public Interest* (1969)

SOURCES AND SELECT BIBLIOGRAPHY

Cmnd 4506 *The Reorganisation of Central Government* (1970)
Cmnd 5014 *Section 2 of the Official Secrets Act, 1911* (Franks, 1972)
Cmnd 5322 *The Dispersal of Government Work from London* (Hardman, 1973)
Cmnd 5460 *The Constitution* (Kilbrandon, 1973)
Cmnd 6151 *Attack on Inflation* (1975)
Cmnd 6386 *Ministerial Memoirs* (Radcliffe, 1976)
Cmnd 6393 *Public Expenditure* (1976)
Cmnd 6440 *Cash Limits on Public Expenditure* (1976)
Cmnd 7057 *Political Activities of Civil Servants* (Armitage, 1978)
Cmnd 7285 *Reform of Section 2 of the Official Secrets Act* (white paper, 1978)
Cmnd 7520 *Open Government* (green paper, 1979)
Cmnd 7797, *Non-Departmental Public Bodies* (Pliatzky, 1980)
Cmnd 8141, *The Value of Public Pensions* (Scott, 1981)
Cmnd 8293, *Efficiency in the Civil Service* (1981)
Cm 2627 *The Duties and Responsibilities of Civil Servants* (Armstrong Memorandum, 1986)
P.P. (1854) xxvii, *Report on the Organisation of the Permanent Civil Service* (Northcote-Trevelyan Report)
P.P. (1854–5) xx, *Papers on the Reorganisation of the Civil Service*
P.P. (1872) xix, *Seventeenth Report of Her Majesty's Civil Service Commissioners*
P.P. (1957–8) v, Estimates Committee, *Sixth Report: The Treasury Control of Expenditure* (HC 254)
P.P. (1963–4) v, Estimates Committee, *Fifth Report: Treasury Control of Establishments* (HC 228)
P.P. (1964–5) vi, Estimates Committee, *Sixth Report: Recruitment to the Civil Service* (HC 308)
P.P. (1972–3) xxiii, Expenditure Committee, General Sub-Committee, *Minutes of Evidence* (HC 226)
P.P. (1976–7) xxxi, Expenditure Committee, *Eleventh Report: The Civil Service* (English Report, HC 535), 3 vols
P.P. (1977–8) xxxv, Expenditure Committee, *Twelfth Report: The Civil Service* (second English Report, HC 576)
P.P. (1979–80) 45, Treasury and Civil Service Committee, *Fourth Report: Civil Service Manpower Reductions* (HC 712) 2 vols
P.P. (1980–1) 11, Treasury and Civil Service Committee, *The Future of the Civil Service Department* (HC 54)
Interim Report of the Reorganisation Committee of the Civil Service National Whitley Council (HMSO, 1921)
Civil Service Statistics (annually from 1970)
Civil Service Staffing (Treasury Occasional Paper 1, 1994)
Committee on Standards in Public Life, *Ninth Report* (2003)

Select bibliography

Publication in London, unless otherwise cited. Listing, for maximum convenience to the reader, is largely by part and typically restricted to works cited more than once.

General

Agar, J., *The Government Machine: a revolutionary history of the computer* (Cambridge, MA: MIT Press, 2003)

SOURCES AND SELECT BIBLIOGRAPHY

Albrow, *Bureaucracy* (Macmillan, 1970)
Bagehot, W., *The English Constitution* (Chapman and Hall, 1867)
Baker, A., *Prime Ministers and the Rule Book* (Politico's, 2000)
Barberis, P., *Elites of Elites* (Aldershot: Dartmouth, 1996)
Barberis, P. (ed), *The Whitehall Reader* (Buckingham: Open University Press, 1996)
Bogdanor, V. (ed), *The British Constitution in the Twentieth Century* (Oxford: OUP for British Academy, 2003)
Chapman, R.A., *The Civil Service Commission, 1855–1991* (Routledge, 2004)
Chapman, R.A. and Greenaway, J.R., *The Dynamics of Administrative Reform* (Croom Helm, 1980)
Craig, F.W.S., *British General Election Manifestos, 1959–1987* (Aldershot: Dartmouth, 1990)
Drewry, G. and Butcher, T., *The Civil Service Today* (Oxford: Blackwell, 1988)
Edgerton, D., *Warfare State: Britain, 1920–1970* (Cambridge: Cambridge University Press, 2006)
Fry, G.K., *The Administrative 'Revolution' in Whitehall* (Croom Helm, 1981)
Fry, G.K., *The Changing Civil Service* (Allen and Unwin, 1985)
Fry, G.K., *Policy and Management in the Civil Service* (Hemel Hempstead: Prentice Hall, 1995)
Heclo, H., and Wildavsky, A., *The Private Expenditure of Public Money* (Macmillan, 1974)
Hennessy, P., *Cabinet* (Oxford: Blackwell, 1986)
Hennessy, P., *Whitehall* (Secker and Warburg, 1989)
Jenkins, K., *Politicians and Public Service* (Cheltenham: Edward Elgar, 2008)
King, A., *The British Constitution* (Oxford: Oxford University Press, 2007)
Marquand, D., *The Unprincipled Society* (Cape, 1988)
Pollitt, C., *Manipulating the Machine* (Allen and Unwin, 1984)
Rhodes, R.A.W. et al, *The Oxford Handbook of Political Institutions* (Oxford: Oxford University Press, 2006)
Rhodes, R.A.W. (ed), *Transforming British Government*, 2 vols (Basingstoke: Macmillan, 2000)
Rhodes, R.A.W., *Understanding Governance* (Buckingham: Open University Press, 1997)
Sisson, C.H., *The Spirit of British Administration* (Faber, 1959)
Theakston, K., *The Civil Service since 1945* (Oxford: Blackwell, 1995)
Theakston, K., *Leadership in Whitehall* (Basingstoke: Macmillan, 1999)
Theakston, K. and Fry, G.K., 'Britain's administrative elite' *Public Administration* 67 (1989) 129–47
Wheare, K.C., *The Civil Service in the Constitution* (Athlone Press, 1954)

Introduction and Conclusion

Andrew, C., *The Defence of the Realm* (HarperCollins, 2009)
Bancroft, I., 'The Civil Service in the 1980s' *Public Administration* 59 (1981) 139–50
Bancroft, I., 'Whitehall: some personal reflections' (LSE, 1983)
Beck, P., *Using History, Making British Policy* (Basingstoke: Palgrave, 2006)
Bevir, M. and Rhodes, R.A.W., 'Searching for civil society' *Public Administration* 81 (2003) 41–62
Bogdanor, V. and Wilson, R., *Civil Service Reform* (Public Management and Policy Association, 2001)
Chapman, R.A., *Ethics in the British Civil Service* (Routledge, 1988)
Dowding, K., 'The Civil Service' in J. Hollowell (ed), *Britain Since 1945* (Oxford: Blackwell, 2003)

Hancock, K. and Gowing, M., *British War Economy* (HMSO, 1949)
Harris, J., 'If Britain had been defeated by the Nazis' in Wm R. Louis (ed), *Still More Adventures with Britannia* (I.B.Tauris, 2002)
Hennessy, P., *The Secret State* (Allen Lane, 2002)
Hoskyns, J., 'Conservatism is not enough' *Political Quarterly* 55 (1984) 3–16
Hoskyns, J., 'Westminster and Whitehall: an outsider's view' *Fiscal Studies* 3 (1982) 162–72
Jeffery, K., *The History of the Secret Intelligence Service, 1909–1949* (Bloomsbury, 2010)
O'Toole, *The Ideal of Public Service* (Abingdon: Routledge, 2006)
Wass, D., 'The public service in modern society' *Public Administration* 61 (1983) 7–20
Wilding, R., *Civil Servant* (Stanhope: Memoir Club, 2006)

Part 1 The Legacy

1854–1916

Barker, E., *The Development of Public Services in Western Europe, 1660–1930* (Oxford University Press, 1944)
Beveridge, Lord, *Power and Influence* (Hodder and Stoughton, 1953)
Bourne, J.M., *Patronage and Society in Nineteenth-Century England* (Edward Arnold, 1986)
Chester, D.N., *The English Administrative System, 1780–1870* (Oxford: Clarendon Press, 1981)
Davidson, R., *Whitehall and the Labour Problem in Late-Victorian and Edwardian Britain* (Croom Helm, 1985)
Davidson, R. and Lowe, R., 'Bureaucracy and innovation in British welfare policy, 1870–1945' in W.J. Mommsen (ed), *The Emergence of the Welfare State in Britain and Germany* (Croom Helm, 1981)
Hanham, H.J., 'Political patronage at the Treasury, 1870–1912' *Historical Journal* 3 (1960) 75–84
Harris, J., 'Society and state in twentieth-century Britain' in F.M. L. Thompson (ed), *The Cambridge Social History of Britain*, vol 3 (Cambridge: Cambridge University Press, 1990)
Harris, J., *William Beveridge* (Oxford: Clarendon Press, revised ed, 1997)
Humphreys, B.V., *Clerical Unions in the Civil Service* (Blackwell and Mott, 1958)
Jenkins, R., *Gladstone* (Macmillan, 1995)
Kitson Clark, G., ' "Statesmen in disguise" ', *Historical Journal* 2 (1959) 19–39
Lambert, R., 'Central and local relations in mid-Victorian England' *Victorian Studies* 6 (1962) 121–50
Lowe, R., *Adjusting to Democracy* (Oxford: Clarendon Press, 1986)
MacDonagh, O., 'The nineteenth-century revolution in government: a reappraisal' *Historical Journal* 1 (1958) 52–67
MacLeod, R.M., *Treasury Control and Social Administration* (Bell, 1968)
MacLeod, R. M. (ed), *Government and Expertise* (Cambridge: Cambridge University Press, 1988)
Matthew, H.C.G., *Gladstone, 1809–1874* (Oxford: Clarendon Press, 1986)
Parris, H., *Constitutional Bureaucracy* (Allen and Unwin, 1969)
Pellew, J., *The Home Office, 1848–1914* (Heinemann, 1982)
Roseveare, H., *The Treasury* (Allen Lane, 1969)
Sutherland, G. (ed), *Studies in the Growth of Nineteenth-Century Government* (Routledge and Kegan Paul, 1972)

Trollope, A., *The Three Clerks* (Richard Bentley, 1858)
Winter, J., *Robert Lowe* (Toronto: University of Toronto Press, 1976)
Wright, M., *Treasury Control of the Civil Service, 1854–1874* (Oxford: Clarendon Press, 1969)

1916–1956

Anderson, G. (ed), *The White-Blouse Revolution* (Manchester: MUP, 1988)
Anderson, J., 'The machinery of government' *Public Administration* 24 (1946) 147–56
Balogh, T., 'The apotheosis of the dilettante' in H. Thomas (ed), *Crisis in the Civil Service* (Anthony Blond, 1968)
Beloff, M., 'The Whitehall factor' in Peele, G. and Cook, C. (eds), *The Politics of Reappraisal* (Macmillan, 1975)
Bridges, E., *Portrait of a Profession* (Cambridge: Cambridge University Press, 1950)
Bridges, E., *The Treasury* (Allen and Unwin, 1964)
Bridges, E., *Treasury Control* (Athlone Press, 1950)
Brown, W.J., *So Far* (Allen and Unwin, 1943)
Cairncross, A. and Watts, N., *The Economic Section, 1939–1961* (Routledge, 1989)
Campion, G., et al, *British Government since 1918* (Allen and Unwin, 1950)
Cato, *Guilty Men* (Gollancz, 1940)
Chapman, R.A., *Leadership in the British Civil Service* (Croom Helm, 1984)
Critchley, T., *The Civil Service Today* (Gollancz, 1951)
Dale, H.E., *The Higher Civil Service of Great Britain* (Oxford University Press, 1940)
Dale, H.E., *The Personnel and Problems of the Higher Civil Service* (Barnett House, 1943)
Fabian Society, *The Reform of the Higher Civil Service* (1947)
Finlayson, G., 'A moving frontier: voluntarism and the state' *Twentieth Century British History* 1 (1990) 183–206
Fry, G.K., *Statesmen in Disguise* (Macmillan, 1969)
Greenaway, J.R., 'Warren Fisher and the transformation of the British Treasury, 1919–1939' *Journal of British Studies* 23 (1985) 125–42
Kelsall, R.K., *Higher Civil Servants in Britain* (Routledge and Kegan Paul, 1955)
Kirby, M.W., *Operational Research in War and Peace* (Imperial College Press, 2003)
Lee, J.M., *Reviewing the Machinery of Government: the Anderson Committee and its successors* (privately published, 1977)
Lewis, J., *Women in England 1870–1950* (Brighton: Wheatsheaf, 1984)
Lowe, R., *The Welfare State in Britain since 1945* (Basingstoke: Palgrave, 3rd ed, 2005)
Lowe, R., 'The Second World War, consensus and the foundation of the welfare state' *Twentieth Century British History* 1 (1990) 152–82
Lowe, R. and Roberts, R., 'Sir Horace Wilson, 1900–1935: the making of a mandarin' *Historical Journal* 30 (1987) 641–62
Martindale, H., *Women Servants of the State* (Allen and Unwin, 1938)
Middlemas, K., *Thomas Jones: Whitehall Diary* 3 vols (Oxford University Press, 1969–71)
Nicolson, I.F., *The Mystery of Crichel Down* (Oxford: Clarendon Press, 1986)
Nottage, R. and Stack, F., 'The RIPA, 1922–1939' *Public Administration* 50 (1972) 281–302
O'Halpin, E., *Head of the Civil Service* (Routledge, 1989)
Parris, H., *Staff Relations in the Civil Service* (Allen and Unwin, 1973)
Peden, G.C., *British Rearmament and the Treasury* (Edinburgh: Scottish Academic Press, 1979)
Peden, G.C., *Keynes, the Treasury and economic policy* (Macmillan, 1988)

Peden, G.C., *The Treasury and British Public Policy, 1906–59* (Oxford: Oxford University Press, 2000)
Reynolds, D., *In Command of History: Churchill fighting and writing the Second World War* (Allen Lane, 2004)
Robson, W.A., *Justice and Administrative Law* (Stevens, 1947)
Robson, W.A. (ed), *The Civil Service in Britain and France* (Hogarth Press, 1956)
Roskill, S., *Hankey, Man of Secrets* 3 vols (Collins, 1970–4)
Savage, G., 'Entering the corridors of power' in J. Burton (ed), *Essays in European History* (Lanham, MD: University of America Press, 1989)
Savage, G., *The Social Construction of Expertise: the English civil service and its influence, 1919–1939* (Pittsburgh, PA: University of Pittsburgh Press, 1996)
Theakston, K., *The Labour Party and Whitehall* (Routledge, 1992)
Thomas, R.M., *The British Philosophy of Administration: a comparison of British and American ideas, 1900–1939* (Longman, 1978)
Turner, J., 'Cabinet committees and secretariats 'in K. Burk (ed), *War and State* (Allen and Unwin, 1982)
Turner, J., *Lloyd George's Secretariat* (Cambridge: Cambridge University Press, 1980)
Zimmeck, M., 'Strategies and stratagems for the employment of women in the Civil Service, 1919–1939' *Historical Journal* 27 (1984) 910–17

Part 2 The Reform Momentum

General

Barnett, C., *The Audit of War* (Macmillan, 1986)
Booker, C., *The Neophiliacs* (Collins, 1969)
Brittan, S., *Capitalism with a Human Face* (Fontana, 1996)
Brittan, S., *The Treasury under the Tories* (Secker and Warburg, 1964), later twice revised as *Steering the Economy* (Secker and Warburg, 1969; Harmondsworth: Penguin, 1971)
Cairncross, A., *The Wilson Years* (Historians' Press, 1977)
Carpenter, H., *That Was Satire That Was* (Gollancz, 2000)
Dorey, P. (ed), *The Labour Governments, 1964–1970* (Routledge, 2006)
Fry, G.K., 'More than counting manhole covers' *Public Administration* 77 (1999) 527–40
Lowe, R. and Rollings, N., 'Modernizing Britain' in R.A.W. Rhodes (ed), *Transforming British Government*, vol 1 (Basingstoke: Macmillan, 2000)
Shanks, M., The Stagnant Society (Harmondsworth: Penguin, 1961)
Shonfield, A., *British Economic Policy since the War* (Harmondsworth: Penguin, 1958)
Theakston, K., *The Labour Party and Whitehall* (Routledge, 1992)
Tomlinson, J., *The Politics of Decline* (Harlow: Longman, 2000)
Ziegler, P., *Wilson* (Weidenfeld and Nicolson, 1993)

Pre Fulton

Cannadine, D., 'C.P. Snow' in Wm. L. Louis (ed), *Yet More Adventures with Britannia* (I.B. Tauris, 2005)
Chapman, B., *British Government Observed* (Allen and Unwin, 1963)
Clarke, R., *The Management of the Public Sector of the National Economy* (Stamp Memorial Lecture, 1964)

Clarke, R., *New Trends in Government* (HMSO, 1971)
Clarke, R., 'Parliament and public expenditure' *Political Quarterly* 44 (1973) 137–53
Clarke, R., *Public Expenditure Management and Control* (Macmillan, 1978)
Conservative Party, *Change or decay?* (Conservative Political Centre, 1962)
Fabian Society, *The Administrators* (1964)
Hunt, N. (ed), *Whitehall and Beyond* (BBC, 1964)
Johnson, N., *Parliament and Administration* (Allen and Unwin, 1966)
Lowe, R., 'The core executive, modernization and the creation of PESC, 1960–4' *Public Administration* 75 (1997) 601–15
Lowe, R., 'Milestone or millstone? The 1959–1961 Plowden Committee' *Historical Journal* 40 (1997) 463–91
Lowe, R., 'Resignation at the Treasury . . . 1955–7' *Journal of Social Policy* 18 (1989) 505–26
Mackenzie, W.J.M., 'The Plowden Report: a translation' in R. Rose (ed), *Policy-Making in Britain* (Macmillan, 1969)
Morton, W.W., 'The Plowden Report III. The management function of the Treasury', *Public Administration* 41 (1963) 25–35
Nicholson, M., *The System: the mismanagement of modern Britain* (Hodder and Stoughton, 1967)
'The Plowden Report: a symposium' *Public Administration* 41 (1963) 1–50
Sampson, A., *Anatomy of Britain* (Hodder and Stoughton, 1962)
Sampson, A., *Anatomy of Britain Today* (Hodder and Stoughton, 1965)
Thomas, H. (ed), *Crisis in the Civil Service* (Blond, 1968)
Thomas, H. (ed), *The Establishment* (Blond, 1959)

Fulton

National Whitley Council, *Developments on Fulton* (1969)
National Whitley Council, *Fulton – a Framework for the Future* (1970)
National Whitley Council, *Fulton – the Reshaping of the Civil Service* (1971)
National Whitley Council, *The Shape of the Post-Fulton Civil Service* (1972)

***

Castle, B., *The Castle Diaries* 2 vols (Weidenfeld and Nicolson, 1980, 1984)
Castle, B., *Fighting All the Way* (Macmillan, 1993)
Davis, J., *Prime Ministers and Whitehall, 1960–1974* (Hambledon Continuum, 2007)
Fry, G.K., *Reforming the Civil Service* (Edinburgh: Edinburgh University Press, 1993)
Garratt, J.L., *The Management of Government* (Harmondsworth: Penguin, 1972)
Garratt, J.L., *Managing the Civil Service* (Heinemann, 1980)
Hennessy, P. and Fry, G.K. (ed), 'Fulton: 20 Years On' *Contemporary Record* 2 (1988) 44–54
Kellner P. and Lord Crowther-Hunt, *The Civil Servants* (Macdonald, 1980)
Radice, G., *Friends and Rivals* (Abacus, 2003)
Rowat, D.C., 'Canada's Royal Commission on Government Organization' *Public Administration* 41 (1963) 193–205
Saint-Martin, D., *Building the New Managerialist State* (Oxford: Oxford University Press, 2000)
Wilenski, P., *Public Power and Public Administration* (Sydney, NSW: Hale and Ironmonger, 1986).

SOURCES AND SELECT BIBLIOGRAPHY

Part 3 The Politics and Planning of Reform

1968–1979

Wider Issues Review Team (CSD), *Civil Servants and Change* (HMSO, 1975)

* * *

Armstrong, W., 'The role and character of the Civil Service' (Thank-Offering to Britain Fund lecture) *Proceedings of the British Academy, 1970* (1972)
Bacon, R. and Eltis, W., *Britain's Economic problem: too few producers* (Macmillan, 1976)
Ball, S. and Seldon, A. (eds), *The Heath Government, 1970–74* (Harlow: Longman, 1996)
Barnett, J., *Inside the Treasury* (Deutsch, 1982)
Benn, T., *Against the Tide* (Hutchinson, 1989)
Blackstone, T. and Plowden, W., *Inside the Think Tank: advising the Cabinet 1971–1983* (Heinemann, 1988)
Blick, A., *People Who Live in the Dark* (Politico's, 2004)
Brittan, S., 'The economic contradictions of democracy' *British Journal of Political Science* 5 (1975) 129–59
Butler, F.E.R. and Aldred, K., 'The Financial Information Systems project' *Management Services in Government* 32 (1977) 24–30
Campbell, J., *Edward Heath* (Cape, 1993)
Chapman, R.A., 'The Vehicle and General affair' *Public Administration* 51 (1973) 273–90
Connelly, P., *Portrait of a Mandarin: the life of William Armstrong* (forthcoming)
Donoughue, B., *Downing Street Diary*, 2 vols (Jonathan Cape, 2005, 2008)
Donoughue, B., *The Heat of the Kitchen* (Politico's, 2002)
Donoughue, B., *Prime Minister* (Cape, 1987)
Draper, P., *The Creation of the DoE* (HMSO, 1977)
Gray, A. and Jenkins, B., 'Policy analysis in British Central Government: the experience of PAR' *Public Administration* 60 (1982) 429–50
Healey, D., *The Time of My Life* (Joseph, 1989)
Heseltine, M., *Life in the Jungle* (Hodder and Stoughton, 2000)
Howell, D., *The Edge of Now* (Macmillan, 2000)
Howell, D., *A New Style of Government* (Conservative Political Centre, 1970)
Howell, D., *Whose Government Works?* (Conservative Political Centre, 1968)
Hurd, D., *An End to Promises* (Collins, 1979)
Morgan, K.O., *Callaghan* (Oxford: Oxford University Press, 1997)
Niskanen, W.A., *Bureaucracy: servant or master?* (IEA, 1973)
Painter, C., 'The Civil Service: post-Fulton malaise' *Public Administration* 53 (1975) 427–41
Pliatzky, L., *Getting and Spending* (Oxford: Blackwell, 1982)
Price, D., *Office of Hope* (PSI, 2000)
Rothschild, V., *Random Variable* (Collins, 1984)
Sedgemore, B., *The Secret Constitution* (Hodder and Stoughton, 1980)
Seldon, A. and Hickson, K. (eds), *New Labour, Old Labour: The Wilson and Callaghan Governments, 1974–79* (Routledge, 2004)
Wass, D., *Decline to Fall* (Oxford: Oxford University Press, 2008)
Wilding, R.W.L., 'The post-Fulton programme' *Public Administration* 48 (1970) 391–403
Windmill, L.A., *A British Achilles: the story of . . . Earl Jellicoe* (Barnsley: Pen and Sword, 2006)

SOURCES AND SELECT BIBLIOGRAPHY

1979–1981

Efficiency Unit, *Making Things Happen* (HMSO, 1985)
National Audit Office, *The Rayner Scrutiny Programmes, 1981–1983* (HMSO, 1986)
Efficiency Unit, *Improving Management in Government: the Next Steps* (HMSO, 1988)

***

Bray, A.J.M., *The Clandestine Reformer* (Glasgow: Strathclyde Papers in Government and Politics, no 55, 1988)
Campbell, J., *Margaret Thatcher* 2 vols (Jonathan Cape, 2000, 2003)
Gilmour, I., *Dancing with Dogma* (Simon and Schuster, 1992)
Heseltine, M., *Where There's a Will* (Hutchinson, 1987)
Hoskyns, J., *Just in Time* (Aurum Press, 2000)
Howe, G., *Conflict of Loyalty* (Macmillan, 1994)
Lawson, N., *The View from No 11* (Bantam Press, 1992)
Lee, J.M., 'Epitaph for the CSD' *Public Administration* 60 (1982) 3–9
Metcalfe, L. and Richards, S., *Improving Public Management* (Sage, 1990)
Prior, J., *A Balance of Power* (Hamish Hamilton, 1986)
Rayner, D., *The Unfinished Agenda* (Stamp Memorial Lecture, 1984)
Thatcher, M., *The Downing Street Years* (HarperCollins, 1993)
Young, H., *One of Us* (Macmillan, 1989)

Part 4 Wider Issues

Whitleyism

CCSU, *The Bulletin* (1981–)
IPCS, *State Service* (1919–)
NSS/CCSU, *Whitley Bulletin* (1966–1981)

***

Beaumont, P.B., 'The obligation of the Government as employer in the British Civil Service' *Public Administration* 56 (1978) 13–24
Callaghan, L.J., 'Whitleyism' (Fabian Society, 1953)
Mortimer, J.E. and Ellis, V.A., *A Professional Union: the evolution of the IPCS* (Allen and Unwin, 1980)
O'Toole, B., *The Ideal of Public Service* (Routledge, 2006)
O'Toole, B., *Private Gain and Public Service: The Association of First Division Civil Servants* (Routledge, 1989)
Parris, H., *Staff Relations in the Civil Service* (Allen and Unwin, 1973)

Training

Bird, D.L., *The Civil Service College* (HMSO, 1995)
Egger, R., 'Civil servants in mid-career' *Public Administration* 54 (1976) 83–98
Grebenik, E., 'The Civil Service College: the first year' *Public Administration* 50 (1972) 127–38
Heaton, R.N. and Williams, L., *Civil Service Training* (CSD, 1974)

SOURCES AND SELECT BIBLIOGRAPHY

Keeling, D., 'Central training in the Civil Service' *Public Administration* 50 (1972) 1–18
Keeling, D., 'The development of central training in the Civil Service, 1963–1970' *Public Administration* 49 (1971) 51–71
Lindley, P.D., *A Short Account of the Administrative Processes which Led to the Setting Up of the Civil Service College* (CSC, 1973)

Gender and race

Brimelow, E., 'Women in the Civil Service' *Public Administration* 59 (1981) 313–36
Fogarty, M.P., *Women in Top Jobs: four studies in achievement* (Allen and Unwin, 1971)
Fogarty, M.P., *Women and Top Jobs: the next move* (PEP, 1972)
Fogarty, M.P., Allen, I. and Walters, P., *Women in Top Jobs, 1968–1979* (Heinemann, 1981)
Hede, A., 'Women managers in the Civil Service: the long road to equality in Britain' *International Review of Administrative Sciences* 61 (1995) 587–600
Lewis, J., *Women in Britain since 1945* (Oxford: Blackwell, 1992)
Tavistock Institute, *Application of Race Relations Policy in the Civil Service* (HMSO, 1978

Computerisation

Agar, J., *The Government Machine: a revolutionary history of the computer* (Cambridge, MA: MIT Press, 2003)
CSD, *Longer-Term Review of Administrative Computing in Central Government* (CSD, 1978)

Secrecy

Crossman, R., *The Diaries of a Cabinet Minister* vol 1 (Hamish Hamilton and Jonathan Cape, 1975)
Crossman, R., *Plato Today* (Allen and Unwin, 1959)
Garrett, J. and Sheldon, R., *Administrative Reform: the next step* (Fabian Society, 1973)
Hennessy, P., 'Open government, Whitehall and the press' in H. Stephenson (ed), *Media Voices* (Politico's, 2001)
Hooper, D., *Official Secrets; the use and abuse of the Act* (Secker and Warburg, 1987)
Ingham, B., *Kill the Messenger . . . Again* (HarperCollins,1991)
Justice, *The Law and the Press* (1965)
Theakston, K., 'Richard Crossman' *Public Policy and Administration* 18 (2003) 20–40
Vincent, D., *The Culture of Secrecy: Britain, 1832–1998* (Oxford: Oxford University Press, 1998)
Young, H., *The Crossman Affair* (Hamish Hamilton and Jonathan Cape, 1976)

Parliament

Benn, T., *Against the Tide* (Hutchinson, 1989)
Bogdanor, V. (ed), *The British Constitution in the Twentieth Century* (Oxford: Oxford University Press for British Academy, 2003)
Crick, B., *The Reform of Parliament* (Allen and Unwin, 1964)
Gregory, A., *The Parliamentary Ombudsman: a study in the control of administrative action* (Allen and Unwin, 1975)

Gregory, A. and Giddings, P., *The Ombudsman, the Citizen and Parliament* (Politico's, 2002)
Gwyn, W., 'The British PCA: ombudsman or ombudsmouse?' *Journal of Politics* 35 (1973) 45–69
Gwyn, W., 'The ombudsman in Britain: a qualified success in government reform' *Public Administration* 60 (1982) 177–95
Kirkham, R., *The Parliamentary Ombudsman: standing the test of time* (www.ombudsman.org.uk 2009) (last accessed December 2009)
Marshall, G., 'The British PCA' *The Annals* 377 (1968) 91–6
Pugh, I., 'The ombudsman – jurisdiction, powers and practice' *Public Administration* 56 (1978) 127–38

The constitution

Bogdanor, V., *Devolution in the UK* (Oxford: Oxford University Press, 1999)
Denman, R., *The Mandarin's Tale* (Politico's, 2002)
King, A., *The British Constitution* (Oxford: Oxford University Press, 2007)
Soames, C., 'Whitehall into Europe' *Public Administration* 59 (1972) 271–9
Young, H., *This Blessed Plot* (Macmillan, 1998)

INDEX

Page numbers in Bold represent major references.
Page numbers followed by n and a number represent end notes.

accountable management 118–19, 135, 183–5, 235, 347, 370; *see also* departmental agencies, Fulton, hiving off
Adams, J. B. 22
Administration Group 139, 142, 147, 259
Administrative Class 47, 50–9, 86–93, 97, 119, 123–5, **137–9**, 407 n40, 413 n103, 417 n30, 427 n20, 436 n50, 439 n71; and women 75, 329–32
administrative law 33–4, 68–9, 73, 78
Administrative Reform Association 20, 30
Allen, D. A.V. (Lord Croham) **196–9**, 211–14, 221, 322, 326–7, 344, 351, 355–6; 424 n88, 447 n134, 451 n164, 463 n61–5, 467 n90, 494 n50, 496 n60; *see also* Croham directive
Allen, P. 122, 125
Anatomy of Britain (Sampson) 84, 89
Anderson, J. 59, 65, 404 n17; Anderson Committee on the Machinery of Government (1942–5) 49–50, 63, 65–7
Armitage Committee on the Political Activities of Civil Servants (1976–8) 222, 294–6, 310
Armstrong, R.T. 11, 220, 263, 271–2, 274, 519 n32
Armstrong, W. 111, **131–4**, 347, 415 n1, 417 n24, 428 n35, 431 n3, 432 n15, 439 n7, 446 n129, 491 n28; 'deputy prime minister' 163, 444 n114–5; management failings 432 n12, 433 n21; and Business Team 173–7, 450 n151; Central Capability 159–66; Europe 375; Fulton 135–54, 429 n38, 436 n49–50, 437 n58;

hiving off 183–6; management challenges 290–2, 319–22, 442 n98 and 100, 492 n36, 519 n36; open government 351–3; ombudsman 367; strike action 303, 457 n12; women 333–7
Askwith, G. 37, 402 n65, 409 n60
Assheton Committee on the Training of Civil Servants (1943–4) 58, 313
Association of Government Supervisors and Radio Staff (AGSRO) 287–8
Atkinson, R. 343–4; Atkinson Report (1971) 340, 342–3, 347; *see also* computerisation
Australia 10, 38, 125, 127, 141, 223, 432 n11, 434 n37, 444 n11, 464 n 62; *see also* Coombs Committee

Bacon, R. 195
Bagehot, W. 49
Baker, K. 455 n191
Balogh, T. 60, 89–95, 407 n 40, 416 n17
Bancroft, I. 153, 165, **196**, 213, 217, 260, 356, 361, 364, 385, 424 n9, **457 n11,** 463 n56, 473 n131, 481 n79, 487 n139; dismissal 269–70; Permanent Secretary's dinner 256–7; and defence of the Civil Service Department, 272–5, 486 n124; devolution 377–9; Rayner reforms 260, 478 n49, 480 n74
Bellinger Committee 132, 173–4, 449 n146
Benn, T. 222, 362, 520 n46, 521 n56
Benthamites 30, 32, 34

INDEX

Berrill, K. 219–20
Beveridge, W. 21–22, 121; Beveridge Report on Social Insurance and Allied Services (1942) 44
Bird Report on job evaluation (1971) 148–50; Investigating Team 139, 142, 145, 148–9; *see also* unified grading.
Bishop, F. 419 n49
Black Book (1970) 157–8, 160–1, 172, 185, 211, 443 n106
Bletchley Park 74, 342
Bligh, T. 419 n49
Board of Trade 21, 23, 26, 32, 40, 57, 103, 171, 402 n63
Bradbury Committee on the Organization and Staffing of Offices (1918–19) 49, 55, 73
Bridgeman Committee of Enquiry into the Post Office (1931–2) 357
Bridges, E. 3, 9–10, 42–79, 83–4, 97, 99, 127, 349, 403 n3 and 8, 410 n64; *Portrait of a Profession* 43
Brittan, S. 89, 91–3, 107, 119
Brook, N. 2, 46, 54, 59, 85–6, 97–8, 106–7, 162, 419 n49, 423 n87
Brown, P. 227
Brown, W. J. 70–1, 73
Bullock, C. 405 n26
Bullock Committee and Report on Industrial Democracy (1977) 209, 281, 290, 294
Bureau of the Budget 106–7, 111, 156–7, 211–12, 214, 224, 236; Office of Management and Budget 271, 274–5, 485 n120
Burrett, G. 286
Business Team 161, 166, **173–9**, 183, 185–7, 189, 462 n49; *see also* Bellinger, management consultants, Meyjes
Butler, F.E.R. 227, 447 n132

Cabinet Office 162, 214, 404 n17, 423 n82, 442 n100; Cabinet Secretariat, creation of 42, 45–6
Callaghan, J. 194, 206–8, 211–15, 232–3, 294, 298, 306, 311; open government 356, 359–60, 364
Carswell, J. P. 334–5
Cash Control Group 229–30
cash limits **224–34**, 242, 266–7, 298, 307, 310
Castle, B. 127, 221

categories 138, 141–4, 148, 151; *see also* unified grading
Caulcott, T. H. 159, 175, 372
Central Capability 157–60, 162–71, 173, 209
Central Policy Review Staff (CPRS) **165–70**, 180, 190, 214–15, 220, 339, 344
Central Statistical Office 46, 57; statisticians 254, 399 n22
Centre of Administrative Studies (CAS) 91, 313–18, 347, 500 n1; *see also* Civil Service College, training
Chadwick, E. 19, 23, 33, 36–7
Channon, P. 238, 242–3, 247
Chapman, B. 89–91, 97, 243–4
Chapman, L. (*Your Disobedient Servant*) 188, 195, 235, 243
Charkham, J. 517 n13
Chester, D. N. 114–15, 122, 428 n32
Chilcot, J. A. 448 n137
child benefit leak (1976) 469 n98, 518 n25
Christopher, A. 287, 299; *see also* Inland Revenue Staff Federation
Churchill, W.S. 21–22, 66
Civil and Public Services Association (CPSA) 281, **283–5**, 288, 292, 302, 304, 308–9; *formerly* Civil Service Clerical Association (CSCA) 70, 72, 415 n117
civil servants; accountability 48, 97, 183–4, 351, 385, 454 n182; 'amateurism' 40, 58, 78, 90, 92, 123, 128, 421 n58; anonymity 35–7, 351, 353, 365, 369, 411 n80; Crown employees 4–8, 512 n106; division of labour 19–20, 24–25, 30–1, 41, 47, 71; enthusiasm, limits to 385, 410 n64, 527 n3; exclusivity **50–60**, 62, 71, 78, 89–90, 92, 124, 137; neutrality 35–6, 41, 59, 79, 295, 410 n64, 524 n85; political influence 59–63, 86, 406 n28; politicisation 418 n41, 468 n92, 527 n1 and n3; specialists 117, 142, 152, 285, 402 n63, 435 n42; vetting 395 n9; *see also* promotion, public service ethos, recruitment, training
Civil Servants and Change (1975) 197
Civil Service 4–12; golden age **9–10**, 42–3, 45, 77–8, 383; industrial civil service 396 n9; international reputation 10, 58, 115, 191, 383, 386, 426 n5; permanence 23, **35–7**, 100, 400 n36; size 6, 202; unification/ departmentalism 19, **27–9**,

544

INDEX

45–50, 64, 71, 462 n56; *see also* dispersal, manpower
Civil Service College (CSC) 40, 117, 135, 137, 262, **313–19**, 347, 403 n75; *see also* training, Heaton-Williams Report
Civil Service Commission 20, 25–7, 52; *see also* recruitment
Civil Service Confederation 70
Civil Service Department (CSD) proposed (1945) 49, 406 n31 (1962) 106, 423 n85; (Fulton) 119–20, 126; established (1968) **136–7**; decline 209–14, 458 n22, 463 n59; demise (1981) **269–76**, 384; *see also* Hawtin-Moore Report
Civil Service Gazette 29
Civil Service Selection Board (CSSB) 52, 317; *see also* recruitment
Civil Service Union (CSU) 283, 287–8
Clarke, R. O. 99–100, 102–3, 108–9, 111, 422 n69 and n76
closed shop 295–6
Committee of Civil Research 46
Compton, E. 365, 367, 522 n66
Comptroller and Auditor General 260–1
computers 6, 74, **340–6**, 470 n111; Central Computer Agency (CCA) 340, 343–6; PRISM 440 n81; earlier mechanisation 73–7, 97; *see also* Atkinson, R., ICL, Longer-term Review
Conciliation and Arbitration Board (1917–22, 1925-) 69, 71
Conn, E. 334
Constitution Unit 374, 377
Coombs Committee (Australia, 1974–6) 10, 125, 429 n45
Cooper, F. 134, 146, 150, 258, 294, 432 n12, 438 n59, 454 n188, 457 n11
Council of Civil Service Unions (CCSU) 281, 283, **289**, 300, 306–9, 337, 483 n102; Major Policy Committee 289, 308; Pay Campaign Coordination Committee 289, 307
Crichel Down affair (1954) 48, 54, 77, 365
Cripps, S. 65–6
Croham directive 350–2, 364, 516 n7, 519 n33; *see also* Allen, D.A.V.
Crossman, R. 127, 370, 522 n66; *Crossman Diaries* 195, 235, 349–50, **358–63**, 370, 379, 384, 518 n25–7
Curtis, M. 414 n110

Dale, H. E. 58, 60–2
Datalink 346; *see also* computers, DHSS
delegated legislation 60, 68–9, 76
departmental agencies 182–3, 186–8, 410 n75, 453 n177; *see also* accountable management, hiving off, Procurement Executive, Property Services Agency
Department of Economic Affairs (DEA) 84, 96, 108, 111–12, 159, 275
Department of Employment 8, 189, 337–8, 396 n13
Department of the Environment 171, 396 n13, 448 n139; *see also* Property Services Agency
Department of Health and Social Security (DHSS) 245, 253, 302, 346, 396 n13, 457 n12, 498 n79; *see also* Datalink
Department of Trade and Industry (DTI) 171–2
Department Training Officers (DTO) 313
Derx, D. 527 n3
devolution 195, 348, 374, 376–9
Dicey, A. V. 69
dispersal 319–24; *see also* Hardman
Donoughmore Committee on Ministerial Powers (1932) 68–9
Donoughue, B. 219, 223, 353, 360, 466 n77
Drake, J. 151–2, 154, 433 n21; *see also* personnel management
Dryden, J. 288, 302, 488 n9; *see also* Society of Civil Servants, National Staff Side
Dugdale, T. 54
Dunnett, J. 115, 122–3, 125

Ecole Nationale d'Administration (ENA) 58, 92, 126, 314, 319; *see also* training
Economic Advisory Council 46
Economic Growth and National Efficiency 85, 99, 103
Economic Section (Cabinet Office 1939–53, Treasury, 1953-) 46, 57, 95, 313–14, 418 n41, 424 n88
Efficiency in the Civil Service (white paper 1981) 249
Efficiency (Rayner) Unit 11, 213, 236–7, 239–41, 243–4, 254, 276, 486 n135; *see also* Rayner, D.
Eltis, W. 195
Employment Policy (white paper 1944) 44
Employment Protection Act (1975) 329
English (Expenditure) Committee 148, 209, 211, 215–217, 269–71, 317, 369, 371

545

INDEX

Equal Opportunities for Women in the Civil Service (NWC) 330
Equal Pay Act (1970) 329, 334
Equality for Women (white paper 1976) 334
Establishment Officers 47, 142–3, 149–50, 153, 293, 315–18, 334–5, 427 n15
Estacode 150, 221–2, 303, 352, 359, 361
European Economic Community (EEC) 195, 348, 374–7, 379
European Interdepartmental Unit (EIU) 374–5
Executive, power of the 95, 183, 365, 370–3, 379

Fabian Society 32, 55, 87, **91–5**, 114; *The Administrators* 91–5, 124
Finance Officers; Principal Finance Officers (PFO) 47, 226, 232–3, 263, 481 n91
Financial Information Systems (FIS) 224–27
First Division Association (FDA) 281, **286**, 305; *formerly* Association of First Division Clerks 70
Fisher, W. 9–10, 42–79, 83, 98, 106, 405 n25–6, 408 n50, 413 n104
Fleming Report on dispersal (1963) 320
Foot, M. 293, 362
Foster, C. 418 n34
France 33–4, 57, 90, 314–15, 368, 510 n92
Francs case (1928) 48, 77
Franks Report (1972) 350, 352–8, 365
freedom of information campaign 358, 364; Freedom of Information Act (2000) 2, 350; *see also* open government
Freud, C. 356
Fry, G. K. 43, 115
Fulton, J. S. 121; Fulton Report (1968) 10–11, 17–18, 83–4, 94–8, **114–128**, 396 n15, 491 n27; implementation **131–155**, 209–10, 290–2, 492 n29, 505 n48; training 312–19; open government 349–52, 516 n2; retrospective reputation 383–6, 441 n89, 492 n36; *see also* Halsey Social Survey, Management Consultancy Group, Joint Whitley Committee

Garrett, J. 115, 125, 127, 209
Geddes Report (1922) 44
Gillman, G. 285, 298–9, 491 n26; *see also* Civil and Public Services Association
Gilmore, B. 315

Gladstone, W. E. 20–2, 28–30, 36, 384
Glassco Commission (Canada, 1960–2) 10, 125, 141, 429 n44–5
Goodman, Lord 361, 520 n44
Graham, A. 289, 307, 488 n8; *see also* Civil and Public Services Association
Grebenik, E. 314, 316–19; *see also* Civil Service College
Grigg, J. 59

Haddow, D. 350–1
Haldane, R. 55, 64; Haldane Report on the Machinery of Government (1918) **63–5**, 75, 78–9, 128, 368, 445 n124
Halls, M. 127, 140, 143–6
Halsey Social Survey of the Civil Service 124, 329, 332, 334, 337
Hancock, K. 2, 12
Hankey, M. 45–6, 409 n60
Hardman, H. 419 n49; Hardman Report on the Dispersal of Government Work from London (1973) 319–23
Hartman, W. F. 335
Hawtin-Moore Report on the future of the CSD (1980) 273
Hayter, W. 20
Head of the Civil Service 42–3, 106–7, 213–4, 400 n38, 404 n15, 405 n22, 463 n56
Healey, D. 211–2, 230, 232, 459 n28, 463 n57, 469 n103
Heath, E. 10, 96–7, 146–8, 157–171, 294, 352–3, 371, 443 n105
Heaton-Williams Report (1974) 313–16; *see also* Civil Service College
Helsby, L. 105, 107–8, 111–12, 114, 355, 359, 424 n87, 428 n34
Henley, D. 227, 229–30
Hennessy, P. 115, 127, 363–4, 397 n28; *see also* Whitehall correspondents
Herbecq, J. 238, 270, 462 n52, 478 n45, 487 n139, 505 n49
Heseltine, M. 242, 246, 255, 262
Hewart, G. 42, 68–9
hiving off 118–19, 171–3, 182–90, 240, 283–4; Hiving Off Steering Group 184
Home Office 23, 27, 35, 337, 402 n72
homosexuality (male) 513 n112
Hoskyns, J. 269, 276, 308–9, 385–6, 485 n128
Houghton, D. 72, 326
Howard, A. 360, 363–4
Howe, G. 250, 265, 327, 373, 506 n58

546

INDEX

Howell, D. 98, 132, 156–7, 160–79, 326, 328, 371–2, 426 n8
Hunt, J. 214, 216, 219, 222, 244, 357, 359–60, 362, 520 n43
Hunt, N. 121–3, 125, 132–46, 154–6, 317, 428 n28, 526 n103
Hurd, D. 181

ICL 341–2, 344–5
Improved Expenditure Decisions by Government (East, Fogg and Meyjes) 176–7
incomes policy 204, 206–7, 297, 301, 307
Industrial Relations Act (1971) 132, 193, 285, 292, 294
Information and the Public Interest (white paper 1969) 352; *see also* open government
Information Officers, 521 n49 and 54
Inland Revenue Staff Federation (IRSF) 206, 287, 302, 309
Inspector General 260, 477 n39, 481 n87, 486 n135
Institution of Professional Civil Servants (IPCS) 70, 206, **285–8**, 302, 345, 448 n142
International Monetary Fund (IMF) 193–4, 196, 211, 219, 222, 224, 355
Investigating Team 139, 142, 145, 148–9; *see also* Bird Report, unified grading

Jay, P. 350
Jellicoe, G. 161, 175, 187, 301, 319–20, 324, 335, 371, 432 n1, 438 n62, 442 n98
Jenkins, R. 122, 127, 220, 355–6, 519 n39
Job Appraisal Review (JAR) 152, 183, 440 n82
Joint Whitley Committee on Fulton (NWCJC) 134, 146–8, 150–2, 288, 290–1; *see also* Fulton, Whitleyism
Jones, P. 289, 490 n19
Jones, T. 46
Jowett, B. 40–1, 401 n46
Justice (International Commission of Jurists) 365–6, 516 n5, 518 n30

Keeling, D. 314, 318
Kelsall, R. K. 51, 407 n38–42, 408 n47
Kemp-Jones, E. 330; Kemp-Jones Report (1971) **331–6**, 347; *see also* women
Kendall, W. 283, 288–9, 299–300, 302, 463 n56, 494 n51, 495 n60, 497 n72, 497 n76
Keynes, J. M. 42–3; Keynesianism 45, 78, 184, 383

Kilbrandon Report on the Constitution (1973) 377

labour exchanges 21–2
Lancaster, D. 336
Lawson, N. 209, 447 n132
Lee, F. 85, 98–9, 103, 107, 213
Lipsey, D. 220, 223,
Lloyd George, D. 50, 61, 65, 78, 86, 218, 403 n1
The Longer-Term Review of computerisation (1978) 345
Lowe, R. 20, 28–30, 37

Macaulay, T. 22, 40–1, 58, 401 n47; report on the Indian Civil Service (1854) 40
MacDonagh, O. 31
MacDonnell Commission on the Civil Service (1912–14) 21, 23–5, 27, 50, 71
Machinery of Government Division (Treasury, CSD, Cabinet Office) 183, 372
Mackenzie, W. J. M. 114, 122, 428 n32
MacLeod, I. 102–3, 109
Macmillan, H. 84–5
Mallaby, G. 359
Management Consultancy Group (MCG) 124–6, 128, 139, 141, 209; *see also* Fulton
Management Consultants 87, 137, 171, 173–4, 175, 227, 244, 255, 259, 429 n43, 437 n56, 441 n95
Management Information System (MINIS) 242, 246, 249, 255
Management Group (Treasury, 1962–8) 109–10, 112
Management and Personnel Office (MPO) 238, 274
Management Projects Cabinet Committee (MPC) 163, 166, 174, 176, 308, 444 n116
manpower policy 199–203, 246–64; cuts 237, 240–3
Manpower Services Commission (MSC) 8, 189, 200, 239, 323, 462 n49
Marples, E. 419 n46, 441 n94, 450 n156
Marre, A. 367
Masterman Committee on the Political Activities of Civil Servants (1948) 72, 295
May Report on National Expenditure (1931) 44

McCall, W. 285–6; *see also* Institution of Professional Civil Servants
McNally, T. 220–21
Megaw Committee on Civil Service Pay (1981–2) 265, 307
Meyjes, R. 161, 173–4, 178–9, 187–8; *see also* Business Team
Ministerial Committee on the Central Capability (MCA) 167, 441 n116
Ministerial memoirs 358–63
Ministerial responsibility 10, **37–8**, 48, **53–4**, 64–6, **160**, 386, 408 n45, 411 n80, 413 n100, 474 n137; *see also* Crichel Down
Ministry of Defence (MOD) 5, 201, 499 n92, 504 n36; *see also* Procurement Executive
'Ministry of Finance' 86, 106, 211–12, 214, 224
Ministry of Industry 171
Ministry of Labour 57
Ministry of National Insurance 74
'Ministry of Programmes' 157–60
Ministry of Technology 84, 89, 96, 171
Morant, R. 37
Morrell, F. 222–3, 468 n96, 469 n101
Morton, W. W. 109

Nairne, P. 258, 375, 526 n1
National Audit Act 373; National Audit Office (NAO) 261, 365, 373
National Economic Development Council (NEDC) 85, 240, 352
National Pay Agreement 204, 206–7, 281, 292–3, 296–8, 300, 305–6, 345; *see also* pay
National Staff Side (NSS) of the Whitley Council 113–4, **282–306**, 431 n7; Committee A 287–8, 308; and computerisation 345–6; dispersal 319–23, 526 n105; pay 204–9; pensions 325; personnel management 151–3, 460 n31; unified grading 140, 143–4, 436 n46; women 333 *see also* Joint Whitley Committee on Fulton
National Whitley Council (NWC) 70, 144–5, 282–3, 287; and women 74, 76, 330; *see also* Whitleyism
Neild, R. 95, 122–3
Next Steps (1988) 1, 4, 17, 115, 155, 182, 324, 379
The New Despotism (Hewart) 42, 68–9

The New Style of Government (1970) 156, 164, 171, 184
New Zealand 368
non-departmental bodies (NDPBs) **237–40**
Northcote, S. H. 21, 36
Northcote-Trevelyan Report (1854) 8–9, **18–29**, 92, 123, 143, 295, 433 n25,441 n132; implementation 31–41, 43–5, 46–63, 77–9, 142; retrospective reputation 17–18, 115, 383–5, 403 n3, 426 n6, 428 n34, 433 n25
Northern Ireland 132, 156, 193, 305, 525 n98; Northern Ireland Civil Service 3, 331, 377–8
Nott, J. 249, 255

Official Information Bill 355–6; *see also* open government
Official Secrets Act (OSA) 12, 53–4, 317, **349–58**; *Reform of Section 2 of the Official Secrets Act* (white paper 1978) 355
ombudsman 356, **365–8**; *see also* Compton, E., Marre, A. and Pugh, I.
open government **348–63**, 368–9, 379; *see also* freedom of information
Operation Vigilant 110
Organisation and Methods Division (Treasury) 55, 65, 74, 109, 125, 340, 342–3, 412 n89, 414 n111
Osmotherly rules 369, 371 see also Select Committees
output budgeting 157–8, 166, 176, 178, 181
Oxbridge 51–3, 55, 76–7, 407 n38; *see also* Administrative Class, recruitment

Padmore, T. 98, 107, 218, 419 n49, 423 n81
Parliamentary Control of Expenditure (Reform) Bill (1983) 373
patronage 20–3, 30, 40–1, 56, 86, 89, 239–40
pay 28, 71, **203–9**, 263–9, 306–7; equality 76–8; negotiations **296–300**, pay research 285, 288, 293, 297–300, 305–6, 310, 460 n37–8; comparability 140–5, 149, 151, 203–4, 207, 229, 231–3, 265, 267, 305–7, 373–9, 461 n46; *see also* National Pay Agreement, Priestley Commission, Megaw
Pay Board 301; anomalies ruling 293–4, 297, 302, 310

548

INDEX

Pay Research Board 11, 461 n40; Pay Research Unit (PRU) 205, 207, 461 n45
Paymaster General's Office (PGO) 225–6
Peart, T. F. 205, 299
pensions 26, 36, 195, **324–9**; inflation-proofing 325–8; Pensions (Increase) Act (1971) 324, 326–7; Principal Civil Service Pension Scheme 324; Public Service Pensioners Alliance 325; *see also* Superannuation Acts
Permanent Consultative Committee 28; *see also* promotion
Permanent Secretaries, role of 100, 119, 186, 256–9; departmental accounting officers 521 n56
personnel management 147, **151–4**, 187, 210, 291–4, 312, 441 n84–6
planning units 119, 126, 451 n166
Plant, C. 287
Playfair Commission on the Civil Service (1875) 24–5, 31
Playfair, E. 414 n111
Pliatzky, L. 181, 215, 238–9
Plowden, E. 484 n116; Report on the Control of Public Expenditure (1961) 85–6, 97–100, **101–5**, 110–112, 230, 312–14, 384, 404 n17
Policy Unit (No. 10) 217–20, 224, 266, 308
Post Office 8, 57, 71, 90, 182, 245, 252, 283; and race 512 n102
Powell, E. 103, 337, 419 n45
press 83, 348–9, 351, 359–60, **363–4**, 371, 379
Priestley, C. 257–9, 320, 372
Priestley Commission on the Civil Service (1953–55) 63, 71, 203–4; 'Priestley principle' 140, 145, 151; *see also* pay
Prime Minister's Office/Department 46, 97–8, 106, 157–60, 162–5, 219, 255, 374; male chauvinism within 509 n82
privatisation 185, 187, 262
Procurement Executive (MOD) 185, 188–9, 474 n5; *see also* departmental agencies
procurement policy 341–3
Programme Analysis and Review (PAR) 166–7, **177–83**, 189–90, 214–16, 244, 252
promotion 26–7, 29, 118, 139, 210, 263, 334, 406 n30, 422 n72; *see also* Permanent Consultative Committee

Property Services Agency (PSA) 188–9, 262; see also departmental agencies, hiving off
Public Accounts Committee (PAC) 39, 87, 199, 274, 365, 369, 372–3
Public Appointments Unit (PAU) 352–3, 364
public expenditure 101–5, 107–10, 157–9, 178–80, 212, 214–15, 224–33, 241–2; cuts 194, 197, 201–2
Public Expenditure Survey Committee (PESC) 85, 99, 101–3, 105, 108–10, 178–9, 202, 226
Public Sector Borrowing Requirement (PSBR) 195, 199, 201, 204, 228, 241, 282
Public Sector Research Unit (PSRU) 96–8, 156–61, 165–6, 169–73, 182, 209, 216–18
public service ethos 9, 10, 30, 286, 397 n22, 433 n26, 455 n191
Pugh, I. 366, 523 n71
Pym, F. 242, 249, 253

quangos *see* non-departmental bodies (NDPBs)
Questions of Procedure for Ministers (1949) 46

race **337–40**; Race Relations Acts (1965, 1968, 1976) 337, 396 n17; Race Relations Board 337–8
Radcliffe Committee on Ministerial Memoirs (1976) 359–60, 362
Radcliffe Report on Security Procedures in the Public Service (1962) 283
Rayner, D.: pre 1979 11, 173, 176–7, 188, 299; post 1979 236, 249, 277–8, 385–6, 403 n74, 459 n29, 527 n5; Civil Service Department 248, 269–75; lasting reforms 246, **256–64**; manpower policy 243, 246–7; projects 237, **242–6**; scrutinies **250–6**, 347; *see also* Procurement Executive, Efficiency Unit
recruitment 52–3, 58, 89, 114, 117, 436 n50, 483 n98; examinations 19–20, 23–25, 29–31, 40, 52, 75–6, 399 n19, 403 n75, 407 n39; interview 52, 78, 398 n15, 407 n40; open competition **20–23**, 36, 75–6, 79; *Recruitment to the Civil Service* (Estimates Committee 1965) 87; *see also* Civil Service Commission; Civil Service Selection Board; Oxbridge
Reisner, A. 415 n117

549

INDEX

The Reorganisation of Central Government (white paper 1970) 131, 135, 157–8, 161, 170, 184, 294
Ridley Commission on the Civil Establishments (1886–1890) 24–5, 27, 31
Robot (1952) 84, 94
Robson, W. A. 69
Rothschild, V. 168–9, 181, 219–20
Royal Institute of Public Administration (RIPA) 55, 97, 314

Sampson, A. 84, 89, 91
Scandinavia 90, 357, 366; Sweden 90, 349–50, 368, 515 n2
Schreiber, M. 161, 164, 167, 173, 441 n94, 443 n108–9, 446 n128, 467 n91
Scotland 283, 305, 322, 348, 376–7, 504 n40
Scott Report on the Value of Public Pensions (1981) 324, 327–8
Sedgemore, B. 209
Select Committees (Parliamentary) 64, 365, **368–73**, 386; Select Committee on Miscellaneous Expenditure (1848) 24; Treasury and Civil Service Select Committee (1979-) 249; Estimates Committee 87–8, 101, 114–15, 117, 124, 143, 369, 371, 416 n13–15, 421 n66; *see also* English Committee, Public Accounts Committee
Senior Policy and Management Group (forerunner to Senior Civil Service) 7, 139, 142, 147
Sex Discrimination Act (1975) 329, 337
Sex Disqualification (Removal) Act (1919) 75–7
sexual equality 5, 73–7, 329–40
Sharp, E. 97–9, 103, 105, 157, 412 n86, 420 n54–5, 519 n35; Sharp Committee (Conservative Party) 159, 162, 170
Shackleton, E. A. A. 140, 144, 333–4, 342, 432 n1, 506 n55
Sheldon, R. 122–3, 132, 274, 352, 457 n8, 463 n59, 503 n34
Short, T. 321, 323
Simey, T. 17, 122
Sisson, C. H. 316, 500 n4
Snow, C. P. 89–90, 123, 419 n43
Soames, A. C. J. 238, 242, 248–9, 255, 259, 266, 268, 300, 525 n89 and 94
Social Contract 193, 204
Society of Civil Servants (SCS) 70, **283–5**, 286, 292, 302, 436 n50, 440 n83, 490 n23; Society of Civil and Public Servants (SCPS) 283, 285, 288, 298, 304–5; *formerly* Second Division Clerks' Association 25–6, 285
special advisers **218–24**, 233–4, 418 n40–1, 441 n94
staff associations *see* National Staff Side, Whitleyism, individual associations
Standing Instruments Act (1946) 68
Stephen, J. 23, 36, 59, 402 n61
St John Stevas, N. 373
Stowe, K. 357, 377, 421 n60, 476 n25
Straw, J. 221, 458 n93
strike action 206–8, 281, 283, 285–6, 288, 297–9, **300–9**; first national strike (1973) 150–1, 257, **301–4**; General Strike (1926) 72; 1981 strike 237, **265–9**, 300, **306–9**, 384; selective action 207, 265, 283, 287–8, 299, 304–10, 488 n8; *see also* winter of discontent
Stuart-Bunning, G. H. 71
Suez 10, 42, 83, 112, 122
The Sunday Times 358–9, 363
Sunningdale; Permanent Secretaries' conference 197–9, 215–6, 420 n54, 438 n63; Spring Sunningdales (with industrialists) 446 n146; site for CSC 318
Superannuation Act (1859) 26, 35; (1972) 293, 324; *see also* pensions
'Super' ministries 159, **170–2**

Tavistock Institute of Human Relations 337
Thatcher, M. 17, **235–78**, 295–6, 300, 307–8, 320, 323–4, 327, 346, 373, 384, 451 n164, 474 n3, 502 n29
Thomas, K. 283, 299, 309, 499 n92–5; *see also* Civil and Public Services Association
Thorneycroft, P. 84
The Times 350, 363
Tomlin Commission on the Civil Service (1931) 6–8, 49, 55–7, 63, 71, 120
Trade Union and Labour Relations Act (1974) 295
Trades Union Congress (TUC) 193, 254, 295; and staff associations 72, 133, 281, 285–6, 298, **495 n57**
Training 19, 40, 56–8, 89, 91–4, 100, 126, 117, 210, 262, **312–19**, 345, 411 n79, 417 n30, 426 n5, 429 n39;Training and Education Division (Treasury) 93, 313; Administration Trainee (AT) scheme

550

147, 210, 317; Administrative Staff College (Henley) 313; Node 313; Osmond Working Party on Management Training 314; Senior Professional Administrative Training Scheme (SPATS) 316; Specialist Training Wing 317; *see also* Centre of Administrative Studies, Civil Service College, *Ecole Natonale d'Administration*,
Treasury: Treasury control **38–9**, 43–5, 47–50, 64, 72, 87–9, 98, 104, 111, 485 n126; critique (pre-Fulton) 84–94, 95–7, 103–5; (1976) 469 n102; rehabilitation (1974–9) **224–33**; reorganisation 86, 98–100, 105–13; Treasury Organisation Committee (TOC, 1961–2) 86, 105, 108–11; Historical Section; 395 n4, 473 n133 *see also* Machinery of Government Division, Management Group, Organisation and Methods Division
Treasury Control of Expenditure (Estimates Committee 1958) 87
Treasury Control of Establishments (Estimates Committee 1964) 87
The Treasury Under the Tories (Brittan) 89, 91
Trend, B. 85, 101–3, 159–60, 166–70, 349, 351, 355, 371, 421 n65, 431 n3, 444 n114, 452 n170, 522 n63
Trevelyan, C. E. 22, 28, 30, 37, 401 n60; *see also* Northcote-Trevelyan Report
Trollope, A. 27, 398 n16, 400 n36, 403 n75
Troup, E. 26

unified grading **118**, 124–7, **132–55**, 182, 187, 190, 209–10, 291–2; *see also* Bird Report, Investigating Team
United States of America (USA) 11, 34–5, 73, 88, 96, 124, 140–1, 341–2, 357, 435 n37 and n39, 456 n4, 501 n16, 517 n22, 523 n79, 523 n79; Hoover Commissions 429 n45

Vehicle and General affair (1971) 286, 365, 454 n187, 474 n137

Vehicle Excise Duty (VED) 201, 211, 213
Vinter, F. R. P. 103

Walker, P. 189, 249
Walters, A. 447 n132, 479 n64
Wass, D. 211, 385, 463 n61, 469 n104, 514 n122
Wardale Report (1981) 259, 263, 274
Waterfield, P. 52
Whitehall correspondents 363–4; *see also* Hennessy, P.
Whitleyism 69–73, 78, 120, 209, **281–311**; *Whitley Bulletin* 136, 139; *see also* Joint Whitley Council on Fulton, National Staff Side, National Whitley Council
Wicks, N. 357
Wider Issues Review 197, 292, 303, 310, 335, 363
Wilding, R. 115, 144–6, 148, 154, 396 n18, 428 n31, 431 n3, 438 n65, 527 n3
Williams, L. 134, 288, 291–2, 297, 302–3, 321–2, 325, 437 n57, 497 n71; *see also* Heaton-Williams Report, National Staff Side, Whitleyism
Williams, M. 195, 219
Wilson, H.; Fulton 121, 127, 131–2, **135–40**, 143–5; Labour Party 94–5; manpower 200–1; open government 351–2, 356, 359, 362–4; special advisers 218–21
Wilson, H. J. 59, 61, 407 n40
winter of discontent (1979) 5, 193, 195–6, 203, 206–8, 233, 237, **304–6**
women 5, **73–7, 329–40**; marriage bar and pay equality 76–8; *Women in Top Jobs, 1968–1979* (PEP) 332; Women's National Commission 508 n68–9, 511 n101; pressure groups (Women in the Civil Service, Civil Service Women's Rights Group) 508 n73, 510 n87; *see also* Kemp-Jones, sexual equality

Yes Minister 218, 443 n109, 518 n29
Younger Inquiry into privacy (1972) 356